An Emotional History of the United States

The History of Emotions Series

EDITED BY
PETER N. STEARNS, CARNEGIE-MELLON UNIVERSITY
JAN LEWIS, RUTGERS UNIVERSITY, NEWARK

An Emotional History of the United States

EDITED BY

Peter N. Stearns and Jan Lewis

New York University Press

NEW YORK AND LONDON

NEW YORK UNIVERSITY PRESS
New York and London

Library of Congress Cataloging-in-Publication Data
An emotional history of the United States / edited by Peter N. Stearns
and Jan Lewis.
p.   cm. — (The history of emotions series)
Includes index.
ISBN 0-8147-8087-3 (clothbound : alk. paper). — ISBN
0-8147-8088-1 (paperbound : alk. paper)
1. United States—History—Psychological aspects.   2. United
States—Social life and customs—Psychological aspects.
3. Emotions—Social aspects—United States—History.   I. Stearns,
Peter N.   II. Lewis, Jan, 1949–   .   III. Series: History of emotion
series.
E179.E54   1998
973'.01'9–dc21   97-33779
                            CIP

New York University Press books are printed on acid-free paper, and
their binding materials are chosen for strength and durability.

Manufactured in the United States of America

10 9 8 7 6 5 4 3 2 1

From Jan Lewis
For Beth Rowley

From Peter Stearns
For Meg

Contents

Varieties of Emotional Expression and Experience: Ethnicity, Gender, Race, Religion

Twentieth-Century Emotional Standards and Emotional Experience: Class and Gender

Emotion and the Consumer Economy

Emotion and Individual Experience in the Twentieth Century

Introduction

Jan Lewis and Peter N. Stearns

Do the emotions have a history? Of course. All human experience has a history, although not every aspect of the human experience has been equally well studied by historians. Yet the nature of historical study has biased historians against the examination of the emotions. From the moment history became a profession in the nineteenth century, it has usually aimed at objectivity and attempted to purge itself of the irrational. Professional historians' epistemology, their underlying assumptions about knowledge and the way it is acquired, has often turned into a set of assumptions about the way people behave. By their choice of topics and the way they have studied them, historians have implied that most people in the past have been more or less rational, which at the very least downplays emotion. Historians have analyzed aspects of human history that tend to validate the assumption that the past is more or less knowable in rational terms. As Raymond Williams has noted, most historical analysis focuses on "relations between . . . produced institutions, formations, and experiences, so that . . . only the fixed explicit forms exist, and living presence is always, by definition, receding."[1]

The history of emotions is then, first of all, an attempt to recover that living presence, to recapture the way history felt. It is to ask what it felt like to be a Puritan immigrant to America, or an Irish one two hundred years later. It is to understand how religious doctrine could work "like strong wine" and make early seventeenth-century Americans' "judgment reel and stagger, who are drunken therewith" and how worship could feel like "joy unspeakable and full of glory" to American Pentecostal women three centuries later.[2] History has been felt; the lives men and women have lived have had an emotional dimension. That dimension has not only given shape to history but also created history, as men and women have acted on their feelings, sometimes knowingly, sometimes not.[3]

To study the history of emotions is also to recognize that the emotions have a history and that, hence, we may never be able to know with certainty whether men and women in the past have felt the same emotions that we experience today, or even whether what we call love or anger or fear is what people in the past understood by those terms. Exploring the complex issues concerning the transferability of emotions over time is, in fact, a chief contribution of the historical approach to the study of emotions generally. Connecting emotional formulations to more familiar developments in war, politics, or economic transformations serves as the principal link between this new field and historical inquiry more generally.

We do know that emotion and its expression have been a persistent concern in American history, that some emotions have seemed particularly troubling and others more desirable at various times in American history. Puritans seemed to find anger particularly threatening, and passion itself has been a concern, particularly to the middle class, for the past two centuries.[4] Conversely, a succession of experts and authorities has instructed Americans about what they should feel, how they should feel it, and how they ought to lead their emotional lives. Much of this effort has focused on the family and on private life; it has attempted to define what is normal—what love between parent and child is, or between husband and wife.[5] In recent years, historians of the emotions have become increasingly sensitive to the disparity between those emotional standards, established and maintained by a succession of writers and other experts, and the lived experience of men and women. Once we distinguish between prescription and description, we can see not only that actual experience sometimes differs markedly from notions about how people ought to behave and feel, but also that these prescriptions for emotional life often have important cultural, social, and political functions. Emotional standards are woven into the fabric of the discourses, belief systems, and ideologies that explain and attempt to structure our lives.

At the same time, the distinction between precept and experience should not be drawn too sharply, for the two are always held in tension; the one is tested against the other, and each is understood only in the context of the other. Historians of the emotions remind us that men and women give shape to their own lives, sometimes attempting to conform to the prevailing standards, sometimes internalizing them, sometimes resisting, but always negotiating between experience and precept, in the process giving history its distinctive, human contours.[6] Historians of the emotions then ask and attempt to answer truly fundamental questions about the human experience, about how history is experienced and how it is created, about the conditions under which we live our lives and our capacity for reshaping those conditions or perhaps even transcending them.

There is more to emotions history, however, than the obvious fact that emotions count: they count, but they also change. Historians dealing with emotion, or accounting for emotion's role in their particular topics, have to place emotion in a specific historical context and explain alterations in context and therefore in emotions' impact in real historical settings. Here, the relationship with more conventional historical topics is interactive. Emotions change in some instances because of familiar historical developments—think of the impact of factory work, for example, on emotional expression, or the interactions between emotional responses to death and the events of the Vietnam War. At the same time, events can reveal the impact of emotional change caused by other, more amorphous forces, including deliberate attempts to manipulate emotional outpourings in the interests of political order or social hierarchy.

The Development of Emotions History

The field of emotions history per se is both old and new. Many historians have evoked emotional context when describing rituals or riots, and of course biographers have often conveyed the emotional characteristics of their subjects. When social history was being created as a field of scholarly inquiry by French historians in the 1920s and 1930s, leaders like Lucien Febvre specifically appealed for work on the nature and impact of emotional change. A host of works, from art histories to explorations of childhood, have yielded relevant materials. Anyone concerned with emotion in the past will find a vast trove of data in a variety of historical inquiries.[7]

The formal study of the history of emotions, however, dates back less than two decades. Conventional historians, dealing with politics or great ideas, rarely treated emotions as more than a footnote. More surprisingly, many biographers shunned too much attention to emotions because of their elusive quality. It was hard, even in dealing with individual people, to know what emotions caused, unless a Freudian perspective was adopted in the style of psychohistory. For their part, social historians in the United States and Britain were initially eager to downplay emotional qualities of the lower classes. Work on social protest, particularly, urged the rationality of crowd behavior and argued that people carefully selected targets according to reasoned expectations about how merchants, landowners, or political leaders should operate.[8]

As it evolved, however, social history helped focus attention on emotions. Family history is a case in point. Many social historians who dealt with the family were particularly interested in birth rates or family structures, and used quantitative materials to establish the domestic settings in which people lived. As this work advanced, however, historians were increasingly tempted to ask additional questions about the emotional qualities of family life. What happened to the emotional relationships between parents and children when the birth rate was reduced, and only a few children competed for parental attention and affection? When marriage began to become less of an economic arrangement, as work moved outside the home, was there any impact on the emotional expectations of husbands and wives? By the 1970s, many historians, dealing with both European and American materials, were beginning to find distinct shifts in emotional aspects of family life, particularly in qualities of affection but also in attitudes toward anger. Expectations about emotional rewards from family life were also subject to change. From this it was a short step to explicit treatment of emotions themselves, with a focus on instances of change and the causes and consequences of change.

Family history was not the only precursor to emotions history. French work that focused on changing hygiene and public health practices led to important conclusions about redefinitions of disgust. Sociological studies of twentieth-century work patterns suggested major shifts from previous employment norms, toward greater emotional manipulability on the job site. An important series of studies of death in Western society strongly connoted points of change in patterns of grief, though the emotion itself was only rarely examined directly. Work on the major shifts in popular beliefs in early modern Europe shed light on changes in emotional values. Rhys Issac,

Jan Lewis, and Philip Greven applied this inquiry to eighteenth-century and early nineteenth-century America.[9]

In a real sense, emotions history resulted from new needs encountered in several branches of social and cultural history. Family relationships, no matter how quantitatively studied, obviously had emotional components, and these components, it began to appear, were susceptible to change. New emotional goals within the family might result from shifts in other family dynamics. One historian has argued, for example, that the decline in the property power and respect of older family members actually opened the door to greater affection for the elderly (particularly grandmothers) during the nineteenth century. Or emotional change might generate other alterations in family behavior: did a move toward more intense emotional attachment to infants cause or result from a lower birth rate? What was the relationship between emotional expectations and rising levels of divorce? The need to probe emotions as part of an expanding research agenda was not confined to family matters alone. Explorations of alterations in religious belief and the role of religion in the lives of ordinary people, for example, led to the first assessments of the changing meaning of fear in European history.

The discovery of the historical importance of emotional variables led to the explicit formation of emotions history per se. If family or religious or work history had a mutual engagement with emotional values and experiences, then emotions must themselves be exposed to direct historical scrutiny. A number of historians, beginning in the early 1980s, began to take up this task, which meshed readily with a growing interest in cultural factors—deeply held beliefs and values—in historical inquiry.

The Analytical Features of Emotions History

Over the past fifteen years, a number of further advances have occurred in the understanding of emotions in history. Additional emotions have been brought into play. Jealousy, for example, gained attention in its transition from a quite general, even admirable emotional concomitant to honor (the traditional view of aristocratic males), to an emotion related more strictly to rivalries for love. This collection extends the reach of emotions history by giving new attention to topics like the historical contexts for joy, for example, or interactions between depression and periods of literary creativity.

Distinctions in the nature of evidence and the degree of contact between professed emotional goals and real emotional experience have improved, as historians of emotion have learned to sort through some prior confusions. Historians seize most readily on written evidence about past emotions, and this evidence in turn is often prescriptive, approving or disapproving of various types of emotions and emotional expressions. Early statements of emotions history, stimulated by the evidence available but understandably hasty in its use, were sometimes crude: it was assumed that changes in stated emotional values equated readily with actual emotional experience. Thus one historian, dealing with the absence of prescriptive recommendations about love in religiously based family-advice literature in Renaissance England, assumed that actual families manifested about as much emotion as one would expect to find in a bird's nest. A dramatic image, but an inexact equation.[10] Historians of emotions have taught us to distinguish between precept and behavior, and also to interpret silences more carefully.

Explicit emotions history, as it has matured, offers a way to clarify the complex interrelationships between expressed emotional values and inner experience. Emotional standards (sometimes called emotional culture, or emotionology) play a distinct role in any society or group. They influence public representations, including law as well as literature. Think, for example, of the underpinnings of no-fault divorce law, instituted in the United States in the 1970s: a potentially searing emotional experience could now, legally, be regarded with cool neutrality. Emotional standards are not public guidelines alone, however. They also affect personal judgments, the second arena for inquiry into the impact of standards on social and individual life. Emotionology shapes the way other people's emotions, and one's own, are perceived and evaluated. A jealous American woman in the nineteenth century, for example, might be regarded as legitimately, if slightly childishly, needing more loving attention from family; her counterpart in the twentieth century, amid a different set of standards, may be essentially required to apologize for her petty possessiveness. Finally, in what is admittedly the hardest area for the historian to penetrate, emotional standards normally mold, without fully determining, the actual incidence and intensity of certain emotions. Thus a group that strongly urges against anger may well experience less of it, thanks in part to childhood socialization according to the desired cultural norms. But emotional experience itself requires some separate assessment, an admittedly difficult task that can, however, be approached through certain kinds of evidence, including self-report. Thus, somewhat hesitantly, historians have returned to discussions of such matters as the changing realities (as well as shifting public definitions) of love.

A central feature in any emotions history—and certainly the essays in this volume—is still the careful examination of the types of evidence used and their relation to stated standards. Historians of emotions must also be tested on the care they use in moving from emotional culture to wider discussions of perception and experience.

Explicit focus on emotions history also draws attention to the causes and effects of change. It was the discovery that aspects of emotional culture shift that stimulated emotions history in the first place, and here historians can claim a leading analytical role. Emotions may alter rarely, but they are not constant—and modern American history may have been unusually productive of redefinitions. The effects of emotions are also important. A tendency in emotions research more generally to regard emotions as an end product is less satisfactory in a historical framework, where connections to other behaviors and institutions can be sought. Links not only to family history but to developments in fields as disparate as law and sports spectatorship have been explored in light of emotional change. Historians of emotions have sought reasons for the redefinitions of emotional configurations (for example, why did anger come to seem increasingly infantile and unacceptable?) and have used emotional change itself as an explanation of wider developments in social and even political history. The history of protest, from this vantage point, must be considered yet again. Once a field for conservative laments over the mindlessness of crowd behavior, protest history shifted to a view of mass protest as a highly rational targeting by groups of people coherently organized and moved by definite goals; now, not surprisingly, this picture has been revised to include an emotional component fit within rational purposes and tactics but vivid and significant all the same. Politics, religion, and even consumerism constitute other fields in which shifting emotional formulations explain, as well as result from, more familiar historical currents. Essays in this volume variously attend to these issues of the causes of change and the impacts of new emotional standards.[11]

Admittedly, it remains more tempting to see emotions as a by-product, a result of larger social forces—indeed, perhaps a means of translating factors such as new economic organizations or altered political beliefs to the personal level. But it is vital, as well, to look to emotional redefinitions as causes of further developments, helping explain even some of the historian's more familiar targets such as changing strike rates or Americans' ambivalence about politicians and political life.

The focus on change moves the historian to attempt to formulate a periodization scheme in which clusters of developments could be coherently located. To be sure, specific processes may spark an independent redefinition of one particular emotion. The decline in infant death rates in the United States beginning in the 1880s inevitably shifted attitudes toward grief and mourning. Often, however, more general turning points can be identified. Work in emotions history to date, centered primarily on the middle classes, has generated considerable agreement on a preliminary periodization, at least in American history. Changes in the decades around 1800 and again around 1920 gain particular attention. Both these turning points involved new ideas—democratic beliefs, or a growing acceptance of leisure plus a new type of psychological expertise. Both involved economic change: the spread of commercial relations and then the rise of corporate management and a service, consumerist economy. Both involved movements toward redefining gender and real changes in male-female social interactions. Alterations in class relations—the result of new cities and concerns for respectability, in the first instance; a consumerist-induced reduction of class-specific behavioral norms around the twentieth-century change point—also played a role. Growing literacy, around 1800, and new media, in the 1920s, added further ingredients to the larger recipes for emotionological and emotional change. This dual periodization requires further testing—the field is far too young for definitive frameworks. Some of the essays in this volume explain how the chronology must be modified for key subgroups in American society. But the pattern is clear enough at least to facilitate good questions as emotions history presses into additional areas; there is no need to start with a blank slate.

A final attribute of emotions history to date involves its initially serendipitous coincidence with a surge of research in related fields. The topic of emotions arose from the expansion of historical concerns associated with the rise of social history— hence the agenda urged by the French pioneers more than half a century ago—and then specific issues raised in family history and other areas. But this historical contribution coincides with growing interest in emotions in several branches of psychology, philosophy, sociology, and anthropology. After a period of interest in emotion inspired by Darwinian concerns (emotions' evolutionary function) and laboratory psychology (as described in the essay by Otniel E. Dror in this collection), explicit attention to emotion had declined. But by the 1970s new concerns about gender, about emotional complexities in contemporary industrial society, and about distinctions between human reactions and those of the instruments of artificial intelligence prompted renewed and varied research. The result poses interdisciplinary opportunities and challenges for historians. Some of the new attention to emotion focuses on presumed physiological or psychological constants, the so-called basic emotions; this approach has little relevance for the historian's interest in change over time. But among some psychologists—admittedly particularly amid a maverick group—and certainly most anthropologists and many sociologists dealing with emotions, an interest in the powerful, but variable, social or cultural construction of emotion lends obvious importance to the historical research agenda. Hence emotions history offers an unusual opportunity to use historians' findings to inform the work of other disciplines, less intrinsically comfortable with change, chronology, and periodization as variables, and a chance as well to incorporate insights as well as explicitly historical research from other sources. The historian's goal, in this field, can be at once to illumine the past and to contribute to an understanding of how emotions actually operate in real human contexts. The work helps explore the boundary line between unalterable features of human nature and the vast array of experiences essentially constructed by a highly variable set of cultural signals.[12]

New Approaches to the Study of the History of the Emotions

Although professional historians have been studying the emotions since at least the early part of this century, the field was not given focus until 1985, with the publication of Peter N. Stearns and Carol Z. Stearns's "Emotionology: Clarifying the History of Emotions." This essay gave retrospective shape to the field by identifying works that had examined the emotions in historical perspective. It also charted a course for future studies by bracketing several of the most nettlesome issues that confront any student of the history of emotions: How can we know what people in the past felt? Do the words they used to describe certain emotions, such as love, anger, joy, for example, have the same meaning today? If people in the past did not write about particular emotions, does this mean they did not experience them? Stearns and Stearns noted that these questions are difficult, if not impossible, for historians to answer: "the finding most obviously desired from a history of emotion—some plausible chart of the rates of love and anger or the experience of sexuality, joy, and grief—is unlikely to emerge with any precision" (824). Much more feasible was the study of "emotionology," a term they coined to denote the "collective emotional standards of a society" and to distinguish those standards from emotional experience (813). By narrowing the historian's task and defining it with precision, Stearns and Stearns gave the new field an important boost, which has led to the publication of a number of new works in the field.[13]

The essays in this volume demonstrate how the field of the history of emotions has developed in the dozen years since the publication of "Emotionology." A number of the essays in this volume follow the path charted in that article by delineating the emotional standards of particular groups outside the white middle class and particular periods, especially the essays by Timothy Kelly and Joseph Kelly, C. Dallett Hemphill, Cas Wouters, David R. Shumway, and Linda W. Rosenzweig. But historians, particularly those influenced by the methods of cultural history and literary criticism, have also developed other methods of studying the history of the emotions.

In his path-breaking methodological essay, Kenneth J. Gergen, a psychologist, maps out the ways psychologists and historians have studied the emotions and argues that the future lies with the approaches most congenial to historians. Until recently, Gergen contends, most psychologists and historians have shared a common set of assumptions: that their subject matter is "given in nature" and independent of human observation and that understanding is objective and cumulative. They have likewise shared an "essentialist view of mind," considering mental processes (including the emotions) part of the independent subject matter they study. This approach, which Gergen calls "history as psychological expression," corresponds to historians' attempts to study emotional experience, which Stearns and Stearns also have warned is problematic. For scholars who use this approach, Gergen notes, "The existence of the emotions . . . is never doubted; their expressions and effects may be controlled, channeled, or suppressed, but the fundament remains fixed." Gergen identifies a second paradigm shared by other historians and psychologists, "history as psychological progenitor," in which mental processes are seen as the "by-products of antecedent historical conditions." In this approach, the focus is shifted to the historical context — whether conditions of labor that may lead to alienation and false consciousness or the social history of romantic love. Although Gergen does not make explicit reference to the concept of "emotionology," clearly it has much in common with Gergen's "historical constitution of the psyche." Both challenge "the essentialism so endemic to psychological science" and both bring into question "the search for transhistorical and transcultural generalizations." Going beyond Stearns and Stearns, Gergen suggests that if we believe that "mentalities are socially constituted" (surely one of the implications of the focus on emotional standards), why study them unless we believe that they may shape human behavior and consciousness in some way? Then it is but a short step to concluding that subjectivity too is "socially constituted." If in the first paradigm, historians had to turn to psychologists for an understanding of the psychological substrate, in the second, psychologists must rely on historians to help them understand how emotional expression has been historically conditioned.

The approach Gergen finds most appealing, one that sees "psychological discourse as history," reflects the influence of poststructuralist and postmodern critical theory. Going one step beyond claiming that "mental events are socially constituted," this paradigm holds that what we call "mental life" is constructed discursively, by particular interpretive communities. Hence it is impossible for us to say whether there is or is not such a thing as "mental life" or "how (if it exists) it is constituted." After all, Gergen points out, from the time of Aristotle, thinkers have offered up lists of what they suppose are fundamental human emotions, yet each list is substantially different.

The most we can say is that at different times, different people have thought that there were different fundamental emotions, not that such emotions exist, have existed, or have been experienced independently of the person who made up the list.

Although he inclines to the discursive paradigm, Gergen recognizes that all approaches have something to offer. In fact, we may have the most to gain from a dialogue among these three approaches. Indeed, this volume may be viewed as precisely that sort of discussion. Most of the contributors to this volume favor the social-constructionist paradigm; as Gergen suggests, it is one naturally suited to historians. Several also employ the discursive methods of literary critics, in particular Otniel E. Dror, David R. Shumway, Kevin White, and Lucia McMahon. Here, the influence of Michel Foucault on cultural historians can also be seen. In a fascinating essay that draws from and modifies Foucault's argument in *Discipline and Punish* (1977), Dror shows how psychologists and physiologists at the turn of the twentieth century discovered that in the very process of being observed, the body changed its constitution: its temperature, its blood pressure, its gastric juices. Faced with an ever changing body that responded through the emotions to the emotions of the observer, turn-of-the-century psychologists and physiologists sought to free the bodies of both the observed and the observer from the operation of the emotions—not to liberate those bodies, but to know and discipline them. Also building on Foucault, Kevin White argues that twentieth-century sexual "liberation" in fact imposed a new discipline on men. David R. Shumway explores the discursive construction of a new ideal of marital intimacy in the early twentieth century, while Lucia McMahon uses the discursive practices of a young couple to discuss the construction of early nineteenth-century subjectivity.

If some contributors have borrowed from cultural studies and literary criticism, others turn to contemporary psychology and psychiatry. W. Andrew Achenbaum asks historians to pay attention to the work of psychologists and gerontologists on Alzheimer's disease and other physiological and psychological changes associated with the aging process. In his work, the emotions of the aging process, like old age itself, become, in Gergen's terms, an independent subject matter, an observable psychological substrate. Yet Achenbaum also urges historians to study the social history of aging and to use their imaginations; that is, historians must be at once medical scientists, social scientists, and humanists. Similarly, Bertram Wyatt-Brown, in his moving study of Reuben Davis, Sylvia Plath, and other twentieth-century American writers who transcended depression through artistic creativity, joins together medical science and literary analysis. Wyatt-Brown accepts the findings of contemporary psychiatrists that certain serious mental disorders have, at the very least, a chemical component. Their illnesses shaped the emotions of artists such as Davis and Plath, yet they turned their sufferings into art; Wyatt-Brown directs our attention to this creative process. Implicitly, he explores another dimension of the history of emotions: the deep empathy of the historian for his subjects. (This empathy is also evident in a number of the other essays, particularly those of McMahon and Jeffrey Steele.) Gergen and Dror question the possibility of scholarly objectivity; the subjects of our study are always mediated and hence altered by our own emotions. Historians like Wyatt-Brown suggest that rather than being the bane of historical analysis, the historian's emotions, when carefully deployed, may lead to new insights and deeper appreciations.[14]

While several of the contributors to this volume connect the history of emotions to psychology, psychiatry, and medicine, others reach out toward politics. Mary H. Blewett and Dolores Janiewski show how passion and its control became important elements in labor strife and racial politics. They reintroduce emotions into protest history, showing how various sides in conflicts tried to manipulate emotions and choose emotionally effective strategies. Jan Lewis deconstructs one of the enduring themes in American emotional history, the notion that private life is emotionally fulfilling while politics is wholly desolate. Neither, she suggests, is "given" in nature; rather, they are part of an ideology, constructed by early national political leaders in dialogue with women. Jeffrey Steele too asks us to examine what might be called emotional ideologies. The rituals and practices of mourning—part of the emotionology of mourning—functioned as ideologies (what Louis Althusser called "ideological state apparatuses") that "helped inculcate American citizens as middle-class 'subjects.'" Steele's suggestion that emotionologies might function as ideologies that were inculcated (or "interpollated," to use Althusser's term) into individuals enables the history of emotions to engage political history (via the concept of ideology) and psychoanalytic theory. In Steele's essay we see individuals—in this case, women and slaves—finding an ideological "terrain on which the damaging aspects of oppressive social conditioning can be engaged and changed." Painting on a smaller canvas, McMahon shows the way two individuals at once resisted and re-created the ideologies of romantic love and sexual difference; she argues that an individual's subjectivity—like gender roles—was constructed in relationship to others.

The essays in this volume thus may be read as precisely the sort of dialogue about methods and underlying assumptions for which Gergen has called.

An Emotional History of the United States: An Outline

If the essays exemplify new methods for the study of the history of emotions, they also suggest a new narrative for the emotional history of the United States. In a series of essays and books, Peter N. Stearns and his collaborators have pointed to key transitions in the history of emotions, one at the beginning of the nineteenth century, and another at the beginning of the twentieth. These transitions correlate and perhaps are in some measure caused by familiar social, economic, and structural changes in the United States: the emergence of a democratic form of government and an egalitarian social ethos, the market revolution, the abolition of certain social hierarchies, and the creation of an American middle class at the beginning of the nineteenth century; and at the beginning of the twentieth, the spread of urbanization and industrialization, the growth and importance of corporations, and the spread of a consumer economy and its attendant ethos. Both periods of change brought with them an emphasis on the management of emotions and an outpouring of prescriptive literature instructing Americans on how to control their emotions.[15]

The essays in this volume suggest, in fact, that the most salient theme in the history of American emotions may well have been a strenuous effort to suppress certain emotions while releasing others. As the essays by Jan Lewis, Mary H. Blewett, Dolores Janiewski, Michael Barton, Otniel E. Dror, and Timothy Kelly and Joseph Kelly suggest, at several points in American history, we can observe concerted efforts to manage, channel, and suppress certain emotions, in particular passion, anger, fear, and even emotion qua emotion. Essays by Susan J. Matt and Peter N. Stearns show that some of the efforts to channel and direct certain emotions can be directly related to the needs of a consumer economy. More important, however, in giving shape to the American emotional style, as the work of C. Dallett Hemphill and Cas Wouters suggests, may be the distinctive class structure and ethos of the United States. Hemphill demonstrates that the first period of change, just after the American Revolution, was part of the emergent middle class's attempt to define itself and prepare to succeed in a more egalitarian social order and competitive, capitalist economy. Similarly, Wouters argues that the absence of a hereditary aristocracy and the diversity of the American population explain Americans' preference for an "easy" social style. Comparing the United States to nations of Western Europe highlights "the specifically American integration process, characterized by relatively open competition, a high level of (status) anxiety, and a comparatively strong reliance on external social controls." The result has been an ongoing process of what Wouters has called "informalization." [16] Yet the easy and informal style so valued by the American middle class was by no means a natural or unmediated expression, but instead required active and vigorous efforts to achieve and maintain. Michael Barton shows how high-status journalism imposed new standards of restraint even as greater informality came to the fore at the end of the Victorian era.

At the same time, recent work in the history of emotions suggests, those strenuous efforts also produced if not the opposite effect, at least countertendencies in which some groups attempted either to resist the dominant emotionology or to reshape it for their own purposes. The clearest examples come from dispossessed groups, the poor women, black and white, who, R. Marie Griffith shows, found joy in Pentecostal Protestantism, and the poor blacks who, according to Kimberley L. Phillips, achieved emotional release through gospel music. When read together, the essays in this volume suggest that American emotional standards and emotional experience must be examined relationally; that is, the emotionalism of gospel music and Pentecostal worship can be understood fully only when placed against the drive for emotional control of mainstream churches, black and white. Likewise, as Blewett and Janiewski suggest, mainstream efforts at emotional control are inexplicable without reference to the perceived emotionalism of women, poor whites, and blacks.

An interest in the workings of gender, like those of race and class, informs many of the essays in this volume. It likewise complicates our understanding of the trajectory of American emotional history, showing us that there is not a unified, single narrative, but rather a set of shifting themes and counterthemes. The essays of David R. Shumway, John C. Spurlock, Kevin White, and Linda W. Rosenzweig may all be read as responses to and commentaries on Cas Wouters's discussion of an

"American habitus." Shumway, Spurlock, White, and Rosenzweig all suggest that a seemingly liberatory new sexual ideology in fact exacted its toll—if in different ways—on men and women. White is the most insistent on this point, arguing that the twentieth century brought (middle-class white) men "not liberation but entrapment." Read together, Shumway and Spurlock suggest that twentieth-century sexual advice literature created a new and elusive, if not impossible, standard of intimacy. And Rosenzweig argues that as "heterosexual interactions [now] took precedence over female friendship," friendships among heterosexual women became more difficult to sustain. White's emphasis on the costs to middle-class white men of the twentieth-century sexual revolution is intriguing. Gender studies have accustomed us to reckoning the costs of changing sexual ideologies to women; it may be a measure of the influence of gender studies on the history of the emotions that they now enable us to problematize the history of masculinity.

Although we can now sketch the rough outlines of an emotional history of the United States, it is clear that different groups have had their own histories. Sometimes those differences have been the product of the different social position of the group under consideration. C. Dallett Hemphill, Lucia McMahon, and Jan Lewis all suggest that the early nineteenth century created a single emotional standard for men and women, which placed a premium on self-control, candor, and affection, for example, at the same time that it maintained certain notions of sexual difference. Necessarily, then, the experience of women was different. Jeffrey Steele makes a similar point about mourning among women and slaves: that their very different social (and political) position shaped the way they enacted the dominant emotionology. In other cases, certain groups created their own emotional standards. Timothy Kelly and Joseph Kelly describe the history of American Catholics' discourse of fear (a discourse that became increasingly less resonant for the twentieth-century laity). And Hasia R. Diner draws our attention to the very different emotional experiences of immigrant Jews and Irish men and women. Diner helps us recover the history of how men and women felt.

The essays in this volume represent a significant step on the path toward understanding the emotional history of the United States and a powerful reminder of the complexity of history and the variety of human experience. They also call attention to the need for further work on issues ranging from emotions in biography to emotions in protest and politics. Even developments in the richly studied early twentieth century—when the complexities of love and consumerism are combined—invite further sorting out. The field reflects but also illumines some of the largest issues in American history.

What makes the study of emotions so stimulating and yet so maddening is the elusiveness of its subject, the knowledge that we can, in fact, never be entirely confident that our interpretations are correct. The shifting sands of human emotion and experience both bedevil and beguile us. As such, the endeavor is much like the object of its focus.

NOTES

1. Raymond Williams, *Marxism and Literature* (Oxford, 1977), 128, quoted in Andrew Delbanco, *The Puritan Ordeal* (Cambridge, MA, 1989), 2. For a discussion of historians' quest for objectivity, see Peter Novick, *That Noble Dream: The Objectivity Question and the American Historical Profession* (New York, 1988).

2. See, for example, the essays by Hasia R. Diner, R. Marie Griffith, and Kimberley Phillips in this volume; Delbanco, *The Puritan Ordeal;* and Perry Miller, "From Edwards to Emerson," in *Errand into the Wilderness* (New York, 1964), 184–203; quotation is on 190.

3. For a recent example, see Frank Costigliola, " 'Unceasing Pressure for Penetration': Gender, Pathology, and Emotion in George Kennan's Formation of the Cold War," *Journal of American History* 83 (1997): 1309–39.

4. See John Demos, *A Little Commonwealth: Family Life in Plymouth Colony* (New York, 1970); and the essays by Jan Lewis, Mary H. Blewett, and Dolores Janiewski in this volume.

5. See, for example, John R. Gillis, *A World of Their Own Making: Myth, Ritual, and the Quest for Family Values* (New York, 1996).

6. See, for example, the essays by Lucia McMahon and Jeffrey Steele in this volume; and Steven R. Stowe, *Intimacy and Power in the Old South: Ritual in the Lives of the Planters* (Baltimore, 1987).

7. Johann Huizinga, *Waning of the Middle Ages* (London, 1927); Lucien Febvre, *A New Kind of History* (New York, 1973), 9; Erik Erikson, *Young Man Luther* (New York, 1958).

8. George Rudé, *The Crowd in History*, rev. ed. (New York, 1981); Charles Tilly, *From Mobilization to Revolution* (Reading, MA, 1981).

9. David Hunt, *Parents and Children in History: The Psychology of Family Life in Early Modern France* (New York, 1970); Lawrence Stone, *The Family, Sex and Marriage in England, 1500–1800* (New York, 1977); Rhys Isaac, *The Transformation of Virginia, 1740–1790* (Chapel Hill, 1982); Jean Delumeau, *La peur en Occident, XIVe–XVIIIe siècles* (Paris, 1978); Randolph Trumbach, *The Rise of the Egalitarian Family: Aristocratic Kinship and Domestic Relations in Eighteenth Century England* (New York, 1978); Philippe Ariès, *Hour of Our Death* (New York, 1981); Robert Muchembled, *Popular Culture and Elite Culture in France, 1400–1700* (Baton Rouge, 1985); Philip J. Greven, Jr., *The Protestant Temperament: Religious Experience and the Self in Early America* (New York, 1977); Paul C. Rosenblatt, *Bitter, Bitter Tears: Nineteenth-Century Diarists and Twentieth-Century Grief* (Minneapolis, 1983); Arlie Hochschild, *The Managed Heart: The Commercialization of Human Feeling* (Berkeley, 1983); Alain Corbin, *The Foul and the Fragrant: Odor and the French Imagination* (Cambridge, MA, 1986); Jan Lewis, *The Pursuit of Happiness: Family and Values in Jefferson's Virginia* (New York, 1983).

10. Stone, *Family, Sex and Marriage;* see also Edward Shorter, *The Making of the Modern Family* (New York, 1975).

11. Peter N. Stearns with Carol Z. Stearns, "Emotionology: Clarifying the History of Emotional Standards," *American Historical Review* 90 (1985): 813–36; John Demos, "Shame and Guilt in Early New England," in Carol Z. Stearns and Peter N. Stearns, eds., *Emotion and Social Change* (New York, 1988), 69–86; Karen Lystra, *Searching the Heart: Women, Men and Romantic Love in Nineteenth Century America* (New York, 1989); Peter N. Stearns, *American Cool: Constructing a Twentieth-Century Emotional Style* (New York, 1994); Cas Wouters, "On Status Competition and Emotion Management," *Journal of Social History* 24 (1991): 699–717.

12. Michael Lewis and Jeanette Haviland, eds., *Handbook of Emotions* (New York, 1993); Rom Harré, ed., *The Social Construction of Emotion* (New York, 1986); Catherine Lutz, *Unnatural Emotions: Everyday Sentiment on a Micronesian Atoll and the Challenge to Western Theory* (Chicago, 1988); L. Abu-Lugbod, *Veiled Sentiments: Honor and Poetry in a Bedouin Society* (Berkeley, 1986).

13. See, for example, Kenneth A. Lockridge, *On the Sources of Patriarchal Rage: The Commonplace Books of William Byrd and Thomas Jefferson and the Gendering of Power in the Eighteenth Century* (New York, 1992); Linda W. Rosenzweig, *The Anchor of My Life: Middle-Class American Mothers and Daughters, 1880–1920* (New York, 1993); Stearns, *American Cool;* Carol Z. Stearns and

Peter N. Stearns, *Anger: The Struggle for Emotional Control in America's History* (Chicago, 1986); Peter N. Stearns, *Jealousy: The Evolution of an Emotion in American History* (New York, 1989).

14. For recent uses of empathy as a historian's tool, one implicit and one explicit, see James Goodman, *Stories of Scottsboro* (New York, 1994); and Thomas P. Slaughter, *The Natures of John and William Bartram* (New York, 1996).

15. See note 11.

16. See Cas Wouters, "Etiquette Books and Emotion Management in the Twentieth Century, Part I," *Journal of Social History* 29 (1995): 107–24; and idem, "Etiquette Books and Emotion Management in the Twentieth Century, Part II," *Journal of Social History* 29 (1995): 325–40.

Chapter One

History and Psychology
Three Weddings and a Future

Kenneth J. Gergen

Psychological science and historical scholarship have not always been congenial companions. For many historians, psychology has been a suspicious enterprise, an uneven fledgling in the intellectual world, disingenuously arrogating to itself the status of a natural science. Further, psychology's implicit agenda is hegemonic. In the present case, if psychological science furnishes foundational knowledge regarding human behavior, and historical study is largely devoted to understanding just such conduct across time, then history stands to be absorbed by the science—ancillary and subsidiary. Psychology's attitude toward history has been equally distant. As a child of cultural modernism, psychological science has treated historical inquiry with little more than tolerant civility. Psychology has been an enterprise struggling to develop general laws through scientific (and largely experimental) methods. Because of its newly fashioned commitment to empirical methods, preceding scholarship of the mind or scholarship about earlier mentalities was necessarily impaired. In an important sense, the past was a shroud to be cast away. Psychologists might scan historical accounts of earlier times in search of interesting hypotheses or anecdotes, but the results would most likely confirm the widely shared suspicion that contemporary research—controlled and systematic—was far superior in its conclusions. From the psychologist's standpoint, historians are backward looking, while the proper emphasis of research should be placed on building knowledge for the future.

Slowly, however, these disciplinary antipathies have begun to subside. With the emergence of new cultural topoi—globalization, ecology, information explosion, multiculturalism, and postmodernity among them—we encounter increased sensitivity to the artificial and often obfuscating thrall of disciplinarity. Division and specialization are falteringly but increasingly replaced by curiosity, dialogue, and an optimistic sense of new and fascinating futures. It is with the shape of this future that the present chapter is concerned. A marriage of history and psychology can take many forms, and reflexive concern over their differing potentials and shortcomings is essential. It is not merely a matter of intellectual and scholarly promise; long-standing traditions hang in the balance—to be strengthened or dissolved accordingly. These traditions are further linked to broader societal practices of moral and political consequence. In choosing our mode of inquiry, so do we fashion a cultural future.

With these concerns in mind, I wish to consider three contrasting orientations to this blending of orientations: history as psychological expression, history as psychological progenitor, and psychological discourse as history. Wherever possible, we shall keep issues of the emotions in the foreground; however, where the literature directs us to other psychological states and conditions, we shall find that the conclusions are also relevant to the emotions. I will not pretend to be impartial in this analysis. Indeed, the issue of moral and political impartiality is central to the discussion. At the same time, I make no claims to clairvoyance in these matters. These remarks are not intended as conclusive—the end of the conversation—so much as invitations to collective reflection on the building of a viable future.

History as Psychological Expression

My chief concern in the present analysis is the set of assumptions traditionally grounding central inquiry in both the psychological and historical domains. These assumptions, I will argue, while inviting certain forms of communication between history and psychology, are also problematic and delimiting in significant respects. Further, within certain forms of historical psychology, these assumptions are giving way to significant alternatives. For many, these latter developments represent important threats to the relevant disciplines. However, as I shall argue, these threats are more than offset by the manifold advantages, both to historical/psychological study and for societal life more generally.

Let us briefly consider several pivotal assumptions that traditionally conjoin these domains. I shall not lay out the terrain in any detail in this essay, as the assumptive paradigm is well elaborated within twentieth-century philosophy of science (as emerging within 1920s positivism and extending through logical empiricism to the Popperian extenuations in critical rationalism), and deeply embedded as an implicit forestructure within the everyday activities of scholars and scientists themselves. Briefly to recapitulate four of the central working assumptions within vast sectors of the disciplines today, we find commitments to the following:

1. *An independent subject matter.* Until recent years, historians and psychologists have virtually assumed the existence of their subject matters independent of the particular passions and predilections of the inquiring agent. This obdurate subject matter—given in nature—is there to be recorded, measured, described, and analyzed. Experience of this subject matter may serve as an inductive basis for the generation of knowledge or understanding. Contrasting accounts of the world may be compared against the range of existents to determine their relative validity.

2. *An essentialist view of mind.* Historians have largely joined psychologists in presuming that among the important subject matters to be explored are specifically mental processes, their antecedents and manifestations. Because human action is based on a psychological substratum (including, for example, emotion, thought, intention, and motivation), an illumination of psychological functioning is essential

for historical knowledge (lest history become a mere chronicle of events). Mental process is the pivotal focus of psychological science.

3. *Understanding as objective and cumulative.* Psychologists have expended great effort to insure the objective assessment of their subject matter. Instrumentation, computer control, experimental design, and test validation studies are only a few of the safeguards to objectivity. Although few historians would claim the world of the past to be transparent, most would agree that through the examination of manuscripts, letters, diaries, and other artifacts, one can construct accounts of the past that shed increasing light on the actual occurrences. Objective understanding may not be fully achievable, but the goal can be approximated in ever advancing degree. Further, in both disciplines objectivity serves as the foundation for cumulative knowledge. With increasing study of a given phenomenon—whether psychological depression or the Great Depression—scholars can achieve more fully detailed understanding.

4. *Value neutrality.* The pervasive tendency in historical and psychological inquiry has been a claim to ideological nonpartisanship. To be sure, scholars and scientists may harbor strong personal values, but these should in no way influence the assaying of evidence or the resulting account of the subject matter. The quest for objectivity in both cases is simultaneously linked to a belief in objectivity as liberation from ideology.

In large measure, these shared assumptions are also responsible for the emergence of a small but robust movement toward a historical psychology. Given broad agreement in metaphysical assumptions, a variegated range of exciting and challenging explorations into the interrelations between psychological process and historical change has emerged. It will be useful for the present analysis to draw several of these enterprises into focus, and then to examine several problematic implications. With these issues in place, we can turn to two further developments that offer alternative weavings of the historical and the psychological.

Assumptions in Action: Historical Psychology

As indicated, the assumptions outlined here essentially prefigure the dominant postures of inquiry. If we presume the existence of psychological process (entities, mechanisms, dispositions, etc.), along with an objectified historical context (that is, a context that exists independently of mental representation), then we are disposed to analyses that causally link mental predicates with historically specific events or actions. Two major forms of inquiry are favored: the first illuminating *psychological origins* of historically located actions, and the second focused on the *psychological outcomes* of specific historical conditions. While interactions between psychological and historical conditions are rare but noteworthy, most research tends to favor one of these causal sequences or the other. In the case of psychological origins, perhaps the premier efforts have been those of psychohistorians (see, for example, DeMause, 1982; Loewenberg, 1983; Brown, 1959), who typically presume the existence of various psychodynamic processes and focus analysis on the ways these processes manifest themselves in various historical events. Such analyses may consider the psychodynamic conditions of people at a given era of history (for example, Fromm, 1941), or the individual psychology of significant historical figures (for example, Erikson, 1975). While Martindale's work (especially 1975, 1990) on psychological motives giving rise to aesthetic appreciation and interests places primary stress on the mind as origin of history, his work is especially interesting in demonstrating that psychological states create context effects that loop back to alter their own character. Thus, for Martindale there are predictable historical trajectories derived from psychohistorical interactions.

Increasingly prevalent, however, is research in which mental states and expressions are positioned as effects of particular historical conditions. This work does not propose that psychological processes are products of these conditions; rather, the analyst presumes the existence of fundamental psychological processes (e.g., cognitive, emotional, motivational, etc.), and views the historical context as shaping their content, character, or expression. In effect, we might say, there is a *historical texturing* of the psychological. Work of this sort has sprung from many sources. There has been a long-standing concern, for example, with the ways processes of child development are situated within particular historical milieus (Aries, 1962; van den Berg, 1961; Kessen, 1990). Wide-ranging works such as those of Elias (1978) on the civilizing process, Ong (1982) on forms of cognition favored by oral as opposed to print cultures, and Elder (1974) on the psychological effects of the Great Depression also stand as important contributions to this form of inquiry. Researchers such as Simonton (1984, 1990) have even attempted to generate means of quantifying historical variables so as to predict historically specific levels of creativity, genius, or leadership. Perhaps the most extensive and concerted work within this domain has been that of Stearns and Stearns, including their history of anger in the American context (Stearns and Stearns, 1986), the evolution of jealousy in recent history (Stearns, 1989), and the fate of Victorian passions in twentieth-century life (Stearns, 1994). Further exemplars of inquiry in these various domains is contained in the volume *Historical Social Psychology* (Gergen and Gergen, 1984).

Approaching the Limits of the Tradition

As we find, each of the traditional assumptions outlined earlier is clearly manifest in these lines of inquiry. Each presumes the independent existence of its subject matter, the psyche as a "natural kind" available to scientific appraisal, research as objective and cumulative, and the research enterprise not itself ideologically invested. A significant enrichment of understanding has resulted from the pursuit of these assumptions, including among them the very development of the social/behavioral sciences as significant disciplines on the cultural landscape; an emerging sense of unity in questions of knowledge, its importance, and how it is to be pursued and taught; and an enormous body of inquiry serving to stimulate the intellect, the imagination, and public practice. Yet while there is much to be said for these endeavors, it is also important to realize their limitations. That we should applaud the traditional efforts is not in question; whether a single paradigm should suffice is yet another matter.

Three critical issues demand attention in the present context. At the outset, it is important to realize that the assumptions giving rise to this form of inquiry are themselves derived from a historically situated intelligibility. The assumptions as articulated give the impression of "first principles," foundations that transcend historical and cultural context. Yet the historically sensitive analyst will draw attention to the social conditions under which these assumptions emerged, and the part they may have played within the political and economic context of the time. The "grounding" assumptions, then, derive their legitimacy not from transcendent verities but from specific conditions of society. And if this is so, then there is no binding necessity for maintaining them to the exclusion of others. Or more positively, because they are optional they may be opened to broad-ranging scrutiny and alternatives invited.[1]

Such scrutiny begins in earnest when it is realized that these pivotal assumptions furnish no means of critical self- reflection. Once they are set in motion, there are no means of questioning their premises or intelligibly raising questions falling outside the ontology they circumscribe. Once it is agreed that knowledge is accumulated through empirical assessment of the world's givens, it is difficult to challenge this assumption. To question it on grounds that did not assume the ontology (e.g., on spiritual grounds) would be irrelevant to the venture (e.g., "mere mysticism"). To put empiricism to empirical test would be equally problematic. It would be conceptual mischief to suppose that empirical methods could prove themselves untrue.

Yet the problem is not limited to an incapacity for self- reflexivity. As we find, once the paradigm is in motion, all questions falling outside the bounded domain of empirical knowledge are placed in jeopardy. In particular, critics have long been concerned with the inability of the traditional orientation to speak to questions of human value. Because the language of value cannot unequivocally be linked to events in the material world, issues of value have been largely removed from discussion. Further, the pursuit of knowledge is concerned with establishing what is (or was) the case, it is said, and not with promulgating a canon of "oughts." Objective inquiry is not in the business of ideological propaganda. Yet, as critics insist, in his or her choice of descriptive terminology, explanatory base, method of exploration, and rationalizing metaphysics, the scientist/scholar is also acting in the world and inevitably shaping its future for good or ill. In spite of erstwhile claims to value neutrality, then, traditional research pursuits are inevitably ideological. Means must be found, it is argued, to restore a sense of moral and political responsibility to such endeavors.

There is a final issue, less profound in implication, but nonetheless significant. This concerns the tensions inhering in the dominant traditions of history and psychology, and the ways they are resolved within various forms of interdisciplinary work. Of particular concern, psychological study has generally, though not exclusively, been a generalizing discipline. That is, the chief attempt is to establish knowledge of human functioning that transcends both time and culture. In contrast, most (but not all) historical analysis has tended to be particularizing, concerned with the unique configuration of circumstances existing at different periods of time. In terms of our preceding discussion, these differences in propensity are not without political significance. For the generalizing disciplines, a conception of human nature as relatively fixed (of genetic origin) tends to prevail. Thus, there is a preference for explaining various social ills (e.g., aggression, poverty, drug use) in terms of individual, inherent tendencies, with an associated preference for strong state controls and political conservativism. ("One cannot change human nature, but only control its excesses.") For the particularizing scholar, the tendency is to view human nature as more mutable and multi-potentiated. Societal problems are more likely to be understood in terms of the particular configuration of circumstances (e.g., economic, attitudes and values, quality of governance), with policy solutions favoring collaboration and creativity over control and punishment.

In this context we find that many of the efforts just described, in their assumption of human action as an effect or expression of a fixed psychological substrate, will tend to privilege the universal over the particular. The existence of the emotions, for example, is never doubted; their expressions and effects essentially constitute the historical. Such expressions may be controlled, channeled, or suppressed, but the fundament remains fixed. Thus, psychological process remains a prevailing force in the generation of historical events, and the history of psychological processes can be written only in terms of the variations on the fundamental theme. We can appreciate these contentions more fully by contrasting this initial orientation with a second.

The Historical Constitution of the Psyche

In important respects, the second line of psychohistorical inquiry represents a more extreme version of the texturing approach just discussed. However, rather than the historical context serving to give content or conditions of expression to an otherwise fixed domain of psychological functioning, here we find that the historical constitutes the mental. That is, mental processes—both the ontology of the mind and the specific manifestations—are by-products of antecedent historical conditions. These conditions may be material: for Marxist historians, psychological conditions of self-alienation and false consciousness are the specific outcome of conditions of labor. The reconfiguration of labor would essentially eradicate these particular states of mind. For the most part, however, scholars have looked to the social conditions as the primary formative agents of psychological process.

This approach has been most inviting for a range of psychological states that are either marginal or controversial to the society more generally. Thus we are not at all discomforted by accounts of the social history of romantic love (for example, Hunt, 1959; Kern, 1992). Possibly because many feel uncertain that they never have or will experience such a state, and possibly because romantic love is essentially problematic to an Enlightenment ideal of a rational and objective functioning of the mind, there is a certain relief attendant on such historization.

However, the intellectual and ideological stakes are raised considerably when such analysis turns to psychological predicates more pivotal to our public institutions. For example, the radical implications of Lev Vygotsky's (1978) views on human development have not been lost on the professional psychologist. For Vygotsky, "There is nothing in mind that is not first of all in society" (142). In effect, for Vygotsky the processes of thinking and memory are not there in nature, prior to culture, but owe their very existence to cultural antecedents. At the same time, this view serves as a strong invitation to historical analysis. The periodist may attempt to locate unique psychological states resonating with the configuration of cultural conditions dominant at a given time. Exemplary is Badinter's (1980) analysis of the mother's "instinctive" love for her child, its genesis traced to particular political and intellectual conditions of the eighteenth and nineteenth centuries. My own work (Gergen, 1991) attempts to link various senses of self (as variously possessing a deep interiority, unity) to earlier eras, and argues for the contemporary (postmodern) erosion of this sensibility. Harre and Finlay-Jones's (1986) explorations of *accidie* and *melancholy* in the early European context are also apposite. Although cross- cultural in its focus, Lutz's work on the social constitution of emotions such as *fago* and *song* in the Ifaluk people of the southwest Pacific is highly compelling. Contributions to Harre's (1986) edited collection, *The Social Construction of Emotions,* add important dimension to the form of study.

It is noteworthy that most of the research on the sociohistorical constitution of mind has not been carried out by empirically oriented psychologists. This is perhaps not surprising, inasmuch as the implications of such work for traditional empirical psychology are little short of devastating. At the outset, such inquiry challenges the essentialism so endemic to psychological science, and so necessary to its claims to be studying "universal man." Not only is the search for transhistorical and transcultural generalizations thrown into question, but the very assumption of the science as cumulative is jeopardized. Today's empirical results, on this account, are indicators not of universal truths, but of historically contingent customs (see Gergen, 1994a). Or in terms of our previous concerns, this form of analysis reverses the privilege of the psychological over the historical. Here psychology becomes a tributary of historical analysis.

When their implications are extended, such analyses also favor a self-reflexive posture. This is primarily so because the analyst comes to appreciate the historical contingency of the very conceptions of human knowledge giving rise to historical study itself. For example, if mentalities are socially constituted, what are we to make of the concept of objectivity as state of mind, and the assumption of an unbiased relationship between a private subjectivity and the objects of study? The very idea of a mind separate from the world, existing within the body, and reflecting the contours of an external world becomes open to historical reflection (see, for example, Rorty, 1979). If subjectivity is socially constituted, then isn't all scientific description and explanation colored by (if not derivative of) the community conventions of the time? A space is opened, then, for self-reflexive dialogue.

Further, a view of minds as historically constituted begins to generate a moral and political sensitivity. In particular, if the mental is socially constituted, then forms of psychological being are essentially optional. And if they are optional, we may inquire into the desirability of existing modes of being, and the potentials inherent in potential alternatives. To illustrate, Averill (1982) argues for anger as a form of culturally situated performance. Anger in Western culture, for example, is not duplicated elsewhere, and what we might wish to term anger in many other cultures scarcely resembles what we take to be anger in our own. Under these circumstances, we in contemporary Western culture can raise questions about the desirability of our current construction of anger. Based on this premise, Tavris (1982) argues for a transformation in our cultural constructions, so as to reduce family violence and other crimes of aggression. More recently, Averill and Nunley (1992) extend these arguments to propose that people should create the emotional forms essential for fulfilling lives.

Finally, we find in this orientation the seeds for a dramatic recasting of the role of historian in matters of psychology. As we found in the preceding analysis, once mentalities are objectified, they will tend to make pivotal demands on all historical analysis. However, if the mental world is historically constituted, then historical understanding is essential to any further analysis of mind. The work of the historian becomes a necessary prolegomenon for further understanding in psychological science. To launch research into any psychological "phenomenon" without a grasp of the textual history giving rise to the very presumption of a phenomenon would be cavalier, to say the least. To carry out research without a sense of the sociocultural forestructure that sets the limits of the project's intelligibility would be myopic.

In spite of the profound implications of inquiry into the historical constitution of the psyche, it must be said that its practitioners have not typically been among the most active in pressing forward its more radical implications. In spite of the tensions, most of this work has proceeded within the traditional metatheoretical thrall. Practitioners have primarily set out to do illuminating historical work, justified in terms of its evidential base and without a particular ethico-political agenda. Such provocation is saved for a third form of psychohistorical inquiry.

Psychological Discourse in Historical Context

The most recent turn in scholarship is a dialogic companion to an array of interrelated movements recently sweeping the humanities and social sciences more broadly. These movements—variously indexed as poststructural, post-empiricist, post-foundational, post-Enlightenment, and postmodern—all tend to converge in their concerns on the construction of meaning through language and within community. That is, in varying ways they draw attention to the multiplicity of ways differing communities construct, typically in language, a local sense of the real and the good. Further, as it is commonly argued, because such constructions create and sustain particular forms of conduct, they simultaneously operate as forces of control or power within society. Most pointedly, as it is proposed, those standing at the margins of such communities may become subject to what, for them, are oppressive if not annihilative consequences of construction.[2]

These have been stirring if not dramatic dialogues, and their implications far-reaching. Of particular relevance to the present chapter, they have stimulated an alternative from of scholarship, devoted in this case to the historical and cultural circumstances giving rise to particular vocabularies in the ordering of social conduct. The argument here is not that mental events are socially constituted, as in the previous case. For most of these scholars the existence of mental life itself is undecidable. That is, whether or not there is "mental life" and how (if it exists) it is constituted are not questions generally felt to be answerable outside the confines of a particular interpretive community. The major concern, then, is with the discourses of mental life, people's actions made apparent or possible through such discourses, and the functioning of these discourses (and associated actions) within society over time.

Emotions as Discourse: An Illustration

To convey the logic of this work, I will illustrate with the discourse of the emotions. Attempts to define the emotions and elucidate their character have ornamented the intellectual landscape for over two thousand years. Two characteristics of this continuing colloquy are particularly noteworthy: first, the presumption of palpability, and second, the interminability of debate. In the former case, until the present century there has been little doubting the obdurate existence of the emotions. In the second book of the *Rhetoric,* Aristotle distinguished among fifteen emotional states; Aquinas's *Summa theologiae* enumerated six "affective" and five "spirited" emotions; Descartes distinguished among six primary passions of the soul; the eighteenth-century moralist David Hartley located ten "general passions of human nature"; and the major contributions by recent theorists, Tomkins (1962) and Izard (1977), describe some ten distinctive emotional states. In effect, in Western cultural history there is unflinching agreement regarding the palpable presence of emotional states.

At the same time, these deep ontological commitments are also matched by a virtual cacophony of competing views on the character of the emotions—their distinguishing characteristics, origins, manifestations, and significance in human affairs. For Aristotle the emotions constituted "motions of the soul"; for Aquinas the emotions were experienced by the soul, but were the products of sensory appetites; Descartes isolated specific "passions of the soul," these owing to movements of the "animal spirits" agitating the brain. For Thomas Hobbes (1651), the passions were constitutive of human nature itself, and furnished the activating "spirit" for the intellect, the will, and moral character. In his *Treatise on Human Nature* (1739), David Hume divided the passions into those directly derived from human instinct (e.g., the desire to punish our enemies), and those that derive from a "double relation" of sensory impressions and ideas. A century later, both Spencer's *Principles of Psychology* and Darwin's *Expression of the Emotions in Man and Animals* attempted to place the emotions on more seemingly certain biological grounds.

This interminability of debate is most effectively illustrated when we consider the "object of study" itself, that which is identified as an emotion. For example, Aristotle identified *placability, confidence, benevolence, churlishness, resentment, emulation, longing,* and *enthusiasm* as emotional states no less transparent than *anger* or *joy.* Yet, in their twentieth-century exegeses, neither Tomkins (1962) nor Izard (1977) recognizes these states as constituents of the emotional domain. Aquinas believed that *love, desire, hope,* and *courage* were all central emotions, and while Aristotle agreed in the case of *love*, all such states go virtually unrecognized in the recent theories of Tomkins and Izard. Hobbes identified *covetousness, luxury, curiosity, ambition, good naturedness, superstition,* and *will* as emotional states, none of which qualifies as such in contemporary psychology. Tompkins and Izard agree that *surprise* is an emotion, a belief that would indeed surprise most of their predecessors. However, whereas Izard believes that *sadness* and *guilt* are major emotions, they fail to qualify in Tompkins's analysis; simultaneously, Tompkins sees *distress* as a central emotion, while Izard does not.

There is a certain irony inhering in these two features of emotional debate, palpability and interminability. If the emotions are simply there as transparent features of human existence, why should univocality be so different to achieve? Broad agreement exists within scientific communities concerning, for example, chemical tables, genetic constitution, and the movements of the planets; and where disagreements have developed, procedures have also been located for pressing the nomenclature toward greater uniformity. Why, then, is scientific convergence so elusive in the case of emotions? At least one significant reason for the continuous contention derives from a presumptive fallacy, namely, Whitehead's *fallacy of misplaced concreteness.* Possibly we labor in a tradition in which we mistakenly treat the putative objects of our mental vocabulary as palpable, whereas it is the names themselves that possess more indubitable properties. Because there are words such as love, anger, and guilt, we presume that there must be specific psychological states to which they refer. And if there is disagreement, we presume that continued study of the matter will set the matter straight. After two thousand years of debate on the matter, one is ineluctably led to suppose that there are no such isolable conditions to which such terms refer.

This latter possibility has become more compelling within recent years, and particularly with the development of ordinary language philosophy. Wittgenstein's *Philosophical Investigations* was the major stimulus in this case, both questioning the referential base for mental predicates and offering an alternative way of accounting for such discourse. As Wittgenstein (1953) asks, "I give notice that I am afraid.—Do I recall my thoughts of the past half hour in order to do that, or do I let a thought of the dentist quickly cross my mind in order to see how it affects me; or can I be uncertain of whether it is really fear of the dentist, and not some other physical feeling of discomfort?" (32e). The impossibility of answering such a question in terms of mental referents for the emotion demands an alternative means of understanding mental terms. This understanding is largely to be found in Wittgenstein's arguments for use-derived meaning. On this view, mental predicates acquire their meaning through various language games embedded within cultural forms of life. Mental language is rendered significant not by virtue of its capacity to reveal, mark, or describe mental states, but by its function in social interchange.

Historicizing Psychological Discourse: Instances and Implications

Arguments of the preceding kind inform a genre of historical work concerned not only with emotion, but also with the full range of discourses on the nature of psychological functioning. The focus of inquiry is variously on the genesis and sustenance of psychological discourse, its modes of functioning within society, and the values and groups that it sustains (and suppresses). Illustrative are Suzanne Kirschner's (1996) exploration of the way contemporary conceptions of psychological development echo the narratives of neo-Platonist theological texts; David Leary's (1990) edited collection on the place of metaphor in the history of psychological theorizing; Gigerenzer's (1991) analysis of the influence of statistical methodology on psychology's emerging conception of cognitive functioning; Hacking's (1995) *Rewriting the Soul,* a historical inquiry into the conceptions of multiple personality and the politics of memory; Spacks's (1995) exploration of the emergence of boredom in the eighteenth century; and Herman's (1992) inquiry into the political roots of the discourse of psychic trauma. A broad sampling of historical work on psychological discourse is also contained in *Historical Dimensions of Psychological Discourse* (Graumann and Gergen, 1996).

This latter work begins to form a significant alternative to the stance of value neutrality pervading both the preceding psychohistorical enterprises. That is, rather than simply reflecting on the nature of the past, these latter inquiries use historical work in the service of moral/ethical critique with the aim of altering the shape of cultural action. This kind of value-based analysis is specifically invited by the assumption that what we take to be human action is neither given as an essence nor fixed within individuals as cultural disposition; rather, human action is woven into the fabric of discursive understandings. Thus, if the scholar can alter such forms of understanding—as in the case of the historicization of psychological discourse— then we enter a clearing in which choice is possible. To understand that the psychologist's conceptions of emotion, for example, are not maps of human nature but the outcomes of cultural tradition enables us to reflect on the relative value of these conceptions in comparison with other possibilities. The discourse is not fixed, but is rendered optional. Particularly illustrative of these concerns are Rose's (1985, 1990) Foucauldian explorations of the role of the discourse and methods of professional psychology in the political "disciplining" of the society; Lutz's (1988) critique of the androcentric biases fostered by the discourse of emotions in contemporary Western culture; and Sampson's (1988) analysis of the individualist ideology sustained by emerging conceptions of mental life.

The implications of this growing corpus of work for more traditional historical and psychological inquiry seem, at the outset, little short of annihilative. From the discursive perspective, it is difficult to locate a subject matter that is independent of the discursive/theoretical projects of the investigating agents. The very idea of an "independent subject matter"—whether the mind or history itself—lapses into incoherence. And with this turn, of course, so do essentialist conceptions of mental events or processes. If anything, these inquiries demonstrate the tenuous (if not tautological) relationship between our language of the mind and its putative referents. Further, the aspiration for an objective science/history begins to whither. Yes, the sense of objectivity may be achieved within a particular community of interlocutors. However, the scientist/scholar loses the warrant for claiming truth beyond community, some privileged relationship between words and world. Similarly, knowledge may accumulate, but only by virtue of the standards shared within an interpretive community.

Yet in the end, the annihilative implications of these arguments cannot be sustained. Should the discursive critic make claims to the truth of his/her critique, then the very grounds from which they issue are removed. More positively, this is to say that discursive inquiry does succeed in avoiding the pitfalls of gainsaying its own rationale. Whereas traditional inquiry has no means of questioning its own premises (e.g., presumptions of objectivity, value neutrality), the discursive scholar is invited into a posture of humility. Thus, the discursive critique of the traditions must itself be viewed as a discursive move, a means of carrying on intellectual life within the scholarly community, and relating this community to the broader society. The arguments essentially serve as an invitation to forms of conversation and relationship that may offer new alternatives for inquiry and new roles for the scholar.

Finally, we find that from the discursive perspective, neither psychology nor history is furnished an ultimate explanatory privilege. Neither psychological nor historical events are celebrated as the generative sources of action. In the discursive account, psychological processes are bracketed, thus seeming to give explanatory privilege to historical analysis. At the same time, one might counter that discourse analysis now replaces mental states as the central focus of historical analysis. However, because psychological discourse is integral to (and not separated from) social process, it is neither a cause nor an effect of social pattern. In effect, discourse both constitutes and is constituted by the historically located conditions of the culture. Neither mind nor material are paramount.

History and Psychology: Is There a Future?

We have surveyed three significant departures in the marriage of historical and psychological scholarship, the first drawing on traditional essentialist assumptions regarding both history and psychology, the second emphasizing the historical constitution of the psychological domain, and the third transforming both history and psychology to discourse. How should we now regard these ventures in terms of future investments? Should the traditional endeavors, still very robust, simply continue unabated in their hegemonic trajectory? Do the emerging alternatives now make it impossible to return to traditional work? Is there some form of amalgam that we should seek? These are complex questions, and discussions should remain open. However, we may draw several conclusions from the preceding discussion that may serve as useful entries into the dialogue.

At the outset, I find myself compelled by the various arguments seeding the discursive turn in social analysis. To be sure, the chief outcomes of historical and psychological scholarship are bodies of discourse—books, articles, lectures, and the like. The extent to which these bodies of discourse are referentially linked to events outside language must always remain in question; word-object relations are forever in motion ("infinite semiosis"), and words themselves are easily objectified even when there are no ostensible referents. Further, when we attempt to describe the world to which discourse could be linked, we again enter the corridors of discourse. To be sure, we may deconstruct this line of reasoning by resorting to its own forms of argument. However, such an act of deconstruction, though certainly valid, simultaneously reasserts the intelligibility of the discursive arguments.

With this said, however, we do not locate within the discursive orientation any foundational arguments against the preceding lines of investigation. Unlike the empirically based traditions, there is no presumption that research may proceed in an unbiased way to reveal what is (or was) the case. Thus, there is no means of discrediting a particular form of inquiry because it fails to participate within the paradigm (e.g., because it fails to employ traditional canons of evidence). Rather than ruling out forms of inquiry, then, the discursive scholar should ideally welcome a range of possible endeavors, each of which would speak for a given community, its traditions and values. The aim should not be to obliterate traditions of language but to enrich them. At the same time, we are sensitized by the logic of discursive inquiry to the potential effects of our study on intellectual, political, and societal life more generally. Thus, while not discrediting any particular form of study out of hand, we should explore the societal implications of all our inquiries, whether oriented around psychological process, historical analysis, or discursive process. To publish work without preliminary attention to the moral and political implications within one's cultural/historical context would, from the discursive standpoint, be arrogant if not inhumane.

What seems favored in the end is a dialogic marriage among equals. With no ultimate grounds of dismissal on any side, it may also be possible to appreciate the interdependencies of these various forms of inquiry, along with complementarities and potential affinities. With respect to interdependency, for example, with all its critique of objectively accurate analysis, discursive inquiry must indeed rely on the rhetoric of objectivity to render its analyses intelligible. Concerning complementarity, analyses favoring both the social constitution and discursive construction of the mind do tend to privilege social change over stability (liberal and transformative agendas over conservative). However, it is very unlikely that any analyst would favor a complete overhauling of all societal investments; absolute change would be the equivalent of absolute chaos. Transformation is possible only against the backdrop of a deep stability. And finally, there are opportunities for coalescence. For example, there is a high degree of overlap between the social constitutionalist and the discursive constructionist efforts. With the former shifting the emphasis from psychological states to culturally situated performances, and the latter embedding discourse within embodied actions, a powerful form of historical analysis would be consolidated. Perhaps within intellectual life, polygamy will prove a superior cultural form to monogamy.

NOTES

1. See Levy (1989) and Modell (1989) for discussions of some of these limitations.

2. For more extended discussion of the emergence of social constructionism, see my 1994 volume, *Realities and Relationships*. For a detailed analysis of the position of historical analysis within these debates, see Novick (1989).

REFERENCES

Aries, P. (1962) *Centuries of childhood: A social history of family life*. New York: Vintage.

Averill, J. (1982) *Anger and aggression*. New York: Springer-Verlag.

Averill, J. R., and Nunley, E. P. (1992) *Voyages of the heart*. New York: Free Press.

Badinter, E. (1980) *Mother love: Myth and reality*. New York: Macmillan.

Brown, N. (1959) *Life against death: The psychoanalytical meaning of history*. Middletown, CT: Wesleyan University Press.

Cohen, E. (1995) Towards a history of European physical sensibility: Pain in the later Middle Ages. *Science in Context*, 8, 47–74.

Corbin, A. (1986) *The foul and the fragrant*. Cambridge: Harvard University Press.

Coulter, J. (1979) *The social construction of the mind*. New York: Macmillan.

Danziger, K. (1990) *Constructing the subject*. New York: Cambridge University Press.

DeMause, L. (1982) *Foundations of psychohistory*. New York: Creative Roots.

Elder, G. H. (1974) *Children of the Great Depression*. Chicago: University of Chicago Press.

Elias, N. (1978) *The civilizing process*. New York: Urizen Books.

Erikson, E. H. (1975) *Life history and the historical moment*. New York: Norton.

Fromm, E. (1941) *Escape from Freedom*. New York: Rinehart.

Gergen, K. J. (1991) *The saturated self*. New York: Basic Books.

———. (1994) *Realities and relationships*. Cambridge: Harvard University Press.

———. (1994a) *Toward transformation in social knowledge*. 2d ed. London: Sage.

———. (1995) Metaphor and monophony in the twentieth century psychology of emotions. *History of the Human Sciences*, 8, 1–23.

Gergen, K. J., and Gergen, M. M. (Eds.) (1984) *Historical social psychology*. Hillsdale, NJ: Erlbaum.

Gigerenzer, G. (1991) Form tools to theories: A heuristic of discovery in cognitive psychology. *Psychological Review*, 98, 254–67.

Gordon, R. (1990) *Anorexia and bulimia*. Cambridge: Basil Blackwell.

Graumann, C. F., and Gergen, K. J. (Eds.) (1996) *Historical dimensions of psychological discourse*. New York: Cambridge University Press.

Hacking, I. (1995) *Rewriting the soul*. Princeton: Princeton University Press.

Hare-Mustin, R. T., and Marecek, J. (1988) The meaning of difference: Gender theory, postmodernism, and psychology. *American Psychologist*, 43, 455–64.

Harre, R. (Ed.) (1986) *The social construction of emotions*. Oxford: Blackwell.

Harre, R., and Finlay-Jones, R. (1986) Emotion talk across times. In R. Harre (Ed.) *The social construction of emotions*. Oxford: Blackwell.

Herman, J. (1992) *Trauma and recovery*. New York: Basic Books.

Hunt, N. M. (1959) *The natural history of love*. New York: Knopf.

Izard, C. E. (1977) *Human emotions*. New York: Plenum.

Kern, S. (1992) *The culture of love: Victorians to moderns*. Cambridge: Harvard University Press.

Kessen, W. (1990) *The rise and fall of development*. Worcester, MA: Clark University Press.

Kirschner, S. (1996) *The religious and romantic origins of psychoanalysis*. New York: Cambridge University Press.

Leary, D. (Ed.) (1990) *Metaphors in the history of psychology*. New York: Cambridge University Press.

Levy, R. I. (1989) The quest for mind in different times and different places. In A. E. Barnes and P. N. Stearns (Eds.) *Social history and issues in human consciousness*. New York: New York University Press.

Loewenberg, P. (1983) *Decoding the past: The psychohistorical approach*. New York: Knopf.

Lutz, K. (1988) *Unnatural emotions*. Chicago: University of Chicago Press.

Martindale, C. (1975) *The romantic progression: The psychology of literary history*. Washington, DC: Hemisphere.

———. (1990) *The clockwork muse: The predictability of artistic change*. New York: Basic Books.

Modell, J. (1989) A note on scholarly caution in a period of revisionism and interdiciplinarity. In

A. E. Barnes and P. N. Stearns (Eds.) *Social history and issues in human consciousness.* New York: New York University Press.

Morawski, J. G. (1985) The measurement of masculinity and femininity: Engendering categorical realities. *Journal of Personality,* 53, 171–97.

Novick, P. (1982) *That noble dream.* New York: Cambridge University Press.

Ong, W. J. (1982) *Orality and literacy.* London: Methuen.

Rorty, R. (1979) *Philosophy and the mirror of nature.* Princeton: Princeton University Press.

Rose, N. (1985) *The psychological complex: Psychology, politics and society in England, 1869–1939.* London: Routledge and Kegan Paul.

———. (1990) *Governing the soul: The shaping of the private self.* London: Routledge.

Sampson, E. E. (1988) The debate on individualism. *American Psychologist,* 43, 15–22.

Sarbin, T. R., and Mancuso, J. C. (1980) *Schizophrenia: Medical diagnosis or verdict.* Elmsford, NY: Pergamon.

Sass, L. A. (1992) *Madness and Modernism.* New York: Basic Books.

Semin, G., and Chassein, J. (1985) The relationship between higher order models and everyday conceptions of personality. *European Journal of Social Psychology,* 15, 1–16.

Shorter, E. (1992) *From paralysis to fatigue: A history of psychosomatic illness in the modern era.* New York: Free Press.

Simonton, D. K. (1984) *Genius, creativity, and leadership.* Cambridge: Harvard University Press.

———. (1990) *Psychology, science and history: An introduction to historiometry.* New Haven: Yale University Press.

Soyland, A. J. (1994) *Psychology as metaphor.* London: Sage.

Spacks, P. M. (1995) *Boredom: The literary history of a state of mind.* Chicago: University of Chicago Press.

Stearns, P. (1989) *Jealousy: The evolution of an emotion in American history.* New York: New York University Press.

———. (1994) *American cool.* New York: New York University Press.

Stearns, C. Z., and Stearns, P. N. (1986) *Anger: The struggle for emotional control in America's history.* Chicago: University of Chicago Press.

Tavris, C. (1982) *Anger: The misunderstood emotion.* New York: Simon and Schuster.

Tomkins, S. (1962) *Affect, imagery and consciousness.* V. 1. New York: Springer.

van den Berg, J. H. (1961) *The changing nature of man.* New York: Norton.

Vygotsky, L. S. (1978) *Mind in society: The development of higher psychological processes.* Cambridge: Harvard University Press.

Wiener, M., and Marcus, D. (1994) A sociohistorical construction of "depression." In T. A. Sarbin and J. I. Kitsuse (Eds.) *Constructing the social.* London: Sage.

Wittgenstein, L. (1953) *Philosophical investigations.* Tr. G. Anscombe. New York: Macmillan.

The Creation of an American Emotional Style
Class, Gender, and Race

Chapter Two

Class, Gender, and the Regulation of Emotional Expression in Revolutionary-Era Conduct Literature

C. Dallett Hemphill

> Fitch's Countenance is not Steady. He has a look of Jealousy, and of Diffidence. He has a look of Conceit, affectation, Suspicion, and Diffidence. His swell. His Puff. Gridley has a stedy and fixed face. His face is expressive. When he smiles his whole face is lighted up. His lips do not show a smile when his Brows are frounding, and his Eye complaining. The Brow, the Eye, the Lips and the Voice all alike affected together.

As a young man John Adams deemed it of crucial importance to observe others' faces.[1] He did so as part of a campaign to improve the mastery of his own. He apparently thought it was necessary to control this potential window into the emotions, and to actively manipulate facial features to convey certain impressions (or deny certain truths) about his emotional inner state. We find these comments on some fellow lawyers among various legal notes of the winter of 1763. Adams had not yet gained fame or elite status, although he had started on the path to both with his Harvard education and fledgling legal career. His diary allows us to follow this man of middling origins as he painstakingly acquired gentility.

Adams's diary is full of such observations, especially in young adulthood. The nature of his comments—especially his minute attention to his own and others' faces, posture, and demeanor—is interesting in light of a new level of concern with control of the body and face that is evident in the period's published advice on proper conduct.[2] Taken together, the changes suggest that notions of genteel behavior were undergoing a subtle but important transformation in the hands of, and for the benefit of, ambitious men like John Adams.

Before the middle of the eighteenth century, most of the printed conduct advice on early American bookshelves consisted of imported Renaissance courtesy works and their English imitations. These works, which described the proper deportment of gentlemen, were intended for and owned only by the elite. By and large the only conduct advice intended for the middling and lower sort was that delivered via Puritan sermons and tracts that circulated in New England; and it was mostly concerned with securing deference to the elite and reinforcing patriarchal order within households. The mid-eighteenth century brought considerable change in this scenario. Far fewer works were directed to the elite alone, and American printers and booksellers from Boston to Philadelphia began to supply a broader group of prosperous Anglo-American families with a new sort of conduct advice, written by some American but mostly British authors of middling social status. Their works remained popular into the first decades of the nineteenth century. The provenance of this literature means that the changes examined here in the American context were part of a transatlantic phenomenon, and the "revolutionary era" referred to in these pages, approximately 1740 to 1820, was that of the larger transformation to modernity at work in Western society, not simply in the new American polity. Owing to American republicanism and the American social structure, however, the "middling" nature of these works had special power here.[3]

In these works, middling authors appropriated the aristocratic code of the older courtesy books and remade it for their own class. Above all, they greatly elaborated on the older code's injunctions for control of the body and face. The middling writers also stamped the code as their own by shedding earlier concerns for hierarchical relations and inscribing a clear disaffection with servile behavior. In presenting a new code that emphasized physical self-control among peers, they gave men of middling origins the tools for convincing others of their individual creditworthiness. The new self-control thereby aided in a new sort of self-presentation increasingly important in the context of rising capitalism.[4] Self-control could also serve as the sign (as well as the means) of one's successful self-madeness. The conduct works thus show the early stages of the evolution of middle-class culture, a culture derived from, but more co-optive than imitative of, aristocratic culture.

In recent decades, scholars such as Stuart Blumin and Mary Ryan have explored middle-class culture in the antebellum period. Karen Halttunen and John Kasson have fleshed out the picture in cultural terms through the use of conduct literature. All these scholars date the emergence of the middle class to the nineteenth century, largely owing to Blumin's socio-occupational definition of the middle class, which is dependent on the emergence of a new white-collar class in that century.[5] But examination of the clear transition in the conduct literature that dates back to the middle of the eighteenth century suggests that the social values that these and other scholars associate with middle-class culture, above all the linked concepts of self-madeness and self-discipline, began to emerge earlier than has been acknowledged. They were bound up with the challenging of aristocratic power and the hold of the traditional social hierarchy at work in Western society, which was in turn part of the long evolution of Western societies of orders into class societies.[6]

This larger cultural sea change—the result not only of the accumulating impact of commercial capitalism but also of Enlightenment thought—went beyond altering the prevailing system of social stratification, bringing all previous inequalities into question. Accompanying the rise of middle-class culture was a revolution in gender relations. Not only did a new basis for gender relations need to be worked out as a result of the cultural revolution against hierarchy, middle-class women had a need similar to that of middle-class men to make their own way in a new competitive world of peers. While the links are not yet fully clear to twentieth-century scholars, it does seem apparent that women, too, were increasingly improving themselves with an eye to more successful performance in a market. The relevant market in their case was not usually that of the economy, but the analogous, and related, one of marriage.[7]

So, along with advice for middling men, conduct writers began to give greater consideration than ever before to proper female behavior. Here they had a large task, for where they had an aristocratic male code to appropriate for men, that code had had considerably less to say about female manners. Both Renaissance courtesy works and Puritan tracts had tended to discuss only the proper behavior of women as wives. Beyond that, the behavior women learned as inferior youth was thought to suit them for life. But now that hierarchy was being thrown out as an ordering principle, proper female behavior had to be considered more fully. Through their conduct advice, the authors took the first steps at integrating women into their vision of the social world, while groping toward new notions of gender difference to accommodate persisting female inequality in the new world of peers.

This essay will consider both the implications of the conduct advice for the history of emotions and the implications of those emotion rules for these larger cultural trends, including gender relations. Obviously, conduct books do not give us access to the history of emotions per se. As explicitly prescriptive sources, they allow only an exercise in what may be called "high emotionology," for they reveal only emotion rules or standards, not the actual experience of emotions.[8] Indeed, their very pre-scriptions tell us that the authors of these works presumed that individuals could control the expression of their emotions, whatever they were feeling inwardly. But conduct works are an excellent source of contemporary ideals for the expression of various emotions before others. They can be especially revealing if one focuses on specific rules for face-to-face behavior rather than the more abstract and moralistic discussions often found in these works. In particular, we find the conduct writers discussing the management of emotion when they considered a person's proper demeanor, facial expression, and conversation with others.

In giving advice on these matters, the authors not only suggest what emotions they were really concerned about—thereby giving a glimpse of the "emotional culture" of their time—they also discuss them in the context of specific relation-ships.[9] The explicitly social contexts of conduct advice can help us see how some of the primary emotions discussed in twentieth-century psychology textbooks might have been combined, construed, and thus experienced in the early modern context. Of all the "basic" emotions, for example, only anger is discussed directly. Other such primary emotions—such as love, fear, anxiety, joy, or sadness—are usually either lumped together in discussions of the overall propriety of emotional expression or so combined and socially situated in face-to-face conduct advice as to become as much attitudes as feelings (not unlike the compound feelings Adams detected in the faces of his fellow barristers). Of chief concern in revolutionary-era conduct literature were the following such socially contingent feelings: pride, "easiness," modesty, reverence, awkwardness, bashfulness, mirth, gravity, familiarity, reserve, and self-possession. Here and throughout, I generally use the authors' own terms, for they suggest not only which feelings the authors were most interested in encouraging or discouraging, but also when, with whom, and how.

So, while strictly normative, the evidence from conduct literature can tell us much about the relationship between contemporary rules for the expression of emotions and social change. Above all, it sheds light on the conjuncture of the history of emotions, the origins of middle-class culture, and the construction of modern gender roles. The rules for face-to-face behavior discussed in these works evoke a new world of individualistic strivers. They suggest that the possibilities of that world depended on one's ability to exert emotional self-control. A smooth facade would allow middling men to both achieve and assert their worth, by keeping vital information from competitors and demonstrating their own worth via gentility. Women could also secure and assert their status through emotional self-control. To a considerable degree, and for the first time, they received advice similar to that dispensed to men. But the market most important to them did have some special requirements. Women were told that a well-balanced modesty would allow them to both attract and restrain potential marriage partners. If anything, their market was the riskier.

John Adams's obsessive concern with control of the body and face in the years he was accomplishing his rise in social status may provide a clue to the huge influence of the most important conduct work of the revolutionary era, Lord Chesterfield's *Letters to His Son.* Chesterfield's work, published posthumously in 1775, immediately became a best-seller in America. The worldliness of his advice prompted criticism, but English and American publishers quickly came out with versions that both excised the most offensive parts and made the conduct rules scattered through the letters more accessible by categorizing them. The work was reprinted dozens of times in these various forms, and passages were borrowed wholesale by other writers through the nineteenth century. What was it that Americans found so compelling about Chesterfield's message? [10]

Chesterfield was an aristocrat, but his work was adapted by middling writers for middling readers. They could do so because he was vague about class distinctions. He often ridiculed pride in rank and place as well as an overbearing attitude toward servants, who in his opinion were equals in all but material wealth. Other revolutionary-era conduct works shared these traits, probably reflecting both the fluidity of a status system increasingly based on wealth alone and Enlightenment thinking about the natural equality of men.[11] Along with the increasing prosperity and literacy of at least some ambitious Americans of middling origins, this class vagueness made the new conduct literature available to a much wider audience than ever before.

More important, Chesterfield's was a manual for strivers. His chief message to his son was that he should work to appear a certain way, regardless of his true character, natural endowments, or inner emotional state. His advice was thus to cultivate appearances, even, when necessary, to dissimulate. While this message has to have contributed to the moral ambivalence middling Americans felt about Chesterfield, it must also explain why they all read him, over and over again, decade after decade. His was advice for those on the rise, those whose class status hinged on their own efforts; his appearance-crafting mantra appealed to those in the process of making themselves. It also had important implications for the expression of emotions.

In contrast with early colonial advice, most revolutionary-era advice concerned relations with equals, not superiors. The little advice that revolutionary-era authors gave concerning behavior with the latter warned the middling not to go so far in showing respect as to appear servile, a caution the authors did not feel compelled to offer the lower sort. Whereas earlier conduct writers had lumped the middling and lower sort together as "ordinary folk" in their prescriptions, the fate of these two groups diverged in revolutionary-era works.[12] This was especially apparent in the period's abundant advice concerning relations with equals. Here, especially, instead of the old gap between the elite and everyone else, the new middling authors included the middling among the potentially genteel by giving them similar advice to that given the elite. This trend was owing, in large part, to the immediate influence of Chesterfield's *Letters* on works for the middle class, but the advice in works that addressed the middling sort was always more extensive and elaborate than advice intended for the elite alone. The elaboration only underscored the central message for middling readers: more than ever before, the new gentility depended on self-possession.

   Certainly the prevailing ideal for one's manner or air in the presence of peers was that expressed by Chesterfield and repeated in works for the middling and elite alike. The striking thing about this advice was the degree to which it prescribed a certain emotional pose, while allowing that such a pose might or even should be different from one's actual inner state. In so doing, these authors were underscoring what was always implied in conduct advice, but it is significant that they drew attention to this demand. In general, one was to conceal one's actual feelings by keeping one's guard up. Specifically, and to use their language, one was to appear "easy and affable" and to strike a balance between formality and familiarity. Chesterfield placed enormous emphasis on this, claiming that an easy manner was initially more important in relations with equals than one's inner talents and virtues, which took more time to be discovered. John Adams confirmed the currency of this distinction between inner worth and outer display when he regretfully confided to his diary that "The Drs. Air and Action are not . . . natural and easy. . . . This however Sub Rosa, because the Dr. . . . is an excellent man." The writers also recommended a degree of reserve with equals, another notion that Adams echoed in his diary. Some authors repeated Chesterfield's suggestion that "the general rule is to have a real reserve with almost everyone, and a seeming reserve with almost no one." This disguised reserve was a new feature of genteel behavior, and thereby hints further at the manipulation (of both self and others) implied in the new self-presentation.[13]

   Writers for the middle class spelled out the emotional implications of this civil and easy manner when they added some more straightforward injunctions against appearing fretful, melancholy, or surly. They also recommended a certain humility in manner, arguing that a haughty air was inconsistent with courtesy. But one was not to be so humble as to fail to preserve one's dignity. Again, one was never to appear servile.

We learn still more about the construction of an "easy" manner and the proper limits of humility—and confront again the influence of Chesterfield—in the frequent warnings to both the middling and the elite against awkward bashfulness. Chesterfield pronounced it shameful if a person could not enter company without embarrassment. He recommended a certain dignity and "exterior seriousness" in manner. But what he stressed over and over was the importance of avoiding awkwardness. Gracefulness, to Chesterfield, was the most important attribute of a person's demeanor. Writers for the middling repeated this advice but warned more emphatically that one's gracefulness should not seem affected. John Adams voiced this concern when he noted that his mentor's "Grandeur" was "diminished by stiffness and affectation." Indeed, Adams often disparaged affectation in others, observing of one acquaintance that "Affectation runs thro the whole Man. His Air, his Gate, his Tone, his Gestures, his Pronunciation." In spurning affectation, the conduct writers were asking for a behavior that was "natural" as well as "easy." But they did not assume that gracefulness came naturally, for they gave extensive advice about how it might be acquired. It was simply never to *appear* contrived. In giving extra warnings about affectation to the middling, then, the conduct writers were really telling them that a convincing performance required work. If one came across as ill-at-ease, one had not practiced enough. Adams's pairing of affectation with "stiffness" was no accident.

Works that addressed the middling also gave similar but more elaborate advice than works for the elite concerning proper facial expression before peers (one author went so far as to prescribe a woman's proper facial expressions when watching a play). As was true of advice regarding body carriage generally, the extra advice to the middling on facial expression urged greater mastery. Again Adams's diary suggests that these concerns were current, as when he regretfully observed of another lawyer that he "has too little command of the Muscles of his face." Some control of the countenance was deemed important for all persons, for the face was thought to reveal one's character and thoughts. Chesterfield recommended "a certain degree of outward seriousness ... and decent cheerfulness" in one's "looks." Both silly smiles and melancholy or sour expressions were to be avoided, as well as "all unnatural distortions of the face." Benjamin Rush accordingly noted that his son Samuel behaved like a perfect gentleman but for his frown.[14]

A host of authors joined Chesterfield in urging both upper- and middle-class readers to avoid laughing aloud, an expression "at all times ungraceful." To our ears this is one of the strangest of revolutionary-era demands. The advice to middle-class readers on this point was again more detailed (do not laugh in church, at table, at your own jokes, etc.), and somewhat varied (a number of authors condemned only "immoderate laughers"), but all the authors agreed that this was a matter of importance, that "nothing shows a genteel person more than laughing decently." Chesterfield said he objected to laughter because it distorted the face and made unpleasant noises. But we might also note historian John Kasson's observation that unrestrained mirth undermined one's proper self-control.[15]

The issue of emotional self-control implicit in all this advice is explicit in Chesterfield's warning, repeated in a number of works for the middling, to beware revealing too much in one's face. The authors urged both the elite and the middling to "Display as much as you can an unruffled and serene countenance" before others. Chesterfield warned that "A man who does not possess himself enough to hear disagreeable things, without visible marks of anger and change of countenance, or agreeable ones without sudden bursts of joy, and expansion of countenance, is at the mercy of every artful knave or pert coxcomb." Chesterfield begged his son to make himself "absolute master" of his countenance, to keep his face "as unmoved and unembarrassed as possible," "whatever you may feel inwardly," for "a tell-tale countenance . . . is a great unhappiness." Abigail Adams agreed when she criticized a man because, among other things, "His countenance plainly speaks the ruling passions of his mind." Only one author offered like advice to the lower sort.[16] These counsels were new; they had no counterpart in earlier conduct advice. Their newness again confirms the importance of manipulation of the outward self in the developing bourgeois version of gentility.

Consistent with this advice on facial expression, both the elite and the middling were urged to stifle all expression of anger in conversation. But works that addressed the middling contained quite a few additional instructions to this end. One was not to be surly or rude to peers. One was not to use contemptuous, reproachful, or abusive language to or about others, especially behind their backs. One was not to take offense at others' contradictions or reproofs. One was to take others' wrongs patiently, acknowledge one's own faults, and ask pardon when one had offended. Disagreements were to be treated gently and with good humor, not as opportunities to speak one's mind. One was to stay calm and not be too eager for victory.[17]

By asking readers to remain thus "unruffled," revolutionary-era conduct writers were asking them to master their feelings, or at least to stifle expression of them. Indeed, one needed to manufacture feelings of calm self-assurance in order to give a convincingly graceful genteel performance. This theme of self-mastery was not entirely new, as it was often the subtext of prescriptions for gentlemen in the courtesy works that circulated in the early colonial era. But Lord Chesterfield made it his central concern, and brushed aside the traditional pieties that one's outward appearance should match one's inner state. Indeed, he openly urged his son to appear better than he really was, to avoid letting others witness any lapses in his self-mastery, and to hide any feelings that others might use against him. The message was so cynical that contemporaries balked at it, but they also made Chesterfield a best-seller. And writers for the middle class only elaborated on his message.

Why was this message so useful to the middling? Why did middling authors embrace and build on the old aristocratic self-control advice in this new more instrumental vein? The rising middle-class man of the revolutionary era (as we shall see, the emphasis on self-control was strongest in advice to men) was one who achieved independence by his own efforts, not by virtue of his membership in a group. Status was now a function of one's personal behavior, as an individual, and thus required self-discipline. Self-discipline entailed, above all, control of physical drives and emotions, hence focus on the body and face. And one had to prove as well

as attain one's status in an ever more competitive marketplace. The visible performance of self-mastery was especially important to middle-class men whose self-
presentation was central to their maintenance of creditworthy reputations. They
needed to appear in control. John Adams bemoaned losing his temper in a political
discussion, for example, berating himself that "A Character can never be supported,
if it can be raised, without a good a great Share of Self Government." [18] Further, one's
feelings conveyed information best kept from one's social, economic, or political
competitors. And the expression of certain feelings, such as irascibility, might put off
a potential client, patient, or customer.

Self-presentation was more important than ever at this time when new men were
asserting their claims to worthiness. It was an infinitely more subtle task than in the
past because these same men were throwing out the old regime of deference. It was
also more difficult because of the continued development of cities and commerce—
one encountered more and more strangers whom one had to convince. Again,
self-control became both the sign and the substance of the message; that is, the
accomplishment of a new more challenging self-mastery both signified and justified
one's inclusion among the genteel.[19]

The other hallmark of revolutionary-era conduct advice, especially that addressed
to the middling, was a new emphasis on peer relations. Apparently ideas were finally
catching up to the social and economic realities that had long been undermining the
old order; the old model of static hierarchy was being washed away and replaced by
a platform on which all could compete, if sufficiently prosperous. But the impact of
this tide was not confined to class relations, for the old hierarchy was modeled on
the patriarchal family. As it crumbled, the question of women's place in the new
order could no longer be ignored.

A clear sign of this concern is the extended discussions of women's education that
were published in the latter decades of the eighteenth century. In a desire to understand women's place in the new order, historians have focused on the descriptions of
women's special role that are embedded in some of these discussions, especially in
the new republics of America and France.[20] An equally important development,
however, has been missed: the more conscious discussion of women's unique role in
the new republic was dependent on the implicit integration of women into what had
previously been regarded as the world of men. New proclamations of women's special
and different role were accompanied by equally new but perhaps less consciously
given conduct advice that asked women to behave just as it asked men to. At the
same time, the integration of women into the new world of individuals made them
vulnerable to new dangers. Manners suggest that their sexual safety, in particular,
was in their own hands. These were the concerns that shaped rules for the expression
of feelings by women.

The new middle-class woman limned by conduct advice, then, while somewhat
different from her male counterpart, was not his opposite. She needed to veil her
sexuality as she stepped on to the stage of society, but step up she did. Manners
indicate that women won a kind of social equality in the new order, at the same time
that they may have been losing influence in the political and economic realms.[21]

Only time would tell if this would be sufficient to bridge the glaring gap between the new ideal of equality and women's continuing legal subordination. In the meantime, manners reflect the ongoing groping of Euroamericans for means to deal with the contradiction.

Revolutionary-era conduct writers began to address more works to women than to men, a dramatic reversal from the early colonial period.[22] While we cannot assume that the actual readership of these books conformed to the gender audience suggested by the authors (diary entries and library evidence readily suggest that this would be a mistake), the works clearly reflect the new interest in female education and women's role in society. The authors of these tracts, like those of the entire body of revolutionary-era conduct literature, were primarily middle-class Englishmen. The cultural trends of both "anglicization" and the beginnings of middle-class culture thus applied to women as well as to men. While perhaps especially salient in the more rapidly democratizing American environment, the changes that were taking place in contemporary thinking about women, like the changes in class relations, were happening on a transatlantic scale.[23]

How did the advice to women proffered by these authors compare with the period's advice to men? While the new middle-class man needed to guard his emotional expression in order to demonstrate his self-control and protect his affairs from competitors, the new middle-class woman needed to guard her emotional expression in order to protect herself from men. This was necessary in order to preserve capital in the marriage market, as many writers warned women that men would be watching for opportunities to take advantage of them and "will always be ready to take more than you ought to allow them." The conduct advice is consistent with historians' observations that women were adopting new self-controls in the area of sexuality and that a double standard of sexual morality was emerging, as older communal controls fell away in this era of growing individualism. But while their market situations were analogous, women had a more delicate emotional balancing act than men, because they needed to preserve a certain pleasing openness to attract the right customer. Moreover, they were not allowed the same degree of emotional dissimulation, for the modest blushes that were supposed to guard them from predators were to be real, not feigned.[24]

These themes are clearest in advice to women that specifically concerned encounters with men. Instead of asking women, as they asked other "inferiors," to show respect for men, they asked them to adopt a somewhat reserved demeanor with men. They claimed that a woman could and should protect herself from men's familiarities by always maintaining a modest and dignified air. If this did not suffice, and a man attempted improper advances, she was to reduce her complaisance. But while some authors encouraged her to treat such a man with an "air of resentment," others urged women to respond with civility. And all the authors agreed that women should never express too much disdain. This was prudery, in their minds an affected modesty, for true modesty allowed women to be gentle and sweet to men. Women were not to be shy or severe in the presence of good men; they were to be relaxed and gay. But they could not be too easygoing, which behavior might be taken as an invitation to impropriety. Young Eliza Southgate of Maine had clearly taken this advice to heart when she wrote to her cousin respecting a new suitor that "I will endeavor . . . to steer between the rocks of prudery and coquetry, and take my own sense of propriety as a pilot that will conduct me safe." It was a fine line to steer.[25]

The authors told women that their facial expressions played an important role in determining men's conduct. As *The Lady's Library* insisted, " 'tis certain a modest Countenance gives a Check to Lust." Women were to wear "*Looks* that Forbid without *Rudeness,* and oblige without *Invitation,* or leaving room for the Sawcy Inferences Men's Vanity suggesteth to them upon the least Encouragements." More than any other quality, a woman's face was to show her modesty. The authors lamented that some women wore bold and forward looks and expressions, or an "unabashed countenance." It was allowable for women to smile in an effort to please men, or even to laugh, but they were not to forget proper delicacy. A number of authors heartily approved of blushing, arguing that a blush was an external sign of a woman's modesty, and thus the most effective reprimand for men's improper talk or actions. These authors denounced the woman who "hath forgotten to blush." But women were not to affect a blush. Women were also to check improper behavior or talk on the part of men by showing a marked disapproval in their faces; they were to frown or to give men a gentle but "awful look." If they failed to do this, the authors warned, men would take it as an invitation to continue their offensive behavior. Women were to have a particular guard over their eyes. Lord Halifax urged his daughter to "have a perpetual *Watch* upon your *Eyes,* and . . . remember, that one careless *Glaunce* giveth more advantage than a *hundred words* not enough considered; the *Language* of the *Eyes* being very much the most significant, and the most *observed.*" Women were to make sure their eyes did not betray a weakness for any man, as this would encourage him to act boldly. A few authors suggested that "when at any time she discourses with men, she must look a little downwards, or on one side, not stare in their faces, lest it be interpreted in the worst sense."[26]

A woman's talk with men was to be imbued with the same qualities as her demeanor and face: it was to be cheerful and gay, but with just the right amount of modest reserve to awe men into proper behavior. Young women were warned not to betray a particular fondness for a man. But severity was appropriate only when a man made truly indecent suggestions; in that case a woman was not to hesitate to reply with firmness.[27]

As far as revolutionary-era conduct writers were concerned, the burden of controlling men's passions lay on women's shoulders. They simply failed to give men any advice asking them to control themselves in this area. This is significant, given the enormous stress on physical self-control in advice to men regarding their behavior in general society. If self-control was the hallmark of the new man, the abnegation of male responsibility in the sexual arena was a way of reminding women that they had not yet earned equal treatment in the moral realm.[28] In fact, the conduct writers' stance reflected a reality of seduction and a sexual double standard that is also refracted through other evidence of the period, whether court records, newspaper accounts, ballads, stories, or novels. More than ever before, a woman was on her own in courtship; the influence of family and community was ebbing with the rise of privacy and individualism.[29] She had to watch out for herself. And her modesty, as expressed through her demeanor, face, and talk, was thought to be her best defense.

Although middle-class men were given more detailed advice encouraging them to exercise control over their bodies and faces, while women were asked to cloak their behavior with modesty, the most significant facet of the new prescriptive literature was the substantial similarity in instructions. This was a dramatic departure from the conduct advice circulating before the mid-eighteenth century, which had very little to say about proper female behavior outside marriage. What this trend amounted to in emotional terms was a narrowing of the gender gap in expectations for emotional self-control.

Most of the demeanor instructions addressed to the middling and upper sort, for example, were addressed to women as well as to men. Both sexes had to present an appropriately cheerful and courteous front to others, avoiding both excessive formality and undue familiarity. Both sexes were urged to maintain a certain reserve with others. The only differences were of degree: the importance of both complaisance and reserve was emphasized a bit more in advice to women (reflecting their somewhat more difficult emotional balancing act) than in advice to men.

Both sexes were urged to have a modest demeanor, and yet to avoid an awkward bashfulness, before peers. There were important gender differences in this advice, but again they were differences of degree. Conduct writers agreed that modesty was the most essential quality in a woman's demeanor. Some implied that modesty distinguished proper female from male behavior by imposing a measure of restraint on the traits that were recommended to both sexes. Modesty was also thought to keep a woman from "robust," "bold," and "masculine" airs. Other writers claimed that modesty in women was an attractive timidity and diffidence, while they urged men to show "a modest assurance." But the authors did not push this; as one warned women, "Do not confound the ideas of modesty and timidity." Far from an awkward bashfulness, some claimed, proper female modesty entailed dignity of manner. Still, women were not to strive for a "confidant ease," while men were; and the authors warned men more frequently than they warned women against awkwardness and bashfulness. All in all, the authors seemed to be encouraging the display of feelings of self-confidence a bit more in men than in women.

But these important nuances should not blind us to the equally important fact that with the possible exception of boldness, the authors did not urge any traits on men that they did not also recommend to women. And they charged both sexes equally with the final challenge of making their demeanor in general society seem artless and unaffected.[30] Conduct writers were searching for ways to distinguish the sexes, but their efforts, working against the stronger and broader trend of gender integration, went only so far.

Much of the period's advice on facial expression in genteel company was directed to both men and women. The authors urged both sexes not to wear frowns or contemptuous expressions. Both were to smile, though not all the time or at anything improper. Both were cautioned about laughter. Both sexes, in other words, were urged not to express ill humor or unrestrained mirth in their faces, but to maintain the same expression of "easy" (read controlled) affability.[31]

Some face advice did vary according to sex, along the same lines as advice on demeanor. Chesterfield and his imitators deplored men's "being out of countenance" and looking embarrassed in company; while authors for women urged them to strive for modest facial expressions. Some authors even commended "shamefacedness" and downcast eyes, though most simply asked women to avoid a "daring," "masculine," "bold," and "unabashed countenance." A number of authors argued that an unaffected blush at improper behavior on the part of others was both an indication of modesty and a "powerful charm of beauty." But the authors did not push the expression of female sensibility. While a few authors believed that a woman's delicacy might sometimes cause her "to melt into affectionate sorrow" or an "effusion of tears," affected weeping and weeping at trivial causes were explicitly discouraged.[32]

Anger constituted another area of overlap and differentiation. The advice writers implored both men and women to avoid all expression of anger, for example, but they gave the sexes different reasons for doing so. They told women that an angry face was unattractive and immodest. "Passion is a prodigious enemy to beauty," declared James Forrester: "it ruffles the sweetest features, discolours the finest complexion, and, in a word, gives the air of a fury to the face of an angel." Another author claimed that "I never knew an angry woman preserve her beauty long." Men had to suppress the expression not only of anger, but also of every other emotion, including distress and joy, and they were to do so on the grounds that it was simply imprudent to display every thought and feeling. As noted above, the period's strongest (and most Chesterfieldian) advice to mask one's feelings was directed to men alone. More than women, men were implored to keep their faces as calm and unmoved as possible.[33]

Rules for conversation in general society conveyed the same themes regarding proper expression of emotion by men and women. Both sexes were to speak with modesty, but this, predictably, was especially recommended to women. Women were to avoid overly "forward," "confident," or "bold" talk, although their modesty was not to be affected. Meanwhile, Chesterfield and his followers stressed the importance of an assured and unembarrassed manner to men.[34] And, consistent with their greater need for self-control, men received more extensive advice on specific ways to avoid contention.[35]

By giving women many of the same instructions that they gave men, revolutionary-era conduct writers showed that they now regarded women as rightful players in the social world. Exactly how far women had come in the writers' minds, however, depends on the meaning of their recommendations of modesty. Why did the writers focus on modesty (an old theme, but one to which they gave new prominence) in their efforts to distinguish the sexes? Then as now, the term had several meanings. In the context of women's encounters with men, the emphasis was on modesty as an expression of sexual propriety. Indeed, a woman's modesty was to be so strong that it would not only keep her from improper sexual behavior, but also prevent men from behaving improperly toward her. This sort of modesty was enjoined on women only. But revolutionary-era authors also used the term "modesty," especially when discussing female behavior in general society, in its other sense: modesty as humility, the avoidance of excessive displays of self-assurance. In this sense, the word could apply to men, especially young men, but there it was more of a qualifier on a stronger injunction to display self-assurance—modesty was to keep men from going too far. In any event, revolutionary-era conduct writers were far more insistent that modesty serve to restrain women's behavior, in both senses just described. Their invocation of modesty was strong and frequent enough to justify the third meaning of the term, then as now: modesty as "womanly propriety." Indeed, most of the time the authors felt no need to define the attribute; they simply prescribed it. Overall, they seemed to be asking women to behave like men were to behave, just in an appropriately feminine (chaste and humble) way.

Besides the greater invocations of modesty in advice to women, the other gender difference in revolutionary-era advice was the greater detail in self-control instructions to men (outside the realm of sexuality). Ambitious men probably had more of a need than did women for the display of self-control because of their greater commercial and political roles. Perhaps this is why, in their efforts to differentiate the sexes, the thrust of the authors' message to women was that they would appear most feminine when not fully sure of their *selves.* Examined together, the conduct advice for men and women suggests that men were the first middle-class subjects, the first individuals in this age of growing individualism. The role of middle-class women followed close behind, but as the relevant market for most of them was the marriage market, the primary focus of their self-control was sexual. Beyond that, the advice to men and women was similar, indicating that women were newly regarded as part of the social world.

Scholars have come to associate the rise of middle-class culture with separate spheres and the domestic female; but the rules for face-to-face behavior did not construct a particularly domestic or even familial role for women (in part because Americans looked chiefly to British authors for conduct advice, the rules construct no "Republican Mothers" or "Republican Wives"). In this period of transition, when women were first gaining entry into the world of men, they appeared first as variations on a male theme.[36] To make this observation is not to dismiss or even diminish their rise, but simply to acknowledge the enormity of the challenge it presented. This is why so much attention was devoted to female education in this period. Conduct writers, male and female, were wrestling with a new role for women. They had an older aristocratic construction to work with for men; but for the new social woman they had to start from scratch.

The revolutionary era was thus a period of transition in gender as well as class relations. Only time would reveal the outcome. Clearly British and American conduct writers were groping toward a place for women in their democratizing worlds. They saw women in their visions of the social scene, but were struggling to come to terms with their presence. They tried to sort out male from female behavior, but their efforts were superficial, belied by the deeper imperative of inclusion in this "enlightened" age. But inclusion raised the specter of equality, which may in turn have fueled the search for difference. The immediate result of this conceptual tug-of-war was a sense of wariness—it seemed that all fathers could do was warn their daughters that their sexual safety was in their own hands. But this was uncomfortable. It underlay the strikingly androgynous emotional guidelines and child-rearing advice that lasted into the 1830s. The search for a better solution would continue in the antebellum decades, when, for better or worse, a different approach was found. That solution would not be greater gender differentiation, as is often assumed of the advice literature, but the striking of an enduring bargain: men would take on the responsibility of self-control in their relations with women and transform seductive gallantry into protective gallantry. Women would acquire social superiority in the resulting system of "Ladies First," but with it the enduring handicap that that superiority was a fiction, a token compensation for their continued inequality in the bourgeois public sphere.

What do we learn about the formation of the modern class and gender system from the changes in emotional standards that accompanied its emergence? We learn that mastering the expression of one's feelings was extremely important. Older beliefs, from humoral medicine, that the body would change according to inner pressures were almost reversed: detailed control of body and face must supersede emotions themselves. To be convincingly genteel in a world of market competition and social flux, one needed to present a smooth facade. This meant a dignified manner with those who were richer or more powerful, an affable and unruffled way with servants, and, most important, a reserved but "easy" manner with peers. Above all, one was never to express strong feelings. This would signal that one had not achieved self-control and would give others an advantage. It was especially necessary for ambitious men to observe these rules. Middling women also had to exercise emotional self-control, but the advice to women was often shaded by the special requirements of the marriage market, that is, relations with men. Women had a difficult emotional task, in that they needed to preserve a certain pleasing and sincere openness at the same time that they were being asked to behave in such a way as to restrain men's passions. The burden this presented reminds us that the social world women were entering was still a man's world. The emotional difficulty of women's social role may explain the different fates of the systems described here in the antebellum era. The culture of self-manufacture sketched in revolutionary-era conduct works could maintain its established trajectory as it developed in the antebellum era and as the middle class acquired social hegemony, while the etiquette of gender relations had to undergo significant changes to arrive at more satisfactory ritual solutions to the problem of gender inequality in a democratic society.

NOTES

1. John Adams, *Diary*, ed. L. H. Butterfield (New York, 1964), 1:242.
2. All inquiry into these matters must acknowledge a debt to Norbert Elias's pathbreaking *History of Manners*, trans. Edmund Jephcott (New York, 1978). Adams's comments on facial expressions can also be read as evidence of his engagement in the "elocutionary revolution" explored by Jay Fliegelman in *Declaring Independence: Jefferson, Natural Language, and the Culture*

of Performance (Stanford, 1993), 2–3 and passim. I do not think these inquiries are mutually exclusive, although analysis of the conduct literature does lead me down the different path of the explicit class and gender analysis attempted here.

3. The impulse to look to England for models of behavior was facilitated by the increasing economic and political involvement with the mother country and spurred by the contemporary belief in the cultural degeneration of colonial society. It was also spurred by the fact that it was often cheaper for American printer/booksellers to import British works or publish pirated editions of those works than to pay American authors for native productions. See Jack P. Greene, "Search for Identity," *Journal of Social History* 3 (1970): 195–219; Cathy Davidson, *Revolution and the Word: The Rise of the Novel in America* (New York, 1986), 36.

4. Toby Ditz discusses merchant male self-presentation in connection with "the cultivation of credible public personas" in "The Instability of the Credible Self: Credit and Reputation among Eighteenth-Century Philadelphia Merchants" (paper presented at the Davis Center Seminar, April 1995), 5.

5. Stuart Blumin, *The Emergence of the Middle Class: Social Experience in the American City, 1760–1900* (Cambridge, 1989); Mary Ryan, *Cradle of the Middle Class: The Family in Oneida County, New York, 1790–1865* (Cambridge, 1981); Karen Halttunen, *Confidence Men and Painted Women: A Study of Middle-Class Culture in America, 1830–1870* (New Haven, 1982); John Kasson, *Rudeness and Civility: Manners in Nineteenth-Century Urban America* (New York, 1990). Kasson also discusses the relationship between manners and emotions in the nineteenth-century context, chap. 5.

6. See C. Dallett Hemphill, "Middle Class Rising in Revolutionary America: The Evidence from Manners," *Journal of Social History* 30, no. 2 (winter 1996): 317–44, for a fuller exposition of this argument, description of the changing literature, and treatment of all, not just emotion-related, conduct advice.

7. Some other scholars are exploring the links between this earlier period of the formation of middle-class culture and gender change; see Jacquelyn C. Miller, "An 'Uncommon Tranquility of Mind': Emotional Self-Control and the Construction of a Middle-Class Identity in Eighteenth-Century Philadelphia," *Journal of Social History* 30, no. 1 (fall 1996): 129–48. Miller finds an interest in emotional self-control on the part of both men and women in the private writings of middling Philadelphians. See also Konstantin Dierks, "The Feminization of Letter-Writing in Early America, 1750–1800" (paper presented at the Second Annual Institute of Early American History and Culture Conference, June 1996).

8. On emotions/emotionology, see Peter N. Stearns and Carol Z. Stearns, "Emotionology: Clarifying the History of Emotions and Emotional Standards," *American Historical Review* 90, no. 4 (October 1985): 813–36.

9. See Peter Stearns, "Girls, Boys, and Emotions: Redefinitions and Historical Change," *Journal of American History* 80, no. 1 (June 1993): 36.

10. One aspect of the offensive worldliness was that Chesterfield turned his back on the Anglo-American tradition of embedding conduct rules in moralistic advice and reinvigorated an older Continental emphasis on the smaller details of behavior and the importance of gracefulness—he was not so much trying to teach his son to be a good person as he was trying to help him get ahead. The most objectionable parts reflected Chesterfield's rather utilitarian attitude toward women. John E. Mason, *Gentlefolk in the Making: Studies in the History of English Courtesy Literature and Related Topics from 1531 to 1774* (Philadelphia, 1935; rpt. New York, 1971), 107, 253, 286, 297, 369; Virgil B. Heltzell, "Chesterfield and the Tradition of the Ideal Gentleman" (Ph.D. diss., University of Chicago, 1925), abstracted in *University of Chicago Abstracts of Theses, Humanistic Series* (Chicago, 1928), 328; Arthur Schlesinger, *Learning How to Behave* (New York, 1968), 10, 11, 79 n. 14; Frank Luther Mott, *Golden Multitudes: The Story of Best Sellers in the United States* (New York, 1947), 303, 304. One widely reprinted version was *Principles of Politeness,* arranged by John Trusler, an English minister (he also added a few rules); Esther Aresty, *The Best Behavior* (New York, 1970), 151–52.

11. Mason, 108; James Mott, *Observations on the Education of Children and Hints to Young People*

on the Duties of Civil Life (New York, 1816), 10, 26; John Burton, *Lectures on Female Education and Manners* (New York, 1794), 59, 60, 165. On changing behavioral prescriptions accompanying changing attitudes toward servants, see Hemphill, 330–32.

12. See Hemphill, 322–24.

13. Examples of the advice described in this and the next two paragraphs can be found in the following sources: L'Abbe d'Ancourt, *Lady's Preceptor, or a Letter to a Young Lady of Distinction upon Politeness*, 5th ed. (Woodbridge, NJ, 1759), 7, 10–11; Phillip Dormer Stanhope, fourth earl of Chesterfield, *Letters to His Son* (New York, 1775), 1:39, 65, 70–71, 72, 86–87, 121, 148, 2:9, 83, 3:38–39, 104, and the revised and abridged edition, *Principles of Politeness* (Philadelphia, 1778); [William Ramesay], *Gentleman's Companion, or, A Character of True Nobility and Gentility in the Way of Essay* (London, 1672), 70; George Savile, marquis of Halifax, *The Ladies New Year's Gift: Or, Advice to a Daughter*, 3d ed. (London, 1688), 124–25; William Penn, *Fruits of Solitude*, 8th ed. (Newport, 1749), 48; John Hamilton Moore, *The Young Gentleman and Lady's Monitor*, 5th ed. (New York, 1787), 18, 19, 21–29, 223, 224–25, 228–30, 249, 255, 265, 280, 282; John Gregory, *A Father's Legacy to His Daughters* (Philadelphia, 1775), 72–73; *The Polite Lady*, 2d ed. (London, 1769), 14, 15, 206; Eleazur Moody, *The School of Good Manners* (New London, 1754), 1, 14, 26; Burton, 70, 163, 165, 169; *The Guide or Counsellor of Human Life* (Springfield, MA, 1794), 41, 57–58; Giovanni Della Casa, *Galateo* (Baltimore, 1811), 51–53, 264, 265, 267, 268, 269, 270, 273; Tommy Trapwit, *Be Merry and Wise* (Boston, 1762), 12, 14; John Bennett, *Letters to a Young Lady* (Hartford, 1791), 2:7, 8, 27, 42; [Jacob Bailey], *A Little Book for Children* (Portsmouth, NH, 1758), 6, 7; Mott, *Observations*, 18, 20; [J. Williams], *Youth's Virtuous Guide* (Boston, 1818), 3; Enos Hitchcock, *Memoirs of the Bloomsgrove Family* (Boston, 1790), 74, 79; *The Female Friend* (Baltimore, 1809), 112–13; Jonas Hanway, *Advice from Farmer Trueman, to His Daughter* (Boston, 1810), 118, 142; John Barnard, *A Present for an Apprentice* (Boston, 1747), 52. Adams, 1:71, 83, 172, 242, 2:375; another Founder of middling origins, William Paterson, wrote in a college essay that "The true gentleman is easy without affectation." Cited in Gordon Wood, *The Radicalism of the American Revolution* (New York, 1991), 202; Benjamin Rush, *Letters of Benjamin Rush*, ed. L. H. Butterfield (Princeton, 1951), 1:251; see also Richard Bushman, *The Refinement of America* (New York, 1992), 371.

14. *Polite Lady*, 114, 207, 208–9; Chesterfield, 1775, 1:71, 86, 148, 2:11, 84; 1778, 38–39; d'Ancourt, 11, 16; Lady Sarah Pennington, "An Unfortunate Mother's Advice to Her Absent Daughters; in a Letter to Miss Pennington," in *The Lady's Pocket Library* (Philadelphia, 1792), 147; Adolf Franz vom Knigge, *Practical Philosophy of Social Life* (Lansingburgh, NY, 1805), 29; Moore, 18, 99, 224, 228, 235, 265, 267; Hitchcock, 74; Bennett, 2:7, 27; John Griffiths, *A Collection of the Newest Cotillions, to Which Is Added, Instances of Ill Manners to Be Carefully Avoided by Youth of Both Sexes* (Northhampton, MA, 1794), 12; Jean Baptiste Morvan, l'abbe de Bellegarde, "Politeness of Manners and Behavior," in The *Ladies Companion* (Worcester, 1824), 27 and the earlier edition, *Politeness of Manners and Behavior in Fashionable Society* (Boston, 1821); Moody, 13; *A Family Book for Children* (Hartford, 1799), 44; William Dover, *Useful Miscellanies Respecting Men's Duty to God and towards One Another* (Philadelphia, 1753), 32, 33; Trapwit, 14; Della Casa, 24–25, 116, 178, 179, 181; *The Polite Academy*, 3d ed. (London, 1765), vi–vii; [Nancy Dennis Sproat], *The Good Boy's Soliloquy* (New York, 1818), 9; [Nancy Dennis Sproat], *The Good Girl's Soliloquy* (New York, 1819), 10; Adams, 1:83; Rush, 2:1011.

15. Chesterfield, 1775, 1:148, 149, 2:11, 83; Halifax, 107, 108; *Polite Academy*, 19–20, 24–25, 34; Countess of Carlysle, "Maxims," in Mrs. M. Peddle, *Rudiments of Taste* (Philadelphia, 1790), 103, 115; Thomas Gisborne, *An Enquiry into the Duties of the Female Sex* (Philadelphia, 1798), 79; Johann Caspar Lavater, *Aphorisms on Man* (Philadelphia, 1790), 11–12; *The Youth's Monitor* (Leominster, MA, 1799), 9, 26; *A Little Pretty Pocket Book* (Worcester, MA, 1787), 108, 113; [William Green], *The School of Good Manners, Containing Rules for Children's Behavior in Every Situation in Life* (New London, 1801), 8; George Brewer, *The Juvenile Lavater* (New York, 1815), 104; Trapwit, 11; Mott, *Observations*, 20–21; Della Casa, 180, 267; Kasson, 165.

16. Chesterfield, 1775, 2:63, 64–65; Knigge, 16; Moore, 245–46; Laban Thurber, *The Young Ladies and Gentleman's Preceptor* (Warren, RI, 1797), 50; Della Casa, 266; *Youth's Monitor*, 18, 19; Mott, *Observations*, 19; Barnard, 54–55. One author objected to the fashion of having "an absolute

command over our features," arguing that only the wicked had the need to mask their feelings. But this author admitted that his was not the popular view; *Polite Lady*, 209–10; Adams, 3:158.

17. Walter Raleigh, *Instructions to His Son and to Posterity*, 2d ed. (London, 1632), 24, 26; Ramesay, 70, 71; d'Ancourt, 12, 34; Chesterfield, 1775, 2:7, 64; William Penn, *Fruits of a Father's Love*, 6th ed. (Philadelphia, 1776), 17; Moore, 246, 247, 274, 275, 279, 280, 284; *Polite Academy*, xx–xxi, 14, 27, 29–31, 34; *Polite Lady*, 88–89, 242–44; Moody, 1–2, 5, 17, 18, 19, 20, 22; Della Casa, 97, 98, 99, 103, 266, 269, 270, 271; Mott, *Observations*, 18, 19, 21; Dover, 33, 34, 36, 64, 65; John Mellen, *A Discourse Containing a Serious Address to Persons of Several Ages and Characters* (Boston, 1751), 16; Bailey, 4, 5, 6, 7; Erasmus Darwin, *A Plan for the Conduct of Female Education* (Philadelphia, 1798), 92.

18. On focus on the individual, see Kasson, 62. On creditworthiness, see Ditz, 5. Adams, 2:76.

19. Karen Halttunen and John Kasson describe many of the rules in the antebellum context and note their role in the increasingly anonymous urban environment of that period. But they neglect the revolutionary-era roots of these rules and exaggerate the ease of reading others in "preindustrial" cities; see Halttunen, 37, 42. Diaries and letters remind us that even though the scale of cities was much smaller, one still encountered strangers on a regular basis in late eighteenth- and early nineteenth-century cities. I am indebted to Peter Stearns for some suggestions on these points.

20. The pioneering discussion on the American side was Linda Kerber, *Women of the Republic: Intellect and Ideology in Revolutionary America* (Chapel Hill, 1980), chap. 9. Subsequent modifications include Jan Lewis, "The Republican Wife: Virtue and Seduction in the Early American Republic," *William and Mary Quarterly* 44, no. 4 (1987): 689–721; Ruth Bloch, "The Gendered Meanings of Virtue in Revolutionary America," *Signs* 13, no. 1 (autumn 1987): 37–58; and Rosemarie Zagarri, "Morals, Manners and the Republican Mother," *American Quarterly* 44, no. 2 (June 1992): 192–215.

21. Zagarri, 210, makes a similar point.

22. Nearly a third of early colonial works were directed exclusively to men, and many works purportedly addressed to all people seemed to address only men; less than one-seventh were addressed exclusively to women. In the revolutionary era, fewer than one-sixth (eleven of seventy-five) of the conduct works were intended exclusively for men. Taken together with works for both sexes that seemingly addressed only men, less than a third of the conduct works of the period were intended for men. More works addressed both sexes equally, and over a third were addressed solely to women (twenty-seven of seventy-five).

23. Rosemarie Zagarri explores the intellectual currents that accompanied the trends in manners that I describe below in her examination of new thinking about women on the part of the civil-jurisprudential school of the Scottish Enlightenment, thereby also stressing the transatlantic nature of the reevaluation of attitudes toward women, 209–10. See also Bloch, 56 and passim.

24. Nancy Cott has argued that the modesty described below was just an act designed by male writers like Gregory and Fordyce for their own pleasure, in contrast to the sexual "passionlessness" that British evangelicals like Gisborne and More were beginning to prescribe; see "Passionlessness: An Interpretation of Victorian Sexual Ideology, 1790–1850," *Signs* 4, no. 2 (winter 1978): 224–26. But there are no big differences in the advice for face-to-face behavior given in these works, and they are accordingly cited together below. In essence, both male and female conduct writers prescribed modest behavior, both warned against affected modesty, and both made it clear that by affected modesty they meant modesty that was not the expression of real chastity (not passionlessness).

25. James Fordyce, *Sermons to Young Women* (Boston, 1767), 1:60, 73–74, 2:192–93; Gregory, 29–30, 35–37, 43, 78; Bennett, 2:27–28, 47, 48, 96, 98, 99, 102–3; Gisborne, 79, 135, 192, 193; *The Mirror of the Graces* (New York, 1813), 156–57, 158–59, 159–60; Halifax, 96, 98, 99, 102–4; d'Ancourt, 8, 20–21, 42; *Polite Lady*, 214–15, 216, 219; Hester Mulso Chapone, *Letters on the Improvement of the Mind, Addressed to a Young Lady* (Boston, 1783), 188; Jonathan Swift, "Letter to a Very Young Lady on Her Marriage," in *Reflections on Courtship and Marriage* (Philadelphia, 1746), 56–57, 66; Hannah Webster Foster, *The Boarding School* (Boston, 1798), 98, 103; *Female Friend*, 83–84, 94–95, 97, 183–84; Hanway, 152; *The American Ladies Preceptor* (Baltimore, 1810), 20–21, 41, 44; Bellegarde, 1821, 76, 105, 106, 107–8, 135. Eliza S. Bowne to Moses Porter, 18 March 1801, in *A Girl's Life Eighty Years Ago*, ed. Clarence Cook (New York, 1887), 47.

26. Halifax, 103; Richard Steele, comp., *The Lady's Library* (London, 1714), 1:197, 207; Gregory, 28, 29, 57, 58–60; d'Ancourt, 19, 20, 23; Pierre Joseph Boudier de Villemert, *The Ladies Friend* (Philadelphia, 1771), 6, 65; Swift, 57; Gisborne, 79; *Female Friend*, 94–95, 98, 183, 184, 186; *American Ladies Preceptor*, 21, 41; Bellegarde, 1821, 76, 107–8; [William Kenrick], *The Whole Duty of a Woman* (Boston, 1761), 25; Fordyce, 1:69–70; *Polite Lady*, 215; Bennett, 2:28, 99, 103; Burton, 110; Darwin, 95; *The American Academy of Compliments* (Philadelphia, 1796), 55.

27. Swift, 66; *American Ladies Preceptor*, 21, 41; Gregory, 29–30, 35, 37, 77–78; Bennett, 2:27–28, 48; Gisborne, 79; Foster, 98, 103, 105; *Female Friend*, 84, 94–95, 97, 98; d'Ancourt, 8, 19–20, 42; *Polite Lady*, 198, 214–15; Burton, 103; Darwin, 95; Bellegarde, 1821, 105, 107–8, 135.

28. I am indebted to Mike Zuckerman for this point.

29. On the double standard as reflected in court records, see Nina Dayton's fascinating "Taking the Trade: Abortion and Gender Relations in an Eighteenth-Century New England Village," *William and Mary Quarterly* 48, no. 1 (January 1991): 21–22, 39 and passim. Jan Lewis argues that these warnings "should not be read solely or simply as transparent and accurate descriptions of behavior," that the era's seduction tales were "a discourse about politics that had implications for women" (namely, symbolic explorations of the fate of virtue in the new Republic); but the conduct writers at least were offering concrete warnings to women, and warnings that are echoed in other sources (not to mention that at least some of the seduction novels were based on true stories); Lewis, personal communication and "Republican Wife," 716–20. That the authors had reason to caution women is suggested by Christine Stansell's research in court records and other sources from New York City, for example, which reveal that "male license for sexual aggressiveness increased" in the late eighteenth century, "especially toward women in public," who were "fair game"; *City of Women: Sex and Class in New York, 1789–1860* (New York, 1987), 23–27. Cathy Davidson also insists that the problem of seduction was indeed the main story of the seduction novels, even though they may also have had metaphorical functions (105–9); on the salience of seduction tales for the marriage decision (although she thinks these issues were not addressed by the conduct books), see 114–23. Some historians see the period's rise in premarital pregnancy rates as female declarations of independence from parental control in marriage making. It is not clear that this was the case, but it is clear that old communal controls were fading; see Daniel Scott Smith and Michael Hindus, "Premarital Pregnancy in America, 1640–1971: An Overview and Interpretation," *Journal of Interdisciplinary History* 5 (1975): 537–70; Robert Gross, *The Minutemen and Their World* (New York, 1976), 100–101, 184–85; Jay Fliegelman, *Prodigals and Pilgrims: The American Revolution against Patriarchal Authority, 1750–1800* (Cambridge, 1982), 120; for an overview of these issues, see John D'Emilio and Estelle Freedman, *Intimate Matters: A History of Sexuality in America* (New York, 1988), 44–45.

30. Ramesay, 70, 77, 100; Barnard, 52; Chesterfield, 1775, 1:39, 65, 70–71, 86–87, 121, 149, 2:9, 83, 84, 3:104; Moore, 18, 19, 21–29, 223, 224–25, 228–30, 249, 282; Della Casa, 51, 52–53, 264, 265, 270, 272, 273, 274; *Polite Lady*, 78–79, 203, 205, 212, 214, 245; Fordyce, 1:71, 164, 2:182, 183, 218; d'Ancourt, 5, 7, 10, 11, 36; Gregory, 26–28, 72–73, 112; Bennett, 2:7, 16, 23–24, 26, 28–29, 42, 43, 47; Carlysle, 103, 105–6; Chapone, 148, 183; Hannah More, *Essays on Various Subjects Designed for Young Ladies* (Philadelphia, 1786), 46, 62; Gisborne, 192, 193, 196; Boudier de Villemert, 65; [Louis Antoine de Caraccioli], *Advice from a Lady of Quality to Her Children* (Newburyport, 1784), 176; Hitchcock, 74. John Adams described his future wife as, among other things, "modest, delicate, soft"; and later praised David Rittenhouse as "soft and modest," 2:133, 188, 3:164.

31. Chesterfield, 1775, 1:86, 148, 149, 2:11, 83, 84; Moore, 99, 224, 254, 265, 267; *Little Pretty*, 108, 112; Dover, 32, 36; Barnard, 52; Lavater, 11–12; d'Ancourt, 9, 11, 16; Fordyce, 1:126; Chapone, 148; Darwin, 86–87, 94; Hanway, 138; Bellegarde, 1824, 27; Halifax, 107, 108; *Female Friend*, 112; Pennington, 147.

32. Chesterfield, 1775, 1:39, 2:11; Moore, 16, 17, 18, 255; Steele, 1:179, 2:43, 168–69; Kenrick, 24; Robert Dodsley, *The Economy of Human Life*, 7th ed. (Boston, 1752), 26, 28; Bennett, 2:41, 42; Fordyce, 1:69–70, 127, 2:182; Gregory, 28; Swift, 57; *Female Friend*, 183–84; *American Ladies Preceptor*, 40–41; Burton, 110; Darwin, 77, 79–80, 89; Francois de Salignac de la Mothe, Archbishop Fenelon, *A Treatise on the Education of Daughters* (Albany, 1806), 173.

33. Steele, 1:258–67; James Forrester, The Polite Philosopher, 15th ed. (New York, 1758), 24; Polite Academy, xx–xxi; Bennett, 2:29; Foster, 55, 56; Louisa Gurney Hoare, *Hints for the Improvement of Early Education and Nursery Discipline* (New York, 1820), 32–33; Barnard, 54–55; Della Casa, 266; Chesterfield, 1775, 2:63, 64, 65; Moore, 245–46; *Youth's Monitor*, 18, 19; Knigge, 16, 197.

34. *Polite Academy*, 34; Chesterfield, 1775, 1:39, 3:104; Moore, 18; Steele, 1:56, 234, 2:43; d'Ancourt, 36; *Polite Lady*, 203, 205; Chapone, 183; Bennett, 2:28; Swift, 57; Fenelon, 195; *Female Friend*, 183–84.

35. Ramesay, 70, 71; *Family Book*, 41, 45, 46; Chesterfield, 1775, 2:7, 64; Moore, 246, 247, 274, 275, 279, 284, 286; Green, 3, 6, 8, 9; Della Casa, 50, 97, 98, 99, 101, 103, 266, 269, 270, 271; Steele, 1:258–67, 2:179; *Polite Lady*, 88, 242–44; More, 62; Burton, 169; Foster, 55–56; Sproat, *Girl's*, 10.

36. Nancy Armstrong argues that "the modern individual was first and foremost a female," but she neglects to examine conduct advice to men. See "The Rise of the Domestic Woman," in *The Ideology of Conduct: Essays on Literature and the History of Sexuality*, ed. Nancy Armstrong and Leonard Tennenhouse (New York, 1987), 103, 107 and passim. I am similarly uncomfortable, from the vantage point of the conduct prescriptions, with Carroll Smith-Rosenberg's suggestion that the middle-class woman "produced her class"; see "Dis-Covering the Subject of the 'Great Constitutional Discussion,' 1786–1789," *Journal of American History* 79, no. 3 (December 1992): 859–61. For the association of middle-class formation and separate spheres, see Ryan. Amanda Vickery notes and criticizes the association of separate spheres with the rise of the middle class in both American and British women's historiography, but she too assumes that separate spheres reigned in advice books; see her valuable review essay, especially with regard to Leonore Davidoff and Catherine Hall's influential *Family Fortunes: Men and Women of the English Middle Class, 1780–1850* (Chicago, 1987), "Golden Age to Separate Spheres? A Review of the Categories and Chronology of English Women's History," *Historical Journal* 36, no. 2 (1993): 383–14. Anthony Rotundo does note the connection between male ideals and economic change in "Learning about Manhood: Gender Ideals and the Middle-Class Family in Nineteenth-Century America," in *Manliness and Morality: Middle-Class Masculinity in Britain and America, 1800–1940*, ed. J. A. Mangan and James Walvin (New York, 1987), 36; he associates both with rising individualism in *American Manhood: Transformations in Masculinity from the Revolution to the Modern Era* (New York, 1993), 3, 15–16, 17, 18, 20.

Chapter Three

"Those Scenes for Which Alone My Heart Was Made"
Affection and Politics in the Age of Jefferson and Hamilton

Jan Lewis

It was almost summer, and Thomas Jefferson was still in Philadelphia. He had told the president in the fall, before his reelection, that he wanted to resign as secretary of state and return to Monticello. The conflict within Washington's cabinet, particularly with secretary of the treasury Alexander Hamilton, had become too intense for Jefferson to bear much longer. Washington, however, was reluctant to let Jefferson quit, and so he consented to stay "perhaps till summer, perhaps autumn."[1] Jefferson would not return to his beloved Monticello until the beginning of the next year, however. In the meantime, he would become embroiled in the controversy surrounding the reckless new French minister, "Citizen" Edmond Genet. Although Jefferson would eventually come to repudiate Genet, who was defying the president's proclamation of neutrality in the war between France and Britain, it was not before Hamilton's allies had questioned Jefferson's patriotism.

In the midst of this tumult, a letter from his friend Angelica Schuyler Church was particularly welcome. Only a few years before, when Jefferson was serving as his nation's minister to France, Mrs. Church had been part of a circle of men and women with whom Jefferson had passed many happy hours. This group—Jefferson called it "our charming coterie in Paris"—included Mrs. Church, Madame de Corny, the Italian-born English miniaturist Maria Cosway, and the American painter John Trumbull. Mrs. Church's letter brought to Jefferson's mind "remembrances which are very dear to it, and which often furnish a delicious resort from the dry and oppressive scenes of business." Jefferson went on to complain about the trials of a life in government. "Never was any mortal more tired of these than I am. I thought to have been clear of them some months ago: but circumstances will retain me a little while longer, & then I hope to get back to those scenes for which alone my heart was made."[2]

Jefferson's great rival Alexander Hamilton was also considering resigning from the cabinet, even though he more than Jefferson had accomplished his aims. "Our own Jacobins have made a violent effort against me, but a complete victory has been gained to their utter confusion." And like Jefferson, he poured his heart out to Angelica Schuyler Church, the beloved sister of his wife, Eliza. In December 1793, he reported to her on the coming political season, which promised "some volcanic exhibitions." "But how oddly are all things arranged in this sublunary scene — I am still where I do not wish to be — I know how I could be much happier; but circumstances enchain me — It is however determined that I will break the spell."[3]

Here were two of the country's most important political leaders, so influential that the nation they helped create still bears their imprint, lamenting that they would rather be somewhere else. The recent acquisition by the Alderman Library of the University of Virginia of the Angelica Schuyler Church Collection, which includes her letters from both men, affords us an opportunity to consider the place of emotion in the politics of the early national era in American history.[4] Despite their significant disagreements on matters of policy and political economy, Jefferson and Hamilton voiced similar views about politics, society, and emotion in their letters to Mrs. Church. Both described a political world that was emotionally unfulfilling. The seat of the government that the American Revolution had created was, for both men, "where I do not wish to be." Instead, both claimed that they would rather be, as Jefferson put it, "liberated from the hated occupations of politics."[5] Were they serious, we ask? Jefferson did resign from the Washington administration, but he returned in 1797 as vice president and remained in public office through 1808. Hamilton also remained in office. It is almost unimaginable that these men — brilliant thinkers and political animals if ever there were — would willingly have returned home to leave the business of government to lesser men. Yet both men, speaking for their generation of political leaders, were deeply serious. It is not so much that they could have left government behind, but that they felt deep ambivalence about a life of public service. Both — Jefferson more than Hamilton, to be sure — had serious misgivings about government. Those reservations about government are part of their legacy to us. When the Founding Fathers gave us our government they gave us also a set of views about it, a sense that the "occupations of politics" were to be hated rather than revered.

This notion that the political life was less than fulfilling, that it left some significant human needs unmet, has become part of our collective political life — and our collective emotional life as well. To some extent, this notion that politics was despicable is part of the republican legacy. Classical republican thought, as adapted by American revolutionaries, held that the power of the state was so inherently corrupting that its offices should be filled not by lifetime politicians, but by men who temporarily and reluctantly abandoned their private pursuits for brief periods of public service. The model was the Roman senator Cincinnatus, who left his plow when his nation called.[6]

Yet if Americans of the revolutionary age maintained the republican distrust of the state and its underlying suspicion of power, they also added new elements to the formulation and in the process changed it. First, they described in exquisite detail the emotional deprivations of a public life. Jefferson, for example, complained that political life was "a dreary scene where envy, hatred, malice, revenge, and all the worse passions of men are marshalled to make one another as miserable as possible."[7] Second, those who were creating the world of American politics in the revolutionary age imagined private life as the reverse image of the despised world of politics. Although republican thought had always feared the corrupting tendencies of public life, it never detailed them as fully as later Americans would; nor did it ever elaborate the fulfillments of private life. Postrevolutionary Americans thought differently than their ancestors about the emotions and emotional life. As precursors to the romantics, Americans of this era thought that emotions had to be demonstrated and, indeed, performed.[8] Hence, they imagined the opposite worlds of politics and private life as stage sets on which men (and women) could act out their emotional lives. For Jefferson, the political world was a "dreary scene," while private life offered "scenes for which alone" the heart was made. Finally, and as a necessary corollary, emotional life itself was valued. The performance of certain emotions—in particular, sympathy and affection—was one of the objects of life; this was the measure of humanity.[9] Protecting this sort of life, one in which men and women realized their humanity by demonstrating their affection, was, in turn, among the chief purposes of politics. In this way, emotion was woven into the fabric of politics. The challenge for political leaders and thinkers of Jefferson and Hamilton's generation was to create a politics that protected the humane emotions without endangering them. Both used their correspondence with Angelica Church to work out this problem.

Of course, both men were wrestling with a difficult problem in political thought, one that goes to the nature of politics itself. Neither devoted much thought to the place of women in this new political world. Yet to speak of political life as unfulfilling and to contrast it to a different and more authentic one in which men like Jefferson and Hamilton believed that they "could be much happier" reverses one of the commonplaces of modern women's and political history. For the past several decades, women's historians have pointed out that women have been excluded from the public world and confined to the private one, and they have suggested that women's exclusion from public life came because women were believed to lack the qualities necessary for successful political engagement. Supposedly less rational than men and incapable of the disinterested discourse that governing required, women had to be kept out of politics for the good of the commonwealth. The exclusion of women from politics and public life, then, is supposedly a necessary consequence of their greater emotion; politics, like the men who participate in it, has been deemed, or so the argument goes, a wholly rational realm. Yet when the men who founded the American system of government complain in this very clear way about political life and long for the world inhabited by women like Angelica Church, we must question the common wisdom.

We might begin by examining in more detail what it was about politics that men like Jefferson and Hamilton found so distressing. It has long been known that American politics in the 1790s was particularly contentious, even violent, as verbal battles sometimes led to duels. This fierce politics was the product of both intense ideological conflict and the structure of politics itself. Federalists and Democratic-Republicans disagreed fundamentally on important matters of economic and foreign policy, and both believed that the very survival of the new nation depended on their pursuing the correct course. In addition, national politics was less stable and more popular than the Founding Fathers had anticipated. Turnover in Congress was high, and newspapers kept the public both informed and agitated. Men who had entered political life in the much smaller arenas of colonial government were unprepared for the wider stage of national politics. They soon learned how to cultivate public opinion, but not how to channel it.[10]

I have argued elsewhere that American politics would not become stable and free from violence until men like Jefferson learned to expect less personally from public life; that is, not until political leaders found other sources for their identity. In Jefferson's case, he came to expect less gratification from politics and public life and more from his family. As a defense against political attacks, he chose to believe that the public never knew him the way his family did. Even on his deathbed, he brooded. "In speaking of the calumnies which his enemies had uttered against his public and private character with such unmitigated and untiring bitterness," Jefferson's grandson reported, "he said that he had not considered them as abusing him; they had never known *him*. They had created an imaginary being clothed with odious attributes, to whom they had given his name." Jefferson was too committed to the government that he helped create to stay away from it for long. In order to cope with its demands, Jefferson split his personality; the public might have his labor, but it could not claim his true self. This was the same distinction that he drew between "the oppressive scenes of business" and "those scenes for which the heart was made."[11]

Although Hamilton, like Jefferson, recoiled from the personal demands of office in 1793 and 1794, unlike Jefferson he did not retire temporarily. Nor was he able to split his self into a public persona, unknown to most of the nation, and a private self, known and loved by friends and family. Hamilton rested his identity on fame, the love and admiration of his nation. He could not imagine living without it, and so he met his death in a duel, attempting to defend his honor before the world.[12] Jefferson, then, represented the future of American politics. In order to survive—literally— American political leaders would have to learn how to develop thick skins. Like Jefferson, they did it by denying the public the ability to hurt them. They learned not to rest their identities completely on the public's approval. Instead, they would look to family and friends for the love and affirmation that public life could not guarantee.

To a certain extent, this is a familiar formulation. At first glance, it corresponds to the picture of separate male and female spheres that women's historians have sketched for us in the past several decades. From them we have learned that in the antebellum period, Americans believed that men and women were fundamentally different, that men were strong and rational and women weak and emotional, that the world beyond the home was stressful and amoral at best and that home was nurturing, restorative, and fundamentally moral. According to the doctrine of separate spheres, as historians have called it, home was the reward for struggle in the world of work: this was where men returned at the end of the day for succor and sustenance. The doctrine of separate spheres, then, served simultaneously to complement and to critique the world of work; it made it possible, by compensating men for their efforts with the rewards of home, and at the same time undermined it, by denying it moral legitimacy and ultimate significance. According to the doctrine of separate spheres, the structure of modern American life—the way work and family life were configured—rested on the belief in fundamental and natural sexual difference: men by their nature were suited for the public sphere, and women by theirs, to repair the damage done to men in their struggles.[13]

Obviously, this formulation bears a striking resemblance to the contrast that Jefferson established between "the oppressive scenes of business" and "those scenes for which alone my heart was made." There is, however, an important difference: according to women's historians, the doctrine of separate male and female spheres developed in the antebellum period, when the early stages of industrialization and capitalist development removed men's work from the home. Jefferson and Hamilton sought refuge not from work—that is, not from participation in the market—but from politics. Both complained to Angelica Church before the economic transformation that women's historians have argued was the source for the doctrine of separate spheres. In fact, Hamilton's economic policy was designed to bring about those changes, while Jefferson's was intended to prevent or forestall them. It was not the world of work that troubled them, but that of politics. Political leaders like Jefferson and Hamilton, then, delineated an emotional distinction between home and politics in advance of the economic transformations that have usually been cited as the source of that distinction.

It was, then, something about politics itself that not only made a life in government ultimately unfulfilling, but also led political leaders to seek refuge in a world for which the heart was made. The revulsion against politics was, at least in part, a perhaps natural reaction to the political violence of the 1790s. It was also grounded in political thought itself. The ideas about government developed by American political leaders in the era of the American Revolution criticized politics and set up a separate sphere—one that these leaders called "society"—as superior.

Perhaps the most succinct statement of this political disparagement of politics—for such it was—was made by Thomas Paine in *Common Sense,* the influential pamphlet he wrote in 1776. In fact, it appeared in the first sentence, and it is the premise on which Paine's call to revolution rested. "Some writers," Paine began, "have so confounded society with government, as to leave little or no distinction between them; whereas they are not only different, but have different origins." This distinction, between society and government, was precisely the one that both Jefferson and Hamilton invoked in their letters to Angelica Church. "Society," Paine continued, "is produced by our wants, and government by our wickedness; the former promotes our happiness *positively* by uniting our affections, the latter *negatively* by restraining our vices. . . . Society is in every state a blessing, but government even in its best state is but a necessary evil." [14]

Government was not an end in itself. Rather, it served to protect society. But what exactly was meant by the term "society"? American revolutionaries like Paine drew much of their thinking about government from John Locke, who in his *Two Treatises of Government* (1690) had asserted that government was a human creation, designed for mutual protection. The contrast that Locke drew most sharply, however, was between government and a so-called state of nature, rather than between government and society. In the century after Locke, however, the development of a robust civic culture and a thriving middle-class urban and town social life gave palpable meaning to the term "society." In the parlance of the eighteenth century, and as developed by philosophers of the Scottish Enlightenment such as Francis Hutcheson and Thomas

Reid, "society" included all those institutions and places where men and women came together; it occupied the space between the solitary individual and government. Society was where men and women realized their human potential. As Pennsylvanian James Wilson, one of the authors of the Constitution, explained, "We are fitted and intended for society, and ... society is fitted and intended for us." Repeating Paine's emphasis on the term "affection," Wilson explained that "We have all the emotions, which are necessary in order that society may be formed and maintained: we have tenderness for the fair sex; we have affection for our children, for our parents, and for our other relations: we have attachment to our friends." Society, then, was both an expression and the realization of human nature. Man—that is, men and women—was created for society, and that meant the expression of certain desirable emotions. As Jefferson put it, "nature hath implanted in our breasts a love of others, a sense of duty to them, a moral instinct, in short, which prompts us irresistibly to feel and to succor their distresses. . . . The Creator would indeed have been a bungling artist, had he intended man for a social animal, without planting in him social dispositions." [15] The purpose of government was to protect this realm, the one in which people exercised their natural affections and expressed their positive emotions. This was what James Wilson meant when he said that government was "instituted for the happiness of society." [16]

It was also why men like Jefferson and Hamilton dreamed about leaving government to return to private life. Public service could never be ultimately fulfilling, for it provided no outlet for what Jefferson called the "social dispositions." When Angelica Church's daughter Catherine congratulated Jefferson on his election to the presidency, he demurred that "the post is not enviable, as it affords little exercise for social affections." [17] These affections—the attachment that men and women felt for each other, as family members and as friends—were the glue that held society together, or, as Hamilton put it, "this great cement of society." Nurtured in the family, the bonds of affection radiated outward, Hamilton explained, as if in concentric circles, from the family to the neighborhood, thence to the community, and finally to government. [18] In fact, the founders of the new national government knew that one of their greatest challenges was to stimulate affection for the new national government, for such attachments were strongest for objects closest to home.

Affection, then, represented not simply the warm attachment of men and women for their families or of good friends for one another, but the cement that held people together in society. Affection was not simply a private or personal emotion, but a social one. It was also the basis for national unity, for the citizens of the nation were to be joined together as if they were members of a loving family. Urging his countrymen to ratify the Constitution in 1787, James Madison asked them not to listen to those who told them that "the people of America, knit together as they are by so many chords of affection, can no longer live together as members of the same family." [19] The family, then, was both the source and model for the nation. It inculcated the feelings of affection and it demonstrated them in practice. Although Federalists like Hamilton hoped to make the nation worthy of affection, they never set the nation up as a substitute for or superior to the family or society, which is another way of saying that there has never been in America a powerful statist tradition. The purpose of government was to protect society, not to serve as an end in itself.

Cut off from society while they served in government, Jefferson and Hamilton used their correspondence with Angelica Church to sustain the bonds of affection that, they believed, made their lives meaningful. Much of every letter that each man wrote her consisted of an invocation of their mutual affection. "I am with you always in spirit: be you with me sometimes," Jefferson wrote in 1788. He told her daughter Catherine that his family's interest in her was not a favor, "but gratifications of our own affections to an object which has every quality which might endear her to us." A letter from her mother "served to recall to my mind remembrances which are very dear to it." Such phrases were repeated again and again in Jefferson's letters, displacing news and opinions and becoming instead the subject of the letter. Although Hamilton was more inclined than Jefferson to discuss politics with Mrs. Church, he too waxed affectionate in his letters. After her visit in 1789, Hamilton asked her to "imagine" what he and his wife "felt." Then, not trusting to her imagination, he told her: "We gazed, we *sighed,* we *wept,* and casting 'many a lingering longing look behind', we returned home [from seeing her off] to give scope to our sorrows, and mingle without restraint our tears and our regrets."

Such expressions of affection were not, as they sometimes appeared, merely the natural outpourings of a warm heart. Rather, they rested on and indeed sustained a particular social vision, one that assigned different emotions to separate realms. When Mrs. Church returned to her homeland from Europe, Jefferson warned her that "you will find that the agitations of Europe have reached even us, and that here, as there, they are permitted to disturb social life: that we have not yet learnt to give every thing to it's proper place; discord to our senates, love and friendship to society." He thought that her "affections," however, would "spread themselves over the whole family of the good, without enquiring by what hard names they are politically called." Affection, especially of the feminine sort, could make society both moral and whole by rewarding the good and ignoring the arbitrary distinctions of politics. Jefferson, after all, was writing to his great adversary's beloved sister-in-law. He entertained the fantasy that her affection could repair the ruptures caused by partisan wrangling.[20]

This sociology of the emotions, which suggested that feminine emotion could not only constitute society but also repair the ruptures of politics, points to another limitation in the historians' paradigm of separate male and female spheres. It has already been suggested that this paradigm is flawed because it links the development of an ideology of sexual difference to the removal of men's work from the home by industrialization. The paradigm also misrepresents nineteenth-century thinking about the public and private realms in arguing that nineteenth-century Americans believed that women were naturally suited for the private sphere of the home and men for the public sphere of business and politics. Several modifications of this notion may be in order. First, the critical distinction for the first generation of American political leaders was between government and society, including the family, rather than between home and the public sphere. Second, this distinction was not predicated on a notion of sexual difference; that is, these were not separate male and female spheres. To be sure, government was a masculine realm. But society embraced both men and women, and hence it was social and political function more than ideas about gender that set the emotional geography.

What are the implications of these statements? Several historians have recently suggested that the liberal state created by the French and American Revolutions rested on and required the exclusion of women from government.[21] Whatever the case may be for France, American government did not necessitate the exclusion of women. Second, because the purpose of American government was to protect society, which included women, to a certain degree, the object of government was the protection of women.[22]

This is not to suggest, however, that men like Jefferson believed that men and women were identical or even fundamentally the same. In fact, political leaders of this generation believed that sexual difference was grounded in nature. "Male and female," Paine wrote in *Common Sense*, "are the distinctions of nature."[23] Women were softer than men, and with a special gift for society. They enjoyed, Jefferson told Mrs. Church, "the happy privilege" of leaving "to the rougher sex, & to the newspapers, their party squabbles and reproaches." Writing to an American female correspondent from Paris in 1788, Jefferson described a "world" gone "politically mad," where "men, women, and children" talked about nothing but politics. "Society is spoilt by it." Jefferson hoped that America would preserve its sanity and that women would remain "contented to soothe & calm the minds of their husbands returning ruffled from political debate." Jefferson was troubled by what he saw in Paris, for he made similar comments to Angelica Church. "The tender breasts of ladies," he told her, "were not formed for political convulsion; and the French ladies miscalculate much their own happiness when they wander from the true field of influence into that of politicks."[24]

Politics, then, was emotionally draining. It dissipated the affections that were created within the family and society. It also stimulated a whole array of undesirable emotions, ones that Jefferson listed from time to time: "jealousies . . . hatred, and . . . rancorous and malignant passions," "envy, hatred, malice, revenge and all the worst passions of men," "cabal, intrigue, and hatred," and, simply, "the bad passions of the heart."[25] Were these, then, the bad passions of men or of the heart? Certainly, they were specific to a certain place—the political sphere, a place where women were rarely if ever found. At the same time that political thinkers in the age of Jefferson described society as a realm comfortably inhabited by men and women both, they described government as one occupied by men only. They left it for later generations to debate, however, whether it was custom or nature that kept women out of the political realm.

This sociology of the emotions, which assigned certain emotions to politics and others to society, was, I have suggested, an integral part of the political thought of the revolutionary era. It was constructed by men like Jefferson and Hamilton and expressed in their letters to Angelica Schuyler Church. Thus far we have examined emotion and politics by reading their letters to her. But what of her replies? Did she understand the relationship among these terms the way her male correspondents did? Did she think of government and society as opposites and disparage government as they did?

She did not. If Jefferson and Hamilton's letters to her were exercises in affection that created and maintained the bonds of attachment that were supposed to sustain society, hers, by and large, were efforts at patronage politics. In 1793, she wrote Hamilton to recommend the vicomte de Noailles, Lafayette's brother-in-law, who was emigrating to America. A year later, she asked him to "extend" his "care," that is, to serve as a patron, to another of her émigré friends, the duke de Liancourt. Her letters to Jefferson were similar, asking his assistance for the vicomte de Noailles and President Washington's for the marquis de Lafayette. These were the sorts of letters that men and women of influence routinely wrote to each other in the eighteenth century, asking the intercession of one friend for another. Mrs. Church used the term "friend" again and again to make it clear that she was talking about a particular sort of relationship. For example, in her letter recommending the vicomte de Noailles to Hamilton, she noted that he was "a friend of mine," that the vicomte knew of Hamilton as "my friend," and that she herself was Hamilton's "faithful friend." The duke de Liancourt, she told Hamilton, came to America "without a friend, unless my brother . . . will extend to [him] his care." The letter asking Jefferson's intercession with Washington on Lafayette's behalf was written "to solicit your friendship for a friend of yours and mine."[26]

This was the language not so much of affection as of patronage. Eighteenth-century Anglo-American and French politics was animated not by interests, as in modern politics, or even some notion of the public good, but by personal connections in which one earned and cemented loyalty by doing favors for friends.[27] When Angelica Church described someone as a friend, she wanted to convey that he was a person to whom she felt the obligation to render assistance. Among friends, such debts of service were interchangeable, so that one of her friends would naturally feel obliged to assist another of her friends; that, after all, was the very purpose of a letter of introduction from one friend to another. When Mrs. Church told her brother-in-law that the duke de Liancourt had no friends in America unless Hamilton would "extend [him] his care," she did not mean that the duke was lacking in social acquaintances; she meant that he had no one to help him out. Women like Angelica Schuyler Church with access to power were more than willing to pursue it in order to assist friends. This was the way eighteenth-century politics worked.

The Revolution, however, ushered in a new sort of politics, one that raised questions about a politics driven by personal connections. Too many inept and corrupt colonial officials had obtained their positions by working the levers of patronage; too many talented colonists had been, it seemed, excluded from the halls of government. Democracy demanded equal access to power, rather than its domination by a small clique of well-connected families. As a result, political leaders in the new nation found themselves having to turn down pleas for assistance that would have been honored several decades earlier. In 1808, Jefferson explained at great length to Catherine Church Cruger why he could not intercede on behalf of her husband and provide him with the license that he wanted. "It would have been a great gratification," Jefferson wrote, "had the occasion permitted me to be useful to you" by assisting her husband. But the procedures and schedule for granting such licenses had been "duly announced" in the newspapers "some months ago," and the deadline was long passed. Moreover,

> living as we do, in a country governed by fixed rules, nothing can be done for one which is not done for every other in an equal case. However gratifying it might be to our private feelings to indulge these by dispensations in particular cases, yet for the mass of society the doctrine of an equal measure to all is of unquestionable value, & I am sure will be approved by our good understanding & disinterested justice, as well as by Mr. Cruger's.[28]

Hamilton offered a similar lesson in democratic politics to his sister-in-law when she asked him to help secure an appointment for her father, that is, Hamilton's father-in-law. "There is no proof of my affection which I would not willingly give you. How far it will be practicable to accomplish your wish reflecting your father is however very uncertain—Our republican ideas stand much in the way of accumulating offices in one family—Indeed I doubt much whether your father could be prevailed upon to accept."[29] This was a particularly unkind cut, for it suggested that men—Hamilton and Philip Schuyler—understood the practices of modern politics much better than a woman like Angelica Church. Moreover, by removing patronage from the obligations of friendship, Jefferson and Hamilton were redefining the term. "Friendship" was divested of its instrumental, political dimension; now it entailed only sociability and affection. Women like Angelica Church were being stripped of the only significant political power they had held, the ability to call friends—in the older meaning of the term—and kinsmen to account. All that they could now command was a return of their affection.

Democratic politics redefined, or, to be more precise, gave a new political meaning to female emotion. Affection was to be encouraged, but it had to be kept in its rightful place. As Jefferson had told Angelica Church, Americans had to learn to put every emotion in its "proper place; discord to our senates, love and friendship to society." By rejecting women's claims on their patronage for male friends and relations, Jefferson and Hamilton were helping to teach Americans that lesson. If it strayed too far—or in too intense a form—from its natural realm, female emotion could undermine democratic politics. Jefferson complained to Anne Willing Bingham that in Paris, women spent too much time away from home, consumed by "the empty bustle of Paris." In America, however, "the intervals of leisure are filled by the society of real friends, whose affections are not thinned to cob-web, by being spread over a thousand objects."[30] Affection, then, could be endangered if it were spread too thin.

And, according to Hamilton, it could also create trouble if it were concentrated too highly. In the *Federalist* number 6, he worried about conflicts among nations that had "their origin entirely in private passions." In elaborating this concern, he made it clear that such private passions all too easily might involve women. He noted that the "celebrated Pericles" had destroyed a city "in compliance with the resentments of a prostitute" and that "the influence which the bigotry of one female, the petulancies of another, and the cabals of a third, had in the co[n]temporary policy, ferments and pacifications of a considerable part of Europe are topics that have been too often descanted upon not to be generally known." He was referring to Madame de Maintenon, who secretly married Louis XIV of France and persuaded him to persecute the Huguenots; the duchess of Marlborough, an advisor to England's Queen Anne, who was involved in numerous intrigues; and Madame de Pompadour, the mistress of Louis XV and another notorious intriguer, who even played a role in selecting ministers and setting policy.[31] Almost nowhere in the *Federalist* are women mentioned, so Hamilton's association of them with "private" and destructive "passions" is significant. The sort of patronage politics practiced by Angelica Church could, if unchecked, lead to international warfare.

This, in a larger sense, was the problem of affection in politics: if it were too intense, men would carry their private attachments into the public realm and put them ahead of the needs of the nation, or they might succumb to the blandishments of women who persuaded them to put those private concerns ahead of the public welfare. On the other hand, if affection were too weak because, as in Paris, women went flitting about until "affections" were "thinned to cob-web," then society would be without its cement. Affection was utterly necessary—but only in the right proportion.

The first generation of American political leaders saw danger all around them. The world had not yet seen a democratic government that had stood the test of time. The deep ambivalence of men like Jefferson and Hamilton, Madison and Paine about government and their conviction that it was not an end in itself combined with their fears for the future of democratic government. How could they sustain a government whose purpose was to protect society and all its members? One of the challenges was to make certain that society, in turn, sustained government. That meant making sure that society continued to sustain the bonds of affection that held the nation together. Those bonds of attachment—the love that men and women felt for others near and far—must be strong enough, not cobweb thin, but never too intense, never too passionate. In fact, it was passion itself that was the danger, for that was what politics stimulated—"rancorous passions," as Jefferson called them. These were men of the Enlightenment, and their ideal was moderation. Society was the solution to the family feuds and dynastic struggles that had convulsed Europe for centuries. Men like Jefferson and Hamilton imagined a social life whose principal emotions were affection, cheerfulness, and, when the occasion required, sadness—but never despair. Women had an important role to play in social—and, hence, political—life, but that role was carefully scripted. Women must love, but not too much. They were to be the antidote to passion, not its source. By no means would political leaders like Jefferson and Hamilton—the men we often refer to as the Founding Fathers—have segregated women in a "separate sphere." Women were at once too necessary—and too potentially disruptive—to the national endeavor to have been left wholly to their own devices.

It remains for historians of American politics and the emotions to determine how much of this formulation has survived into the modern era. To a certain extent, the early national period was a unique moment in American history, a transition between the classical style of the Enlightenment and the romanticism of the Victorian era.

Politics was in transition, from a hierarchical system with limits on popular participation to a democratic one that drew in all (white) men, regardless of their wealth or status. Simultaneously, ideas about gender were changing dramatically, as men and women came to believe that sexual difference was a fact of nature.[32] Yet if, as I have tried to suggest, the historians' paradigm of separate spheres has probably exaggerated and delineated too sharply the differences that earlier Americans saw between men's and women's spaces and their natures, it is possible also that we have assumed too readily that they believed that male and female emotions were fundamentally different. Recent work in the history of the emotions by Peter Stearns and Carol Zisowitz Stearns, C. Dallett Hemphill, and Lucia McMahon suggests that certain nineteenth-century emotional standards—those for anger and love, for example—were the same for middle-class women and men.[33] Affection, too, was the province of both men and women.

Yet for American political thinkers like Hamilton and Jefferson, affection was not simply an emotion, a particular kind of love. It was also a term laden with political and social meaning. Affection was what held men and women together in society and in the nation both. And once a simple human emotion was made a critical term in political thought, it would necessarily have implications for both politics and emotional life, and the way they are held in tension. The twinned notions that public life cannot be emotionally fulfilling and that private life must of necessity be wholly gratifying are, in fact, the creations of a moment in history, ones that the history of emotions enables us to question.

NOTES

1. Quoted in Dumas Malone, *Jefferson and the Ordeal of Liberty* (Boston, 1962), 9.

2. Quoted in Dumas Malone, *Jefferson and the Rights of Man* (Boston, 1951), 70; Jefferson to Angelica Schuyler Church, June 7, 1793, Angelica Schuyler Church Papers, Alderman Library, University of Virginia.

3. Alexander Hamilton to Angelica Schuyler Church, December 27, 1793, Church Papers. A year later Hamilton told Church that he still planned to resign from Washington's cabinet. Hamilton to Church, December 8, 1794, in Harold Syrett, ed., *The Papers of Alexander Hamilton*, 27 vols. (New York, 1961–87), 17:428.

4. I am indebted to Karin Wittenborg, University Librarian, Alderman Library, University of Virginia, for making photocopies of the Angelica Schuyler Church Papers available to me. Much of the collection has already been published, in Syrett, ed., *Papers of Hamilton*, and in Julian P. Boyd et al., eds., *The Papers of Thomas Jefferson*, 26 vols. to date (Princeton, 1950–). Some of the letters in the collection, such as Jefferson's to Church's daughter Catherine, have not, however, been previously published.

5. Jefferson to Angelica Schuyler Church, November 27, 1793, in Merrill Peterson, ed., *Thomas Jefferson: Writings* (New York, 1984), 1013.

6. See Garry Wills, *Cincinnatus: George Washington and the Enlightenment* (Garden City, NY, 1984).

7. Jefferson to Martha Jefferson Randolph, February 8, 1798, in Edwin Morris Betts and James Bear, Jr., eds., *The Family Letters of Thomas Jefferson* (Columbia, MO, 1966), 155.

8. Jay Fliegelman, *Declaring Independence: Jefferson, Natural Language, and the Culture of Performance* (Stanford, CA, 1993). See also Gerald N. Izenberg, *Impossible Individuality: Romanticism, Revolution, and the Origins of Modern Selfhood, 1787–1802* (Princeton, 1992).

9. Consider Thomas Haskell, "Capitalism and the Origins of the Humanitarian Sensibility, Part I and Part II," in Thomas Bender, ed., *The Antislavery Debate: Capitalism and Abolitionism as a Problem in Historical Interpretation* (Berkeley, 1992), 107–60.

10. John R. Howe, "Republican Thought and Political Violence in the 1790s," *American Quarterly* 19 (1967): 147–65; Marshall Smelser, "The Federalists Period as an Age of Passion," *American Quarterly* 10 (1958): 391–419; Richard Buel, Jr., *Securing the Revolution: Ideology in American Politics* (Ithaca, 1972); Drew R. McCoy, *The Elusive Republic: Political Economy in Jeffersonian America* (Chapel Hill, NC, 1980); Jack N. Rakove, "The Structure of Politics at the Accession of George Washington," in Richard Beeman, Stephen Botein, and Edward C. Carter II, eds., *Beyond Confederation: Origins of the Constitution and American National Identity* (Chapel Hill, NC, 1987), 261–94; Joanne B. Freeman, "Dueling as Politics: Reinterpreting the Burr-Hamilton Duel," *William and Mary Quarterly*, 3d ser., 53 (1996): 289–318; Jan Lewis, " 'The Blessings of Domestic Society': Thomas Jefferson's Family and the Transformation of American Politics," in Peter S. Onuf, ed., *Jeffersonian Legacies* (Charlottesville, VA, 1993), 109–46.

11. Sarah N. Randolph, *The Domestic Life of Thomas Jefferson* (1871; reprint, Charlottesville, VA, 1978), 369; Lewis, "Blessings of Domestic Society."

12. Lewis, "Blessings of Domestic Society"; and Freeman, "Dueling as Politics." For the importance of fame in this era, see Wills, *Cincinnatus*; and Douglass Adair, "Fame and the Founding Fathers," in *Fame and the Founding Fathers* (New York, 1974), 3–26.

13. See, for example, Nancy F. Cott, *The Bonds of Womanhood: "Women's Sphere" in New England, 1780–1835* (New Haven, 1977); Kathryn Kish Sklar, *Catharine Beecher: A Study in American Domesticity* (New Haven, 1973); Barbara Welter, "The Cult of True Womanhood, 1820–1860," *American Quarterly* 18 (1966): 151–74; Mary P. Ryan, *Cradle of the Middle Class: The Family in Oneida County, New York, 1790–1865* (New York, 1981).

14. Thomas Paine, *Common Sense* (1776) (London, 1976), 65.

15. James Wilson, *Lectures on Law*, in *The Works of James Wilson*, ed. Robert Green McCloskey, 2 vols. (Cambridge, MA, 1967), 1:233; Thomas Jefferson to Thomas Law, June 13, 1824, in Peterson, ed., *Writings*, 1337.

16. Wilson, *Lectures on Law*, 1:85–88.

17. Jefferson to Catherine Church, March 27, 1801, Church Papers.

18. Hamilton, "The Federalist No. 17," in Jacob E. Cooke, ed., *The Federalist* (Middletown, CT, 1961), 107.

19. Madison, "The Federalist No. 14," in Cooke, ed., *The Federalist*, 88.

20. Jefferson to Angelica Schuyler Church, August 17, 1788; Jefferson to Catherine Church, January 11, 1798; Jefferson to Angelica Schuyler Church, June 7, 1793; Hamilton to Angelica Schuyler Church, November 8, 1789; and Jefferson to Angelica Schuyler Church, May 24, 1797, Church Papers.

21. See in particular Joan B. Landes, *Women and the Public Sphere in the Age of the French Revolution* (Ithaca, 1988).

22. Jan Lewis, " 'Of Every Age Sex & Condition': The Representation of Women in the Constitution," *Journal of the Early Republic* 15 (1995): 359–87.

23. Paine, *Common Sense*, 72.

24. Jefferson to Angelica Schuyler Church, May 24, 1797, Church Papers; Jefferson to Anne Willing Bingham, May 11, 1788, in Peterson, ed. *Writings*, 922; Jefferson to Angelica Schuyler Church, September 21, 1788, Church Papers.

25. Jefferson to Martha Jefferson Randolph, June 8, 1797; February 8, 1798; Jefferson to Mary Jefferson Eppes, February 15, 1801; and Jefferson to Martha Jefferson Randolph, January 16, 1801, in Betts and Bear, eds., *Family Letters*, 146, 155, 196, 191.

26. Church to Alexander Hamilton, February 17, 1793, and September 19, 1794, in Syrett, ed., *Papers of Hamilton*, 14:89, 251–52; Church to Thomas Jefferson, August 19, 1793, and February 17, 1793, in Boyd et al., eds., *Papers of Jefferson*, 26:722–23, 25:215.

27. Gordon S. Wood, *The Radicalism of the American Revolution* (New York, 1992).

28. Jefferson to Catherine Church, December 15, 1808, Church Papers.

29. Hamilton to Angelica Schuyler Church, January 31, 1791, Church Papers. See similarly Hamilton's exchange with Catherine Greene, the widow of Revolutionary War General Nathanael Greene, in Syrett, ed., *Papers of Hamilton*, 6:448–50, 7:457–58, 8:165–66.

30. Jefferson to Anne Willing Bingham, February 7, 1787, in Peterson, ed., *Writings*.

31. Cooke, ed., *The Federalist*, 29–30. See Cooke's annotation.

32. Thomas Laqueur, *Making Sex: Body and Gender from the Greeks to Freud* (Cambridge, MA, 1990); Nancy F. Cott, "Passionlessness: An Interpretation of Victorian Sexual Ideology, 1790–1850," *Signs* 4 (1978): 219–36.

33. Carol Zisowitz Stearns and Peter N. Stearns, *Anger: The Struggle for Emotional Control in America's History* (Chicago, 1986), 46; also see the essays in this volume by C. Dallett Hemphill and Lucia McMahon.

Chapter Four

"While Our Souls Together Blend"
Narrating a Romantic Readership in the Early Republic

Lucia McMahon

Rachel Van Dyke, a seventeen-year-old New Brunswick, New Jersey, resident and student, loved to visit a grove of trees along the brook at the "mile run." There, Rachel enjoyed reading the poetry and prose that her teacher and friend Ebenezer Grosvenor (whom Rachel referred to as Mr. G——) left for her on their "favorite tree." On September 18, 1810, Rachel recorded in her journal a visit to her retreat: "[D]etermined to postpone no longer my walk to mile run. . . . I crossed the brook without any difficulty and at last to my great joy arrived at my old favorite tree, my rural throne." She found her surroundings "tranquil" and "delightful." "I believe Mr. G—— has visited it very often since the evening Abbey [Condict] and me were there with him. The bark of [the tree] is covered with poetical lines from different authors." Rachel "wrote on it a few lines" of her own composition: "They will suffice to let him know I have been there." Perhaps Rachel told Mr. G—— of her visit, for later that same day she noticed "Mr. G—— direct his steps towards the mile run."[1]

A few weeks after these visits to the mile run, Mr. G—— composed and submitted the following poem to the *Rural Visiter,* a Burlington, New Jersey, newspaper that he and Rachel avidly read:

> There is a spot—I love its pensive shade;
> Where scarce a foot save mine, e'er treads the bending grass:
> . . . .
> There creep a stream, on whose untrodden shore,
> A Sycamore's huge roots in folds fantastic twine:
> Where many a thought, in sweet poetic lore,
> In characters uncouth, forms many a crooked line.
>
> There oft I've found with pleasures ever new,
> The roughly-penciled thoughts of a congenial mind—
> Thoughts there inspired, and which, or ere they flew,
> Were to Sibylline tablets, on the bark consigned.
> . . . .
> And here so oft the tear of pleasure steals,
> That, *Pensive Pleasure's Nook,* I've nam'd the fav'rite place.[2]

It was, undoubtedly, Rachel's "roughly-penciled thoughts" and "congenial mind" that Mr. G—— spoke so highly of in his poem. When Rachel "discovered" this piece in the *Rural Visiter,* she immediately "knew it to be his," yet few readers would realize that the anonymous author of "Pensive Pleasure's Nook" was Mr. G——.[3] By anonymously publishing a poem about their retreat in the *Rural Visiter,* Mr. G—— was using a very "public" medium to communicate "private," shared sentiments to Rachel. Although other readers might appreciate the poetic charm of Mr. G——'s publication, perhaps only Rachel would have recognized both the author and the spot described. And certainly no one but Rachel could encourage Mr. G—— to change the name of his "fav'rite place." She informed him that, before reading his poem, she had begun referring to the mile run as Vaucluse—she took the name from the retreat of one of her and Mr. G——'s favorite authors, the Italian philosopher Petrarch. Mr. G—— agreed that "Vaucluse shall be its name." [4]

Ostensibly for the purpose of appreciating nature, a visit to Vaucluse was capable of generating strong emotional reactions—Rachel and Mr. G—— used words such as "joy," "delightful," "love," and "pleasure" to describe moments at their retreat. But more than a "delightful," solitary retreat for contemplation, Vaucluse served as the site of romantic and intellectual exchange between Rachel and Mr. G——. Although Rachel and Mr. G—— rarely visited Vaucluse together, they used this space to communicate with one another, by carving into the tree original poetry or the works of their favorite authors. In addition to their communications at Vaucluse, Mr. G—— and Rachel exchanged journals, poetry, and books on several occasions, creating areas of written "conversation" between them—or what I term a "romantic readership." At once emotional and intellectual, Rachel and Mr. G——'s romantic readership blurred the boundaries between private and public, between courtship and print culture, between desire and intellect, between love and learning.

As a case study in the history of emotions, Rachel and Mr. G——'s romantic readership illuminates new patterns and standards of friendship and romantic love emerging in the nineteenth century. As individualism and the "culture of sensibility" took hold in early nineteenth-century America, new emotional standards for intimate relationships were enacted.[5] Individualism asserted that one's "true" or "inner" self was unique, private, and concealed from the outer world. But to assert and validate one's individuality, it was perhaps necessary—and desired—to realize a sense of connection with other individuals. A key goal of nineteenth-century friendship and romantic love, then, was the achievement of a shared selfhood through sincere and candid communication. As Karen Lystra argues, "If to reveal one's 'true self' was a central convention of nineteenth-century romantic love, it was also a process of strengthening, and sometimes even creating, a role best called the 'romantic self.' " [6] This "romantic self," according to Lystra, represented the immersion of one's self with another—the idea that one's sense of self could be defined only in relation to one's romantic partner.

This emphasis on sharing feelings and emotional similarity occurred within a world that simultaneously assumed and insisted on certain kinds of gender differences. Prescriptions for early nineteenth-century gender roles were crafted from the related ideologies of separate spheres and sexual difference.[7] Separate spheres ideology bound women to the "private" sphere of home and domesticity, while assigning to men the more "public" realms of work and politics.[8] The basis for these assumptions about separate spheres and gender roles was the construction of and belief in natural, biologically innate, fundamental differences between the sexes.[9] Prescriptive literature repeatedly asserted that men and women were dissimilar beings whose differences, "though forming in themselves an evident contrast, serve to illustrate each other."[10] In other words, femininity and masculinity were defined in opposition to one another. Women who repudiated their "natural" feminine traits were defined as "masculinized," while men who failed to live up to standards of masculinity were deemed "effeminate." Neither of these characterizations could be considered positive in a culture that placed a high premium on clearly defined and delineated gender roles. And as French historian Genevieve Fraisse has shown, writers who crafted the doctrines of separate spheres also insisted that sexual attraction and compatibility ultimately depended on these innate sexual differences.[11] Article after article in the prescriptive literature suggested that any "sameness" between men and women would threaten sexual relations by creating rivalry and competition.

Like other nineteenth-century couples, Rachel and Mr. G—— mediated their emotional experiences against cultural standards and prescriptions of friendship and romantic love.[12] But for individuals like Rachel and Mr. G——, the emotional standards prescribed by separate spheres ideology were not the models by which they defined their relationship, but rather the models *against which* they crafted alternate visions of romantic love, courtship, and marriage. Through their romantic readership, Rachel and Mr. G—— sought to transcend the world of separate spheres and achieve "the truest sort of friendship."[13] Against prescriptions of sexual difference, Rachel and Mr. G—— crafted and expressed new standards of emotional experience based on intellectual and emotional "sameness."

Rachel and Mr. G——'s romantic readership, then, was as much a romantic "writership" of experimentation that "narrated" their relationship's progression from a teacher/student interaction to friendship to romance. In choosing what stories to record, and then share, about their relationship, and especially through their journal exchanges, Rachel and Mr. G——sought to shape and maintain control over their own love story. By scripting their emotional narrative, Rachel and Mr. G——hoped to perfect the practice of romantic love while transcending tragic, unhappy fates represented by authors like Petrarch (who, for example, spent decades engaged in an unrequited love affair with Laura, a married woman).[14] On the pages of Rachel and Mr. G——'s romantic readership, a narrative of emotions unfolds.

Rachel Van Dyke, born in 1793, was the youngest daughter of Frederick Van Dyke (1751–1811) and Lydia Cole Van Dyke (1760–1823). Frederick Van Dyke, respected member of the growing city of New Brunswick, New Jersey, lived with his family in a home on Albany Street and owned and operated a farm a few miles outside town. Rachel's playful anecdotes and journal entries indicate that she enjoyed good relationships with her family. Her siblings, James, John, Augustus, and Lydia, were frequently absent from the Van Dyke household; the young men pursued educational or career opportunities and Lydia conducted extended visits with out-of-town relatives and friends.[15] Although the youngest daughter in the Van Dyke family, Rachel was not subject to overwhelming demands of housework that characterized many early republican households.[16] Rachel sometimes helped prepare pies, cakes, dinner, or tea parties, but she was not expected to do so: "Mama never wishes us to be always at this kind of work," Rachel wrote. "She only wishes us to be able to do it—and to direct others if we should ever have occasion."[17] In no small way, it was the presence of these "others" (African American servants) performing household duties that freed Rachel to pursue her own interests.[18]

The Van Dykes' social and economic position can be placed at the moment of transition between two cultures: although the family could not be considered a member of the eighteenth-century gentry class, a coherent middle class had not yet emerged. Rachel noted the growing class distinctions that marked the early nineteenth century, locating her experiences between her friend Jane DuMont's privileged class position and her friend Maria Smith's lower class status. Jane, "Fortune's chosen favorite," experienced "no want," and enjoyed her family's "respected" position, while Maria and her family "struggl[ed] under Poverty" and the "pangs of Misery." The experiences of Rachel and her family, located economically and socially between these boundaries, point toward larger patterns of white middle-class formation that characterize the early nineteenth century.[19]

As a young adolescent, Rachel attended Miss Hay's boarding school in New Brunswick, receiving what many emerging middle- class families considered a standard and sufficient education. Boarding schools provided young women the basic rudiments of reading, writing, arithmetic, and geography, while also offering "ornamental" subjects such as music, drawing, and sewing intended to "refine" future wives and mothers.[20] But at the time she began her journals in 1810, Rachel was attending the Female Academy, an advanced school for young women recently established in New Brunswick by board members of Queens College and the First Dutch Reformed Church. More comprehensive than boarding schools, institutions like the Female Academy provided "young Misses a more accurate and extensive education than is usual." The school's focus was purely academic; it offered no domestic skills or fine arts. Its trustees firmly insisted that applicants exhibit "some considerable progress in reading and writing . . . in order to [gain] admittance."[21] To distinguish the Female Academy from typical boarding schools, the board members entrusted the pupils to a male, college-educated teacher.

It is unclear when Rachel began studying with Mr. G——, but by the spring of 1810 she was his student at the Female Academy, and in June 1810 she began attending his small, advanced Latin class for young women.[22] Ebenezer Grosvenor was born on July 26, 1788, in Pomfret, Connecticut, the third son of Lemuel Grosvenor (1752–1833) and Eunice Putnam Avery Grosvenor (1756–1799). (His mother was the youngest daughter of Revolutionary War general Israel Putnam.) An 1807 graduate of Yale College, Mr. G—— arrived in New Brunswick in April 1808, where he "commenced the instruction of a school of young misses in this place."[23] While in New Brunswick, he boarded with Dr. Ira Condict and his family.[24]

In his journal entry for May 31, 1808, Mr. G—— described his motivations for coming to New Brunswick. He left his hometown of Pomfret "very willingly indeed," for it contained "no society at all which I could be happy with." At the age of twenty, Mr. G—— came to New Brunswick to teach, before returning home to study and practice law: "Young as I am, it will be of no disadvantage I hope if I spend one or even two years in teaching or in some other employment, before I finish my professional studies."[25] Mr. G—— was one of many young men of his generation who migrated to other geographical areas, in search of educational or career opportunities, before embarking on the full path of manhood—defined by early nineteenth-century standards as career, marriage, family.[26] By May 1810, when Rachel's journals began, Mr. G—— had been teaching in New Brunswick for a full two years.

As her male instructor, Mr. G—— culturally stood in a dual position of hierarchy over Rachel. If Mr. G—— and Rachel had conformed to cultural prescriptions, their relationship might never have progressed beyond a friendly, but formal, unequal status between teacher and student. But Mr. G—— and Rachel's friendship sought to transform this hierarchical model. Mr. G——'s behavior and attitudes may have facilitated the transformation, especially his "sentiments on the female sex," which Rachel noted were "generous in the extreme."[27] Perhaps, then, Mr. G—— was no ordinary teacher—and Rachel no ordinary student. In any case, it is fairly clear that by the opening of Rachel's journals in May 1810, Rachel and Mr. G——'s relationship had progressed beyond that of teacher and student, and had crossed into the realms of friendship and romantic love. As Rachel's regular school term with Mr. G—— was about to end in May (and at this time she had no idea that she would later join his advanced Latin class), her journal entry suggests that an emotional attachment had developed between her and Mr. G——:

> After school was out this morning—as I was putting on my hat, Mr. G—— said to me—"Is it then irrevocably fixed? Are you not coming to school any longer than this week?" "I believe it is," I answered, "I believe this week will be the last." "I am very sorry for it," said he looking down and playing with his penknife. I walked to the door and said "I am very sorry too."—These were the very words which passed between us—I shall not forget them. His conveyed to my mind a mixture of sorrow and pleasure. They awakened my sorrow by reminding me how soon I was to leave school— and I felt pleased perhaps I ought to say vain—that he so sincerely regretted it. I regret it no less than he does—yet I feel a pleasing satisfaction in reflecting that since I have been under his tuition—I have gained his esteem—and that he wishes to retain me as his pupil."[28]

One perhaps could be tempted to interpret their mutual regret at Rachel's leaving school strictly in terms of scholarly interest: as an intelligent young woman, Rachel may have been upset because she did not foresee any future opportunities to further her education; while as a caring teacher, Mr. G—— may have regretted that a capable student was unable to continue her studies. But the awkwardness of this moment (as recorded by Rachel), coupled with evidence that Rachel and Mr. G—— were spending time together socially, suggests more than scholarly interest. Rachel and Mr. G——'s mutual "sorrow and pleasure" had romantic as well as intellectual origins.

As Rachel and Mr. G——'s relationship progressed to friendship and then romance, they implicitly confronted cultural standards governing relationships between the sexes. Aware of the power dynamics inherent in their relationship—both in

terms of gender and in terms of their teacher/pupil status—Rachel and Mr. G——
sought to lessen them through "the truest sort of friendship." (But it is significant
that throughout their relationship, Rachel referred to him as "Mr. G——"—not
"Ebenezer.") "True" friendship, according to prescriptive literature, existed between
equals, exhibited mutuality of thoughts, emotions, and sentiments, and depended
upon confidence, sincerity, and candor in communications. Friendship, according to
one writer's summary, was "an affectionate union of two persons, nearly of the same
age, the same situation in life, the same dispositions and sentiments, and, as some
writers will have it, of the same sex." [29]

The notion that true friendship could exist only between individuals of the same
sex reflected ideas about men's and women's contrasting natures. As Carroll Smith-
Rosenberg has argued, the ideologies of sexual difference and separate spheres
formed the basis for a social framework that led to the "emotional segregation of
men and women." [30] Women crafted a "female world of love and ritual" for intimacy
and emotional fulfillment that seemed nearly impossible to obtain in male-female
relationships. Men, E. Anthony Rotundo suggests, also sought same-sex romantic
friendships for emotional support and intimacy, but mainly during a particular phase
in their life cycle: as young men, single, in their twenties, establishing careers (that is,
the life cycle phase Mr. G—— occupied). [31]

Against cultural models of sexual segregation, friendship and courtship rituals
common among members of the emerging white middle class reveal a thriving realm
of heterosocial youth culture. [32] Alone or with friends, heterosocial friends and
courting couples attended parties, teas, and singing schools, took "romantic" walks
along the river, and spent casual evenings together. Rachel and Mr. G—— spent
typical summer evenings socializing with one or two other friends: "We talked,
played, laughed, walked in the garden and amused ourselves in the swing." In
addition, Mr. G—— and Rachel passed many evenings in her family's parlor, playing
backgammon and enjoying "good—long—sociable—uninterrupted conversation." [33] As Ellen Rothman notes, "male-female socializing did not depend on special
occasions, but was integrated into the routine of everyday life." Much of this socializing took place in the absence of parental or communal control, as "youths expected
and experienced considerable autonomy in courtship." [34]

This fluid sphere of heterosocial interaction, coupled with cultural ideals of
friendship (sincerity, candor, and intimacy), also served as the basis of companionate
marriage in the early Republic. As Jan Lewis has argued, the model "republican
marriage," which in turn served as political metaphor for the young Republic, was
"friendship exalted." [35] The author of an essay "On Matrimonial Happiness" captured
this ideal of early republican marriage: "No happiness on earth can be so great, nor
any friendship so tender, as the state of matrimony affords, when two congenial souls
are united." [36] Despite the rhetoric of separate spheres and sexual difference, then,
heterosocial friendship and marriage were celebrated as sites where "congenial souls"
could experience rich, satisfying relationships.

While their flirtatious encounters at school and evenings socializing mirrored
friendship and courtship practices of the early Republic, it was through their romantic readership that Mr. G—— and Rachel sought the shared experiences and affinity

that would strengthen significantly their relationship.[37] We can trace the chronology of their romantic readership through Rachel's journals. Rachel began to keep a daily journal on May 7, 1810, under the advice and encouragement of Mr. G——. As her teacher, Mr. G—— may have suggested that Rachel begin her journal as an intellectual and educational endeavor. But two weeks later, Mr. G—— made a request of Rachel that suggests he had an ulterior motive in mind:

> I have passed the day at school as usual. Mr. G—— this evening said he expected to have the privilege of perusing one of my journals. *I don't think you will Sir.* I flatter myself that it will never be in the power of anyone to laugh at this nonsense. . . . [T]he privilege you claim Mr. G—— requires some consideration. Therefore I will now defer giving an answer and if you please will think on the matter at my leisure.[38]

Significantly, Rachel's "response" was written in her "private" journal but addressed directly to Mr. G——, a curious gesture from one who denied the possibility of his readership. In denying Mr. G——'s request, Rachel attempted to claim her journal strictly for her use and reflection, and not to give another individual the "power" to read her innermost thoughts—to read her "self." But Rachel's reply to Mr. G—— ended with equivocation, not an outright rejection of his request. Although she would "defer" the matter for nearly six weeks, in July 1810 she and Mr. G—— began exchanging journals. In the six-week interim between Mr. G——'s initial request and Rachel's agreement to exchange journals, they began the first stage of their romantic readership: sharing sentimental and romantic books and poetry.

"Reader response" to particular authors and works validated Rachel and Mr. G——'s individual feelings within a framework of shared communications.[39] As its title suggests, M. Zimmerman's *Solitude Considered with Respect to Its Influence upon the Mind and Heart* was a perfect bridge between the intellectual and romantic strands of their relationship.[40] Zimmerman, a German romantic writer about whom little is known or written, extolled the virtues of solitary reflection and scholastic pursuits of literature. When Mr. G—— lent this book to Rachel, she responded enthusiastically: "[Zimmerman] addresses himself only to those who possess 'sufficient energy to drive away the dread of being alone—to those whose hearts are susceptible of the pure and tranquil delights of domestic felicity.' To me, then, I suppose that he addresses himself. . . . Retirement I love, Solitude is my delight."[41]

Rachel responded to Zimmerman by identifying completely with him. She imagined herself as his ideal reader, in complete understanding of his thoughts: "I feel a secret satisfaction—when reading his sentiments—which heretofore no serious author could bestow."[42] Her reaction to this book was active and "intensive." As Robert Darnton argues, "Reader and writer communed across the printed page, each of them assuming the ideal form envisioned in the text." This form of intensive reading broke down barriers between the author and the reader, as the reader was urged to achieve complete identification and emotional affinity with the author and book read. The reader aimed to "absorb [the book] into his inner world, and to express it in his daily life."[43]

When Mr. G—— lent Rachel a book of poetry by James Montgomery, she spent an entire day reading it, to the neglect of her studies and housework. She justified

her actions by claiming that Montgomery's poetry fully absorbed her attention—
that it in essence seduced her. She compared her response to Montgomery's poetry
to that an "adoring lover" would have to the "enticing charms" of "a lady exquisitely
beautiful and truly fascinating." As a "lovestruck" reader, Rachel wondered, "And
may I not with as much truth say it was the simple melody of the poems which won
my attention—my admiration—and caused me to neglect my work."[44] Rachel was
so enthralled by Montgomery that, "with a little alteration," she copied one of his
poems into her journal. Rachel's poem appears on the left, and Montgomery's
original on the right (her alterations appear in italics):

And yet *my* Pillow! yet to me,	And yet O Pillow! yet to me,
My *wish'd* for friend *exists* in thee:	My gentle Friend survives in thee:
On thee, in pensive mood reclin'd,	On thee, in pensive mood reclin'd,
I've pour'd *my* contemplative mind,	He pour'd his contemplative mind,
Till over *my* eyes with mild control	Till o'er his eyes with mild control
Sleep like a soft enchantment stole,	Sleep like a soft enchantment stole,
Charm'd into life *my* airy schemes	Charm'd into life his airy schemes
And realized *my* waking dreams.	And realized his waking dreams.

On thee, Oh Pillow! now I'll rest
And Sleep shall calm my troubl'd breast
Sleep shall my weary eyelids close
And hush my thoughts to sweet repose.[45]

What is perhaps most striking in this evidence of reader response is the "alteration" Rachel made to Montgomery's poem. Although "The Pillow" contained a
description of a deceased friend, Rachel selected and altered passages that instead
reflected what were undoubtedly her romantic musings about Mr. G——. Significantly, she substituted Montgomery's line "My gentle friend survives in thee" with
the more romantic text "My wish'd for friend exists in thee." She then reworked the
stanza on "pensive" thoughts to reflect her own fondness for "waking dreams,"
rather than the author's fond tribute to a departed companion. Rachel's response to
Montgomery's poetry included, then, an effort to make sense of her romantic feelings
for Mr. G——. She experienced similar responses to the romantic poetry of Cowper,
Ossian, Thomson, and Young. She read these works repeatedly, noting that "there
are some books which you cannot read too often—the better you are acquainted
with them—the more you admire them."[46]

This process of intense, enthusiastic response to and identification with certain
authors was mediated by Rachel's relationship with Mr. G——: books gained symbolic value as a reflection of the giver.[47] Through their romantic readership, Rachel
and Mr. G—— participated in reciprocal exchange rituals in which books became
symbols—and tools—of friendship and romantic love. Rachel was also an active
participant in these exchanges, frequently recommending and/or lending books to
Mr. G—— that she identified with or enjoyed reading. "When I first got the life of
Miss Elizabeth Smith," Rachel wrote, "I told Mr. G—— of it and said he must read
it. He . . . begged me to mark out the passages which pleased me best—or which I
wished him to take notice (as we always do in books we read together)."[48] Marking

passages was a way of providing interaction between their individual acts of reading. Pointing out particularly interesting, relevant, or moving passages to one another helped assure that their reader response would be truly mutual.

Rachel's intense response to Zimmerman, Montgomery, and other authors also was enhanced by the idea that Mr. G—— had responded similarly to these works. By mutually admiring certain authors and works, and appropriating sentimental and romantic language, Rachel and Mr. G—— forged reading—normally a solitary, individual act—into a collective process, a process that forged a shared sense of self while strengthening the intellectual and romantic bonds between them. As Mary Kelley notes in her discussion of nineteenth-century women's collective reading: "Sharing books both literally and figuratively, [women] recommended volumes, exchanged ideas, and celebrated the pleasures of reading."[49] Collective reading validated educated women's sense of self, while also providing a source of connection among women. Implicit in Kelley's argument is the notion that nineteenth-century women were capable of sharing identities through reading because they shared some common sense of self as *women*. But in collective reading processes that took place between men and women, the common sense of self had to come from somewhere else—or be built through the common experience of reading itself.[50] Rachel and Mr. G——'s romantic readership was thus an attempt to script an ideal shared self that simultaneously denied/transcended their sexual difference, while also highlighting their romantic attraction for each other.

On July 9, 1810, Rachel and Mr. G—— exchanged journals for the first time, beginning perhaps the most intimate form their romantic readership took. Exchanging journals was a key means of sharing their innermost thoughts and emotions with one another, to the extent that the other committed them to paper. A "private" journal is often thought of as an emotional repository where an individual asserts his/her own unique self.[51] But for Rachel and Mr. G——, their journals were also the vehicles for narrating and refining the emotional state of their relationship. In her journals, Rachel constructed (through her writing) and revealed (through the journal exchanges with Mr. G——) a sincere, likable character—and expected the same of Mr. G—— when she read his journals.

When Rachel received Mr. G——'s journal the morning of July 9, 1810, she at first was disappointed with its contents: "I declare he has cheated me—it does not contain half so much as mine does. . . . Sometimes he fills *one whole* page in four days." Rachel felt "cheated" by Mr. G——'s journal, apparently because it failed to convey to Rachel a proper self-representation of its author. Its short entries and sparse content did not fit Rachel's model of a personal journal: "Why positively it is nothing more than an Almanac," she complained. In Rachel's opinion, her own journal more accurately portrayed a true and sincere representation of the self: "To read my journal I may almost say that with a few exceptions you read my heart." But Mr. G——'s journal, Rachel felt, was "merely a register of time."[52]

Rachel's disapproval of Mr. G——'s journal almost caused her to retract her promise to exchange journals with him. When Mr. G—— visited Rachel that evening at home to receive her journal, she complied "with reluctance and at the same time abused his because there was so little of it."[53] On the front cover of her journal fascicle, she wrote the following instructions to Mr. G——: "You are to read this journal but once through—You are not to copy *any* of it—or to impart the least of its contents even to your best friend—Upon these conditions, proceed—and read this *important book*."[54] In setting the conditions under which the journal exchanges could take place, Rachel was attempting to maintain some control over Mr. G——'s response to her journal. As the author of this "important book," Rachel directed her reader (Mr. G——) to read carefully, but she attempted to set clear limits on Mr. G——'s reaction. In his reply to Rachel's mandate, however, Mr. G—— found a loophole that she had not anticipated: "Upon reading this *Law*, with all the legal sagacity of which I am master I can discover nothing in it which forbids me learning *by rote* (rather, by *heart*) the whole book. This has been my endeavour."[55]

Although Rachel's command to Mr. G—— expressly forbade him to copy any of her journal, she did not hold herself subject to the same "law." Instead, Rachel copied several passages of Mr. G—— 's journal into her own journal: "All that I intend to copy is about myself. It looks something like vanity," Rachel admitted, "but still I will do it."[56] In recording her responses to passages from Mr. G——'s journal, Rachel seemed flattered but hesitant to trust fully his opinion or her own vanity:

> He speaks of me once again as follows—
>
> "Spent the evening at Miss Van Dikes. . . . She is indeed accomplished before any girl I know in the literary point of view."
>
> Here again I intend to scribble an answer. It shall be this—"I must believe that these are your thoughts, or you would not have written them—where you little expected I would meet with them—but don't imagine that because *you think* so *I receive* it as a truth."[57]

Reading such passages, in which Mr. G—— also referred to Rachel as "the best girl extant," was a source of ambivalence for Rachel. Considering that his comments were made in the privacy of his own journal, "when he did not expect that any one would ever see it," Rachel reasoned that "he writes what he thinks," but she was reluctant to believe (or admit) that she was "so vain as to believe what he thinks is true." Rachel conceded that Mr. G——'s private "thoughts" were undoubtedly sincere and authentic, or he would not have written them in his private journal. But in order to square her belief in the sincerity of his private word with her own skepticism of Mr. G——'s opinion of her, Rachel was left to question the validity—but not the sincerity—of his ideas. Thus, she could avoid accepting his sincerity as "truth," but with the error resulting not from any poor or insincere character: "I only conclude that he is a poor Judge and entertains erroneous ideas of my abilities."[58]

The idea, as Jay Fliegelman argues in *Declaring Independence*, that private writings were more sincere and "more frank than public utterance" found ambivalent expression once Rachel and Mr. G—— made their private "utterances" "public" to each other. Individuals continually sought the "public revelation of a private self," but strove to ensure that public communication reflected one's true self, and not a public mask or persona. Thus, in the effort to make public the private—and hence true and authentic—self, individuals had to guard against the danger of misrepresenting their private selves through public communication. The result, as Fliegelman suggests for the context of public speaking, was a "paradoxical mutuality of self- assertion and self-concealment."[59]

Mr. G—— and Rachel sought to bridge this gap between private sincerity and public artifice, communicating to each other through the "private" medium of their journals. Although the possibility of each other's readership undoubtedly altered the "private" nature of their journals, Rachel and Mr. G—— repeatedly insisted that each other's journal writings must be true, sincere, and candid—or else they would not have been recorded in the "privacy" of their journals. Moreover, Rachel and Mr. G—— both insisted that their journal exchanges represented the ultimate expression of their trust in one another. They relied on each other's assurances that "private" writings would not be revealed to others, an act that would compromise that trust.

Yet the act of entrusting another person with one's emotions and "inner self" was a risky element of nineteenth-century individualism and romantic love that placed individuals in vulnerable positions. Issues of power and vulnerability thus surfaced frequently during the journal exchanges. As Mr. G—— noted in a journal exchange that took place on September 14, 1810:

> The manner in which I have spent this (Friday) evening—reading and remarking on your journal, fills my head with a thousand queer thoughts—that I suffer my journals to pass beneath any eye but my own! . . . No one but yourself has ever read the journal of a day of mine. I need not tell you that it seems odd when I reflect that all these thoughts are no longer my own—no longer in my own power.[60]

Mr. G—— remarked on a central element of their journal exchanges. Surrendering his "thoughts" to Rachel, Mr. G—— also surrendered his own "power" over his emotions and his inner self. And as we have seen, Rachel shared Mr. G——'s concern about making her self vulnerable to another's power. But at the same time, this concern with vulnerability had an unmistakable thrill and attraction to it—as evident by their repeated journal exchanges. By relinquishing their power over their own selves and self-representations, Rachel and Mr. G—— gained an element of power and control over their relationship. Having confronted each other's true self in the "privacy" of one another's journals, Rachel and Mr. G—— then could assure themselves that the "self" revealed to each other during intimate conversations and social encounters was also a true, sincere character. Thus, Rachel felt increasingly confident in her encounters with Mr. G—— in the classroom and in her parlor: "I really talk to him with less restraint—with less fear that what I say should be repeated—than to any other friend I have—and I believe—nay I am sure he does the same to me. It was only this evening that he told me he had never shown his journals or his poetry to any one except me—and what *he* says I believe."[61]

As Rachel and Mr. G——'s emotional encounters grew more and more intimate, they used their journal exchanges to narrate and, in a sense, "review" their relationship. In scripting their emotional narrative, Rachel and Mr. G—— related stories, encounters, and emotions that validated their sense of connection to each other's inner self. Descriptions of shared flirtatious events or veiled romantic musings sparked romantic and erotic "conversations" between Rachel and Mr. G—— in the margins of her journals. One journal conversation alluded to an evening Rachel and Mr. G—— spent alone together. On September 14, 1810, while "no one was left" in the house but Rachel, "Mr. G—— stopped as he came from school and passed a couple of hours with me." Rachel admitted in her journal that the visit left her "in a strange humour." Upon later reading her journal, Mr. G—— agreed that it was a special evening: "I can remember no time that I have ever spent at your house so perfectly well as this couple of hours. I know not *why*—But it seems as if I can almost *realize* them now—how it rained ~~~,~~~,~~~." Mr. G—— and Rachel exchanged journals that evening, "as he appeared to desire it so much."[62] Their journal exchange that evening seemed to serve as an erotically charged substitute for sexual exchange.

Taking Rachel's journal home with him the evening of September 14, Mr. G—— read her "romantic" description of a moonlit evening: "I don't think I ever saw the sky look so lovely," she wrote. "I could have gazed the whole evening—for . . . every moment I discovered new beauties." Mr. G—— referred Rachel to the entry "August 25 in my book," where presumably she would find his similar description of this evening. "Is it possible," he wondered, "that *accident* should have turned our thoughts at the same instant of time so exactly into the same channel—I remember this evening perfectly for its own sake, but this circumstance will render it indelible."[63] In this erotically charged "conversation," Mr. G—— noted that their thoughts were often identical, even when apart—suggesting that the bond between them was more than "accident." Implicitly, Mr. G—— was suggesting that their identities had become so connected that shared experiences and reactions to moonlit evenings were inevitable.

Through "conversations" in their journal exchanges, Rachel and Mr. G—— grew closer to complete identification with each other and to a shared identity that joined two separate selves into one unified "romantic" self. Perhaps nowhere is this process more evident than in their journal exchange of September 4, 1810. On this occasion, Mr. G—— managed to extract from Rachel her current journal. When she complained that doing so left her with no way of keeping her journal up to date, he took the liberty of "writing" her journal for two days. In authoring her journal, Mr. G—— engaged in an ultimate act of assuming and assimilating Rachel's identity. Although he used humor to conduct this symbolic ritual of role reversal, his writings highlight their efforts to construct a shared sense of self:

> He staid, as he always does, till I was ready to send him away. I believe he forgets, when he comes here, that he is not *at home* and if there was no *clock* to drive him away, I believe he would stay till *hunger* did. However, he says he never makes a visit any where else and so I suppose he cannot measure time so well as if he was more in the habit of doing it. I gave him some poems which I had promised him, and chang'd journals with him again. I got two, or am to have another tomorrow, in addition to the one which I got tonight in exchange for mine: for when he sees there is any prospect of getting one of mine, he seems to lose his usual circumspectness and agrees, almost without hesitation, to exactly such terms as I choose to fix. I laughed heartily after he was gone, to think that he should be so foolish as to change two journals for one.[64]

In this playful passage, Mr. G—— suggested his own vulnerability in the act of exchanging journals with Rachel. Although he suggested the practice, he felt that his eagerness to see her journal allowed Rachel to chose "exactly such terms" as she desired. In an amusing tone, he assumed that Rachel reveled in her privileged position, "laugh[ing] heartily" over his "foolish" willingness to "change two journals for one." Vulnerable in the act of being "read" by one another, Rachel and Mr. G—— also experienced a certain thrill and pleasure in the process of sharing their selves—and narrating their relationship—with each other.

When Mr. G—— took home Rachel's current journal on September 4, he had the opportunity to read and respond to very recent events in Rachel's life. By ghostwriting Rachel's journal, Mr. G—— was able to shape and narrate particular events as they occurred. In the first entry of the fascicle that Mr. G—— carried home on September 4, Rachel described a visit she made to the mile run, where she "carved letters on the trees."[65] The day after she gave this journal to Mr. G——, Rachel returned to the mile run, correctly surmising that after Mr. G—— read her journal, curiosity would lead him to seek out her carvings. Thus, part of Mr. G——'s journal entry for September 5, 1810, includes "his" version—in Rachel's voice—of her actions:

> In p.m. I walked with M. Lawrence out to the farm. I was careful to stop on my return just at dusk and deface the names which I had cut on the tree at the Mile Run for I was sure that Mr. G—— would go there to see them, the first moment he had time—and I love, above all things, to tantalize him. I did but just affect my purpose this time, for I had just got the names destroyed and got to the road, when I saw Mr. G—— walking in the opposite road. He went directly to . . . where I had been at work. The wound was still fresh, still weeping ~~and in this I could well nigh have joined it for mere vexation~~— *I forgot myself here completely for a moment and imagined I was writing in my own journal.* I was extremely careful to destroy every vestige of a letter, as to leave him in perfect uncertainty.[66]

By suggesting that Rachel's actions were deliberately designed to tease him, Mr. G—— was scripting this event in light of his own "vexation"—a viewpoint Rachel may not have included in her own narration. Upon reading this entry, Rachel agreed almost completely with Mr. G——'s version, noting in the margin of her own journal that it was "as true and exact as if I had written it myself." But Rachel also recast the narrative, revising her motivations and actions to reflect Mr. G——'s implicit critique. She made it a point to edit her own journal, noting that her actions were conducted "not with a view to tantalize him," but rather because she "really feared he might see the initials of a name which he would have known instantly."[67] Although Mr. G——'s appropriation of Rachel's "self" brought them closer to a shared sense of identity (after all, Mr. G—— succeeded at capturing Rachel "as true and exact" as herself), Rachel also viewed the narration of their romance as a process open and subject to revision.

Throughout their romantic readership, Rachel and Mr. G—— were engaged in what Lystra calls an "intensely dramatic and exciting period of interaction," or the ritualistic "testing" of romantic love. The most important scenes of their courtship, including daily encounters at school, intimate conversations, and romantic musings, implicitly were moments of both anticipation and anxiety.[68] Rachel and Mr. G—— took a very active role, not just performing but also narrating these scenes, hoping to maintain some control over the potential outcome of their relationship. Their close proximity facilitated this measure of control. But in November 1810, Rachel learned that Mr. G—— had plans to return to Connecticut at the end of the school term. Although they both knew that physical separation was approaching, it was a subject they treated vaguely and wrote about with reservation. On November 5, 1810, Mr. G—— asked Rachel to exchange journals with him: "I could not refuse him. I thought, perchance, it might be [the] last time we would be near enough to do it."[69] During this last journal exchange, Mr. G—— refused to treat his impending departure as an ending to their romantic readership: "I anticipate a time when I shall see B[runswick] and my friends in it again. Then too I shall hope to be indulged with the perusal of these books which have already afforded me so much and so exquisite gratification."[70]

Shortly after this last journal exchange, Mr. G—— fell seriously ill, and was unable to hold school or visit Rachel. Mr. G—— left New Brunswick on December 7, 1810, returning home to Pomfret to recover fully his health and then resume his law studies. Although her journals began to express more fully her sadness and melancholy at Mr. G——'s departure, Rachel sought to bridge the physical distance between them by focusing on the emotional attachment and affinity they could experience still. "I have thought a great deal of Mr. G—— since he has been gone," Rachel wrote shortly after his departure. "I supposed he was wrapped up—sitting on the deck looking at the moon. I enjoyed a kind of pleasure in imagining that tho' far distant—we might still at the same moment be viewing the same object—and perhaps- -said I to myself—he also may be thinking of his friend Rachel."[71] Like the moonlit evening that had turned their "thoughts at the same instant of time so exactly into the same channel," Rachel and Mr. G—— could continue to delight in separate—though shared—experiences.[72] "Tho' far distant," Rachel and Mr. G——'s identities remained fully connected. Thus, they could envision and imagine each other's thoughts and emotions to provide a source of "pleasure" to ease the pain of separation.

Now that they were separated by distance, the written word became an even more central means of communication between Rachel and Mr. G——.[73] In an effort to continue their romantic readership, Mr. G—— and Rachel began a monthly correspondence. Rachel eagerly awaited Mr. G——'s letters, reading them "over and over again." She found writing to Mr. G—— was "rather a pleasure than a hardship. . . . I am afraid I send him a great deal of nonsense but . . . he knows how to excuse it, he knows that I write to him just as I would talk, without fear or restraint: considering him . . . as my truest, my best, my ~~~ friend."[74] Rachel and Mr. G——'s letter writing paralleled the experiences of other nineteenth-century romantic couples, who, as Lystra notes, "often read and wrote love letters as if they were in a conversation that might be overheard."[75]

Both Lystra and Rothman suggest that letters offered a "safe, in some cases, the only way" for men and women separated by distance to communicate, yet Mr. G——

and Rachel found other means of maintaining their romantic readership.[76] In his letters, Mr. G—— asked Rachel for her recommendation of reading material: "Mr. G—— is reading Camilla upon my recommendation—How flattering to me is the deference he pays to my judgement."[77] Rachel, in turn, was pleased to receive the February 11, 1811, issue of the *Rural Visiter*: "It contains . . . one piece of prose more *valuable than all the rest—because Mr. G—— was its author*. He told me before he went away, that he did not expect to write any more for the *RV [Rural Visiter]* unless *RVD* [Rachel Van Dyke] would give him a subject. I requested . . . a few remarks on his '*waking dreams*' . . . and this is the promised—expected piece." As with his earlier poem on "Vaucluse," Mr. G—— submitted a composition that would be readable to a general audience, but understood fully only by Rachel.[78]

In response to Mr. G——'s composition on waking dreams, and after receiving his monthly letter, Rachel composed and submitted a poem for publication. Once again, the *Rural Visiter* became the means by which Rachel and Mr. G—— communicated "privately" through a very public vehicle. The last three stanzas of her poem appear below:

> What rapt'rous pleasure still to gaze
>   Thinking some dear absent friend
> Then views that spot, those very rays
>   While our souls together blend.
>
> Then, fairy Fancy, busy pow'r,
>   Building castles high in air,
> With thee I pass the fleeting hour,
>   Forming future prospects fair.
>
> Waking, I dream—I dream of bliss:
>   "Waking dreams" are dear to me;
> Though (experience teaches this)
>   "Gilded poisons" they may be.[79]

By publishing—and publicizing—their "private" sentiments in the *Rural Visiter*, Rachel and Mr. G—— extended the boundaries of their romantic readership into the public realm of print culture. In the process, Rachel and Mr. G—— both framed and subverted the traditional boundaries of courtship in print. Traditional courtships often were validated in newspapers, through the printing of marriage banns or announcements. Unlike marriage banns, which publicly validated a relationship to a larger community, Rachel and Mr. G——'s publications secretly displayed in public a relationship that was validated only in the confines of their private letters and journals.[80] In one sense, Rachel and Mr. G——'s publications echoed the concerns over secret and private communications articulated by a young Thomas Jefferson: "We must fall on some scheme of communicating our thoughts to each other, which shall be totally unintelligible to every one but to ourselves."[81] While Jefferson worried that his communications with John Page might fall into the wrong hands, Rachel and Mr. G—— seemed to enjoy a certain thrill and delight in conducting a "private" communication and courtship in "public." Conducting their romantic readership across a spectrum of printed sources—journals, books, poetry, carvings at Vaucluse, and publications in the *Rural Visiter*—their "congenial mind[s]" experienced "pleasures ever new."

*

The romantic readership of Rachel Van Dyke and Ebenezer Grosvenor indicates a complex periodization and categorization in the history of emotions. This case study suggests that cultural standards of expressive sincerity and emotional intimacy generally associated with the mid- to late nineteenth century were developing by the early nineteenth century.[82] But certain elements of early nineteenth-century emotional standards seem distinct from later developments. Since gender and middle-class ideology was still in the process of formation, there was perhaps more room for flexibility and an active reworking of individual expectations. In particular, Rachel and Mr. G——'s willingness to engage in a romantic readership emphasizing both emotional unity *and* intellectual compatibility suggests that, at the very least, notions of gender differentiation were perhaps less important and more easily overcome than would be true later in the nineteenth century. Upon further research we may even have to revise our notions about the relationship between emotional standards and individual experience for the latter part of the nineteenth century as well.

If Rachel and Mr. G——'s romantic readership is at all typical, we need to consider more closely how the relationship between courtship and print culture intersects with the emotional standards created by the ideologies of separate spheres and sexual difference. If print culture was the site of Rachel and Mr. G——'s expressive sincerity, it was also the space used to construct and explain men and women's contrasting reason, morality, manners, and disposition. Separate spheres ideology insisted that attraction between the sexes was generated by a sense of compatibility through these "natural" differences. But Rachel's romantic readership with Mr. G—— enabled her to envision a partnership between two individuals that challenged prevailing views of gender relations and marriage:[83]

> When . . . I am married, I intend that my deary shall build me a neat little cottage, in some retired, romantic place . . . and there we will live like—like—Oh Bless me I can't find anything to which I may compare such happiness. Like two turtle doves? No, no that would be too loving. Like two affectionate friends—Yes, that will do better. We would live like *true* friends—our thoughts, our wishes should be known to each other. We would share equally each other's joys and griefs—nay, our very souls should be one.[84]

In accord with cultural prescriptions, Rachel envisioned marriage as two individuals experiencing a "true" friendship. But Rachel's vision of romantic love and marriage was divested of the sexual difference, as well as the hierarchy and power relations, that marked companionate marriages. Companionate marriage stressed friendship, intimacy, and affinity, but ultimately, cultural standards called on women to subordinate their own interests for the sake of a happy, loving marriage. As Lewis argues, when marital conflict arose, "the wife, in order to maintain domestic tranquillity, was expected to defer."[85]

Against prescriptive literature and prevailing emotional standards, Rachel celebrated not female submission, but "affectionate" equality, as an alternative for marital happiness and fulfillment. Rachel developed her own emotional standard, in which

individuals experienced a shared identity through intellectual and emotional sameness, not from prescriptive literature, but from her romantic readership with Mr.
G——. Thus, Rachel's ideal marriage more closely mirrored Zimmerman's writings,
which emphasized the pleasures one could gain from "enlightened friendship" between two individuals expressing similar "sentiments mutually interchanged and
equally sincere":

> Casting a retrospective eye on the time that has passed, the happy pair mutually exclaim
> with the tenderest emotions, "Oh! What pleasures have we not already experienced,
> what joys have we not already felt!" . . . Day after day, they communicate to each other
> all that they have seen, all that they have heard, all that they feel, and everything they
> know.[86]

Rachel and Mr. G——'s romantic readership served as a bridge between private
and public, between courtship and print culture, between romance and reading. The
assertion and validation of one's individualism, especially one's "inner self," occurred
at the nexus of these sites. In effect, authentic expression and communication were
the desired effects of both romance and reading, intended to draw individuals (as
authors/readers or as friends/courting couples) closer to a shared sense of self.
Readers sought to achieve intensive, emotional reader response to sentimental and
romantic works, while couples sought to achieve a unified romantic self through
communion of "true selves."[87] Through their romantic readership, Rachel and Mr.
G—— merged these two aims: seeking complete identification with sentimental
literature not just as an end in itself, but as a means to the end of achieving complete
identification with one another.

The idea that reading and romance were areas in which individuals experienced a
sense of complete identification and communion with one another raises interesting
questions regarding the construction of identity and "selfhood."[88] The importance
of emotionally fulfilling (homo- or heterosocial) relationships to men and women's
self-fashioning suggests that one's individualism or sense of self—like gender roles
themselves—was constructed primarily in relationship to others. In other words, an
individual encountered and made sense of his or her identity primarily in relation to
other individuals, and particularly those individuals with whom he or she experienced close, intimate relationships. For individuals sharing several common characteristics—age, race, socioeconomic position, intellectual interests—gender could
serve as either another category of "sameness" (for individuals sharing gender) or
perhaps a key marker of "difference" (for heterosocial couples).[89]

The existence of heterosocial friendships and courtships like Rachel and Mr.
G——'s suggests that men and women confronted—perhaps embraced—the tensions inherent in achieving emotional and intellectual "sameness" against cultural
prescriptions of gender and sexual "difference." Rachel and Mr. G—— crafted a
unified standard of emotions (a denial of sexual difference) that was not incompatible with their ardent attraction for one another (which, in a heterosexual context,
would highlight sexual difference). In contrast to prescriptive literature that evoked
natural, irrefutable differences between the sexes, Rachel and Mr. G——'s romantic
readership suggests that a relationship based on intellectual parity and emotional

sameness could enhance and intensify—not detract from—sexual desire and attraction. Mr. G—— and Rachel's shared intellectual pursuits created not rivalry and competition, but affinity and fellowship.

But in a culture that inscribed fundamental gender and sexual differences as normative, the possibility of true intimacy and union between the sexes was a thrilling prospect indeed. Rachel Van Dyke and Ebenezer Grosvenor aspired to create such a heterosocial world, sharing emotions and sensibilities and incorporating each other's identity so that their "very souls should be one."[90] Bridging the boundaries between courtship and print culture in their search for an expressive, sincere form of communicating the self, Rachel and Mr. G—— scripted new standards for individualism and emotional expression. In the process, they experienced a romantic readership that both denied and affirmed sexual difference, at once diffusing and embracing the erotic tension between them.[91]

NOTES

Earlier versions of this chapter were presented at the Philadelphia Center for Early American Studies and the Annual Meeting of the Society for Historians of the Early American Republic.

1. Journals of Rachel Van Dyke, September 18, 1810, Special Collections, Alexander Library, Rutgers University, New Brunswick, New Jersey; hereafter cited as RVD, with date of entry. Rachel's journals consist of twenty-three numbered fascicles (each between forty-four and forty-eight pages), and cover the period from May 1810 through July 1811. The first book, covering May 7–19, 1810, is lacking. Throughout this chapter, Ebenezer Grosvenor will be referred to as Mr. G——, consistent with Rachel's journals. Spelling and punctuation appear as in the original text (except a few revisions for clarity).

2. The *Rural Visiter [sic]* (Burlington, NJ), October 8, 1810. The poem was submitted by Mr. G—— under the initials M. R.

3. RVD, October 9, 1810. Mr. G—— was following the well-established practice of publishing one's work anonymously. See Michael Warner, *The Letters of the Republic: Publication and the Public Sphere in Eighteenth-Century America* (Cambridge: Harvard University Press, 1990).

4. RVD, October 9, 1810. Rachel and Mr. G—— learned about Petrarch from many sources, especially Susannah Dobson [Dawson], *Life of Petrarch* ([18??]; reprint, Philadelphia: Mitchell and Ames, 1817).

5. For the rise of individualism and sentimental expression in the early nineteenth century, see especially Jan Lewis, *The Pursuit of Happiness: Family and Values in Jefferson's Virginia* (Cambridge: Cambridge University Press, 1983); G. J. Barker-Benfield, *The Culture of Sensibility: Sex and Society in Eighteenth-Century Britain* (Chicago: University of Chicago Press, 1992); Jay Fliegelman, *Declaring Independence: Jefferson, Natural Language, and the Culture of Performance* (Stanford: Stanford University Press, 1993); John Gillis, "From Ritual to Romance: Toward an Alternative History of Love," in Carol Z. Stearns and Peter N. Stearns, eds., *Emotion and Social Change: Toward a New Psychohistory* (New York: Holmes and Meier, 1988), 87–121; Karen Halttunen, *Confidence Men and Painted Women: A Study of Middle-Class Culture in America, 1830–1870* (New Haven: Yale University Press, 1982); and Thomas Haskell, "Capitalism and the Origins of the Humanitarian Sensibility, Part 2," in Thomas Bender, ed., *The Antislavery Debate: Capitalism and Abolitionism as a Problem in Historical Interpretation* (Berkeley: University of California Press, 1992), 136–60.

6. Karen Lystra, *Searching the Heart: Women, Men and Romantic Love in Nineteenth-Century America* (New York: Oxford University Press, 1989), 27. Although she focuses largely on mid- to late nineteenth-century America, Lystra provides a useful discussion of courtship practices and the search for shared subjectivities through print (namely, letter writing). To argue that nineteenth-

century individuals believed in the ideal (or the emotional standard) of a "true self" is not the same as arguing for the existence of or belief in a "true self" per se. Rather, my aim here is to explore the belief systems and performative processes that individuals such as Rachel and Mr. G——enacted in an effort to meet a historical and cultural standard of individuality. In other words, it is perhaps less important to ponder whether Rachel and Mr. G—— in effect realized their "true selves" with one another, than the idea that they strove to and believed that they had.

7. For a review of the scholarship and a useful analysis of how the concept of separate spheres has affected the historiography of nineteenth-century America, see Linda Kerber, "Separate Spheres, Female Worlds, Woman's Place: The Rhetoric of Women's History," *Journal of American History* 75 (June 1988): 9–39. Important works employing the model of separate spheres to describe and analyze prescriptions for and experiences of women's lives in the early to mid-nineteenth century include Nancy Cott, *The Bonds of Womanhood: Woman's Sphere in New England, 1780–1835* (New Haven: Yale University Press, 1984); Linda Kerber, *Women of the Republic: Intellect and Ideology in Revolutionary America* (Chapel Hill: University of North Carolina Press, 1980); Suzanne Lebsock, *The Free Women of Petersburg: Status and Culture in a Southern Town, 1784–1860* (New York: Norton, 1984); Mary Ryan, *Cradle of the Middle Class: The Family in Oneida County, New York, 1700–1865* (New York: Cambridge University Press, 1981); and Carroll Smith-Rosenberg, "The Female World of Love and Ritual: Relations between Women in Nineteenth-Century America," *Signs* 1 (autumn 1975): 1–29, and reprinted in her *Disorderly Conduct: Visions of Gender in Victorian America* (New York: Oxford University Press, 1985), 53–76.

8. Positing a sharp divide between public and private, historians employing a separate spheres analysis often contend that men and women led very different lives in distinct spheres (see n. 7). Recently, however, historians of women's and gender history have uncovered a fluid interaction between the lives of men and women, and between the spheres of public and private, although the metaphor of separate spheres continues to serve as a dominant conceptual framework for antebellum America. For the purposes of this essay, "separate spheres" is best understood as an ideology (and less as a description of actual behavior) that attempted to define and articulate gender roles based on the presumption that men and women inhabited distinct, divided realms.

For a useful discussion of the uses and limitations of separate spheres and public/private frameworks, see Susan M. Reverby and Dorothy O. Helly, "Introduction: Converging on History," in *Gendered Domains: Rethinking Public and Private in Women's History* (Ithaca: Cornell University Press, 1992). For examples of historians of the nineteenth century who have charted a fluid interaction between public and private, or who have attempted to reconceptualize this framework, see Paula Baker, "The Domestication of Politics: Women and American Political Society, 1780–1920," *American Historical Review* 89 (June 1984): 620–47; Karen Hansen, *A Very Social Time: Crafting Community in Antebellum New England* (Berkeley: University of California Press, 1994); Nancy Grey Osterud, *The Bonds of Community: The Lives of Farm Women in Nineteenth-Century New York* (Ithaca: Cornell University Press, 1991); and Mary Ryan, *Women in Public: Between Banners and Ballots, 1825–1880* (Baltimore: Johns Hopkins University Press, 1996).

9. For discussions of the deployment of sexual difference, see Joan Wallach Scott, "Gender: A Useful Category of Analysis," in *Gender and the Politics of History* (New York: Columbia University Press, 1988); and her latest book on French feminism, *Only Paradoxes to Offer: French Feminists and the Rights of Man* (Cambridge: Harvard University Press, 1996). A provocative and useful discussion of sexual difference, situated in the context of the French Revolution, is Genevieve Fraisse, *Reason's Muse: Sexual Difference and the Birth of Man,* trans. Jane Marie Todd (Chicago: University of Chicago Press, 1994). Articles that discuss the broad implications of discourses about gender in the early Republic include Norma Basch, "Marriage and Morals in the Election of 1828," *Journal of American History* 80 (December 1993): 890–918; Ruth Bloch, "American Feminine Ideals in Transition: The Rise of the Moral Mother, 1785–1815," *Feminist Studies* 4 (June 1978): 100–126; Nancy Cott, "Passionlessness: An Interpretation of Victorian Sexual Ideology, 1790–1850," *Signs* 4 (winter 1978): 219–36; and Jan Lewis, "The Republican Wife: Virtue and Seduction in the Early Republic," *William and Mary Quarterly* 44 (October 1987): 689–721.

10. "On Masculine Manners in the Fair Sex," *Boston Weekly Magazine,* May 5, 1804, 109.

11. Fraisse, *Reason's Muse,* esp. chap. 1.

12. As Peter N. Stearns and Carol Z. Stearns argue, historically defined emotional standards—or emotionology—affected individuals' expressions and experiences of emotions. Peter N. Stearns and Carol Z. Stearns, "Emotionology: Clarifying the History of Emotions and Emotional Standards," *American Historical Review* 90 (October 1985): 813–36. Also see introduction to Stearns and Stearns, eds., *Emotion and Social Change,* 1–21. See Francesca M. Cancian, "The Feminization of Love," *Signs* 11 (summer 1986): 692–709 for the argument that the rise of separate spheres led to gendered assumptions about ideals of love (especially the notion that women were more prone than men to be loving and emotional).

13. RVD, September 16, 1810.

14. As Gillis argues for early modern love, Rachel and Mr. G—— regarded their emotional experiences as a script, "something to be negotiated, acted out, worked on, with a public as well as a private dimension." See Gillis, "From Ritual to Romance," 91.

15. Background material on Rachel Van Dyke and her family compiled from Introduction to Journals of Rachel Van Dyke; Cemetery Records of the First Dutch Reformed Church; and New Jersey Historical Society Genealogy Files, Special Collections, Alexander Library, Rutgers University, New Brunswick.

16. In *Cradle of the Middle Class,* Ryan discusses the demands placed on daughters in middle-class households. For a useful gender analysis of women's housework in the early Republic, see Jeanne Boydston, *Home and Work: Housework, Wages, and the Ideology of Labor in the Early Republic* (New York: Oxford University Press, 1990).

17. RVD, November 2, 1810.

18. RVD, August 17, 1810. From comments in Rachel's journals, I infer that the African American servants in the Van Dyke household were slaves. The 1810 census for New Jersey noted that there were 10,851 slaves in New Jersey (out of a total state population listed as 245,562). Figures for North-Brunswick (including New Brunswick) were 3,980 total population, 203 slaves.

19. RVD, November 8, 1810. For middle-class formation, see Stuart Blumin, *The Emergence of the Middle Class: Social Experience in the American City, 1760–1900* (Cambridge: Cambridge University Press, 1989); and Ryan, *Cradle of the Middle Class.*

20. RVD, June 5, 1810, February 28, 1811. According to a 1799 advertisement for Miss Hay's boarding school in New Brunswick, Rachel would have learned French and English grammar, geography, writing, arithmetic, "every branch of needlework," music, and dancing. *Guardian* (New Brunswick, NJ), April 30, May 7, May 28, 1799. Although "standard" boarding school education remained popular in the early Republic, advancements in women's education proliferated. As noted by Kerber and other historians, improvements in men and women's education in the early Republic are most commonly associated with republicanism. See Cott, *Bonds of Womanhood;* Cathy N. Davidson, *Revolution and the Word: The Rise of the Novel in America* (New York: Oxford University Press, 1985); Kerber, *Women of the Republic;* William Gilmore, *Reading Becomes a Necessity of Life: Material and Cultural Life in Rural New England, 1780–1835* (Knoxville: University of Tennessee Press, 1989); Mary Kelley, *Private Women, Public Stage: Literary Domesticity in Nineteenth-Century America* (New York: Oxford University Press, 1984); and idem, " 'Vindicating the Equality of the Female Intellect': Women and Authority in the Early Republic," *Prospects* 17 (1992): 1–28; Lewis, "Republican Wife"; and E. Jennifer Monaghan, "Literary Instruction and Gender in Colonial New England," *American Quarterly* 40 (March 1988): 18–41. The classic descriptive study on women's education in the nineteenth century (including the shift from boarding schools to female academies) is Thomas Woody, *A History of Women's Education in the United States* (1929; reprint, New York: Octagon Books, 1980).

21. *Guardian,* April 18, 1811. Advertisements for the Female Academy appear in the *Guardian* throughout 1811–13 (earlier copies of the paper are not extant). See April 18, May 2, October 17, 1811, April 12, May 7, June 25, 1812, for sample advertisements. In his classic study *A History of Women's Education in the United States,* Woody estimated that, between 1749 and 1829, most of the subjects offered by the Female Academy were available in over 75 percent of advanced educational institutions for women. See chapters 7–9, esp. chart on 418. Percentages for subjects were as follows:

reading (89 percent), writing (75 percent), arithmetic (86 percent), English grammar (89 percent), composition (50 percent), and geography (82 percent). In her journal, Rachel also noted that she began more advanced studies with a Mr. Preston in 1807, and that she also studied, for a brief time, with a Mr. Cady (it is unclear whether these instructors were affiliated with the Female Academy). See RVD, June 5, 1810, February 28, 1811.

22. Complete copies of New Brunswick newspapers for the period 1808–10 are unavailable, and thus, to date I have been unable to locate advertisements listing Ebenezer Grosvenor as an instructor at the Female Academy. Rachel's journal begins when she was already attending school with Mr. G——.

23. Journal of Ebenezer Grosvenor, Special Collections, Alexander Library, Rutgers University, New Brunswick, April 25, 1808. Background material on Ebenezer Grosvenor is compiled from Clarence Winthrop Brown, *The History of Woodstock, Connecticut: Genealogies of Woodstock Families* (Norwood, MA: Plimpton Press, 1935), 6: 283–84; Franklin Bowditch Dexter, *Biographical Sketches of the Graduates of Yale College* (New Haven: Yale University Press, 1912), 6: 117–18; and Eben Putnam, *The Putnam Lineage* (Salem, MA: Salem Press Company, 1907), 87–88, 184–85. Mr. G—— is also a relation of the Grosvenor family involved in Cornelia Dayton's article describing an eighteenth-century abortion case. See Cornelia Dayton, "Taking the Trade: Abortion and Gender Relations in an Eighteenth-Century New England Village," *William and Mary Quarterly*, 3d ser., 48 (January 1991): 19–49.

24. Ira Condict was the preacher of the First Dutch Reformed Church and a board member of both Queens College and the Female Academy. Both Mr. G—— and Rachel attended services at the First Dutch Reformed Church.

25. Grosvenor journal, May 31, 1808.

26. For a description of the life cycle of young men, see E. Anthony Rotundo, "Romantic Friendship: Male Intimacy and Middle- Class Youth in the Northern United States, 1800–1900," *Journal of Social History* 23 (fall 1984): 1–25; and idem, *American Manhood: Transformations in Masculinity from the Revolution to the Modern Era* (New York: Basic Books, 1993).

27. RVD, July 17, 1810.

28. RVD, May 22, 1810.

29. "On Friendship," *Lady's Magazine and Musical Repository* (New York), November 1801, 245.

30. Smith-Rosenberg, "Female World of Love and Ritual," 60.

31. Rotundo, "Romantic Friendship"; and idem, *American Manhood*.

32. The courtship practices described by Lystra, *Searching the Heart* and Ellen Rothman, *Hands and Hearts: A History of Courtship in America* (New York: Basic Books, 1984) suggest fluid interaction between men and women. Also see Hansen, *A Very Social Time*, for further evidence of heterosocial interaction in antebellum America.

33. RVD, July 5, August 31, 1810

34. Rothman, *Hands and Hearts*, esp. chap. 1. Quotes appear on 23–26.

35. Lewis, "Republican Wife," 707. See Edmund Leites, "The Duty to Desire: Love, Friendship, and Sexuality in Some Puritan Theories of Marriage," *Journal of Social History* 15 (spring 1982): 383–407 for the argument that Puritan society also operated under the notion that marriage was "pure friendship."

36. "On Matrimonial Happiness," *Visitor, or Ladies' Weekly Miscellany* (New York), December 17, 1803, 4.

37. The importance of male-female friendship and shared intellectual and romantic interests is implicitly evidenced in several of the courting couples discussed by Lystra, *Searching the Heart* and Rothman, *Hands and Hearts*. In addition to these general sources on courtship, the overlap of intellectual pursuits and male-female friendship and courtship can be gleaned from a variety of sources. In his biography of Margaret Fuller, Charles Capper discusses Fuller's network of male and female friends, including her intimate, "Romantic" friendships with George Davis and James Clarke. See Charles Capper, *Margaret Fuller: An American Romantic Life: The Private Years* (New York: Oxford University Press, 1992). In his study on the diffusion of knowledge and development

of nineteenth-century print culture, Richard Brown includes a chapter on women readers that briefly mentions evidence of shared reading practices between courting men and women. See Richard Brown, *Knowledge Is Power: The Diffusion of Information in Early America, 1700–1865* (New York: Oxford University Press, 1989), 160–96. And Andrew Burstein, *The Inner Jefferson: Portrait of a Grieving Optimist* (Charlottesville: University Press of Virginia, 1995), esp. 49, 61–62, briefly discusses Jefferson's shared reading habits with his wife.

38. RVD, May 21, 1810.

39. For an overview of reader response theory in the context of nineteenth-century history and literature, see James L. Machor, ed., *Readers in History: Nineteenth-Century American Literature and the Contexts of Response* (Baltimore: Johns Hopkins University Press, 1993), especially essay by Susan K. Harris, "Responding to the Text(s): Women Readers and the Quest for Higher Education." For historical applications of reader response theory, see Robert Darnton, "Readers Respond to Rousseau: The Fabrication of Romantic Sensibility," in *The Great Cat Massacre: And Other Episodes in French Cultural History* (New York: Vintage Books, 1985), 215–56; Davidson, *Revolution and the Word;* Carlo Ginzburg, *The Cheese and the Worms: The Cosmos of a Sixteenth-Century Miller,* trans. John and Anne Tedeschi (1976; reprint, New York: Penguin, 1980); Mary Kelley, "Reading Women/Women Reading: The Making of Learned Women in Antebellum America," *Journal of American History* 83 (September 1996): 401–24; and Janice Radway, *Reading the Romance: Women, Patriarchy, and Popular Literature* (Chapel Hill: University of North Carolina Press, 1991).

40. M. Zimmerman, *Solitude Considered with Respect to Its Influence upon the Mind and Heart,* trans. J. B. Mercier (New York: Mott and Lyon for Evert Duyckinch, 1796).

41. RVD, May 26, 1810. Quote that Rachel refers to appears on page 8 of Zimmerman, *Solitude.*

42. RVD, July 8, 1810. This process—and the attraction—of achieving intense identification between authors and readers is discussed in several histories of sentimental and romantic literature. Frequently, this identification between author and reader was directed primarily at female readers and the cultivation of "feminine" sensibilities. For useful discussions, see Barker-Benfield, *The Culture of Sensibility;* Darnton, "Readers Respond to Rousseau"; Cathy N. Davidson, "The Novel as Subversive Activity: Women Reading, Women Writing," in Alfred F. Young, ed., *Beyond the American Revolution: Explorations in the History of American Radicalism* (DeKalb: Northern Illinois University Press, 1993), 283–316; and idem, *Revolution and the Word.*

43. Darnton, "Readers Respond to Rousseau," quotes appear on 239, 249. Discussion of "intensive" reading practices also appears in David D. Hall, "The Uses of Literacy in New England, 1600–1850," in William L. Joyce et al., eds., *Printing and Society in Early America* (Worcester: American Antiquarian Society, 1983), 1–47.

44. RVD, June 6, 1810. For a discussion of the seductive power of print/language, see Darnton, "Readers Respond to Rousseau"; and Fliegelman, *Declaring Independence.*

45. RVD, June 6, 1810. James Montgomery, *The Poetical Works of James Montgomery,* vol. 1 (1806; reprint, Boston: Little, Brown, 1858), esp. 83–88. In Montgomery's original poem, the first stanza appears four pages before the second stanza.

46. RVD, July 19, 1810. Poetry read by Rachel included William Cowper, *Poems,* 2 vols. (Philadelphia: B. and T. Kite; T. and G. Palmer, 1809); Ossian, *The Poems of Ossian,* trans. James Macpherson (London: J. Walker, 1812); James Thomson, *The Seasons* (London: C. Whittingham, 1802); and Edward Young, *Young's Night Thoughts* (1717; reprint, London: Cassell, Petter and Galphin, 1873).

47. The symbolic value of books as gifts is discussed in Ronald J. Zboray and Mary Saracino Zboray, "Books, Reading, and the World of Goods in Antebellum New England," *American Quarterly* 48 (December 1996): 587–622.

48. RVD, August 2, 1810. The book referred to by Rachel was Elizabeth Smith, *Fragments, in Prose and Verse, with Some Account of Her Life and Character by H. M. Bowdler* (Burlington, NJ: D. Allison, 1811 [1810]).

49. Kelley, "Reading Women/Women Reading," 417–20. As Kelley suggests, women readers shaped books to their own purposes, fashioning identities for themselves based largely on the "learned women" whose biographies, histories, and works they read and with whom they closely

identified. The parallel process of validating masculinity through shared intellectual pursuits is discussed in Konstantin Dierks, "Letter Writing, Masculinity, and American Men of Science, 1700–1800" (paper presented to the Philadelphia Center for Early American Studies, 1996).

50. Rachel and Mr. G——'s reading habits mirror many of Ronald Zboray's findings for the 1850s, including the existence of wide varieties of reading patterns for both men and women and shared heterosocial reading patterns. See Zboray, *A Fictive People: Antebellum Economic Development and the American Reading Public* (New York: Oxford University Press, 1993), esp. 156–79.

51. For a theoretical discussion of self-representation through diaries and autobiographies (many feminist scholars maintain that diary writing is a gendered form of autobiography), see *Prose Studies*, special issue on autobiography and gender, 14, no. 2 (September 1991), especially introduction by Shirley Neuman, "Autobiography and Questions of Gender: An Introduction," and essay by Rebecca Hogan, "Engendered Autobiographies: The Diary as a Feminine Form."

52. RVD, July 9, 1810.

53. Rachel never repeated the complaint about Mr. G——'s "almanac" style in subsequent exchanges, so presumably he heeded Rachel's admonition and began to portray a more accurate and complete sense of self in his journals. This suggests that Rachel's reading of Mr. G——'s self produced changes in his manner of self-presentation and self-construction (much as his reading of her journals was reflected in *her* journals). Although there are no extant journals of Mr. G—— during the period of their exchanges, we can presume that his self-representation also was altered by Rachel's perusal of his journals.

54. RVD, July 9, 1810. During this exchange, Rachel gave Mr. G—— her journal book 3, covering the period June 10–23, 1810.

55. RVD, front cover of journal book 3 covering June 10–23, 1810. Mr. G——'s comments added during journal exchange that took place July 9, 1810.

56. RVD, July 9, 1810. The passages copied by Rachel provide us with the only fragments of Mr. G——'s journal in existence from the period of their exchanges. During subsequent exchanges, Rachel copied entries from Mr. G——'s journals onto separate pieces of paper (which have not survived), not directly into her journal.

57. RVD, July 9, 1810. Mr. G——'s comments as recorded by Rachel in her journal.

58. RVD, July 9, 1810.

59. Fliegelman, *Declaring Independence*. Quotes appear on 2–3, 24.

60. RVD, August 25, 1810. Mr. G——'s comments added during journal exchange that took place September 14, 1810.

61. RVD, August 31, 1810.

62. RVD, September 14, 1810. Mr. G——'s comments added during journal exchange that took place November 5, 1810. On September 14, 1810, Rachel gave Mr. G—— her journal book 7, covering August 12–25, 1810.

63. RVD, August 24, 1810. Mr. G——'s comments added during journal exchange that took place September 14, 1810.

64. RVD, September 4, 1810. Journal entry written by Mr. G—— during journal exchange that took place September 4, 1810. During this journal exchange, Rachel gave Mr. G—— her journal book 8, covering August 26–September 6, 1810.

65. RVD, August 26, 1810. This was the first entry in the journal Rachel exchanged with Mr. G—— on September 4, 1810.

66. RVD, September 5, 1810. Journal entry written by Mr. G—— during journal exchange that took place September 4, 1810. Italicized text is used to emphasize Mr. G——'s handwriting for this line, which was distinct from and smaller than the rest of the entry. Strikeout (by Mr. G——) appears in original.

67. RVD, September 5, 1810. Rachel made the revisions to her journal on September 6, 1810, after Mr. G—— returned her journal.

68. Lystra, *Searching the Heart*, 157–91. Although Lystra maintains that women tested more "intensely" and "routinely" than men, Rachel and Mr. G——'s romantic readership suggests intense mutual "testing."

69. RVD, November 5, 1810.

70. Mr. G——'s comments at end of Rachel's journal book 9, covering September 7–20, 1810, added during journal exchange that took place November 5, 1810.

71. RVD, December 10, 1810.

72. Mr. G——'s comments in RVD, August 24, 1810, added during journal exchange that took place September 14, 1810.

73. See Zboray, *A Fictive People,* 110–21; and Burstein, *Inner Jefferson,* esp. 267 for the importance of letter writing as a form of communication across distance.

74. RVD, January 26, February 2, 1811.

75. Lystra, *Searching the Heart,* 4.

76. Rothman, *Hands and Hearts,* 12.

77. RVD, January 26, 1811.

78. RVD, February 13, 1811. Mr. G——'s piece appeared in *Rural Visiter,* February 11, 1811, 148–49.

79. *Rural Visiter,* April 1, 1811. RVD, March 7, March 8, April 3, 1811. Rachel submitted the poem under the name Augusta—after her brother Augustus, who encouraged her to submit the poem for publication. The phrases "waking dreams" and "gilded poisons" were set in quotes to denote references to the composition that Mr. G—— had previously published.

80. Gillis, "From Ritual to Romance," esp. 100, discusses how each stage of early modern courtship (betrothal, banns, marriage) required ritual publicity. Love "made public" was considered more credible than private declarations of same.

81. Quoted in Fliegelman, *Declaring Independence,* 120. Burstein also discusses Jefferson's desire for a secret means of communication with Monroe and Page. See *Inner Jefferson,* 69, 137.

82. For mid- to late nineteenth-century emotional standards, see Halttunen, *Confidence Men;* Lystra, *Searching the Heart;* Rothman, *Hands and Hearts;* and Rotundo, *American Manhood.*

83. For discussions of women's ambivalent attitudes toward marriage, see RVD, May 31, 1810; Lystra, *Searching the Heart;* Rothman, *Hands and Hearts;* and Virginia Lee Chambers-Schiller, *Liberty: A Better Husband: Single Women in America: The Generations of 1780–1840* (New Haven: Yale University Press, 1984).

84. RVD, September 5, 1810.

85. Lewis, "Republican Wife," 712–13.

86. Zimmerman, *Solitude,* 17–23.

87. For discussion of sincerity and candor in print culture and in reading practices, see Darnton, "Readers Respond to Rousseau"; Fliegelman, *Declaring Independence;* and Warner, *Letters of the Republic.*

88. Scholarship on subjectivity and identity formation has proliferated in the last decade or so, especially in the hands of feminist theorists. A useful summary of how this scholarship affects the writing of women's and gender history can be found in Scott, "Gender: A Useful Category." Rather than provide a lengthy list of citations, I point the interested reader to two anthologies that provide useful summaries of the direction and status of this field of scholarship: Gisela Bock and Susan James, eds., *Beyond Equality and Difference: Citizenship, Feminist Politics, Female Subjectivity* (New York: Routledge, 1992); and Deborah Rhode, ed., *Theoretical Perspectives on Sexual Difference* (New Haven: Yale University Press, 1990).

89. See Kelley, "Reading Women/Women Reading," and Dierks, "Letter Writing," respectively, for discussions of how cultural notions of femininity and masculinity were validated in shared reading and intellectual habits that took place between women or between men.

90. RVD, September 5, 1810.

91. An afterword: readers of earlier versions of this essay have understandably been curious about the ending of Rachel and Mr. G——'s romantic readership. Unfortunately, the sources have yet to uncover a complete end to their story. I present the facts as I know them, but much is left to speculation. Rachel's journals end abruptly in July 1811, after the death of her father. At the time, she and Mr. G—— were writing regularly to one another. But fragments of Mr. G——'s extant journals for 1812 contain no direct mention of Rachel. On May 3, 1815, he married his first cousin

Harriet Wadworth Putnam. It is perhaps significant to note that in 1812, Mr. G—— was teaching his cousin Latin—suggesting his continued efforts to merge intellectual and romantic pursuits. (See Diary of Ebenezer Grosvenor, Manuscripts and Archives, Sterling Memorial Library, Yale University, New Haven, Connecticut, 1812, especially entries for September 27, October 14, October 18, November 7, 1812.) On November 10, 1817, at the age of thirty, Ebenezer Grosvenor died. Sources for Rachel prove more elusive. Her parents and siblings have been accounted for, but to date, I have not been able to locate/confirm information on Rachel's marital status or death. She may have left New Brunswick after her father's death to live with relatives or friends. She may have married— but if so, did a marriage occur before or after Mr. G——'s?

Could Rachel and Mr. G——'s romantic readership have led to a formal engagement and marriage? Their experiences clearly mirror the pattern of friendship-courtship-engagement-marriage described by Rothman in *Hands and Hearts*. At the time of Mr. G——'s departure from New Brunswick, Rachel was only seventeen and he was only twenty-two; perhaps they were too young to think of marriage, but hoped that their courtship could continue through letter writing (a common practice in both Rothman and Lystra's studies). Perhaps, then, circumstances beyond their control led them to lose touch with one another. Or Mr. G——'s marriage to his first cousin could have been arranged and somewhat out of his control—a not unheard-of occurrence, even by the early nineteenth century (he did belong to an old New England family with somewhat patriarchal tendencies—note the actions of his male relatives in Dayton's "Taking the Trade" article). Unfortunately, however, the evidence I have uncovered to date does not allow me to privilege one speculation over another.

Chapter Five

The Gender and Racial Politics of Mourning in Antebellum America

Jeffrey Steele

Death was a familiar visitor for the generation of American writers who reached maturity in the 1840s and 1850s, the era just before the onset of the Civil War. During this period of primitive health care and high mortality rates, few individuals avoided the traumatic losses of one or both parents and beloved siblings. When Nathaniel Hawthorne was a young child, his father, a sea captain, died in South America. Ralph Waldo Emerson lost his father when he was eight, his first wife when he was twenty-seven, and a beloved brother during the year he was finishing his first book, *Nature*. Herman Melville's father, Allan Melville, went bankrupt and then died two years later, when Herman was twelve. Edgar Allan Poe's father deserted his family shortly after Poe's birth; his mother died when he was two; and his wife Virginia suffered from a lingering, fatal illness during the period when he was completing many of his most famous works. In the case of all these writers, the deaths of parents led to dramatic shifts in personal finances, consigning these authors to genteel poverty or economic dependence on others. For each author, issues of inheritance, independence, and authority were inextricably entwined with themes of mourning.

The record is just as stark in the case of prominent women writers during the antebellum period. Catharine Sedgwick (the author of *Hope Leslie,* one of the most popular American novels in the early nineteenth century) endured both the mental illness and the premature death of her mother, who died when Sedgwick was seventeen. The mother of Lydia Maria Child died when Child was twelve, and she was sent to live with a married sister. Susan Warner, the author of the 1850 best-seller *The Wide, Wide World,* was born in 1819 after her parents lost their first child and "was doubly precious to her parents ... when, after her birth, they lost two more children in succession."[1] Warner's mother died when she was nine, and she was raised in large part by her father's sister. Sarah Josepha Hale, a prolific author and editor of the highly influential *Godey's Lady's Book,* lost both her mother and a sister when she was in her early twenties and was so affected by the death of her husband in 1822 that she wore black mourning dress for the rest of her life. Sara Payson Willis Parton (better known as "Fanny Fern") lost her mother, first child, and husband during a two-year period in the 1840s—a series of catastrophes recounted in her autobiographical novel, *Ruth Hall.* As I have argued elsewhere, the writing career of

Margaret Fuller was precipitated in part by a delayed mourning reaction to the death of her father.[2] During her childhood and youth, Fuller experienced the deaths of her infant sister, Julia (who died when Fuller was three) and her sixteen-month-old brother, Edward (who died in her arms when she was nineteen). As in the case of their male contemporaries, this intimate acquaintance with death and mourning deeply molded the lives and consciousness of antebellum women writers. Since most women during this period were economically dependent upon relatives, each death also served as a graphic reminder of the material precariousness of women's lives.

By midcentury, the culture of mourning had pervaded every area of life in America.[3] Living in an age when life expectancy was much shorter and when funeral arrangements were made at home, most Americans before the Civil War assumed that existence would have an elegiac—if not tragic—tone. But the cemetery lay closest to the daughters, wives, and mothers of America, for men and women were positioned differently within the culture of mourning. The attire, social decorum, and physical movement of mourning women were all carefully prescribed within complicated mourning rituals; while the "question of men and how they mourned is little mentioned in the literature of the period. . . . Judging from surviving artifacts and from the literature, the burden of mourning fell primarily on women."[4] Reflecting women's position "as the pillar of home and society," the material practices and public rituals of mourning were "symbolic of woman's place in the world."[5]

In both England and America, the female mourner became the most familiar symbol of grief. In eighteenth-century England, stylized representations of mourning women were duplicated on numerous objects, ranging from architectural elements to household items.[6] After the death of George Washington in 1799, similar images of female mourners were popularized in America, as European and American mourning customs were blended together.[7] By the advent of the Civil War (and well before the death of Queen Victoria's husband, Prince Albert, in 1861), "mourning customs were well established" as countless images were reproduced of women draped over the tombs of departed children, husbands, and fathers.[8] In private academies, such as Mary Balch's school in Providence, young women practiced their artistic skills by duplicating images of mourning women in needlework samplers.[9] These images were originally modeled on James Akin and William Harrison's famous print of a female America mourning at the tomb of George Washington. Over the years, the representation of Washington's tomb was replaced by a variety of funeral urns, but the mourning woman (occasionally accompanied by other family members) remained the central figure.[10] Although such mourning samplers fell out of fashion by the 1830s (when their imagery began to be mass-produced by printmakers), they are indicative of significant differences in the ways women and men were trained to mourn.[11] Women, by and large, received most of the training in observing mourning rituals, ranging from specific forms of dress to patterns of social decorum and the preparation of food for grieving families. No similar training existed for young men, who lacked the same direct connection to the icons and rituals of mourning.

In the terminology of Louis Althusser, the family and religious rituals, educational practices, and iconography of mourning all represented "ideological state apparatuses" that helped inculcate American citizens as middle-class "subjects."[12] This process of social indoctrination was most apparent in the case of white middle-class women, who were habituated to standards of passivity that invisibly meshed with familiar images of female mourners draped over tombs. Stereotyped notions of women's emotionality (as opposed to rationality) were replicated by women who occupied traditional mourning roles. As the designated "heart" of America, women were expected to perform the emotional work of mourning that helped support prevailing notions of gender difference. This is not to say that men did not mourn, but—as we shall see—they were often much less comfortable with the role. In texts by prominent white male writers during the antebellum period, mourning was often defined as a transitory state, to be passed through as quickly as possible. Periods of prolonged or "disordered" mourning were seen as pathological, preventing the assumption of adult authority and even threatening to fixate the male subject in a dangerous, "feminized" position.[13] According to Neal Tolchin, such was the popular response to Melville's *Moby-Dick* (1851). Contemporary readers, Tolchin argues, refused to accept the morbidity of Captain Ahab's excessive mourning—an emotional excess that seemed to duplicate "the social role ascribed to the female mourner."[14]

It is striking that Kathleen Woodward has identified a similar male stance toward mourning in Sigmund Freud's influential essay "Mourning and Melancholia" (1917). Freud's essay, Woodward argues, "casts the difference between mourning and melancholia in clear-cut binary terms": "Freud defined mourning as a way of divesting ourselves of pain, of getting it over and done with," while melancholia—"a denial of the reality of loss"—is defined as "pathological," as "failed, or unsuccessful, mourning."[15] In these stoic terms, "the work of mourning is the healing of a wound," so that the mourner can get back to the demands of life. But recent revisions of Freud—as well as studies of prominent American writers—have tended to blur the strict line between mourning and melancholy by arguing that mourning is not a terminable process but persists in the somber tinges of melancholy. We see this development clearly if we compare Ralph Waldo Emerson's apparent disavowal of mourning in his first book, *Nature* (1836), with the melancholic rhythms of his later works.

Emerson's early works, written before the death of his five-year-old son, Waldo, in 1842, seem to substantiate the idea (later popularized by Freud) that "normal" mourning has a clear limit. Issuing his fervent appeal for American creativity in *Nature*, Emerson found unavoidable the father's tomb, which suggested the weight of literary and theological tradition he hoped his contemporaries could surpass. Calling for the development of new, American cultural forms (free from European influence), Emerson eloquently implores his readers to establish their own, independent connection to the "natural" energies contained both within the self and in the external world. Strikingly, the route to such independence leads through the father's grave:

> Our age is retrospective. It builds the sepulchres of the fathers. It writes biographies, histories, and criticism. The foregoing generations beheld God and nature face to face; we, through their eyes. Why should not we also enjoy an original relation to the universe? Why should not we have a poetry and philosophy of insight and not of tradition, and a religion by revelation to us, and not the history of theirs?

We have worshipped at the tombs of the fathers long enough, Emerson asserts; now it is time to put away our grief and get on with manly living.[16] In this paradigm, emotional and cultural maturity is measured in terms of the capacity to terminate a process of "mourning" that links one to the past. Attending too long to the accomplishments of the dead deflects attention from the pressing need to establish a new "relation" to life. Personal and national independence, Emerson suggests, will transpire far away from the dependent (and presumably feminizing) relations situated at the foot of graves.

After the death of his son Waldo, Emerson's essays present a more sustained engagement with death and loss, reflecting an unfinished "dialogue with death" at the heart of his work.[17] Mark Edmundson has argued that Emerson's career progresses from an early disavowal of mourning to the acceptance, after Waldo's death in 1842, of the persistence of melancholia or what Kathleen Woodward has described as a life "still in mourning but no longer exclusively devoted to mourning."[18] Sharon Cameron's careful reading of Emerson's "Experience" elaborates this new logic of melancholy, at the same time that it suggests the distance between Emerson's vision of mourning and those of his female (and African American) contemporaries.[19] Mourning and (later) melancholia in Emerson's works are intensely *personal* affairs. To the extent that he implicates others in his essays, he does so by projecting representations of his own development as universal paradigms that present the vicissitudes of white male middle-class subjectivity as a normative model. In other words, Emerson does not grieve for the losses experienced by others; instead, his mourning is focused through the lens of individual development. We might identify this as an "Oedipal" model of mourning and melancholia. The "successful" conclusion of mourning—in these terms—facilitates the son's accession to paternal power. Conversely, the failure to terminate mourning (resulting in a state of "disordered" mourning or melancholia) is perceived as a threat to manhood and one's assumption of authority.

This is precisely the dynamic we encounter in the fiction of Emerson's contemporaries, Melville and Hawthorne, who both focus on the personal aspects of mourning in "Oedipal" scenes dramatizing the contest with dead father figures for personal and cultural power. The most striking of such combats, Captain Ahab's pursuit of the white whale in *Moby-Dick,* is tinged by the specter of Ahab's (and Melville's) dead father. In his depiction of Ahab's "larger, darker, deeper, part," Melville projects a model of the psyche fixated—at the core—on the paternal image within:

> Winding far down from within the very heart of this spiked Hotel de Cluny where we here stand . . . and take your way, ye nobler, sadder souls, to those vast Roman halls of Thermes; where far beneath the fantastic towers of man's upper earth, his root of grandeur, his whole awful essence sits in bearded state; an antique buried beneath antiquities, and throned on torsoes! So with a broken throne, the great gods mock that captive king; so like a Caryatid, he patient sits, upholding on his frozen brow the piled entablatures of ages. Wind ye down there, ye prouder, sadder souls! question that proud, sad king! A family likeness! aye, he did beget ye, ye young exiled royalties; and from your grim sire will the old State-secret come.[20]

At the heart of the (male) psyche, Melville suggests, lies the specter of the dead father, who continues to haunt the present.

In his evocative reading of Melville's prolonged grief over his father's bankruptcy, insanity, and premature death, Tolchin locates Ahab's grief in "Melville's sense of his mother's conflicted grief for his father."[21] But while Ahab's (and Melville's) obsessive mourning partly meshed with the feminized mourning culture of nineteenth-century America, its fixation on issues of personal "dismemberment" embodied what Tolchin identifies as a typical *male* response to grief. Male images of "dismemberment" internalize grief as a *personal* (not social) loss, stressing a castrating threat to one's bodily integrity and sense of authority (central themes in *Moby-Dick*).

In contrast to such masculinized narratives of mourning, the grief studies cited by Tolchin suggest that women often express their grief through a "sense of abandonment"—a response that highlights the *social* dimension of grief by attending to the severing of important social bonds with others.[22] Although men were indeed deeply hurt by the deaths of parents or spouses, their sense of vulnerability rarely carried the same economic and material connotations. Death, in the case of men, did not hold the same threat that it did for women, who could find themselves homeless after the loss of a father or husband. It is important to consider such differences, as well as to recognize that nineteenth-century men's use of the feminized signifiers of mourning could not carry the same value as women's use of them. Because of their different locations within nineteenth-century culture, men's and women's mourning—even if they resembled each other—carried different ramifications. While we must recognize the danger of any universalizing theory of the emotions, it is striking that this contrast correlates nicely with the gender dynamics of grieving in antebellum American literature.

One of Nathaniel Hawthorne's most haunting stories, "Roger Malvin's Burial" (1832), helps us understand such gender differences. This troubling tale replicates the individualized grieving we found in Emerson, but it does so in negative terms. While Emerson's speaker in *Nature* found a way to escape from the dependent relation of mourning, the protagonist of Hawthorne's tale is tied to the grave. Set during the French and Indian Wars, this story focuses on the psychological history of Reuben Bourne, a young man who, because of the gravity of his own wounds, was forced to abandon in the wilderness the dying (and unburied) Roger Malvin, the father of Reuben's fiancée. Reuben survives, makes it back to the settlement, and marries Malvin's daughter Dorcas; but his failure to properly bury and mourn this father figure has serious psychological and social repercussions. Haunted by "an unburied corpse ... calling to him out of the wilderness," Reuben becomes a gloomy and quarrelsome man who fails to free himself from the ghosts of the past.[23] Unable to locate his "father's" grave, he is trapped in a cycle of unresolved and disordered mourning that prevents him from occupying a secure masculine role in his society.

Hoping to start over again, Reuben leads his wife and their fifteen-year old son, Cyrus, out into the wilderness to build a new homestead for themselves. Lured by unconscious psychological processes that he cannot control, he takes them to the very site where he had abandoned the dying Roger Malvin. Leaving Dorcas behind in camp, Reuben and Cyrus go out to hunt in "the vicinity of the encampment." At the foot of the very rock where he had left the dying Roger Malvin years before, Reuben mistakes his son for a deer and shoots him. Although the stone looks like "a gigantic gravestone" with "an inscription in forgotten characters," it seems that the forgotten inscription of mourning becomes legible in the sacrifice of Reuben's son at the foot of his "father's" grave, for at the end of the story, "His sin was expiated— the curse was gone from him."[24] In this passage, Hawthorne validates popular assumptions about the efficacy of successful mourning for men, at the same time that he represents patterns of psychological obsession and repetition that call this process into question for Reuben Bourne. On the whole, Hawthorne depicts male mourning as being an intensely private and personal affair that disrupts the performance of public, communal responsibilities.

But Hawthorne complicates this troubling tale by shifting the viewpoint, at the climax, from Reuben to Dorcas. We hear the report of Reuben's gun once again through her ears, and we follow the action up to her discovery of her son's corpse lying at the foot of her father's "tomb." The effect of this narrative displacement is to highlight Dorcas's location within a different economy of mourning. Throughout the story, Reuben's actions were measured on a scale in which the act of successfully mourning the "father" (whether or not it is actually accomplished) signified the necessary step from dependence to personal independence. But there is no suggestion that mourning has any comparable efficacy for Dorcas. By the end, she is so overwhelmed by grief that all she can do is sink "insensible by the side of her dead boy."[25] Indeed, Dorcas is not even allowed the consolation of conscious mourning; instead, we are left with the image of a woman whose dependence on her husband has trapped her in a world of loss with no exit. Presumably, when Dorcas recovers consciousness she will be trapped forever in the familiar cultural role of female mourner.

Hawthorne's tale reminds us that representations of mourning carried very different meanings for men and women in the nineteenth century. Women writers found it much more difficult to leave behind the sepulchre of the father. And in contrast to Hawthorne, they measured the disturbance of mourning less in terms of the failure of *personal* independence than in terms of the losses experienced by groups whose pain needed to be addressed and resolved. In their works, mourning became a representative posture that facilitated the articulation of *collective* loss and grievance. Although many theorists of mourning fail to distinguish male from female mourning, it is important to consider whether women—especially in the nineteenth century—had the same capacity to liberate themselves from the emotional and ritual demands of mourning. Thus, the excessive mourning perceived as "disordered" in the case of men may have been closer to the norm for women.

Such is the argument made by Luce Irigaray in her evocative critique of Freudian theory. Like other contemporary psychoanalysts (most notably Nicolas Abraham and Maria Torok), Irigaray regards the capacity to mourn as a sign of mental health, especially in the case of a woman who might use the act of mourning to focus her sense of "grievance at being excluded as 'subject.' "[26] Many women, she argues, have been "mutilated, wounded, humiliated, overwhelmed by a feeling of inferiority that can never be 'cured' " (or effectively mourned).[27] "And if you reread 'Mourning and Melancholia' in this perspective," Irigaray argues, "you will be struck by the way the libidinal economy of the little girl . . . crosschecks with the symptoms of melancholia: profoundly painful dejection, . . . abrogation of interest in the outside world, . . . loss of the capacity for love, . . . inhibition of all activity, . . . fall in self-esteem."[28] In contrast to theorists who normalize Freud's account of melancholia as a disordered mourning that cannot be successfully terminated, Irigaray suggests that the conditions of many women's lives may motivate an unlocalized melancholia that "cannot be worked through by mourning."[29] Unable to define the precise cause of the loss that they feel, such women are overwhelmed by "a loss that radically escapes any representation. Whence the impossibility of mourning it."[30] The dilemma confronted by such women, according to Irigaray, is that cultural inscriptions of female "fault" and "deficiency" provide them "too few figurations, images, or representations" with which to depict themselves.[31]

Such theories resonate with historical accounts of women's lives in antebellum America. Lacking the same agency, freedom of movement, economic rights, and political power as their male contemporaries, many women lived in a world that was greatly circumscribed and that they did not control.[32] But it is important to recognize that some antebellum women writers began to locate and control their pain by displacing the prevalent signifiers of mourning from specific losses to a more general sense of grievance. Some of the most prominent women writers of the period discovered that they could actively *mourn* the ways in which the limited conditions of individual lives reflected losses experienced by other women. Such acts of mourning differed markedly from the personalized narratives of mourning and melancholy we found in Emerson, Melville, and Hawthorne; they defined a cultural grief-work devoted to collective processes of social reform.

In a culture in which everyone mourned, it was not easy to define the barrier separating the grief and pain of others from one's own sense of bereavement. It was difficult to resist what Karen Sánchez-Eppler has characterized as the tangible appeal of tears that had the potential to cross gender, class, and racial boundaries.[33] The fluidity of mourning, as well as the overdetermination of the many signifiers of grief, prevented the easy containment of grieving within a specific set of cultural forms. Thus, it is difficult to accept the argument (made by one critic) that the "emotions" of nineteenth-century mourners "were kept within strict bounds," because "the codes of Christianity and gentility conspired to regulate and formalize bereavement."[34] This would be true only if American society were a closed system with stable mourning rituals imposed uniformly on all who grieved. But what if there was not one culture of mourning, but multiple cultures that overlapped and intersected in a variety of ways? Because they crisscrossed the lives of all Americans and thus bridged social and racial gaps, representations of mourning came to play an increasingly important role in the discourses of antebellum social reform.

Middle-class expressions of grief for others were easily displaced and expanded to include persons outside one's social circle. Among the staples of the emerging sentimental novel were scenes of pathos in which middle-class readers mourned the plight of orphans, the dying, and the destitute. While such narrative moments had the capacity to reinforce existing class boundaries, confirming a smug sense of middle-class distance and comfort, they were destabilized by the prevalence of tears. For example, women and African American writers of both sexes began to exploit the middle-class demand for sentimental pathos by expanding the group of suffering victims. Taking advantage of structures of sentiment that luxuriated in the outpouring of mournful sympathy, they shifted attention from individual victims to groups of suffering individuals cut off from America's democratic promise.

In many instances, the rhetoric of antebellum social reform depended on dramatizations of middle-class readers as prospective mourners, grieving for the losses suffered by the destitute, the imprisoned, the mentally ill, and the enslaved. Embodying the assumption that reform efforts could be effectively motivated through the transmission of sentiment, these reformers often resorted to familiar tropes of mourning. For example, John R. McDowell's 1830 annual report of the New York Magdalen Society (devoted to rescuing women who had "fallen" into prostitution) expressed the object of "pour[ing] consolation into the hearts of parents, mourning the ruin of beloved and once hopeful children."[35] In similar fashion, Dorothea Dix mobilized her readers' grief for the institutionalized mentally ill through her presentation of "the saddest pictures of human suffering and degradation."[36] "I come," Dorothea Dix proclaimed in her 1843 report to the Massachusetts legislature, "to present the strong claims of suffering humanity"—"the condition of the miserable, the desolate, the outcast."[37] As Dix and her contemporary reformers recognized, these claims were often most recognizable when presented through the familiar signifiers of sentimental mourning.

One of the most striking representations of this reform rhetoric of mourning occurs near the end of Harriet Beecher Stowe's *Uncle Tom's Cabin*. In this paradigmatic moment, Stowe links the capacity to mourn for private losses to a politicized grieving for those trapped in slavery:

> By the sick hour of your child; by those dying eyes, which you can never forget; by those last cries, that wrung your heart when you could neither help nor save; by the desolation of that empty cradle, that silent nursery,—I beseech you, pity those mothers that are constantly made childless by the American slave-trade! And say, mothers of America, is this a thing to be defended, sympathized with, passed over in silence?

Using the most familiar and clichéd of situations, a mother's grief for her dead child, Stowe displaces personal grief into the public context of racial oppression. This political move is made possible by the overdetermination of maternal mourning as a culturally familiar—if not unavoidable—site. By 1852, evocations of "dying eyes," "last cries," and the "empty cradle" had appeared in numerous periodicals. Nearly every reader in America had encountered poetic dramatizations of maternal sorrow. Presumably there were female readers of this passage who had not lost children, but Stowe could tap the sentiment of maternal mourning as if it were universally available. Every reader of this passage, she assumes, knew what it meant to mourn.

Appealing to a widespread sense of sympathy for the bereaved, Stowe's text bridges racial and class boundaries that other antislavery writers found much more formidable. For example, William Lloyd Garrison's voice of indignation and moral outrage lacked such an emotional solvent and, as a result, was much less appealing. While we should not overlook the important role of moral argumentation in antebellum reform movement, we must also take seriously Ronald Walters's conclusion that "the importance of antislavery (or any antebellum reform) came through . . . [the] ability to help the public perceive situations, or institutions like slavery, in a new, emotionally charged way."[38] In order to create this necessary emotional charge, reformers borrowed images and narrative situations from the emotional discourses of the day. The literature of bereavement provided such a storehouse of available emotional forms.

The gender and racial politics of mourning began to crystallize in the 1840s, while both the advocates of woman's rights and abolitionist leaders were adapting the forms of sentiment to new political ends. Indeed, the signifiers of mourning often gained their greatest political efficacy in the hands of those who challenged middle-class values, especially in their inscription of specific gender and racial roles. As pioneers and the most prominent practitioners of this new political rhetoric of mourning, Margaret Fuller and Frederick Douglass deserve special attention. While Fuller's texts highlight many of the gender differences we have been examining above, Douglass's writing opens a window onto a much less familiar terrain—the *racial* politics of mourning in antebellum America.

Both Fuller and Douglass construct literary personae that are both the object and agent of politicized mourning. Mourning losses experienced by their past selves, they position themselves as representative victims, generating sympathy for the oppression they (or others who share their suffering) have experienced. In Fuller's writing, for example, acts of mourning are linked to the pain of groups who have not realized the full promise of American citizenship. Her representations of mourning either portray her grief as a representative American woman struggling to overcome gender oppression, or they focus on groups who have experienced a similar disenfranchisement. Thus, in *Woman in the Nineteenth Century,* when Fuller observes that the great women of the past "had much to mourn, and their great impulses did not find due scope," this expression of sorrow includes Fuller herself among the group of talented women whose lives were unduly constricted.[39]

In similar fashion, Frederick Douglass's mournful recollection of the slave songs that he heard as a child implicates him as one of the suffering victims of slavery who were also "within the circle."[40] We encounter a similar tone of grief in Douglass's scathing oration "What to the Slave Is the Fourth of July?"—a text that disrupts the public celebration of national independence with the evocation of "the mournful wail of millions, whose chains, heavy and grievous yesterday, are to-day rendered more intolerable by the jubilant shouts that reach them."[41] Douglass's authority here, as elsewhere, resides in part in his capacity to mourn the effects of slavery, which have scarred both his life and those of countless others. "My feet have been so cracked with the frost," he exclaims in the *Narrative,* "that the pen with which I am writing might be laid in the gashes."[42] Mourning his own representative losses, Douglass—like Fuller—positions himself as the object of the reader's mournful sympathy.

But by inscribing themselves as the *agents* of mourning, both Fuller and Douglass generate patterns of cognition that enable them to rise above their pain. "I did not, when a slave," Douglass observes, "understand the meaning of those rude and apparently incoherent songs. I was myself within the circle; so that I neither saw nor heard as those without might see and hear. They told a tale of woe which was then altogether beyond my feeble comprehension."[43] How was Douglass (or Fuller, for that matter) able to move "outside" the circle of oppression and pain? To answer this question, we must consider what it meant to be "within the circle." In addition to humiliation and physical hardships, each writer testifies to the experience of internalized forms of oppression that were still harder to overcome. Fuller's term for this condition is "idolatry." "I wish woman to live, *first* for God's sake," she exclaims in *Woman in the Nineteenth Century;* "Then she will not make an imperfect man her god, and thus sink to idolatry."[44] Frederick Douglass also testifies—in *My Bondage and My Freedom*—to the ways he was bound by his idolatrous worship of the masters who had enslaved his mind as well as his body. "Trained from the cradle up," he reflects, "to think and feel their masters are superior, and invested with a sort of sacredness, there are few who can outgrow or rise above the control which that sentiment exercises."[45] By placing their masters on a higher ontological plane, as if they were a different order of being, the slaves detached their pain from any accessible cause. Their "idolatry" perpetuated the ideological fiction that their masters were distant, godlike beings whose destructive actions could not be effectively mourned.

To slip into the theological framework that Douglass occasionally uses, the slaves' position was analogous to that of the fallen Adam and Eve exiled from the garden, trapped in a position of permanent guilt. In the 1845 *Narrative,* for example, he described the godlike Colonel Lloyd, who employed "all kinds of stratagems to keep his slaves out of the garden," including "tarring his fence all around." The slaves, he observes, kept out of the garden, since they "seemed to realize the impossibility of touching *tar* without being defiled."[46] But their lives, we see, had already been defiled by the "tar" of slavery, which kept them in a fallen position. Ten years later, in *My Bondage and My Freedom,* Douglass makes the theological pattern even more explicit, when he describes Colonel Lloyd as a "fearful and inexorable *demi-god* whose huge image haunted my childhood's imagination."[47] The slaves, he recalls, were exiled from the "sacred precincts of the great house," which possessed an almost "Eden-like beauty."[48] One of the reasons the slaves were exiled from "Eden," he argues, is because their beings had been invaded by an alien consciousness—that of their masters who had inculcated a primordial subservience.

Julia Kristeva's analysis of abjection in *The Powers of Horror* helps us understand this condition. "I experience abjection," Kristeva argues, "only if an Other has settled in place and stead of what will be 'me.' Not at all an Other with whom I identify and incorporate [as we shall see, 'introject' would be a more precise term], but an Other who precedes and possesses me, and through such possession causes me to be."[49] The structure of Douglass's personal narratives suggests the efficacy of mourning in helping him overcome this position of abjection, which he demonstrates is the posture of a "slavish" soul.[50] He makes it clear that such slavishness extends far beyond the Mason-Dixon Line, since it is the posture of any person whose being has been invaded by an ideology that he or she cannot control.[51] Although it was impossible for Douglass to control all the ideological pressures affecting his readers, he was able to highlight the ways in which the ideology of slavery had infected the minds of those within the system, as well as the intellects of those who uncritically supported such servitude.

Aiming to transform the structure of "public sentiment," Douglass punctuates his autobiographies with scenes that dramatize the "claims of humanity," claims that are focused through his readers' capacity to mourn for the victims of slavery.[52] Each of his great mourning scenes dramatizes his own movement from such abjection, at the same time that each scene attempts to free his readers from the ideology of slavery that has possessed them. These scenes of mourning enable both Douglass's narrators and his readers to avoid the incoherence and silence of melancholy (which threatens to perpetuate their subjection to the ideology of slavery). When melancholy can be turned into grievance, he shows us, it can be mourned. In his 1845 *Narrative,* the three most striking mourning scenes are the description of the mournful slave songs Douglass listened to as a child, his lament for the abandonment and death of his grandmother, and his anguished soliloquy near the Chesapeake Bay after being pushed to the edge of submission by the slave driver Edward Covey. The significance of these three narrative moments is highlighted and strangely duplicated ten years later when Douglass embeds each of them in his second autobiography, *My Bondage and My Freedom.* Let us pause to consider one of these—Douglass's complicated treatment of the slaves' songs.

In an important paragraph in his 1845 *Narrative,* Douglass had posited the capacity to hear the mournful lament of these songs as a sign of the capacity to understand the psychological effect of slavery. As a slave, he had found the songs "rude, and apparently incoherent," telling "a tale of woe which was then altogether beyond my feeble comprehension." Only later, he argues, did he realize that they were "tones . . . breathing the prayer and complaint of souls boiling over with the bitterest anguish." As Douglass continues, he generalizes his own response as a politicized model of mourning. "If any one wishes to be impressed with the soul-killing effects of slavery," he concludes, "let him go to Colonel Lloyd's plantation, and, on allowance-day, place himself in the deep pine woods, and there let him, in silence, analyze the sounds that shall pass through the chambers of his soul,—and if he is not thus impressed, it will only be because there is no flesh in his obdurate heart."[53] In these terms, a tender and feeling heart, capable of mourning the anguish caused by slavery, will motivate both Douglass and his readers to resist the source of such pain.

Ten years later, in *My Bondage and My Freedom,* Douglass returned to the slaves' songs, citing verbatim the earlier paragraph from his *Narrative.* Quoting his own mournful reconstruction of the past (in the *Narrative*), he sets up structures of mourning within mourning, receding back to the original—and perhaps inexpressible—trauma of slavery. In 1855, Douglass mourns the pain embodied in his 1845 narrator, who mourns the pain of his precursor, the slave Frederick Douglass. In a sense, this textual maneuver allows Douglass to authenticate his own pain, by taking his former self (the 1845 narrator) as an authoritative mourner, able to grieve for the losses experienced by all those within slavery. Douglass prefaces his excerpt from his 1845 *Narrative* with several paragraphs that make even more explicit this dynamic of mourning. The slaves' songs, he adds in 1855, "were mostly of a plaintive cast, and told a tale of grief and sorrow." Even in "the most boisterous outbursts of rapturous sentiment," he adds, "there was ever a tinge of deep melancholy."[54] In both texts, the capacity to be impressed (to receive an impression) from the slaves' songs depends on the imaginative reconstruction of their *mournful* wail. Only at the moment when such grief and melancholy could be focused through self-conscious acts of mourning could the sources of that pain be addressed.

A new element in the 1855 autobiography helps clarify the importance of this effort to shape the fog of melancholy into mourning. In *My Bondage and My Freedom*, Douglass first analyzes his "life-long standing grief" at his separation from his mother.[55] Rarely allowed to see her and absent at her death and burial, he was not allowed the consolation of those "scenes of sacred tenderness, around the death-bed, never forgotten"—a luxury only accorded the "free" (and novelists, like Stowe, working in the sentimental tradition). The "heartless and ghastly form of *slavery*," he laments, "rises between mother and child, even at the bed of death."[56] The pervasive specter of slavery cut the young Douglass off from the emotional consolations of mourning and left him "without an intelligible beginning in the world," for his mother's death, like her grave, was "unmarked."[57] In many respects, *My Bondage and My Freedom* represents Douglass's effort to locate his mother's grave, as well as the graves of all those like her who perished in slavery. This process of localization is a crucial element of his politics of mourning. Just as he needed to escape the unfocused abjection of the idolatrous slaves, unconsciously worshipping their masters, Douglass needed to fix his anguish onto specific images that could be mourned. Although his mother's grave was "unmarked," Douglass's account of this fact enabled him to bring his mother's death into his text, a process that began to localize and thus counteract the "ghastly form" of slavery that threatened to seep into a pervasive and disabling melancholy.

But Douglass's own painful recollections of childhood traumas suggest that his mourning might not be terminable; the "gashes" remained, the specters of the past (such as his dead mother) continued to haunt him. We see this haunting most clearly in his account of his grandmother. In both the *Narrative* and *My Bondage and My Freedom*, he laments the abandonment of his "poor old grandmother," who—at the end of her usefulness—was turned out to die. In an uncanny way, Douglass's grandmother (who is certainly dead by 1855) is cast into the role of posthumous mourner. Her specter haunts both of Douglass's texts, as the epitome of a mournful consciousness that he cannot escape: "If my poor old grandmother now lives, she lives to suffer in utter loneliness; she lives to remember and mourn over the loss of children, the loss of grandchildren, and the loss of great-grandchildren."[58] At this moment, Douglass mourns himself through the figure of his dead grandmother—a specter incorporated within his psyche. But the effect of this repetition is to incorporate the absent voice of the grandmother within the reader as well, as a structure of ethical consciousness channeled through our capacity to hear and feel the tones of her grief.

This structure of incorporation has been analyzed most thoroughly by Nicolas Abraham and Maria Torok, French psychoanalysts who have become our most sophisticated theorists of mourning. In recent years, a number of scholars and critics have begun to notice the importance of Abraham and Torok's radical revision of Freud's model of mourning, especially their original distinction between psychic incorporation and introjection.[59] Deriving the term in part from Sandor Ferenczi, Maria Torok defines "introjection" as a healthy process of psychic growth akin to Freud's reality principle. "Like transference," she explains, "introjection is defined as the process of including the Unconscious in the ego through objectal contacts"; "broadening and enriching the ego," introjection is "mediated by the object," a process that allows instinctual drives to "exist and unfold in the objectal sphere."[60] But such healthy psychic investments, Torok argues, can be short-circuited by traumatic losses that resist normal mourning (a form of introjection). At such moments, a lost object (which cannot be directly mourned) is hidden within a psychic "tomb" that possesses its own power and agency. We detected this process in Douglass's incorporation of his dead grandmother's grief for him and his other relatives trapped in slavery—a situation in which (to use the words of Abraham and Torok) "the 'I' stages the words, gestures, and feelings" of a loved one "who mourns his [or her] forever 'dead' object."[61] In summary, moments of traumatic loss can result in "inexpressible mourning" that "erects a secret tomb inside the subject," an "unspeakable scene" that could not be directly mourned but only addressed through the phantasmic and compulsive repetition of another person's grief.[62]

The terror of slavery, Douglass came to realize, was that such traumas reinforced the psychological hold of the slaveholders, manifested in the slaves' idolatry. In the terminology of Abraham and Torok, the idolatrous slaves had installed (or encrypted) an alien presence within their psyches, an imaginary structure molding their subservience. The only way out of such "inclusion," they argue, is through a process of "genuine mourning" in which "fantasies of incorporation can be transformed into ... the acceptance and assimilation of loss."[63] By expressing *his own* grief for his dead grandmother (as opposed to merely repeating the signs of her grief), Douglass began to dissolve the crypt that had been erected by the trauma of her mistreatment. Although an alien consciousness (namely, the psychological terrorism of the slaveholders) had once invaded his abject self, this psychic invasion—he shows us—could be identified as a "wound" and mourned. This act of mourning dissolved idolatry, for it made visible the alien ideology of slavery that had initially traumatized the abject and "slavish" self.

But such slavish "idolatry" was only an extreme form of the ideological position of Douglass's (as well as Fuller's) readers, many of whom had absorbed their society's oppressive values. It is an illusion to believe that our own critical consciousness places us outside such ideological interpellation. Even before birth, Althusser observes, each person is "always-already a subject, appointed as a subject in and by the specific familial ideological configuration in which [he or she] is 'expected' and conceived."[64] Although they cannot escape ideology, subjects can recognize various points of contradiction and overlap between the various ideological patterns shaping them. In nineteenth-century America, one such area of agency emerged in literary works that utilized the overdetermined signifiers of mourning. These texts teach us to recognize the multiple ideological patterns crisscrossing the self and, thus, to avoid the trap of believing in a liberated being beyond the social imaginary. It is intriguing to consider whether patterns of mourning, which—in some accounts—have been interpreted as constraining, do not possess this liberatory potential from the beginning. The act of mourning the dead, especially those who have intimately shaped one's life, promises to make visible those complicated networks of dependence and filiation within which each person gains subjectivity and learns to deal with loss. At the same time, the process of mourning the losses experienced by others often bridges the social barriers perpetuating their grief. As Fuller, Douglass, and other antebellum writers show us, the variable and overdetermined signifiers of mourning provide a terrain on which the damaging aspects of oppressive social conditioning can be engaged and changed.

NOTES

1. Jane Tompkins, afterword to *The Wide Wide World* (rpt., New York: Feminist Press, 1987), 587.

2. Jeffrey Steele, "The Call of Eurydice: Mourning and Intertextuality in Margaret Fuller's Writing," in *Influence and Intertextuality in Literary History,* ed. Eric Rothstein and Jay Clayton (Madison: University of Wisconsin Press, 1991), 271–97.

3. According to Martha Pike and Janice Armstrong, "No convenient assumption explains the character and complexity of nineteenth century American mourning. It comprehends life, death, family structure, social behavior and religion." Prologue to *A Time to Mourn: Expressions of Grief in Nineteenth Century America,* ed. Martha Pike and Janice Gray Armstrong (Stony Brook, NY: Museums at Stony Brook, 1980), 13.

4. Martha Pike, "In Memory Of: Artifacts Relating to Mourning in Nineteenth Century America," in *Rituals and Ceremonies in Popular Culture,* ed. Ray B. Browne (Bowling Green, OH: Bowling Green University Popular Press, 1980), 310.

5. Pike, 310, 312.

6. According to Anita Schorsch, images of mourning women were duplicated on "earthenware . . . plaques, cameos, patch boxes, opera glasses, fans, ceilings, arches . . . the knops of tea pots . . . architectural decoration . . . drawings . . . [and] memorial tablets." *Mourning Becomes America: Mourning Art in the New Nation* (Clinton, NJ: Main Street Press, 1976), no pagination.

7. Schorsch.

8. Pike and Armstrong, prologue, 13.

9. Martha Pike and Janice Gray Armstrong, "In Memoriam," in *A Time to Mourn,* ed. Pike and Armstrong, 67. In *Confidence Men and Painted Women: A Study of Middle-Class Culture in America, 1830–1870* (New Haven: Yale University Press, 1982), Karen Halttunen observes that "During this same period, roughly from 1780 to 1840, school girls were turning out mourning pictures based on the same design, but with a significant addition: a woman who wept over the urn, the lines of her drooping figure conforming to those of the willow" (126).

10. Betty Ring, *Let Virtue Be a Guide to Thee: Needlework in the Education of Rhode Island Women, 1730–1830* (Providence: Rhode Island Historical Society, 1983), 158–89.

11. Pike and Armstrong, "In Memoriam," 67–68.

12. Louis Althusser, "Ideology and Ideological State Apparatuses (Notes toward an Investigation)," in *Lenin and Philosophy and Other Essays,* trans. Ben Brewster (New York: Monthly Review Press, 1971), 174.

13. See "The Domestication of Death" in Ann Douglas, *The Feminization of American Culture* (1977; rpt., New York: Avon Books, 1978).

14. Neal L. Tolchin, *Mourning, Gender, and Creativity in the Art of Herman Melville* (New Haven: Yale University Press, 1988), 118.

15. Kathleen Woodward, "Freud and Barthes: Theorizing Mourning, Sustaining Grief," *Dis-*

course: Journal for Theoretical Studies in Media and Culture 13:1 (Fall–Winter 1990–91): 94, 95.

16. Ralph Waldo Emerson, *Nature, Addresses, and Lectures,* ed. Robert E. Spiller and Alfred R. Ferguson (Cambridge: Harvard University Press, 1979), 7. *Nature,* like Emerson's other essays, advocates a strong masculinity that might avoid the taint of "effeminacy."

17. George Sebouhian, "A Dialogue with Death: An Examination of Emerson's Friendship," *Studies in the American Renaissance* 1989: 238.

18. Mark Edmundson, "Emerson and the Work of Melancholia," *Raritan* (Spring 1987) 120–36; Woodward, 96.

19. Sharon Cameron, "Representing Grief: Emerson's 'Experience,'" *Representations* 15 (Summer 1986): 15–41.

20. Herman Melville, *Moby-Dick,* ed. Harrison Hayford and Hershel Parker (New York: Norton, 1967), 161.

21. Tolchin, 118.

22. Tolchin, 117. Tolchin attributes his terminology to the Harvard Study of Bereavement.

23. Nathaniel Hawthorne, "Roger Malvin's Burial," in *The Celestial Railroad and Other Stories* (New York: New American Library, 1963), 17.

24. Hawthorne, 23, 27.

25. Hawthorne, 26.

26. Luce Irigaray, *Speculum of the Other Woman,* trans. Gillian C. Gill (Ithaca: Cornell University Press, 1985), 88.

27. Irigaray, 57.

28. Irigaray, 66–67.

29. Irigaray, 57.

30. Irigaray, 68.

31. Irigaray, 71.

32. Barbara Welter's essay "The Cult of True Womanhood" provides a classic characterization of this position. In *Dimity Convictions: The American Woman in the Nineteenth Century* (Athens: Ohio University Press, 1976).

33. Karen Sánchez-Eppler, "Bodily Bonds: The Intersecting Rhetorics of Feminism and Abolition," in *The Culture of Sentiment,* ed. Shirley Samuels (New York: Oxford University Press, 1992), 100.

34. Tolchin, 13.

35. John R. McDowell, "New York Magdalen Society," in *The Reform Impulse, 1825–1850,* ed. Walter Hugins (New York: Harper and Row, 1972), 44.

36. Dorothea Dix, "The Strong Claims of Suffering Humanity: Dorothea L. Dix," in *The Reform Impulse, 1825–1850,* ed. Hugins, 70.

37. Dix, 69.

38. Ronald G. Walters, *American Reformers, 1815–1860* (New York: Hill and Wang, 1978), 100.

39. *The Essential Margaret Fuller,* ed. Jeffrey Steele (New Brunswick: Rutgers University Press, 1992), 267.

40. *Narrative of the Life of Frederick Douglass,* in *The Classic Slave Narratives,* ed. Henry Louis Gates, Jr. (New York: Mentor, 1987), 263.

41. Frederick Douglass, *My Bondage and My Freedom* (with supporting texts), ed. Philip S. Foner (New York: Dover, 1969), 442.

42. Douglass, *Narrative,* 271.

43. Douglass, *Narrative,* 263.

44. *The Essential Margaret Fuller,* ed. Steele, 346.

45. Douglass, *My Bondage and My Freedom,* 251.

46. Douglass, *Narrative,* 264.

47. Douglass, *My Bondage and My Freedom,* 45.

48. Douglass, *My Bondage and My Freedom,* 107, 67.

49. Julia Kristeva, *Powers of Horror: An Essay on Abjection,* trans. Leon S. Roudiez (New York: Columbia University Press, 1982), 10.

50. Douglass, *My Bondage and My Freedom*, 95.

51. We see this, for example, in Douglass's discussion in his *Narrative* of "the slaves of the political parties" (262).

52. Douglass, *My Bondage and My Freedom*, 62, 79. William Andrews has argued that Douglass developed emotionally expressive modes of narration "so that the reader could be shown not just the incident or what the incident signified but how to *feel* about the incident." *To Tell a Free Story: The First Century of Afro-American Autobiography, 1760–1865* (Urbana: University of Illinois Press, 1986), 103.

53. Douglass, *My Bondage and My Freedom*, 99.

54. Douglass, *My Bondage and My Freedom*, 98.

55. Douglass, *My Bondage and My Freedom*, 57.

56. Ibid.

57. Douglass, *My Bondage and My Freedom*, 60.

58. Douglass, *My Bondage and My Freedom*, 180.

59. Cameron, 35; Angela Moorjani, "Kathe Kollwitz on Sacrifice, Mourning, and Reparation: An Essay in Psychoaesthetics," *MLN* 5 (December 1986): 1116; Kenneth Reinhard and Julia Lupton, "Shapes of Grief: Freud, *Hamlet*, and Mourning," *Genders*, no. 4 (Spring 1989): 51; Woodward, 99.

60. Maria Torok, "The Illness of Mourning," in *The Shell and the Kernel*, ed. Nicholas T. Rand (Chicago: University of Chicago Press, 1994), 113.

61. Nicolas Abraham and Maria Torok, " 'The Lost Object—Me': Notes on Endocryptic Identification," in *The Shell and the Kernel*, 148.

62. Abraham and Torok, "Mourning *or* Melancholia: Introjection *versus* Incorporation," in *The Shell and the Kernel*, 130. Idem, " 'The Lost Object—Me,' " 145.

63. Abraham and Torok, "Mourning *or* Melancholia," 137.

64. Althusser, 176.

Emotional Expression and Emotional Control in the Transition to the Twentieth Century

Chapter Six

Passionate Voices and Cool Calculations
The Emotional Landscape of the Nineteenth-Century New England Textile Industry

Mary H. Blewett

"Anger at work" indeed "has a history" of both continuity and change.[1] Corporate policies that suppressed strong feelings among both workers and townspeople, especially hostility, contempt, and passionate rage at uncontrollable economic change, shaped nineteenth-century New England textile industrialization. The style of emotional expression varied with perceptions of power wielded by capitalists and the efforts by workers and their middle-class allies to curb industrial might through reform legislation or organized opposition. Public anger at corporate power was revealed or concealed in accordance with perceived advantages and circumstances.

When in the 1810s Boston capitalists first tried to organize a distinctly republican form of industrial production, they carefully planned to avoid the miseries, deprivations, and excitements of English textile centers. Textile capitalists also successfully persuaded politicians and the public to give them a tariff and send their daughters into the new brick textile mills of Waltham and Lowell, Massachusetts.[2] Watchful eyes would provide moral control and work discipline. Later, paternalism gave way to more coercive means of emotional discipline in, for example, the post–Civil War mills of Fall River, Massachusetts.

In antebellum mills and boardinghouses, paternalism served not only to secure the loyalty of the workforce, but also to influence the community's economic and social life. In Lowell the goal was absolute managerial control over the rationalization of production.[3] To make profits, managers and workers alike had to accept the smooth, harmonious workings of integrated and mechanized production. Disruptions threatened failure in an infant industry; feelings upset by the riptide of economic transformation had to be stifled.[4] Control over local expressions of anger that might lead to organized strife reflected the power of the textile capitalists. Before 1860, ambivalence—relatively quiet ambivalence—was the primary attitude of most native-born textile workers toward industrial change.[5] The paternalism of early New England industrialization successfully concealed most but not all negative responses by workers and townspeople alike.

The scarcity of primary sources on the private lives of nineteenth-century working people, in contrast to the employing middle class, means that historians who study the history of emotion in the workplace must examine the public record of labor struggles to understand the emotional landscape of the New England textile industry. The Lowell mills, financed by the Boston Associates, a group of wealthy merchants looking for profitable investment, rose in the early 1820s on the Merrimack River with limitless water power to drive textile machinery. The imperious Kirk Boott, an American-born Anglophile and trained engineer who had served in the British military during the Napoleonic Wars, was given complete control over the construction of canals and mills by the Boston capitalists, to whom he was carefully deferential. His unquestionable power in Lowell unleashed his haughty contempt for Americans and his arrogant impatience with delays. Sleepy bobbin boys felt the lash of his riding crop. East Chelmsford farmers, who had unwittingly sold their farmland cheap to Boott, felt cheated, expressing their disgust in a popular rhyme:

> There came a young a man from the old countree,
> The Merrimack river happened to see.
> What a capital place for mills, quote he. . . .
> And then all these farmers, so [a]cute,
> They *gave* all their land and timber to Boott.
> Ri-toot, ri-toot, ri-toot, ri-toot, rumpty ri-tooten.[6]

One Fourth of July, Boott's flagpole sported the British flag above the Stars and Stripes. In his absence, his Yankee neighbors switched them.[7] Boott's combative and antagonistic style was unique. Other managers and mill agents in Lowell cautiously hid their heated debates and crucial decisions on wages, dividends, and profits behind the doors of countinghouses and at stockholders' meetings. This pattern of avoiding public confrontation with disgruntled workers and townspeople while concealing decision making took hold throughout the region.

The "turnouts" or strikes by Lowell factory women in the early 1830s and the New England ten-hour petition campaign of the 1840s, led by mill worker Sarah Bagley among many others, tested the mills' policy of public silence. The initially astonished but unintimidated reaction of the agents to the early strikes and denunciations shouted in the streets was to dismiss these activities as aberrant and hire other workers. The high turnover rate among the factory operatives (few remained in the mills more than four years) undermined collective unrest.[8] Sarah Bagley disappeared from labor activity by 1848.[9] As the mills began in the 1850s to hire immigrant Irish workers, religious bigotry among Yankee women workers prompted them to act as strikebreakers during a strike by female frame spinners in 1859.[10] Divide the workforce and dismiss the leaders became the watchword of New England mill agents. Anger would turn to fear, and fear to submission. This policy was followed in other textile centers, especially in the mills of Fall River, which exploded with growth after the Civil War.

The nineteenth-century records of the Fall River mills revealed characteristics of what economist Werner Sombart called "modernity," markers of modern capitalism: "a capacity for abstraction, rationality in relating means to ends, impersonality, unending search for production efficiency, and the separation of business and other goals in the course of operations."[11] One of those "other goals" was emotional expression, especially anger. The textile industry of Fall River, which reached its peak development during a "hyper-expansion" between 1865 and 1873, provides a case study of continuity and change in emotional responses and the repression of anger-provoking political memories, especially among English immigrant workers.[12]

Fall River capitalists rejected Lowell's pre–Civil War paternalism but not its goals of control and discipline. The mill managers intended to amass enough productive power to dominate the domestic market for their chosen product: cheap print cloth. Although an ample and relatively docile workforce was essential, most managers paid no attention to the morality, housing, sanitation, working conditions, political traditions, or work experiences among their native-born or immigrant workers. This policy, hardly confined to Fall River, was expressed baldly by an unidentified Fall River mill agent in 1855 and reported with great indignation in 1868 to a Massachusetts Senate committee by a former mill agent turned labor reformer. The Fall River agent had said,

> As for myself, I regard work people just as I regard my machinery. So long as they can do the work for what I choose to pay them, I keep them, getting out of them all I can. What they do or how they fare outside my mills I don't know, nor do I consider it my business to know. They must look out for themselves as I do for myself. When my machines get old and useless, I reject them and get new; and these people are part of my machinery.[13]

This approach to the workforce contradicted the political and moral values of many experienced immigrants from Lancashire and Yorkshire, England.

During the early 1870s, English textile workers poured into the textile centers of southeastern New England and seized control of labor politics in Fall River and throughout the region. English men and women had immigrated in successive waves before and after the American Civil War.[14] Unlike many immigrants to nineteenth-century America from preindustrial societies, these Lancashire people, both English and Irish-born, came with industrial skills, urban experience, class consciousness, and a rich heritage of the expression of popular radicalism. They brought with them customs and traditions, which included the outspoken rhetoric of mule spinners and weavers; the practices and rituals of public demonstrations and censure of misbehavior; the varying uses of both defiance and deference as public expression; expectations about working conditions and respectable manhood and womanhood; and the deeply felt responsibilities of sons and daughters to fathers and mothers who embodied the radical politics of the Lancashire past. At the same time that Fall River capitalists were attempting to dominate the market for print cloth, they sought to purge their English workers of "their chronic insubordination."[15] The resulting conflicts over the expression and viability of Lancashire anger and other legacies significantly influenced the direction of late nineteenth-century New England labor politics.

The nineteenth-century heritage of these Lancashire working people included ritualized, harmonious collective bargaining with English employers, worked out during the mid-Victorian compromise of the 1850s. Mutual advantage repressed public anger. Part of this compromise defined working-class manhood as rational, sober, and conciliatory and relations between employer and worker as respectful.[16] These negotiations excluded women workers. Complex mutual behaviors worked out among men in the Lancashire textile industry, composed of many small, individually owned, single- process firms (unlike New England's giant, integrated mills), secured the respectability of workingmen.[17] Once in post–Civil War Fall River, where such behaviors were scorned by employers, Lancashire workingwomen contributed in deeply provocative ways to the meanings of manhood and womanhood by their voiced expectations, their activism and successes, their memories of history, and their views on politics.

Significant cultural conflicts developed within the Fall River working class over the utilization of this political memory and the expression of public anger as a viable strategy. The most crucial issue workers confronted was the power of mill agents to influence the market for their goods. This power, if unopposed, gave employers the authority to alter wages and working conditions in the mills that affected standards of living and union strength. From the moment Lancashire workers landed in Fall River, the managers of the mills systematically challenged customary measures of skill and strength. The mill agents used the cheapest raw cotton and the best machinery, paid the lowest wages in the region, and demanded ever more intense physical exertions from their operatives—especially mule spinners—to produce massive quantities of inferior cloth, the defects in which the printing process would conceal. They controlled the domestic market for print cloth by having the capacity to glut it with the cheapest possible goods. Suppression of opposition was vital. In turn, English workers regarded the Fall River agents with open contempt as "shoddyites" with "shoddyite morality." Fall River became known among operatives as "the hardest place for work and the meanest place for wages" in New England.[18] The city began to fill with emotional and political tension.

After scouring New England for workers, Fall River managers actively and heedlessly recruited additional Lancashire workers with promises of good wages. The workforce more than quadrupled between 1865 and 1875. The Fall River mills and the scale of their operations had outstripped Lowell and Lawrence. Immigrants faced ruthless managers who found themselves responsible during the industrial depression of 1873 for paying off very heavy corporate debts from land speculation, new buildings, and imported machinery. These burdens added urgency to the need to suppress and control any opposition. Relying on managerial and financial skills acquired in commerce, most mill agents were unfamiliar with and contemptuous of English work traditions and labor protest. Many mill owners, who both feared and despised their Lancashire-born workers, regarded their mannered courtesy, doffed caps, and references to their employers as "masters" as marks of unmanly servility.[19] In American experience, only black slaves had masters. Lancashire workers faced both their employers' immense market power and a dismissive, open contempt for their deferential behavior. Still, for the sake of negotiation, they carefully hid their anger.

A strike in the summer of 1870 after a general wage cut demonstrated the failure of concealed emotion and respectful deference as a strategy to draw the mill owners into negotiations. Representatives of the 420 male mule spinners, speaking for the

7,000 other operatives thrown out of work with the stoppage of spinning operations, offered to compromise. The agents never even acknowledged the mule spinners' offers. Strike leader and Lancashire immigrant William Isherwood, who in 1867 had been blacklisted in Lowell for ten-hour reform activity, called their actions "silent contempt."[20]

During the strike in 1870, David Anthony Brayton, treasurer of the Durfee Mill, broke ranks with the other textile capitalists and became publicly enraged with strikers, to his regret. Brayton, reared on a farm and trained as a lawyer, was new to the textile business. In 1866 he became the manager of the family-controlled factory and four years later was supervising the building of a second mill, funded by undistributed profits. Brayton personally owned nearly one-third of the mill's stock. The 1870 mule spinners' strike became his first confrontation with quietly defiant but politically experienced, skilled workingmen. The shutdown threatened his company's expansion. Unlike the other textile managers, who relied on their wealth and power and refused to speak with any strikers, the inexperienced Brayton reacted passionately to the situation.

Early in the strike, which began in July, while Brayton was driving out of the millyard in his carriage, he was approached by two striking spinners, trying to get him to talk about the wage cut. He refused, but then went on:

> I said further: I think you should be thankful we don't have to cut down [wages] again; ... One of them commenced arguing the case. ... Finally he spoke of the high price of beef here and in England, to which I replied that it was very high here, but not so high as to prevent any honest laboring man from having it on his table three times a day. "Well," said he, "we can't have salmon." At that I got a little excited and answered: By thunder! if you are going to count on salmon I can't stand here to argue with you.[21]

Brayton was outraged to be stopped inside his own millyard to discuss what was likely to appear on his workers' supper tables. Goaded by his insulted dignity and his responsibility to get that second mill built, Brayton attempted long before the others to reopen his mill. He thus made himself and his property the target of the strikers and their supporters. His uncontrolled emotions got him into trouble with everyone.

When one of his strikebreaking spinners was severely beaten up, Brayton, in an angry panic, sprang to his defense, notified the police to escort the worker home, and gave the injured man a pistol. Then Brayton went to the mayor, insisting that a crisis existed that called for action. When Mayor Samuel M. Brown tried to calm him down, Brayton threatened to go to the governor's office for state troops. Brown finally agreed to so something. The next evening as the Durfee replacement workers were leaving the mill, the city marshal, armed only with a little whip, tried to part the jeering crowd to let the workers through. Brayton was furious and disgusted: "it was like switching grasshoppers." If the city would not act decisively, he would.

In his own words, "[n]ow greatly excited," Brayton, armed with a loaded pistol, set off the fire alarm, bringing onto the turbulent scene the textile mills' private firefighting force. He directed them to drench the crowd and drive them out of the street in front of the mill. His forthright action turned ridiculous, because the hoses' stream reached only 130 feet. The crowd, with much hissing and hooting, simply stood in defiance beyond the water's reach. Thrown into a rage by the impotence of his actions, Brayton drew his pistol, intending to force his workers through. Before this could happen, the mayor arrived and, ignoring Brayton's pleas for mass arrests, ordered the people in the name of the Commonwealth to disperse. They did. Brayton's actions made him look a fool. The next day, in an overwhelming show of force, two hundred special police, four companies of militia, and a contingent of state police arrived, thus controlling both Brayton and the strikers.[22]

Treasurer Brayton was learning the hard way about the strategy of Fall River's mill agents during strikes: refuse to talk, sell their inventories, starve out the strikers, and blacklist the leaders. His excited emotions resulted from inexperience, confrontations with workers that left him feeling humiliated, emasculated, and powerless, and his failed expectations of an immediate and decisive response from city officials who had already learned to respect the wise strategy of the mill owners. Thereafter, he fell into line.

In contrast to Brayton, the strikers carefully avoided any association with acts of anger or violence. The union represented its position as "repeatedly and respectfully" entreating the mill owners to negotiate, while peaceably offering strikebreakers train fares back home. Lawbreaking or violent confrontations in the streets by union men might justify their employers' refusal to negotiate. Instead, spinners enlisted sympathetic striking weavers (both men and women) and the spinners' own families to confront strikebreakers. The spinners' union thus implicitly endorsed public activity for women that involved rude and violent behavior: yelling, pummeling strikebreakers, and throwing stones, behavior inappropriate for respectable working-class men. Their women could—at the direction of the men on whom they depended for support and leadership—exhibit violent behavior to support the strike.[23] Class needs encouraged female activism.

The only significant incident of violence in 1870 toward a strikebreaker illustrates how this worked. The victim was Brayton's spinner, Isaiah Sanderson, a Scottish immigrant farmer who had worked in a mill for only three years. Sanderson had refused to join the spinners' union but expected trouble and afterwards named no attackers. To make an example of him to others, a noisy crowd waiting outside the mill kicked and stoned him and gave him "a tremendous pounding" as he quit for the night after two days at work.[24] The street crowds who surrounded Sanderson were mostly women and children. They supplied the howls and jeers, the fists and blows, to humble him. These crowds were backed up by the female tenants of corporation housing nearby, armed with stones and dirt clods concealed under their aprons and ready to shower the strikebreakers at a signal.[25] Peaceable male behavior and female acts of violence served class politics.

Using the local press, mill agents tried to goad the strikers into an emotional response by denigrating spinning as an unmanly trade and claiming that elsewhere in Massachusetts, "girls run mules easily and successfully." In reaction, the spinners argued that they worked harder and faster at their machines than anywhere else in New England, walking twenty-five miles and more per day over eleven hours with only one young boy to help piece up broken yarns: "a pretty good day's work for any man."[26] However peaceable they remained in 1870, the mule spinners' leaders could not persuade the agents to negotiate. Protest strategies based on respectable deference might have offered hope in Lancashire, but they did not work in Fall River. After two months, workers slowly returned to the mills. To strike fear into the rest, managers blacklisted union leaders and forced them from their corporation tenements. Other strikers felt the humiliation of signing antiunion contracts.[27] Meanwhile, the spinners organized in secret, and the weavers waited for reinforcements from Lancashire.

Failing to locate sufficient labor for the twenty-two new cotton mills built in a frenzy of construction between 1870 and 1872, Fall River managers recruited more English workers. According to a well-known local story, one Fall River manufacturer confided to an overseer his eagerness to employ "green horns" from Lancashire. "Yes," the overseer replied, "but you'll find that they have brought their horns with them."[28] Yet Fall River agents believed that they could dominate these historically unruly people as easily as the national market for print cloth. Heavy immigration in the early 1870s swelled the numbers of Lancashire workers in the rapidly expanding city. Weavers entering the Fall River mills grumbled over working conditions, long hours, and tyrannical overseers unknown to them since the 1840s.

The 1873 depression intensified the mill agents' anxieties and the operatives' resentment over increased workloads and wage cuts. The pace of work drove mule spinners beyond endurance. New England mill agents refused to supply their spinners with the help of adult male piecers (customary in Lancashire); the supervisory aspects of the job had helped define spinning as man's work. Skilled men now supervised mere boys, who helped piece up or repair the multiple strands of flimsy yarn spun from cheap cotton as the spinner drove the huge frames back and forth. These pressures produced a "Fall River walk," brisk and quick. Few spinners, even the younger, vital ones, had the stamina to work out the full month of six-day weeks, eleven hours a day, without laying off as "sick" for several days each month to regain their strength. Substitutes on a "sick spinners" list routinely filled the jobs of these exhausted men. An employer's decision to define a spinner's work as just beyond the extent of a man's physical powers, an abuse the operatives called the "grind" or "lashing the help," challenged his pride in strength and skill.[29]

Humiliations followed workers inside their homes as wage cuts showed on the family supper table. English workers had legendary appetites for beer and beef. Hard times meant less money to spend on food to sustain overtaxed strength and vitality. After a sweating mule spinner walked his daily twenty- five miles and more, back and forth in a brutally hot spinning room, beer supplied carbohydrates for his thirsty body and anesthetic for overstrained muscles and nerves. Ashamed English workers hid dinner pails with cheese and bread rather than the customary cold meat, and spinners refused to substitute salmon for beef, that traditional New England means of feeding apprentices cheaply.[30] Despite local temperance opinion, a man's physical well-being, especially under the exhausting terms he faced in Fall River factories, required red meat and plenty of beer.

In contrast to English practice, overseers in the Granite Mill posted the daily work records of each spinner to provoke shaming, competitive behavior. They thus tried to humiliate men over their work capacities in addition to manipulating the piece rate. Overseers denied spinners their customary time to oil and clean their machines by setting the piece rate for spinning yarn so low as to require almost total concentration on machine operations. The power of the Granite Mill agents to define the pace of work proved deadly. In September 1874, the accumulation of cotton waste on and near mules whose unoiled gears scraped metal against metal caused a disastrous fire that destroyed Granite mill 1. The official inquest criticized as cowardly the behavior of mule spinners who saved themselves while the women and illegally employed children, some as young as eight, were trapped on the upper floors and either were "roasted alive" or jumped to their deaths. Workers laid the blame on the short reach of the hook and ladder companies and on the totally dry pails and stand pipes in the mills.[31] Tensions continued to build.

This accumulated rage and contempt broke loose in 1875. In late 1874 the mill agents decided to stimulate prices in the depressed print cloth market by limiting production. But when other New England textile mills began to manufacture print cloth to meet the shortfall, Fall River factories returned to full capacity in January 1875 and cut wages by 10 percent. They intended to flood the market and defeat their upstart competitors. This wage cut, in addition to a 10 percent cut one year before, made hard times worse. Male weavers, however, in a January 6, 1875, meeting that excluded women weavers, accepted the additional cut until the market improved. The women weavers' reactions prevented this acquiescence by male weavers and mule spinners. Inspired by their heritage of Lancashire popular radicalism, they organized to oppose vehemently any further capitulation as bad politics. They shamed and pushed their reluctant male coworkers into the only successful weavers' strike in the city in the nineteenth century.[32]

There were two major strikes in 1875: the first in the spring, a success; the second in the fall, a disaster. Labor politics in Fall River revealed the emerging differences among activist men and women and between the eight thousand weavers and two thousand mule spinners over the styles of expression and the direction of labor protest. The successful challenge to male leadership by workingwomen and the weavers' strike tactics that used passionate emotional expression produced intraclass, intercultural, and gender conflict. The historical and political traditions and customs of Lancashire provided the cultural framework for this struggle.

In 1875, women represented about one-third of the striking weavers, and about half of the weaving workforce. These female strikers demanded that the men, both weavers and spinners, act quickly and decisively to halt recurrent wage cuts, as in Lancashire. In public, they angrily denounced deference and conciliation as cowardly and unmanly. Female strikers organized themselves across skill, gender, and ethnic lines. As one activist put it, "We have not been men or women enough to stick to our rights . . . and must sink all national differences in the one great question of [their] preservation."[33] Led by Lancashire women weavers, the strike included native-born Americans and French-Canadian immigrant females.

Never a part of deferential policies in Lancashire, women workers ignored the midcentury compromise in the old country and its language of respectability, paternalism, and the family wage. Instead they reached back to early nineteenth-century forms of popular radicalism that included angry and violent crowd action to uphold a moral economy with customary, mutual responsibilities. This radical tradition, the women believed, was more appropriate to the ruthless nature and overweening power of Fall River–style textile capitalism. They cited historic examples of the long-term effectiveness of resistance—win, lose, or draw—the relationship between labor and capital. Activist females used the lessons of the Preston, Lancashire, strike in 1854: suspend work at the three mills whose agents had instigated the wage cut, while allowing the other mills to make cloth, meet their contracts, and pay their workers, who contributed to the strike fund.[34] The lessons of history and politics were plain to them and shaped both their expectations about working-class manhood and their protest strategy.

In a public call for action, the women weavers revealed the source of their anger: their exclusion from decision making and their disapproval of deferential male behavior. "Writhing under the cruel and oppressive effects of the late reduction, and dissatisfied with the dilatory, shilly-shally and cowardly action of many of the chief conductors of our late meetings, we, the female operatives have decided to meet together and speak and act for ourselves."[35] This meeting reverberated with direct challenges to working-class manhood. Addressing their complaints to the only man present, Henry Sevey, editor of the Fall River *Labor Journal*, they shouted insults: "Come on, you cowards! You were [be]got in fear, though you were born in England."[36] They were reminding the male weavers that they were the sons and grandsons of the handloom weavers of Lancashire who had fought tenaciously and boldly for their rights. It was time for the sons, like their fathers, to show their "horns" with bold action and imaginative strategy. They ascribed to masculinity the qualities that they themselves were exhibiting: open aggressiveness and loud defiance. For them, New England was a new Lancashire where the old battles needed to be refought.

Before joining the women's strike, however, the male weavers, discouraged by past failures and hard times, took their caps in their hands and on January 17 approached the treasurer of the Crescent Mill.

> A delegation of 6 tall, blond, blue-eyed Englishmen, they held their hats in their hands and their tongues in their mouths until the Treasurer spoke to their leader when he stepped respectfully to the counter and said in a marked North Country accent: "Wael, I suppose ye're awaere we are come to see ye, sir, about our little grievances, and thaet's about the figger thaet we think will bring us back t'our looms."

When Richard Borden, Jr., protested that the manufacturers suffered more than the weavers from hard times, their barely concealed anger flared briefly.

> "More of a hardship, sir?" interrupted a giant bearded Yorkshire man, with a flushed pale face and tears standing in his eyes. . . . "We haeve to live upon our daily wages," another said in a low suppressed voice, "and back of thaet we've no money, sir; while you've plenty to back-set you, I hope."

As the men went away disappointed, the *Boston Globe* reporter remarked to Borden, "That's a gentlemanly set of strikers." "Yes," Borden replied, "I make them gentlemanly."[37] The next day, the male weavers and the mule spinners made the strike successful.

The issue of supporting the women's actions created immediate dissension among Lancashire men that touched the emotional core of their manhood. Labor reformer Thomas Stephenson, whose *Lawrence Journal and Citizen* competed with Henry Sevey's *Labor Journal* for the support of New England textile operatives, sharply criticized Sevey's support for the women strikers as another "Adam in the garden of old" who had been manipulated "as the weaker vessel" by "babbling Amazons. . . . Let us have family altars, not demoralizing harems." His belief that Sevey lacked "ordinary manly courage and determination" may have echoed the views of many male workers. At issue were the prerogatives of sober and careful men weighing the tactics of labor protest against other men who might be misguided and emasculated by emotional, rebellious Eves. But some Lancashire men agreed with the women about the lessons of history and politics and found in defiance a genuinely satisfying, if more unruly, physical expression of manliness. As editor Sevey put it, "If a man cannot knock down his oppressor, you at least like to see him try; and if you cannot knock the tyrant down who would oppress you, you can at least give him a welter!"[38] To some, perhaps many, active defiance felt right.

Once the strike was won in April, the weavers and their confrontational style controlled local labor politics. Their aggressiveness and unexpected success had empowered labor protest and defeated the arrogant employers. Quickly the weavers began to organize a regional association of textile operatives, call for a standard list of wages, and in coalition with labor reformers agitate for ten-hour laws that would make New England the Lancashire of America.[39] This prospect sent waves of alarm throughout the region's textile interests.

The success of the first strike in 1875 created a dilemma for mule spinners. An alliance with the weavers represented a tantalizing prospect of powerful combinations against the mills that might lead to union recognition, but it might also undermine the spinners' leadership of labor politics. Furthermore, many of the native-born workers, male and female, valued geographical mobility, not persistent confrontation, as a measure of personal liberty. Since the early nineteenth century, New England workers had been told that their working conditions and political rights were superior to those of the factory slaves of England. Many of them, whether as Civil War veterans or just westward dreamers, rejected as spiritless and un-American the claims of immigrants to a right to work in their trade in their chosen community. In contrast, Lancashire textile workers regarded their emigrations as collective, not individual, acts. When their countryfolk decided to return to Lancashire, they were sent off with distinctive public fanfare.

Some American workers believed that "[Lancashire weavers] know only weaving, and nothing else, and regard it as their only work . . . and they will starve rather than do anything else. . . . They will work and growl, and when they can they will strike again. . . . I cannot help but think the American would show the greater pride and independence in his course."[40] Lancashire traditions appeared alien, rash, foolhardy. Earlier English immigrants had developed connections with native-born workers and labor reformers, understanding and using the rhetoric of Yankee rights and republicanism. Post–Civil War English immigrants, however, viewed Yankee willingness to move about looking for better work as naive foolishness, playing into the hands of hostile employers. Lancashire operatives described the byword of Fall River as "If you don't like it, get out," and spoke of the American as "proverbial for his submission."[41] These differing strategies and attitudes proved divisive and explosive.

During the summer of 1875, as the weavers organized throughout southern New England, the Fall River mill agents decided that continuing competition from Rhode Island mills—which threatened their control of print cloth production—required them once again to glut the market with cheap cloth. They cut wages severely and threatened a general lockout if the weavers struck any mill. The unusual ferocity of this struggle over industrial power exposed the ire of both employers and workers. The weavers responded by applying the Lancashire custom of a moral economy that rejected the amoral or "mammonite" marketplace ideology of supply and demand.[42] On July 31, most weavers, spinners, and carders collectively withheld their labor from the mills. They meant to influence the print cloth market for their own purposes. They agreed that if other manufacturers could pay more for the work, then "they have the best right to it," and the Fall River mills "must stand their chance of being burst up." Convinced that the mills would inevitably be forced to halt overproduction, the workers seized control of the timing of the shutdown for the summer months, when their cost of living was relatively low.[43] This defiant collective act denied the existence of a morally neutral market run by natural economic laws, which masked the power of the mills. It exposed the employers' ideology as immoral and fraudulent. This decision represented an extraordinary challenge to the power of the mill agents to control production and dominate the market. Class antagonism hardened.

By early August, thirty-five mills and fifteen thousand operatives stood idle, while Fall River weavers led an intensified effort to institute a ten-hour day in Rhode Island.[44] Together, the mill owners in Fall River became determined to crush this unprecedented threat to their power, whatever the cost. After weeks of no work and no price increase in the market, the operatives abandoned their efforts. The mill agents, however, eager to demolish any hope for a New England Lancashire, decided to lock out their employees for another month and starve them into submission. Mill owners particularly wished to destroy Lancashire-style protest discipline: "Up goes a hand and out goes the help!"[45]

After several weeks of trying to live on potatoes and bread, the operatives submitted and the mills reopened. On September 27, returning workers discovered to their fury that they were again, as in 1870, being forced to sign antiunion contracts. As fifty-year-old spinner Thomas Stamson, an immigrant from Preston, Lancashire, in 1857, put it, this was unthinkable: "we mun ask for oor roights the same as thae gie em in Englan'."[46] Hunger and the knowledge that the mills would employ only the utterly defeated produced a response by enraged Lancashire workers that harked back to the bread riots of the late eighteenth century. Seventy-five-year-old former Lancashire handloom weaver Jonathan Biltcliffe reminded a mass meeting to great sensation about late eighteenth-century food riots in England and Wales. To thousands of strikers, a fuming Biltcliffe insisted, "while there was bread in the town I would go take it." Hundreds of men and women strikers then marched to City Hall, cheering and yelling "Bread!" "Tyranny!" Twenty boys bore poles on which were impaled loaves of bread stolen from a bakery. An American flag, carried upside down as a distress signal, preceded a sign that read, "15,000 white slaves for auction," topped with a loaf of bread (see fig. 6.1). Lancashire workers had long been incensed at American pretensions to freedom and democracy in contrast with the tyranny thrust on them.

To underscore her disgust at being told to return to work or face the misery of the state poor farm, one woman struck the mayor on the head with a loaf of bread.[47] The mayor neither literally or figuratively knew what hit him. The historic and cultural significance of the food riot behavior that gave form and direction to the turmoil in the streets was clear to Lancashire people, but baffling to all others involved in the strike. Only the editors of the conservative press in Boston and Providence recognized the revolutionary implications of Manchester-style bread riots in New England, while Boston labor reformer Jennie Collins appreciated the disciplined, ritualized crowd action during the tumult.[48]

The spectacle and incipient violence of the massive demonstration split the textile operatives into confused and hostile camps and alarmed many labor reformers. To the uninitiated, these customary rituals appeared to be "hideous" and "incendiary" conduct by a riotous "mob."[49] The local French-language newspaper denounced the demonstration as ridiculous.[50] Labor reformers lectured the defeated workers that "rioting and violence are not the true American way of settling a difficulty."[51] These cultural divisions and the crushing defeat of the labor with-holding strategy convinced the mule spinners that the weavers' union with its contingent of female agitators had led the strikers into total disaster. The spinners concluded that uncontrollable women had provoked riotous actions and that their emotional, public displays of outrage and dependency had emasculated the male weavers. The mule spinners would no longer cooperate in strikes with the weavers. Passion had overcome reason.[52]

With the Lancashire past rendered perilous and angry expressions feminized in late 1875, the mule spinners turned toward moderation and caution. Their union secretary, Lancashire immigrant Robert Howard, won acceptance as a leader who first tamed his men and made them "as obedient and docile and harmonious as the parts of a mule frame."[53] The union adopted policies that restored a proper sense of respectable manhood but offered no real means to confront the power of their employers to set wages and working conditions. The spinners succeeded, however, using cautious cooperation and exclusionary policies, in achieving union recognition. Yet they lost an important strike in 1879, highlighted by uncontrollable outbursts of wrath that led to the brutal stoning of strikebreaking French-Canadian families arriving from Quebec.[54] In the midst of a losing fight, passion momentarily superseded caution. By 1880, the national mule spinners' union led by Howard advocated an ideal family wage paid to respectable, dispassionate trade union men who supported their homebound wives and children. Adopting the motto "Defense not Defiance," the union endorsed the exclusive control of spinning by men (who were faced with deskilling by the new technology of ring-spinning) and the acceptance of

State militia quelling the strikers' activities, including (bottom right) placards and boys carrying loaves on poles. "The Labor Riot at Fall River, Massachusetts," *New York Graphic: An Illustrated Evening Newspaper*, October 2, 1875: p. 713.

market forces to determine wage levels—with special provision for themselves.[55] Later, the national union became central to craft conservatism in the Knights of Labor and the American Federation of Labor.[56]

During the winter of 1881–82, Robert Howard brought social reformer Lillian Chace Wyman to Fall River to interview blacklisted mule spinners. Howard and Wyman visited the home of English immigrant "Mr. W." Poverty had forced him to sign away his union membership, promise to remain silent about grievances, and never again participate in strikes. Remembering this shameful abandonment of his heritage of union activity, he sprang to his feet and cried out, "I'm humiliated,—I'm less of a man than I was!"[57] Mr. W's sense of loss reflected the defeat of Lancashire radicalism that was the aftermath of that bitter decade of class struggle in Fall River. It also revealed the desperation of a man unable to act on either outraged feelings or political legacies.

In nineteenth-century New England textile communities, anger was always present, expressed or unexpressed, often varying in intensity according to previous work experiences and cultural traditions. It arose primarily out of disappointed expectations, perceptions of injustice, and differing cultural and class values. For many Fall River textile workers in 1875, open emotional expression had first empowered and then disempowered their organized opposition. Anger had always been a shifting instrument of protest, but for mule spinners its suppression as a policy seemed a reasonable choice after that devastating September defeat, when old styles appeared useless and new tactics necessary. But this choice divided spinners from weavers for the rest of the century and weakened organized opposition to employer power. The expression and suppression of public anger remained deeply political and contingent. It also operated as a field on which the qualities of manhood and womanhood were defined and redefined. These events make Fall River an important case study for the history of emotion.

Mill owners and the press supported the spinners' abandonment of the weavers and their angry radical tradition for cautious calculation. Even the editor of the pro-labor *Boston Herald* called for moderation and the conduct of Fall River strikes as "matters of clear, cool business, not of enthusiasm or temporary excitement." The *Providence Journal*'s conservative editor endorsed the new, dispassionate mode of behavior. The basis of strikes should be

> a cold-blooded business one.... If ... Mr. Howard will enlarge the scope of [his] calculations, ... including all of the circumstances of time, capital invested, risk and prospective demand and supply of labor and product, and advise the operatives to strike or not strike in a "cool business manner," no one need complain.... [T]here should be no boycotting of workers who want to work, no mobbing or violence committed upon the industrious and producent; because these things are not "business," but criminality. No excitement and the general public may feel a relief from ... anxiety.[58]

For the rest of the century, textile employers and the leaders of skilled mule spinners embraced the same emotional patterns of dispassionate and conservative coexistence. The American Federation of Labor would do the same.

NOTES

1. Carol Zisowitz Stearns and Peter N. Stearns, *Anger: The Struggle for Emotional Control in America's History* (Chicago: University of Chicago Press, 1986), 1. This pathbreaking work on the history of emotions concentrated its analysis on work in the twentieth century and suggested that changes in "emotionology" originated largely within the family and marriage. There was little attempt to formulate a pattern of control for anger during nineteenth-century industrialization, 110–12. E. Anthony Rotundo, *American Manhood: Transformations in Masculinity from the Revolution to the Modern Era* (New York: Basic Books, 1993) did not include the experience of a northern industrialist. For an exploration of prescriptive literature on middle-class anger and masculinity, see Peter N. Stearns, "Men, Boys and Anger in American Society, 1860–1940," in J. A. Mangan and James Walvin, eds., *Manliness and Morality: Middle-Class Masculinity in Britain and America, 1800–1940* (Manchester: Manchester University Press, 1986), 75–91.

2. Thomas Dublin, *Women at Work: The Transformation of Work and Community in Lowell, Massachusetts, 1826–1860* (New York: Columbia University Press, 1979); and Robert F. Dalzell, Jr., *Enterprising Elite: The Boston Associates and the World They Made* (New York: Norton, 1987).

3. Hannah Josephson, *The Golden Threads: New England's Mill Girls and Magnates* (New York: Duell, Sloan and Pearce, 1949), 8.

4. David Zonderman, *Anxieties and Aspirations: New England Workers and the Mechanized Factory System, 1815–1850* (Oxford: Oxford University Press, 1992).

5. Charles Sellers, *The Market Revolution: Jacksonian America, 1815–1846* (Oxford: Oxford University Press, 1991).

6. Harriet H. Robinson, *Loom and Spindle: Or, Life among the Early Mill Girls* (1898; reprint, Kailua, HI: Press Pacifica, 1976), 6.

7. Ibid.

8. Dublin, *Women at Work*; and Teresa F. Murphy, *Ten Hours' Labor: Religion, Reform, and Gender in Early New England* (Ithaca: Cornell University Press, 1992).

9. Helena Wright, "Sarah G. Bagley: A Biographical Note," *Labor History* 20 (1979): 398–413.

10. Dublin, *Women at Work*, 206–07.

11. Paul F. McGouldrick, *New England Textiles in the Nineteenth Century: Profits and Investments* (Cambridge: Harvard University Press, 1968), 204–6.

12. Thomas Russell Smith, *The Cotton Textile Industry of Fall River, Massachusetts* (New York: King's Crown Press, 1944), chap. 2.

13. Henry K. Oliver, *Report*, Massachusetts Senate Document no. 21, 1868, 23.

14. On English immigrants in America, Rowland T. Berthoff, *British Immigrants in Industrial America, 1790–1950* (Cambridge: Harvard University Press, 1953); Charlotte Erickson, *Invisible Immigrants* (Ithaca: Cornell University Press, 1990); John T. Cumbler, *Working-Class Community in Industrial America: Work, Leisure, and Struggle in Two Industrial Cities* (Westport: Greenwood, 1979); and Cynthia Shelton, *The Mills of Manayunk: Industrialization and Social Conflict in the Philadelphia Region, 1787–1837* (Baltimore: Johns Hopkins University Press, 1986).

15. *Fall River News*, March 6, 1875 (hereafter cited as *News*).

16. Patrick Joyce, *Work, Society, and Politics: The Culture of the Factory in Later Victorian England* (Brighton: Harvester Press, 1980); and Neville Kirk, *The Growth of Working Class Reformism in Mid-Victorian England* (Urbana: University of Illinois Press, 1985).

17. William Lazonick, "Competition, Specialization, and Industrial Decline," *Journal of Economic History* 41 (March 1981): 31–38.

18. *Providence Sun*, February 27, 1875; *Boston Herald*, February 24, 1875.

19. *News*, October 22, 1875.

20. On the 1870 strike, see Massachusetts Bureau of Labor Statistics [MBLS], *Second Annual Report* (Boston, 1871), 49–93; *News*, July 21–September 16, 1875; *Boston Herald*, August 26–30, 1870.

21. MBLS, *Second Annual Report*, 49.

22. Ibid., 52.

23. Keith McClelland, "Some Thoughts on Masculinity and the 'Representative Artisan' in

Britain, 1850–1880," *Gender and History* 1 (summer 1989): 164–77; and A. James Hammerton, "The Targets of 'Rough Music': Respectability and Domestic Violence in Victorian England," *Gender and History* 3 (spring 1991): 23–44.

24. MBLS, *Second Annual Report*, 57–62.

25. Ibid., 68–74, 84.

26. *News*, August 8, 1870.

27. *News*, September 9, 1870; MBLS, *Second Annual Report*, 90.

28. *News*, January 18, 1875.

29. MBLS, *Second Annual Report*, 482; Lillian Chace Wyman, "Studies of Factory Life: Black-Listing at Fall River," *Atlantic Monthly*, November 1888, 661; *News*, August 8, 1875; MBLS, *Thirteenth Annual Report* (1882), 348–54.

30. *New York Herald*, September 26, 1875; MBLS, *Second Annual Report*, 49, 469–70, 476–86; MBLS, *Sixth Annual Report* (1875), 284–90; *News*, March 6, 1875; MBLS, *Thirteenth Annual Report*, 209, 219, 254–60.

31. *Labor Journal*, September 26, October 3, 1874; MBLS, *Sixth Annual Report*, 142–77.

32. *News*, January 7, 11, 1875; *New York Times*, January 23, March 15, 1875; *Boston Globe*, February 23, 1875.

33. *Providence Sun*, January 18, 1875.

34. *News*, January 18, February 22, March 8, 17, 1875; *Commercial Bulletin*, August 28, 1875.

35. *News*, January 18, 1875.

36. *Boston Globe*, February 22, 1875.

37. *Boston Globe*, January 18, 1875.

38. *News*, February 22, 1875.

39. *News*, April 5, 1875; *Providence Sun*, August 21, 1875.

40. *News*, February 19, 1875; MBLS, *Thirteenth Annual Report*, 300; *New York Herald*, October 19, 1875.

41. *New York Herald*, October 13, 1875; MBLS, *Thirteenth Annual Report*, 338, 224.

42. *News*, July 19, 22, 24, 30, 1875; Edward P. Thompson, "The Moral Economy of the English Crowd in the Eighteenth Century," *Past and Present*, February 1971, 76–136.

43. *News*, August 2, 1875; *Providence Sun*, August 7, 1875, suggested that the weavers were also applying Luddite lessons from British protest traditions in an attempt to limit output.

44. *Providence Sun*, August 14, 21, 1875; *Commercial Bulletin*, August 28, 1875.

45. *New York Herald*, September 29, 1875; *News*, October 22, 1875.

46. *New York Herald*, September 26, 1875.

47. *New York Herald*, September 25, 26, 27, 28, 1875; *News*, September 25, 27, 28, 29, October 2, 1875; *New York Times*, September 28, 29, 1875. Also see John Bohstedt, *Riots and Community Politics in England and Wales, 1790–1810* (Cambridge: Harvard University Press, 1983), 7; on the importance of memories about the triumph of the customary over the market, see Andrew Charlesworth and Adrian J. Randall, "Morals, Markets and the English Crowd in 1766," *Past and Present*, 1987, 200–213.

48. *Providence Journal*, September 29, 1875; *Commercial Bulletin*, October 2, 1875; *Boston Globe*, October 4, 1875.

49. *News*, September 27, 1875.

50. *L'Echo du Canada*, October 2, 1875.

51. *News*, October 1, 1875.

52. Lancashire immigrant Robert Howard, secretary of the Mule Spinners' Union in 1877, cited in "Progress in the Textile Trades," in George E. McNeill, ed., *The Labor Movement: The Problem of To-Day* (1887), argued that during the 1870 strike "reason triumphed over passion," while he represented the weavers' strikes in 1875 as dangerous conflagrations raging out of control, consuming and destroying, 219, 223.

53. *Boston Globe*, August 18, 1879.

54. MBLS, *Eleventh Annual Report* (1880), 53–68.

55. Cumbler, *Working-Class Community,* 173–94.

56. David Montgomery, *The Fall of the House of Labor* (Cambridge: Cambridge University Press, 1987), 157, 164.

57. Wyman, "Studies of Factory Life," 605–12.

58. *Boston Herald* and *Providence Journal* reprinted in *News,* March 15, 1881.

Chapter Seven

The Reign of Passion
White Supremacy and the Clash between Passionate and Progressive Emotional Styles in the New South

Dolores Janiewski

During periods of political and economic crisis like the 1890s, when the conservative monopoly of political power came under threat, politicians and journalists sought to restore the comfortable binaries that structured their conception of the social order. Inflaming the emotions of others, often through incitement to racial hatred, "codings of criminalization," and the legitimation of "grotesque and murderous rage," they identified the source of disruption with one or another vulnerable target. Projecting blame on the groups designated "moral aliens," powerful men recruited others to defend the status quo and used an emotionally laden terminology of race and gender that drowned out the competing claims of class-based appeals. White supremacists spoke in the name of "virtuous homes, purer citizenship, and decent government." Rhetorically assigning their adherents to the ranks of the respectable classes of the "imperial middle," they consigned "negroes," radicals, and other enemies to the degraded classes defined as treasonous, criminal, and immoral.[1]

Because North Carolina was the site of challenges to conservative rule, it offers a suitable historical context in which to examine the interaction between emotional styles and the contest for power. The relative weakness of planters gave yeoman and laboring groups more scope for maneuver, and the regional balance between a black-majority east, a racially mixed center, and an overwhelmingly white western area made the outcomes of political battles more unpredictable than in most southern states. The potential for a class-based alliance between poorer whites and blacks was realized through the election of a coalition between the white Populists and the Republican Party in 1894. In addition, the relative openness of the power structure stimulated debate concerning economic, political, and social questions. As a consequence, North Carolina writers produced works of political commentary in essay and fictional forms that attracted national attention. The writers who will be discussed in this essay commented on the emotional climate—the "reign of passion"—that inflamed the electoral contests of the 1890s but was by no means unique to North Carolina.[2] Examining the state's mixture of politics, passion, and political commentary provides insights into the emotional and political culture of a region where a passionate emotional style was facing a new challenge from those advocating a cooler, more restrained style.

A prominent theme in the political language of the tumultuous 1890s was the manly defense of sexual honor as presented in a white supremacist context, a specific instance of the larger processes that create normative models of gender and sexuality. Combining real and imaginary terrors into a narrative of sexual danger, conservative politicians and editors intensified fear and provoked anger in the service of a political cause. As the righteous defenders of white womanhood, southern white men gained permission to indulge sadistic pleasures, lustful murder, and necrophilia in defense of "morality" and a white supremacist system.[3] The love and devotion signified by "chivalry" and the bloodlust incited and justified by the lynching narrative reinforced the emotional and ideological connections between sexuality and politics in a potent fusion that turned fear into anger against political rivals represented as sexual predators.

The white supremacy campaigns of 1898 and 1900 in North Carolina produced a striking example of the incitement to anger in the service of a political cause. Political leaders of the Democratic Party and their editorial allies utilized one of the most potent weapons in their rhetorical armory. Editorially and oratorically disseminating what Judith Walkowitz has called "popular narratives of sexual danger," the architects of the Democratic strategy created a monstrous image of "negro rule" to incite white male voters into violent opposition to the political coalition between the Republicans and the Populists. Warnings that political power gave black men unholy and danger- ous potency proliferated in written, oral, and visual forms. Images of well-dressed white women being inspected by black politicians illustrated the "power conferred upon a negro politician" to exert authority over "white ladies." The violence of rape and the dangers of seduction became vivid expressions of sexualized and racialized politics with their explicit references to sexual intercourse and black male violence. In the words of Ida Wells- Barnett, these authors of the "lynching plot" invented the excuse that "Negroes had to be killed to avenge their assaults upon women" in order to "assume a chivalry which they do not possess." This "distinctive sexual script"— at once "terrifying and titillating"—helped organize "emotional and erotic experi- ence.[4] As the campaign would demonstrate, the ability to elicit powerful emotional responses from the audience offered Democratic strategists an enormous advantage over their opponents.

Democratic editors spearheaded the campaign through verbal and—in the case of the leading party organ, the *Raleigh News and Observer*—visual appeals. Tightly coordinated editorial strategies circulated similar stories from newspaper to newspaper across the state while building emotional tension to a crescendo just before the climactic elections. Cartoons and the translation of strident editorials and sensational news stories into oral form provided a way for a print medium to communicate beyond the literate members of the public. The passionate emo- tional style that was simultaneously assumed, reinforced, and celebrated in the words and images reached a more diverse audience than could the advice books and other reading matter accessible primarily to a middle-class audience. As a means of communication, therefore, newspapers were indispensable to the promotion of a form of passionate politics that its opponents found difficult to resist.

In countering a strategically developed emotional onslaught, the Democrats' political opponents, who challenged the deeply rooted racial divisions built into the structure of southern society, faced a daunting task. The enormity of the challenge was only intensified by the need to rewrite a narrative concerning gender and sexuality as well as race. The ability to create a panic around the dislocation of gender identities and relations was a major advantage for white supremacists. Outnumbered and underresourced in the contest between newspapers, their opponents also lacked the orators white supremacist forces could muster. The need to defend alliances between poorer whites and blacks was hard to satisfy with the constrained educational and intellectual resources that such groups could muster. It was, therefore, not surprising that defenders of Fusion between Populists and Republicans might try to emulate rather than combat the Democrats' tactics. The *Progressive Farmer,* for example, had already published a cartoon of Grover Cleveland's welcoming of Frederick and Helen Douglass to the White House. The cartoon included a caricature of Josephus Daniels, the editor of the *Raleigh News and Observer,* introducing Cleveland to "Fred Douglas and wife." Admitting that Daniels had not really been present, the *Progressive Farmer* charged him with endorsing Cleveland "year after year," an example of the Democrats' failure to uphold white supremacist principles. Later cartoons depicting Democrats forcing poor white women to work beside black men made similar accusations of hypocrisy.[5] Simultaneously reinscribing white supremacist assumptions while battling their Democratic adherents, Republican and Populist editors confused their message and failed to blunt their opponents' attack.

After the initial victories for the white supremacist cause, critics of the "reign of passion" faced the difficult task of cooling the emotional fervor in the name of a "politics of reason." But disgust at the deliberate manipulation and dismay at the bloodthirsty ferocity convinced some North Carolinians, both inside and outside the state, of the need to advocate an alternative emotional and political style. They challenged a central assumption of the passionate emotional style that anger was an essential attribute of masculinity that spurred men to "actions necessary to competition or social justice."[6] Seeking to rein in angry white men, the proponents of restraint simultaneously criticized the political ends to which passions had been directed and sought to persuade southern men of the desirability of self-restraint. Arrayed against Josephus Daniels, Charles Brantley Aycock, leading Democratic orator, and Thomas Dixon, Jr., whose novel *The Leopard's Spots* celebrated the victory of the "Anglo-Saxon," were Alex Manly of the *Wilmington Record,* John Spencer Bassett in the *South Atlantic Quarterly,* Charles Chesnutt in *The Marrow of Tradition,* and Walter Hines Page in *The Southerner,* all of whom sought to damp down the "flames of antipathy" lit by demagogues. Handicapped by their confinement to a medium more limited in circulation and readership than that boasted by the Democratic press, these men promoted a progressive emotional style more conducive to rational political debate than the flamboyance and emotional extremes engendered by their opponents.

The Vocabulary of Fear and Anger

These reformers found themselves involved in verbal combat with conservative orators and editors who had taken a leading part in energizing and shaping a moral and gender panic by stereotyping their opponents as monsters, "taking up . . . absolutist positions," calling their followers to mount barricades, and advocating the "imaginary solution" of lynchings and violence against political opponents. Through suggestive words and images, conservatives continued to mobilize a constituency of angry white men for action. Sexual danger—the bestial rapist stalking the pure victim, the verbally proficient seducer or the unnaturally aggressive female—would trigger "a set of psychosexual and political fears," that is, a "visceral analogue to the epistemological incoherence and political disorientation threaten the body politic." Conservatives portrayed opponents' activities as unnatural and unholy alliances that placed immoral men in positions of power and undermined the moral, racial, and gender order—a powerful formulation that reformers found difficult to challenge, and white supremacists unwilling to relinquish.[7]

These narratives of sexual danger also responded to men's fears about women's entrance into arenas formerly considered exclusively masculine terrain as well as threats to "white supremacy." Beneath the surface of chivalrous claims to protect white women, narratives of rape and lynching conveyed a "veiled hostility toward women in a patriarchal society" with potent appeal to men threatened by women's movement into wage labor and political life. Black women's designation as "libertines" or viragoes allowed white men to express their "obsessive concern over white women's sexuality" without allowing those fears to "percolate up to the conscious level." Even as they punished the crime of rape when committed by a black man, white men gave themselves permission to rape or otherwise exploit women who had been defined as "outside the moral system" of evangelical Protestantism that constrained their relations with "respectable" white women.[8] African American women served as useful targets for an unarticulated fear of female sexual power and political aspirations, while their vulnerability warned white women about the dangers of asserting themselves and forgoing white male protection.

The black rapist, the chivalrous white male protector, and the white female victim were the major characters in a long-running political melodrama that demonstrated the " 'pornographic' aspect of racism" which allowed its white heroes to "injure and humiliate" through "rituals of hurting" as desire became expressed as bloodlust. By projecting lust and sexual violence onto the black rapist, the chivalrous myth repressed the knowledge that white men lusted, loved, raped, and fathered across the color line. "Combative, prone to seek popularity," and "moved by basic feelings of insecurity that led them into hard drives for power," Alfred M. Waddell and other fire-eating white supremacists found an unending supply of "devils" to combat to demonstrate their masculinity and their potency. White women, pressed into service in the fields or sent into the mills, experienced a similar insecurity that could be molded into politically useful emotions. Racial antagonism offered a vent for women seeking "safer targets for their frustrated outrage" than husbands or fathers. According to a contemporary scholar, "Southern white woman's hate and loathing of the new negro" was so intense as to be "unspeakable," an asset for an ideological practice that gave white women and men permission to indulge their more violent feelings. Anger could find acceptable release in the emotional fervor of a revival, a rally, or a lynching frenzy while assuaging women's fear of sexual attack. Presented with a racial other, a "black beast" or an insolent, foul-mouthed strumpet, the white audience could vent anger on a politically useful object.[9] Beset by economic insecurity, especially in the depression-blighted 1890s, frustrated white women and men welcomed an explanation in human form for the problems that bedeviled them. It would take great emotional sophistication to develop a suitable psychological substitute for the "negro scarecrow" that Democrats had erected in the political field.

Opponents were handicapped by their own immersion in the same cultural milieu. Few questioned the gender and sexual imperatives that shored up the masculine sense of self. Although some critics accused the Democrats of hypocrisy for assuming a chivalrous pose, few contemporaries actually questioned the definition of men as women's "natural protectors." Populist, Republican, and African American papers revealed shared assumptions about manhood. Describing the transition of the "race" from "vileness and dishonor to chastity and integrity," George Stevens in the *A.M.E. Zion Quarterly Review* called on men to shield "womanhood that it may cradle a race invincible in character, unchecked in growth, and massive in power." Like their white counterparts, black journalists masculinized and rendered plural "the negro" who must "compel the world to respect their rights." Men showed "race love and patriotic blood" by courageously enlisting in the political battle.[10] A belief in masculine assertiveness and feminine vulnerability, masking an underlying fear of female activity and dominance, structured the common understanding of gender relations despite ideological and racial differences. By consistently and stridently upholding the cultural ideal of masculinity affirmed by men of all political faiths, the Democrats possessed a major political and emotional advantage.

As editor of the leading Democratic newspaper in the state capital, Josephus Daniels was a key architect of the Democratic campaign in association with Furnifold Simmons, the chairman of the Democratic Party machine. A series of cartoons commissioned by Daniels began in August 1898 with a depiction of a fist extending from a sleeve marked "honest white man" striking at an overdressed, diamond-bedecked black man in a hat labeled "Negro Rule"; the caption read, "Get Back! We will not Stand It." Appealing to the "manhood of the people," the menace of "Negro Rule" appeared as a "Vampire that hovers over North Carolina" clutching at white womanhood and manhood with its hairy claws. Another cartoon showed a spat-clad foot labeled "the negro" crushing a sprawled, overall-clad figure labeled "white man." The caption asked the reader, "A Serious Question—How long will this last?" Each image appealed to white Democrats to take back the power dangerously bestowed on a dandified "town negro" or "negro politician" who leered at "white ladies" vulnerably exposed to his gaze and subjected to his authority. Highly emotive and direct, the cartoons made vivid the narratives of black dominance and aggression as they appealed to class envy and sexual rivalry.[11]

Editorially, Daniels described the "negro" as the "aggressor." His paper interspersed political news with reports on lynchings as punishment for the "nameless crime." Repeated phrases and stereotyped reports reinforced the message that the "nameless" or "usual crime" was occurring more frequently. The images and the emotive stories called "upon all white men who are truly white to vote with their color" as they tied together black political power, sexual danger, and criminality.[12] Black men and women were figured as modern versions of the "folk devil," whose polluting presence endangered the purity of the white "race."

Wilmington, where black political power and economic success had reached their zenith in the 1890s, became a prime example of "unbridled lawlessness" and "political corruption" as the local newspapers portrayed the dangers of "negro domination" in a city where "insolent, arrogant, insulting negros, male and female, seem to think the city belongs to them." According to the Democratic press, "saucy and overbearing" African Americans hunted trouble, and found "pleasure in being impudent," and did not spare the delicate ears of "white ladies" from "filthy, coarse and profane language." Wilmington represented the depraved example of the excesses of "Radicalism." The *Wilmington Messenger* referred to "the conceits and swellings of Negrodom." When "white skins began to hobnob with negroes," the *Messenger* predicted a descent to "the level of the lower animal" and the "lowest deep of political depravity." Fusion was a "pitiful burlesque, a contemptible betrayal of virtue and education," which turned over the "government of a free people into the hands of half-educated and completely illiterate savages." Eliding the distinction between miscegenation and political alliances, the *Messenger* used all the means at its editorial command to support its demand for the "restoration of white supremacy and pure, upright, manly, honest, conservative government" as it linked together manhood, morality, and whiteness.[13]

Elsewhere the *Messenger* recounted incident after incident to support its claims that the rule of the "vicious and ignorant" hung like a "black cloud" over North Carolina and the entire South. It decried the "desperation and savagery of the brutes who assault white women and little girls" and regretted that "lynchings would never cease until the black devils were all hanged or their brutalities ended." New Bern witnessed rampant "Negroism" as "young negro men" took over the sidewalks of black-ruled cities and refused to let white ladies pass. When one woman chose to "leave the walk" to pass around one such obstruction, "one of the brutes" allegedly "slapped her in the face." A young lady—"One of the loveliest of Southern womanhood"—appropriately dressed in white, passed a "negro woman" who took offense at her superior manner. In retaliation, the black woman poked the white woman in the side with her umbrella. In Tarboro, young men were "impudent and loud while the young women are very saucy and impertinent." Streets in Raleigh were "guarded to prevent more rioting by Negroes," while "unadulterated deviltry and general violence among the negroes," according to the *Messenger,* increased throughout the areas where blacks dared to exercise political power. It predicted that the men of the "great race which God Almighty had created the masterful, dominating, civilizing race of the world" would soon "rise in their strength and majesty and throw off the despotism" of "a negro government."[14] Certainly its reports were intended to achieve that very result.

In Wilmington itself, repeated rumors of a negro uprising, threats, and coercion supplemented by a steady drumbeat of stories of outrages, insolence in the street, and crime impressed on the white inhabitants a hellish depiction of their city. Advising "all white men to arm and be ready to defend themselves," Democrats used "fiery orators to help inject their fire upon the audience," while nightly meetings kept the "town bubbling over with excitement." White men who refused to sign the White Government pledge were told to leave the city, while "drunken Red Shirts" terrified "everybody they could."[15] Indeed, a reign of terror existed in Wilmington, but the terrorists, sometimes called the Rough Riders or the Ward Five Regulars, were white Democrats rather than the "savages" so often depicted.

The *Wilmington Messenger* predicted that the "fight will be made . . . on the basis of a White Man's government" because "white men shall be masters here" while "good order" would be reestablished "under the rule of real white men." Thomas Clawson, the elderly editor who remained strongly influenced by proslavery beliefs, insisted that the "white man" would never abridge "lawful rights," yet no "decent, honorable, upright worthy white man in all North Carolina is so fallen in his manhood as to be willing to be overruled and mastered by the negro race." Labeling white Fusionists as "lowdown white ingrates" who allied with "black fools," he accused them of using "the negroes for the injury and oppression of the true whites." B. F. Keith, who refused to join the White Government Union, was accused of favoring "amalgamation" and denounced by the *Messenger* for that crime against the purity of the race. Keith became the recipient of anonymous letters arriving "in every mail, with coffins, skulls, etc drawn on them advising him to leave [Wilmington] at once or join the Red Shirt club." A "frenzied excitement," instigated, in part, by the two newspapers, the *Messenger* and the *Wilmington Star,* combined with local organizations to create an atmosphere in which men like Keith became the targets of threats. Clawson asked him, "On which side, Mr. Keith, do you draw your lance and couch your blade in this magnificent fight for 'civilization vs. barbarism'? There is no middle ground upon which white men may stand." Accompanied by acts of ostracism, boycotts, and physical intimidation, the newspapers pressed their editorial message home.[16]

The *Messenger* warned that "the lawless element lurks in the negro race" because "Sambo has never been able to ascertain the true meaning of liberty but thinks it means sweeping lawlessness and without restraint." It had been a"crime" to award the franchise to men possessing such tendencies. Clawson thus narrowed the definition of "lawful rights" and expanded the meaning of criminal conduct to include any extension of political rights or power to black men. Warning of an "element among the negroes whos inspiration, hope and purpose are to bring about the amalgamation of the races," Clawson cited "Old Fred Douglass" as an example of the dangerous lusts that would soon populate the land with a "mongrel, hybrid crowd."[17]

A Counterattack and Its Reception

A nearby target of Clawson's diatribes became the most outspoken critic of the passionate brand of politics preached by the Wilmington editor and his editorial allies across North Carolina. Alex Manly, the editor of an African American newspaper in Wilmington, was dragged into the political maelstrom stirred up by his editorial adversaries. Witnessing the campaign of harassment, threat, and vicious propaganda directed against the people of his community, Manly, the illegitimate grandson of the last Whig governor, found it impossible to keep prudently silent. As the product of a white man's illicit sexual desires, he read the attacks on miscegenation that poured from the pen of Thomas Clawson and the other Democratic editors as blatant hypocrisy. In August 1898, after having read Rebecca Felton's vehement defense of lynchings to protect white women's honor, Manly expressed his resentment in an episode that revealed the presence of an emotional "color line." A fateful editorial attacked Democrats as a "lot of carping hypocrites" who cry "aloud for the virtue of your women when you seek to destroy the morality of ours. Don't think that your women will remain pure while you are debauching ours." Violating the taboo against besmirching white women's sexual reputation, Manly claimed, "The women of that race are not any more particular in the matter of clandestine meetings with colored men than the white men with colored women." Perhaps a touch of boastfulness colored his claims that "white girls of culture and refinement" had sometimes fallen in love with men like himself. He ended with what may have been a veiled reference to his own heritage: "You sow the seed. The harvest will come in due time."[18] Beyond refuting Felton's arguments, Manly had challenged white men's assertions of white women's racial fidelity and suggested that he had personal experiences across the color line. The editorial was fuel to the raging emotional fires already ignited by the *News and Observer,* the *Messenger,* and Democratic politicians.

Anger had driven Manly to violate the sexual, racial, and emotional double standard. Denying white men their chivalrous masquerade as the "superrational superego" who restored order by killing the "black beast," Manly sought to make them confront the consequence of their own erotic desires. The son who had been denied his paternal heritage called on the father to recognize him. It was a daring but dangerous attempt to rewrite the lynching script by recasting the "white hero" as a lecher and hypocrite, endowing the white lady with romantic if not carnal desires, and asserting that "love" could transcend the emotional color line.[19]

Furnifold Simmons, chief strategist for the Democratic campaign, quickly decided that the "article would make it an easy victory for us" if he could prevent immediate retaliation. It would light victory fires by arousing the anger of white men. Showing his skillful tactical sense and his concern to avert federal or state intervention in the election itself, he told the Wilmington Light Infantry "to try and prevent any riot until after the election." The militia put forth its "best efforts" and prevented "the people from lynching" Manly during the campaign. Better to rub rhetorical salt into psychological wounds than avenge the alleged insult on white women's honor immediately. Shrewdly, Simmons and his political allies calculated the best way to keep hot-blooded emotions simmering at the necessary level to achieve ultimate victory without bringing the federal government in to punish his supporters. Following the plan, the Democratic press turned the editorial into rhetorical ammunition for the campaign, which would call white men to take political and physical vengeance for the insult to white women's sexual reputation.[20]

Rushing to the attack, the *Messenger* interpreted the Manly editorial as an insult to the "character of every white wife in the South." Clawson accused Manly of excusing rape for allegedly claiming that "negro rapists" are "beguiled by poor white women and are fallen in love with by the young ladies in higher circles" rather than describing them as "brutal and savage" criminals. Manly had defamed the virtue of "poor white women" by claiming that their morals were as low as those of "negro women." The editor asked "white men—particularly the white married men and especially the sons of white mothers" what "they think of such dirty defamation," which excused the "black brutes who commit rape at the expense of the character of every white wife in the South." Screeching "vile and villainous," Josephus Daniels reprinted three hundred thousand copies of the editorial to distribute throughout the state. Making sure that his readers made the link between sexual predation and political power, he observed, "Give the negro political superiority and he will rage inwardly that he is not given social equality." The Manly editorial offered the Democratic press the evidence that confirmed their claims about black men's desires to violate the antimiscegenation taboo.[21]

According to the *Messenger*, the "villainous editorial in the nigger organ" exemplified the "depravity and swaggering boldness" that should "make every decent man's blood boil" unless "manhood is gone and with it Anglo-Saxon loyalty to the pure and noble white woman of our land." The editor urged his readers to "strike for the protection of your home against prowling, incarnate devils," for "your personal freedoms," and for "God and your native land." Repeatedly, the Manly editorial would reappear, usually on a front page as an illustration of the "dishonor" that would befall white men who allowed power to go to the head or other vital parts of the "black radical." The "nigger organ" in both meanings of that phrase would play a prominent part in the campaign. The *News and Observer* argued that "Republicanism" was responsible for "slanders of white women" would make the "negro brute" think he "had license to outrage white women." It condemned the African American ministers who supported Manly in the *Record* as endorsing a "paper that was upholding negro fiends and traducing in the vilest manner the white women of the State." Accusing Manly of "excusing rapists," the editors directed their fire against Manly's depiction of white women's sexual desires and stoked white men's sexual jealousy.[22]

Seeking to deflect the force of the attack, the *Progressive Farmer*, the organ of the North Carolina Farmers' Alliance, asked female readers, "Is it not time for the women of this and every other State, to take up the matter, and to treat it according to the facts as they stand, not on the written page, for that is often exaggerated, when not absolutely false, but as they stand within our certain knowledge?" Interpreting Manly's editorial as primarily aimed at exposing the immoral behavior of white men, the *Progressive Farmer* restated the black editor's argument: "Sin is sin, and the difference in color between a white man and a black one does not make the sin any blacker or any whiter." In order to arouse white women's indignation against men's sexual behavior, the editor referred to "those houses which are 'the way to hell' " and suggested that women should boycott male sinners. A narrative of male sexual betrayal and an appeal to white women's sexual jealousy became an emotional defense against the Democrats' attempts to use anger and bloodlust. Simultaneously, a cartoon equated Daniels and Manly as "twin defamers," because the former had reprinted the editorial and thereby given the insulting editorial greater circulation even as he zealously but hypocritically denounced its author.[23]

Voting and Rioting

But the *Progressive Farmer*'s strategy was not emotionally powerful enough to override the Democratic onslaught. The Democrats understood that women's emotions as well as men's could be mobilized in support of the white supremacy campaign. The Democratic series of urban outrage stories rendered it difficult to rewrite the lynching narrative into a story of white male lust and hypocrisy. Over and over, the Democratic press rammed home the point to its female readership concerning the threat to "refined" womanhood from the "indolent and saucy" residents of Wilmington and other places afflicted by "negro domination." "Negro boys" insulted "young ladies," and "negro girls" pushed white women off the sidewalks. Meanwhile an "innocent white woman" was dragged into a "dirty dive" for trial before a "negro constable" in New Bern, where an "orgie of crime" occurred under "negro magistrates." "Young male negroes" jostled "white ladies on the streets," used "vulgar and infamous language in public places," and were assisted by "females" who "follow the lead of the males." "Colored women" appeared in confrontations with "white youths" whom they "insolently shoved" into ditches, unleashed "a filthy tirade of abuse," and placed a dark elbow "into the face of a white gentleman." A young white woman who called on white men of Lenoir County in "the names of their wives and daughters" to destroy the "black vampire hovering over our beloved old North Carolina" was only one of many women urging their men to protect "us with your vote."[24]

When election victory gave the Democrats control of the North Carolina legislature, the *Wilmington Messenger* celebrated the end of "lying and slander and misrepresenting attempts to place the White People, men and women and children, under the cruel, detestable, unbearable domination of the niggers." It did not denounce the postelection riot that resulted in the destruction of Manly's press and the death of unknown numbers of black residents. The usual editorial was absent on the day after the riot because "our proprietor, staff, and mechanical force were on the street with their Winchesters."[25] Returning to his post, Clawson applauded the banishment of white Republicans and African Americans from the city and expressed few regrets for the deaths of those who had failed to escape the wrath of the mob. The victory for white supremacy would soon usher in disfranchisement: two years later, using the same emotional and narrative strategy, the Democrats successfully campaigned for an amendment to the state constitution imposing a literacy qualification for suffrage.

On a hot summer day in North Carolina in 1900, Charles Brantley Aycock, the Democratic nominee for governor, retold the story of the Wilmington riot that had climaxed the 1898 campaign. Aycock's speech elicited a response that revealed the emotional division of labor among whites. According to Josephus Daniels, who reported on the event, the candidate's eloquence "made the faces of the women whiten with fear while the cheeks of men burned red with anger and indignation." Aycock's words came "sharply and rapidly, like hailstones in a storm" as he lashed the emotions of the crowd to a fury. Aycock reported that he had seized a gun to take to Wilmington, a gesture any "real man" would have replicated. "In the applause that greeted these words fierce passion thundered and rushed and turmoiled about the speaker." In Aycock's version of the 1898 events, the African American victims of the mob became "men who were leading the riot." White rioters disappeared, and there was no indication that white men had done all the killing. Corpses lay "cold in death" as though by divine intervention. Guilt and innocence, victim and perpetrator changed places in a heroic saga of manly courage triumphing over cowardice. The Democratic standardbearer concluded by asking the voters in his audience to give him the "power that shall execute the will of every white man in the State and shall safeguard every woman."[26] Aycock's familiar words were skillfully orchestrated to elicit the same anger from his listeners that had produced the violent explosion in Wilmington fourteen months earlier.

Depicted in speeches, news stories, editorials, novels, histories, and film, successive generations of heroes—angry white men—rode on horseback, on bicycles, and, eventually, in cars—to punish the unrighteous violators of the codes of honorable conduct. They dispensed a "rough" justice that punished activities, often redefined as sexual crimes, that posed threats to the prevailing relations of power. As was the case in 1900, vigilantes, despite their passionate disregard for the normal rules of civilized conduct and the judicial system, received the approbation of respectable politicians and editors. Speeches and editorials, authored by those Charles Chesnutt called "excusing voices," transformed the victims into perpetrators whose actions had provoked white men into angry reaction. African American men and women— and those who could be ideologically "blackened" due to their political or sexual deviations—faced "the full sexualized perniciousness of white racism" with its use of "black" men and women "as targets for projecting its own most demeaned private fears and longings." Only real "white" men could legitimately express their anger and dispense justice. White women must display the "purity" and the submissiveness that gained for them the "compassion and pity for the helpless and dependent," which the "strong, the brave, and the powerful" inevitably felt unless provoked to anger by rebellion. The volatile combination of race and sexual danger linked "cultural forms of emotional meaning with much broader political and economic structures" in the service of the "large scale organization of power."[27]

As indicated by the approving reference to "fierce passion" in the tumultuous response to Aycock's retelling of the Wilmington story, passion received a vastly different evaluation depending on who displayed the emotion and against whom it was directed. When it was associated with black men and women or "immoral" whites, it connoted a set of perjorative meanings describing these people as "weak," "brutish," "savage," and "antisocial." Such people could be legitimately excluded from positions of power and responsibility because they were prey to raw, wild, and primitive forces that revealed them as uncivilized, irrational, immature beings. The "fierce passion" of heroic white men, who killed in the defense of the reputation of white women, received another, more positive evaluation. Passion for power in the hands of the "masters of superior minds, information, and morality" was essential to maintaining social order; thus, sexuality and politics were linked in a complex interplay. In effect, passion acted like an ideological practice that gave emotional color to a complicated, violent, and brutal series of political battles "over the meaning of events, over rights and morality, over control of resources." The authors of the political language and the promoters of the passionate emotional style of politics both discussed aspects of social reality and created that reality as they wrote and spoke their emotionally inflected version of the white supremacist victory and praised the men who had used violence to achieve political ends.[28]

Dissenting Voices

In Wilmington as elsewhere in North Carolina, it was dangerous to dissent from the version of the 1898 events told by Aycock and other Democrats. Witnessing the fate of at least a thousand people like the persecuted Alex Manly, others knew the cost of speaking out. A white woman in Wilmington wrote a version of the events in the form of a letter to the editor of the *Independent,* which she apparently never dared to send. Although her conscience reproached her for not writing "the truth for publication," Jane Cronly feared that "I might be asked to leave town if I were found out." Intimidated by the "spirit of evil" that "entered into some of our best citizens," she dared not speak aloud.[29] The ability to silence their opposition was one of the most powerful weapons in the white supremacist arsenal. But further away from Wilmington, John Spencer Bassett, a young historian teaching in Durham, Walter Hines Page, a North Carolina–born editor based in New York, and Charles Chesnutt, who had left North Carolina in the 1880s to embark on his writing career, were more willing and able to assume the risks that came from challenging the ideological and political power of the men who now dominated North Carolina under the rule of the "white man's government."

Seeking to escape the racial limitations that denied a "colored man" the full realization of his talents, Charles Chesnutt had left Fayetteville in the early 1880s. Reversing the usual racial conventions, Chesnutt believed that an honest portrayal of "colored" life could contribute to "the elevation of the Whites." In his view, subservience to "the unjust spirit of caste" prevented the "moral progress of the American people." Realizing that an "appeal to force" would be unlikely to achieve the necessary changes, he hoped for "a moral revolution" in racial attitudes and practices, to which he could contribute by demonstrating the capacities of a "negro." Schooled in the emotional restraint that had enabled a man of his abilities and his color to survive in

North Carolina, Chesnutt created characters who negotiated the unstable and shifting middle ground between the races. In life as in art, he described the dangers that befell those who gave vent to their passions.[30]

Despite the relative freedom and prosperity he achieved in Ohio, Chesnutt never escaped the sense of being "oppressed by the fear that this line or this sentiment would offend somebody's prejudices, jar on somebody's American-trained sense of propriety." At the same time, he refused to cater to views that described a "drop of black blood" as a "taint." Like the archetypal seventh son, his work bore the traces of emotional repression and the "double-aimed struggle" of the black artist seeking to overcome the legacy of "ridicule and systematic humiliation" that denied him the same scope afforded to the racial sensationalism of Thomas Dixon, Jr., and other white authors.[31] In form, content, and popular reception, Chesnutt's work revealed the consequences of the emotional double standard that denied black men and women the same right to express their passions that white men reserved for themselves.

Chesnutt passed the initial test. His first major publication, *The Wife of His Youth and Other Stories of the Color Line,* received the praise of the *Atlantic*'s editor W. D. Howells for its "passionless handling" of its subject matter. Ironic and emotionally detached, the narrator in the collection's title story provided no emotional clues to his racial identity. Aware of the author's racial ancestry, Howells placed Chesnutt in the "middle world which lies next, though wholly outside, our own," to which he had secured admission through his demonstration of emotional restraint and literary talent. Chesnutt had crossed the color line into a "department of literature." He had also successfully disciplined his emotions and his expression so that his words did not "jar on somebody's American-trained sense of propriety."[32] Such restraint, however, was difficult to sustain for an author who cared deeply about racial injustice.

The same events that caused Manly to violate the emotional and ideological color line exerted a similar effect on Chesnutt, who knew people in Wilmington terrorized by the mob. Having discovered that his editor, Walter Hines Page, had also come from North Carolina, Chesnutt wrote a series of letters to Page in which he revealed his reaction to the "outbreak of pure, malignant and altogether indefensible race prejudice" that made him feel "humiliated and ashamed for the country and the State." But he wanted to do more to inform the northern public about a place "where no Negro can enjoy the blessed privilege of free speech." Indignant about the "outrageously unjust and unconstitutional law" proposed in North Carolina to disfranchise African Americans, Chesnutt decided to write a novel that would encourage white readers to consider "both sides of the matter—if there can be two sides to it."[33] It was a decision that would put his literary ambitions at risk.

Recognizing that he occupied the "weaker side in point of popular sympathy," Chesnutt was convinced that he stood on the "stronger side in point of justice and morality." Employing "irony, masquerade, and chicanery," he induced his readers to see the events as black people in Wilmington had experienced them. But the proximity of the events and his own passionate engagement prevented him from exercising the same restraint that had characterized his earlier writing. His irony grew sharper as he wrote about the activities of a fictional editor of a southern newspaper who sought to stir up racial passions in men "capable of anything which will humiliate self-respecting colored people." Chesnutt's anger could not be entirely disguised beneath his cool and ironic prose.[34]

Featuring a mulatto hero and heroine, *The Marrow of Tradition* placed the heroes, and therefore the white reader, in the "no man's land" between the races. The "staring signs" that faced Dr. Miller on his trip to Wilmington reminded "him continually that between him and the rest of mankind, not of his own color, there was by law a great gulf fixed." Prosperous African Americans "must have their heads cut off, figuratively speaking" while those who "fell beneath the standard set had their necks stretched, literally enough.[35] As Chesnutt described it, the leaders of a political party decided to convince white men that the "darker race" was "an incubus, a corpse chained to the body politic," and a "danger to the state." Seeking a pretext, they pounced on an editorial in an African American newspaper, a "frank and bold discussion of lynching and its cause." The editor had audaciously violated one of the key tenets of "an unwritten law of the south"—making "our women" the "subject of offensive comment." The editor decided to broadcast the editorial to "fire the Southerner heart," which, along with "red shirts and shotguns," would "scare the negroes into fits." Predicting that the African American newspaper would be destroyed and "so will the editor," the plotters cynically began a propaganda campaign to stir up an emotional firestorm to serve their political ambitions.[36] Obviously Chesnutt or his informants had closely observed the actual sequence of events and the strategy pursued in the 1898 campaign, which he only thinly disguised in his fictional plot by changing the names of the newspaper and the conspirators and naming the city Wellington.

Aroused by the drumbeat of propaganda, a lynch mob gathered to punish an innocent black man for a crime committed by a white man in blackface. Editorials in the *Morning Chronicle* proclaimed the need to "protect the white women of the south against brutal, lascivious, and murderous assaults at the hands of negro men." A special edition contained "all the old shopworn cant about race purity and supremacy and imperative necessity." Warning that the "whole white womanhood of the South is in danger," the newspaper urged the mob to strike. The preparations for a "burning" were deliberately set "to take place early in the evening so that the children might not be kept up beyond their usual bedtime." Young men discussed which "portions of the negro's body they would prefer for souvenirs" as they might discuss a picnic frolic. Describing the mixture of calculation, emotional manipulation, and savagery, Chesnutt stripped away the mask of chivalry to reveal ignoble motives and sadistic pleasures. Bloodlust and political opportunism were the forces behind the violence as he portrayed it.[37]

But Chesnutt was not content merely to expose the duplicity of white southerners. Apparently he had been angered by the sympathetic response from many northerners to the riot in Wilmington and the overthrow of the city government. Undoubtedly he had read comments that explained the "primal cause" of conflict in North Carolina as the "unstatesmanlike endeavor to establish universal suffrage in the South without respect to either intelligence or character." His descriptions of the mob that had marched on Manly's press as a "gathering of white men who were determined to teach a lesson—a lesson that should be practical and contain no element of doubt" was a pointed response that did not spare northern sensibilities. He described a visit to the fictional Wellington by gullible northerners who accepted too readily the views of their southern host. These men, "a new generation, who knew little of the fierce passions which had played around the negro in the past epoch and derived their opinions of him from the 'coon song' and the police reports," naively accepted at face value the racial views of their manipulative hosts. In both the North and the South "venal and self-seeking politicians" dulled "the public conscience by a loud clamor in which the calm voice of truth was for the moment silenced."[38] Chesnutt's controlled but critical narration implicitly criticized the views held by many of his potential readers. It was not a strategy likely to achieve the popularity awarded to Thomas Dixon's *Leopard's Spots: A Romance of the White Man's Burden—1865–1900*, which Walter Hines Page had also chosen to publish the same year *The Marrow of Tradition* appeared in print.

Taking direct aim at northern apologists, Chesnutt wrote a dramatically different version of the events in Wilmington that had been "dignified subsequently as a 'revolution' " in northern journals and southern newspapers. Instead of noble and dignified Anglo-Saxons, Chesnutt described "crowds of white men and half- grown boys, drunk with whisky or with license" who "raged through the streets, beating, chasing, or killing any negro so unfortunate as to fall into their hands." Rather than a solid phalanx of liberty-loving revolutionaries, the crowd was "merely a white mob thirsting for black blood." The smouldering ruins of Wellington bore "melancholy witness" to the "thin veneer" of civilization, "which cracks and scales off at the first impact of primal passions." Depicting white men as "a mob of primitive savages, dancing in hellish glee around the mangled body of a man," Chesnutt transformed the "fierce passion" of a proud Anglo- Saxon race into bloodlust and other licentious passions that rendered them oblivious to "the calm voice of truth."[39] He chose to claim for his narrator, and thus for himself, the role of the accusing voice of an angry but restrained prosecutor.

Although more cautious and circumspect than Manly, Chesnutt displayed unacceptable emotions as he stripped away the rhetorical camouflage that masked white supremacist appeals to brutal passions. As he later acknowledged, *Marrow* was "criticized as being bitter." The public disliked books whose principal characters were "colored people" and whose author expressed "sympathy with that race." F. L. Barnett, the husband of Ida Wells-Barnett, commiserated with Chesnutt because "the subject of your excellent work is not one that will commend it to the general public." The "truths you portray so faithfully are unwelcome ones." A sympathetic W. D. Howells, after commenting on the "bitterness," welcomed the literary evidence "of the sort of negro equality against which no series of hangings and burnings will finally avail."[40] Heartened by such support, Chesnutt continued his battle against the passions that were celebrated and inspired by Dixon's *Leopard's Spots,* which more perfectly accorded with "public opinion on the race question" than did Chesnutt's critically subversive text.[41] Rather than paying in blood and economic destruction like Manly and other black Wilmington residents, Chesnutt lost his chance for popular acclaim because he criticized the passions to which Dixon played.

Outraged by Dixon's success, Chesnutt circulated *The Marrow of Tradition* to political leaders, hoping to persuade them to oppose Dixon's racial views. Referring to "southern claptrap" about miscegenation—one of the themes the two novels had in common—Chesnutt asserted that "such intermingling as there has been, and there has been a great deal, has been done with the entire consent and cheerful cooperation of the white race, and I am unable to see any disastrous results that have followed so far." Perhaps aware of Dixon's unacknowledged half-brother, whose mother was the family cook, Chesnutt described the author as a typical North Carolinian obsessed by the "race feeling" that has "been very acute in that state."[42] Seeking to encourage sober and serious reflection, Chesnutt battled against "race feeling" and the appeal of the passionate emotional style that gave the white suprema-cist cause an intensity he was not supposed to exhibit on his side of the literary color line.

Temporarily abandoning the effort to convey his beliefs in the "passionless" disguise of ironic fiction, Chesnutt published an essay that explained the "true secret of the virulent Southern hostility" toward black men's rights. "Rather than any stagnation or retrogression" on the part of the "negro," the cause was resentment over the advancement of "colored" men like himself. Criticizing the north for abandoning African Americans to the "tender mercies" of hostile southerners, Ches-nutt attacked the reconciliation between the regions, which had been consummated at the cost of a people's democratic rights. He denounced the "excusing voices" who defended lynchings and other acts of brutality and implored his readers to listen to the "accusing voices" of an almost "silent white South." Although those voices might be "scarcely audible above the clamor of the mob," their "numbers and their courage [would] increase" with sufficient encouragement from outsiders. Continuing his crusade against the "unjust spirit of caste" through essays and membership in the National Association for the Advancement of Colored People (NAACP), Chesnutt reluctantly abandoned his literary efforts after the failure of another novel published the same year Dixon produced another best-seller, *The Clansman*.[43] In an emotional and literary climate where Dixon's sensational appeals to racial hatreds could find an enthusiastic audience, Chesnutt found himself unable to exercise sufficient restraint so that his views would not grate on the sensibilities of a white audience.

Undeterred by Chesnutt's difficulties, two white North Carolinians joined his protest against "the clamor of the mob." John Spencer Bassett, who had studied with Dixon at Johns Hopkins, criticized *The Leopard's Spots* as stylistically "commonplace" and the product of a "sensational politician" who lacked a "serious sense of mission." The book's suggestion that the "negro" should be removed or killed was a "great wrong," a violation of "the fundamental principles of the constitution," and a recipe for economic disaster in a region that needed its "laboring population." Chiding Dixon, the former minister, for his "unchristian tone," Bassett concluded his review in the *South Atlantic Quarterly* by referring to an article by Walter H. Page, which had praised Booker T. Washington. Dissenting from Dixon's claims that the "over-educated negro" represented a "danger and menace to America," Bassett and Page asserted that education offered a better way to deal with the "negro problem" than the violence that the other North Carolinian had justified.[44] Bassett did not point to the irony that Page had published Dixon's novel.

As one of the first generation of professionally trained historians, Bassett had returned to North Carolina in 1894 "to do God's work in the field of history" just at the time of the Fusion victory. Writing in the aftermath of the 1898 election, Bassett disagreed with "most of my fellow Anglo-Saxons on the negro question." He described the Democratic press as having "opened up on the negro question" with a "violent" attack that "vilified, abused, denounced" the "negro" as an "unclean thing." Distastefully labeling the campaign as "one of passion," he explained events in Wilmington as "a riot directly due to the 'white man's campaign,' " in which a mob had killed innocent men in a "miserable affair." Alarmed by the fearful consequences of violence and passion, Bassett revealed himself as an advocate of political and emotional restraint in his letters to his mentor, Herbert Baxter Adams.[45]

Determined to "cause men to think," Bassett decided to "set a limit to this wildfire of prejudice" sparked by the Democratic press and politicians. He asked Adams to inform northern philanthropists about the solution to the "negro problem." "The way to help the negro" would be to educate "the Masses in the South." Education was needed to combat the deleterious effects of political propaganda, which educated "our people that it is right to lie, to steal, & to defy all honesty in order to keep a certain party in power." Protesting against politically induced racial hostility, Bassett believed that knowledge would inoculate poor whites against the appeals to prejudice, passion, and vanity that he saw as essential elements in the Democratic strategy.[46]

Moving from private dissent to public debate, Bassett began to publish the *South Atlantic Quarterly* to provide a vehicle for his critique of passion and demagoguery. Denying that chivalrous motives explained lynching, John Carlisle Kilgo insisted that the practice was rooted in a "jealous regard of personal honor," the "deification of woman as a social being," and "temporary social insanity." Kilgo, the president of Trinity College, advocated a new form of masculine emotional restraint based on the recognition that "excitability is the mark of weakness." Politicians and journalists who catered to the "passions of ignorance" would ultimately fail because a solidly based patriotism must be "founded in truth, not in myths."[47] The first issues of the fledgling *Quarterly* revealed its intention to take direct aim at white supremacist orthodoxy and the passionate style that provided its emotional sustenance.

Bassett's essay "The Reign of Passion" made explicit his editorial agenda. Blaming slavery, aristocracy, illiteracy, and the war as inciting "passion" and "bitterness" among white southerners, Bassett criticized political campaigns conducted by fraud and a "one-sided press," which pandered to "pauperized" intellects and incited race hatred. Concerned about the lack of reaction to the essay, Bassett deliberately raised the rhetorical temperature in another article on the same subject. In "Stirring Up the Fires of Race Antipathy," Bassett audaciously declared that Booker T. Washington was "the greatest man, save General Lee, born in the South in a hundred years." Democrats made "sensational appeals to the race feeling of the white man, awakening a demon in the South." Bassett predicted racial equality at some point in the future, and in a reference to the red-shirted men on horseback who had served as the shock troops of the Democratic campaign, he predicted that "Some day the white man will beat the negro out of his cowardice and then 'red shirts' will exist no more."[48] Succeeding in gaining attention to his article and his arguments, Bassett also revealed that his conception of masculinity shared the same attachment to the manly ideal held by Red Shirts and their editorial champions, Josephus Daniels and Thomas Clawson.

Bassett's article enraged Josephus Daniels, who had already been embroiled in an ongoing battle on behalf of state-funded education against Trinity College and its association with the American Tobacco trust. Bassett was "under the spell of ne-grophilist hypnotism" and prayed "with his face turned toward Tuskegee." The "fulsome eulogy of a smart negro" created a "fiction out of nothingness." Other newspapers followed the *News and Observer*'s lead by labeling Bassett "a burning shame and disgrace to the Anglo-Saxon blood" of his "good Christian mother." Privately, some members of the Trinity College board of trustees joined in the criticism. John F. Bruton claimed that Bassett should have refrained from putting "pen to words" that might encourage the "lawless element among this race, the best of whom are children in mental and moral stamina."[49] Trustees like Bruton and Furnifold Simmons agreed with the Democratic papers who called for Bassett to resign or be forced out of Trinity College.

During the height of his public pillorying, Bassett received support from another graduate of Johns Hopkins, Walter H. Page, who shared his distaste for the "Southern bully," who with "his oaths and 'honor' . . . has strutted through all the quiet ways of Southern life, calling himself 'the South,' writing and speaking of 'our people,' and now [leading] mobs to avenge 'our women.' " Page sent him "one of many words of encouragement" received from "intelligent and thoughtful Southerners of the younger generation." As the target of a "large mass of angered men whose leaders are politicians," Bassett vowed to resist the "mob in this state." As he explained to Page, whose brother was also a Trinity trustee, he wanted to "prove to the world" that one institution in the South offered a refuge from the "regime of passion which has weighed us down for seventy years." Defining themselves as the embattled exponents of a New South, the two men agreed that a passionate emotional style and demagogic politics prevented the New South from severing its retrogressive attachment to antebellum culture.[50]

Despite the furor whipped up by Daniels, a majority of the trustees voted to allow Bassett to retain his position, influenced no doubt in part by the previous attacks made against Trinity from the same quarter. George S. Bradshaw of Greensboro accused the *News and Observer* of opening "its cold-cruel mouth" to "spit the warm blood of a fellow man." Already upset at Bassett's reprieve, Daniels grew outraged when he heard that he had been hanged "in effigy" by Trinity College students celebrating Bassett's victory. The students had committed an "overt and lawless act seeking to destroy the liberty of the press." He accused them of "mob tyranny" for their symbolic lynching of "one who utters timely criticism." Rallying around Daniels, the North Carolina Press Association "passed a resolution condemning the hanging of Mr. Josephus Daniels in effigy." Blurring the distinction between symbolic and actual violence, the white supremacist version of manly "honor" turned words and gestures into a more deadly form of assault than the actions of men who silenced, exiled, or killed. Unable to burn the press of a white man, the Democrats sought to silence him by other means.

Recognizing the link between rhetorical and actual violence, Bassett and his supporters celebrated the defeat of the leading exponent of the passionate political style, but it was by no means a final victory. A year later Bassett published two articles that marked the end of his editorial duties as he fell victim to the same silencing that ended Chesnutt's literary career. Unorthodox critics understood the "numbing effect on intellectual integrity of continually cringing before the dominion of adverse public opinion." Bassett concluded his editorial career with the essay "An Exile from the South," describing those driven into exile by "the spirit of intolerance." Having briefly chosen "utterance" over "acquiescence," Bassett announced his retirement from the editorial fray. Deciding to choose history over a continuing campaign to influence public sentiment, Bassett departed for the "peaceful atmosphere" at Smith College far away from the rantings of Daniels and his allies.[51] In contrast to Chesnutt, who continued his activities with the NAACP against southern demagogues and the pernicious influence of white supremacist ideology, Bassett ceased his active opposition against the "reign of passion" as he became another exile from North Carolina.

Seven years after he had published Chesnutt's *Marrow of Tradition* and Dixon's *Leopard's Spots*, Walter Hines Page anonymously published *The Southerner* as his own contribution to the cause for which Manly, Chesnutt, and Bassett had risked so much by their public defiance of the "southern bully." Through the protective camouflage of anonymity, Page objected to the obsession with the "negro question" on the part of white supremacists and those susceptible to their exhortations. A whole people had "lost their minds on one subject." The "negro-in- America" had become a "form of insanity that overtakes white men." Sheltering his iconoclasm behind the pseudonymous pun of Nicholas Worth, Page was yet another "accusing" voice from the "silent South." Insightfully he analyzed the 1898 election in a fictional North Carolina in which "race hatred" became the "staple of the campaign." Democratic orators depicted a state of society that everyone knew "to be a horrid lie." But in the throes of emotionalism, the followers believed it. As he observed, "men are easily frightened if you lead them to the edge of this dark and unfathomable abyss—this difference of race." A panic-induced fear rose "as children's in the dark." Constant reiteration convinced many of the truth of what they heard. "The Negro was a savage, a brute, a constant menace. Educate him? Then you only make him more cunning for evil. He must be put down." As his narrator lamented, "unnatural emotions" had taken possession of the "mind of a whole people," leading them to "fear impossible things."[52] Concurring with Kilgo and Bassett in their diagnosis of mass hysteria, Page deplored the association between passion and power—a combination so strong and seductive that reason appeared to have little chance to break the connection. Perceptively, Page analyzed the tactics of the white supremacists and the emotions they manipulated, but found himself unable to subvert an emotional and ideological strategy that transformed fear into hatred and anger directed to political ends. Like Chesnutt's effort, Page's novel never attracted the audience Dixon's novels received nor the fame that came with their cinematic reappearance as D. W. Griffith's film *The Birth of a Nation.*

Change and Continuity

Despite their inability to find popular support, Chesnutt, Bassett, and Page advocated an emerging ideological practice that would gradually claim adherents as business elites began to challenge planters for political supremacy in the South. The passionate style continued to depict the "negro" as immoral, sexually depraved, and hypermasculine—a danger to pure white womanhood and the white community unless kept firmly subordinated by the righteous anger of white men. The alternative favored by Bassett and Page, which would later be described as "civility" or the "progressive mystique," advocated reliance on white courts and "white man's justice" rather than the "rough justice" of the lynch mob. Welcoming women's involvement in a reform coalition, proponents of civility softened the stark polarities between men and women, good and evil, black and white, vice and virtue, as they sought to moderate the "aggressive" masculinity of the "white man." Undoubtedly reflecting the evolution of national cultural style, the progressive variant emphasized the issue of control over passions that had been an inherent but neglected aspect of the Victorian emotional style as it was manifested in a politicized white masculine culture in the South.[53] As intellectual fashion shifted from biological determinism toward a culturalist emphasis on developmental potential, in which education and opportunity could transform human emotions, behavior, and intellect, the views that received little support in the early 1900s might find a more receptive audience a decade later.

Militant critics like the NAACP and more daring representatives of African Americans within North Carolina took advantage of the wartime demand for black labor to warn white southerners that they risked losing their labor supply if they refused to moderate their white supremacist excesses. Seizing the opportunity, Charles Hunter, editing the *Raleigh Independent,* expressed the hope that "every man in N.C." might get "an absolutely square deal regardless of his color and condition" when he congratulated the newly elected governor, Thomas Bickett, in 1916. Affirming the willingness of "every Negro North Carolinian" to support the war effort, he added, "We are embarrassed by the situation into which we are thrown by the continued assaults upon our rights as citizens and as human beings." Black North Carolinians seized an opportune moment to persuade white elites that loyalty should be appropriately repaid. Hunter became active in the NAACP to protest riots, lynching, and other forms of violence against African Americans. Even as he covertly worked with the NAACP, he pressed state officials and Senator Furnifold Simmons to secure "for N.C. Negroes the recognition to which they are justly due." When African American soldiers resumed from the war to "don the freedom of civil garb," the NAACP took the lead in combating "bigotry and injustice" as it began a concerted drive against lynching and other forms of discrimination against African Americans.[54]

As political and economic leadership in the South passed from planters to urban professionals and industrialists, the South gradually offered a more receptive milieu for a new emotional style. Without the same direct stake in direct forms of racial domination required on a plantation, whose workforce must be compelled to submit to an authoritarian regime, New South elites patterned their attitudes and behavior on the cooler and more restrained emotional style of the modern businessman. Having succeeded in the task of disfranchising black male voters and no longer facing a credible threat to their economic interests, such men may have been more willing to eliminate the violent excesses that gave their region a reputation for lawlessness, brutality, and backwardness. A new generation began to respond to criticisms from the NAACP and to proposals for change from the Commission for Interracial Cooperation that involved a modification, if not an abandonment, of older forms of racial domination.

Emphasizing the control of the self rather than an obsession with honor and social reputation as the essence of a mature masculinity, adherents of a progressive ideological practice began to gain support at the same time that Prohibition tried to improve the moral tone of the nation. The *Raleigh News and Observer* and other North Carolina newspapers adopted a "progressive" political and emotional style that suited the reform commitments of Josephus Daniels and other editors. A new model of masculine emotional restraint along with greater moderation in racial attitudes appeared in some sectors of the popular press. Antilynching reformers agitated for federal legislation against the crime, gathered information about its occurrence, and refuted the usual justifications for the crime. Locally, African American men and women embarked on an educational campaign to influence public opinion. They lobbied politicians, wrote letters to editors, and placed lynching on the agenda of the Committee for Interracial Cooperation. The NAACP's strong base in Durham among the officials of the North Carolina Mutual Insurance Company, led by a group of men who still remembered the horrors of 1898, was a particularly vital asset in the campaign against mob violence. The campaign included undercover endeavors by insurance agents to discover the cause of lynchings and locate, if possible, the perpetrators. Anxious to avoid federal intervention, North Carolina elites "aroused sentiments against lynching that otherwise would have taken a century to accomplish" as journalists contributed to an emerging critique of demagogic appeals to bloodlust and the "reign of passion.[55]

White journalists signaled their conversion to the new ideological dispensation. Criticizing both lynchers and rapists, editorials combined a white supremacist emphasis on the "bestial negro" with a reformist condemnation of "unlawful" violence and the alcohol that turned white and black men into beasts. The *Raleigh Evening Times* referred to a 1918 lynching as a "disgraceful episode" while calling the "killing of a fellow-man, no matter how degenerate that fellow-man may be" an act "nothing short of savagery." That same month the *Greensboro Daily News* condemned the "Dutch courage" of a "gang of excitable and irresponsible youth turned anarchists" who embarked on "promiscuous shooting and terrifying of blacks." Shifting from the first to the third person as it referred to "white people," the Greensboro paper distanced itself from white supremacist conventions. A year later the *News and Observer* condemned "mob law" as the "usurpation of the organized law," while finding it "shocking to think that our womanhood . . . must be at the mercy of brutes in human form." It ascribed such crimes to whiskey and the need for "better educational and church facilities [to] teach the negro to be law-abiding."[56] Beginning to accept the "progressive" argument that blacks could be taught to obey the law rather than the white supremacist assertion that they were irredeemably criminal, the *News and Observer* rewrote the lynching narrative it had previously constructed in the campaign spearheaded by Daniels two decades earlier. No longer emphasizing depravity and violent emotions as innate, natural, and unchanging, editors now spoke of education as a method for modifying undesirable impulses, a process that might be needed for "savage" white men as well as black "brutes."

These trends became more visible in the battle between "progressive" Governor Thomas Bickett and the newly revived Ku Klux Klan in the war's aftermath. Bickett attacked the Klan for harking back "to the lawless time that followed the civil war" and to "the terrors of those dark days." Instead of "hatred or suspicion between races," he advised North Carolinians to follow the "best and wisest men in both races [who] are working to strengthen the ties of friendship and of peace and lay broad and deep foundations of an enduring peace and prosperity for both races." Bickett publicly opposed the Klan by saying that the "man or order that encourages hatred or suspicion between races in North Carolina is the mortal enemy of both races." His attack, labeled the "first made by any Southern governor on this organization," denied the Klan's assertions that it would "protect our country from lawless invasions," "protect the women of our South," and prevent "riots and disorders." Bickett condemned a lynching that took place in his home county as a deed that put "to open shame our boasted white civilization and make[s] the name of Southern chivalry a byword and a reproach." Soon Bickett acquired a media image as the "bold, justice-loving chief executive," while North Carolina acquired a "progressive" reputation as its governor demonstrated a new model of masculinity and a more tempered emotional style.[57]

As another indication of the new, "progressive" style, the *Elizabeth City Independent* attacked the claims of chivalry as a defense of lynching in words that repeated arguments for which Alex Manly had paid dearly: "But what do mobs care about the sanctity of womanhood? You will find the average mob made up largely of men who don't scruple about cohabiting with negro women. And these lousing lechers are the loudest in talking about the sanctity of womanhood." The fact that "American citizens right here at home" were "deprived of the right of trial by jury and lynched by hellish mobs" scandalized this editor.[58] Characterizing the lynchers as evildoers, the editor rewrote the sexual and racial script within the context of an ideological practice that preached emotional restraint rather than appealing to passion and included African Americans among the citizenry who had earned their place by fighting in the war.

As testified to by Bickett's stance on lynching, the adherents of the "progressive alternative" exuded self-confident mastery. Bickett had proclaimed that "the negro above all others is entitled to the protection of the law" because "all the power and all the processes of the law are in the hands of white men." As a consequence, white men must guarantee that a "white man's justice" prevailed in the state. The same self-confidence allowed progressive men to relinquish some aspects of the patriarchal control over women embodied in chivalrous mythology. White women joined men in reform organizations, assumed some official positions in state government once they had received the vote, participated in party politics, and commented on political affairs. The progressive ideological and emotional style did not require the same emphasis on disorder, passion, and intensity that projected on the racial "other" all that was most terrible and most arousing and required that white women play the part of the virgin and victim. The mob—a literal reenactment of the carnivalesque loss of control—could be relinquished as a political method and an emotional catharsis by men who felt themselves unassailably in control, emotionally, politically, and economically.[59]

Yet that confidence might prove as short-lived and fragile as the economic prosperity of the war years. Bickett left the governor's mansion just as North Carolina's economic situation was beginning to deteriorate. The agricultural crisis of the 1920s, precipitated in part by the boll weevil and the declining fortunes of the textile industry, might prove just as conducive to volatility in the political system as had the depression- plagued 1890s. Furthermore, the confidence of businessmen, textile executives, and tobacco manufacturers might arise out of the very conditions that rendered other groups of white men more insecure. The decline in farm incomes and the growth of an industrial working class increasingly threatened by unemployment, managerial demands for increased productivity, and the erosion of mill village paternalism made it difficult for large numbers of white North Carolinians to experience the same sense of mastery that Bickett expressed. The growth of the "redneck" stereotype used by upper-class whites to describe benighted, bigoted, and backward poor whites may have emerged from just such a class-based division in masculine cultures. As the more economically secure adopted the progressive style, workers, small farmers, sharecroppers, and other members of the white laboring classes may have felt the same need for mastery expressed in the familiar rituals of the more brutal forms of racial domination.[60]

Having suffered at the hands of lynch mobs and rioters, African Americans undoubtedly preferred the newer, "progressive," business-suited version of masculinity to the more irrational and brutal forms of white supremacy. Both approaches to racial politics denied African Americans freedom of action, but the "soft" or progressive version gave greater scope for initiative and offered greater safety from the violence with which they were all too well acquainted. The genteel heirs to a fortune built on crude and bombastic origins might revert to their more primitive ancestral type during a crisis, but the softening of the brutal, masculinist politics of the past was an improvement nevertheless.

Overly optimistic hopes that the stronghold of the "southern bully" had been leveled, however, were dashed when Cameron Morrison, who began his career during the 1898 campaign, became the Democratic candidate for governor in 1920. Although a letter-writing campaign warned that his election would disturb the "peace and tranquility" of the state and might "cause unrest with the colored laborers of the State," white voters gave Morrison the required support. Democrats in the Simmons machine kept "chanting the same old song of 'Nigger, Nigger, Nigger.' " A dismayed Charles Hunter listened to the election speeches. "It sounded to me like weird, discarded canticles from some far off ghost-land." Using words that echoed those written by Walter Hines Page, John Spencer Bassett, and Charles Chesnutt, Hunter wrote that the old "nigger-bashing" trick was being used to "conjure intelligent, Christian white people"; he admitted that it "did have some effect." He decided to keep silent because he could not make "any effective resistance under the circumstances" where Republicans were "lily white" and Democrats embraced only the "white man." Hunter's decision all too closely resembled those made earlier by Page, Basset and Cronly. Although insisting that "thoughtful sensible Negroes can and will be heard," Hunter recognized the persistent power of an ideological practice that allowed white men to take "real pleasure in their power over their terrified victims" as violence retained its "erotic charge."[61] The new emotional style and ideological practice, although increasingly visible among urban professionals, state political officials, and the leading newspapers of North Carolina, had not supplanted the older brand of politics despite the disappearance of the lynch mob for most of the 1920s.

Fomenting a "moral panic" whenever their power appeared to slip, white men of the older middle and upper classes restored a sexual and racial order that secured their position at the top. They appealed to a "common manhood" to resume "a racially commanding presence" at the top of the social order as they associated whiteness with male dominance. Reared in a sexually repressive evangelical culture, men atoned for their own "impurities" by ruthlessly punishing the sexual sins of their subordinates. An "obscene, perverse imagery" projected the menace of sexual danger onto other people while white men vainly sought to keep "the affairs of their own heart and conscience and home, as well as the community, 'under control.' "[62] Updated versions of the lynching narrative continued to be deployed. Anger fueled political passions and lit victory fires as politicians relied on appeals to savage emotions in their determination to keep power. The "progressive" emotional style had not gained ascendancy in North Carolina, but its fledgling presence gave some degree of protection to those threatened or coerced into silence by the grotesque and murderous rage of the mob.

The role of emotion in political contests is not easy to pinpoint. It is not a constant, for particular issues and configurations carry much greater than average emotional potential. Race, in American history, unquestionably bears a disproportionate emotional load. Yet emotion itself helps cause political reactions, as it emanates from large numbers of voters or rioters and as it can be manipulated by clever leaders who themselves share the emotional assumptions. Clearly, the clashes in North Carolina before 1900 cannot be understood apart from the special emotional context. Reformers realized this, as they tried to develop a more controlled emotional approach. Cases of this sort ultimately invite a wider typology of emotional reactions as they emerge from, and shape, political and social controversy.

NOTES

1. Judith Walkowitz, *City of Dreadful Delight: Narratives of Sexual Danger in Late-Victorian London* (London: Virago, 1992), 8, 9; Lynn Segal, *Straight Sex: The Politics of Pleasure* (London: Virago, 1994), 277, 248; Catherine A. Lutz, *Unnatural Emotions: Everyday Sentiments on a Micronesian Atoll and Their Challenge to Western Theory* (Chicago: University of Chicago Press, 1988), 72; "5000 Hear Aycock Speak," *Raleigh News and Observer,* 25 July 1900; Nancy MacLean, *Behind the Mask of Chivalry: The Making of the Second Ku Klux Klan* (New York: Oxford University Press, 1994), 187.

2. John Spencer Bassett, "The Reign of Passion," *South Atlantic Quarterly* 1: 4 (October 1902): 301–9.

3. See, for example, Segal, *Straight Sex,* 269; Deborah Cameron and Elizabeth Frazer, *The Lust to Kill: A Feminist Investigation of Sexual Murder* (London: Polity Press, 1987), ix, x, 5, 19, 35, 66; MacLean, *Behind the Mask of Chivalry;* Jacquelyn Dowd Hall, "The Mind That Burns in Each Body: Women, Rape, and Racial Violence," in Ann Snitow, Christine Stansell, and Sharon Thompson, eds., *Powers of Desire: The Politics of Sexuality* (New York: Monthly Review Press, 1983), 328–49; Peter N. Stearns, *American Cool: Constructing a Twentieth-Century Emotional Style* (New York: New York University Press, 1994), 43.

4. Walkowitz, *City of Dreadful Delight,* 2, 85; David R. Roediger, *The Wages of Whiteness: Race and the Making of the American Working Class* (London: Verso, 1992), 56, 57; Dolores E. Janiewski, *Sisterhood Denied: Race, Gender, and Class in a New South Community* (Philadelphia: Temple University Press, 1985), 52; Sherry B. Ortner and Harriet Whitehead, introduction to Sherry B. Ortner and Harriet Whitehead, eds., *Sexual Meanings: The Cultural Construction of Gender and Sexuality* (Cambridge: Cambridge University Press, 1981), 5; Jane F. Collier and Michelle Z. Rosaldo, "Politics and Gender in Simple Societies," in Ortner and Whitehead, *Sexual Meanings,* 275–329, 297; Ida Wells-Barnett, *A Red Record* (Chicago: Donohue and Henneberry, 1895), as quoted in Gerda Lerner, *Black Women in White America: A Documentary History* (New York: Vintage Books, 1973), 202, 203–4; Frank Mort, *Dangerous Sexualities: Medio-Moral Politics in England since 1830* (London: Routledge and Kegan Paul, 1987), 9.

5. Segal, *Straight Sex,* 269; *Progressive Farmer,* 12 March 1895; *Union Republican,* 27 October 1898.

6. Stearns, *American Cool,* 4, 29.

7. Walkowitz, *City of Dreadful Delight,* 121, 198; Simon Watney, *Policing Desire: Pornography, AIDS, and the Media* (Minneapolis: University of Minnesota Press, 1989), 40, 43.

8. Jacquelyn Hall, *Revolt against Chivalry: Jessie Daniel Ames and the Women's Campaign against Lynching* (New York: Columbia University Press, 1979), 147–48; Nell Irvin Painter, " 'Social Equality,' Miscegenation, Labor, and Power," in Numan V. Bartley, ed., *The Evolution of Southern Culture* (Athens: University of Georgia Press, 1988), 50, 58.

9. *Raleigh Sentinel,* 24 August 1867; Painter, " 'Social Equality,' " 64; Mort, *Dangerous Sexualities,* 83; Joel Williamson, *Rage for Order: Black/White Relations in the American South since Emancipation* (New York: Oxford University Press, 1986), 184–86; Roediger, *Wages of Whiteness,* 56, 57; Janiewski, *Sisterhood Denied,* 52; Ortner and Whitehead, introduction, 5; Collier and Rosaldo, "Politics and Gender," 275–329, 297; Williamson, *Rage for Order,* 184–86; LeeAnn Whites, "Rebecca Latimer Felton and the Problem of 'Protection' in the New South," in Nancy A. Hewitt and Suzanne Lebsock, eds., *Visible Women: New Essays on American Radicalism* (Urbana: University of Illinois Press, 1993), 41–61, 45, 46; Robert Watson Winston, "An Unconsidered Aspect of the Negro Question," *South Atlantic Quarterly* 1: 3 (July 1902) 265–68, 266.

10. *A.M.E. Zion Quarterly Review* 3: 4 (July 1893): 454; *Raleigh Gazette,* 27 February 1897; *A.M.E. Zion Church Quarterly* 4: 5 (December 1894): 494; James B. Dudley, "How to Teach History," *A.M.E. Zion Church Quarterly* 3: 1 (October 1892): 39.

11. *Raleigh News and Observer,* 3 August; *Raleigh News and Observer,* 27 September 1898; "A Serious Question—How Long Will This Last?" *Raleigh News and Observer,* 13 August 1898; *Raleigh News and Observer,* 8 September 1898; "Jim Young, the Negro Politician, Inspecting Apartments in White Blind Institution," *Raleigh News and Observer,* 19 August 1898.

12. *Raleigh News and Observer*, 8 August 1898; "Negroes Exalted—White Folks Must Stand Aside," *Raleigh News and Observer*, 16 August, 1898; "A Strong Antagonism to the Negro," *Wilmington Messenger*, 16 May 1898; "A United Democracy," *Wilmington Messenger*, 21 May 1898; "The Conceits and Swellings of Negrodom," *Wilmington Messenger*, 23 July 1898; Bennet L. Steelman, "Black White and Gray: The Wilmington Race Riot in Fact and Legend," *North Carolina Literary Review* 11: 1 (Spring 1994): 70–82, 75; "What Radicalism Means in Wilmington," *Raleigh News and Observer*, 19 August 1898; F. B. Arendell, "Negro Control in Wilmington," *Wilmington Messenger*, 11 August 1898; "The Crime and the Remedy," *Wilmington Messenger*, 22 July 1898; "Negro Control in Wilmington, Unbridled Lawlessness," *Wilmington Messenger*, 12 August 1898; "White Man Friend to Negroes," *Wilmington Messenger*, 19 August 1898; *Wilmington Morning Star*, 8 September 1898; *Wilmington Messenger*, 7 September 1898.

13. "Negro Control in Wilmington"; *Wilmington Messenger*, 4 September 1898; "The Crime and the Remedy"; "A United Democracy"; "The Official Call to Democratic Electors," *Wilmington Messenger*, 23 March 1898.

14. *Wilmington Messenger*, 18 September, 21 September, 1 October, 9 September 1898.

15. B. [Benjamin] F. Keith, *Memories* (Raleigh: Bynum, 1922), 98, 99, 100.

16. "A Strong Antagonism to the Negro"; "A United Democracy"; "Conceits and Swellings of Negrodom"; Keith, *Memories*, 62, 67, 97, 98, 99; "The Crime and the Remedy"; "Negro Control in Wilmington"; "White Man Friend to Negroes"; *Wilmington Morning Star*, 8 September 1898; *Wilmington Messenger*, 7 September 1898.

17. "The Lawless Elect—A Lesson to Sambo," *Wilmington Messenger*, 20 August 1898; "The End of Negro Scheming in Amalgamation with Whites," *Wilmington Messenger*, 11 October 1898.

18. "Mrs. Felton's Speech," *Wilmington Record*, 18 August 1898, reprinted in "Look at This Trio," *Wilmington Messenger*, 4 September 1898.

19. Quoted in Steelman, "Black White and Gray," 76; "A Negro Defamer of the White Women of North Carolina," *Wilmington Messenger*, 21 August 1898; "Mrs. Felton's Speech."

20. Association of Wilmington Light Infantry, "Meeting," Lumina, Wrightsville Beach, 14 December 1905, North Carolina Collection, Wilson Library, University of North Carolina, Chapel Hill; hereafter, WLI/NCC.

21. *Wilmington Messenger*, 21 August, 4 September 1898; "Vile and Villainous," *Raleigh News and Observer*, 24 August 1898.

22. Steelman, "Black White and Gray," 76; "Condemns Editor Manly," "Bearing Its Fruit the Slanderous Article of the Wilmington Negro Paper," *Raleigh News and Observer*, 25 August 1898; "A Legitimate Result," 25 August 1898; "A Base Slander," *Wilmington Messenger*, 23 August 1898; "Who Is Manly?" *Wilmington Messenger*, 28 August 1898; "Slander of White Woman by Negro Editor," *Wilmington Messenger*, 1 September 1898; *Wilmington Messenger*, 4 September 1898; "Remember the 6," 18 August 1898, Wilmington Race Riot, North Carolina Collection, Wilson Library, University of North Carolina, Chapel Hill. "Republicanism Responsible for Slanders of White Women," *Raleigh News and Observer*, 25 August 1898.

23. *Progressive Farmer*, 8 November 1898; Mort, *Dangerous Sexualities*, 117, 118.

24. "The Negro in New Hanover," *Charlotte Observer*, reprinted in *Raleigh News and Observer*, 8 September 1898; "New Bern's Plight," *Raleigh News and Observer*, 10 September 1898; "The Vicious Are Upheld," *Raleigh News and Observer*, 8 October 1898; "Cases of Negro Insolence," *Raleigh News and Observer*, 12 October 1898; "Banner for the Victors," *Raleigh News and Observer*, 9 October 1898; *Durham Sun*, 21 July 1900.

25. Let the People Rejoice," *Wilmington Messenger*, 10 November 1898; "A Revolution," *Wilmington Messenger*, 11 November 1898.

26. "A Splendid Day for the Democracy in Wake County," *Raleigh News and Observer*, 14 July 1900.

27. Charles Chesnutt, "The Disfranchisement of the Negro," in *The Negro Problem: A Series of Articles by Representative American Negroes of Today, Contributions by Booker T. Washington, W. D. Burghardt DuBois, Paul Lawrence Dunbar, Charles W. Chesnutt, and Others* (New York: James Pratt, 1903), 79–124, 113, 117–18, 124; Segal, *Straight Sex*, 261, 257, 255, 254; George Fitzhugh, "Southern

Thought," in Drew Gilpin Faust, ed., *The Ideology of Slavery: Proslavery Thought in the Antebellum South, 1830–1860* (Baton Rouge: Louisiana State University Press, 1981), 295, 293; Marjorie Garber, *Vested Interests: Cross-Dressing and Cultural Anxiety* (New York: Routledge, 1992), 271; Walkowitz, *City of Dreadful Delight*, 6, 7.

28. Lutz, *Unnatural Emotions,* 64, 65, 62, 4, 5, 10.

29. Jane Cronly to editor, *Independent;* Jane Cronly, untitled memoir (written within week of 10 November 1898), box 21, Cronly Family Papers, Manuscripts, Perkins Library, Duke University, Durham.

30. Charles W. Chesnutt, "Notebook," 16 March 1880, Charles Chesnutt Papers, Special Collections, Fisk University, Nashville, Tennessee (hereafter Chesnutt/Fisk); as quoted in Sylvia Lyons Render, *Charles W. Chesnutt* (Boston: Twayne, 1980), 22; Charles W. Chesnutt, "Notebook," 3 January 1881, Chesnutt/Fisk; W. E. B. Du Bois, *The Souls of Black Folk* (New York: Signet, 1969), 45; Charles W. Chesnutt, "Notebook," 3 January 1881; Charles W. Chesnutt to Robert E. Park, 19 December 1908, Chesnutt/Fisk; as quoted in Render, *Charles W. Chesnutt,* 22, 23; Charles W. Chesnutt, "Notebook," 3 January 1881, Chesnutt/Fisk.

31. Charles W. Chesnutt to George W. Cable, 5 June 1890; George W. Cable to Charles W. Chesnutt, 17 June 1890, Chesnutt/Fisk; Du Bois, *Souls of Black Folk,* 46, 50.

32. W. D. Howells, "Mr. Charles W. Chesnutt's Stories," *Atlantic Monthly,* May 1900, 699–701; Chesnutt to Cable, 5 June 1890.

33. Charles W. Chesnutt to Walter Hines Page, 11 November 1898; Page to Chesnutt, 14 November 1898; Chesnutt to Page, 22 March 1899, Chesnutt/Fisk.

34. Charles W. Chesnutt to Booker T. Washington, November 1901, in Louis R. Harlan and Raymond W. Smock, eds., *Booker T. Washington Papers* (Urbana: University of Illinois Press, 1977), 6: 288; Joyce Pettis, "The Marrow of Tradition: Charles Chesnutt's Novel of the South," *North Carolina Literary Review* 1: 1 (spring 1994): 108–21; Chesnutt to Page, 22 March 1899; Houghton Mifflin to Chesnutt, 24 March 1900; Thomas J. Garrison to Chesnutt, 9 November 1901; Chesnutt to Houghton Mifflin, 14 December 1899; Chesnutt to Mrs. E. E. Henderson, Indianapolis, 11 November 1905; Victoria Richardson to Chesnutt, 30 January 1901; James Dudley, A & M College, Greensboro, to Chesnutt, 18 February, 20 March 1901; J. E. Garford, Office of the Collector of Customs, Wilmington, 2 April 1901; Chesnutt to Page, 22 March 1899, Chesnutt/Fisk.

35. Charles W. Chesnutt, *The Marrow of Tradition* (1901; reprint, Ann Arbor: University of Michigan Press, 1969), 49, 56, 57, 60, 61.

36. Ibid., 79, 80, 85, 86.

37. Ibid., 178, 185, 190, 194, 212, 219, 227.

38. A. J. McKelway, "The North Carolina Revolution Justified," *Outlook,* 31 December 1898, 1057–59; Kelly Miller, "A Negro's View," *Outlook,* 31 December 1898, 1059–63; Harry Litchfield West, "The Race War in North Carolina," *Forum,* January 1899, 578–91; Chesnutt, *Marrow of Tradition,* 238, 239, 248.

39. Chesnutt, *Marrow of Tradition,* 110, 113, 114, 115, ,310, 212.

40. Charles W. Chesnutt to Sallie Henderson, 11 November 1905; Charles W. Anderson to Chesnutt, 11 December 1901; Francis J. Garrison to Chesnutt, 13 February 1902; F. L. Barnett to Chesnutt, 5 November 1901, Chesnutt/Fisk; W. D. Howells, "A Psychological Counter-Current in Recent Fiction," *North American Review,* December 1901, 882; W. E. B. Du Bois to Chesnutt, 8 March 1902, Chesnutt/Fisk.

41. As quoted in James T. Rostar, "Walter Hines Page: Editor, Publisher, and Enlightened Reformer," *North Carolina Literary Review* 11: 1 (spring 1994): 102–7, 106; Robert M. Farnsworth, introduction to Chesnutt, *Marrow of Tradition,* xiv, xvi; Thomas Dixon, Jr., "Historical Note," in *The Leopard's Spots, or a Romance of the White Man's Burden* (New York: Doubleday, Page, 1902), vi; Glenda Elizabeth Gilmore, "One of the Meanest Books: Thomas Dixon, Jr. and *The Leopard's Spots*," *North Carolina Literary Review* 11: 1 (spring 1994): 87–101, 87; Pettis, "Marrow of Tradition," 112.

42. Farnsworth, introduction, vii, xiv; E. D. Crumpacker, to Charles W. Chesnutt, 5 May 1902; Chesnutt to E. D. Crumpacker, 9 May 1902, Chesnutt/Fisk.

43. Chesnutt, "Disfranchisement of the Negro," 79–124, 80, 81, 113, 117–18, 124.

44. "The Leopard's Spots by Thomas Dixon, Jr.," *South Atlantic Quarterly* 1: 2 (April 1902): 188–89; quoted in Gilmore, "One of the Meanest Books," 96.

45. Bruce Clayton, "Southern Critics of the New South, 1890–1914" (Ph.D. diss., Duke University, 1966), 40; John Spencer Bassett to Herbert Baxter Adams, 16 January 1896, in Herbert Baxter Adams, Letters, 1891–1913, taken from extensive correspondence of Herbert Baxter Adams at Johns Hopkins University, in Manuscripts, Perkins Library, Duke University, Durham, hereafter Adams/DU; Bassett to Adams, 26 September 1897, 31 July 1895, 26 September 1897, 24 January 1898, 15 November 1898, Adams/DU.

46. Bassett to Adams, 15 November, 16 December 1898, 18 February 1899, Adams/DU.

47. As quoted in Hugh Talmage Lefler and Albert Ray Newsome, *A History of a Southern State: North Carolina* (Chapel Hill: University of North Carolina Press, 1972), 597; "Editor's Announcement," *South Atlantic Quarterly* 1: 1 (January 1902): 1–2, 2; John Carlisle Kilgo, "An Inquiry Regarding Lynching," *South Atlantic Quarterly* 1: 1 (January 1902): 4–13, 4, 5, 7, 11, 13; idem, "The Christian Basis of Citizenship," *South Atlantic Quarterly* 1: 2 (April 1902) 118–27, 127.

48. "The Reign of Passion," *South Atlantic Quarterly* 1: 4 (October 1902): 301–9; John Spencer Bassett to Walter Hines Page, 14 December 1903, Walter Hines Page Papers, Harvard University, photocopies in Manuscripts, Perkins Library, Duke University, Durham, hereafter Page/DU; Bassett to Page, 8 December 1903, Page/DU; "Stirring Up the Fires of Race Antipathy," *South Atlantic Quarterly* 2: 4 (October 1903): 297–305.

49. "The Tobacco Farmers Are Robbed," *Raleigh News and Observer*, 20 October 1903; "Prof. Bassett Says Negro Will Win Equality," *Raleigh News and Observer*, 2 November 1903; "Political Intolerance in North Carolina," *Raleigh News and Observer*, 2 November 1903; "Playing with Fire," *North Carolina Christian Advocate*, quoted in *Raleigh News and Observer*, 6 November 1903; "Kindling Flames of Indignation," *Raleigh News and Observer*, 3 November 1903; *Goldsboro Argus*, 2 November 1903; "Spirit of the Press," *Charlotte News*, as quoted in *Raleigh News and Observer*, 4 November 1903; "Almost Beyond Belief," *Wilmington Messenger*, as quoted in *Raleigh News and Observer*, 5 November 1903; John F. Bruton to James H. Southgate, 14 November 1903, James Southgate Papers, Manuscripts, Perkins Library, Duke University, Durham, hereafter Southgate/DU; George Fredrickson, *Black Image in the White Mind: The Debate on Afro-American Character and Destiny, 1817–1914* (Middletown: Wesleyan University Press, 1971), 282.

50. Walter Hines Page, "The Last Hold of the Southern Bully," *Forum* 16 (1893): 313–14; Josiah Bailey to Walter Hines Page, 30 July 1902, 23 December 1903, Josiah William Bailey Papers, Manuscripts, Perkins Library, Duke University, Durham; John Spencer Bassett to Page (confidential), 7 November 1903, Page/DU; "Call Murder Murder," *State Chronicle*, 6 October 1883.

51. George S. Bradshaw, Greensboro, to James Southgate, 4 December 1903, Southgate/DU; John Spencer Bassett to Walter Hines Page, 2 December, 8 December 1903, Page/DU; "The Task of the Critic," *South Atlantic Quarterly* 3: 4 (October 1904): 297–301. "An Exile from the South," "The Editor's Announcement," *South Atlantic Quarterly* 4: 1 (January 1905): 82–90, 91; Clayton, "Southern Critics," 119; John Spencer Bassett to William E. Dodd, 7 May 1907; Bassett to William K. Boyd, 2 January 1912, quoted in Clayton, "Southern Critics," 111.

52. Nicholas Worth [Walter Hines Page], *The Southerner: A Novel* (New York: Doubleday, Page, 1909), 46, 47, 59–60, 194, 247, 253, 265, 266, 268.

53. Lutz, *Unnatural Emotions*, 64, 65, 62, 4, 5, 10; Fitzhugh, "Southern Thought," 293, 292; Evelyn Brooks Higginbotham, "African American Women's History and the Metalanguage of Race," *Signs* 17: 2 (winter 1992): 251–74, 263, 266–67; Wendy Saravasy, "Beyond the Difference versus Equality Policy Debate: Postsuffrage Feminism, Citizenship, and the Quest for a Feminist Welfare State," *Signs* 17: 2 (winter 1992): 329–62, 333; William H. Chafe, *Civilities and Civil Rights: Greensboro, North Carolina and the Black Struggle for Freedom* (New York: Oxford University Press, 1981), 7, 8; MacLean, *Behind the Mask of Chivalry*, 19; Stearns, *American Cool*, 42.

54. Charles N. Hunter to T. W. Bickett, 11 November 1916, Bickett to Hunter, 15 November 1916; D. J. Jordan to Hunter, 30 July 1917; C. N. Hunter, "The Negro's Call to World Service," 15 November 1917, Hunter/DU; James Weldon Johnston to Hunter, 17 December 1917, 8 February 1918;

Jane S. McKimrnon to Hunter, 19 February 1918; Hunter to Furnifold Simmons, 7 May 1918; John Paul Lucas to Hunter, 16 May 1918, Hunter/DU; John Hope Franklin, *From Slavery to Freedom: A History of Negro Americans* (New York: Knopf, 1980), 345, 347, 351; "Democracy Betrayed by the South," *Star of Zion*, 17 January 1918; "Prejudice Dragging Anchor," *Star of Zion*, 12 September 1918; "Reid to Be Deposted," *Star of Zion*, 8 August 1918; Julius F. Taylor, "The Lynching Record for 1917," *Star of Zion*, 21 February 1918; *Star of Zion*, 12 September 1918; Joanna De Groot, " 'Sex' and 'Race': The Construction of Language and Image in the Nineteenth Century," in Susan Mendus and Jane Rendail, eds., *Sexuality and Subordination: Interdisciplinary Studies of Gender in the Nineteenth Century* (London: Routledge, 1989), 89–128; Alexander Saxton, *The Rise and Fall of the White Republic: Class Politics and Mass Culture in Nineteenth-Century America* (London: Verso, 1993), 89, 152, 149–50.

55. A. M. Rivera to Walter White, 28 February 1922; Rivera to James Weldon Johnson, 18 December 1922, Branch Files, box 147, National Association for the Advancement of Colored People Papers, Library of Congress, Washington, DC, hereafter NAACP/LC.

56. Bickett Denounces Lynchers of Green," 29 December 1920, "Lynching," box 363, NAACP/LC; *New York World*, 29 December 1919; Janiewski, *Sisterhood Denied*, 92; Rivera to White, 28 February 1922; A. M. Rivera, President, N.C. Medical, Pharmaceutical, and Dental Association, to James Weldon Johnson, 18 December 1922, NAACP/LC; *Raleigh Evening News*, 11 November 1918; "The Trouble at Winston-Salem," *Greensboro Daily News*, 19 November 1918; see also "Winston-Salem Scene of Disorder and Bad Riot," *Raleigh News and Observer*, 18 November 1918; "Troops No Longer Needed," *Raleigh News and Observer*, 20 November 1918, 21 August 1919.

57. "Gov. Bickett Attacks Loyal Order Klansmen," *Raleigh News and Observer*, 30 June 1919; *Charlotte Sunday Observer*, 8 June 1919, quoted in *Southwestern Christian Advocate*, 26 June 1919; Edward Ayers, *Vengeance and Justice: Crime and Punishment in the Nineteenth-Century American South* (New York: Oxford University Press, 1984), 28, 272; *Norfolk Journal and Guide*, 2 July 1919; *St. Louis Argus*, 11 July 1919; *Baltimore Commonwealth*, 11 July 1919; "Prominent Carolinians Denounce Clan Activities," *Detroit Leader*, 11 July 1919; *Raleigh Evening News*, 11 November 1918; see Bruce Clayton, *The Savage Ideal: Intolerance and Intellectual Leadership in the South, 1890–1914* (Baltimore: Johns Hopkins University Press, 1972), 90–92; *New York Tribune*, 30 December 1919; "Bickett Denounces Lynchers of Green"; *Birmingham Age-Herald*, 3 August 1920; *Shreveport Journal*, 19 July 1920.

58. *Elizabeth City Independent*, reprinted in "Lynching Epidemic Causes Alarm and Indignation among Southern Whites," *Norfolk Guide and Journal*, 24 July 1920.

59. "Bickett Denounces Lynchers of Green"; Earl Black and Merle Black, *Politics and Society in the South* (Cambridge: Harvard University Press, 1980), 180; Sander L. Gilman, *Disease and Representation: Images of Illness from Madness to AIDS* (Ithaca: Cornell University Press, 1988), 1–5.

60. Janiewski, *Sisterhood Denied*, 106–8, 122–26; Chafe, *Civilities and Civil Rights*, 6–9.

61. Charles N. Hunter to W. Lee Pearson, 10 July 1920, Hunter/DU; MacLean, *Behind the Mask of Chivalry*, 163.

62. Nina Silber, *The Romance of Reunion: Northerners and the South, 1865–1900* (Chapel Hill: University of North Carolina Press, 1993), 154, 156, 167, 168, 174, 175; Lillian Smith, *Killers of the Dream* (Garden City: Anchor Books, 1963), 126.

Chapter Eight

Journalistic Gore
Disaster Reporting and Emotional Discourse in the New York Times, 1852–1956

Michael Barton

Some years ago my son and I were watching the evening news on television. The reporter was describing an accident—a fatal car crash, as I recall. Jonathan wrinkled his brow as he heard the story, and at the end he simply asked, "Why aren't they sad?" He could not understand why the reporter was talking so matter-of- factly about such a lamentable event. I gave Jonathan what was undoubtedly the right answer—something about the impersonality of mass society and the standards of professional journalism—but I don't think my five-year-old got it.

A few months ago I was reading a newsmagazine article about an airplane crash in western Pennsylvania. The accident was especially dreadful because the plane had dived almost straight into the ground. Inspectors had cordoned off the crash site to look for clues to the accident and to collect the remains of the passengers. The article went into detail on this last point. It mentioned that body parts were scattered all over; flesh even had to be retrieved from trees. I was taken aback by such explicit reporting in the mainstream press.

I saw on television recently an advertisement for a videotape of exciting accidents. Much of the footage had been shot by amateur videographers. One could watch boats capsizing, planes crashing, and cars careening into raceway walls. The viewer could rubberneck as long as he liked without getting in the way of rescuers, and without feeling embarrassed for being entertained. There was no explicit bloodletting in the ad, but "graphic footage" was promised in the complete spectacle.

Those are three modern, mediated representations of disaster—the television reporter's affectless description of a deadly accident, the newsmagazine's grisly examination of body parts, and the advertisement's exuberant commodification of catastrophes. You can see that these representations are quite different from one another. An emotional response is suppressed in the first instance, emotional distress is forced in the second instance, and, finally, there is a flood of permissible emotional stimulation. As representations, they carry confusing lessons about the nature of disaster and conflicting messages about the proper response to it. These troubling representations signify, in other words, modernity.

The difficulty with this interpretation, besides its subtle pomposity, is that it presumes that the past must have been quite different. It presumes that the treatment of disasters in the media used to be less troubling because the culture used to be kinder and gentler. But we need to test that presumption. Before we overinterpret the meaning of the contemporary representation of disaster (including the torrent of disaster movies being currently visited upon us), we should examine the media's treatment of disaster in the past and analyze the emotional discourse that went with it.

To start on that project, we will study here the *New York Times*'s reportage on disasters from before the Civil War to after World War II. Our method will be to sample issues of the *Times* at random to see how "minor" disasters were reported. We will also be looking specifically at the coverage of "major" disasters, treating those events as checkpoints to see whether the qualities of that kind of coverage change. Of course, we cannot simply treat the *Times* and its disaster reportage as typical of all newspapers, and we should not generalize fearlessly from what we find in reporters' discourse to most citizens' discourse. But my approach here, I think, is the most convenient and suggestive way to open the questioning on this subject.

In analyzing the past editorial practices of newspapers, we hope to discover more about the pertinent American "feeling rules" and "emotion talk" that once prevailed—rules and talk about feeling afraid, stoical, saddened, brave, terrified, or stunned.[1] The extreme conditions presented by disasters are likely to provoke the application of these rules by reporters and editors. To be sure, the emotional style of newspaper disaster stories is not a perfect reflection of the culture's emotional style, but it makes sense to see how the two relate. In any case, we know that newspapers pay attention to disasters, and readers pay attention to disaster stories.[2] (Cynics say the media's motto is "If it bleeds, it leads.")

Ellery Sedgwick, writing in 1905 for *Leslie's Monthly Magazine,* called America "the land of disasters." He asserted that between 1853 and 1904 there had been "Fifty years of wreckage and murder!" "For five months this Magazine has been printing plain English about the hideous responsibility for accidents by land and water," he wrote. He blamed the directors of the railroads and steamship lines for their negligence. When they and their stockholders saw the cost of accidents, Sedgwick predicted, then there would be reforms. Already an accident in a New York Central train tunnel led a jury to value a single life "at a hundred thousand dollars, the highest price ever paid for an American life."[3] His articles provided graphs showing that in 1904, "the banner year," 3,367 railroad employees were killed and 43,266 injured; as for passengers, 420 had been killed, 8,077 injured. Also, 5,000 "trespassers" died that year. "Whoever heard a party of drummers chatting in a smoker without listening to the personal story of a wreck? . . . Everywhere people are talking about it. Everywhere newspapers are discussing it."[4]

Indeed, Sedgwick's dates, 1853 to 1904, spanned a terrific amount of disaster. The *New-York Daily Times* (precursor to the *New York Times*) published on June 11, 1853, a list of the locations of 117 earthquakes that had been recorded in the 455 days between January 1852 and March 1853. A few months later, on January 17, 1854, the *Times* reported that 1853 had been "a year of wrecks":

The wreck of the *San Francisco* recalls the fact that the past year has been one of unusual calamity on the sea. In the brief space of twelve months, one hundred and thirty vessels, of all descriptions, have been totally lost, involving a heavy amount of damages and the loss of nearly *two thousand lives*. We believe that no year within the last half century has been so fruitful in marine disasters as the one just passed.

Twelve years later came the most serious marine disaster in American history, the explosion of the *Sultana,* a Mississippi River steamer carrying Union soldiers just freed from Confederate prison camps. It blew up near Memphis, Tennessee, on April 27, 1865, killing 1,547.[5] On June 15, 1904, only six months before Sedgwick wrote his article in *Leslie's Monthly,* an excursion steamer, the *General Slocum,* burned in the East River at New York City; 1,021 lives were lost. It was the worst harbor accident in American history.[6]

The country's deadliest fire started in a forest and then destroyed the town of Peshtigo, Wisconsin, on October 8, 1871, killing 1,152 persons. Another fire that same day in Illinois was less deadly but more famous: the Great Chicago Fire, which killed 250. The worst blizzard struck the eastern United States on March 12, 1888; about 800 persons died. The infamous Johnstown flood on May 31, 1889, left more than 2,200 dead. Galveston, Texas, was hit by the nation's worst hurricane and flood on May 8, 1890, and 6,000 were killed.

If we go beyond Sedgwick's time span by just a few years, we find the San Francisco earthquake, the country's worst, which struck on April 18 and 19, 1906. The worst single coal mine disaster happened on December 6, 1907, when 362 men were killed in an explosion near Monongah, West Virginia. Two weeks later, 239 miners died in a gas explosion at the Darr Coal Mine in Jacob's Creek, Pennsylvania. The worst year for coal mine disasters was 1909, when there were twenty accidents with fatalities.[7]

In sum, reporters had a horde of tragedies to cover in the last half of the nineteenth century and the early years of the twentieth. For our purposes, the data base is rich. Their assignment included the same kinds of natural disasters that were chronicled in the Bible and ancient histories—fires, floods, hurricanes, tornadoes, earthquakes, and tidal waves. But the age of industry would be the age of industrial accidents, so reporters also became witnesses to what could be the bloodier results of railroad, steamship, and mining calamities.

How did the *New York Times* talk about emotions in Sedgwick's "land of disasters"? The *Times* began publishing in 1851. The paper had a special place for announcements of disasters, a column at the top of the front page entitled "Latest Intelligence," later known as "News by Telegraph" in 1859. Let us sample both the minor and major disaster coverage of the 1850s, so as to establish a baseline for the rest of our analysis. The issue of January 19, 1852, announced "Fire and Loss of Life at Buffalo," and in three inches it compressed much emotional detail:

> About one o'clock this morning, a fire broke out in the saloon under the brick building occupied by P. G. Vought & Co. . . . Mr. Bean was sitting up with the corpse of his child, and would not leave the building until the corpse was removed. . . . By the death of Mr. Smith the city loses a most active and useful citizen. He leaves a wife and six children.

In the far right-hand column of the same issue's front page was a story from the *Savannah Republican,* with even more detail and pathos:

> It is with the deepest regret that we announce that the steamer *Magnolia* . . . was blown up on her return here Friday. . . . the scene was one of a most distressing character. In addition to the killed, a number had their arms and legs broken, and others were badly maimed. . . . But the most melancholy reflections suggested by this painful calamity are those connected with the family of Capt. McNelty. A wife and five children . . . are left to mourn the loss of a kind husband and affectionate father, to whom they daily looked for every temporal want. . . . When the sad intelligence was first communicated to his family yesterday, the scene, as described by an eye witness, was most heart-rending.

When accidents were reported, which was often, this sort of story, with this sort of detail, was not unusual in the *Times* of the 1850s. The reporter's empathy with the tragedy and its victims appears total. Readers do not have to imagine that the event was sad; they are specifically told it was "sad." They are not left to imagine how survivors felt; they are specifically told that survivors "mourn." And the reporter includes his own emotions in the story, his "melancholy reflections" on this "distressing" and "painful" event and its "heart-rending" conclusion. For readers, the emotional investigation and modeling are fairly thorough.

The *Times* of October 11, 1852, had no accidents on its front page that day, but there were other emotional narratives. In a story at the top of the page, "Walks among the New-York Poor," the reporter told of walking through Five Points with a missionary. An "open door showed a crowd of low women in a small dirty room, gathered in great glee around some poor fellow they were plucking." In the next doorway were some children: "Something in the expression of one—perhaps a look of such sad want—struck me . . . the children rushed forward, recognizing Mr. Pease, and clung to his hand most affectionately." At the end of his walk, the reporter proclaimed, " 'God help them!' say I, from my heart, for Man seldom will." Such an outpouring of emotion in a newspaper today could be found only in the work of a columnist, but there is no columnist today who works that way.

A brief story in the far right-hand column of the *Times* that day, under the heading "Townalities," told of one group's emotional state:

> Amusement for the Mad People—Messers Appleton and Co. have just made a donation of two hundred volumes of pleasant books to the Bloomingdale Asylum for the Insane. . . . the insane patients seldom read, but they are almost without exception violently attached to pictures . . . if they were once to get fairly entangled amid the mazes of metaphysics or the monstrosities of modern romance, they would be very likely to become more incurably mad than ever.

According to this report, even the books given to the emotionally disturbed possessed, in themselves, an emotional state—pleasantness.

Lower in the same column, under the heading "Mother Eve," was the observation that

> A very beautiful and expressive group of statuary with this title may be seen in the window of No. 547 Broadway. The position of Eve, with her hands clasped despairingly across her knees, and the two babies nestling in her lap, is well chosen. . . . The

expression of the two children's faces is intensely sorrowful, but the mother's face is weak. The grouping of the limbs and the general pose are full of grace, repose, and dignity.

In a culture that feels strongly about, and commonly instructs its members in, the intricacies of emotional release and containment, I suppose we should not be surprised to find the emotional states of statues taken seriously on the front page of a mainstream daily newspaper. Call this tendency romanticism, Victorianism, sentimentalism, Dionysianism, or simply emotionalism, it was one of the defining characteristics of American public and private expressive life in the 1800s. This was the tendency that would allow the *Times* to publish, as if it were a weather report, the following "Latest Intelligence" item at the top of the front page on April 22, 1853: "Fatal Accident. Pawtucket, R.I., Thursday, April 21. Samuel Wood, a manufacturer at Central Falls, was instantly killed and horribly mutilated by being caught in the gearing of his water-wheel this evening."

A *Times* reporter showed his skill at writing disaster prose on August 27, 1853, when he described the burning of the steamship *Cherokee:*

> In a marvelously short time . . . the hull of the ship was a sheet of flame. The red-tongued element burst out ferociously from the port-holes, crawled up the timbers, went down the beams, flickered about the masts, ate up the cordage, waved to and fro, and set off the rigging and the hull in fine relief against the clouded sky. We have rarely seen a more beautiful sight—always divesting the subject of its more melancholy features—than the ship at the moment when the flames had thoroughly enwrapped her.

The *Times* of January 16, 1854, devoted its entire front page to reporting the fate of the steamship *San Francisco,* which had been swamped in a great gale after many of its crew and passengers had been felled by cholera. In this instance, while giving "additional details of the sad disaster," the newspaper also provided "interesting statements by survivors." These revealed the culture's penchant for emotionalism even as the survivors declined to provide emotional accounts:

> We must fail to describe their joy at the change they experienced—removed from the cramped little bark to the roomy, comfortable quarters of the *Lucy Thompson.*

> We shall not attempt to portray the feelings of the rescued sufferers, or to measure the joy with which they were welcomed.

> When the sea struck the vessel, it precipitated itself into the lower cabin, where the passengers were still engaged in prayer, and instantly there were three feet of water in that part of the vessel. The horror of this moment cannot be described.

> The hardships which the officers and men endured cannot be described.

> I have thus endeavored to give the details of our shipwreck in the simplest *matter-of-fact* language, without attempting to describe the sufferings of those on board. . . . No language can adequately describe the scenes of danger and terror through which we have passed.

But occasionally the emotions displayed aboard the *San Francisco* were described: "Some were praying. The children were screaming lustily, but the ladies were almost universally calm. The camp women, however, were shrieking a great deal, but the ladies were clinging to each other and the little ones, and were calm and speechless."

The *Times* of April 22, 1854, told on its front page the story of the "Loss of the Powhattan." It did not avoid mentioning mortal details. The story began with testimony from Captain Jennings, the "wreckmaster": "I went down on the beach where the bodies were being washed on shore. Women and children came on shore first." One wonders whether any reader caught, or the captain intended, that irony of chivalry. The paper continued with its own account:

> The clothing of another of the victims, about 20 years of age, showed her to belong to the wealthy class of Germans. She was a beautiful looking creature, even as she lay in death. On her fingers she wore two rings—one plain and the other having a heart attached to it. They were marked "P.S." and "B.S.," 1854. . . . About fifty bodies have been taken to Smithville for interment. Most of the people here, says an eye-witness, are afraid to touch them. . . . The bodies of nearly all are badly bruised, and some of them could not have been recognized by their most intimate friends. One interesting little girl, about 11 years of age, was in her bare feet; her right eye was knocked out . . . a little boy came alongside of her. His face was swollen up to twice its natural size. A man . . . had his skull broken. The bodies had the appearance of having been dashed against the wreck.

A *Times* reader that day looking for more morbidity could have spotted, tucked away at the bottom of the front page, just below a story of the first session of the Thirty-third Congress, an account of the "Execution of James Quinn":

> Wilkesbarre, Friday, April 21. James Quinn, the murderer of Mahala Wiggins, by cleaving her skull with an axe, last Fall, on a canal boat, was executed here today. He was brought out of his cell at 1 1/2 o'clock, when, running eagerly up the steps of the scaffold, he looked around with apparent unconcern and composure, and smiled and bowed to his acquaintances during prayer. A few minutes before 2 o'clock the Sheriff bid him farewell, the drop fell, and he died after but few struggles, and without having made any confession.

Over in the far right-hand column of the paper were short paragraphs of advertisements, fitting in their technique:

> "Gas! Gas! Gas!"

> "Tea! Tea! Tea!"

Was the *Times* being typical of newspapers or unusually sensationalist in its employment of this morbid, emotional style? In its very first issue on September 18, 1851, the editor Henry J. Raymond announced his policy: "We do not mean to write as if we were in a passion, unless that shall really be the case; and we shall make it a point to get into a passion as rarely as possible." The *Times*'s own history, written by staff member Elmer Davis in 1921, contrasts its style with the revolutionary practices of James Gordon Bennett's *New York Herald*, most famous of the sensationalist "penny press": "There was a field for a sane and sensible newspaper in New York in 1851," Davis wrote. Still, he implied that the differences between the *Times* and the *Herald* were not vast. If Bennett's paper was thought "obscene" in its time, Davis opined that it was "not so very terrible, judged by the more elastic standards of our time"; credit the *Herald*, Davis wrote, because it still "respected certain reticences."[8] Speaking for itself in the 1850s, however, the *Times* was quite sure it was a better class of newspaper than the *Herald*, the *Sun*, and the other scandal sheets. At the end of its first year of publication, Raymond editorialized that the *Times* represented "the best portion of our citizens," and that it did not "pander to any special taste, least of all to any low or degrading appetite."[9] To answer the question, then, we are dealing with a paper that was sensational only from our modern point of view. Actually, it was among the least sensational of its day, and it believed it was sober.[10]

As for the emotional climate, as well as the accident context, that the *Times* reporters worked in, David Reynolds has shown that the 1850s was a sensation-filled era. He quotes the observations of our major writers: Edgar Allan Poe wrote in 1846 that the sensationalism of the press was having an effect "probably beyond all calculation"; Ralph Waldo Emerson wrote in his journal in May 1852 that Americans were "reading all day murder & railroad accidents"; Henry David Thoreau wrote in his journal of the "startling and monstrous events as fill the daily papers." Reynolds observes that Walt Whitman "noted the special scurrility of American newspapers," that Nathaniel Hawthorne was a "lifelong addict of popular newspapers" (Hawthorne's son called it a "pathetic craving"), and that Herman Melville "kept a close eye on the sensational press, which often featured bizarre or freakish images," such as ship disasters.[11] What the *Times* seems to be revealing, then, in its moderately sensationalist way, is the kind of emotional discourse that prevailed in the 1850s.

Later that year, in a front-page story about a Susquehanna Railroad wreck near Baltimore, there is more gore. The edition of July 6, 1854, reported the results:

> Awful Catastrophe. Horrible Accident. . . . The scene was most dreadful. . . . The rear car passing entirely through the foremost one, and both being filled with passengers, the destruction of life and limb was almost unprecedented. . . . Among the dead was Mrs. Roberson, a young and beautiful woman. . . . In removing the cars Mrs. Roberson's body was literally torn to pieces.

Of course, this style of discourse could be called realism as well as sensationalism. To repeat, the age of industrialism was also the age of industrial accidents. Reporters may have been perfectly honest in saying, at first, "the destruction of life and limb was almost unprecedented." They were facing what amounted to battlefield scenes. Under these circumstances, a certain journalistic excess might be excusable, if its honest purpose was to warn readers about the dangers of transportation technology. Of course, that is the defense penny press editors would have immediately given for their immoderation. Bennett of the *Herald* had promised "to give a correct picture of the world—in Wall Street—in the Exchange—in the Police office—at the Theatre—in the Opera—in short, wherever human nature and real life best display their freaks and vagaries." Benjamin H. Day, editor of the *New York Sun*, was even more realistic: "We newspaper people thrive best on the calamities of others."[12] But was it necessary to describe in detail all the injuries—"Wm. Bridges. His injuries consist of a wound in the side, the mashing of his right arm. . . . . Harriet Burleigh, an aged colored woman, had one of her legs horribly mangled by a splinter . . . a gentleman passenger from the West, whose name we did not obtain, had one hand mashed"—while spending only one sentence on the probable cause: "the train was thrown off the track by the misplacement of the switch by some person unknown." [13] Or, if three lines about an entire accident is all the space that can be spared, must they read, "A powder mill in Spencer, Mass. blew up yesterday afternoon, and Wm. Bixby, one of the workmen, was torn in pieces"? [14]

From 1855 to 1860, the samples drawn from the *Times* show the same pattern: accidents and assaults on the front page, with sensational details, the items often imported from outside New York City.

> Ormsbee took out a pistol and shot him, mutilating his face terribly.
> [from Cincinnati, January 16, 1855]

> Bloody Work at Sebastopol
> [from Liverpool, England, April 23, 1855]

> Portions of the body of a colored woman were discovered today. . . . It is supposed she was butchered by her husband.
> [from New Haven, October 11, 1855]

> Railroad passengers frozen. . . . the poor fellow suffered intense pain. The passengers have terrible stories.
> [from Cleveland, January 16, 1856]

> Insurrection of the Negroes—Dreadful Butchery
> [from Venezuela, July 16, 1859]

> The Slaughter of Senator Broderick
> [from Cincinnati, October 11, 1859]

Now let us consider at more length the *New York Times*'s coverage of some particularly stunning American disasters, beginning with the Johnstown flood of June 1889. We should be slow to accuse the *Times* of sensationalizing its reportage on Johnstown, because the disaster was in fact spectacular. The Chicago fire of 1871 was a great conflagration, but there were relatively few deaths. The Johnstown flood caused the devastation of both the city and its citizens. When the *Times* first headlined the event on June 1, 1889, as "A Waterspout's Dreadful Work in Pennsylvania . . . A Lake on the Neighboring Hills Bursts its Barriers and Sweeps Everything Before it," that was no exaggeration.

The coverage for the first two days was generally factual and sober. The paper noted calmly the unavoidable facts: how many bodies were seen floating downstream, and how many had piled up with the flood debris. There were anecdotes of individual survivors and victims, but they tended to be written with verbs rather than adjectives—that is, the emphasis was on what happened, not on what people looked like or how they felt. There are a few reminders of 1850s-style reportage on June 2 ("the coffin factories of this city are working as they never worked before"; "clinging to the debris were men, women, and children shrieking for aid"; "the most awful culmination of the awful night was the roasting of a hundred or more persons in mid flood"), but straight reporting was more typical.

On the third and fourth days of coverage, the adjectives and the "piteous" scenes increased:

> The Hungarians were out for plunder. . . . when a bloody finger of an infant, encircled with two tiny gold rings, was found among the plunder in the leader's pocket, the cry went up "Lynch them!" [15]

> A sad feature was when Joseph Smith, a man of extraordinary size and strength entered . . . he went from corpse to corpse, lifting the stained and muddy coverings of the dead. At last he came . . . to his daughter. . . . and then with a voice of the most unutterable agony cried: My Maggie, my little Maggie!

> In one case a couple were found locked in each other's arms.

On June 4, a *Times* reporter managed to find a happy story. In the Church of the Immaculate Conception, which had been completely flooded, a statue of the Blessed Virgin Mary was found "unsullied as the day it was made. The flowers, the wreaths, the lace veil, were undisturbed and unsoiled. . . . The miracle has caused a tremendous sensation." On June 5, 1889, the last day of full coverage of the flood on the front page, a reporter unsoberly declared, "The town is one vast charnel house!" Details had to do with the estimates of the number dead and the disposition of the decomposing bodies.

What we see in the *Times*'s coverage of the Johnstown flood in 1889, I believe, is a newspaper considering emotional restraint. Perhaps the reporters simply lacked enough gory details at first to write "interesting" stories, but the reportage the first two days almost sounded like a modern voice speaking matter-of-fact, declarative sentences.

It is Michael Schudson's judgment that the *Times* established its modern voice by 1896, when Adolph Ochs took over the paper. Ochs announced his policies on August 19, 1896: he would publish "a high-standard newspaper, clean, dignified and trustworthy . . . in language that is parliamentary in good society." [16] Let us see, by sampling coverage of minor disasters in 1904, whether Ochs followed that pledge. On January 4, a box to the left of the newspaper's name on the top of the front page declared that the reader would find "All the News That's Fit to Print," but the bottom half of the front page was filled with little dramas. "Car Rolls Down Mountain" was a legitimate story of a train accident near Baltimore; but it also contained the detail that "An unknown woman was so wedged in the wreckage that her dead body is unrecognizable." Next to that was a story from Paris: "Alleged Hypnotic Murder." At the top of the front page was a story about an explosion at a New Jersey inn. If the word "explosion" did not attract the reader's attention, perhaps the sub-headlines did: "500 Dancers in Panic and Men Trample on Women to Escape. Lightly Clad Merrymakers Rush from Wrecked Building Into Heavy Snowstorm at Keasbey." On

March 7, 1904, the *Times* told on the front page about a "Woman Danced to Death"; Mrs. Joseph Sailer of St. Louis, who had just won the first prize and was one of the "most conspicuous characters on the floor . . . suddenly threw up her hands and sank to the floor dead from heart disease." Below that was the story "Greenwich Girl Elopes . . . Friend of the Carnegies," and next to that was an item from Philadelphia—"Scalded Friend to Death," about two men playing in a Turkish bath. On September 20, 1904, news fit to print on the front page included "Slept on Ledge in Midair. Passer-by Shuddered at Window Cleaner Eighteen Stories Up," and the less humorous story, "Dream of Tragedy Came True. Aunt Says She Had a Vision of Her Nephew's Suicide. . . . her dream was fulfilled in almost every detail." Ochs's *Times* may have started using a modern voice in 1896, but it was a voice still willing to speak sensationally.

The burning, explosion, and grounding of the *General Slocum* near New York City on June 15, 1904, presented the *Times* with its greatest disaster to report. The paper gave more coverage to the burning of the *Slocum*—almost five complete pages on June 16—than to any other tragedy in its fifty-year history. "The disaster stands unparalleled," it declared. Most of the one thousand dead were women and children who had taken an excursion trip sponsored by St. Mark's Evangelical Lutheran German Church. The description of events and emotions was both matter-of-fact and ghastly. As the reporters simply told about the "pathetic incidents" they saw, sensationalism was beside the point. Scenes "have seared themselves in the brains of the survivors never to be effaced," the reporter wrote at the beginning of the story. Columns of the story were set aside for "Tales of Horror Told by Survivors." Several men's heroism—and one's "absolute callousness"—was frequently mentioned, as was the shrieking and hysteria of women and children. One witness said, "the band kept on playing in an effort to quiet the people." Another blamed the crew for "neglecting to prevent a panic"; he condemned their "mad desire to escape themselves." Those looking for the bodies of loved ones were "a mad excited crowd, frenzied with grief, to a point that meant self-destruction if unrestrained." There was "pathos" at the police station—one man who came to identify relatives "lost his reason entirely," and another man's stammering returned "because of the fright he had been subjected to. He was forced to write what he had to say." It was noted that two husbands, when they found out their families were dead, killed themselves. On the last page of coverage, after the names of the dead, the *Times* presented a history of "Disasters Similar to the Slocum Horror." An editorial called the event, in "sad literalness . . . a holocaust." In the end, two things are striking about the first day's coverage, which was nearly all words and no pictures: its emphasis on the emotional chaos that attended the disaster and the relative lack of graphic detail about injuries that were suffered.

Now let us sample the paper again for minor disasters in 1913. The *Times* still offered dollops of sensationalism on the front page, as it had in 1904. On March 22, 1913, in Seneca Falls a crash killed a "Man and Girl . . . Haist was crushed to death, but Miss Voorhees was drowned. Miss Freeman was rescued just as she was about to give up the fight to keep her head above water." The front-page stories beneath the fold on June 6, 1913, include the following: "Weds Man Who Hurt Her"; "Skirt

Wrecks Aeroplane"; "Bees Infest a Church"; "Shoots at His Wife"; and perhaps the story of greatest moment, "Police Eye Split Skirts. Indianapolis Women Mustn't Wear Them Without Undergarments," said the sub- headline. The front page of September 2, 1913, kept up on the issue of the split skirt: "Cries Down Split Skirts. True Women Will Not Wear Them, Says Bishop Luther B. Wilson." The front page also told of what might happen to women inclined to wear split skirts and the like:

> Mob a Woman Bather. Mrs. Lanning Beset by 200 Men at Atlantic City. . . . handled roughly by rowdies on the beach. . . . She wore a bright purple bathing suit with a short skirt which was slit on either side from the hem to the waist. She had been on the beach but a short time when some excursionists saw her and began to throw handfuls of sand at her. In a moment she was surrounded by some 200 men. The life guards . . . formed a flying wedge and broke through the mob.

The samples of coverage from 1913, like those of 1904, suggest that Ochs's *Times* does not yet have a consistently "dignified" voice in its coverage of minor disasters. Reporting on the major disasters, however, has a certain gravity.

The sinking of the *Empress of Ireland* on May 29, 1914, provides us with another checkpoint to see how a major disaster is covered. The British ocean liner had collided with the *Storstad* while steaming on the St. Lawrence River in a fog. More than a thousand passengers and crew were killed. The *Times*'s main coverage was an epilogue to the accident. First, in its front- page sub-headlines, the paper testified to the passengers' emotional self-control: "Faces Show Little Fear. The Dead Seem to Have Met Their Fate Bravely," said one column; of the commanding officer, another column said, "No Panic After Crash." Then the paper offered what we have seen before—a kind of reportorial gawking—and also a good deal of class-conscious, heroic melodrama:

> Photographs of the faces of the dead were taken by railway photographers at Rimouski today to aid in the work of identification, which is expected to be difficult in many cases. . . . the sight was heartrending. Many of the dead stared heavenward with wide-open eyes, some with horror in them, and others with an air of puzzled surprise. There was but little attempt to cover the corpses, and for the most part they lay practically as they had been taken out of the water, some half dressed and others nearly naked. . . . There is among the dead the body of a well-dressed woman, on whose fingers there are diamonds. . . . The mother who held the body of her dead child to her breast wore a gold chain bearing a gold cross.

More prominent on the front page, however, was the stirring account of how Laurence Irving, "the actor," had died with his wife "in unflinching courage":

> When the collision occurred, Mr. Irving and his wife, Mabel Hackney, rushed on deck, scantily clad. The ship settled down in the water, and a wave swept across the deck. Mr. Irving clasped his wife in his arms in an endeavor to save her, but the two were swept overboard. There was one fleeting glimpse of them, arms entwined, before they sank.

In another version of the story, passenger F. E. Abbott testified that Irving "calmly" asked him, "Is the boat going down?" Then Irving told his frightened wife, "Keep cool." When Abbott asked if he could help the couple, Irving replied, "Look after yourself first, old man; but God bless you all the same." The last time Abbott saw Irving, "He was kissing his wife. And as the ship went down, they were clasped in each other's arms." What the reporter no doubt had in mind was the mythic heroism of the *Titanic* disaster.

If it can be said that the *Times* had moved somewhat in the direction of modernity in disaster reporting since the 1850s—toward more information than story, more sobriety than empathy, more discretion than gore—then it must be said there was backsliding on July 26, 1915, when the newspaper reported on the capsizing of the *Eastland* in the Chicago River. The excursion steamer tipped over into the water at its pier because of faulty loading of the ballast and the overloading of 2,500 passengers. Like the Johnstown flood, it was a dreadful event, and even a modern editor would ask a reporter for details that would bring that reality home. But the details in Chicago were not handled modernly.

The headline asserted that "1,800 Drown." The *Times* figured that this made the *Eastland* accident the deadliest ship disaster ever, but a later count showed there were less than half that many deaths. It was a kind of statistical sensationalism, and there were other examples of excess. Prominent at the top of the front page of the Sunday paper was the story "Scenes Drive Diver Mad": "A city diver engaged in the work of taking bodies from the Eastland became violently insane tonight, after several visits to the hold of the vessel. . . . He discarded his suit, and, raving, started to run across the hull of the boat. He was overcome and placed in a patrol wagon and taken away." Coverage took three full pages and concentrated on personal testimony and "thrilling" stories (the word was used three times): one man's coat was caught on a nail and he was held above the water; a woman held on to her daughter but "with arm benumbed, she finally had to let the daughter go." Henry Vantak, who lost a wife and three children, said, "Someone grabbed me around the neck and kept dragging at me. It was a woman, but I could not save her." The reporter did not ask him whether he tried.

Harlan E. Babcock, a reporter for the *Chicago Herald*, witnessed the capsizing and provided a "graphic narrative" on page 2 that was the epitome of melodrama:

> Solemnly the stretcher bearers walked down the hull of the steamer to the pier with their inanimate burdens of humanity that a brief half hour or hour before had scurried laughing to the death craft. . . . Wild-eyed, half hysterical, and trembling, [a mother] watched every form that was brought up. . . . Finally a tiny bit of clay was brought up to the street. "Oh, maybe that's him!" she moaned. Before they could prevent her she had snatched the blanket away from the cold, white face of the child. Yes, it was her baby. They lifted her up with the little body clutched in her arms, but she knew nothing of what was transpiring. She had swooned, but she had her baby, at last.

Elsewhere in the paper the most vivid—better said, morbid—details were provided: "By pinching the throat of each victim with his fingers the physician determined how he had met death—whether by drowning or suffocating." Reporters did not resist metaphors—"Wee infants floated about like corks" (that was also a subheadline), and "When the boat toppled on its side those on the upper deck were hurled off like so many ants being brushed from a table."

Gretchen Krohn, "a woman writer of Chicago," provided her writerly observations "Special to the *New York Times*." These went beyond melodrama into the macabre:

> All the bodies carried past were so rigid that poles to carry them by seemed superfluous. ... has it ever been your unhappy lot as a youngster to drown a batch of particularly unwelcome kittens? Or have you ever plunged a wire rat trap into water? Imagine that expression of trapped animal terror transferred to the face of a human being, and then so firmly stamped by death that the pattern has set.... And as I duly counted the bodies it seemed that human beings were killed as easily as flies, after all.

It is not apparent why the coverage of the *General Slocum* disaster was so stylistically different from the *Eastland* stories. Perhaps in this instance the *Times* was mainly a conduit for Chicago reporters and their sensibility. This discrepancy underscores other variations that appear in disaster reporting. We know there are variations from publisher to publisher. As for race and culture, catastrophes that happen thousands of miles away receive notice in the *Times* but they do not preoccupy the paper. This could be evidence of bias, or it might also be a demonstration of the psychological principle that we cannot give every human problem equal emotional treatment. We have seen that minor disasters are treated differently from major disasters; the former stand the chance of being used as a kind of cheap thrill in the paper, while the latter can be presented as tantamount to hell. There might also be regional variations in disaster coverage. The story of disaster stories, in other words, admits of much complexity.

The sinking of the British steamer *Vestris* off the coast of Virginia in a gale on November 12, 1928, provides another checkpoint, albeit smaller, where we find melodrama. There was, apparently, no opportunity here to record the appearance of the dead. Instead, the *Times* printed the contents of the ship's last radio messages. One could say this was both a more objective and a more dramatic journalism. The sub-headlines told readers what to look for in the messages. One column read, "How Ship Begged Aid Recorded by Radio. Frenzied Calls Broadcast at Intervals Until Order to Take to Lifeboats. 'Oh, Please Come!' Was One." Another column read, "Liner Radios Frantic Appeals Before Final 'Good-Bye.' " In addition to the original data the paper provided, another indication of its growing modernity was a story at the conclusion of the coverage titled "Sea Disasters Recalled." Here were brief, factual descriptions of thirteen sinkings going back to 1841. This was the first time the paper had offered its readers a historical perspective on the event.

For the last random sample of minor disasters, let us look at reportage from one week in May 1931. All the accidents have been moved to the inside of the paper; there are no more spurts of sensation on the front page. There is still emotion-laden scandal—"Dancer Kills Wife in Lawyer's Office" (May 3, 1931, p. 3); "Ends Life, Killing Her Son" (May 4, p. 14); "Slays Wife, Self After Bank Theft" (May 5, p. 25)— but the graphic details have been suppressed and there is no reportorial gawking. On May 6, an Armenian earthquake was reported that killed almost five hundred and injured more than eleven thousand. The story was placed on page 6. Its few details tried to convey the human impact of the disaster: "It was a strange scene—groups of men, women and children hunched over the few belongings they had managed to salvage, incredibly terrified." But the story essentially distanced itself from the reader. The numbers of horses, cattle, sheep, and goats killed were given right after the human casualties were counted. On May 3, 1931, the *Times* published a story on accident statistics, as it had on June 11, 1853, but in this case the type of conveyance and the tone were different: "258 Deaths, One to Each 219,000 Miles Flown. . . . Only two persons were killed in scheduled air services during the six months, both in the same accident. This gave a new safety mark for American air operations." The *Times* was making a transition, and so was the country. From Victorian "passion" before the Civil War, the newspaper had moved to a modern "cool" style after World War I.[17]

Let us check two more major disasters to confirm this change. The cruise liner *Morro Castle* burned off the coast of Asbury Park, New Jersey, on September 8, 1934. The *Times*'s coverage now looked quite professional. The details of the disaster were told, a map and an entire page of photographs were furnished, all the passengers were listed, poignant or penetrating observations were made, and stories were collected from survivors. The estimated number of casualties was handled carefully— "200 to 250 Are Listed as Dead or Missing" (the final death toll was 134). The participants' emotions were also covered. It was "a story of heroism and panic," the paper's opening paragraph said. There were "Frantic Efforts to Flee," "Frightened passengers were crowded aft in the vessel," "women were weeping and praying," and "men and more courageous women" banded together to sing songs to "bolster the courage of the rest." On shore, "Throngs at Piers Wait Anxiously," there are "Some Joyful Reunions," and "Others Cling to Slender Hope."

Note that the descriptions of emotion include gender distinctions. It is assumed that women will be frightened or panicky, but they will be praised for bravery as they sacrifice for their children. But gender rules could be deactivated too—stewards blamed part of the death toll on women who were too "modest" and "waited in their cabins to dress." Also, "Reluctant Women" were "Pushed Overboard or into Boats." Some women were stronger swimmers than their husbands and watched them drown. Men, especially the ship's crew, are expected to be brave in the first place, and their manliness is ruined if they are cowardly or hesitant or lose their self-control.

The *Times* was now detached enough in its reporting to notice ironies and coincidences. A New York insurance broker had cancelled his reservation at the last minute. A father and his sons are sleeping in separate places and thus do not know that the mother is dead; they will be told in the morning. But the coverage is not so detached that it does not mention injuries: "Men came by, dragging burned friends or wives whose screeches of pain chilled the hearts"; rowers' hands were "lacerated and blistered." What is pertinent for us about the *Morro Castle,* however, is not only the thoroughness of the reporting but what is missing from it. Emotions are surely brought out, but nothing particularly gruesome or hideous is stared at. The photographs of the rescued passengers show them all cheerful and relieved; only one man is labeled "dazed."

The collision of the *Andrea Doria* and the *Stockholm* forty-five miles off Nantucket Island on July 26, 1956, shows how disaster coverage had fully evolved at the *Times.* Photographs show both ships before and after the accident, and then the *Andrea*

Doria taking its "final plunge." The issue of July 26 transcribes the final radio messages, gives background data on both vessels, and surveys experts on the causes of the accident. Each reporter is identified by name, which was not done for the *Slocum* and *Eastland* coverage. There is the usual article on the history of ship disasters, but this time Chinese and Japanese sinkings are given their due seriousness. The *Times,* always a paper for the "better portion of our people," showed pictures of the "Notables" who were aboard, and safe.

The second day's coverage on July 27, 1956, is even more thorough. Final figures show that there are 1,117 survivors from the *Andrea Doria*—7 dead, 52 missing, and 1,652 saved altogether from both ships. Stories are collected and told: "Passengers Tell of Fear in Night," but "Survivors Also Recount Heroism." "Frightened women and children wept," but "there was no mass panic." Finally, I find two especially modern items in this coverage. First, the paper noted that some passengers had immediately filed a formal complaint charging that there had been "abhorrent disregard" for safety procedures. Second, considerable space was given to announcing that "Federal and City Officials Relax Regulations to Help Collision Survivors Enter U.S."

As for the dead, they are simply . . . dead.

How do these findings match up with my observations at the beginning? My son was right to observe the significance of the television reporter's lack of affect. This is the modern "cool" style, clearly. There can be a current of sympathy in the anchorman's voice (indeed, there must be, but not too much), and he may even open with the remark, "Sad news in the mid-state today." But he or she is a professional, not a penny press reporter. Sentimental stories are usually presented, and excused, as sentimentalist, and melodrama is mocked as melodramatic. Straight news is delivered straight, if not flat. When Walter Cronkite announced on television that President John Kennedy was dead, he turned his head slightly sideways, adjusted his eyeglasses a little, and then went back to work. We could tell how he felt, and that was enough.

The easiest way to tell the difference between a modern, informative, "cool" journalist and his storytelling, passionate ancestor is to look at their vocabularies. Modern journalism simply does not use the words "pathos," "heartrending," "melancholy," "or "piteous," just as religious phraseology is no longer present. *Times* reporters no longer mention the jewelry corpses wear, or describe victims as "mangled" or "torn to pieces." Bodies and body parts are usually "remains" nowadays. Indeed, it would be interesting to run a search to see when that euphemism took over. I think these are not only changes in etiquette; they also signal changes in feeling rules and emotion talk.

As for my own observations, they were partly right. I still think journalistic gore (certainly the particulars of sex crimes) has increased lately. It is also important to note that the emotional evolution of mainstream journalism created a new niche for separate, more emotionally and viscerally engrossing journalistic genres—a new division, twentieth-century-style, between the respectable and the disreputable. But I admit now that the modern newsmagazine does not yet copy the lurid penny press style. I am nearly convinced when two of my journalist friends tell me that modern reporting is not journalistic gore. Professor Peter Parisi of Hunter College, formerly a working reporter, told me that he is impressed with what he calls the relative "chastity" of journalists. They do not say nearly what they could, Peter told me. Michael Barber is a reporter in Seattle who followed the serial killings of Ted Bundy. He insists that the ghastly details of those murders were highly sanitized before the public read them.

Finally, I know I am right to point out the present carnival of disaster films and videos. But I did not realize until I finished my research how successfully disaster was commercialized in the past. John Kasson has described the restaging of disasters at Coney Island at the turn of the century. The great amusement park re-created Pompeii's destruction by Vesuvius, the Galveston flood of 1890, and the Johnstown flood of 1889. Thousands of visitors each day watched "Fire and Flames" in the island's Luna Park, which featured firemen dousing the flames in a four-story building and victims jumping into safety nets. Later, "Fighting the Flames" was performed at Dreamland, in a six-story building with two thousand performers, on a stage 250 feet long by 100 feet deep. The crowd was a part of the event. Other historians following Kasson have found that the modern disaster film starts at the turn of the century.

Kasson believes that disaster, "in its very horror . . . conferred a kind of transcendent meaning to its victims' lives," and thus the audience at the re-creation experienced a "horrible delight" at the thought of their own vulnerability and a "vicarious sense of this transcendence."[18] I would not go that far. It sounds like scholarly sensationalism, which is said to be increasing.

NOTES

I want to acknowledge the invaluable detective work as well as clerical labor that my assistant, Renee Jackson, contributed to this project. When I posted a message on H-amstdy, an internet discussion group, asking for help in my research, I was given timely encouragement and more learned advice than I could use by Renee Sentilles, Edward M. Griffin, Lt. Col. Elliott G. Gruner, Tom Chambers, Gert Buelens, Carl Smith, Stuart C. Hobbs, Kenneth D. Pimple, Jay Mechling, Sue Currell, Lynne Adrian, Joseph Heathcott, Andy Grossman, Susan Tornatore, Sarah Chinn, Marc Singer, and Hank Greenspan. From the Journalism History Discussion Group, jhistory, which Peter Parisi put me in touch with, Christopher Harper and Mary A. Hamilton were also helpful.

1. On the concept of "feeling rules" and the management of emotions, see Arlie Russell Hochschild, "Emotion Work, Feeling Rules, and Social Structure," *American Journal of Sociology,* 85 (1979): 551–75. For a discussion of "emotion talk" and general background on the sociology of emotions, see Rom Harre and W. Gerrod Parrott, eds., *The Emotions: Social, Cultural, and Biological Dimensions* (London: Sage, 1996), especially the essay by Paul Heelas, "Emotion Talk across Cultures," 171–99. An excellent introduction for historians is Peter N. Stearns, with Carol Stearns, "Emotionology: Clarifying the History of Emotions and Emotional Standards," *American Historical Review* 90 (October 1985): 813–36. John F. Kasson uses "feeling rules" in *Rudeness and Civility: Manners in Nineteenth-Century Urban America* (New York: Hill and Wang, 1990), esp. chap. 5, "Emotional Control."

2. As for modern newspapers, our common sense tells us that they emphasize disaster coverage out of proportion to straight news, and now social science research backs that up. See Eleanor Singer and Phyllis M. Endreny, *Reporting on Risk: How the Mass Media Portray Accidents, Diseases, Disasters, and Other Hazards* (New York: Russell Sage Foundation, 1993), esp. chap. 3.

3. Ellery Sedgwick, "The Land of Disasters, 1853–1904," *Leslie's Monthly Magazine,* January 1905, 350–51.

4. Sedgwick, "Charting the Land of Disasters," *Leslie's Monthly Magazine,* March 1905, 469; idem, "The Case for the People," *Leslie's Monthly Magazine,* April 1905, 711.

5. This disaster has recently received its complete history. See Gene Salecker, *Disaster on the Mississippi: The Sultana Explosion, April 27, 1865* (Annapolis: Naval Institute Press, 1996); and Jerry O. Potter, *The Sultana Tragedy: America's Greatest Maritime Disaster* (Gretna, LA: Pelican, 1992).

6. See William Peirce Randel, "The Flames of Hell Gate," *American Heritage* 30 (October–November 1979): 62–75.

7. For information on disasters that occurred between 1853 and 1909, see Stuart Flexner, with Doris Flexner, *The Pessimist's Guide to History* (New York: Avon, 1992). As a professional historian, I was chagrined to find that the most comprehensive and best-organized history of disasters was this "entertaining" paperback. See also Jeremy Kingston and David Lambert, *Catastrophe and Crisis* (New York: Facts on File, 1979). Summary information on mining disasters came from the U.S. Department of Labor, Mine Safety and Health Administration, MSHA Fact Sheet no. 95–8.

8. Elmer Davis, *History of the New York Times, 1851–1921* (1921; reprint, New York: Greenwood, 1969), 6–9, 19–21.

9. Quoted in Meyer Berger, *The Story of the New York Times* (1951; reprint, New York: Arno Press, 1970), 16.

10. For more on the penny press in New York and the characteristics of sensationalism, see James L. Crouthamel, *Bennett's New York Herald and the Rise of the Popular Press* (Syracuse: Syracuse University Press, 1989), 24–26; Dan Schiller, *Objectivity and the News: The Public and the Rise of Commercial Journalism* (Philadelphia: University of Pennsylvania Press, 1981), chap. 2; *Journalism History* 12 (autumn–winter 1985), Special Issue on Sensationalism; Hans Bergmann, *God in the Street: New York Writing from the Penny Press to Melville* (Philadelphia: Temple University Press, 1995); Hazel Dicken- Garcia, *Journalistic Standards in Nineteenth-Century America* (Madison: University of Wisconsin Press, 1989), 82–96, 202–5; John D. Stephens, *Sensationalism and the New York Press* (New York: Columbia University Press, 1991); Edwin Emery, *The Press and America: An Interpretive History of Journalism,* 2d ed. (Englewood Cliffs, NJ: Prentice Hall, 1962), chaps. 11, 19; and Frank Luther Mott's familiar tome, *American Journalism: A History: 1690–1960,* 3d ed. (New York: Macmillan, 1962), chap. 13 and p. 442, where Mott speaks of sensationalism as reportage that stimulates "unwholesome emotional responses" and adds that "Anything which answers to fundamental and primitive human desires can belong to no single period." Most useful as a survey and most convincing to me was Michael Schudson, *Discovering the News: A Social History of American Newspapers* (New York: Basic Books, 1978), which describes sensationalism as "the chief development in newspaper content" (5) in the nineteenth century; he describes the rise of the *New York Times* as a paper that develops the "information model" over the "story model."

11. David S. Reynolds, *Beneath the American Renaissance: The Subversive Imagination in the Age of Emerson and Melville* (New York: Knopf, 1988), 171. An excellent cultural history of the meaning of urban disasters in the late nineteenth century is Carl Smith, *Urban Disorder and the Shape of Belief: The Great Chicago Fire, the Haymarket Bomb, and the Model Town of Pullman* (Chicago: University of Chicago Press, 1995).

12. Bennett and Day are quoted in Crouthamel, 24–25.

13. *New-York Daily Times,* July 10, 1856, 1.

14. *New-York Daily Times,* July 17, 1854, 1.

15. David McCullough, in *The Johnstown Flood* (New York: Simon and Schuster, 1968), finds that "there was scarcely any truth" to these stories of Hungarian looters. He also points out that the *Times* coverage was more cautious than that of most eastern newspapers, which went "heavy on the horrors," publishing "distortions, exaggerations, and outright nonsense." See especially chap. 8, "No Pen Can Describe."

16. See Schudson, especially his comparison of the *World* and the more conservative *Times,* in chap. 3, "Stories and Information: Two Journalisms in the 1890s."

17. See Peter N. Stearns, *American Cool: Constructing a Twentieth-Century Emotional Style* (New

York: New York University Press, 1994), esp. chap. 2, "The Victorian Style." Stearns speaks of a Victorian emotional culture that emerged in the 1840s and yielded in the 1920s to a modern emotional culture. Those are the same dates that this research finds effective.

18. John F. Kasson, *Amusing the Million: Coney Island at the Turn of the Century* (New York: Hill and Wang, 1978), 71–72. See also Andrea Stulman Dennett and Nina Warnke, "Disaster Spectacles at the Turn of the Century," *Film History* 4 (1990): 101–11 for the history of early disaster films.

Chapter Nine

Creating the Emotional Body
Confusion, Possibilities, and Knowledge

Otniel E. Dror

The relationship between emotions and bodies has a long and rich history in Western tradition, stretching back to the early pre-Socratic philosophers, the Hippocratic treatises, and the early biblical texts.[1] Yet, as ancient as this tradition is, and as apparent as the power of emotions seems to be, it was only during the closing decades of the nineteenth century that physiologists (and psychologists) systematically introduced emotions into the new *arrivés*—the physiological and psychological laboratories.[2] Here, the physiologist and psychologist applied their new experimental methods and instruments to emotions: generating, releasing, inducing, amplifying, curtailing, prolonging, purifying, measuring, quantifying, temporizing, tracing, identifying, purging—controlling and manipulating the phenomenon called emotion. Their travails made emotions an object of the laboratory, one more biological life process among others.

It was in the early 1880s, when the Italian physiologist Angelo Mosso began his laboratory investigations of emotions, that the beginnings of a systematic and modern program of laboratory-based physiological investigation of emotions can be identified.[3] His work emphasized the measurable, recordable, and quantifiable physiological effects of emotions: he recorded and calculated the exact temperature fluctuations in the bodies of his laboratory animals that were due solely to their emotions; reported that his own thermometer-measured rectal temperature changed with his spontaneously evoked emotions (by 0.7 degrees centigrade); and designed specific laboratory manipulations and instrumentation for determining the exact effects of emotions on the circulation.

Preceding Mosso's systematic program of researches on emotions were the early laboratory observations of Claude Bernard, who had applied Marey's new cardiograph to trace the heart during emotion (1865).[4] By translating the heart's "intimate functions" into omnipresent and permanent graphs on paper, Bernard literally "read in the human heart."[5] The slightest sincere emotion, he explained, produced a reflex impression in the heart, "imperceptible to all, but for the physiologist" and his instrument.[6] The heart, Bernard proclaimed, "betray[ed]" the body.[7] Following in Bernard's footsteps was the Russian physiologist M. E. Cyon (1873). The heart, he concurred, was both a mechanical pump and a "mirror" of the spirit.[8] Each emotion immediately, reflexively, and involuntarily activated the heart. Each emotion left its own "peculiar and characteristic" curve on the graphic paper issued forth by the physiologist's new machine.[9] The new physiological instruments could now just as well serve psychological ends. In the organ of the heart, physiology was psychology.

The rise of these nineteenth-century laboratory-centered physiological investigations of emotions marks the departure point of our essay. At first sporadic, isolated, and centered in European laboratories, these investigations soon proliferated and during the course of the twentieth century shifted significantly to the United States. One of the important developments that the early nineteenth-century European physiologists signaled was the impending twentieth-century reversal of what Peter Stearns has characterized as the Victorian "spiritualizing of key emotions"—their "fascination with emotional fervor," on the one hand, and their "bent on disciplining the body through demanding clothing, posture requirements, and sexual constraints," on the other hand.[10] During the twentieth century the Victorian penchant to disembody emotions, to make emotions "more abstract," would be rejected as emotions were *re*-embodied. By the early twentieth century an emotion was, for the physiologist, a concrete set of rapid bodily changes, a dynamic materialization of multiple and fleeting body states, or, as one author explained in the *Reader's Digest,* an internal bodily "explosion."[11] For the moderns the body was inseparable from emotion.

The embodiment of emotions and the emotionalization of the body were implicated in a wide and comprehensive reconceptualization that went beyond the laboratory, the clinic, or the body proper. In this essay we will attempt to characterize some aspects of this larger and emergent twentieth-century emotional perspective. Instead of a narrative that emphasizes evolution over time, we will examine numerous case studies that exemplify the new possibilities and the emerging tensions surrounding this novel re-emotionalized body.[12] William James's famous late nineteenth-century essays on emotion exemplify one of these tensions. Although in the first of his essays on emotions (1884) he had argued for the organic basis of *all* emotions, James, under the sway of his critics, retreated in 1890 to a classification that clearly distinguished between the "coarse"—organically based—emotions on the one hand, and the "subtler"—nonorganically based—emotions on the other hand.[13] The challenge to Victorian conceptions of the body and to their canon of knowledge is one of our themes.

For the moderns the body was in very important ways an emotional phenomenon. Physiologists, psychologists, and clinicians of the late nineteenth and twentieth centuries discovered that the material body under examination was an effect of the immediate and local emotions produced, so to speak, on site. The manipulations of the examination; the emotional ambiance of the clinic, hospital, or laboratory; the emotional relationships between examiner and examinee; and the capricious nature of emotions all literally reconfigured the body from one moment of the examination to the next, or from one examination to the following one. With each emotion, the body would shift and flow, alternating between numerous material possibilities. In the eyes of these investigators, these multiple and fleeting substantiations of the body were proof of the embodiment of emotions. For the Victorians, emotions "came from the spirit." [14] For the moderns, these new discoveries about the nature of the body—as continuously in motion—raised the specter of a nonstandardizable, non-normalizable, and uncontrollable body, and challenged the project of modernity. [15] Troubled by this specter, experimenters and clinicians developed a science and an art of emotional manipulation, whose goal was to fixate and congeal the body's flowing interiors. The theme that united the various emotional technologies proposed by these protagonists was the de-emotionalized body. Once de-emotionalized, the protagonists argued, the individual's body would remain stable through time—could be standardized, normalized, and replicated universally—and made into an object of scientific knowledge.

In its new guise as a psychological entity, the body would serve as a window into the "spirit"—the body could now speak its mind. The transparency of the individual's emotional interiors, visible by means of the new emotion-gauging technologies, would prompt a call by some for the resurrection of the Rousseauite dream of a transparent society—a society of Truth. This transparent body would also reflect, in a very concrete and recordable manner, the ethereal emotional networks and fields that implicated and contained individuals. Physiologists, psychologists, and clinicians ventured with their body-gauging technologies into the public domain and discovered that emotions permeated the world. On the physical (and social) nature of the world they superimposed a rich and variegated emotional dimension, a dimension that was visible in, and through the mediation of, the material body. These moderns could now carve up the physical world into a dense mosaic of emotional spaces. This reconceptualization of spaces, instruments, manipulations, and even their own material bodies—as emotional rather than physical entities—marginalized the physical nature of the world. An emotional perspective had emerged.

We will begin our examination of this new emotional body, its larger cultural context, and the emergence of an emotional perspective by focusing on what Foucault called "the procedures that constitute the individual as effect and object of power"—the examination. [16] But contrary to Foucault, who emphasized its discipline and knowledge, we will emphasize its confusion and emotions.

Multiple Possibilities of the Body

In the late 1880s Dr. Morton Prince, a physician for nervous diseases at the Boston City Hospital, presented a paper on the incidence of "mitral" heart murmurs in routine medical examinations of job applicants. [17] The high incidence (twenty-six out of seventy-seven) of this supposedly pathological finding in young and presumably healthy men raised serious questions for the clinician. How did these signs of organic heart disease come to inhabit the bodies of the young, healthy, and strong? To the consternation of some of the attending physicians, Prince argued that the murmur was not pathological at all, but was a "normal," "functional" product of the encounter between Prince, the physician, and his medical clientele. [18] The murmur, Prince contended, literally materialized in bodies during his examinations, and vanished as the physician-applicant encounter dissolved. [19] The physical liaison between physician and patient, that quintessential element of modern medical practice writ large, directly induced the seepage of blood through the cardiac valves, audible as a murmur.[20] The physicians attending Prince's presentation had varied opinions on that score. Some concurred with Prince, and reported an occasional encounter with the murmur; others retorted that they had only rarely found a body with a "mitral" murmur. One physician observed that bodies examined as part of a job or life insurance application were rich in murmurs. Another rejoined that in the hospital, or in the outpatient department, the body rarely murmured. Prince noted that since he had begun to record systematically his preliminary impressions, the frequency of the murmur had more than doubled. Perhaps the activity involved in transforming first impressions into aggregated and reliable knowledge created murmuring hearts, he implied. Dr. E. G. Cutler suggested that the absence of the murmur in the setting of the outpatient department was because the patients "don't fear some accidental thing that may throw them out from making a living."[21] And Prince reflected that perhaps "my business-like way [in tabulating the data] made it an ordeal for the subjects" and was responsible for the murmur.[22]

As their discussion unfolded, and as each of the participants contributed from his own local clinical knowledge, a collective and conflicting set of bodies seemed to emerge. Instead of *a* body, each physician experienced a different set of bodies. The difference between these conflicting sets of bodies, they agreed, depended on the "conditions" and "circumstances" of the medical examination. And, they further assented, the discrepant reports would all harmonize if one adopted Prince's original suggestion and interpreted the murmur as the embodiment of the examinees' emotional excitement, if the medical encounter was reconceived from its emotional perspective—as an emotional encounter. The conundrum of the members of the Boston Society for Medical Improvement was resolved. The sudden and capricious materialization of "phantom" heart murmurs was the pure and simple effect of the mechanics of emotionally excited bodies.[23] The murmur was an effect of the power of emotion.

In the 1930s, the massive routine screening of young and healthy military recruits evinced and gave the force of numbers to this early pointed discussion of "phantom" heart murmurs, materialized excitement, and the multiple possibilities of the body. The "emotional factor on first examination" of military recruits elevated their blood pressures. These "phantom" elevated blood pressures materialized in the bodies of the new recruit, and vanished on subsequent medical examinations. As one physician explained, "the Royal Air Force Board in recent years . . . practically disregard[s] this figure in young candidates for the Service."[24] Or as another physician put it, criticizing the "present degree of prejudice" of American actuarial figures, these elevated blood pressures were merely the product of "transient emotion."[25] They were not true manifestations of the clinically relevant body. The true body, these British physicians implied, was absent on "first" examinations. The physician would have to wait for a subsequent examination, for only then would *the* body of the recruit materialize and appear in its normal (i.e., unemotional) guise. Or alternatively, as some proposed, the physician could take ten consecutive blood pressure readings in those cases where the blood pressure of new recruits was "found to be abnormal."[26]

Experience had shown that the physician would encounter a different body with the mere repetition of the examination. The repetitive manipulation rid the body of its "phantom" high blood pressure. This alternative method obviated the need to wait for a future examination and accelerated the process of de-emotionalization.

The medical encounter was ostensibly between the physician and only one of the various possible bodies of the examinee. As Armstrong, summarizing his discussion, proclaimed, each aspect of the medical examination was accompanied by a different emotion.[27] The final body facing the physician would depend on the sum total of these diverse emotions—on the emotionally situated self/body. The individual body of the recruit (e.g., his blood pressure) was literally constituted as the "effect . . . of power."[28] Emotional power. Or as Walter Alvarez observed in 1915, "I frequently find sugar in the urines of nervous people on their first visit to the office and then only."[29] The bodies of ("nervous") people were different during "first visits" to the physician's office. The physician would necessarily schedule a second patient-physician encounter—expecting that the patient's body would then de-emotionalize and reveal its true self.

During the first five decades of the twentieth century these "phantom" changes in emotional bodies would constitute a vast collection of body possibilities. Measurable changes during emotion would be observed in body temperature, blood pressure, white and red blood cell counts, clotting times, gastric secretions, intestinal motility, gastric motility, bladder motility, levels of enzymes, thyroid functions, visual acuity, pupil size, perspiration, spleen size, blood acidity, caliber of airways, adrenaline levels, blood sugar levels, blood fat levels, metabolic rates, bile secretion, muscle tension, voice tremor, somatic reflexes, saliva secretions, nose secretions, blood flow in the gastric mucosa, various endocrine "glands" (pituitary, parathyroid, and sex glands), respiration, and heart rate.[30] As one physician explained in the *Ladies' Home Journal,* "the whole body changes with every emotional wave."[31]

Rejecting the Victorian Body

It is during these early decades of the twentieth century that we find the somewhat paradoxical denunciation of the Victorians for their neglect of emotions. If the body was emotional, as these moderns perceived, then the current tables, figures, and facts—the known body created during the Victorian era—were wrong. The quantified, canonical, textbook bodies had been formulated by an emotion-oblivious physiology. M. Dresbach, for example, published in 1910 his series of blood pressure measurements in sheep. He had discovered that his own values for sheep blood pressures were lower than the canonical, textbook figures for "normal" sheep blood pressures. A sheep, he explained, became emotionally excited during its encounter with the human experimenter. This excitement was produced exactly at the moment of measurement and deflected its blood pressure from its true value.[32] Dresbach had succeeded in circumventing this excitement and had procured the real, correct reading of the body—the new body. Other physiologists reported similar observations on the values of the "normal."[33] Adopting an iconoclastic stance, these new emotio-physiologists rejected the Victorian body of knowledge. The Victorians, they argued, had mistaken the emotionally excited organism, the transient and "phantom" body, for its truer, real self. As one prominent emotio-physiologist declared, "all the early determinations of the 'normal' content of sugar in blood which has been drawn from an artery or vein in the absence of anesthesia, are of very doubtful value."[34] The normal was the de-emotionalized, "anesthetized" body.[35]

"The Psyche of the Physician Works on the Soma of the Patient"

In the clinical setting, where the physician could not pharmacologically anesthetize the patient during each examination, alternative formulas for de-emotionalizing were suggested. Some clinicians attempted to formalize the physician-patient interaction, in what might be called an emotional etiquette.[36] This was a standard of conduct whose sole purpose was to de-emotionalize the patient, so that his body would conform to its "normal" state, its emotionally "indifferent" configuration. This emotional etiquette was only one of a series of emotional technologies. As Dr. Esther M. Greisheimer explained, "if the patient is afraid or is antagonistic toward the observer, the [blood] pressure will be increased. Thus, one should avoid emotional stress when blood pressure determinations are being made. In order to rule out fear, the method of taking the blood pressure should be explained briefly to one who is unused to the process."[37] The patient-physician encounter, it was argued, should include a series of manipulations whose ultimate target was the patient's body. The physician had to create the proper (de-emotionalized) body state.

One could try to incorporate Greisheimer's emphasis on a "humane" interaction into the general interwar development of a clinical humanitarianism. At first glance, this interpretation would be appropriate, and would fit well into recent historiographical arguments on the rise of a humanitarian, patient-centered, holistic approach in clinical medicine during the first several decades of the twentieth century.[38] However, in the context of our analysis, and of Greisheimer's text, this humanitarianism requires a different interpretation. Emotional etiquette should be viewed as a strategic step meant to control the internal confusion and the multiple possibilities created by the (emotional content of the) examination itself. Should the physician stray from this humanitarian prescription, our protagonists argued, she would encounter the emotionally excited body of the patient, not his normal self. The physician's demeanor was, thus, a resource in the hands of the physician—a tool for establishing and maintaining in the patient's body his normal self. It configured the patient's interiors to their measurement-appropriate values.

The emphasis on providing information to the patient should also be viewed within this general framework. Information was not volunteered for the purpose of elucidating, teaching, or enlightening the patient, but rather served as a means of reducing emotional excitement and bringing the body closer to its "normal" state.[39] The physician could thus literally play with the material state of the patient's body: inducing, reducing, affecting both the flow and the final state of numerous interior variables. As Frank Beach somewhat cynically summarized the notion of the psychosomatic relationship, "the psyche of the physician works on the soma of the patient."[40] This was more than a play on words. The "stress interview," one of various emotio-technologies, is an example par excellence of the examiner's role in fashioning the examinee's body through emotion. The "stress interview" was used in the setting of the clinical laboratory for investigating the relationships between "life-situations," emotions, and the body. It is best described by one of its prominent advocates, Dr. Stewart Wolf:

> the pattern was: first of all we would talk for a few minutes with the patient about "ships and shoes and sealing wax, cabbages and kings" and this was the so-called neutral period. Then, the stress period was to bring up for discussion, usually with a question, often with an attitude of not just inquiry, but a touch of skepticism, [the upsetting topic] and then the patient would do most of the talking. I wouldn't talk much, but I would prompt here and there in the discussion. This would go on, then, for a specified length of time. The length of time was usually governed by the nature of the physiological change you were measuring. Some things happen quickly; others develop slowly. So, it was that period, the stress period. And then it was the period of reassurance. . . . And that involved a switch of the interviewer's attitude to one of "Oh, now I understand." . . . and strong reassurance.[41]

As the physician chose the topics for discussion, the body of the examinee would change.

The new emphasis on emotions in clinical medicine might also be presented in the classic form of a case. Usually, the case would exemplify the omnipresence of emotions during the patient-physician encounter, and would illustrate the important role that these often ignored emotions played in the way the body of the patient presented itself to the clinician. Walter Bradford Cannon would tell his correspondents the amusing anecdote of

> a recent case of Raynaud's disease operated upon at the M.G.H. . . . Some days after the operation the surgeon took a group of medical students to see the patient, and to his chagrin her fingers were as blue as ever. The next day he went to see her alone and they were again pink. One of my former associates was present and interpreted the anomalous blueness to the excitement caused by the medical students."[42]

A more direct attack on the role played by emotions in fashioning the body during the examination took place in the experimental setting, where one hoped to "isolate" and trace the emotional vectors of specific clinical manipulations. The critical task was to separate those changes in the body that were due to the physico-chemical effects of the manipulation from those changes that were due to emotional ones.[43] The same body, Harold G. Wolff reported from his laboratory, "demonstrated" a "markedly different [skin temperature] in the presence of Dr. A and in the presence of Dr. B . . . Dr. B had, on previous occasions made the patient feel uneasy in his presence."[44] The particular history of encounters between examiner and examinee played a decisive role in constituting the examinee's body during its present examination. Again, as the reach of these various investigations expanded during the interwar years, the obviousness of *the* body was increasingly problematized. The trivia of the patient-physician encounter could instantly re-create the examinee's body (through emotion). As the psychologist William Marston discovered, blood pressure readings depended on the sex of examiner vis-à-vis examinee. Higher readings were recorded in the same body when the examiner and examinee were of the opposite sex (for both men and women).[45]

The Sculpted Body: Emotional Spaces

This focus on emotions and the body extended well beyond the immediate instant of patient-physician interaction and included the clinical (and laboratory) settings themselves as emotional environments. Frequently, these spaces were depicted as shielding the human—or laboratory animal—from the burdens of the extramural emotional milieu. Thus, George Draper, a physician at Presbyterian Hospital, would argue in the mid-1930s that the relief of "peptic ulcer patient's pain" during hospitalization could be compared to the emotionally/stress-"protected" animal in the laboratory.[46] Or the sudden deterioration of a hospitalized diabetic patient on receiving news (from the outside) of an impending possible layoff exemplified the emotional divide between inside and outside, the protection afforded by this emotional enclave, and the cost to the body of its violation.[47] For these physicians, then, the hospital-situated body was potentially different from its public-sphere self. The difference in emotional milieu translated into a difference in bodies.

This emotional topography of spaces and its transformative power over bodies was almost idolized in discussions of peptic ulcer. The high incidence of peptic ulcer in industrialized nations, coupled with the significant shift in the male-to-female ratio, marked peptic ulcer, in the eyes of some physicians, as a paradigm disease of the "modern" emotional milieu.[48] Peptic ulcer, so these clinicians argued, had once been a disease commonly found in men and women in equal numbers. Since the turn of the century, statistical evidence had shown a dramatic rise in male patients. A minority of clinicians advanced the view that the incidence of the disease correlated with the degree of emotional development on the evolutionary scale of nature: " 'Peptic' ulcer has never been found in the lower animals. . . . 'Peptic' ulcer occurs very rarely in the Negro race. . . . The Mexican Indians are free from ulcer," and "the few females that develop ulcer often show some masculine traits."[49] The explanation was attributed to nature: "the negro race in its evolutionary ascent has not, as yet, acquired the habit of worry so peculiar to the white race under pressure of routine civilized living." The "hereditary differences of psychological structure and function" explained why these races were emotionally "immune" to this disease.[50] The emotional "privilege" of the white man was his capacity to worry.[51] But it was not just any sort of "worry." It was the worry inherent to participation in the complexities of civilization, with its demanding responsibilities and burdens.

Most physicians, however, opposed this emphasis on innate racial and gendered (though not necessarily anthropometric) characteristics in explaining peptic ulcer, and focused exclusively on the emotional milieu.[52] As Steigman explained, the statistical evidence reflected not heredity, but rather differences between the "industrial" and "urban" centers of the North and the "agricultural" and "rural" centers of the South. The emotions were differentiated along a geographical divide between

North and South. Southern blacks were more "indifferent," while northern blacks, like their white brethren, were more worried, stressed, and under strain.[53] Or, as another clinician, supporting the emphasis on environment, argued, "Negroes of all types were deliberately chosen [for the study] ... most of them, of course, still represented the slow-moving, easy-going type, untouched by aspiration for culture." The absence of disease in these "slow-moving" individuals was contrasted with the "toll" in health paid by "those who choose to run" in the "race" of "modern life, with its ever-increasing rapidity of progress."[54] This geo-emotional map of the United States was reflected in bodies (by the differential incidence of peptic ulcer) and reified the cultural gap between North and South, whites and blacks. It also validated the multiple possibilities of the body. This was most evident in the analyses of the incidence of peptic ulcer in southern-born blacks who migrated to the North. The clinician superimposed on their geographical migration an emotional migration, which explained the increase in peptic-ulcerated bodies among these migrants (now living in the North). Their bodies exemplified how the emotional milieu sculpted the body.[55]

A similar emotio-topographical approach was adopted to explain the low inci-dence of peptic ulcer in women. On top of the domestic-public sphere distribution of bodies was superimposed an emotional one. "Why is a period of rapid change more costly to males than to females?" Harold G. Wolff had rhetorically queried, answering that it is because the man "is the buffer making initial and major adjust-ments both inside and outside the family."[56] The bodies of women were protected from the emotional milieu of modern civilization by the emotional enclave of the domestic sphere at the price of men's bodies. As other historians have argued, the domestic sphere had been promulgated and represented since the nineteenth century as an emotionally protected domain vis-à-vis the public sphere.[57] The body could now testify to these differences in emotional content and the price paid by men.

The Emotional Order

This discovery of the power of the emotional milieu over bodies led some clini-cians, implicitly if not explicitly, to abandon the search for a standard—fixed, stable, *one*—body. A deeper layer of emotional bodies now confronted the physician. For even when the physician could control the local emotional milieu and the immediate physico-emotional encounter with the patient (in her office), the body, she discov-ered, could nevertheless succumb to larger emotional currents. As one physician discovered, the body could follow an emotional rhythmic pattern of recurrent fluc-tuations over the extent of the week. There was a cyclic oscillation of its materiality that obeyed the work-weekend cycle, irrespective of the immediate examination or the local emotional milieu of the clinic, hospital, or laboratory. The recurrent "emotional upset" of the weekends sent blood pressure readings up from their lower values during the "routine" of work, one physician commented on his patient's fluctuating blood pressure. "Now we see that those [blood pressure estimations] taken on Monday cannot always be compared with those taken on Friday," another physician concluded.[58] The emotional order of a society (work versus weekend) could determine, to a certain extent, what the body would be, and what the physician would see on examining the patient during different days of the week. The illusion of isolation created by the secluded and walled physical boundaries of the clinic did not fool the body. These observable and concrete blood pressure rhythms reflected the social order in the interiors of bodies. They attested to the constitutive effect of the socioeconomic order in bodies (mediated by emotions), and gave a material substantiation to the intangible notion of social order.

These clinical and laboratory representations of the body resonated with wider public conceptions. Here, for example, the flux of the body would reify both the emotional bonds sustaining the social order and the body's emotionally inscribed flux. As one newspaper reported, the new "Kiss-O-Meter" could measure objectively, through the body, the infatuation of two lovers during a kiss. The instrument, constructed by the Armour Institute of Technology, had been tested on various couples. The results showed a steady decline in the intensity of the kiss with age and years of marriage. The article also reported that "ten husbands were persuaded to kiss their mothers-in-law. Here the highest that the machine was able to register was six [on a scale of 0 to 120] . . . and observers remarked that it might be interesting to add a minus scale to the dial."[59] The ethereal emotional networks/fields that implicated humans had a very concrete and substantial presence in the body.

The scope of these numerous findings extended well beyond what might be perceived as the obviously emotional. The body, via emotions, was also an effect of aesthetics. Thus, as Alvarez analyzed the variations observed in the intestinal contractions of one of his nurse-fed patients, he explained the change in intestinal contractions by appealing to "something about [the nurse's] ministrations that annoyed" the patient—but not before he had rejected an alternative possibility by observing that "the nurse was not unattractive."[60] For Alvarez and fellow emotio-clinicians and physiologists, aesthetics had their corporeal side too. These aesthetics should not be interpreted in a narrow sense. They could include anything from Alvarez's "not unattractive" nurse to "a careful consideration of the use of martial music in warfare . . . to reinforce the *bodily changes* that attend the belligerent emotions," to an understanding of "why the sight of a well-ordered dining room aids digestion, why our food and our dining room should be made attractive, why fusses should be undertaken only after digestion is complete" and to the observation that technical music and the Bible (Luke 6:18–49) were boring (i.e., do not produce significant bodily changes).[61] Mediating between the body and aesthetics was emotion. This bio-aesthetic connection was often accompanied by an implicit or explicit valuation that reflected an aesthetics of health and disease. "In the serving of food. . . . the little attentions to esthetic details—the arrangement of the dishes, the small portions of food, the flower beside the plate—all," Cannon explained, promoted changes in the body that helped in digestion and promoted health.[62] Or as Thurman B. Rice explained, "there is a real reason why dining tables should be clean and well arranged. . . . why food should be . . . pretty . . . and why the dishes and silver should gleam and sparkle. . . . Under such conditions we can digest well."[63] A list of dos and don'ts, befitting the aesthetic values of the physician, would be supported by the body. The body could now mirror, prescribe, and inform about aesthetics and the emotional-social order.[64]

The Confessions of the Body: A Society of Truth

In its new guise as a psychological entity, the body would also serve as a window into the interiors of the individual's "spirit." Numerous observations on the body, ranging from the changes due to a visit by an examinee's mother-in-law (which changed the amount of his nasal secretions) to a "young Jew. . . . concerned over an election of the B'Nai Brith" (which arrested his stomach), would all confirm this general representation.[65] At times, these observations would take on a more reflexive form as investigators monitored their own bodies during life's ordinary daily activities. The capricious behavior of their body-heat regulatory processes, Goodell and her colleagues reported, followed the capricious events of their individual emotional lives.[66]

One could also follow John Whitehorn, a psychiatrist at McLean Hospital, who monitored his patients' changing heart rates as he experimented with the different possibilities of establishing rapport. He engaged his patients in both a question-answer type of interview and a more friendly open-ended discussion. Whitehorn could now consult his patients' heart rates to gauge their emotional responsiveness to these different types of interaction.[67] He discovered, via the organ of the heart, that emotional rapport was best established through a friendly discussion. It was now the body, as the inscriber of emotions, that could itself serve as an emotio-meter.[68] Through it, the examiner could know of the examinee's worry and joy, fright and rage, love and disappointments.[69] In engaging this body, the physician did not necessarily renounce the patient's experiences or her words.[70] Yet the private emotional experiences of the examinee were now defined by the body, independent of the patient's words, will, or knowledge. As Otto Veraguth, expounding on the psychogalvanic reflex during the early years of the twentieth century, explained, "we cannot prevent the electric confession of our skins."[71] Whitehorn's conclusion from his experiments in rapport had, once again, demonstrated the collapse of emotion with knowledge during the examination. The examination's quintessential "play of questions and answers" reconstituted the body (changed the patient's heart rate).[72] The process of extracting and constituting knowledge was an emotional one.

These clinical and laboratory observations on the uses of the psychological body also resonated with wider public conceptions. The primordial suggestions of the late nineteenth-century physiologists were taken up with vigor and stirred the twentieth-century imagination. Alternatively known as "lie detectors," "polygraphs," "affecto-meters," or "deceptometers"—these portable laboratory and clinical instruments invaded the public domain as they measured and recorded, through the medium of the body, the most intimate of emotions.[73] This science of exteriorizing and visualizing emotions—of creating the transparent individual—led some of the protagonists to argue for the imminence of a utopian and transparent society, a society of Truth founded on the new technology of the mobile emotion detector.[74]

What Is the Truth (about the Body)?

Such observations of the shifting nature of the body during the first several decades of the twentieth century would become practically limitless: spectators in football games, students taking examinations, people testifying on witness stands, bank employees under suspicion, participants in parlor games, condemned criminals; or reading the Bible, reading your own personal mail, watching a movie, dreaming, listening to nonsense syllables, "conjuring up" various memories, malingering, food tasting, and numerous other banal daily activities—all produced phantom bodies.[75]

The body seemed doomed to a life of perpetual flux, an inexorable multiplicity of existences.[76] How could the physician ever define the true body? Under what conditions would the physician encounter the body's truth? Certainly not during a patient's first visit to the clinic; nor, so it seemed, when the examinee applied for a job, a (military) position, or life insurance;[77] nor, and this is a crucial point, when the physician was "busy," examining, tabulating and collecting information—trying to know and canonize the body. Should the nurse be attractive or unattractive? Should the readings be taken on Mondays or Fridays? Should the physician avoid examining the patient when the patient's mother-in-law was in town? Was the patient permitted to think about emotionally significant situations during the examination? Should the sex of the physician and patient be the same or different? Should the physician engage the patient in a friendly conversation or a question-answer type of interview? Should the physician examine the patient alone or with students? Should the body be examined in the North or the South? In each of these instances, our protagonists argued, the physician would encounter a different set of "phantoms" in the body.[78] Where could the physician find the Truth?

The Animal's Body

The parallel developments taking place in the physiologist's laboratory during the first half of the twentieth century highlight the wide reach of these representations. In the laboratory, as in the clinic, the invisible "routines" or "common . . . procedures" of the experimenter were discovered to be the rabbit's, cat's, and dog's emotional significants.[79] Similar to the encounter of humans with their physicians, here too first encounters in the laboratory were misleading. Cats required "a week" in order to get accustomed to the laboratory, a week for their emotional bodies to de-emotionalize.[80] Physiologists, like their fellow clinicians, had also discovered the permeability of the laboratory space. The infinitesimally small intrusions of the public sphere on the laboratory had profound effects, mediated by emotions, on the bodies of their animals.[81] Hargis and Mann, working with dogs in the mid-1930s, published their own experience with these emotional intrusions on the laboratory, and proposed a series of maneuvers aimed at emotionally isolating their laboratory from the world. They had observed that a reflex emotional change in the spleen was "so easily induced in many of the animals that . . . in many instances it was found necessary to carry on the observations [on the spleen] in a closed room from which all extraneous noises had been excluded. Even this was not sufficient with some of the animals, and in these cases investigations had to be carried on at night when the laboratory was very quiet."[82]

The physiologist, like her fellow psychologist and clinician, had discovered through the mediation of the animal's body that an emotional dimension overlaid the physical dimensions of the laboratory. This new understanding of the laboratory—as an emotionally rich space—was alien to the physiologist's conception of the laboratory as an emotion-free or emotion-controlled enclave. The physiologist, like the clinician, strove to arrest these emotions qua bodily flows, and began to investigate the motions of the laboratory—not for their mechanical expediency, but rather for their emotional content. The physiologist engaged in an emotional content-analysis of the experimental movements, spaces, and instruments. He discovered that the routine displacement of the animal from the kennels to the experimental space produced a measurable phantom increase in its body temperature, due solely to the animal's emotions.[83] Or he reconceptualized space as he discovered that the animal pound could no longer be conceived along the old physicalist perspective—as simply a storage house for animals—but was now an emotional space. Though the caged cats and dogs in the pound were physically isolated one from the other, they interacted emotionally while in the pound (e.g., the pound was a fear-rich space for the cats). This pre-experiment emotional interaction would produce confusion once these animals were brought into the laboratory space.[84] The animal pound had a tangible emotional content.

As in the clinic, various suggestions for ridding, compensating, or controlling emotions would be made. Some animals (rabbits in particular) were simply "discard[ed]" "as entirely unsuited" for physiological work (e.g., on blood sugar levels). The physiologist could not succeed in controlling, stabilizing, and disciplining the interior fluctuations of their bodies—their emotions. At times, the physiologist would discard only the more emotional individuals in a cohort of animals—those animals whose bodies perpetually fluctuated.[85] The physiologist could also adopt a number of emotional technologies that we have already examined in the setting of the clinic and during the human-human interaction. Animals, like new military recruits, could be "trained" for the procedure: "dogs are easily trained for this work and quite readily learn the routine . . . ; the trained animal will remain perfectly contented for a long time, frequently sleeping while the observations are being made."[86] Perhaps the most "clinical" and revealing proposal concerned the animal-human interaction. Questions centering on the proper conduct between experimenter and animal came to the fore. What was the correct etiquette when one interacted with an animal in the laboratory? The nature of this interaction would determine the state of the animal's body. Would the body spin out of control? Or could the physiologist, like the clinician, succeed in stabilizing the interior? Here, as in the clinic, a humanitarian human-animal interaction was recommended, not as an affirmation of the contemporary, women-led, rising antivivisection agitation, but "quite apart from any humanitarian considerations."[87] It was but a means of manipulating the animal's interior body. Or, as a "precaution against excitement, an attendant, from whom the animals were accustomed to receive food, brought them to the laboratory and assisted throughout the preparation of the animal and the collection of blood," ensuring that the body of the animal would configure itself to the requirements of the experimental protocol.[88] This invisible participant played an emotio-somatic role. His bodily presence—absent from published protocols— maintained the right configuration in the animal's body (i.e., its de-emotionalized state).[89]

The Body: Created in Their Own Image

The production of this de-emotionalized body—as the clinical and experimental ideal of the "normal" and "standard"—brings us back to the larger cultural resonance of this new body. As Philip Pauly has argued, the late nineteenth and early twentieth centuries saw the "importation of the strategy and tactics of artifice into the core of biology. The most exciting 'game' was to get organisms to do and be new things. . . . when serious biologists began to see themselves as designers and inventors of new things, the conceptual and practical significance of 'nature' began to evaporate."[90] Thus, at a time when the modernist's penchant for artifice trivialized nature, the normal itself was an artifice of the laboratory's creation. While emotions permeated the world, the laboratory ideal of the normal body was a de-emotionalized one—an ideal normal that materialized only as the body was confined and conformed to the ideal de-emotionalized laboratory. And this ideal of an emotionally controlled or de-emotionalized laboratory (science) was itself created in the image of the emotional imagination of our historical actors, as Charles Darwin, William James, Walter B. Cannon, and Walter C. Alvarez all testify. "Scientists . . . look on their material dispassionately, much as a physician looks many times a day on disrobed men and women whom he must examine. . . . [T]o a scientist things that might seem disgusting or obscene to a layman mean nothing but objects of study," Alvarez testified.[91] As Walter Cannon argued, "flowery language and dramatizations are out of place in scientific exposition . . . for the facts presented should be convincing without an appeal to feelings."[92] Or take William James: "the 'marvels' of Science, about which so much edifying popular literature is written, are apt to be 'caviare' to the men in the laboratories. And even divine Philosophy itself . . . is too apt to the practical philosopher himself to be but a sharpening and tightening business, a matter of 'points,' of screwing down things, of splitting hairs. . . . Very little emotion here!"[93]

In fact, the practice of science itself was a numbing or anesthetizing experience. "There was a time," Cannon confessed in his autobiography, "when the Boston Symphony concerts were a source of pleasure, but for me, as was true of William James, they gradually lost their charm."[94] And Darwin complained, "in one respect my mind has changed during the last twenty or thirty years. . . . [A] lamentable loss of the higher aesthetic tastes. . . . My mind seems to have become a kind of machine for grinding general laws out of large collections of facts."[95] The ideal image and the private experiences of science were of a de-emotionalized or at least de-emotionalizing endeavor. The ideal normal/standard (de-emotionalized) body, created in the ideal (de-emotionalized) enclave/image of the laboratory, was created, we can suggest, in the ideal de-emotional self-image of science and the scientist.[96]

This essay argues for the emergence of a new emotional perspective in physiology, psychology, and medicine and locates the body at its center. In this new perspective, physiologists, psychologists, and clinicians reconceived spaces, instruments, motions, manipulations, and bodies as emotional—rather than purely physical—entities. The new understanding of the body as an emotional entity and of emotions as objective corporal phenomena played a significant role in the emergence of this new perspective. The measurable, mappable, evokable, quantifiable, visualizable, and very tangible aspects of the emotional dimension in the body played an important role in supporting this transformation. The laboratory and clinic contributed in important ways to the construction and extension of this new modern view of the body.

Implicated in the emergence of this new perspective was a set of wide-ranging conceptual shifts. These include the discovery of the multiple possibilities of the body; the modern paradoxes of the "examination" as both an emotional and a knowledge-producing encounter; the body's new role as literally an objective mirror of the social order and of the individual spirit; the bio-aesthetics of health and disease; the increased attention to the powerful effects of the infinitesimally small and physically insignificant on the body; the accommodation of a mechanistic approach to the body with an emphasis on emotions; the creation of the de-emotionalized body as the normal; and the development of technics of emotional-physiological manipulation. This cluster of changes, it has been argued, was embedded in the broader sociocultural transformation of the late nineteenth and early twentieth centuries.[97]

We may also suggest a modern revision of Foucault's analysis of the gaze. When Michel Foucault published his study of the Panopticon and described the interrelationships between power, vision, and architecture, he paid but little attention to the emotional realm.[98] Though Foucault hinted in one passing allusion to an "anxious awareness of being observed," he did not elaborate on the relationships between vision (the gaze), its power, and emotions.[99] This absence seems enigmatic—particularly as the Panopticon's most diabolical effects best worked through the creation of a "state of *conscious* ... visibility." [100] "He who is subjected to a field of visibility, and *who knows it*, assumes responsibility for the constraints of power," Foucault had proclaimed.[101] Perhaps his silence on the issue of emotions merely reflects the obvious: that Foucault took for granted the play of emotions in the workings of the gaze.

The modern physiologists, psychophysiologists, and clinicians that we have studied discovered the power of the gaze not in the external "gesture," but in the interiors of the new emotionalized body. They attributed its powerful effects on bodies to emotion, and held that emotion was inherent to the power of the gaze. Yet unlike Foucault, for them the gaze qua emotion that disciplined and normalized the "gesture" created a dynamic materialization of multiple and fleeting body states, and a body independent of, and severed from, its subjecting cerebral connections.[102]

Gazed-excited bodies, they argued, "resisted" both discipline and knowledge.[103] Foucault, in contrast, had focused exclusively on the "gesture" and had neglected to examine the significance of the emotional component of the gaze for the modern bodies of the Panopticon's inmates: their urine sugar levels, their metabolic rates, their blood pressures, their cardiac rhythms, or their intestinal contractions.[104]

This explains why the moderns rejected the classic structure of the Panopticon with its emotionally suffused gaze. These moderns set out to construct a de-emotionalized gaze, an emotion-free variant that would allow them to discipline and know the modern body interior. Maintain the gaze, they would say, maintain the cage, but curb the emotions. These moderns had discovered that the classic structure of the gaze was suffused with emotion and therefore its power to discipline and know the modern body was nothing but a superficial observer's illusion.[105]

NOTES

I would like to thank John Carson, Gerald Geison, Jan Lewis, Elizabeth Lunbeck, Michele Rivkin-Fish, Peter Stearns, and especially Elizabeth Kronzek for their helpful comments on earlier drafts.

1. H. M. Gardiner, Ruth Clark Metcalf, and John G. Beebe-Center, *Feeling and Emotion: A History of Theories* (New York: American Book Company, 1937). For other traditions, see Joel Marks and Roger T. Ames, eds., *Emotions in Asian Thought: A Dialogue in Comparative Philosophy* (Albany: State University of New York Press, 1995).

2. On the development of experimental physiology during the nineteenth century, see William Coleman and Frederic L. Holmes, introduction to William Coleman and Frederic L. Holmes, eds., *The Investigative Enterprise: Experimental Physiology in Nineteenth-Century Medicine* (Berkeley: University of California Press, 1988). For its development in the British context, see Gerald L. Geison, *Michael Foster and the Cambridge School of Physiology: The Scientific Enterprise in Late Victorian Society* (Princeton: Princeton University Press, 1978). For its development in the American context, see G. L. Geison, ed., *Physiology in the American Context, 1850–1940* (Baltimore: Waverly Press, 1987); and Saul Benison, A. Clifford Barger, and Elin L. Wolfe, *Walter B. Cannon: The Life and Times of a Young Scientist* (Cambridge: Harvard University Press, 1987). On the rise of experimental psychology during the late nineteenth and early twentieth centuries, see Kurt Danzinger, *Constructing the Subject: Historical Origins of Psychological Research* (Cambridge: Cambridge University Press, 1994 [1990]).

3. See, e.g., Angelo Mosso, *Fear*, 5th ed., trans. E. Lough and F. Kiesow (London: Longmans, Green, 1896); and Ugolino Mosso, "Influence du système nerveux sur la température animale: Recherches," *Archives Italiennes de Biologie* 7 (1886): 306–40, esp. 337–40. The publication of Charles Darwin's text on the expression of emotions and Douchenne de Boulogne's intensive laboratory investigations of human facial expression all point to the early years of the latter third of the nineteenth century as an important juncture in the study of emotions. See Charles Darwin, *The Expression of the Emotions in Man and Animals* (New York: D. Appleton, 1872); and G. B. Duchenne (de Boulogne), *Mécanisme de la physionomie humaine ou analyse électro-physiologique de l'expression des passions applicable à la pratique des arts plastiques* (Paris: Jules Renouard, 1862).

4. Claude Bernard, "Sur la physiologie du coeur et ses rapports avec le cerveau," in *Leçons sur les propriétés des tissus vivants,* collected, edited, and published by M. Émile Alglave (Paris: Germer Baillière, 1866), 421–71. The cardiograph's principle was based on mechanical transmission: a stethoscopic drum was placed on the chest of the examinee, above the heart; the pulsation of the heart would be transmitted from this drum and registered in the form of a curve. (All translations from the French are my own.)

5. Bernard, "Sur la physiologie du coeur," 437. On the history of graphic methods in physiology

and medicine, see Robert G. Frank, Jr., "The Telltale Heart: Physiological Instruments, Graphic Methods, and Clinical Hopes, 1854–1914," in Coleman and Holmes, eds., *The Investigative Enterprise,* 211–90. See also Frederic L. Holmes and Kathryn M. Olesko, "The Images of Precision: Helmholtz and the Graphical Method in Physiology," in M. Norton Wise, ed., *The Values of Precision* (Princeton: Princeton University Press, 1995), 198–221. For a general review of the rise of medical technologies during the nineteenth and twentieth centuries, see Stanley Joel Reiser, *Medicine and the Reign of Technology* (Cambridge: Cambridge University Press, 1978), esp. 91–121. On my use of "translation," see Bruno Latour, *The Pasteurization of France,* trans. Alan Sheridan and John Law (Cambridge: Harvard University Press, 1988).

6. Bernard, "Sur la physiologie du coeur," 469–71, 469.

7. Ibid., 458–60. This metaphor of "betrayal" by the body in the context of emotions was common in the twentieth century. See, e.g., Hugo Münsterberg, *On the Witness Stand: Essays on Psychology and Crime* (New York: McClure, 1908), 111–33.

8. M. E. Cyon, "Le coeur et le cerveau," *Revue Scientifique de La France et de L'étranger* 21 (November 22, 1873): 481–89. Both Bernard and Cyon attribute an active role to the heart in contributing to the emotion itself. Their essays are, in fact, an argument for the reciprocal relationships between science and art, the *savant* and the *artiste,* reason and emotion, positivism and inspiration, the brain and the heart.

9. Ibid., 487. For the quote, see Fernand Papillon, "Physiology of the Passions," *Popular Science Monthly,* March 1874 (4): 552–64, 559. See also Charles Darwin, who concludes his book on the expression of emotions by suggesting that "our subject.... deserves still further attention, especially from any able physiologist." Darwin, *Expression of the Emotions,* 366.

10. Peter N. Stearns, *American Cool: Constructing a Twentieth-Century Emotional Style* (New York: New York University Press, 1994), 66–68, 67.

11. For emotion as an "explosion," see, e.g., Walter B. Pitkin, "Take It Easy," *Reader's Digest* 28 (January 1936): 101–3, 101.

12. Space limitations will allow only a brief examination of the various issues involved.

13. William James, "What Is an Emotion?" *Mind* 9 (1884): 188–205; and idem, "The Emotions," in *Principles of Psychology,* chap. 25 (New York: Henry Holt, 1890). Both are in Carl Georg Lange and William James, *The Emotions* (Baltimore: Williams and Wilkins, 1922).

14. Stearns, *American Cool,* 67.

15. On the connections between standardizability, control, and modernity, see Wise, ed., *Values of Precision.*

16. Michel Foucault, *Discipline and Punish: The Birth of the Prison,* trans. Alan Sheridan (New York: Vintage Books, 1979), 192.

17. "Reports of Societies: Boston Society for Medical Improvement," *Boston Medical and Surgical Journal* 120, no. 5 (January 31, 1889): 109–14. This was an open discussion of papers presented by Morton Prince and J. H. McCollom. See Morton Prince, "The Occurrence and Mechanism of Physiological Heart Murmurs (Endocardial) in Healthy Individuals," *Medical Records* 35, no. 16 (April 20, 1889): 421–28.

18. "These murmurs must ... be physiological—not pathological" (109). Some of the discussants did not concur with Prince's normalization of heart murmurs. On the rise of a functional and physiological approach in medicine, see Knud Faber, *Nosography: The Evolution of Clinical Medicine in Modern Times,* 2d rev. ed. (New York: Paul B. Hoeber, 1930), 59–93, 112–208.

19. Though Prince directly discussed only the appearance of the murmur, his argument makes it clear that the murmur dematerialized as the encounter subsided.

20. On the history and rise of the physical examination, see Roy Porter, "The Rise of Physical Examination," in W. F. Bynum and Roy Porter, eds., *Medicine and the Five Senses* (Cambridge: Cambridge University Press, 1993), 179–97. For an interesting illustration of the epistolary nature of the doctor-patient interaction during the early eighteenth century, see Barbara Duden, *The Woman beneath the Skin: A Doctor's Patients in Eighteenth-Century Germany,* trans. Thomas Dunlap (Cambridge: Harvard University Press, 1991).

21. "Reports of Societies," 113.

22. Ibid., 114.

23. "Excitement" led to increased heart rate and blood flow, which led to seepage of blood through the valves.

24. Harry G. Armstrong, "The Interpretation of Normal Blood Pressures and Pulse Rates in Routine Physical Examinations," *Military Surgeon* 80, no. 6 (June 1937): 456–62, 460.

25. H. A. Treadgold, "Blood Pressure in the Healthy Young Male Adult," *Lancet* 1 (April 8, 1933): 733–40, 739.

26. Ibid., 735: "Three readings [were taken] during the medical examination, three more at the end, three before rotation . . . and one after, making ten in all."

27. E.g., "A strange environment (uncertainty, apprehension). . . . Bodily exposure (resentment, embarrassment)," etc.; see Harry G. Armstrong, "The Blood Pressure and Pulse Rate as an Index of Emotional Stability," *American Journal of the Medical Sciences* 195, no. 2 (February 1938): 211–20, 213.

28. Foucault, *Discipline and Punish*, 192.

29. Walter Alvarez to Walter Bradford Cannon, July 21, 1915, folder 1514, box 110, Walter Bradford Cannon Papers, Rare Books and Manuscripts, Francis A. Countway Library of Medicine, Boston (hereafter cited as WBC).

30. This list is a compilation of numerous articles culled from the Anglo-American literature, appearing during the first five decades of the twentieth century. They support the argument that the body was "different." The literature describing these changes is rich in adjectives such as "dramatic," "profound," "violent," and so forth. It is important to emphasize that the literature on bodies that we are examining should *not* be confused with the literature on emotions and disease. Our discussion focuses on what numerous physicians, psychologists, and physiologists considered to be perfectly normal changes. These emotional-corporeal changes were not of the "traumatic" type. We are not dealing with the literature of "traumatic neuroses" or "nervous shocks." Nor have we discussed unconscious conflicts, childhood traumas, psychoneurosis, psychopaths, or psychotic episodes. The bodies that we are dealing with are the normal, not the pathological. I do not intend to cover the field of emotions and disease in this essay. Much, but not all, of the literature dealing with the *normal* perceived emotional bodies as serving a largely functional and utilitarian role. In large, it adopted an explicitly Darwinian perspective in physiology and medicine. According to this perspective, emotions and multiple bodies were the outcome of the Darwinian process of natural selection. They thus served useful/adaptive purposes. On this Darwinian physiology and medicine, see, e.g., M. Foster, *A Textbook of Physiology*, part 1, 5th ed. (London: Macmillan, 1888), 179–81; Charles S. Sherrington, *The Integrative Action of the Nervous System* (New Haven: Yale University Press, 1906), 235–68; and George W. Crile, *The Origin and Nature of the Emotions: Miscellaneous Papers* (Philadelphia: W. B. Saunders, 1915).

31. Luther Halsey Gulick, "Emotional Storms in Women," *Ladies' Home Journal* 25 (January 1908): 24.

32. M. Dresbach, "Observations upon the Blood Pressure of the Sheep," *American Journal of Physiology* 25, no. 7 (March 1, 1910): 433–38; and idem, "Some Observations upon the Blood Pressure of the Sheep under Local and General Anesthesia," *American Journal of Physiology* 26 (1910): 17.

33. For peristalsis, see John Auer, "The Course of the Contraction Wave in the Stomach of the Rabbit," *American Journal of Physiology* 23, no. 3 (December 1, 1908): 165–73; For blood sugar levels, see Ernest Lyman Scott, "The Content of Sugar in the Blood under Common Laboratory Conditions," *American Journal of Physiology* 34, no. 3 (June 1, 1914): 271–311. See also Mosso, "Influence du système nerveux."

34. Walter B. Cannon, *Bodily Changes in Pain, Hunger, Fear, and Rage: An Account of Recent Researches into the Function of Emotional Excitement*, 2d ed. (New York: D. Appleton, 1929), 73.

35. This drive for standardization should be understood in the context of the general drive for standardization in the Western world during this period. See Wise, ed., *Values of Precision*.

36. Though I am emphasizing this one particular aspect of the doctor-patient interaction, there were numerous other interesting and substantial aspects. For example, "emotional etiquette" was

important for retrieving intimate knowledge from the patient, or as part of therapy, or because the patient "was a person," and so forth. For a different perspective on this interaction, see Christopher Lawrence, "Incommunicable Knowledge: Science, Technology and the Clinical Art in Britain, 1850–1914," *Journal of Contemporary History* 20 (1985): 503–20; and John Harley Warner, "Ideals of Science and Their Discontents in Late Nineteenth-Century American Medicine," *Isis* 82 (1991): 454–78.

37. Esther M. Greisheimer, *Physiology and Anatomy*, 4th ed. (Philadelphia: Lippincott, 1940), 487–88.

38. See the papers presented at the conference on "The Holistic Turn in Western Biomedicine, 1920–1950," McGill University, Montreal, May 4–6, 1995.

39. Nonetheless, the patient was enlightened.

40. Stewart Wolf and George B. Jerzy Glass, "Correlation of Conscious and Unconscious Conflicts with Changes in Gastric Function and Structure: Observations on the Relation of the Constituents of Gastric Juice to the Integrity of the Mucous Membrane," in *Life Stress and Bodily Disease* (Baltimore: Williams and Wilkins, 1950), 674.

41. Interview with Stewart Wolf, M.D., head of Totts Gap Institute, August 8, 1995, Philadelphia. I thank Dr. Wolf for the opportunity of this interview. These "stress interviews" were followed, "somewhat later," by a post-experiment interview, in which Wolf would talk with the patient to find out how the experience "sat with him." The majority of interviewees had a positive reaction to the interview.

42. The patient with Raynaud's disease would suffer from recurrent bouts of sudden constriction of the blood vessels supplying the hands, which caused the hands to become "blue." Surgical treatment consisted in removing the nerve supply that was responsible for these recurrent constrictions. Walter Cannon to J. C. Whitehorn, May 29, 1933, folder 1799, box 128, WBC.

43. This was done by calculating the amount of change in the body due to all the known physico-chemical forces and attributing the residual changes to emotion.

44. Harold G. Wolff, "Hypertension and Coronary Disease" (oral presentation, n.d.), unmarked folder (9th in box), box 11, Harold G. Wolff Papers, New York Hospital-Cornell Medical Center Archives, New York (hereafter cited as HGW).

45. William Moulton Marston, "Bodily Symptoms of Elementary Emotions," *Psyche* 10, no. 38 (October 1929): 70–86, 81.

46. George Draper to Walter B. Cannon, February 4, 1936, folder 1738, box 124, WBC.

47. Walter B. Cannon, "Cinquieme conference: Troubles emotifs des fonctions de l'organisme," folder "Lectures on Emotion [in French] by WBC, Paris, 1930, IV–V," box 179, WBC (this was part of a series of lectures given in French by Walter B. Cannon during his visit to Paris).

48. There were various alternative explanations for peptic ulcer.

49. Samuel C. Robinson, "On the Etiology of Peptic Ulcer," *American Journal of Digestive Diseases and Nutrition* 2 (August 1935): 333–43, 333, 342.

50. Ibid., 342.

51. On disease as "privilege," see Susan Sontag, *Illness as Metaphor and AIDS and Its Metaphors* (New York: Anchor Books, 1990), esp. 26–36: "TB was one index of being genteel, delicate, sensitive," during the late eighteenth and nineteenth centuries (28); Ann Jessie Van Sant, *Eighteenth-Century Sensibility and the Novel: The Senses in Social Context* (Cambridge: Cambridge University Press, 1993), 3 n. 8; and Janet Brown, "Darwin and the Expression of the Emotions," in David Kohn, ed., *The Darwinian Heritage* (Princeton: Princeton University Press, 1985), 307–26, n. 14.

52. Other "systemic" variables also contributed to the development of the disease, e.g., general health.

53. Frederick Steigman, "The Peptic Ulcer Syndrome in the Negro," *American Journal of Digestive Diseases and Nutrition* 3, no. 5 (July 1936): 310–15. Steigman mentions a list of authorities who do not subscribe to race as a factor in the etiology of peptic ulcer. Steigman was from Chicago.

54. Andrew B. Rivers, "Clinical Consideration of the Etiology of Peptic Ulcer," *Archives of Internal Medicine* 53, no. 1 (January 1934): 97–119, 107–8. For the heredity/environment debate during this period in the United States, see Carl N. Degler, *In Search of Human Nature: The Decline*

and Revival of Darwinism in American Social Thought (New York: Oxford University Press, 1991); and Daniel J. Kevles, *In the Name of Eugenics: Genetics and the Uses of Human Heredity* (New York: Knopf, 1985).

55. For the notion of emotions as shaping the body, see Thure von Uexküll, *La Médecine psychosomatique,* trans. Rémi Laureillard (Paris: Gallimard, 1966), 47.

56. Harold G. Wolff, "Change and Adjustment," notes for Hawkes Lecture, 1955, folder 14, box 10, HGW.

57. See, e.g., Peter N. Stearns, "Anger and American Work: A Twentieth-Century Turning Point," in Carol Z. Stearns and Peter N. Stearns, eds., *Emotion and Social Change: Toward a New Psychohistory* (New York: Holmes and Meier, 1988); and Stearns, *American Cool.*

58. Selma C. Mueller, "Hourly Studies of Blood Pressure in Cases of Hypertension and of Normal Subjects," *Proceedings of the Staff Meetings of the Mayo Clinic* 4, no. 21 (May 22, 1929): 163; and G. E. Brown, "Determinations of Blood Pressure Carried Out Three Times Daily by the Patient over a Period of Three and a Half Years in a Case of Essential Hypertension," ibid., 163–65, 165.

59. Young lovers usually rated between 100 and 110. Newspaper clipping, n.d., folder "clippings," carton 7, John Augustus Larson Papers (BANC MSS 78/160z), The Bancroft Library, University of California, Berkeley.

60. Walter Alvarez, "Ways in Which Emotion Can Affect the Digestive Tract," *Journal of the American Medical Association* 92, no. 15 (April 13, 1929): 1231–37, 1231.

61. It is important to stress that Cannon's reference to the connections between the aesthetics of music and the body was distinct from any discussions of motivation. The effect was on the state of the body. For martial music, see Cannon, *Bodily Changes,* 237–38 (my italics). On digestion, see John B. Watson, "The Heart or the Intellect?" *Harper's Magazine* 156 (February 1928): 345–52, 348. On technical music and the Bible, see Carney Landis, "Studies of Emotional Reactions II: General Behavior and Facial Expression," *Journal of Comparative Psychology* 4, nos. 5–6 (October–December 1924): 447–509.

62. Cannon, *Bodily Changes,* 7–8, 7.

63. Thurman B. Rice, "The Mood We Eat," *Journal of the Outdoor Life* 30 (November 1933): 397–98, 397.

64. This mirroring should not be confused with either the "Spencerian" or the "Cannonian" body-politic: Herbert Spencer promulgated analogies between social and biological *structures,* while Walter B. Cannon emphasized analogies between *processes.* See Stephen J. Cross and William R. Albury, "Walter B. Cannon, L. J. Henderson, and the Organic Analogy," *Osiris* 3 (1987): 165–92.

65. "Psychosomatic Medicine," *Society of the New York Hospital Quarterly,* April 1945, 1–6; Walter Alvarez to Walter Bradford Cannon, August 16, 1927, folder 1516, box 110, WBC.

66. Helen Goodell, David T. Graham and Harold G. Wolff, "Changes in Body Heat Regulation Associated with Varying Life Situations and Emotional States," in *Life Stress and Bodily Disease.*

67. Whitehorn was working with schizophrenic patients who did not communicate their inner emotions. The measurement of the heart enabled Whitehorn to distinguish between the "outer emotional talk and behavior and the inner emotional reaction. . . . the heart rate record provides an indication of the inner emotional reaction" (315). John C. Whitehorn, "Emotional Responsiveness in Clinical Interviews," *American Journal of Psychiatry* 94, no. 2 (September 1937): 311–15.

68. During the first half of the twentieth century there was an extensive literature on using the body for detecting the inner emotions. Space permits only a brief examination of this literature, and only in its capacity to illuminate the argument that the body was a mirror of the spirit.

69. The controversy over the specificity of bodily changes in each particular emotion generated much literature throughout our period of study. It centered around the famous "James-Lange" theory of emotions, which also served as a focus for discussions on the peripheral versus central origin of emotions. See, e.g., Lange and James, *The Emotions;* and Walter B. Cannon, "The James-Lange Theory of Emotions: A Critical Examination and an Alternative Theory," *American Journal of Psychology* 39, nos. 1–4 (1927): 106–24.

70. In fact, it was particularly that group of physicians who paid attention to the patient's words, who emphasized the body-emotional.

71. Otto Veraguth, "Measuring Joy and Sorrow," *Scientific American Supplement* 67 (February 6, 1909): 87.

72. On the "case" as a process of extracting and constituting knowledge through questions and answers, see Elizabeth Lunbeck, *The Psychiatric Persuasion: Knowledge, Gender, and Power in Modern America* (Princeton: Princeton University Press, 1994), esp. 133–44.

73. On the mobility of the polygraph, see William Moulton Marston, *The Lie Detector Test* (New York: Richard R. Smith, 1938), 98: "[Larson] combined the blood-pressure and breathing instruments in a neat, oblong box which could be carried conveniently, like a suit case." It is important to emphasize that the lie detector was, in fact, an emotion detector (usually detecting "fear"). This was accepted and articulated by most of the major protagonists of this machine. See, e.g., Leonarde Keeler, "The Detection of Deception," n.d., folder Scientific Crime Detection Laboratory, Correspondence, 1934–1935, n.d., box 79 (J. H. Wigmore, General Correspondence), Northwestern University Archives, Evanston. The use of ambulatory emotion detectors in different domains and for various purposes is a vast subject in and of itself. It is mentioned here only in passing and as an illustration of our argument concerning the body, emotions, and technology.

74. For a clear statement of this future utopian society permeated by emotion detectors, see Marston, *Lie Detector Test*, 10–11, 144–46. On the Rousseauite roots of the transparent society, see Michel Foucault, "L'oeil du pouvoir," interview with Jean-Pierre Barou and Michelle Perrot, in Jeremy Bentham, *Le Panoptique* (Paris: Pierre Belfond, 1977), 16.

75. See, e.g., Landis, "Studies of Emotional Reactions"; David Brunswick, "The Effect of Emotional Stimuli on the Gastro-Intestinal Tone: I. Methods and Technique," *Journal of Comparative Psychology* 4, no. 1 (February 1924): 19–79; and idem, "The Effects of Emotional Stimuli on the Gastro-Intestinal Tone: II. Results and Conclusions," *Journal of Comparative Psychology* 4, no. 3 (June 1924): 225–87.

76. Whether emotions were bodily changes, were the cause of bodily changes, or were caused by bodily changes (or various other intermediate proposals) absorbed a not insignificant amount of the protagonists' time and energy. These controversies will not concern us here, especially as practically all the protagonists agreed on the immanence of bodily *change*. Some of the important texts are Lange and James, *The Emotions;* Sherrington, *Integrative Action of the Nervous System*, 235–68; and Cannon, *Bodily Changes*.

77. For a similar argument concerning job positions, see Walter Alvarez, "The Blood Pressure in 6225 Prisoners and 422 Guards," *Proceedings of the Staff Meetings of the Mayo Clinic* 4, no. 45 (November 6, 1929): 321–23.

78. Parallel with this narrative of change and instability was an important literature on the body's stability and equilibrium. These two discourses were not mutually exclusive. On this second current and its history, see Frederic L. Holmes, "La Signification du concept de milieu intérieur," in *La Nécessité de Claude Bernard* (Paris: Méridiens Klincksieck, 1991), 53–64; Christiane Sinding, "Du Milieu intérieur à l'homéstasie: Une Généalogie contestée," in ibid., 65–81; and Cynthia Eagle Russett, *The Concept of Equilibrium in American Social Thought* (New Haven: Yale University Press, 1966).

79. Scott, "Content of Sugar."

80. Ibid., 278.

81. Not through their physico-chemical effect, but through emotions.

82. Estes H. Hargis and Frank C. Mann, "A Plethysmographic Study of the Changes in the Volume of the Spleen in the Intact Animal," *American Journal of Physiology* 75, no. 1 (December 1925): 180–200, 191.

83. For a very early argument, see Mosso, "Influence du système nerveux."

84. Cannon, *Bodily Changes*, 173.

85. Scott, "Content of Sugar," 283. The difference between individual animals of the same species was a common and important observation among these emotio-physiologists.

86. Hargis and Mann, "Plethysmographic Study," 183.

87. Scott, "Content of Sugar," 296. For a similar approach, see W. B. Cannon and D. De La Paz, "Emotional Stimulation of Adrenal Secretion," *American Journal of Physiology* 28 (1911): 64–70. For

psychology, see Brunswick, "Effect of Emotional Stimuli on the Gastro-Intestinal Tone: I." It is interesting to note the concurrent rise of the antivivisection movement in the United States (spearheaded by women), which also argued for a humanitarian approach to animals, but not for the scientist's utilitarian ends. On the antivivisection movement in the Anglo-U.S. context, see Richard D. French, *Antivivisection and Medical Science in Victorian Society* (Princeton: Princeton University Press, 1975); Benison et al., *Walter B. Cannon;* and Susan E. Lederer, "The Controversy over Animal Experimentation in America, 1880–1914," in Nicolaas A. Rupke, ed., *Vivisection in Historical Perspective* (London: Routledge, 1990 [1987]), 236–58. On women and the antivivisection movement, see Judith R. Walkowitz, *Prostitution and Victorian Society: Women, Class, and the State* (Cambridge: Cambridge University Press, 1980), 129.

88. Scott, "Content of Sugar," 285.

89. For another example of the effect of the "keeper" on the animal's physiology, see J. Barcroft and J. G. Stephens, "Observations upon the Size of the Spleen," *Journal of Physiology* 64 (1927–28): 1–22.

90. Philip J. Pauly, "Modernist Practice in American Biology," in Dorothy Ross, ed., *Modernist Impulses in the Human Sciences, 1870–1930* (Baltimore: Johns Hopkins University Press, 1994), 272–89, 286. For the connections between modernist and artifice, see David A. Hollinger, "The Knower and Artificer, with Postscript 1993," in ibid., 26–53. See also Philip J. Pauly, *Controlling Life: Jacques Loeb and the Engineering Ideal in Biology* (Berkeley: University of California Press, 1990 [1987]).

91. Affidavit sworn by Walter Alvarez in the case of censorship of the Kinsey Institute, April 30, 1957. See Nancy F. Wechsler to Walter Alvarez, April 22, 1957, folder "Alvarez/90.2/Greenbaum, Wolff & Ernst/2," box Alvarez/BMS/C 90.2/G-O, Walter C. Alvarez Papers, Rare Books and Manuscripts, Francis A. Countway Library of Medicine, Boston.

92. Walter Bradford Cannon, *The Way of an Investigator: A Scientist's Experiences in Medical Research* (New York: Norton, 1945), 40.

93. James, "Emotions," 122.

94. Cannon, *Way of an Investigator,* 203.

95. Darwin lamented his loss of musical and poetical appreciation. See Francis Darwin, ed., *The Autobiography of Charles Darwin and Selected Letters* (New York: Dover, 1958 [1892]), 53–54. On Darwin as "anaesthetic man," see Donald Fleming, "Charles Darwin, the Anaesthetic Man," *Victorian Studies* 4, no. 3 (March 1961): 219–36.

96. And we could point to their possible larger resonance with that wider social contemporary movement that made Americans emotionally "cool." See Stearns, *American Cool.*

97. For a more extended discussion of these and other themes, see Otniel E. Dror, "Modernity and the Scientific Study of Emotions, 1880–1950," dissertation in progress, Department of History, Princeton University.

98. Foucault, *Discipline and Punish,* 135–228.

99. Ibid., 202.

100. Ibid., 201 (my italics).

101. Ibid., 202–3 (my italics).

102. One physician elegantly used a common late nineteenth- and twentieth-century metaphor to refer to the body during emotion: "an escape of the [spinal] cord from the control of the brain." Walter Alvarez to Walter B. Cannon, August 27, 1927, folder 1516, box 110, WBC. For an overview of the history of the hierarchical structure of the brain, its different functional levels, and the notion of "release," see Roger Smith, *Inhibition: History and Meaning in the Sciences of Mind and Brain* (Berkeley: University of California Press, 1992); and Anne Harrington, *Medicine, Mind, and the Double Brain* (Princeton: Princeton University Press, 1987).

103. On the notion of "resistance," see Foucault, "L'oeil du pouvoir."

104. Or any of the numerous bodily phenomena of emotions that we have seen.

105. The moderns therefore challenged the classic structure of the examination: this quintessential process of extracting knowledge was inherently an emotional one. This notion of going beyond the superficial was a central theme in the physiological investigation of emotions. See, e.g., Cannon, *Bodily Changes,* 2–3; Bernard, "Sur la physiologie du coeur"; and Cyon, "Le Coeur et le cerveau."

Varieties of Emotional Expression and Experience
Ethnicity, Gender, Race, Religion

Chapter Ten

Ethnicity and Emotions in America
Dimensions of the Unexplored

Hasia R. Diner

Conflicting emotions—pride and shame, chauvinism and self-hatred, loyalty to the place and group of one's birth and a desire to escape the shackles of the past and embrace the new, engaging American culture, resistance of the new and guilt over rejection of the old—cannot be disentangled from the fundamental processes endured by millions of immigrants who have, since the seventeenth century through the closing years of the twentieth, transplanted themselves physically and "became" American. Immigrants who envisioned a permanent move to America and those who intended merely to sojourn there went through a series of emotional negotiations between old and new, between imagined expectations and the reality of outcomes.

What did it "feel" like for women and men to leave their ancestral homes and establish new communities in a strange land? Did immigrants feel guilty about abandoning not only places, but people, to whom they felt a deep loyalty and whom they might never see again? What kinds of emotions did the newcomers endure as they became strangers in a relatively unknown place? What about their children? How did first-generation Americans balance love of parents and their parental cultures with a sense of personal awkwardness as they moved beyond the protected immigrant enclave and into the American mainstream? What feelings engulfed them, and what behaviors did they manifest as they dealt with these conflicted emotions? How did they negotiate on the emotional level the line between two worlds? How have immigrant/ethnic emotions changed over time and how did the very nature of the migration shape the kinds of emotional response toward acculturating to America on an emotional level?

We know precious little about the emotional lives of immigrants and their offspring, the new Americans. We know that immigrants and their children learned English. They learned how to use the political system for their own purposes. They picked up and adopted American attitudes about race. We need to also ask, by what means did immigrants learn to express their feelings in American styles? How did they come to internalize the emotions deemed appropriate by the native-born, largely Protestant, American mainstream? How did individuals negotiate living in two worlds, each with its own appropriate ways of feeling and expressing those feelings?

In a profound sense, the history of immigration and ethnicization *is* a history of emotions.[1] Such a drastic change in individuals' lives could not have taken place without serious emotional involvement. How could people born and nurtured in one society leave, usually for good, and not respond on an affective level? While such emotions may analytically have been subsumed under the category of "assimilation" and all its adjustments, immigrants were, after all, real men and women, individuals who felt happy or sad, lonely or fulfilled, ashamed or proud, guilty or self-satisfied with the decisions they made.

Certainly the imaginative literature produced by immigrants—novels, poetry, short stories, plays spoke eloquently—if often in highly stylized ways, about such poignant emotions as loneliness, discomfort, shame, awkwardness, anger, and pride, both in the group and in the personal accomplishments of the protagonist, often the stand-in for the immigrant author. Immigrant fiction also probed perhaps the most profound question attendant on the immigration process. Was it worth it? Abraham Cahan opened the final chapter of the classic immigrant text *The Rise of David Levinsky* with exactly such a formulation, as the once impoverished student of Talmud, now a highly successful clothing manufacturer who has triumphed in the American realm of material acquisition, asks,

> Am I happy?
>
>   There are moments when I am overwhelmed by a sense of my success and ease. I become aware that thousands of things which had formerly been forbidden fruit to me are at my command now. . . . I recalled . . . people whom I used to fear and before whom I used to humiliate myself because of my poverty. . . . At this moment, as these memories were filling me, I felt as though now there was nobody in the world who could inspire me with awe. . . . And yet . . . I feel a peculiar yearning. . . . My sense of triumph is coupled with a brooding sense of emptiness and insignificance. . . . I am lonely. . . . No, I am not happy. . . . I can never forget the days of misery. I cannot escape from my old self. My past and my present do not comport well.[2]

Cahan was not alone among immigrant authors, or writers whose parents had transplanted themselves in America, in structuring their work around emotional questions about the meaning of migration and the personal discomfort of being outsiders in America. On a basic level, all immigrant fiction dealt with this central problem in one way or another.

Writers of the first American-born generation also focused on the emotional tension of being pulled in one direction by parents who represented the Old World and in the other direction by the seductive lure of America. The remembered experiences of the immigrants' children centered on journeys away from the comforts of home to the larger, less hospitable, but much more attractive world of America. Literary critic Irving Howe described his childhood in New York in exactly these terms.

> The thought of bringing my friends home was inconceivable, for I would have been as ashamed to show them to my parents as to show my parents to them. . . . The worldly

manner affected by some of my friends would have stirred flames of suspicion in the eyes of my father; the sullen immigrant kindliness of my parents would have struck my friends as all too familiar; and my own self-consciousness, which in regard to my parents led me into a maze of superfluous lies and trivial deceptions, made it difficult for me to believe in a life grounded in simple good faith. . . . So we walked the streets.[3]

So too the more sensitive of American observers, people like Jane Addams, for example, recognized the emotional gulf that stretched out between foreign-born parents and American children. Her *Spirit of Youth and the City Streets* (1909) saw this chasm as a cause of much of the tension in the immigrant homes in her Hull House neighborhood and beyond. Writing about the proliferation of public entertainment and its negative impact on young people, Addams asked her readers, "Who is responsible for its [the city's] inadequacy and dangers?" She then proceeded to answer her own rhetorical questions: "We certainly cannot expect the fathers and mothers . . . who have emigrated from other lands to appreciate or rectify these dangers. We cannot expect the young people themselves to cling to conventions which are totally unsuited to modern city conditions . . . we cannot hope that they will understand the emotional force which seizes them and which, when it does, does not find the traditional line of domesticity."[4]

Historians who have grappled with the multiple aspects of immigration and the creation of ethnicity in America, phenomena so crucial to the understanding of American history, have shied away from the realm of the emotional and have hesitated to explore the feelings immigrants endured and the meanings they invested in their experiences. The grand narrative of emigration and immigration has been told primarily from a structural, economically driven perspective. The dominant paradigm in the scholarship has focused on the causes of the migration and the institutional accommodation of immigrants, regardless of where they came from, and regardless of the historic moment.

Most of what we know about this phenomenon involves the social and economic forces that compelled women and men to leave their ancestral homes, places of diminishing economic prospects, and the forces at work in America, which in one way or another satisfied the migration's economic goals. By and large, American opportunity, economic, social, and cultural, has provided the analytic context for understanding immigrant behavior. America offered abundant material rewards—as measured against previous levels of subsistence—and high rates of personal autonomy, in contrast to the highly regulated community life of premigration villages and towns.

We also know that Americans articulated a range of attitudes toward immigrants in general, and toward specific groups in particular. Immigrants and their children maneuvered around restrictions where Americans imposed them, and created communal infrastructures to provide for members' needs. The production of ethnic culture, including newspapers, theaters, houses of worship, literature, and benevolent associations, buffered the immigrants from the hostile outside. These institutions waxed and then waned, as the immigrants and their descendants lived through changing social and economic conditions.

But all these observable, measurable, and tangible elements of immigrant adaptation to America can be—and ought to be—considered on the emotional level as well. They must have come with an emotional price tag. What *did* it cost? How much *did* ordinary women and men pay in order to become American?

It is not that the historiography is utterly devoid of attention to the emotional issues of immigration and ethnic adaptation. The two pioneering historians of the field, Marcus Hansen and Oscar Handlin, did in fact pose their work directly in terms of emotional concerns; in part because of how they framed the issues, subsequent scholars have eschewed grappling with them any further.

Hansen, a student of Frederick Jackson Turner, himself the child of immigrant parents, can rightfully be called the first historian to legitimate the study of immigration. Although his remarkably nuanced essays of the 1920s and 1930s pointed to the complexity inherent in studying this "mingling of social systems,"[5] when he delved into the zone of feelings, generalizations and speculations took over.

Few concepts have proved more durable in American history than Hansen's "third generation law," which he developed in a lecture, "The Problem of the Third Generation Immigrant," delivered in 1937 at the Augustana Historical Society in Rockford, Illinois.[6] Here he surveyed the emotional lives of three generations—the immigrant grandfather, the American-born son, and the very American grandchild. In Hansen's schema, the first American-born individual in this family chain, the literal middle man, played the pivotal emotional role. The immigrant had been too caught up in the struggle for daily bread to worry about feelings. He lived his life in an immigrant enclave into which American ideas penetrated little and offered few challenges to his emotional stability.

But the son of that immigrant felt shame and discomfort at the foreignness of his father as he, the product of the New World, moved out into the American landscape and recognized the "otherness" of his ways. He developed a kind of loathing, and self-loathing, of everything that smacked of his Old World patrimony. He assertively opted to forget tradition in order to fit in to the American mold. Yet his son, a member of the second generation of Americans, distant enough from the premigration experience and comfortable enough in his American pedigree, sensed a kind of loss and developed a nostalgic relationship to that which he had never known. This representative of the third generation then engaged in an effort to reclaim his heritage by reinventing tradition. He fondly remembered what his father had forgotten out of shame. As Hansen formulated it, "What the son wishes to forget the grandson wishes to remember."

Oscar Handlin, like Hansen, was the first of his family to be born in America. He too, in his self-proclaimed "Epic Story of the Great Migrations That Made the American People," focused on the emotional experience of immigration, the process of being "uprooted."[7] He too created an immigrant archetype. Handlin's uprooted peasant found himself emotionally ill equipped to endure the rigors of life in a new and alien culture. Handlin peppered his prose with such words as "alienated," "dazed," "lonely," and "disoriented." The mere act of moving found him "exhausted—worn out ... emotionally by the succession of new situations that had crowded in."[8] An emotional wreck, the immigrant faced America with no inner supports. "Every element of the immigrants' experience since the day they had left home added to this awareness of their utter helplessness."[9]

At various moments in his narrative Handlin actually switched to italicized type when he granted himself literary (historical?) license to re-create an immigrant's inner thoughts. One of the grimmest of *The Uprooted*'s chapters, that on families and their utter breakdown in America, began with the ominous ruminations of an immigrant woman, unable to sleep. *"All else has passed away with our passing from that place. But this will never change. By holy matrimony he has made me wife and mother to his family. That (fiercely) we can hold intact."* Readers knew in advance that she was wrong. The emotional disruption caused by leaving "that place" predestined the marriage and the family, like every other facet of her existence, to fall apart.[10]

Handlin owed much to the Chicago school of sociology. In *The Uprooted*, he employed many of the concepts of Robert Park, Louis Wirth, and the others of that scholarly tradition of the 1920s and 1930s who emphasized marginality and its attendant emotional upheavals.[11] Their ideas about social alienation and disorganization, by-products of urban life, industrialization, and migration, found a comfortable berth in *The Uprooted*, where among the immigrants, "all relationships became less binding, all behavior more dependent on individual whim."[12] Handlin saw immigration as a fundamentally disruptive phenomenon, less of economic or social patterns than of the emotional balance that had been intrinsic to traditional life.

The ways Handlin and Hansen posed these problems in essence tainted the subject. First, neither Handlin nor Hansen backed up their assertions about emotions with evidence; their conclusions were apparently intuited from their own experiences as the products of immigrant homes. In the increasingly evidence- oriented field of social history, this sort of intuitive inference from personal experience became increasingly suspect.

The historians who followed Handlin and Hansen by and large rejected their invention of a paradigmatic "immigrant" who stood for the diverse millions who had made the journey. Immigration history since the 1960s has been based on the idea that each group had its own story and no single group encapsulated the entire experience of all. Each migration took an idiosyncratic form because each grew out of specific premigration conditions. Some immigrants migrated with the desire to return to their homes with a nest egg earned in America; others opted for a permanent home in the United States. In some cases men predominated among the migrants, while in others men and women migrated in equal numbers. The practitioners of immigration and ethnic history concerned with delineating specific group experiences rejected any analysis based on such sketchy data. They looked to study that which could be documented and measured.

Immigration/ethnic history emerged as a subfield within social history. As such it owed its underlying framework to the idea of human agency, particularly as articulated by the British historian E. P. Thompson and his American disciple Herbert Gutman.[13] According to Thompson and Gutman, immigrants knew what awaited them long before they stepped off the boat. They planned and organized themselves to facilitate the migration. They migrated not as strangers, alone and disoriented, but along chains of family and friends, who provided jobs, housing, and, most important from the point of view of undermining the Handlin- Hansen theses, emotional support. The immigrants themselves set the terms of their adaptation to America. What they liked they accepted; what they disliked they rejected. They found a myriad of ways to accommodate their preferences into a new way of life. Their children by and large negotiated comfortably among the various options around them. Balance and continuity rather than disorientation and the emotionally wrenching process of forgetting characterized the perspective of immigration history.[14] If Oscar Handlin named the emotionally drained peasants of his grand synthesis "the uprooted," John Bodnar, an exemplar of the new immigration history, dubbed his "the transplanted."[15]

Because the practitioners of immigration/ethnic history have worked on the a priori assumption of accommodation and communal support, they have mostly shied away from exploring the feelings that immigrants experienced. Or if they have addressed them, they tend to present the emotional component as something outside or independent of the structural. When they have treated the process of assimilation, they have done so in a largely mechanistic, unilinear way. Over time, immigrants and their children became more like the Americans around them. Public schools may have been the agency of change, or mass culture and public entertainment. Politics, trade unions, or participation in the army all have been offered up as engines of acculturation. But few historians have really tried to play with the notion, obvious as it might be, that undergoing these acculturative activities involved an emotional reaction. It had a feel to it, and ordinary women and men sensed the changes. How did they respond on an affective level?

By and large, scholars who have amply documented the ways Americans represented the immigrants and their children (usually pejoratively) have not gone the next step. They have not asked how various groups made sense of those negative portrayals. Such groups became the subject of stereotypical portrayals in advertisements, early movies, novels, newspaper cartoons, widely circulating jokes, and other forms of American mass rhetoric. How did immigrants and their children, the ones who made the forays into American culture, engage with these images, or with the serious, political debate over the merits or demerits of particular groups? How did it feel to sit in the darkness of a movie house and see someone of "your" group mocked in the flickering images on the silver screen? How did immigrants and their children respond when they picked up the morning's newspaper and read about the efforts to exclude immigrants, in general or their own kind in particular, because of their imputed degraded moral and mental abilities?

By avoiding the emotional, scholars have missed many opportunities to come to terms with migration and adaptation as cultural as well as social processes.[16] After all, each part of the journey, literally, raises a host of possible questions that can be understood only if the emotional realm receives the kind of attention it deserves.

Regardless of time or place, scholars of immigration have given their concerns a kind of tripartite analysis, and each one of these parts would benefit greatly from being engaged with problems of the emotional. Our understanding of immigration and ethnic history has focused first on the causes of migration and the nature of premigration life, basically, the "push" factors that propelled people outward. Second, scholars have rightly considered it crucial to understand the migration experience itself, the physical process of movement, the stage between emigration and settlement in a new home. Finally, the literature has focused on, in largest measure, the American experience, the "pull" factors that drew people to America and then shaped the nature of settlement, institution building, and adaptation.

Immigration/ethnic history, as social history, has sought out aggregate experiences. It has looked for large concentrations of Polish, or Chinese, or Swedish, or Cape Verdean newcomers in particular places and has delineated their mass experiences. Biography has not been a particularly popular genre in this field, since questions of typicality and representativeness cloud its usefulness to inform about group process. A biography, after all, tells only one individual's story. Yet it would be precisely in the realm of biography that we might learn more about the range of emotional reactions to these movements.

It might be through biographies that we could learn how immigrants "felt" about their decisions to leave. We might find out if they felt differently about the process of leaving home and going far away, if they believed that they would return, as did Greeks or Italians, as opposed to Jews or the Irish. How did this feeling change over time, as technology made it possible to return for visits? What did it mean on an emotional level that some immigrants had been persecuted minorities in their native lands and as such despised those places? Did immigrants endure different kinds of emotions if they were part of a migrant pool consisting of primarily single young women, as in the case of the Irish, or of relatively intact families, as in the case of Jews? What difference did it make in how they felt about leaving if the clergy back home preached against the migration? How might feelings of guilt at leaving their compatriots engaged in struggle against outside oppression, in for example, Ireland or Poland, shape the political behavior of these women and men once they settled in the United States? Did men and women within an ethnic community struggle with different kinds of emotional reactions to their anomalous place in the world around them? Might there be some relationship between the level of shame and anxiety that immigrants and their children endured and their levels of economic mobility? How did immigrants internalize the stereotyping and negative portrayals of them that appeared on the stage, in film, or in print? Did they reject it as racist claptrap or did they internalize some of those objectionable stereotypes and come to believe them themselves?

Even with the overwhelming reticence of ethnic historians to tangle with these issues, it is possible to sketch out some tentative lines of inquiry about ethnicity and emotions. Keeping in mind that a subject of such magnitude still awaits the systematic attention of *many* scholars, studying a range of groups, I want to offer two preliminary portraits of the ethnicization of emotions, portraits that should be taken as suggestive for future research rather than definitive.

The histories of Irish and Jewish immigration to America represented two radically different narratives of migration and adaptation. In the first case, over the course of the mid- to late nineteenth century, women came to outnumber men in this permanent exodus to America.[17] Among Jews, men and women migrated in roughly equal numbers and, except for a statistically insignificant minority, they never considered the possibility of going back. Both groups engaged immediately in the process of creating a complex institutional network to facilitate adaptation. They had no alternative to plunging into America by creating their own ethnic worlds.[18]

These two groups experienced fairly different rates of economic mobility and hence differing patterns of contact with the mainstream institutions of American society. Although this essay cannot explain why, it is sufficient to note that Jews, either those who migrated during the period from 1820 to 1880 from central Europe or the later arrivals from eastern Europe, beginning in the 1870s through the 1920s, found their niche in the American economy with greater ease and speed than had the Irish. Economic mobility brought with it contact with American institutions; schools in particular played a key role in the Jewish emotional encounter with America.

The Irish experienced more sluggish rates of economic mobility and ventured into the mainstream in more measured ways. Only very slowly did Irish American men move beyond their fathers' educational and occupational profile, and not until the early decades of the twentieth century did a sizable middle class constitute the Irish majority. The Irish pursued the option of creating ethnic schools under the aegis of the Catholic Church in a way unmatched by Jews, who opted for public education instead.

Because of the speedier upward economic mobility and the fact that the Jewish migration, although dramatically smaller in number, took place over a full century, Jews had within their fold a more variegated class structure. Well-off, comfortably adjusted Americanized Jews of central European origins, for example, met the massive floods of Jewish newcomers from eastern Europe. Whatever the nature of that greeting (and that indeed may prove to be a key variable in the Jewish reaction to America), Jewish immigrants at the height of the migration encountered a host of ready-made institutions of "help."

Yet in other ways, Irish and Jewish immigrants shared some salient characteristics that might indeed have contoured their emotional responses to America. They arrived poor, compelled to migrate because of the untenable nature of life back home. Massive dislocations of traditional economic and social arrangements in the lands of their birth disrupted life as it had been lived. They had confronted the stirring of modernization before reaching America.

Americans harshly stigmatized both groups. Nineteenth- century Americans considered the Irish a separate and degraded race. Drunken "Pat" and dim-witted "Bridget" entertained American audiences. "No Irish Need Apply" graced many job advertisements. Anti-Irish hostility fueled nativist politics in the mid- to late nineteenth century, while the reform-minded advocates of temperance and public schools sought to transform Irish newcomers and their children into sober—and Protestant—citizens.[19]

Americans likewise viewed Jews as "other." American street talk resounded with the taunts of "kike" and "Hebe." Hook-nosed peddlers and the cunning, avaricious, and dirty ragpickers infused the American popular imagination. There was a connection between "stereotype" and discriminatory behavior. Jews endured street attacks, a few times by organized mobs, and even a few lynchings. Impoverished farmers of the Midwest and South and elite New Englanders shared an antipathy to the Jews. As public debates raged about the Jews, they found themselves excluded from further entry to America after the passage of the 1924 Johnson Act.[20]

How did the women and men of these two groups who came to America experience their new homes on the emotional level? How did they come to terms with what they "knew" Americans thought of them? What kinds of emotional reactions did they undergo as they sought access to life in America beyond the immigrant enclaves? How were those emotional reactions shaped by the kinds of communities they lived in, which themselves made demands on their sons and daughters?

Jewish Shame

In a profound way, modern Jewish history *is* a history of emotions. They provide *the* central tension in the Jewish confrontation with modernity, regardless of where it played itself out. Starting in the late eighteenth century and the age of revolution, Jews lost their separate corporate status. As they came out of their enforced separate existence, they engaged in a complex, tortured confrontation with the various societies in which they lived. Everywhere they lived, in Europe and in the United States (although Jews never had to be formally emancipated in America), emancipation came with a price tag. In order to gain access to the proffered bounties of the outside, larger society, Jews had to learn to conform to new rules of behavior.

In central Europe this actually found its way into the law and into policy. Emancipation was offered in Prussia, for example, to those Jews who spoke German, who did not engage in peddling, the classic ghetto occupation, and who could demonstrate their worthiness to the society. In short, they were told that their behavior was uncivil and they had to civilize themselves.

Elsewhere, including America and England, while the law did not require that Jews prove their acceptability in order to reap the benefits of citizenship, social practices distinguished between those who were "too Jewish" and those who had picked up the accoutrements of gentile behavior and could be tolerated. All Jewish men in the United States, with a few minor, local exceptions, had access to the benefits of civic equality vis-à-vis voting, office holding, jury duty, and the like. But social approval, admission to colleges, universities, and schools of professional training, certain areas of employment and places of leisure and recreation demanded that Jews shed that which seemed Jewish—and hence, offensive—and learn to act American.

They had to learn to negotiate as individuals with the non-Jewish world around them. As a previously ghettoized "nation within a nation" whose members dealt on an emotional level only with each other, Jews in France, Germany, Austria, Italy, and elsewhere in Europe, for the first time, faced the possibility that as individuals they could enter the mainstream.

How to do that? How did access to the gentile world complicate their ties to the

Jewish one? How could one be a Jew and an Englishman? How did looking and acting American distance one from the inner life of the Jewish world?

One writer of the Jewish enlightenment, the *haskalah,* offered a piece of advice that in its simplicity indicated the depth of the emotional entanglement brought by the possibility of emancipation. The Vilna-born poet Yehuda Leib Gordon (1831–1892) wrote in 1863 in an appropriately titled poem, "Awake My People,"

> To the treasury of the state bring your strength,
> Take your share of its possessions, its bounty.
> Be a man abroad and a Jew in your tent,
> A brother to your countrymen and servant to your king.[21]

However dense all four of these lines, the third one expressed the emotional conundrum inherent in the process. In the street, in public, in the neutral realm of the outside, he advised his people, be "a man," fit in, act like other men. Jewishness should be reserved for the confines of "the tent."[22] Essentially Gordon and several generations of Jewish modernists advocated the cultivation of a kind of Jewish split personality, a Janus-faced existence of a bifurcated consciousness, whereby Jews would hang up their Jewish hats before they exited their homes to go "abroad," and leave their "manliness" (or probably better, humanity) on the threshold before they entered into the comfort of their tents. Jews were told to, and probably did, compartmentalize their lives into the outside world of the public and the inside, Jewish world of the private.

In his poem, Gordon did not spell out precisely what he meant by outside and inside. Perhaps he could not. The blurriness of that line of demarcation proved indeed to be the zone of emotional conflict, the place where Jews who attempted to be both "man" and "Jew" struggled on a deep personal level to figure out where they were and what they should be.

At least four issues suggest themselves immediately to indicate how imprecisely Gordon's inside/outside, tent/abroad dichotomy might have presented itself to a nineteenth-century Jew attempting to navigate these two shores. Jewish tradition demanded that Jews separate themselves out from non-Jews in the matter of food. Jewish dietary observance made it virtually impossible for a Jew to sit down and eat with a non-Jew, while the civility of shared common space created multiple opportunities for coworkers, fellow students, and friends to sit down and share a meal. If "you are what you eat," then what, and with whom, should the Jew, who wants to be true to Judaism and fit in with gentile acquaintances, eat? Likewise, if "clothes make the man," then how did Jewish men, required by *halachah* (Jewish law) to cover their heads and refrain from shaving, present themselves in public as just like anyone else, when other men were clean-shaven and bareheaded? Similarly, what names should they carry, both first and last? Those that grew out of their tradition and marked them as "other," or those that resonated as familiar and normal to gentile ears?[23] How about the weekly and annual calendar? What to do in a world where others worshipped and recreated on Sunday while for Jews Saturday had long been marked off as sacred time? How could Jews negotiate the world around them when they organized their year around holidays different from those of the Christian majority?

The negotiation of these practical, behavioral matters took a heavy emotional toll on those Jews who had to decide what to do. These were not mere matters of preference and taste; Jewish tradition considered them divinely mandated law, not to be negotiated for purposes of convenience. Some Jews did not even brook the question. Tradition could not be modified to accommodate to gentile modernity, and these resisters probably did not experience emotional upheavals. At the other end of the spectrum, the most assimilated blended into the majority and converted to Christianity. They too may have escaped inner struggles with identity and feeling, in part to avoid the emotional problems of juggling personae.[24]

The vast majority did neither. Rather, they struggled with place and identity. As they ventured out into the upper rungs of German life—and by extension in other places as well—they felt humiliated by the vestiges of their pre-emancipation lives. They struggled to remake themselves in the light of others' perceptions of them.[25]

Historians of the Jewish experience in the modern world have paid attention to the emotional realm. They had to. Without it, much of the Jewish cultural and political reaction, including the rise of Reform, modern Orthodox, and Conservative Judaism could not be understood. The emergence of Zionism and the Jewish embrace of Marxism grew directly out of the conflicted emotional Jewish reaction to emancipation. For example, one of the key goals of Zionism was "the normalization of the Jewish people."

As immigrants to America, only Jews came with a legacy of having endured de-ghettoization as a legal and cultural process. Scholars concerned with American Jewish history have had to focus on the emotional, albeit in a lesser degree than their colleagues who have studied European Jewry. The process in America took more subtle and indirect forms. But by contrast, they have focused on the emotional price of acculturation to a degree unmatched by those who have studied other groups of newcomers to the United States.

The very conditions of Jewish immigration to America invite us to explore the emotional. For Jews, for example, there was no going back if America did not work out. That from the start differentiated them from Italians, for example, who could return if they so chose; many intended to, and about one-third of them actually did. Italian immigrants had a safety net into which they could fall if disappointment, loneliness, and even generational conflict got too overwhelming.

Jews seem to have experienced a more rapid and intense interaction with American culture than did other immigrants; Italians again are a useful group for purposes of comparison.[26] Jews had no choice but to come to terms with America, and with their own marginal status in it.

The drawn-out process of coming to terms with their new environment meant that their discomfort at being in America was felt that much more sharply. Knowing that they had no "out" and that they were, by definition, not "in" heightened their sense of otherness and made shame, sometimes labeled "self-hatred," a leitmotif of communal culture.

Sociologist Louis Wirth's 1928 study *The Ghetto,* for all its analytic shortcomings, identified the emotional process that came with mobility. In this first work of academic scholarship to probe the impact of American life on the Jews, Wirth wrote,

As long as he remains in the ghetto the Jew seldom becomes conscious of his inferior status. He emerges from the ghetto and finds himself surrounded by a freer but less comfortable and less homely and familiar world. He flees from his people in order to escape from the bonds by which, whether he wills it or not, he is tied to his group.[27]

The overwhelming evidence of several decades now of historical scholarship on rates of ethnic mobility, as defined in terms of education, occupation, or income, points to significant differences between Jews and most other immigrants, particularly the Italians and the Irish. While the Jewish adaptation to America was more complicated than the mythic, single-generational jump from "rags to riches," Jews did experience a more rapid move from the ranks of the working class, where they struggled as immigrants as either manual laborers or petty merchants, to the middle classes.

With that economic mobility came a movement closer to the center of American society. Jews who could, for example, afford the luxury of keeping their children in school had among their ranks a larger percentage of daughters and sons exposed to the values and idioms of American culture, than, for example, the Italians, for whom economic mobility and school attendance took place at a slower rate, or the Irish, who also experienced an excruciatingly sluggish movement out of poverty. In essence then, a critical mass of the American Jewish population, by the 1910s and 1920s, consisted of American-exposed and American-educated young people who felt keenly the distance between the world of home, the Jewish world, and the world of America, that of the streets and the schools.[28]

We know that by these same decades Jewish students clamored for admission to America's colleges and universities. By the 1930s, when Jews made up about 3.5 percent of the American population, they accounted already for 10 percent of its college students.[29] They sought admission to colleges in large enough numbers that those institutions of higher learning began to ponder "the Jewish question," how to deal with the problem of too many (as they defined it) Jews seeking to enter Harvard, Yale, Columbia, and the like. The surge in Jewish applications to these schools perhaps threatened the Anglo-Protestant gatekeepers, who instituted explicit quotas and other discriminatory practices to keep Jews out.

Not surprisingly, much of the manifestation of, and certainly discussion about, Jewish shame took place in the realm of higher education. It was on the campuses that young Jews found themselves exposed to behaviors and styles so unlike their own and where they struggled to be like the gentiles with whom they studied and sometimes lived. In 1926 the *Jewish Tribune* posed the question, "Do Jewish Undergraduates Attempt to Distinguish Their Jewishness?" It answered itself in the affirmative with vignettes from students at a number of colleges, all expressing discomfort at being known among their fellow students as Jewish.[30] A 1941 Jewish graduate of Yale University remembered, "We walked on eggshells … tried to conform. Because the more you conformed, the less you stood out."[31] Stories abounded of students who pretended to be something other than Jewish. Another Yale alumnus of the 1930s mentioned that among his classmates he saw "a good deal of incipient student Marranism," the reference being to the Jews of Spain, the Marranos, who in public "passed" as Christians, but practiced Judaism in secret.[32]

Unlike, however, the secret Jews of Spain, those of the Ivy League did not face torture and execution for their Jewishness. They faced instead the possibility of social ostracism and for that they felt shame, shame at their behavior and at the fact of their Jewishness.

The handful of Jews who secured teaching positions at American colleges in the decades before World War II confirmed the overwhelming sense of shame that haunted the Jewish students they met. Horace Kallen, for example, the social philosopher who taught at Harvard, helped create in 1906 the first Jewish student organization in America, the Menorah Society, designed specifically for the purpose of "liberating the Jewish student from his feeling of inferiority." Kallen, reminiscing about his early years in academia, estimated that almost all the Jewish students he met at Harvard felt "openly ashamed of Jewishness" and sought to distance themselves from their origins.[33]

Henry Wolfson, also an anomaly, a Jewish professor at Harvard in the interwar years, recognized as well the depths of shame endured by the Jews on his campus, and indeed, the depths of shame and discomfort endured by all Jews eager to embrace modernity.[34] In a 1921 article, aptly entitled "Escaping Judaism," he admitted with resignation that "when a young man comes to me complaining about the narrowness, the dryness, the intellectual poverty of Judaism, I do not argue with him." The discomfort they felt with Jewishness, Wolfson believed, could not be countered with any rational argument.[35]

For those eager to be American, Jewishness proved to be a burden. Importantly, though, very few American Jews went as far as shedding their Jewishness by formally converting to Christianity. Rather, many (or so I infer from a wide reading of biographies, autobiographies, memoirs, fiction, journalism) struggled with the shame of being Jewish, yet were unwilling to go the final step and actually become Christian. Instead American Jewish sources point to a wide array of tactics to cover up, particularly in public, manifestations of Jewishness.

Without, in all likelihood, having read Y. L. Gordon's advice about being a "man" on the street, American Jews heeded it. They sought out ways to make their Jewishness less obvious. Name changing seems to have been rampant.[36] Jews, women in particular, underwent surgery, enduring the famed "nose job," so celebrated in the fiction of Jewish male authors like Philip Roth, to appear less Jewish.[37]

Jews' discomfort with themselves focused heavily on questions of language. Sander Gilman has delineated this anxiety for German Jews in his study *Jewish Self-Hatred*, although no American Jewish historian has tried to tackle its manifestation in America. Yet literary sources point to language as a source of Jewish discomfort in public. In his classic novel of the immigration, *Call It Sleep*, Henry Roth dichotomized between the Yiddish of the home and the English of the streets. Efforts to eradicate Jewish accents consumed the energies of immigrants and their children. Even so affirmative and traditional a Jewish institution as the Jewish Theological Seminary of America employed on its staff from its founding in the 1890s a non-Jewish teacher of speech and elocution, working to eradicate the foreign-sounding accents of the mostly immigrant (and children of immigrant) students.[38] Ethnolinguist Joshua Fishman noted that Jewish immigrants themselves developed a complicated relationship with Yiddish, their mother tongue. To many, eager to become American, it served as a "badge of shame." Rather than seeing it as a language like any other, they rather saw it as "the 'jargon' of the ignorant. . . . It was the despoiler of American accents."[39]

The ways Jews acted out their shame about public presentations of their Jewishness was captured in a 1944 essay by Hayim Greenberg, an intellectual and professional activist in the Labor Zionist movement. In a piece that explored the inner Jewish debate over the question whether American Jews actually lived in the diaspora, Greenberg wrote,

> The Italian who sells newspapers in my neighborhood is naturally uninformed about . . . disputations among Jewish intellectuals. He may or may not look upon himself as an exile from Italy . . . ; but he lives in America, and knows that his Jewish customers ought to be treated with proper "delicacy." When a man buys an English and a Jewish newspaper from him, the vendor, scrupulously observing the ethics of his profession, quickly wraps the Jewish paper inside the English, making the former invisible, and inoffensive to the eye.[40]

It may be that the purchaser of the Jewish newspaper wanted the Jewish text hidden by the American so as to not elicit any hostility from potential anti-Semites. The Jewish patient who chose to shorten and uplift her nose may have done what she did less because of revulsion at her own Jewishness than because she knew that without it, a sought-after job could be denied her on account of her obvious Jewish appearance. So too the Jew who changed her name or struggled to change his accent. Jews did calculate the existence of real anti-Semitism and decided that a small cover-up of obvious Jewishness was worth it.[41]

Such defensiveness is clearly not a matter of shame or self-hatred but rather a rational response to real, or sometimes possibly imagined, hostility. Yet to ascribe such behavior totally to anxiety over anti-Semitism discounts much of the inner communal rhetoric that resounded among American Jews through at least the first six decades of the twentieth century, a communal rhetoric that recognized that as Jews came into contact with non-Jewish society, they measured their own behavior and background against that of others, and found themselves wanting. They *knew* that even with cover-ups and camouflages they would always remain Jews, and that made them ashamed.

Probably the complex of shame, self-hatred, and the inability to really overcome it was best captured by the Jewish social psychologist Kurt Lewin, who in a series of articles in the 1930s explored the "nearly unavoidable inner conflict" faced by Jews, youth in particular, in America. Lewin had been trained in Germany and fled to America on the eve of the Nazi takeover of his homeland. Influenced by the German-Jewish philosopher Theodor Lessing, who in 1930 coined the phrase "self-hatred," *Judische Selbsthass*, Lewin applied and refined Lessing's ideas for American Jewry. Lewin was also influenced by the literary works of Ludwig Lewisohn, an American Jewish writer who himself had once converted to Christianity in order to secure a teaching appointment and then returned to Judaism. Lewisohn went on to write a series of novels that probed the tangled psyches of various Jewish characters who hated themselves because of their Jewishness and who further hated themselves because of that hatred.

Jewish self-hatred, a form of shame, took many forms. Lewin saw it playing itself out in a number of directions, ranging from the Jewish "inferiority complex," wherein the Jew always saw that which was Jewish as degraded, to Jewish "escapism," that is, a reluctance on the part of some Jews to venture out into the larger world for fear of being discovered and having to deal with the consequences of marginalization. "This hatred," which really amounted to shame, Lewin wrote, "is so blended with other motives that it is difficult to decide in any one particular case whether or not self-hatred is involved." [42]

Clearly the subject of Jewish shame cannot be disentangled from the intense process of Jewish acculturation to America. Jews *had* to acculturate and wanted to. In the process, although they had never in America faced a legally sanctioned ghetto, they found themselves moving outward from a familiar world where they interacted primarily with other Jews, into a far larger and, from their point of view, more attractive outside world of the mainstream.

It was at this point that they faced a series of decisions about behavior and a series of emotional reactions to who they were, where they had been, and where they were going. The closer they came to some kind of American mainstream, the more tortured and complex the emotional overlay of those negotiations.

Irish Guilt

Like the Jews, the Irish came to America for good. They too evidenced little return migration. Yet their permanence in America can be seen as different from that of Jews, and it helps explain the Irish emotional reaction to America. Theoretically, Irish immigrants could have gone back, particularly the legions of young women who increasingly made up the majority of the migrants in the decades after the 1850s, once the dislocations immediately caused by the great famine of the late 1840s subsided.

It would have made perfect sense for the hundreds of thousands of "girls" who came to America from Ireland to work in domestic service to have returned once they had earned their own dowries. They had the ability to make the return voyage, with money in their pockets, find an unmarried man — since bachelors came to predominate in the Irish countryside — and get married. But they did not do this. They stayed in America, and probably up to half of them never married. Although they continued, as long as they worked and remained single, to fulfill their obligations to family left behind, they made no effort to take that same cash and go back again themselves. In a way, they sent the money as a substitute for sending themselves. [43]

Although in the most profound sense they abandoned Ireland, the historian Kerby Miller has convincingly argued in *Emigrants and Exiles* that the Irish who left before, during, or after the famine considered themselves in exile. They could not reconcile themselves to the reality of having left and never returning. In his masterful study of immigrant letters, ballads, poetry, and similarly emotional sources, Miller juxtaposed the Irish sense of exile and abandonment with the reality of the permanent move to America. Despite the behavior of no-return, Miller convincingly asserted, they held out against fully assimilating into America and never reconciled themselves to modernity.

Miller referred to their migration as an "involuntary" exile. From a structural point of view he was correct. Post- famine Ireland contained within itself a centripetal dynamism; by its very nature it sent out its young, and it prospered over time because those young had left, thus raising the economic level of those who stayed, at the same time that those young sent back vast amounts of money, facilitating the ratcheting up of the Irish economy.

Social historians looking backward can see that the youth of Ireland had no choice but to leave for this involuntary exile. But at the time, individuals could not discern the inevitability of this process. To them, their behavior involved a matter of personal decision making and as they saw it, they were choosing their own futures and their own mobility over staying put and helping out at home. They may have known on an intellectual level that they had to go, but on an emotional or visceral level, they believed that they had agency, and that they had chosen America over Ireland.

The implication of this was that the emotion that loomed largest among the Irish was guilt, a feeling of having behaved wrongly, of having turned their backs on personal responsibility, of having abandoned all those who held them dear. While they might, once settled in America, send money back home in the form of remittances, they never went back themselves.

They embarked on their one-way journey to America after the ritual of the tearful "America wake," the highly charged send-off that resembled the preparation for a funeral as much as a farewell party. The inner logic of the "America wake" assumed that this would indeed be the last time that parents would see their children, that kin would all be together. Crying, keening, drinking, and mournful music dominated the rite, the event that marked emigrants' last hours on "the ould sod."

Emotionally the Irish went through a process by which they knew they had to leave, but also understood that by doing so they were breaking up their families and communities. Caught between the reality that they could not stay in Ireland and the feeling that by going to America they were abandoning it, they experienced a deep and profound sense of guilt. Much of the popular culture surrounding the emigration confirmed the widely shared emotion of guilt. One widely sung ballad, heard on both sides of the Atlantic, may have encapsulated the inevitability of the migration and the guilt that went along with it:

> God keep all the mothers who rear up a child,
> And also the father who labors and toils.
> Trying to support them he works night and day,
> And when they are reared up, they then go away.[44]

Irish priests thundered against the migration. They foretold only doom and destruction for the young people who left, and went so far as to call them traitors to their people. America, they predicted, would bring about the "moral murder of countless virtuous maidens";[45] they lambasted the "selfish" ones who abandoned family, community, and "Holy Ireland."

The nearly universal decision of the Irish youth to leave their homes forever and the intense, emotional Irish rhetoric against the (inevitable) emigration caused the Irish in America to experience guilt, an overwhelming and inescapable sense that even though Ireland sent them out, they had somehow betrayed it.[46] The fact that they understood their emigration as exile explains the sense of remorse endured by the Irish as they fashioned for themselves an Americanized ethnic identity.

Politics compounded this feeling of guilt. Not coincidentally, the most massive exodus to America took place at the same time as the most intense struggles for national liberation. In essence, and obviously overstated here, the Irish people who stayed home endured poverty and fought, in one way or another, against continuing British rule. Others went to America and earned money. This reality, like that of the permanent, self- imposed exile, produced a kind of collective, ethnic sense of guilt. The American Irish had pursued their own material goals and left the battle against the hated enemy to those back home.

That guilt can be marshalled to explain the intensity of the Irish American involvement in the nationalist movement. In every phase of the nationalist struggle, the Irish in the United States tended to side with the most extreme factions and to support the least compromising elements in the effort to ease Ireland's political suffering. They sent vast amounts of money back to Ireland, not just to their own families trying to upgrade their meager farms, but also to the political factions and movements seeking to free Ireland of British rule. They organized parades and mammoth rallies and even attempted, in the Fenian movement, to attack British forts in Canada in the 1870s. While the size of nationalist societies rose and fell, growing at moments of greatest crisis in Ireland, throughout the history of the Irish in America they manifested their anti-British feelings to a high degree. It became a kind of definition of what it meant to be Irish American. Having decided to become permanent, voluntary exiles, the Irish in the United States compensated for their guilt by become hyperpatriots for a cause whose results they would never have to live with.[47]

Little, however, in the extant literature indicates that shame of Irishness or embarrassment about Catholicism was common among the Irish immigrants and their children. While individual biographies emphasized shame about past poverty, unlike Jews, Irish Americans by and large wore their Irishness with pride. Over time, they became more assertively and affirmatively Irish, if only on a symbolic level. Indeed, the more American they became, the more they flaunted their Irishness. St. Patrick's Day parades, visible, voluble, and demonstrative, came in the latter decades of the nineteenth century to dominate the Irish American calendar, as the Irish took to the streets to strut their Irishness. A purely American invention, the parade enabled the Irish of New York, Philadelphia, Boston, and countless smaller communities to prove to themselves, to the people back home, and to their American neighbors that they had not given up their Irishness in exchange for America.

As the Irish became more American, they became more intensely Catholic. Despite the tremendous anti-Catholicism of nineteenth-century America and the assiduous efforts of Protestant evangelicals to convert them, the Irish who came to America relatively unchurched heightened their involvement, loyalty, and identification with Catholicism the longer they lived in America. In the first generation the services of a priest sufficed for the Irish immigrants. Within a generation, parochial schools, church societies, and recreational activities for every age group mushroomed as parish life and community life became one and the same.[48]

There is no body of scholarly or memoir literature that indicates any trend toward passing, name changing, or assiduously trying to weed out distinctively Irish behavioral traits, as defined by the hostile, American world. As the Irish settled themselves into America, amidst an intense public rhetoric about their degraded character, they became more overtly Irish in their behavior.[49] Even those Irish who made the move into the better-off classes, the "lace curtain" Irish, did not express self- loathing over their Irishness. They may have opted for American—that is, middle-class, Protestant—living styles, and they may have manifested behaviors of respectable decorum. But they did not try to "pass" as something other than Irish Catholics out of shame at who they were or where they came from.

Some commentators at the time of immigration and settlement and subsequent historians have attributed the high levels of Irish drinking and the public flaunting of it, at a time when Protestant Americans came to view drinking as immoral and dysfunctional, to the Irish need to mark off their distinctiveness in Yankee society. John Francis Maguire, a major figure in Irish nationalist circles in America, himself a critic of Irish drinking, recognized that despite its pathology it served an ethnic, emotional purpose. "The Irishman," he wrote in 1868, "more impulsive, more mercurial, more excitable, will publish his indiscretion on the highway, and will himself identify his nationality with his folly."[50]

Over the course of the mid- to late nineteenth century, the Irish in America, despite impressive statistics on participation in, for example, the Civil War, the Spanish-American War, or even World War I, developed what might be seen as a kind of oppositional relationship to American culture. While Jewish rhetoric sought to prove the points of confluence between traditional Judaism and liberal Americanism, the Irish staked out a kind of confrontational relationship with America, its emphasis on "progress," and its individualistic culture of materialism and acquisitiveness. Irishness, as distinct from Americanness, had to be proven and vindicated.

It may be that their guilt at having left, and left for good, held the Irish back from pretending to be something other than what they were. They worked out their sense of guilt at having abandoned Ireland by accentuating their Irishness as they constructed it. Real remorse at the sense of having betrayed Ireland at its moment of need pushed them into behaviors that indicated their deep guilt. Indeed, the more Americans—Protestant, Yankee—derided them, the more demonstrably they presented themselves as Irish.[51]

These two, less than equal sketches, that of the Irish and that of the Jews, are just that. I am offering them here as a kind of preliminary salvo to historians of immigration and ethnicity, challenging the field to tackle the emotional. No doubt, the Irish and Jewish reactions to America must have involved emotional engagements more complex than just guilt on the part of one, and shame felt by the other. We should explore what they were.

It *is* possible to explore the emotional dimension of migration and ethnicization without falling into the pitfall of glittering generalities. Historians can continue to employ the concept of human agency and recognize the multiplicity of ethnic experiences, and still explore the emotional contours of immigration. They are not mutually exclusive. Indeed, these themes need to be analytically joined. After all, the women and men we study *felt* as much as they worked; they experienced emotions as well as strikes, crowded neighborhoods, and mass entertainments. Just as they learned to "act" American, they also learned how to "feel" American. We owe it to them, as well as to the field of historical scholarship, to focus on them.

NOTES

1. I use the term "ethnicization" as opposed to "Americanization" for very specific reasons. First, "ethnicization" avoids any of the politically charged reactions associated with such terms as "Americanization" or "assimilation." Second, it indicates a process that scholars have long alluded to, namely, that immigrants accommodated simultaneously to America and to a new entity, the ethnic group. Previous to migration, with some exceptions, they did not have a clear sense of belonging to a particular nation or group but rather manifested feelings of loyalty to family, village, or region. Only upon arrival in a modern, complicated, multiethnic society with a strange, dominant culture did they develop a consciousness of and a set of institutions based on this identity. Indeed the process that propelled individuals and families out of traditional communities into the process of migration coincided with the emergence of national identities at home, under the influence of the rise of capitalism. I am indebted to Ewa Morawska, *Insecure Prosperity: Small-Town Jews in Industrial America, 1890–1940* (Princeton: Princeton University Press, 1996) for this term.

2. Abraham Cahan, *The Rise of David Levinsky* (New York: Harper and Brothers, 1917), 525–30.

3. Irving Howe, *World of Our Fathers: The Journey of the East European Jews to America and the Life They Found and Made* (New York: Harcourt Brace, 1976), 262–63.

4. Jane Addams, *The Spirit of Youth and the City Streets* (New York: Macmillan, 1909), 15.

5. Marcus Lee Hansen, *The Immigrant in American Life* (New York: Harper and Row, 1940), 206.

6. Reprinted in Peter Kivisto and Dag Blanck, *American Immigrants and Their Generations: Studies and Commentaries on the Hansen Thesis after Fifty Years* (Urbana: University of Illinois Press, 1990), 191–203.

7. Oscar Handlin, *The Uprooted* (New York: Grosset and Dunlap, 1951).

8. Handlin, *Uprooted,* 62.

9. Handlin, *Uprooted,* 107.

10. Handlin, *Uprooted,* 227.

11. See, for example, Robert E. Park, "Human Migration and the Marginal Man," *American Journal of Sociology* 33 (May 1928): 881–93; Louis Wirth, *The Ghetto* (Chicago: University of Chicago Press, 1928).

12. Handlin, *Uprooted,* 155.

13. E. P. Thompson, *The Making of the English Working Class* (Harmondworth: Penguin, 1968).

14. For the best statement of this, see Virginia Yans-McLaughlin, *Family and Community: Italian Immigrants in Buffalo, 1880–1930* (Urbana: University of Illinois Press, 1971).

15. John Bodnar, *The Transplanted: A History of Immigrants in Urban America* (Bloomington: Indiana University Press, 1985).

16. Matthew Frye Jacobson, *Special Sorrows: The Diasporic Imagination of Irish, Polish, and Jewish Immigrants in the United States* (Cambridge: Harvard University Press, 1995) provides an exception to the lack of a cultural orientation of immigration history.

17. Hasia Diner, *Erin's Daughters in America: Irish Immigrant Women in the Nineteenth Century* (Baltimore: Johns Hopkins University Press, 1983).

18. Hasia Diner, *A Time for Gathering: The Second Migration, 1820–1880* (Baltimore: Johns Hopkins University Press, 1992); Gerald Sorin, *A Time for Building: The Third Migration, 1880–1920* (Baltimore: Johns Hopkins University Press, 1992).

19. Dale Knobel, *Paddy and the Republic: Ethnicity and Nationality in Antebellum America* (Middletown, CT: Wesleyan University Press, 1986).

20. Leonard Dinnerstein, *Antisemitism in America* (New York: Oxford University Press, 1994).

21. Translation in Paul Mendes-Flohr and Jehuda Reinharz, eds., *The Jew in the Modern World* (Oxford: Oxford University Press, 1980), 312–13.

22. The use of "man" may have been articulated in the universal voice by Gordon. Some scholars of modern Jewish history have studied the ways the process of emancipation specifically focused on Jewish men. Emancipation began with concerns of the state and citizenship and addressed men and men's concerns. The public debate about remaking the Jews, their *Bildung*, highlighted the problems of Jewish manliness. Women's issues were of a secondary and subsidiary nature as Jews faced the possibility of normalization. See Paula Hyman, *Gender and Assimilation in Modern Jewish History* (Seattle: University of Washington Press, 1996).

23. See, for example, William Zvi Tannenbaum, "From Community to Citizenship: The Jews of Rural Franconia, 1801–1862" (Ph.D. diss., Stanford University, 1989), 187–200 on changes in Jewish naming patterns that went along with emancipation.

24. Conversion to Christianity did not ipso facto eliminate the emotional anguish. Witness the career of Heinrich Heine, who converted to Lutheranism but toward the end of his life, bitter over his own behavior and the failed promise of emancipation, returned to Judaism. See Hugo Bieber and Moses Hadas, *Heine: Biographical Anthology* (Philadelphia: Jewish Publication Society, 1956).

25. Naomi Cohen, *Encounter with Emancipation: The German Jews in the United States, 1830–1914* (Philadelphia: Jewish Publication Society of America, 1984); Jacob Katz, *Out of the Ghetto: The Social Background of Jewish Emancipation, 1770–1870* (Cambridge: Harvard University Press, 1973); John Murray Cuddihy, *The Ordeal of Civility: Freud, Marx, Levi-Strauss, and the Jewish Struggle with Modernity* (Boston: Beacon Press, 1974); Michael Meyer, *The Origins of the Modern Jew* (Detroit: Wayne State University Press, 1967); Sander L. Gilman, *Jewish Self-Hatred: Anti-Semitism and the Hidden Language of the Jews* (Baltimore: Johns Hopkins University Press, 1986).

26. I have chosen not to include Italian immigrants in this essay, but would like to note that their immigration and adaptation also suggest a series of emotional reactions that should be probed by other scholars. In an interesting social-psychological study done in the late 1930s in New Haven, Irvin Child looked at the American-born sons of southern Italian immigrants. He found that some—not a majority—of these boys and young men felt uncomfortable with the Italian culture and endeavored to make themselves over into "ordinary" Americans. See Irving Child, *Italian or American? The Second Generation in Conflict* (New Haven: Yale University Press, 1943). Likewise Leonard Covello, the highly influential principal of a heavily Italian high school in New York's East Harlem, wrote a doctoral dissertation at New York University in the 1940s, "The Social Background of the Italo-American School Child: A Study of the Southern Italian Family Mores and Their Effect on the School Situation in Italy and America." In it he noted some—although not high—levels of inferiority and shame among the children. These and a few other random references point that this could be another fruitful area in the study of immigrant and ethnic emotions.

27. Wirth, *Ghetto*, 261.

28. On comparative ethnic school attendance and achievement, see Joel Pearlmann, *Ethnic Differences: Schooling and Social Structure among the Irish, Italians, Jews and Blacks in an American City, 1880–1935* (Cambridge: Cambridge University Press, 1988).

29. Henry Feingold, *A Time for Searching: Entering the Mainstream, 1920–1945* (Baltimore: Johns Hopkins University Press, 1992), 14.

30. Cited in Mordecai M. Kaplan, *Judaism as a Civilization: Towards a Reconstruction of American-Jewish Life* (New York: Thomas Yoseloff, 1934), 525. Reconstructionism, Kaplan's project and movement, itself can be viewed as an effort to reconcile the emotional chasm endured by modern American Jews, who felt discomfort at inhabiting two civilizations that were fundamentally at odds with each other.

31. Dan A. Oren, *Joining the Club: A History of Jews and Yale* (New Haven: Yale University Press, 1985), 73.

32. Oren, *Joining the Club,* 106.

33. Horace Kallen, "The Promise of the Menorah Idea," *Menorah Journal* 49, 1–2 (autumn–winter 1962): 13.

34. See Susanne Klingenstein, *Jews in the American Academy, 1900–1940: The Dynamics of Intellectual Assimilation* (New Haven: Yale University Press, 1991) for an extensive biographical, organized treatment of Jews, American universities, and the unease the Jews experienced in this world that they so eagerly sought to enter.

35. Henry Austryn Wolfson, "Escaping Judaism," *Menorah Journal* 7, 2 (June 1921): 161.

36. This subject has never been studied and deserves a full and extensive analysis.

37. Again, no historian has tackled this subject, with the exception of the highly suggestive study of assimilating German Jews in Sander L. Gilman, *The Jew's Body* (New York: Routledge, 1991), esp. chap. 7.

38. Hasia R. Diner, "Like the Antelope and the Badger: The Founding and Early Years of the Jewish Theological Seminary, 1886–1902," in *Tradition Renewed: A History of the Jewish Theological Seminary,* Jack Wertheimer, ed. (New York: Jewish Theological Seminary, 1997), 3–42.

39. Joshua A. Fishman, "Yiddish in America," *International Journal of American Linguistics* 31, 2, pt. 2 (April 1965): 52.

40. Hayim Greenberg, *The Inner Eye: Selected Essays* (New York: Jewish Frontier Association, 1953), 341.

41. Dinnerstein, *Antisemitism in America.*

42. Kurt Lewin, *Resolving Social Conflicts: Selected Papers on Group Dynamics* (New York: Harper and Brothers, 1948), esp. 145–58, 186–200.

43. Diner, *Erin's Daughters.*

44. Kerby A. Miller, *Emigrants and Exiles: Ireland and the Irish Exodus to North America* (New York: Oxford University Press, 1985), 562.

45. Quoted in Diner, *Erin's Daughters,* 34.

46. For a provocative discussion of Irish American guilt and what the author sees as a kind of ethnic, emotional discomfort with success, see John Duffy Ibson, *Will the World Break Your Heart: Dimensions and Consequences of Irish-American Assimilation* (New York: Garland, 1990).

47. Thomas N. Brown, *Irish-American Nationalism, 1870–1890* (Westport, CT: Greenwood, 1980); David Brundage, " 'In Time of Peace, Prepare for War': Key Theme in the Social Thought of New York's Irish Nationalists, 1890–1916," in Ronald H. Bayor and Timothy J. Meagher, eds., *The New York Irish* (Baltimore: Johns Hopkins University Press, 1996), 321–34.

48. Jay Dolan, *The Immigrant Church: New York's Irish and German Catholics, 1815–1865* (Baltimore: Johns Hopkins University Press, 1975).

49. For that very public discussion on the defects of the Irish, see Knobel, *Paddy and the Republic.*

50. John Francis Maguire, *The Irish in America* (reprint, New York: Arno, 1969), 285.

51. See, for example, the discussion of actor James O'Neill, father of dramatist Eugene O'Neill, in Louis Sheaffer, *O'Neill: Son and Playwright* (Boston: Little Brown, 1968), 26–27.

Chapter Eleven

"Joy Unspeakable and Full of Glory"

The Vocabulary of Pious Emotion in the Narratives of American Pentecostal Women, 1910–1945

R. Marie Griffith

I will turn their mourning into joy, I will comfort them,
and give them gladness for sorrow.

— Jeremiah 31:13

I have a home, it's made of gold;
Its wealth and grandeur is untold;
Eye hath not seen, ear hath not heard,
To the heart of man it hath not occurred.
In that bright home no pain, no death,
No poisonous air, no tainted breath,
No sin, no sorrow, want or care,
But joys eternally are there.

— Mrs. W. P. Fenlason, in *Word and Work*, 1915

In 1877, nineteen-year-old Carrie Judd was struck with a raging fever that soon turned into hyperaesthesia, an excruciatingly painful illness that affected the nerves in her spine, hips, knees, and ankles and made even the slightest touch all but unbearable. Doctors could not seem to ease her agony, and Carrie lay bedridden at her home in Buffalo, New York, for many long months, as death crept forward to claim her. One day, her father read a newspaper article describing the experiences of Mrs. Edward Mix, an African American woman in Connecticut who had been healed of tuberculosis in answer to her prayers and who now in turn offered her prayers for the healing of others. Carrie's mother urged her daughter to write to Mrs. Mix asking her for prayers. Though anxious that Mrs. Mix was too far away to pray for her and fearful that she would not reply, Carrie dictated a letter through her sister Eva imploring the woman to help her.

In "what seemed an incredibly short time" after Carrie's plea was put in the mail, a letter of response arrived from Mrs. Mix, encouraging Carrie by quoting a passage from the book of James: "The prayer of faith shall save the sick." This was a passage

Carrie, though a confirmed Christian, "had never noticed in the Bible before" but that Mrs. Mix assured her was a promise meant explicitly for her. In order to receive this promised healing, Mrs. Mix proclaimed, Carrie must "leave off all remedies, and not trust in the arm of flesh, but trust in God alone, that He might have the glory." Her letter described a particular day and time that had been set for Mrs. Mix and the members of her "female prayer-meeting" to pray for Carrie's healing and asked Carrie "to unite with them at that time." The letter closed with the appeal to "Write soon," an appeal that, Carrie said, "greatly encouraged me, for I said to myself: 'she believes that I will be healed or she would not tell me to write soon.' "

Indeed, during the very hour that Mrs. Mix had promised to pray for her, Carrie stood up for the first time in a year and, helped by her nurse, walked several steps to a chair without pain. Over the next several days and weeks she gained weight, as she began once again to eat solid food, and grew stronger than ever. But "the greatest joy," she later wrote, "was of a spiritual nature, as my soul which had been so hungry for God, was now filled with a satisfaction hitherto unknown, and inexpressible worship constantly arose in my heart." She continued, "My father and mother were filled with unbounded joy and gratitude to God. My pastor, who had been very faithful in his ministry at my bedside, rejoiced with me, as also did the members of our church. . . . When I first walked out on the street, I felt a desire to express my joy to all I met." The story of Carrie's healing through the prayers of Mrs. Mix was published in newspapers across America and England, and Carrie received hordes of visitors and hundreds of letters from "sufferers" requesting her prayers for them. Affiliated with the Episcopal Church, the Salvation Army, the Christian and Missionary Alliance, and the Pentecostal movement, Carrie Judd Montgomery spent the rest of her long life as a minister and magazine editor expounding and illustrating the power of prayer.[1]

The script that Carrie Judd Montgomery employed, steeped in idioms of vivid emotion and shaped by the rhythms of prayer, links her narrative to assorted strands of the American evangelical tapestry, past and present. Since the revivals led by George Whitefield and John Wesley, the evangelical tradition has accentuated an experiential piety of ardent feeling and devotion, in which realization of God's love and power ignites the passions of saint and sinner alike. Wesley's report that his heart felt "strangely warmed" has been echoed, amplified, and particularized by myriad women and men seeking the fire of religious experience, the security of faith and eternal life, and the consolations of a relationship with a divine parent. The assemblage of intense feelings aroused in and through this form of revivalistic piety in sundry times and places has been depicted as evidence of God's presence and benevolent activity, helping to create for evangelicalism a broad appeal to women and men across boundaries of class, race, region, and nationality. God's promise to the people of Israel, recounted in the book of Jeremiah, encapsulates the hope of later believers: "I will turn their mourning into joy; I will comfort them and give them gladness for sorrow."

During the latter decades of the nineteenth century, as the most insistently experiential parties of American evangelicalism refused to subdue what their opponents decried as the excesses of "enthusiasm," the radical wing of the Holiness movement split off from its largely Methodist forebears to form new associations and denominations across the country. Some of these pious offshoots appropriated the designation "Pentecostal" for themselves, narrowly constricting its formerly ample uses for describing unrestrained evangelical piety to a markedly singular article of faith.[2] What distinguished these latter groups as expressly Pentecostal was a marked insistence on the import of speaking in tongues as an initiatory religious experience signaling the baptism in the Holy Spirit, the pinnacle of the believer's quest for divine approbation and intimacy. The distinction, then, was not simply a theological one; more notably, it signaled a quarrel about practice and the precise boundaries of ecstatic experience. What may seem to outsiders like minute doctrinal hairsplitting between nearly identical pietistic religious groups was—and has, in many quarters, remained—a crucial distinguishing feature between Pentecostals and nonpentecostals and a source of recurrent friction between them. For those defending the "tongues" position, the matter represents the difference between a faith that is "cold," "dry," and generally meager and one that is passionate, abundant, and ceaselessly exhilarating.

A chief hallmark of Pentecostalism, then, was the insistent avowal of rapturous happiness made by each devoted worshiper; a later Pentecostal leader hailed this set of believers as "the happiest people on earth."[3] What was historically distinctive about the Pentecostal version of this avowal in the late nineteenth and early twentieth centuries was its widespread embeddedness in a developing theology of illness and divine healing that resisted conventional American medicine—sometimes denouncing it as quackery, more often as atheistic—yet solemnized a form of positive thinking that would burst onto the scene some years later as the so-called Gospel of Health. The experience of illness recounted by young Carrie Judd resonated widely among her readers, while her description of miraculous bodily healing and its accompanying satisfactions—the "greatest joy" being that of spiritual communion with God—was intended to draw others into the evangelical fellowship of believers by inspiring them with the hope that their sufferings could be alleviated and their mourning transformed into joy if they would only surrender their burdens and their doubts to God. The promise of happiness that had long lured potential Christians to the faith thus took on particular meanings for some groups in late nineteenth-century America, suffused with expectations of complete freedom from disease and dreams of vigorous health accompanied by undiluted earthly bliss.

Now at the end of its first century of existence, Pentecostalism claims over fifty million adherents throughout the world; its churches and believers are spread out over most areas of the globe. Countless Pentecostal denominations have emerged in North America and elsewhere, while the "charismatic movement" in Roman Catholic and Protestant churches has widely disseminated the Pentecostal emphasis on ecstatic experience among those who once scorned the "tongues doctrine." The success of modern Pentecostalism—materially represented in vast television ministries like that of Oral Roberts and the ever growing megachurches in metropolitan areas around the world—could hardly have been envisioned by the self-described plain and lowly folks, rural and urban, who were Pentecostalism's original constituents. Careful attention to these early Pentecostal adherents and their distinctive form of piety will not only shed light on a vast subculture, or cluster of subcultures, that would otherwise remain largely invisible, but will also help explain the persistent appeal of Pentecostal piety across cultures throughout the twentieth century and, doubtless, beyond.

Analyzing Pentecostalism in terms of the emotions the movement has sought to provoke and sustain in believers is relevant also for aims pertinent to this volume. Scholars working in the burgeoning field of emotions history have thus far paid little close attention to religion, neglecting the ways in which religious belief and practice create, inflect, and channel feelings and so work to constitute instrumental cultural attitudes and shape complex socioeconomic patterns. The few studies in this field that have treated religious emotion have tended to focus rather unilaterally on the theme of religious fear, a theme that merits close attention yet hardly covers the vast spectrum of devotional experience and sensibility.[4] Likewise, while American historians have written finely nuanced histories of emotions such as anger and jealousy, there has been no sustained attempt to write a social or cultural history of joy, perhaps owing—if Peter Stearns's characterization of late twentieth-century fixation with restraint is correct—to the embarrassment that the ardency of this sentiment evokes among those in the best position to write such a history.[5] Nor have psychologists, ever more concerned with anxiety than with felicity, devoted extensive analytic attention to the rhetorical and practical workings of joy, a lack evinced by the paucity of sources on the subject since George Van Ness Dearborn's seventy- page monograph, "The Emotion of Joy," was published in 1899.[6] Indeed, it may not be wholly implausible to imagine that the explanations for these scholarly lacunae, one pertaining to religious emotion and the other to the history of mirth, might be inextricably related: a highbrow antipathy toward things religious commingled with a matching distaste—dread?—for excessive, uninhibited, potentially turbulent delight.

In any event, religious emotions represent a crucial ingredient of a comprehensive history of emotion, as the story of Carrie Judd only begins to suggest. Such a history overlays histories of gender and race, love and family and civic life, devotional transmission between and across geographic regions, literacy and books and practices of reading. In this particular case, because of the sources available, the main characters of the story are women, the predominant writers of testimonies and prayer requests in early Pentecostal newspapers. Men, too, converted to Pentecostalism during this period, but their articulated concerns often diverged from those of women and were differently expressed, requiring additional analysis that is beyond the scope of this essay. I have chosen to focus only on women's testimonies here in order to underline the particular, gendered emotional style that these texts helped forge and that has defined Pentecostalism since that time.

The characters in this study are also largely southern, rural, and poor, reflecting a significant proportion of early Pentecostal converts (though by no means all of them). Early Pentecostal leaders often emerged from this social class of people, giving the movement as a whole a distinctively southern feel. Yet by the 1930s, Pentecostalism had gained as much of a hold on northern and western urban areas as southern, rural ones. The risk of focusing on southern farmer-laborers and mill workers is to reinforce old stereotypes of Pentecostalism as a crude movement of hillbillies and country bumpkins, attracting the lowly or "disinherited" who sought compensation for their poor lot on earth in a theology of divine reward.[7] Yet it remains undisputed that the hard economic conditions of the industrializing American South, coupled with the long tradition of Baptist and Methodist piety throughout the southern states, made the area fertile soil for the emergent Pentecostal movement in the early decades of the twentieth century. The source materials analyzed here make for riveting evidence of exactly why this was the case.

Just as Carrie Judd's faith was strengthened, her healing enacted, and her mourning turned to joy through the promised prayers of another woman, so other evangelical, Holiness, and Pentecostal women sought healing and happiness through the prayers of their Christian sisters. Denominational magazines and newspapers published in the first half of the twentieth century provided weekly forums for readers in need to ask for prayers as well as spaces wherein believers testified with exuberance to prayers divinely answered, sufferings alleviated, and lives restored. These sensational and often minutely detailed accounts required responsive action from Pentecostal readers, who were urged by writers as well as editors not merely to skim through the prayer requests sympathetically but to "tarry before the Lord" in diligent and prayerful supplication for all requests. The practices around prayer described in such accounts—praying for one another's needs, sending anointed handkerchiefs or other objects as signs of grace, and continually assuring one another of the ardent prayers sent out on their behalf—enabled the formation of a Pentecostal community, composed predominantly of women, that transcended the ordinary bounds of geography and social location, imparting comfort, benevolence, and recognition to the suffering hopeful across the land.

Examining the personal narratives of this network of Pentecostal women during the early decades of the twentieth century, and the ways in which they occasioned and sustained a particular vocabulary of religious emotion, focuses our attention on the ways women cut off from local networks of support found access to sympathy and healing from women known only through mediums of print. Such an analysis may also help clarify the dynamic relationship between evangelical religion and therapeutic culture during the early decades of this century, elucidating the logic of Pentecostal women's resistance to emerging therapies of their day (along with all forms of modern medicine) in light of the wider cultural themes of satisfaction and emotional fulfillment embedded in their narratives and condensed in expressive sentiments of joy.[8] This essay first charts the idioms of pain and suffering elaborated in written Pentecostal narratives from periodicals in the early decades of the twentieth century (particularly the 1930s), concentrating on those idioms that help fashion experiences of illness, fear, and loneliness. Next I turn to the class of emotions pertaining to praise, gratitude, and exuberant happiness, analyzing the role of these sensibilities in constructing a "correct" testimony and separating Pentecostal insiders from all others. Finally, I remark on the more recent trajectory of this vocabulary of pious emotion among Pentecostal women in contemporary American culture.

Sickness, Fear, and Loneliness in Appeals for Prayer

In 1910, the Church of God, with an approximate membership of one thousand people, began publication of the *Evening Light and Church of God Evangel* (shortened in 1911 to *Church of God Evangel*), a religious weekly awash with zestful declarations of the numberless signs that were thought to augur the imminent, long anticipated return of Christ to earth.[9] In 1917, the Pentecostal Holiness Church—a merger of B. H. Irwin's Fire- Baptized Holiness Church, the Holiness Church of North Carolina, and the Tabernacle Pentecostal Church of South Carolina—began publishing its own weekly organ, the *Pentecostal Holiness Advocate,* from its Georgia headquarters.[10] Similar in doctrine (derived from the Wesleyan/Holiness roots of the two churches) and in form, these periodicals were widely circulated among the rural southerners who made up the majority of Pentecostalism's constituency until well into the 1940s. Throughout these decades and beyond, believers wrote frequent letters to the papers, sharing their burdens and sorrows even as they gave witness to the miraculous work of God in their daily lives and urged others to seek the joyous experience of Spirit baptism.[11]

Even as they ended on a tone of triumphal victory and joy in Christ, women's printed narratives often treated pain in the starkest terms, focusing the reader's attention on the severity of life's trials. Appeals for prayer, elaborated profusely throughout Pentecostal weeklies in testimonies, obituaries, and sections entitled "prayer requests," were most commonly written by women and often centered on familial concerns such as a child's illness, injury, or otherwise dangerous situation.[12] Countless mothers wrote dramatic accounts to denominational organs like the *Church of God Evangel* (published in Cleveland, Tennessee) and the *Pentecostal Holiness Advocate* (published in Franklin Springs, Georgia) of children struggling to overcome tuberculosis, measles, pellagra, influenza, or diabetes, often intensifying their requests for healing prayer with laments over a child's unsaved condition. Accounts of the ineffectiveness of doctors and prescriptive medicines were routine, as were diatribes against the faithlessness of those who sought help from such sources rather than trusting God as the "Great Physician" and only true healer.[13] An Oklahoma woman wrote to the *Pentecostal Holiness Advocate* in 1935 imploring readers to pray for her son to be healed from his drug addiction, explaining mournfully, "He is a confirmed dope fiend, and God only can save him."[14] Concerns about children's health and survival took a different form during the early 1940s, as letters poured in to devotional magazines from distraught mothers of U.S. servicemen begging their readers to "pray for my son overseas." A Texas woman's request for prayer, sent to the *Church of God Evangel* in 1944, was typically poignant and brief, as she asked readers to pray for "[m]y two sons in the Armed Forces—one in France and one in New Guinea; me."[15]

The most repeatedly articulated grievance for women, however, was not sick children but wayward husbands, and female writers frequently urged readers to intercede prayerfully for the restoration of their marriages. In July 1930, Mrs. J. L. Tolley of Purcerville, Virginia, wrote to the *Advocate* that her "husband was once saved, but is not saved today, and keeps going deep into sin," requesting "earnest prayer and fasting for his salvation." One month later, Mrs. Tolley wrote a more frantic letter informing her readers that her husband had abandoned her: having told her he was going to find work and would call her soon, he failed to do so and simply disappeared without a trace. In December of that year Mrs. Tolley wrote a rather subdued testimonial to the same magazine, not mentioning her husband's abandonment or whether he'd returned to her but thanking God for "the times He has healed me and my children, and for answering prayer." Once again, she asked readers to "Fast and pray for my dear husband, he is deep in sin, and ask the Lord to save Him in some way, and spare his life that we may have a happy Christian home."[16] Letters from Mrs. Tolley to her sympathizers were printed several more times during the next few years, keeping the community up to date with her situation and thanking them for their constant prayers.

Wayward companions were, not surprisingly, a problem for many other women as well. In 1930 the editor of the *Advocate* asked readers to "Pray again for Mrs. Earnie Tumblin of Laurens, S.C., who is in trouble over her husband who has left her. She wants him to come back."[17] The next year a North Carolina wife and mother, hospitalized for a year with what she called "sleeping sickness," told of her husband leaving her and their two young children; her wish too was for readers to "pray for him to come back."[18] In the same issue the *Advocate* editor wrote of an Ontario, Canada, woman in "deep distress" and desiring prayer that her husband be healed of alcoholism.[19] Perhaps an even worse situation was endured by a South Carolina woman who beseeched prayers "that her husband may get out of jail to earn bread for the home."[20]

Such extreme cases were cited from time to time but were less common than the frequently articulated petition to "pray for my unsaved husband," a plea included in a sizable proportion of testimonies. While some of these accounts involved supposedly "backslidden" Christian men, the majority suggested that their husbands had never undergone conversion and were weary of their wives cajoling them to examine their sinful souls and attend church. Wives in this situation often undertook to warn younger readers not to fall into this perilous situation. A South Carolina woman, describing the "awful mistake" she had made of "marrying into an ungodly home," wrote, "The pangs that have seized my soul by doing this can never be told. I want to say just here, be careful girls whom you seek for life's companion."[21] Whether alcoholic, violent, unfaithful, or simply irreligious, unsaved husbands provoked many Pentecostal women to seek solace and divine help from fellow readers around the country, many of whom well understood the pain of their situations and could be counted on for prayer.

Numerous women focused on the theme of their own felt isolation, describing themselves in their letters as shut-ins or afflicted in some way that prevented them from attending church services regularly and cut them off from ordinary social contacts. Some delivered plaintive appeals for companionship, like Miss Onie Winn from Watonga, Oklahoma, who called herself "a cripple girl" and wrote, "I would be glad if anyone would write me as I am lonely, no one to talk about Jesus with."[22] Miss Minnie Coleman of McKenzie, Alabama, after a typically cheerful testimony in which she praised God for bringing her "more real happiness than [she] ever saw before," concluded her letter with a similar entreaty for a Christian pen pal: "Will some one who read [sic] this please write to me as I live in a place where there are no Pentecostal people. I would be glad to get letters, also pictures of some of the young Christians. I get lonesome sometimes, so please write me."[23] Mrs. R. A. Flurrty, a "shut-in" from Perkinton, Mississippi, thanked her fellow readers of the *Church of God Evangel* for their comforting testimonies, then asked, "Dear Christians—unseen friends—keep praying for me—this old grandmother in a wheel chair."[24] Such women as these, isolated from companionship by location, religion, or illness, sought to cure their "lonesomeness" through a community of people to whom they had access only through the prayer columns of weekly magazines.

In some cases writers craved more than just prayer and made requisitions to their readers for material goods. Mrs. Iva Cockrell of Middlesex, North Carolina, began one written testimony—one of at least fifteen by her printed in the *Advocate* in three and a half years—commenting, "I want to ask a favor of the dear sisters through The Advocate paper." Reporting her long illness during the previous year, she recalled asking others to "fast and pray" for her. "The dear Lord heard their prayers, touched my body and I was made able to help work some this fall; but I am worse again now." Mrs. Cockrell lamented her lack of strength to work, as well as her husband's equally bad health and incapacity to obtain "any job except picking cotton," then wrote,

> If any of you sisters have a little extra money that you don't need please send part of it to this poor sick sister not able to do anything. . . . If any of you who read this have anything to part from for me or any of my family, please mail it to me and the Lord will bless you.

She concluded, "The dear Lord told me to write this request."[25]

Two months later, in February 1931, Mrs. Cockrell wrote again to say, "I want to thank you dear people wherever you all may be, and tell you how much I appreciate your kindness, for answering my request. . . . We thank every one of you that answered in any way. May the dear Lord bless you is my prayer."[26] In April she wrote yet another desperate letter asking for help, begging, "Please help me pray as I feel so little myself, and I am depending on the Lord for all I need. . . . All who reads [sic] this please pray that the Lord will direct you, and if He tells you to help me any, do His will, not mine."[27] Eleven more detailed letters from Mrs. Cockrell were printed in the *Advocate* during the next three years, many of them expressing gratitude for the gifts, letters, and prayers offered to her by women who learned of her plight from the *Advocate.* The letters also continued to dramatize Mrs. Cockrell's increasingly dire situation and to coax and beseech her readers to send more.[28]

While most were not as prolific as Iva Cockrell, many writers wrote some time after their original requests to thank others for responding to their appeals. Miss Onie Winn, the "cripple girl" who had requested letters, wrote back the next month:

> Greetings in Jesus' dear name. I felt led to send in a testimony this beautiful evening. Many thanks to every one who wrote to me. Dear brothers and sisters, Jesus only knows

the joy and encouragement that your good letters brought to my soul. . . . Your writing was not in vain at all, I wish each one knew how my heart was made to rejoice when I received your letters.[29]

Mrs. Bart Williams from Goodwater, Alabama, sent a special note to the *Church of God Evangel* offering her gratitude: "I thank each and every one of you who has prayed for me, also thank you for encouraging letters, tracts and get-well cards. I wish I could write each one but received so many letters I feel much better. Keep praying for me."[30] During the early 1940s, when so many sons and grandsons were off to war, women sent in their boys' addresses overseas, in hopes that fellow Christians would not only pray for them but would also comfort them through direct mail. That readers complied with such appeals is apparently evidenced in the number of servicemen who wrote back to the paper and thanked *Evangel* readers for their prayers and thoughtful letters.[31]

Not all requests for prayer were as detailed as those I have cited thus far. Quite a few women wrote to ask for prayer simply for "special unspoken requests" or "urgent unspoken requests." Miss Lucile Nash from Thomson, Georgia, appealed to her readers for "God to undertake for me and heal my body." Rather than detailing her illness or illustrating it graphically as many other writers did, Miss Nash merely explained, "He knows my condition."[32] Similarly vague, Mrs. Gladys Roberson from Odum, Georgia, wrote, "Please pray a special prayer for me, I'm in so much trouble. God knows all about my trials. I believe in praying for one another and when we are going through a trial is when we need help, so please pray a special prayer for me."[33] Nora Bolin of Blacksburg, South Carolina, conveyed most forcefully her own fear and desperation when she begged her readers, "Please get on your knees right when you read this and pray for this is urgent."[34]

At times, the despair of writers was so acute that editors intervened, as when the editor of the *Pentecostal Holiness Advocate* wrote, "Some mother, who fails to give her name, seems to be in much trouble, and writes that we request prayer for her salvation, for the salvation of her home, for her husband to find work to make the family bread, and sundry life requests."[35] Editors emphasized the exigency of prayer in other ways; this same editor often sermonized at the end of the "requests for prayer" section: "If there are any of The Advocate readers who are wanting to do work for the Lord, here is your opportunity. Go alone, get on your knees, and spread out the above requests before God. Here is some real work to which God is calling you."[36] In at least one case the editor strengthened this injunction with a warning: "Brethren, these are serious matters. These people need help, and they have called on every reader of The Advocate to pray for them. Do not forget them. Remember that it may be you or one of your family next."[37] In an effort to motivate those whose prayer lives might otherwise be thin, editors importuned people to be active purveyors of God's grace by doing the "real work" that God demanded of them.

A common practice reported in the letters printed in Pentecostal devotional materials, whether directed to mostly white or to mostly black audiences, was the use of "anointed handkerchiefs" in procuring physical healings. This practice found scriptural basis in the nineteenth chapter of Acts: "And God did extraordinary miracles by the hands of Paul, so that handkerchiefs or aprons were carried away from his body to the sick, and diseases left them and the evil spirits came out of them."[38] In a typical narrative, Blanche Guthrie from Lepanto, Arkansas, gave an account of receiving one such handkerchief from a Church of God evangelist, placing it carefully on her ailing lungs, and being healed of tuberculosis.[39] Mrs. Frank Colville from Erwin, North Carolina, told a similar story of being healed from phlebitis and "untold agonies" after wearing "an anointed handkerchief that Sister Maxwell sent" her.[40] Such handkerchiefs, always at hand and easily transported, might be monogrammed, embroidered, or plain; people used whatever they happened to have at the time. If one did not own handkerchiefs, she could obtain them from special services; an advertisement in the African American Pentecostal periodical *Whole Truth* reads, "For olive oil and anointed cloths, Write the Field Editor . . . send a donation to keep a supply."[41] A handkerchief was the simplest of items, usually associated with wiping away tears or sweat or mundanely blowing one's nose, and its cleansing function was easily extended into the realm of divine healing.

Sometimes writers described sending their own ordinary handkerchiefs to powerful Pentecostal preachers and evangelists, who would anoint these cloths with oil and prayer and send them back. At other times writers such as Della Tuttle simply begged their readers, "Will somebody send me a handkerchief?"[42] One woman sent a letter to the *Advocate* directed to the "Falcon Prayer Band," noting, "I received the letter with the anointed handkerchief and wonderful blessings I received after I placed one to my body. . . . I surely do feel so much better."[43] Sister L. Banks from Fresno, California, likewise wrote to the *Whole Truth*,

> I received the letter and anointed cloths from you, for which I thank the Lord. My heart rejoiced and the power of God came upon me as I applied the cloth to my breast. I could feel the affected part being drawn, and when I applied the second cloth it completely left. I have not felt the hurting any more. I thank the Lord for being healed.[44]

As sacramental objects saturated with fervent prayer, anointed handkerchiefs could substitute for the physical presence of one whose prayers were sought, healing the sick when there was no one there to lay hands on her. Signs not simply of divine grace but even more of human kindness and generosity, these handkerchiefs were important material articles in the economy of Pentecostal emotion, often holding tremendous healing power for those who obtained them.

In other cases, these Pentecostal letter writers reported using the devotional newspapers themselves as sacramental prayer objects. Sister Happy Smith testified to the power of the *Church of God Evangel*, saying that "every member of our family has been healed by laying on the Evangel." Once, apparently dying from an asthma attack that even "a room full of people . . . praying" could not abate, Sister Smith testified, her pastor "laid the Evangel on me and God wonderfully came on the scene."[45] A Louisiana woman similarly described how only the night before, her young son "took real sick and I took the Evangel and laid it on him and asked Jesus to heal and let the child rest and, glory to His name, the work was done."[46] These magazines, filled with testimonies of divine healings and with promises of prayer, became carriers of hope and so too of healing. Women unable to receive personal prayer from the magazine writers could secure some of that healing power from the material substance in which the testimonies were printed, transforming the magazines, like the anointed handkerchiefs, into sacramental objects, suitable tools that could be utilized to impart divine healing power to those with faith.

Throughout the prayer requests and the testimonial accounts of prayers fulfilled and sorrows healed, writers continually emphasized the power of communal prayer. Like the healing of Carrie Judd, which occurred after Mrs. Mix had promised to pray for her with other women all the way from Connecticut, Pentecostal healings most often transpired in the wake of prayers offered up by fellow Christians. One correspondent, praising God for the healing of her body, spoke for many when she told of having sent in a request to the *Evangel* some time ago and testified, "I know the saints of God prayed for me because I'm healed of a disease that I had ever since I was a child and I haven't taken any medicine for a long, long time."[47] Again and again writers mentioned the formation of small "prayer bands" or "bands of praying sisters" in their region, groups that met for intensive sessions of healing prayer. The women who led and participated in such groups drew others into their midst because they promised them solace from affliction, room to speak, relief from loneliness. As historian Edith Blumhofer has noted about the appeal of the famous Pentecostal evangelist Aimee Semple McPherson, these ordinary praying women "made people feel safe and loved."[48]

Yet the vast majority of letter writers complained that they were bereft of the companionship of Holiness and Pentecostal believers in their own geographic area. For many women who had no lasting or desirable local community, the writers and readers of these denominational periodicals provided their only opportunity for a stable, caring fellowship, along with constant affirmation of the power of healing prayer. So many felt, as one woman put it, that "There is no one here to pray for me and it seems my prayers are weak."[49] The combined prayers of the Pentecostal community, however, seemed strong. Readers whose unsaved husbands or personal afflictions prevented them from attending regular Pentecostal services continually described their gratefulness for this community of readers, like Mrs. D. T. McGraw from Radford, Virginia, who wrote, "As I am afflicted in my body so that I am a shut in I am glad that I can speak through The Advocate to people that I couldn't otherwise speak to."[50]

The rural, predominantly southern women who wrote testimonial letters to the *Pentecostal Holiness Advocate,* the *Church of God Evangel,* and a wide variety of similar publications prayed for the same things Christian women have long prayed for, though in forms and rhythms bequeathed to them by their particular Holiness/Pentecostal heritage and the pages of Pentecostal periodicals. For these particular women, frequently isolated in far-flung mountain communities, mining areas, and mill towns, congregational life was at best fragile and more often unavailable. Like later generations of Pentecostal women, urban and rural, who participated in Women's Aglow Fellowship and sent myriad testimonies and prayer requests to the wide readership of *Aglow* magazine, these letter writers focused their prayer narratives on sick children, wayward husbands, and feelings of loneliness, reaching out for sympathy, healing, and community through the prayers of women near and far.[51] Narrating their own lives not primarily in terms of their own sin, which was most often relegated to accounts of the past, but more in terms of unmerited pain and illness, these women assured one another that healing was obtainable through faith (if not absolutely predictable), that sufficient prayer worked miracles, and that the ultimate earthly result of their petitions would be a passionately emotional closeness with the loving God.

"Praise God!": Hearts of Joy, Gratitude, and Peace

Surrounding the countless appeals for healing prayer that emerged in Pentecostal periodicals were assurances of the joy and peace that accompany salvation, sanctification, and the baptism of the Holy Spirit, as well as declarations of the happiness that follows daily obedience to God. Indeed, words of praise for God's goodness and love and assertions of the everlasting delight that such love brings to the believing saint invariably framed these Pentecostal testimonies, regardless of their content. In typically euphoric style, Mrs. Arthur Watson opened her letter of 1930, "Dear little flock. Greetings in the holy name of Jesus to one and all. This beautiful morning as I sit here reading and meditating upon the words of Jesus, praise His dear name, the sunshine of glory is streaming down upon my soul." Mrs. Watson continued her rapturous declarations and assured her readers that such happiness would follow their own compliance with God's commands, the surrender to which would lead not only to intimacy with God but also to relief from life's hardships. "Praise God, I am not tired of the way. It grows brighter and sweeter all the time, and Jesus is more real to me each day. The clouds get dark and heavy sometimes, but there is sunshine just behind the cloud, and it doesn't take long to pray the clouds away." After asking readers to pray for her home, the writer illustrated the vision of heaven so common in these narratives:

> Some sweet day very soon we are going home with Jesus, the feast of the bride groom to share. When we meet each other in the kingdom of God we shall sit together at His table and Jesus will come forth and serve us. There will be shouting and singing and we shall see Him as He is, for we shall be like Him. Glory to His name.[52]

Basking elatedly in the hoped-for celestial future, Mrs. Watson sought to lift her readers out of their own despair, promising that "sunshine just behind the cloud" could be acquired in this life and pure, carefree delight in the next.

The ecstatic, visionary hope articulated by Mrs. Watson, echoed repeatedly by other writers throughout these texts, vividly elucidates the Pentecostal vocabulary around the emotional complex of joy and suggests some of the meanings embedded in this broad lexicon. Metaphors of light and biblically derived images of sweetness, feasting, singing, shouting, and intimacy with Jesus fused to create a perfect counterpoint to the fear, despair, and loneliness that are elsewhere ascertained to characterize ordinary life. The cure for every sorrow, worry, and longing was elaborated as not merely a sober profession of belief in Jesus as the hoped-for Savior of the world but a livelier and more expressive gratitude for every aspect of this life and the next. The quotidian substance of such appreciation was part of its very power and appeal: "I want to praise the Lord for His blessings this morning. I praise Him for being saved, sanctified and baptized with the Holy Spirit," wrote a woman in line with this devotional pattern. Another writer asserted, "It is with joy I sound a note of praise for my blessed Savior who has done so much for me. I never have been able to tell what Jesus is to me, but I mean to keep trying to tell it." [53]

Asserting that the emotional power of God's love is so great as to be beyond words is a common trope in these narratives, sometimes entwined with profoundly sensual depictions of the power of God. In the early years of the Pentecostal movement, one woman described her spirit baptism thus:

> While looking at [Jesus], I felt a peculiar life coming from His body into my own, and I was so filled with His presence it seemed I could not contain it. Then He said, "this is your baptism." There was such a wonderful awe and sweet sacredness about it, that I was not able to speak of it for weeks afterward, but His presence was continually with me. [54]

Even as they emphasized the indescribability of these spiritual experiences, however, Pentecostals struggled to put their emotions into words.

> To the honor and glory of God I desire to witness to what the Lord has wrought in me. My hungry soul has received the Comforter! It was at the close of the day, Easter Sunday, 1908, that the Holy Spirit came in and filled my life. I can never fully describe the ecstasy and the glory of those three hours, as I was prostrated under the mighty power of God. Even now, as I write of it, tears of joy flow so that I can hardly see, and the Holy Spirit fills and thrills my entire being. [55]

Committed to witnessing to what seemed by nature marvelously unutterable, Pentecostal women employed an erotic terminology of penetration, abundance, and sensate fulfillment, suffused with desire for a divine invasion of the physical body.

The sexual undertones of this language suggest the tactile quality of religious experience and also point to the relationality at the heart of Pentecostal theology. God is no abstract, transcendent being in these narratives but a living, immediate presence; likewise, Jesus plays an intimate role in the lives of believers, conversing with them on the most ordinary of subjects and acting as a sympathetic, affectionate companion to them in their times of loneliness. Like other Christian women who have interpreted Jesus quite literally as a lover or husband, these women intentionally cultivated a daily relationship with Jesus, one that they believed could be damaged by betrayal, bolstered with gifts, and nurtured through communicative prayer. Their interpretation of this relationship emerged out of their experience of earthly kinship, particularly familial ties, but it also represented an ideal by which they could measure those earthly relationships and a standard of affinity that they hoped these could attain. [56]

One of the most common images of God and Jesus in these Pentecostal testimonies, and one that reverberates throughout evangelical history, is of a holy friend. Echoing a religious litany, Mrs. Lavada Bogan soliloquized, "Though my friends despise, forsake me, and on me this world looks cold; I have a Friend that will stand by me, when the pearly gates unfold. . . . Jesus is the truest friend, Bless His name." [57]

The determined hope here expressed is one of the most strikingly poignant aspects of these narratives, articulated by women whose lives, as already shown, seemed in disarray. Another wrote, in equally heartfelt terms, "It is a glorious thing that I now have to praise God for He is a personal friend of mine."[58] At other times, authors simply alluded to diffuse kinds of divine affection and its consequences: "I am happy in the Savior's love." "Our home is a happy one since Jesus came in as the head of the same." "I praise the Lord for a deep settled peace in my soul."[59] Pentecostal worshipers clung to the intense feeling of God's tenderness toward them, letting that love color their dreariest moments with gratitude, eager anticipation, and inward tranquillity.

Throughout this Pentecostal culture, weeping acted as a crucial sign of sincerity, if not its sine qua non. In printed narratives, surrendering to God was very often accompanied by crying; heartfelt feelings of repentance, sorrow, and joy were marked with tears. Tears, of course, have a long history in evangelical piety as signs of true heartfelt piety, and worshipers have frequently made correspondences between, in the words of one historian, being "bathed in tears and being washed in the blood of Christ."[60] As an emblem of candor, weeping has been presumed in such settings to be a natural and unaffected act, the outward expression of an otherwise invisible and unknowable heart. Closely associated as well with notions of traditional femininity, tears elaborated and refined the possibilities of healing and transformation for Pentecostal women, in part by enabling them to enter more fully into a practice of female identity that could make them feel "real."

Just as tears assumedly evinced authenticity, a customary means of emphasizing the feelings of happiness and relief that accompanied salvation and obedience was to testify earnestly to the spiritual "hunger" that earlier characterized one's life. The pastor of one of the early Pentecostal churches in Chicago described his "anguish of soul" before being baptized in the Holy Spirit. "I now understand that God in His goodness will at times seem to withdraw from one's life in order to make him more hungry for God, and also to let him realize what he would be without God."[61] Some years later, a woman elaborated this same point:

> How thankful I am for the peace in my heart. . . . How well I remember the hunger that was in my heart when a child. How hungry I was for spiritual food even before I was old enough to know what I wanted. I know that God is love. I am so thankful that He saw the hunger in my heart and satisfied it with heavenly manna.[62]

Reconstructing her life before receiving God's "heavenly manna" as one of constant yearning and discontent enabled this woman, like so many others, to interpret the existence of all people outside the inner fold as miserable, desolate, and overwhelmingly in need of Christian testimony.

Not only God but also the texts themselves are sources of joy: "I read the Bible and its pages glow with light and love all the day," exclaimed one woman who called herself "a cripple" and the only one in her family who was "saved."[63] The magazines too gave pleasure, and many writers declared them to be "food to my soul." Mrs. Mettie Lamm averred, "I could not get along without [the Advocate]," while another woman effused, "I praise the Lord for the good messages I receive through The

Advocate each week. I can hardly wait for it to come."[64] A few male writers also wrote about the role of the newspapers in their lives; as one man explained, "There is something that goes with the *Evangel* that just seems to open the glory world and heaven seems to kiss the earth; even the trees seem to be glad and the glory of God just floods our souls as we read its pages."[65] Another woman, renewing her subscription, gratefully mused, "I enjoy reading the paper so much. I get almost down and out at times, but when I get the Advocate and read it I feel greatly encouraged."[66]

Some of the greatest joys of all were declared to have emerged from the conversion of sinners in revivals. As Mrs. W. E. Beard wrote of a newly founded church, "The Lord certainly did set His approval on it. Eight or ten would be rejoicing under the power at one time. It was joy unspeakable and full of glory."[67] Especially because fresh believers had been brought into the fold, bringing the world ever closer to the expected second coming of Christ, these were times of great hope, times in which the Kingdom of God seemed imminent. The emotional displays that occurred in these settings, characterized by a quintessentially revivalistic sort of feverish urgency, were also an attempt to ensure that the happiness received from living in the love of God would be evident to all outside observers. Other joyous occasions occurred around physical healings. A woman healed of tuberculosis wrote that when God began to work, "His power came down and struck my body like a bolt of lightning, it seemed. . . . I could not sit still. The power reached my feet and I danced for joy."[68] Rescued from pain and the expectation of immediate death, worshipers who believed themselves to have been divinely healed witnessed to their gratitude through the vocabulary of gladness, exultation, and triumphal victory.

The constancy of this scripted language of rapturous joy and encouragement indicates the dual role of impassioned emotions as both a sign of God's loving approval and an indicator of one's own true piety. While those outside the faith were described as "cold" or "spiritually dead," criticisms of "lukewarm" Christians were also common. Cultivating a sharply defined "ethic of separation," in Edith Blumhofer's words, early Pentecostals denounced those outside their religious boundaries and rejected most traditional/mainline organizational forms as "backslidden."[69] As one man wrote, "I believe with all my heart we have too many cold hearted Christians. Bless God, we don't have to be cold and dry, and lukewarm."[70] One woman spoke for many when she noted reproachfully, "So many are at ease in Zion, and not burdened for lost souls."[71] Again and again, writers suggested that true Christians must be constantly "on fire" for God, ardently spreading the message of divine power to unsaved men and women of their communities and demonstrating sincerity through their passion for holiness. Thus these Pentecostal believers implied that fervent zeal, accompanied by tears, shouting, and other assumed signs of authenticity, was an attendant condition, if not the very evidence, of genuine, vigorous faith.

Such an assumption must have rendered everyday life, with its inevitable irritations and disappointments (not to mention its tragedies), very challenging indeed—what if one failed to uphold the emotional scripts to which one was bound? Some narratives treated this dilemma in consoling terms, exposing the careful exegesis that these ideas about emotion often required. In 1913, for instance, Mrs. Ellen Winter described being "so happy in my new-found joy that I wanted everybody to taste for themselves and see how good the Lord is." When she spoke to "a dear brother who was unsaved" about becoming a Christian, he apparently became angry and told her to mind her own business and leave him alone. Rather than responding to him with Christian love, however, Mrs. Winter wrote that she "answered him in the same spirit." She continued,

> Instantly a horror that no words can express filled my soul. I could not tell for a moment which emotion predominated—grief or astonishment. . . . I had believed there was nothing in my heart but love and purity until those angry words were spoken. From what source did the anger spring? I had never expected to be angry again for . . . I had been made a new creation in Christ Jesus.

Thrown into confusion and despair over her "sin," Mrs. Winter realized that God did not expect perfection from her but only repentance of all such errors. "My burden rolled away and once more the peace of God that passeth all understanding filled my heart." From this she received "the inner evidence of joy, peace, divine reality and an inspiration unspeakable and full of glory," concluding that the continual revelation of God's goodness "makes living a continual delight."[72] She left her readers with the comforting message that while negative feelings like anger were eschewed, they did not necessarily indicate a permanent fall from grace.

While for Mrs. Winter and countless other Pentecostal women, emotions of joy provided evidence that God had truly entered their hearts and saved them, some writers challenged the notion that emotion functioned as a sign. In 1914, Leila Conway wrote of her struggle to feel "some great marvelous manifestation of converting grace" and her distress when none had come. When she finally gave her life to God, she "had not a particle of feeling," and although she testified to her salvation to others, she had to work hard to resist the doubts that flooded her consciousness because of her lack of zealous emotion. As a reward for her persistent faith, God eventually gave her "a deluge of glory to my soul." She described it thus: "O the bliss! 'the rapturous height of that holy delight which I felt in the life-giving blood!' Earth's pleasures were of no comparison. I yearned that 'all the world might taste and see the riches of His grace,' while with a heart overflowing with joy I exultingly sang." Her message to readers left no apparent room for doubt, urging them not to mistake the lack of feeling as a lack of change in their hearts: the feelings themselves are not the sign of faith, she insisted, but rather its glorious reward.[73]

Yet her strenuous assurance itself is revealing of the conflicts around emotion that could arise within this system. Indeed, the intent to persuade evident in so many of these narratives begins to indicate how very bewildering Pentecostal notions of experience and emotion could be for ordinary people. Leila Conway's testimony attests to the fact that boundaries between those considered "cold" and those "on fire" were hardly stable; indeed, they were continually being redrawn, inscribing anew the limits of doctrinal and behavioral acceptability and frequently challenging those within their own ranks who either claimed "new revelations" from God or held too rigidly to the older restorationist vision.[74] Moreover, as the annals of Pentecostalism attest, believers long upheld assumptions of doctrinal unity within their ranks,

234 R. MARIE GRIFFITH

making dissent even on small points into a painful breach of "family harmony."[75] In one historian's words, "unblinking conformity was simply presupposed" in early Pentecostalism, and most forms of deviation from theological or behavioral norms "were crushed without a second thought."[76] Among laypeople less prone to the constant factional wrangling among church leaders, conflict and difference might be suppressed, resembling what folklorist Jody Shapiro Davie has called "a semblance of tacit consensus" necessary for maintaining harmonious unity within religious communities.[77] In the case of religious experience and the emotions that structured them certainty was crucially important and so generated repeated commentary.

Conclusion

The vocabulary of pious emotion that emerges in these Pentecostal texts from the early decades of the twentieth century has hardly faded in subsequent years; if anything, it has become more thoroughly concretized in ever more therapeutically tinged narratives. Originally a grassroots movement whose leaders came from the same social classes as adherents, early Pentecostalism attracted people impatient with traditional church authorities and unwilling to submit to them, expecting instead a community where "the old stratifications were razed and a new order erected."[78] Still professing belief in the priesthood of all believers and in the capacity of all to receive prophetic gifts, Pentecostals soon underwent a dramatic and rapid process of institutionalization, as leaders built vast educational networks for the training of ministers and missionaries, formally codified religious doctrines, and constructed divisions between leaders and laypeople that were not always welcomed by the latter. Tensions rose as the giants of the independent healing revivals—William Branham and Oral Roberts, for instance—began attracting old-line Pentecostals as well as more affluent Americans into the Pentecostal fold, compelling denominational leaders to buttress their authority against these seeming upstarts whom they saw as "commercializing on [sic] the healing ministry."[79]

The long-term effects on actual practices of Pentecostal institutionalization, and of changing socioeconomic patterns among Pentecostals in general, have been significant, as many historians have observed; most often cited is the de-emphasis within many classical Pentecostal communities on ecstatic experiences of the Holy Spirit such as speaking in tongues, divine healing, and prophetic utterances. Yet such experiences survive in the testimonial accounts given witness by Pentecostal letter writers, who recalled leaders to their Pentecostal heritage again and again. Through vivid accounts of supernatural healings and other occurrences, these networks of writers sought to resist the routinization of their faith they saw happening all around them, even in the very periodicals that provided a vehicle for Pentecostal witness. While participating in a practice made possible by church-financed editors, writers could make it their own through the expressive power of their own unique witness to life in the Spirit. Putting their prayers into print gave their stories permanence and, more significantly, the dependable and enthusiastic corroboration of the larger community. Such corroboration provided a kind of assurance, affirming God's intervention in people's lives so that they were freed from the agony of wondering later if they had simply been fooling themselves. As with the efficacy of prayer, one's own discernment might be weak, but that of the trusted community was surely strong.

More recently, devotional accounts published by such groups as Women's Aglow Fellowship, a contemporary organization of Pentecostal and charismatic Christian women, demonstrate attention to a similar range of emotions evident in the earlier Pentecostal narratives, but sometimes with an altered vocabulary.[80] Like their spiritual forebears, these latter-day Pentecostal women have described coming to feel healed, inwardly transformed, and outwardly "set free" from suffering through the power of the Holy Spirit. Recounting, in far more explicit detail than earlier Pentecostal narratives, events such as physical or sexual abuse that left them, in their terms, angry, disappointed, despairing, fearful, ashamed, self-hating, and even suicidal, these women have similarly articulated their desire for God's loving presence, discerning heavenly embraces to be almost as tangible as those of the women with whom they pray in intimate settings. Enveloped in what they feel to be Jesus' loving forgiveness and affirmation, contemporary Pentecostal women have publicly professed joyous release from bondage and deliverance from shame, again and again.

The capacity for feeling healed, transformed, and liberated in all these settings is informed by shared theological beliefs as well as by culturally informed assumptions about the dynamics of suffering and restoration. However natural and authentic these experiences and emotions may have felt to those who recount them, they are patterned after narrative accounts told by other women and so are generated out of a social context that defines what have been called "emotion rules." To analyze the emotions that have accompanied Pentecostal worship and adherence is by no means to deny their power or reality—to the contrary, it is to take their power as social and cultural codes very seriously, ascertaining the values that help create and frame these emotions in specific narrative forms.[81] Those women who have chosen to participate in the highly expressive practices of worship cultivated in Pentecostal meetings and recounted in printed narratives must reconstruct their own life stories and refashion themselves according to these available forms, forms flexible enough to allow variant meanings yet sufficiently restricted to sustain the authority of the narrative itself, elicit correct attitudes and feelings, and produce disciplined religious selves.

Pentecostal beliefs about the emotions have never fit into a simple or transparent scheme; rather, they form an overlapping and contested set of ideas with multiple aims. Primarily, of course, the religious emotions pertaining to joy and the practices of praise and gratitude that accompanied these emotions intended to assure believers of the enduring vitality of their faith in the midst of a hostile, jeering world. In this way, these pious feelings worked as cultural dividers between the "cold" and the "hot," the order of God's plan and the disorder of the world, saints and sinners, the saved and the damned. They created and sustained expectation of relief from the burdens of everyday life and hope in the paradisiacal world to come. For women, they opened the way for triumph over illness, wayward husbands, and disobedient children and ensured "victory over sin and shame." Analyzing these emotions, through the record of narrative practices such as written testimony, and situating them within the broader narrative traditions of Pentecostalism and evangelicalism may yield fresh meaning on old questions pertaining to the historical intertwining of religion and gender in American life, enabling us to see more clearly how and why women have prayed together.

NOTES

1. Carrie Judd Montgomery, "Under His Wings: The Story of My Life," in *The Life and Teachings of Carrie Judd Montgomery* (New York: Garland, 1985), 55–60. See also her original account of her own healing, "The Prayer of Faith" (esp. chap. 1), published in 1880 and reprinted in *Life and Teachings.*

2. The history of the Holiness movement has been recounted in Timothy L. Smith, *Revivalism and Social Reform: American Protestantism on the Eve of the Civil War* (Baltimore: Johns Hopkins University Press, 1980 [orig. pub. by Abingdon Press, 1957]); Melvin E. Dieter, *The Holiness Revival of the Nineteenth Century* (Metuchen, NJ: Scarecrow Press, 1980); and Charles Edward Jones, *Perfectionist Persuasion: The Holiness Movement and American Methodism, 1867–1936* (Metuchen, NJ: Scarecrow Press, 1974). On Pentecostalism, see Robert Mapes Anderson, *Vision of the Disinherited: The Making of American Pentecostalism* (New York: Oxford University Press, 1979); Edith L. Blumhofer, *Restoring the Faith: The Assemblies of God, Pentecostalism, and American Culture* (Urbana and Chicago: University of Illinois Press, 1993); Donald W. Dayton, *Theological Roots of Pentecostalism* (Peabody, MA: Hendrickson, 1987); David Edwin Harrell, Jr., *All Things Are Possible: The Healing and Charismatic Revivals in Modern America* (Bloomington: Indiana University Press, 1975).

3. Demos Shakarian, as told to John Sherrill and Elizabeth Sherrill, *The Happiest People on Earth: The Long-Awaited Personal Story of Demos Shakarian* (Old Tappan, NJ: Chosen Books, 1975).

4. See, for instance, Jean Delumeau, *Sin and Fear: The Emergence of a Western Guilt Culture, 13th–18th Centuries,* trans. Eric Nicholson (New York: St. Martin's, 1990); and Robert Muchembled, *Popular Culture and Elite Culture in France, 1400–1750,* trans. Lydia Cochrane (Baton Rouge: Louisiana State University Press, 1985). On the American side, Jan Lewis devoted considerable attention to religious emotion in chapter 2 of *The Pursuit of Happiness: Family and Values in Jefferson's Virginia* (Cambridge: Cambridge University Press, 1983), exploring the changing place of evangelicalism among the Virginia gentry around the time of the American Revolution. See also Philip Greven, *The Protestant Temperament: Patterns of Child-Rearing, Religious Experience, and the Self in Early America* (New York: Knopf, 1977). An exception to this approach is Gareth Matthews, "Ritual and the Religious Feelings," in *Explaining Emotions,* ed. Amélie Oksenberg Rorty (Berkeley: University of California Press, 1980), 339–53; unfortunately, Matthews's essay is more of an Augustinian apology for the effectiveness of religious ritual than a sophisticated analytic treatment of it.

The best historical treatment of religious emotion that I have seen is Gary A. Anderson, *A Time to Mourn, a Time to Dance: The Expression of Grief and Joy in Israelite Religion* (University Park: Pennsylvania State University Press, 1991). Recent sociological work on contemporary religious groups is also useful; see *De L'Émotion en religion: Renouveaux et traditions,* ed. Françoise Champion, Daniele Hervieu-Léger, et al. (Paris: Centurion, 1990).

5. Carol Zisowitz Stearns and Peter N. Stearns, *Anger: The Struggle for Emotional Control in America's History* (Chicago: University of Chicago Press, 1986); Peter N. Stearns, *Jealousy: The Evolution of an Emotion in American History* (New York: New York University Press, 1989); Stearns's argument for restraint is most fully elaborated in idem, *American Cool: Constructing a Twentieth-Century Emotional Style* (New York: New York University Press, 1994).

6. George Van Ness Dearborn, "The Emotion of Joy," in *The Psychological Review,* vol. 2 (New

York: Macmillan, 1899). This is Dearborn's Ph.D. thesis from Columbia University. For a psychological rendering of joy that focuses exclusively on its neurological aspects, see Silvan Tomkins, "Enjoyment—Joy," in *Shame and Its Sisters: A Silvan Tomkins Reader,* ed. Eve Kosofsky Sedgwick and Adam Frank (Durham: Duke University Press, 1995), 81–105.

Obviously, the devotional literature on joy is far beyond the scope of Pentecostalism (and this essay); a classic religious text, arguing both that joy is a "reasonable feeling . . . capable of cultivation" and that to hide or deny one's joy is to sin gravely, is Arthur Wells Hopkinson, *Be Merry: Some Thoughts on Mirth as a Christian Duty* (London: A. R. Mowbray, 1925), refs. on 6, 3.

My own investigation of this topic have been most influenced by the "social constructionist school" of emotions theory; a coherent explication of this body of theory, including the variations and disputes among scholars in this field, is *The Social Construction of Emotions,* ed. Rom Harré (Oxford: Basil Blackwell, 1986). I have been guided also by the collected essays in *Language and the Politics of Emotion,* ed. Catherine A. Lutz and Lila Abu-Lughod (Cambridge: Cambridge University Press, 1990), and by the example of Lutz, *Unnatural Emotions: Everyday Sentiments on a Micronesian Atoll and Their Challenge to Western Theory* (Chicago: University of Chicago Press, 1988).

7. This notion held long sway in studies of Pentecostalism, capped by Anderson, *Vision of the Disinherited.* A classic version of this argument is Liston Pope, *Millhands and Preachers* (New Haven: Yale University Press, 1942), a sociological study of cotton mills and churches in Gaston County, North Carolina. Recently, historians such as Edith Blumhofer are beginning to refocus attention on Pentecostalism in urban settings, especially New York, Chicago, and Los Angeles.

8. The rise of therapeutic culture and its relation to American religion has been the subject of much discussion; see, for instance, E. Brooks Holifield, *A History of Pastoral Care in America: From Salvation to Self-Realization* (Nashville, TN: Abingdon Press, 1983); T. J. Jackson Lears, "From Salvation to Self-Realization: Advertising and the Therapeutic Roots of the Consumer Culture, 1880–1930," in *The Culture of Consumption: Critical Essays in American History, 1880–1980,* ed. Richard Wightman Fox and T. J. Jackson Lears (New York: Pantheon, 1983); idem, *No Place of Grace: Antimodernism and the Transformation of American Culture, 1880–1920* (Chicago: University of Chicago Press, 1981); Donald Meyer, *The Positive Thinkers: Religion as Pop Psychology from Mary Baker Eddy to Oral Roberts,* 2d ed. (New York: Pantheon, 1980); David Harrington Watt, *A Transforming Faith: Explorations of Twentieth-Century American Evangelicalism* (New Brunswick: Rutgers University Press, 1991), esp. 137–54; and Robert Wuthnow, *Sharing the Journey: Support Groups and America's New Quest for Community* (New York: Free Press, 1994).

9. On the history of the Church of God, see Mickey Crews, *The Church of God: A Social History* (Knoxville: University of Tennessee Press, 1990). A more celebratory, "insider" history is Charles W. Conn, *Like a Mighty Army: A History of the Church of God, 1886–1976,* rev. ed. (Cleveland, TN: Pathway Press, 1977).

10. On the history of the Pentecostal Holiness Church, see A. D. Beacham, Jr., *A Brief History of the Pentecostal Holiness Church* (Franklin Springs, GA: Advocate Press, 1983); and Vinson Synan, *The Old-Time Power: A History of the Pentecostal Holiness Church* (Franklin Springs, GA: Advocate Press, 1973). Both are written by PHC insiders.

11. While we know much about women's devotional narratives and prayer networks in the eighteenth and nineteenth centuries, we know far less about twentieth-century Pentecostal women's devotional lives and the printed texts that helped sustain and expand these, particularly after 1920. The dearth of attention to African American Pentecostal women (and to black Pentecostalism more broadly) has been particularly lamentable. Fortunately, several studies are now being undertaken that examine both white and black women's devotional lives, taking account at last of the complex racial dynamics that accompanied the rise and trajectory of Pentecostalism in America as well as the dynamics of particular devotional practices.

Studies of black Pentecostal women undertaken by Cheryl Townsend Gilkes and Felton O. Best are welcome examples, though it should be noted that Best focuses primarily on women in leadership roles. See Gilkes, " 'Together and in Harness': Women's Traditions in the Sanctified Church," *Signs* 10, no. 4 (summer 1985): 678–99; and idem, "The Role of Women in the Sanctified

Church," *Journal of Religious Thought* 43, no. 1 (spring–summer 1986): 24–41. Also Best, "Loosing the Women: African-American Women and Leadership in the Pentecostal Church, 1890–Present" (paper presented at the Society for Pentecostal Studies annual meeting, Wheaton, IL, November 1994).

Few materials written by black Pentecostals are readily available from this period. Only scattered issues of the organ published by the African American Church of God in Christ, the *Whole Truth*, survive; and here there are far fewer letters and testimonies written by women than in the organs of the predominantly white Pentecostal denominations such as the Pentecostal Holiness Church and the Church of God (Cleveland). The Church of God has always had black members but separated them into segregated black churches for most of the denomination's history. There appear to be few or no blacks in the Pentecostal Holiness Church for much of its history. On the failure of white Pentecostal historians to deal adequately with issues of race and racism, see Anthea Butler, "Walls of Division: Racism's Role in Pentecostal History" (paper presented to the American Society of Church History, January 1996).

12. The flurry surrounding the seeming eruption of Pentecostal activity in the early years of this century was almost immediately channeled into weekly periodicals, their distribution lent urgency by adherents' fervent belief in tongues as the evidence of spirit baptism (the doctrine that separated them from their estranged Holiness cousins) and the sign of the end times, along with the concomitant impulse to evangelize the world before it was too late. Using names like *Apostolic Faith*, *Gospel Witness*, *Herald of Light*, *Latter Rain Evangel*, *Upper Room*, and *Way of Faith*, spirit-baptized editors sought to spread the full gospel across the land through accounts of Azusa Street and other revivals, sermonic editorials, articles outlining Pentecostal doctrine, and personal testimonies sent in by faithful believers. The rapid success of some of these periodicals is remarkable: for instance, the Los Angeles–based *Apostolic Faith* (there were several magazines with the same title), begun in 1906 and initially published by the Azusa Street mission, reached a circulation of forty thousand per month by the end of 1907 and eighty thousand a year later; see Anderson, *Vision of the Disinherited*, 74.

13. Early Pentecostals held various views of the medical establishment. Some, like A. J. Gordon and A. B. Simpson, discouraged the use of medicine but allowed it in extreme cases, whereas the more radical John Alexander Dowie (the notorious founder of Zion, Illinois) rigorously forbade it. Similarities between the more radical Pentecostals and their perceived foes, particularly Christian Scientists, are evidenced in the frequent diatribes against the latter found in denominational editorials. See Blumhofer, *Restoring the Faith*, 19–24.

14. *Pentecostal Holiness Advocate*, May 23, 1935, 14 (hereafter cited as *PHA*).

15. *Church of God Evangel*, July 29, 1944, 11 (hereafter cited as *CGE*).

16. *PHA*, July 10, Aug. 14, Dec. 4, 1930.

17. *PHA*, June 19, 1930, 13.

18. *PHA*, May 28, 1931, 15.

19. *PHA*, May 28, 1931, 15.

20. *PHA*, June 5, 1930, 15.

21. *PHA*, Dec. 11, 1930, 14.

22. *PHA*, June 5, 1930, 14.

23. *PHA*, Sept. 4, 1930, 15.

24. *CGE*, Sept. 12, 1942, 9.

25. *PHA*, Dec. 4, 1930, 12.

26. *PHA*, Feb. 5, 1931, 15.

27. *PHA*, April 30, 1931, 15.

28. See *PHA*, May 21, 1931, Feb. 11, March 31, July 28, Sept. 8, 1932, Jan. 26, March 2, May 11, Sept. 28, 1933, Feb. 1, June 14, 1934. See also Jan. 21, Aug. 18, and Dec. 15, 1932, where the editor mentions that Mrs. Cockrell has written a new letter but does not print it. An earlier letter by her is in *PHA*, July 17, 1930.

29. *PHA*, July 17, 1930, 13.

30. *CGE*, June 26, 1943, 11.

31. *CGE*, April 29, 1944, 11. Male prisoners also frequently wrote to request Christians to encourage them and to thank them for their prayers; see *CGE*, May 27, 1944, 13.

32. *CGE*, June 26, 1943, 11.

33. *CGE*, April 9, 1938, 12.

34. *CGE*, April 9, 1938, 12.

35. *PHA*, June 5, 1930, 14–15.

36. *PHA*, April 14, 1932, 16.

37. *PHA*, April 23, 1931, 15–16.

38. Acts 19:11–12, *RSV.*

39. *CGE*, Dec. 17, 1938, 13.

40. *PHA*, March 22, 1934, 15.

41. *Whole Truth*, February 1934, 18 (hereafter cited as *WT*).

42. *PHA*, May 7, 1931, 13.

43. *PHA*, Nov. 9, 1933, 15.

44. *WT,* May 1933, 2.

45. *CGE*, Dec. 5, 1942, 12–13.

46. *CGE*, April 8, 1944, 12.

47. *CGE*, April 9, 1938, 7.

48. Edith L. Blumhofer, *Aimee Semple McPherson: Everybody's Sister* (Grand Rapids, MI: Eerdmans, 1993), 18.

49. *CGE*, Dec. 19, 1942, 11.

50. *PHA*, May 21, 1931, 13.

51. See R. Marie Griffith, *God's Daughters: Evangelical Women and the Power of Submission* (Berkeley: University of California Press, 1997).

52. *PHA*, Dec. 4, 1930, 12–13.

53. *PHA*, July 17, 1930, 14; June 19, 1930, 12.

54. *Latter Rain Evangel*, November 1908, 23 (hereafter cited as *LRE*).

55. *LRE*, March 1909, 10.

56. For parallels with contemporary Pentecostal women, see Griffith, *God's Daughters.* On Catholic women's relationship with humanized saints, see Robert A. Orsi, *Thank You, St. Jude: Women's Devotion to the Patron Saint of Hopeless Causes* (New Haven: Yale University Press, 1996).

57. *PHA*, June 19, 1930, 12.

58. *PHA*, Aug. 7, 1930, 11. See also *PHA*, Feb. 20, 1936, 11.

59. *PHA*, March 26, 1936, 12; Jan. 9, 1936, 14–15.

60. Leigh Eric Schmidt, *Holy Fairs: Scottish Communions and American Revivals in the Early Modern Period* (Princeton: Princeton University Press, 1989), 79. On other meanings (excluding the religious) of tears, see Anne Vincent-Buffault, *The History of Tears: Sensibility and Sentimentality in France* (Basingstoke: Macmillan, 1991).

61. *LRE*, October 1908, 3.

62. *PHA*, Feb. 20, 1936, 12.

63. *PHA*, Jan. 9, 1936, 15.

64. *PHA*, Jan. 23, 1936, 14.

65. *CGE*, March 1, 1924.

66. *PHA*, March 26, 1936, 12.

67. *CGE*, April 28, 1934.

68. *CGE*, March 14, 1936.

69. Blumhofer, *Restoring the Faith*, 98–99.

70. *PHA*, July 31, 1930, 12.

71. *PHA*, April 23, 1936, 13.

72. *LRE*, May 1913, 8–9.

73. *LRE*, April 1914, 24. This writer delivered a longer version of the same message two years later; see *LRE*, July 1916, 19–24.

74. Prominent instances include the so-called oneness controversy in the Assemblies of God in

1922 as a result of a minister's claim of divine revelation; conflicts over religious pacifism during the two world wars; and internal debates over changing standards for female dress.

75. Blumhofer, *Restoring the Faith,* 13.

76. Grant Wacker, "The Functions of Faith in Primitive Pentecostalism," in *Modern American Protestantism and Its World: Historical Articles on Protestantism in American Religious Life,* vol. 11, *New and Intense Movements,* ed. Martin E. Marty (Munich: K. G. Saur, 1993), 213.

77. Jody Shapiro Davie, *Women in the Presence: Constructing Community and Seeking Spirituality in Mainline Protestantism* (Philadelphia: University of Pennsylvania Press, 1995), 3.

In the case of an edited publication, of course, "consensus" is more than tacit; it is more or less enforced. The editorial authority of people like A. J. Tomlinson and George Floyd Taylor, founding editors, respectively, of the *Church of God Evangel* and *Pentecostal Holiness Advocate,* was extensive yet largely invisible to most readers, past and present. The power of these editors obviously raises questions about the kinds of testimonies found in these periodicals. How might letters have been pared down or, alternatively, embellished for the edification of their readership? How many letters did not make it into these publications, and for what reasons? From time to time, as with Iva Cockrell, editors inform their readers that they are omitting letters, excusing such omissions by referring to the sheer volume (and in this case, repetitiveness) of letters received. Testimonies were undoubtedly more likely to be printed if they accompanied financial contributions (and many such contributions were recorded in print), while the vast number of letter writers who praised various denominational leaders, missionaries, and the church at large suggests that writers may have thought that such praise would help get their testimonies into print. These and other devices pertaining to the composition of a "correct" testimony, one likely to be printed and to receive communal affirmation, need further examination.

78. Wacker, "Functions of Faith in Primitive Pentecostalism," 209.

79. COG Supreme Council, *Minutes,* March 5, 1953, 23–24; cited in Crews, *Church of God,* 152.

80. See Griffith, *God's Daughters.*

81. As Catherine A. Lutz argues, an emotion concept is "an index of a world of cultural premises and of scenarios for social interaction; each is a system of meaning or cluster of ideas which include both verbal, accessible, reflective ideas and implicit practical ones." Lutz, *Unnatural Emotions,* 210–11. The term "emotion rules" is from Arlie R. Hochschild, "Emotion Work, Feeling Rules, and Social Structure," *American Journal of Sociology* 85 (1979): 551–75.

Chapter Twelve

"Stand by Me"

Sacred Quartet Music and the Emotionology of African American Audiences, 1900–1930

Kimberley L. Phillips

I hear the railroad cry
Gonna ride that train, oh pretty mama
Get on board that sweet little mama
She can rock me, too, pretty mama
I board in Birmingham about half past four
Tell your daddy where I've been gone so long
I've been in Cleveland, I've been sad and gone
Tell the world I'm running wild.
—Dunham Jubilee Singers,
My Mama's Baby Child," c. 1928

By the time Arthur Turner and the other members of the Dunham Jubilee Singers recorded "My Mama's Baby Child" in 1928, they had frequently performed throughout the Deep South and the urban Midwest. The quartet sang tight harmony and a diverse repertoire of African American folk songs, spirituals, blues, and gospel. The quartet, along with a number of other Jefferson County groups, such as the Birmingham Jubilee Quartet and the Ravizee Singers, performed for African American audiences in southern and midwestern cities who were hungry for ecstatic music. Gospel did not become the dominant form of sacred music in African American churches until after 1945, but throughout the 1920s it was heard alongside secular music. The Dunham Jubilee Singers, for example, combined sanctified syncopations with blues songs.[1] In a single program the quartet answered the ironic songs of despair in the secular blues with sacred songs of hope. Their song "My Mama's Baby Child" depicted fears about migration, but the group's rendition of the Charles Albert Tindley hymn "Stand by Me" reminded audiences that "the Lord, he heard my cry / And pitied every groan."[2] By the late 1920s, many of these quartets began to sing just sacred music, primarily gospel. Ecstatic and passionate, gospel songs allowed performers and listeners to release intense emotions; in the context of a congregation, these emotional releases were accepted and validated.[3]

The popularity of quartet singing demonstrated that it had become an important sacred and secular form of expression for African American men and women living and working in Jefferson County, Alabama. As early as 1915, gospel quartet singing had emerged and flourished in the steel and coal camps of Jefferson County. Though influenced by quartet music in the black colleges and normal schools of the turn-of-the-century South, its refashioning by black working people for their own worship linked it with older traditions of black sacred expressive culture and the new forms of popular culture, such as blues. Beginning at the turn of the century, the ecstatic worship in the rapidly expanding Holiness and Pentecostal churches infused its music with an emotional intensity drained from other forms of African American sacred music. This new musical style was perceived as low-down music, music too coarse and sexual to be embraced as middle-class entertainment or in middle-class worship. But in the self-organized, all-black settings, working men and women articulated through song and performance style some of their most deeply held beliefs and desires. Drawing on a rich musical heritage of sacred expressiveness, they presented a Jesus who provided divine intervention, offered redemption, and loved all his children. At the same time, this music drew on instrumentations and rhythms that were crafted in blues and jazz and re-created within the context of the black Sanctified churches.[4] That such expressiveness had ties to secular music was equally consistent with tradition: always there had been a fine line between the sacred and the secular, between Saturday night and Sunday morning.[5]

The audiences for this new sacred music, which came primarily from the African American working class, helped create and entrench this new religious music. Though the term "gospel music" was not popularized in the national mindset until the early 1930s, it was a term heard as early as 1921 when the black evangelical minister and composer Charles Albert Tindley published his hymnal *Gospel Pearls*. These hymns were intended to arouse and express religious fervor that many black congregants felt while worshiping in the new Holiness and Pentecostal churches that soon usurped the older traditional black denominations. As African Methodist Episcopal and many Baptist congregations stepped up their attempts to diminish or eradicate expressive worship that had been acceptable in the nineteenth century, the newer denominations encouraged them: the body manifested God's presence through loud vocalizations and a range of physical movements. Music in these new churches was equally expressive, allowing for dancing and shouting. Gospel offered good news, and the passion that it expressed in its content and presentation was intended to incite passion in its audiences. Such intense religious emotion was variously described as great joy, heartfelt love, and "singing in the heart." In the context of this new musical genre, black working people—as performers and listeners—rejected the black middle class's insistence that musical worship had to be emotionally restrained and distinct from secular music. By the late 1930s, gospel music began to preempt other forms of black sacred music and its rhythms were barely distinguishable from blues.

Gospel music emerged in the midst of protracted historical processes that forever reshaped black people's lives and communities. Though Arthur Turner did not migrate out of the South until 1929, like other African Americans, he had witnessed the drama of mass migration, the spread and intensification of Jim Crow, the increased importance of city life to advance black goals, and the diminished role of agricultural wages. Gospel music, therefore, was music of southern migrants as they moved between rural and urban, agricultural and industrial settings. This new music shared aspects of the older traditions in African American sacred music, reinterpreting spirituals and congregational hymns. Its lyrics and modes of presentation demonstrated the immediate impact of the social and economic changes affecting black people's lives. At the same time, like the older sacred music and the new secular music, gospel offered important critiques of the larger society: segregation, economic inequality, and the limits on black agency were reoccurring themes. Gospel music's rousing, emotional, and participatory nature reveals how African American working-class men and women experienced, understood, and mediated the dramatic changes taking place in their everyday lives.

While the history of emotion is now receiving overdue attention from social historians, the shifting contours of African American emotional life in general and religious emotions more specifically have only recently been examined.[6] Those scholars who have examined African American expressive culture have noted the demise of emotion in sacred worship over the course of the twentieth century. They have argued that the influence of European music, the gains in literacy, and the entrenchment of middle-class values eroded the older sacred traditions of slavery.[7] In this argument, gospel music, while central to worship practices by the mid-twentieth century, was less emotionally rich than the spirituals. This conceptual approach, with its primary focus on loss, misses the struggle that many African Americans undertook to maintain the right to raise their voices in ecstatic sacred praise. Even as many black churches eradicated or diminished emotional worship and music from their religious services, other congregations continued to value such expressions. Indeed, gospel quartets were denounced and kept out of churches in the South because of the emotionality they displayed and incited. Even as gospel singing began to make inroads into some black churches after World War II, because of ties to an expressive secular culture, gospel quartets continued to be excluded from Sunday morning services.[8] Ray Pratt has described spirituals as "oppositional creativity" because of slaves' insistence on engaging in religious behavior and expression despite efforts to discourage or ban their independent worship. Though such efforts to ban gospel did not come from outside black communities, the description helps us understand the tension surrounding gospel's formation and presentation. The separate and highly expressive religiosity that gospel reflected and incited reveals an emotional culture and a set of values that African American workers crafted for themselves, sometimes in oppositional settings, sometimes in settings that coexisted with those dominated by the black middle class. Using a variety of descriptions of and recordings by early gospel quartet performances, this essay seeks to examine gospel quartets and their audiences within the larger context of shifting attitudes toward and expressions of religious emotions in African American life.[9]

By the turn of the century, African American churches had a variety of sacred music styles. The lined-out hymns, known in some congregations as Dr. Watts hymns (after Isaac Watts), old hymns, or Wesley hymns, were the most prominent; in addition, congregations still sang nineteenth-century black spirituals and European-style congregational Protestant hymns. A leader, typically a preacher or deacon, lined out the text two lines at a time using a short formulaic chant. The congregation responded, using a slow, a cappella tempo. Humming and moaning were quite common. Noble Sissle, whose father, Reverend George A. Sissle, was a Methodist minister, described the lined hymns he heard as a child: "I used to get a great thrill when my father or some member of the congregation would lead us in hymn, reading off the lyrics ahead of us. Then everyone would join in and every foot would keep time, and soon the whole church would be swaying in rhythm or patting their hands and feet. Whenever I sing a rhythm song—even today—I still pat my feet in the same way." [10] Many congregations still sang older spirituals. At the turn of the century, Mary White Ovington reported that she heard slave spirituals sung in rural Alabama "as they were originally sung, primitive music, great group singing." [11]

In the Missionary Baptist congregations, four-shape-note and seven-shape-note singing were widely practiced. The introduction of shape-note music in the mid-nineteenth century diminished the use of musical instruments such as guitars, banjos, or harmonicas. Yet hand clapping and foot stamping remained central in religious performances. Seven-shape-note singing allowed for more vocal ornamentation. This rural sacred music culture, like the Watts hymns and spirituals, was transmitted orally and depended on the whole congregation's participation. [12] In the devotion service, which consisted of songs, lined hymns, and a prayer, the congregation typically began with the Lord's Prayer, which became a personal prayer and song, using familiar poetic lines from the Psalms and well-known melodies. Participants often covered their faces. Bernice Johnson Reagon and Lisa Pertillar Brevard have noted that the praying and singing in the devotional services were both "public and private." As the congregation made a public prayer, their moans "provide[d] a kind of inside space for the prayer and intensifie[d] the energy within the worship service." [13]

Throughout the last decades of the nineteenth century and well into the first half of the twentieth century, ecstatic, expressive worship remained central to the religious lives of African Americans. In Sunday services and weekday prayer meetings, African Americans had abundant opportunities to give voice to their experiences through sermons, prayers, testimonies, and political speeches. In the numerous meetings and informal activities, African Americans spoke without scrutiny from white society. [14] W. E. B. Du Bois observed at the turn of the century that "the stamping, shrieking, and shouting, the rushing to and fro and wild waving of arms, the weeping and laughing, the vision and the trance" had a "firm hold" in many blacks' worship expressions. These were more than rapturous expressions: Du Bois conceded that many believed that "without this visible manifestation of the God there could be no true communion with the Invisible." [15] As late as the 1930s in the rural areas of coastal Georgia, African practices could still be seen, ranging from spirit possession to ring shouts. [16] In this context, ministers claimed their authority because they were "called to preach" rather than educated to preach. Those who could " 'raise the

Spirit' through the artful manipulation of 'the Word' " were considered to have great skill. Congregations expected their ministers to "respond, engage, and raise spiritual energies during the performance of a sermon."[17]

Throughout this period an expanding group of educated ministers and congregants attempted to alter the worship practices in black churches. In the aftermath of slavery, white and black missionaries from northern churches insisted that the loud prayers and shouts they observed in the church services of the freedpeople were indications of "moral and intellectual weakness," not encounters with the Lord. While sympathetic to the conditions of slavery and post-emancipation that had limited blacks' access to education, these missionaries from the North insisted that religion practiced in freedom demanded emotional restraint and quiet. While certain emotions, such as fear and grief, could not be controlled, they argued that conversion and religious worship did not depend on ecstatic responses. Memoirs from middle-class blacks typically included a reference to their religiosity as "private," "quiet," and "subdued."[18]

In short, expressive worship was viewed as a primitive response. Many educated black church leaders hoped that once blacks gained literacy, some of these practices would dissolve. But the shift in the valuation of quiet and private, not public and demonstrative, expression of blacks' sacred experiences inaugurated what one historian recently described as the "divesting of cultural values" rooted in Africa and the slave experience for values rooted in Europe and the Anglo-American culture of self-restraint.[19] Yet Du Bois viewed the end of passionate expression of faith not as the outcome of European influences, but as a result of the profound dilemmas confronting African Americans at the beginning of the twentieth century. The double-consciousness that he claimed many blacks experienced gave rise to a "painful self-consciousness." As African Americans vigorously combated Jim Crow that relegated them to a marginal political and social status and subjected them to murder and other violent acts, their traditional cultural moorings became unstable. In this context, Du Bois concluded, the inner emotional life of African Americans had entered its own turmoil. The struggle over the color line that marked the beginning of the twentieth century had launched "a time of intense ethical ferment, of religious heart-searching and intellectual unrest" for black folk. If religion had been a source of comfort in the context of slavery, from Du Bois's perspective it no longer provided it in the twentieth century. Instead, a sense of "impotence" and "pessimism" made black "religion a complaint and a curse, a wail rather than a hope, a sneer rather than faith." He hoped, however, that African Americans who retained their "deep religious feelings" would withstand the storm, turning their great "pent up vigor" toward challenging racial oppression.[20] Few other black middle-class observers were as generous.

That the valuation of emotional worship was under concerted attack from within the black communities underscores the creeping gains in the value of emotional restraint in religious practices. As debates swirled among African American elites about how best to combat white supremacy and advance black equality in economic, social, and political life, an equally vibrant debate took place within the black churches about how to best present themselves as dignified people. Most of this second debate focused on the behavior of a black working class that many elites believed violated middle-class notions of decorum. Under attack, then, were the forms of expressive culture—defined as worship styles, secular music, dance, and dress—that reinforced stereotypes of black people as childlike, irrational, shiftless, and sexual.[21] As Michael Harris has reminded us, for African Americans anxious to assimilate into "mainstream American culture, singing was one way they could demonstrate that they deserved a place in the white culture to which they were still denied access."[22]

Though critiques and remedies were advanced, churches remained critical locations for African American social and cultural life.[23] As Evelyn Brooks Higginbotham has rightly noted, African American community building in the South was centered in the mainline churches. More to the point, black churches in the last years of the nineteenth century and the first decades of the twentieth took on a public character within the framework of Jim Crow, "afford[ing] African Americans an interstitial space in which to critique and contest white America's racial domination." The black church, Higginbotham has asserted, did not become

> the embodiment of ministerial authority or of any individual's private interests and pronouncements, but . . . the social space for discussion of public concerns. During the late nineteenth and early twentieth centuries, the church came to represent a deliberative arena, whose character derived from the collective nature of the church itself, namely, as a body of many diverse members, and from race-conscious feelings of nationalism.[24]

In a study on Norfolk, Earl Lewis noted that urban churches sometimes served as a "bedrock" in African Americans' "efforts to thwart white racism and promote advancement in the home sphere." Many denominations, for example, implicitly and explicitly joined in the rejection of the derogatory images of African Americans as inferior, immoral, and childlike.[25]

While churches remained important to African Americans' struggle for equality between 1880 and 1920, the alternative images the black middle class advanced increasingly set them at odds with working-class women and men. Ministers, often backed by middle-class congregants, denounced a variety of working-class secular behaviors and worship practices because they considered them both immoral and detrimental "to the race." Higginbotham has noted that religious spaces and religious language allowed for African Americans' creation and internalization of alternative representations. At the same time, even as blacks rejected white public opinion, their endeavors were often bound up in African American self-help, Victorian ideology, and middle-class values. On the one hand, they denounced the "hedonism and materialism" of the elite; on the other hand, women not only cautioned against the "vice and idleness of the poor," but they vigorously pursued the eradication of this vice.[26] Other women joined in efforts to end dancing, drinking, and gambling, for example.[27] Within churches, ministers sought to downplay ecstatic worship and infuse intellectual content into sermons.[28]

Particularly within the urban industrial setting, black churches followed the patterns found in secular social organizations and developed along class lines. Privately and publicly, middle-class blacks described the black poor (and transgressing working people) in terms that sounded not much different from whites committed to Jim Crow.[29] Sarah Rice, whose father was the pastor for an impoverished A.M.E. congregation in Birmingham, Alabama, during the 1910s, learned early that color and class distinctions among African Americans did not often allow for sympathy for poor people's efforts to assert themselves inside and outside the community. When Rice attempted to physically defend her much younger brother from the taunts of better-dressed middle-class black children, she (and later her mother) was chastised by other black women for transgressing their roles as "preacher's kin," and instead displaying characteristics of low-down Negroes. Rice later remembered, "As minister's children, we were not allowed to fight. We had to take everything they put on us, because we were supposed to be examples. That was hard for me, because I always felt like self-defense was my priority."[30]

More than behavior was under attack. Since emancipation, how African Americans expressed their experiences was no longer validated. As Elsa Barkley Brown has observed of Richmond during the post-emancipation years, "the church provided more than physical space, financial resources and a communication network; it also provided a cultural base that validated emotion and experience as ways of knowing, and drew upon a collective call and response, encouraging the active participation of all." In these settings, prayers, songs, testimonies, and debates enabled all members of the community to voice their experiences and participate in constructing solutions. No one individual claimed authority as knowing what was best for the community.[31] As participation in the political sphere became more rigidly defined along gender and class lines, some blacks in the middle class claimed new authority. Thus traditional values and modes of presentation came under attack.[32]

As the traditional worship practices were variously eradicated or diminished, African Americans in the South began to leave the Baptist and Methodist churches and join first the Holiness and then the Pentecostal churches. The Holiness church— the Church of Christ (Holiness)—was the first denomination to emerge in the 1890s; it largely appealed to Baptist ministers and congregations attracted by its belief in personally received faith. The way to become a saint was to receive the Holy Ghost— to have a personal vision and be saved. Certainly the focus on glossolalia as an ideal appealed to African Americans whose ancestors had believed and practiced spirit possession. In 1907, a schism in the church led to the formation of the Pentecostals, or the Church of God in Christ. This new denomination emphasized personal testimony in which great feeling was a hallmark of salvation. Moreover, prayers of all the saints could play a potent role in "petitioning the Lord" to intervene on an individual's behalf.[33] As Peter Goldsmith observed, church members were obligated to actively participate in church services. "[S]aints are expected to be able to 'testify' in the course of a service, to initiate songs, to pray over an offering and to carry out other ritual functions. Saints cannot attend a church for long without being expected to demonstrate these skills, and they must be ready and willing to demonstrate them on the spot."[34] In rural churches, such an active participation by all members was critical since many congregations did not have full-time ministers.

Though the "inspiration of the spirit" determined events in services, such verbal displays were at once formulaic and improvisational, drawing on older African American worship practices. All services began with prayers, followed by songs and testimonials. The pastor or a designated member preached; the service concluded with shouting and dancing. Often song was the dominant form of expression, ranging from hums, grunts, and moans to rhythmic chants, shouts, and melodic hymns. Through most of the church services, which lasted several hours, members could initiate and lead favorite or improvised prayers and songs. Prayers could either be spoken or sung, relying on a call-and- response pattern that had long shaped African American sacred expressions. Such patterning allowed for an open-endedness to them; at the same time, the initiator of the prayer or song could substitute more appropriate lyrics that spoke to personal experiences of either the singer or members of the congregation. Long before the pastor began to preach, the congregation had set the tone of the service.[35]

But a good preacher was one who had a strong singing voice, setting a rhythm and repetition that at once responded to the congregation yet called them to new emotional heights. An observer of a rural church in Black Belt Georgia during the 1930s described one such sermon, noting how the pastor asked the congregation a question "and they would answer 'Huh.'" Soon the quiet call-and-response between the pastor and the congregation gave way to ecstatic agreement denoted by the stamping of feet and their shouting voices. The repetition of these rhythms "urged him on to greater heights until his shouting voice not only seemed to fill the church but to reverberate from wall to wall." While the observer concluded that this expressiveness acted as a great emotional purge, Jon Michael Spencer has suggested that the testifying in black Holiness and Pentecostal churches provided members with "confirmation, protection, and sustenance." He noted that "Black worshipers have long sung, spoken, and enacted the positive and therapeutic involvement of God in their lives, thereby intensifying their individual faith and their community strength as they endure the ways of the world." Standing, swaying, trembling, and other physical movements were motivated by joy, love, bliss, and sorrow. Ministers' tendencies in these congregations to deliver sermons in quasi-metrical units, thump lecterns, and stomp their feet reinforced the congregations' permission to continue in their own vocalizations. The participatory character of Pentecostal churches provided members with direct personal contact with ministers and each other.[36]

The continued insistence by many African Americans on practicing ecstatic worship became a large countermovement in the cities. William Montgomery has reminded us that the number of African Americans joining these new churches remained small until after 1920 because rural and small-town churches in the mainline black denominations retained the more ecstatic expressiveness. The explosion in Sanctified and Spiritualist churches occurred *after* blacks migrated to first the urban South, and then the urban North. These new denominations attracted migrants in the urban South dissatisfied with the increasingly staid Baptist and Methodist worship practices. By the 1930s, in most cities throughout the United States, the number of black women and men who claimed affiliation with these new churches rivaled the numbers in either the African Methodist Episcopal or Baptist churches.[37] Zora

Neale Hurston explained why so many blacks from the Deep South abandoned the mainline black Protestant churches for the Sanctified churches:

> There is great respect for the white man as law-giver, banker, builder, and the like but the folk Negro do not crave his religion at all. They are not angry about it, they merely pity him because it is generally held that he just can't do any better that way. But the Negro who imitates the whites comes in for spitting scorn. So they let him have his big solemn church all to himself while they go on making their songs and music and dance motions to go along with it and shooting new life into American music.[38]

In these worship settings, shouting was an emotional response to religious experience: "a sign of special favor from the spirit." In her studies of ecstatic worship in the Sanctified churches, Hurston described shouting as a collective response stimulated by rhythm. It was "a community thing. It thrives in concert. After [the first shout] they are likely to sweep like fire over the church."[39] But, as Hurston suggested, the participation in these churches was not one of escape, but rather a critique of a black middle class imitating the staid worship practices of whites.[40] Most important, African Americans insisted that the encounter with the spirit was "experiential rather than a cognitive movement." Iain MacRobert has demonstrated that African Americans who helped shape the worldwide Pentecostal movement "shared an understanding and a practice of Christianity which had developed in the African diaspora out of a syncretism of West African primal religion and culture with Western Christianity in the crucible of New World slavery."[41]

In these new Sanctified denominations, members practiced a music style that would eventually have a tremendous impact on the development of gospel music. The saints called secular music "devil's music," but inside their churches they practiced a lively and highly emotional music punctuated by chants, shouts, weeping, and dancing. Horace Boyer has described this music as "nothing less than ecstatic with forceful and jubilant singing, dramatic testimonies (often delivered as chants), hand clapping, foot stamping, and beating of drums, tambourines, and triangles (pots, pans, and washboards when professional instruments were not available)."[42] Raised as a Baptist, Mahalia Jackson determined that the Holiness churches in her New Orleans neighborhood had a much more interesting style of music and worship practices. "Those people had no choir or organ. They used the drum, the cymbal, the tambourine, and the steel triangle. Everybody in there sang, and they clapped and stomped their feet, and sang with their whole bodies."[43] Preachers in both the black Church of God (Holiness) and the Church of God in Christ (Pentecostal) composed stirring gospel music for their congregations that would add to the emerging forms of ecstatic worship. Their compositions, Horace Boyer notes, were written in the aftermath of a failed Reconstruction. Their songs "move directly to the feeling and expressions of a group of people who, even after having been freed from slavery by law, still find no possible solution to problems on this earth, but who dismiss this earth and turn to the one still believable source of recompense: God in Christ."[44]

A particular concentration of migration streams from rural areas to urban centers of the Black Belt South impacted the shape of gospel quartet music. The decline in cotton prices after 1900 propelled young black men and women north into Jefferson County's expanding industrial workplaces. The county, which included the cities of Birmingham and Bessemer, provided African American migrants with wage work in the coal mines, numerous steel mills, and the factories that produced steel products. When African Americans from southeast Alabama met African Americans from central Alabama in the steel camps and coal mines of Jefferson County, neither had much of a tradition in either country or city blues music. Why? One scholar has argued that in southeast Alabama the predominance of Missionary Baptists, who forbade secular dancing and other forms of secular, popular culture, helped prevent the influx of blues. By the first decade of the twentieth century, much of the secular entertainment was religious music. Why Jefferson County and Birmingham had a weak blues presence is not easily answered. Unlike northwest Alabama, which had a tradition of blues (and was the birthplace of W. C. Handy), central Alabama had less of a tradition. Birmingham had a large industrial working class, but it "lacked the kind of wide-open red-light district found in other urban centers that had a rich blues tradition." The city was home to blues pianist Cow Cow Davenport and blues singer Bessie Jackson, but both went on to live and perform elsewhere. Gospel quartets like the Birmingham Jubilee Singers and the Dunham Jubilee Singers "recorded more titles than did all of the city's blues musicians put together." Thus, the gospel tradition in the area overshadowed Birmingham's early blues milieu.[45]

Though forged in the steel and coal camps, gospel quartet singing had roots in shape-note singing, Watts hymns, folk music, minstrel quartets, and college jubilee singing in the Civil War and Reconstruction-era South.[46] Of these influences, historians have considered the male jubilee quartets first heard at Fisk University and later Tuskegee the most important to the development of sacred quartet singing. Jubilee, a term used to describe the emancipation celebrations (from the day of jubilee when the slaves were set free in the Book of Leviticus) was derived, perhaps, from the Bantu words "diuba" and "juba"—meaning to pat and to beat time. These terms had merged to describe juba dancing as a lively solo dance of hand-clapping and foot-tapping.[47] While jubilee singing built on older African American slave music traditions, it also rejected or refined these performance strategies, styles, and contents. Most important, while the university-based jubilee choirs and quartets performed spirituals, they did so in a European manner. The men who sang in these quartets fanned out into rural and urban schools, transmitting quartet singing into secular settings.[48]

While black quartet singing was not confined to any particular group in the late nineteenth century, it remained most popular among black workers in the first decades of the twentieth century. These men and women migrating to Birmingham tended to belong to smaller rural Baptist churches or the emerging Holiness and Pentecostal churches where spirited singing and emotional worship were still valued. Moreover, many belonged to denominations that had discouraged participation in secular dances and music. During breaks from the mills and mines, quartets performed and perfected their styles in the segregated steel and coal camps. In these autonomous settings away from the gaze of middle-class reformers and white bosses, unskilled workers became skilled singers. As they began to perform, they matched their style to accommodate enthusiastic responses to the music. In these early performances, Horace Boyer has suggested, quartets created a folk style that allowed rhythmic movements, vocal embellishments, and greater vocal ranges common in churches, thereby departing from the style of the university- trained quartets. Most important, sacred music and secular music fused to become acceptable forms of entertainment, furthering the tendencies in black cultural life for special events to take on elements of church services.[49]

Arthur Turner and the other members of the Dunham Jubilee Singers were trained and influenced by R. C. Foster, who had formed the first male quartet in Bessemer, Alabama, after he began working in the mines there in 1915. The Foster Singers sang spirituals and the new gospel hymns published in Charles Tindley's *Gospel Pearls*. By the time the Dunham Jubilee Singers formed their quartet in 1924, the development of local radio programs and the success of traveling black musicians broadened the group's repertoire to include secular music as well. Over the next several years, the Dunham Jubilee Singers sang gospel, folk music, spirituals, blues, and work songs in northern and southern cities. Like most groups, the Dunham Jubilee Singers were a four-part a cappella quartet: Turner sang bass and three other men sang second bass, tenor, and baritone. Known for their tight harmonies, these quartets mesmerized listeners through great skill and meticulous control. Though quartet singing allowed for call-and-response, an emphasis on close harmony meant that few could tell the voices apart. Arthur Turner recalled that the harmony of groups like the Dunham Jubilee Singers was so good, "seems as if the notes could be heard in the room the next day. It was that good."[50]

Though committed to singing "for the Lord," quartets who hoped to make it as professionals also competed for audiences. In order to take advantage of the various radio, recording, and performance opportunities, many of these quartets performed both sacred and secular music. Though some had musical training and in the later years quartets would rely on printed music, the earlier compositions relied on spirituals and the musicians' own personal experiences. Turner recalled that Charlie Dunham crafted lyrics from the "general conversation," and the music came "from the soul." Did these patterns of creativity resemble those of blues? In the end, as Lawrence Levine has concluded, gospel music in style and presentation returned to "black church music the sounds and structure of the folk spirituals, work songs, and nineteenth- century cries and hollers; [gospel singers and composers] borrowed freely from the ragtime, blues and jazz of the secular black world."[51]

Because of their ties to secular music (whether they sang it or not), quartets could not sing in churches. Arthur Turner, whose uncle pastored at the large Sixth Avenue Baptist Church in Birmingham, declared quartet singing "too much entertainment." Further, the spirit wasn't with them. Many groups perceived themselves as entertainers, and did not edit raunchy tunes from their repertoire. The Dunham Jubilee Singers, for example, thought of and presented themselves as entertainers who sang sacred music. Other gospel singers moved back and forth between sacred and secular music, often changing names for each genre. Reverend J. M. Gates recorded gospel songs in the late 1920s, filled with moans and growls in such tunes as "Down Here, Lord, Waiting on You." But Reverend Gates also recorded "Dead Cat on the Line," "These Hard Times Are Tight Like That," "Mannish Women," and "Somebody's Been Stealing." Other singers, not from Alabama necessarily, shared these tendencies. Blind Willie Johnson, perhaps the greatest early gospel soloist, also played the country blues circuit. From Texas, Johnson began such gospel tunes like "Let Your Light Shine on Me" with delicate falsetto and quiet country guitar licks, but he slowly increased the tempo, driving the rhythm with a tapping foot and thumping pats on his guitar. His voice soon roughened, with the painful growls typical of blues singers. The growling, repeated refrain "Shine on, let it shine on" soon dominated, letting the guitar almost fall away. He often played on Texas radio, "praying up a storm." Johnson's "If I Had My Way" is a pure example of the growling, moaning gospel blues that must have terrified traditional ministers used to the sedate Protestant hymns. As one listener recalled, "that's a scary singer." [52]

Because gospel quartets tended to draw members from several congregations, rather than the same church, and since so many performed around work camps or began to travel, singers were exposed to a variety of sacred and secular styles of music presentation. Thus gospel songs rose out of the sacred folk music of the Holiness churches and the many small independent black churches. These songs, which echoed the rhythm of the country blues and drew on the content of religion, were filled with tales of redemption and the triumph over worldly temptation. Moreover, they lacked the condemnation of personal behavior directed at so many blues and gospel singers, and the lives of so many working- class black people. John Spencer has argued that the lines between sacred and secular music were very thin. Often, Spencer has pointed out, blues singers were former preachers, or they later became preachers. In whatever direction these singers moved, they brought sermon-like qualities to secular music, or the driving blues to gospel. Both genres, however, drew on the spirituals or the turn-of-the-century Protestant hymns. Mississippi Bracey's blues tune "I'll Overcome Someday" was apparently *intentionally* titled after the popular hymn of Charles Albert Tindley, the Methodist Episcopal minister of Philadelphia. Later, "We Shall Overcome" became an important gospel/civil rights song. [53]

While sacred quartets sought to be entertaining, they also hoped to spread a religious message. Thus we should be careful not to blur the lines between the intent of sacred music and that of secular music. We would underestimate the struggle that congregations and singers waged within themselves. More to the point, the distinctions that participants and audiences made between sacred and secular music would be ignored. Whether in a sacred or secular setting, a quartet's success was measured in how it could " 'shout' its audience—move it into a jubilant state of ecstasy, with some people 'falling out.' " [54]

Did gospel music advance an African American social and cultural ethos similar to that found in the spirituals created during slavery? Certainly analysis of the gospel songs themselves would provide contradictory responses to this question. According to Lawrence Levine, while gospel music revealed the retention of older black sacred traditions, it also announced the diminution of those traditions.

There were few songs about the Old Testament heroes, few songs portraying victory in this world. Ultimate change when it came took place in the future in an otherworldly context. Christ, with His promise of a better tomorrow was the dominating figure upon whom Man was wholly dependent. No longer were temporal and spatial barriers transcended. This world had to be suffered; one had to take comfort from the blessings one had and from the assurances of the Almighty.[55]

The emphasis on the Lord was more pronounced in gospel music than in the spirituals, but the new music did not overemphasize men's and women's dependency. Rather, gospel music reminded participants and audiences that once saved they could act on their own behalf. Every quartet—amateur and professional—who sang the Tindley hymn "Canaan Land" sang a hymn that merged images of salvation and migration in a driving rhythm. Calls and shouts were part of the performance as the repeated "Over there" was answered with "I'll meet my mother." In the spirituals, Canaan was often meant to mean escape to the North. In the gospel version, migration, which demanded that blacks leave loved ones or enabled them to be reunited with family and friends, was linked to conversion experiences. Gospel reminded listeners that they need not travel alone; at the very least, the fears of the unknown could be offset by spiritual joy.

In more subtle ways, many of the new gospel songs offered emotional release for its listeners living in a secular world where personal and communal relationships had been significantly altered by migration. While the blues often presented despair and resignation as the final outcome of personal relationships, gospel hymns were far more hopeful. In "Mother's Prayers Followed Me All the Way," children were cautioned to respect their parents, especially their mothers. Washington Phillips spoke directly to the shifting class relations in which less-educated blacks were now viewed as marginal: "You can go to college, You can go to School / But if you don't have Jesus, then you're an educated fool / But you better have Jesus, I tell you that's all." Such moralizing reminded listeners that in heaven, class, like race, had no place. "It's right to stand together, it's wrong to / stand apart. / 'Cause none is goin' to enter, but the pure / in heart."[56]

Equally evident, gospel hymns offered more overt political expressions framed in an African American prophetic tradition. The vision of a militant and triumphant Jesus Christ over egregious sins or sinners demonstrated gospel hymns as open critiques of the larger, secular society. Robin Kelley has argued that historians like Gayraud Wilmore might be correct that "the period after World War I witnessed a 'deradicalization' of the black church as well as a simultaneous secularization of black radicalism. [But] nevertheless, a radical interpretation of Christianity continued to thrive outside the organized church."[57] African Americans' efforts to organize in unions, radical politics, and civil rights struggles often included gospel music that dispersed fear and validated action. The Golden Gate Jubilee Quartet's "Stalin Wasn't Stallin'" praised the Soviet Union for its willingness to take on the devil Hitler. The "Yanks," in contrast, dragged their feet, underscoring the belief among African Americans that the commitment to Jim Crow by the U.S. government made a mockery of any triumph over Nazism. Equally popular, the Norfolk Jubilee Quartet's "My Lord's Gonna Move This Wicked Race" announced God's retribution against those who practiced segregation.[58] In the private settings where these songs were performed and received, African Americans could shout and clap their approval without white sanction. More to the point, audiences heard these songs in the 1940s as challenges to segregation became commonplace on buses and in the streets.[59]

In more personal ways, however, gospel quartets and their audiences advanced new conceptions of themselves as sacred people. African American men presented images of elegant men, challenging the now dominant image of them as dangerous and deviant. Only a minority of quartet singers were black women, but they too challenged images of them as unskilled. Indeed, women took on male voices as tenors, basses, and baritones, challenging definitions of ladylike behavior advanced by middle-class black women. Most important, the sacred quartet singing that continued outside Sunday morning rituals—and outside middle-class churches—advanced a working-class congregational autonomy. By the late 1930s, the resistance against gospel music in the older denominations eroded, often because they faced competition from other congregations and denominations that had embraced gospel.[60] While gospel choirs and soloists became increasingly prominent, gospel quartets continued to remain outside the Sunday morning worship. Instead, they typically performed in afternoon and evening services. Others led the midweek prayer services, held special programs to raise money for church buildings, or celebrated ministers' and congregations' anniversaries. Many quartet singers appreciated the autonomy that such divisions provided: quartet singers could push the boundaries of decorum when they performed outside church rituals. As many quartets began to sing only gospel songs, members typically began their programs with testimonials of their salvation from sin and their faith "in Jesus." Gospel quartet singing provided men and women the opportunity simultaneously to preach and entertain. Arthur Turner put it simply: by singing gospel he "could lead a Christian life."[61]

Instead of cleaving to models of middle-class decorum that discouraged emotion as essential to worship, African American working-class men and women advanced their own conceptions of what was permissible to express and where such religious emotions could be expressed. As ministers proclaimed in print and from the pulpit that "God didn't need to hear all that shouting," many black church people thought otherwise. Whether in the Pentecostal churches or the separate performances of sacred music, many blacks demonstrated that religious experience was emotional, not merely cognitive. Such experiences, therefore, could not be separated from the secular. Even as other blacks denounced secular urban music, African American working men and women sifted through this popular culture and linked it to their sacred music. In turn, this music simultaneously reflected and intensified their religious emotions. As they sang "I'm so glad / I'm so glad / Trouble don't last always," hardworking, holy, well-dressed men and women shook, shouted, sweated, and harmonized for the Lord. It was all right for the audience to shout, sweat, and shake, too. By paying close attention to the shifting emotionology of African Americans during the first half of the twentieth century, social historians can begin to better understand the meaning of religious expressions in the everyday lives of working-class blacks.

NOTES

1. Personal interview with Arthur Turner, May 18, 1996.

2. Ibid.; *Birmingham Quartet Anthology: Jefferson County, Alabama (1926–1953)*, Clanka Lanka CL 144.001/002; Anthony Heilbut, *The Gospel Sound: Good News and Bad Times*, 4th ed. (New York: Limelight Editions, 1992), 45.

3. I am borrowing this concept from Earl Lewis, *In Their Own Interests: Race, Class, and Power in Twentieth Century Norfolk, Virginia* (Berkeley: University of California Press, 1991).

4. Bernice Johnson Reagon, "Pioneering African American Gospel Music Composers: A Smithsonian Institution Research Project," in *We'll Understand It By and By*, ed. Bernice Johnson Reagon (Washington, DC: Smithsonian Institution Press, 1992), 3–6.

5. The literature on these links is extensive; see Lawrence Levine, *Black Culture and Black Consciousness: Afro-American Folk Thought from Slavery to Freedom* (New York: Oxford University Press, 1977); Jon Michael Spencer, *Blues and Evil* (Knoxville: University of Tennessee Press, 1993); Alan Young, *Woke Me Up This Morning: Black Gospel Singers and the Gospel Life* (Jackson: University Press of Mississippi, 1997), 9–10.

6. A discussion of African American emotional attitudes, expressions, and values has been largely absent from recent work on the history of emotions. See Peter N. Stearns and Carol Z. Stearns, "Emotionology: Clarifying the History of Emotions and Emotional Standards," *American Historical Review* 90 (October 1985): 813–36. For a discussion of the paucity of attention to religious expressions of joy, see the chapter by R. Marie Griffith in this volume.

7. Levine, *Black Culture and Black Consciousness*, 155–58; William E. Montgomery, *Under Thy Own Vine and Fig Tree: The African-American Church in the South, 1865–1900* (Baton Rouge: Louisiana State University Press, 1993), 266. The most important discussion of African American religion during slavery remains Albert J. Raboteau, *Slave Religion: The "Invisible Institution" in the Antebellum South* (New York: Oxford University Press, 1978).

8. Michael W. Harris, *The Rise of Gospel Blues: The Music of Thomas Andrew Dorsey in the Urban Church* (New York: Oxford University Press, 1992); Kip Lornell, *"Happy in the Service of the Lord": Afro-American Gospel Quartets in Memphis* (Urbana: University of Illinois Press, 1988); Ray Allen, *Singing in the Spirit: African-American Sacred Quartets in New York City* (Philadelphia: University of Pennsylvania Press, 1991); Young, *Woke Me Up This Morning*, 52–66.

9. For an important discussion of the study of emotion, see Stearns and Stearns, "Emotionology"; Shula Sommers, "Understanding Emotions: Some Interdisciplinary Considerations," in *Emotion and Social Change*, ed. Peter N. Stearns and Carol Z. Stearns (New York: Holmes and Meier, 1988), 23–38. Also helpful are John Blacking, "Expressing Human Experience through Emotion," in *Music, Culture, and Experience: Selected Papers of John Blacking*, ed. Reginald Byron (Chicago: University of Chicago Press, 1995), 31–53; and Ray Pratt, *Rhythm and Resistance: The Political Uses of American Popular Music* (Washington, DC: Smithsonian Institution Press, 1990), 47–69.

10. Robert Kimball and William Bolcolm, *Reminiscing with Sissle and Blake* (New York: Viking, 1973), 26.

11. Mary White Ovington, *The Walls Came Tumbling Down* (New York: Harcourt, Brace, 1947), 71.

12. Doris Jane Dyen, "The Role of Shape-Note Singing in the Musical Culture of Black Communities in Southeast Alabama" (Ph.D. diss., University of Illinois at Urbana-Champaign, 1977), 95.

13. Bernice Johnson Reagon and Lisa Pertillar Brevard, liner notes, *Wade in the Water: African American Congregational Singing*, vol. 2, Smithsonian Folkways SF40073; Clifton H. Johnson, ed., *God Struck Me Dead: Voices of Ex-Slaves* (Cleveland: Pilgrim Press, 1993), 4.

14. Montgomery, *Under Thy Own Vine*, 253–306.

15. W. E. B. Du Bois, *Souls of Black Folk* (1903; reprint, New York: Penguin, 1995), 212.

16. Georgia Writers' Project, *Drums and Shadows: Survival Studies among the Georgia Coastal Negroes* (1940; reprint, Athens: University of Georgia Press, 1986); Johnson, *God Struck Me Dead*, 2–12.

17. Gerald L. Davis, *I Got the Word in Me and I Can Sing, You Know: A Study of the Performed*

African-American Sermon (Philadelphia: University of Pennsylvania Press, 1985), 9; Jon Michael Spencer, *Sacred Symphony: The Chanted Sermon of the Black Preacher* (Westport, CT: Greenwood, 1987).

18. Montgomery, *Under Thy Own Vine*, 267–75. For examples of such claims in the autobiographies of middle-class blacks, see Daniel A. Payne, *Recollections of Seventy Years* (Nashville, 1888); and Du Bois, *Souls of Black Folk*, 210–11.

19. Harris, *Rise of Gospel Blues*, 5; T. J. Jackson Lears, *No Place of Grace: Anti-Modernism and the Transformation of American Culture, 1880–1920* (New York: Pantheon, 1981).

20. Du Bois, *Souls of Black Folk*, 221–22.

21. See, for example, W. E. B. Du Bois, "The Problem of Amusement," *Southern Workman* 26 (September 1897): 181–84.

22. Harris, *Rise of Gospel Blues*, 3.

23. Elsa Barkley Brown, "Womanist Consciousness: Maggie Lena Walker and the Independent Order of St. Luke," *Signs* 14 (spring 1989): 610–33; Lewis, *In Their Own Interests;* Robin D. G. Kelley, " 'We Are Not What We Seem': The Politics and Pleasures of Community," in *Race Rebels: Culture, Politics, and the Black Working Class* (New York: Free Press, 1994), 35–54.

24. Evelyn Brooks Higginbotham, *Righteous Discontent: The Women's Movement in the Black Baptist Church, 1880–1920* (Cambridge: Harvard University Press, 1993), 10.

25. Lewis, *In Their Own Interests*, 70–71.

26. Higginbotham, *Righteous Discontent*, 180–96; Kenneth K. Gaines, *Uplifting the Race: Black Leadership, Politics, and Culture in the Twentieth Century* (Chapel Hill: University of North Carolina Press, 1996).

27. Alabama Women's Baptist State Convention, *Minutes*, Ninth Annual Session (Montgomery, AL, 1894), 8.

28. Montgomery, *Under Thy Own Vine*, 291–93.

29. See, for example, Geraldine Moore, *Behind the Ebony Mask* (Birmingham: Southern University Press, 1961).

30. Sarah Rice, *He Included Me: The Autobiography of Sarah Rice* (Athens: University of Georgia Press, 1989), 5–6.

31. Elsa Barkley Brown, "Negotiating and Transforming the Public Sphere: African American Political Life in the Transition from Slavery to Freedom," *Public Culture* 7 (1994): 121. For a similar argument about the role of some churches during the modern civil rights movement, see Aldon D. Morris, *The Origins of the Civil Rights Movement: Black Communities Organizing for Change* (New York: Free Press, 1984), 4–16.

32. Gaines, *Uplifting the Race;* Peter Rachleff, *Black Labor in Richmond, 1865–1890* (Urbana: University of Illinois Press, 1989), 192–93.

33. On the growth of Holiness and Pentecostal churches, see C. Eric Lincoln and Lawrence H. Mamiya, *The Black Church in the African American Experience* (Durham: Duke University Press, 1990); Iain MacRobert, *The Black Roots and White Racism of Early Pentecostalism in the USA* (New York: St. Martin's Press, 1988); Peter D. Goldsmith, *When I Rise Cryin' Holy: African-American Denominationalism on the Georgia Coast* (New York: AMS Press, 1989), 69–190. For the appeal of Pentecostalism, see Harvey Cox, *Fire from Heaven: The Rise of Pentecostal Spirituality and the Reshaping of Religion in the Twenty-first Century* (Reading, MA: Addison-Wesley, 1995); James S. Tinney, "William J. Seymour: Father of Modern-Day Pentecostalism," in *Black Apostles: Afro-American Clergy Confront the Twentieth Century,* ed. Randall K. Burkett and Richard Newman (Boston: G. K. Hall, 1978), 213–25.

34. Goldsmith, *When I Rise*, 95.

35. Ibid., 107–9; Georgia Writers' Project, *Drums and Shadows*, 170.

36. Georgia Writers' Project, *Drums and Shadows*, 170; Jon Michael Spencer, "The Ritual of Testifying in the Black Church," in *Celebrations of Identity: Multiple Voices in American Ritual Performance,* ed. Pamela R. Frese (Westport, CT: Greenwood, 1993), 72.

37. Montgomery, *Under Thy Own Vine*, 350.

38. Zora Neale Hurston, *The Sanctified Church: The Folklore Writings of Zora Neale Hurston* (Berkeley: Turtle Island, 1981), 107.

39. Ibid., 91–92. Hurston noted that there were two types of shouters: silent and vocal. The silent type shake with violent retching and twitching motions. Sometimes they remain seated, sometimes they jump up and down and fling the body about with great violence. Lips tightly pursed, eyes closed. The seizure ends by collapse. The vocal type is the more frequent. There are all gradations from quiet weeping while seated, to the unrestrained screaming while leaping pews and running down the aisle. Some, unless restrained, run up into the pulpit and embrace the preacher. (92) Both of these descriptions differ significantly from the ring shout, common among West African religious practices, and nearly replicated among African American slaves. Nonetheless, Hurston's description focuses on the communal aspect of the shout and its origins in the African "possession by the gods."

40. Ibid. Hurston's conclusion is quite different from other social scientists who have viewed black Pentecostalism as "escapist" and "otherworldly." See, for example, J. B. Holt, "Holiness Religion: Culture Shock and Social Reorganization," *American Sociological Review* 5 (1940): 740–47; Hans A. Baer and Merrill Singer, *African-American Religion in the Twentieth Century: Varieties of Protest and Accommodation* (Knoxville: University of Tennessee Press, 1992), 171–78. For an alternative view, see Goldsmith, *When I Rise;* Cheryl Townsend Gilkes, " 'Together and in Harness': Women's Traditions in the Sanctified Church," *Signs* 10 (summer 1985): 696–99.

41. Iain MacRobert, "The Black Roots of Pentecostalism," in *African-American Religion: Interpretive Essays in History and Culture,* ed. Timothy E. Fulop and Albert J. Raboteau (New York: Routledge, 1997), 299; and idem, *Black Roots and White Racism of Early Pentecostalism.*

42. Horace Clarence Boyer, *How Sweet the Sound: The Golden Age of Gospel* (Washington, DC: Black Belt Communications Group, 1995), 19.

43. Quoted in Viv Broughton, *Black Gospel: An Illustrated History of the Gospel Sound* (Dorset, England: Blandford, 1985), 53.

44. Boyer, *How Sweet the Sound,* 21.

45. For a description of music culture in northwest Alabama, see Willie Ruff, *A Call to Assembly: An American Success Story* (New York: Penguin, 1991), 15–21; William Barlow, *"Looking Up at Down": The Emergence of Blues Culture* (Philadelphia: Temple University Press, 1989), 198–202; interview with Turner; personal interview with Catherine McKenzie, July 21, 1996.

46. Lornell, *"Happy in the Service of the Lord,"* 11–17; Boyer, *How Sweet the Sound,* 29–35.

47. For a description of the terms "jubilee" and "juba," see Richard M. Raichelson, "Black Religious Folksong: A Study in Generic and Social Change" (Ph.D. diss., University of Pennsylvania, 1975), 235–44.

48. Boyer, *How Sweet the Sound,* 29–31.

49. On the widespread participation in male quartet singing, see James Weldon Johnson and J. Rosamond Johnson, *The Books of American Negro Spirituals* (New York: Viking, 1940), 35–36; and Kerrill Leslie Rubman, "From 'Jubilee' to 'Gospel' in Black Male Quartet Singing" (M. A. thesis, University of North Carolina at Chapel Hill, 1980), 34–35. On male quartet singing in work camps, see Lornell, *"Happy in the Service of the Lord,"* 19; Boyer, *How Sweet the Sound,* 32–33; Dyen, "Role of Shape-Note Singing," 114; and interview with Turner.

50. Interview with Arthur Turner; Lornell, *"Happy in the Service of the Lord,"* 22.

51. Levine, *Black Culture and Black Consciousness,* 186.

52. Young, *Woke Me Up This Morning,* 9–10; Tony Heilbut, liner notes, "The Gospel Sound," (CK, CT 57160).

53. Spencer, *Blues and Evil,* 44.

54. Interview with Turner; Goldsmith, *When I Rise.*

55. Levine, *Black Culture and Black Consciousness,* 176–77.

56. "Denomination Blues, Part 2," in *Preachin' the Gospel Blues,* Columbia Legacy CK 46779.

57. Gayraud Wilmore, *Black Religion and Black Radicalism: An Interpretation of the Religious*

History of Afro-American People, 2d ed. (New York: Orbis Books, 1983), 11–12; Robin D. G. Kelley, *Hammer and Hoe: Alabama Communists during the Great Depression* (Chapel Hill: University of North Carolina Press, 1990), 107.

58. *The Gospel Sound,* Columbia Legacy, C2K 57160; Young, *Woke Me Up This Morning,* 55; Kelley, *Race Rebels,* 41–43; Brenda McCallum, "Songs of Work and Songs of Worship: Sanctifying Black Unionism in the Southern City of Steel," *New York Folklore* 14 (1988): 9–33; Kerran L. Sanger, *"When the Spirit Says Sing!": The Role of Freedom Songs in the Civil Rights Movement* (New York: Garland, 1995).

59. For an important discussion of African Americans' resistances to Jim Crow on public transportation, see Kelley, *Race Rebels,* 55–75. For a preliminary discussion of instilling resistance against discrimination within the context of nondenominational church services, see Kimberley L. Phillips, "Making a Church Home: African-American Migrants, Religion, and Working Class Activism," in *Labor Histories,* ed. Eric Arnesen, Julie Greene, and Bruce Levine (Urbana: University of Illinois Press, forthcoming). Far too often scholars have accepted religious theology without exploring fully how individuals and congregations have insisted that the "otherworldly" must influence their everyday lives. Religion demanded on a daily basis that practitioners make choices, and these choices had consequences.

60. Harris, *Rise of Gospel Blues,* 241–71.

61. Interview with Turner.

Chapter Thirteen

American Catholics and the Discourse of Fear

Timothy Kelly and Joseph Kelly

Catholic missionary preachers traveled from parish to parish all across America around the turn of the twentieth century trying to raise the religious fervor of practicing Catholics and to bring those who had left the church back into the fold. Standing before the gathered laity in churches often packed to full capacity, the preachers repeated the message most certain to bring results. In one example of what historian Jay Dolan suggests was a typical missionary sermon, parishioners heard from the pulpit that God called to them "in a loud, earnest voice. Repent, repent. Delay not to be converted to me, and put it not off from day to day, for my wrath will come upon you on a sudden and in the time of vengeance I will destroy you." [1] Dolan argues that this was no mere aberration, but rather part of a conscious strategy to scare Catholics into virtuous behavior, to move them through fear to the good life. In fact, one missionary articulated the intention quite bluntly. Again, from Dolan, we get Walter Elliott's sermon to Catholics:

> And so tonight it is that same dire necessity which makes it my miserable business to concentrate in a single sermon all the threatenings of any angry God, to bring forward what has so far been the dark background of every picture for your sole consideration by a more particular description of the torments of the lost. And brethren, if we knew of no hell to preach of, if we had only the sentiment of honor, or gratitude to appeal to, we should never give any missions: they would all be failures. Ah! but when the sinner hears of a fire which is never going to be quenched, of a gnawing worm which shall never die, it strikes terror to his soul, you will see his face turn pale, you will see the tears start unbidden to his eyes. [2]

These mission efforts to instill fear derived from a broader Catholic emphasis on the suffering that sinners brought on themselves. American Catholics inhabited a world that the official hierarchical church infused with fear from at least the late nineteenth century to the middle of the twentieth century, a world in which Catholics learned regularly of the dire earthly and otherworldly horrors that they would undoubtedly endure if they continued in their current, inevitably sinful ways.

In the middle of the twentieth century the official church began to reject its strong embrace of fear, however, and move toward the ideals of love and intellectual assent in efforts to mold Catholic behavior. Though much work has been done on various changes in the American Catholic Church during this period, no one has approached this period with an explicit focus on emotional culture. In the pages that follow we focus on this dramatic transformation in Catholic emotionology. We explore the widespread reliance on fear through the first half of the twentieth century and the conscious rejection of it as the church headed toward the Second Vatican Council.

Students of emotionology will note that in rejecting fear Catholics seem to have followed the same pattern as other Americans in the twentieth century. Peter Stearns suggests in his discussion of the emergence of a very broad post-Victorian emotional culture that the American middle class came to reject completely a set of emotions they once considered only suspect. Stearns argues that by the 1960s middle-class Americans understood fear to have "no positive function" in their new emotional culture, and that they had begun this total rejection of fear as early as the 1920s. Though American Catholics clearly ended up at the same place as other middle-class Americans, they did not begin their movement away from fear as early, or come to reject it as completely, as Stearns suggests for the broader culture.[3] Part of American Catholics' movement away from fear no doubt derives from their immersion in the broader American culture that saw fear as no longer useful.

Official Catholic View of Fear

Because we are interested ultimately in changes in the way the church used fear to shape behavior, we must explore how the hierarchy understood the role fear ought to have played in people's lives. Theologians, bishops, and priests rarely argued that fear was in and of itself good or virtuous. In fact, they more often stated formally their concerns about fear resulting in sinful behavior. But church officials implicitly endorsed fear as a good means to virtuous ends through their efforts to shape Catholics' behaviors. And when they addressed fear explicitly, Catholic officials reserved the right to use fear to guide ordinary Catholics down the path of sinless lives.

The hierarchy clearly saw fear as an emotion that arose "from awareness of something seen as an imminent danger affecting oneself," and further understood fear-based behaviors to fall sort of halfway between free will and force.[4] Individuals act of free will and maintain responsibility for their behaviors, except when forced to do something against their will. The church did not hold those forced to act in specific ways responsible for those actions. Fear interferes with free will because it is an emotion that one experiences independently of choice, but because it "arises within the agent" it differs from force. When we act to alleviate fear "we are led to do what we do, not because of the fear itself, but in order to avoid the evil that is feared." We choose our strategies to alleviate the fear, and so we act voluntarily and positively to a certain degree. The *New Catholic Encyclopedia* concludes that there is "a mixture of voluntariness and involuntariness in what is done." Further, "the element of involuntariness shows some goodness in the will, even if the action is an evil one, and to that extent diminishes culpability."[5]

Fear could therefore push people to do evil acts, though people remained at least partially responsible for the evil they did. But could fear cause people to do good, and was this kind of fear therefore good itself? The answer to this question, though carefully qualified, was clearly yes. Ignatius's meditation on hell begins with this prelude: "Here it will be to ask for a deep awareness of the pain suffered by the damned, so that if I should forget the love of the Eternal Lord, at least the fear of punishment will help me to avoid falling into sin."[6] Clearly Ignatius held that freely choosing the good was better than shying away from punishment, though if the will was not properly oriented, then fear was a valid motivator. Even more positively, fear of the Lord was good, though this was in theory "filial, not the servile fear whose concern is punishment; it causes the soul to turn not only from sin but also from every tendency to refuse God anything."[7] People could become priests out of fear, or marry out of fear, both essentially good acts, though the fear constituted grounds for nullification.[8] But further still, authority could *justly* induce fear if the victim deserved the evil threatened, the agent had the right to threaten harm, and the threats were made "in a way provided by law."[9] One American theologian likened this to the use of fear by a "father or a judge who threatens us with just punishment for misdeeds."[10] So church officials maintained that fear was not always bad, and might even be good if used by right authority in the right way.

Many Catholics had long maintained that to live in the state of grace was a matter of discipline, and discipline could be elicited by fear. Fear could be elicited by meditation on the final things: death, judgment, hell, and heaven. As early as the sixth century, St. Benedict advocated fear of hell as a method of exacting obedience in his famous Rule. Two of his "instruments of good works" were fear of Judgment Day (instrument 44) and fear of hell (45). Instruments 47 through 49 are "To see death before one daily," "To monitor one's actions ceaselessly," and "To know for certain that God sees all everywhere."[11] St. Ignatius too relied on fear in his *Exercises* for Jesuits. The *Exercises* is a manual that advises spiritual directors on how to conduct retreats. The Ignatian retreat was meant to last four weeks, and during the first week the exercitant meditates on the sinful nature of man. The crowning exercise of this week, the fifth exercise, is a meditation on hell. The exercitant is instructed "To see in imagination the great fires, and the souls enveloped, as it were, in bodies of fire. To hear the wailing, the screaming, cries.... To smell the smoke, the brimstone, the corruption, and rottenness.... With the sense of touch to feel how the flames surround and burn souls." The exercitant goes through all this "so that if [he or she] should forget the love of the Eternal Lord, at least the fear of punishment will help [him or her] to avoid falling into sin."[12]

In both Benedict's Rule and Ignatius's *Exercises,* fear plays a fairly small, if memorable, role in controlling behavior. Jean Delumeau explores the far more central role that fear played throughout Catholic culture in Europe from the thirteenth to the eighteenth centuries, and in many ways the emotionology that we discuss in the twentieth century resembles this much older tradition.[13] We are not prepared in these pages to suggest an uninterrupted persistence across time and continents to early modern Europe, but we find the twentieth-century American Catholic discourse of fear remarkably like that which Delumeau described for the early period. We do know that in the era that stretches between the First Vatican Council (1870) and the Second (which opened in 1962), the American church was particularly fond of using fear to discipline the laity. The church exercised this fear through a rigid, authoritarian hierarchy. As a matter of fact, what had been recognized as a defective or less desirable method of eliciting proper behaviors in Ignatius's day became the preferred method in the early twentieth century. Church officials set themselves apart from the laity as agents who had a right (through apostolic tradition) to threaten harm. As the church hierarchy framed them, normative behaviors and beliefs implicitly recognized both this prerogative and their authority. A Catholic's obedience to his or her priest was as natural as a child's obedience to his father. (Pre-Vatican II literature always characterized filial fear as fear of the father, who was considered the undisputed head of the household. Mothers, apparently, were not to be feared.) Implicit in the official use of this fear was the hierarchical belief that lay Catholics should live in a world of fear—fear justly established and maintained, but fear nonetheless.

Theologian Avery Dulles recalled from his youthful experiences in the early twentieth century that the "church stood for centralized authority, tradition, and discipline," and that ordinary Catholics "did not publicly, or even in most cases privately, question the decisions of their popes, bishops, and pastors."[14] Psychologist Eugene Kennedy reported that the church "operated in a frankly authoritarian manner and, in a huge effort to hold itself together against the challenges of history, it imposed elaborate and effective controls on the lives of its subjects." Kennedy further argued that this mode of operating made Catholics deferential to all authority, civil as well as ecclesiastical, and came at an "enormous psychological price."[15] One price, of course, was the limited exercise of free will. Another casualty was the development of a personal conscience. Theodore Hesburgh, a Holy Cross priest and longtime president of Notre Dame University, recalled that the church in this period placed a very heavy emphasis on authority: "Authority was a force to be reckoned with in the closed church. The reckoning was simple: authority commanded and you obeyed; no questions asked; no reasons given; only the statement, 'You do it because I say do it; do it or get out.' "[16] The threat of isolation from the church, Hesburgh's "do it or get out," struck fear into Catholics. Eugene Kennedy reflected that the threat of formal expulsion from the Catholic community, excommunication, carried heavy consequences.

> So powerful was the social identification of [twentieth-century] immigrant Catholics with the acceptable doctrines and disciplines of the Church that families would shun members who departed, through marriage to a non-Catholic, for example, from the rigid expectations on their behavior. Excommunication was a doomsday weapon on the immigrant Church, for it cut a person off from his or her roots, family, and community.[17]

These Catholics remembered a climate of fear that the hierarchy established and maintained in order to shape lay behavior to conform to those ideals church officials believed would lead to ecclesiastical survival, social cohesion, and personal salvation.

But fear was more than the occasional threat of the rod. Implicit in the official use of this fear was the hierarchy's belief that this world was inherently corrupt. Because the world was so dangerous and enticing, the hierarchy took on the responsibilities of establishing and maintaining a permanent and pervasive sense of fear in lay

Catholics. The church attempted to regulate behavior, then, not only through explicit threats but also by shaping Catholics' experience of life itself, which meant immersing the laity in what a literary critic might call the "discourse" of fear.

A discourse is a system of representations, a network of cultural references that together weave a coherent attitude toward a particular issue. This attitude would be so fundamental that the members of the culture would not even recognize that it is an attitude. To them it is simply the way things are—an unquestionable fact of nature. Invisible as the air and habitual as breathing, a discourse conditions our experience of life. Typically, such attitudes are questioned only when they come into contact with another discourse—when we recognize that someone else's "the way things are" contradicts our own.

This discourse reflected Catholic attempts to both regulate behavior through fear and shape Catholic experiences of fear itself. By constructing and maintaining this discourse of fear, and insisting that its members join, the church created a world in which fear was normative. Our focus is on both the construction of that world (and therefore necessarily the degree to which hierarchical intentions bore fruit—the degree to which lay Catholics acquiesced in that climate of fear) and the transformation of that world to one of intellectual assent. Catholics chose to behave in specific ways in the fearful world because they sought to allay their fear through obedience to hierarchical authority; they chose to behave in particular ways in the post-fear world because they understood those behaviors to be consistent with ideals arrived at through scriptural, theological, and historical discernment. One could not live in both worlds at once, and American Catholics had already begun to reject the former by the middle of the twentieth century.

The Discourse of Fear

Catholicism is a culture as well as a religion, and the hierarchy controlled many of the means of reproducing this culture, from formally recognized liturgical practices to the parochial schools through which so many Catholics passed as they grew to maturity. Not the least of the cultural influences over which the hierarchy exercised extensive control were various popular manuals, especially those aimed at adolescents, young adults, and parents, that prescribed proper Catholic behavior. Official books told Catholic boys and girls how and whom to date and told young adults whom not to marry, how to act in their most intimate relations, and how to raise their children. American Catholics could draw on an extensive prescriptive literature available to guide them at critical moments in their lives.

In the present study we have focused primarily on this prescriptive literature because the texts survive in their original form and are therefore more accessible than most other cultural expressions, such as Sunday sermons and lectures in the confessional box. We can see a discourse most readily in texts, and we proceed under the assumption that the texts reflect the discourse from which they emerged. We have directed our focus to those manuals that direct sexual behavior, especially divorce and the use of birth control, for two reasons: sex seems to be the category of behavior that the hierarchy most ardently sought to control (and for which they most regularly relied on fear); and because other data exist that indicate how Catholics actually behaved relative to the prescriptions the hierarchy offered.

The Dangerous World

We looked at prescriptive literature spanning sixty years, from 1921 to 1982, and our analysis has yielded some interesting results. As we suspected, the earlier tracts threatened damnation, though in terms less colorful than the meditations on hell we mentioned above. These threats tail off in the 1950s, and after the Second Vatican Council they are nearly abandoned altogether. But more interesting are the subtle changes in Catholic ideology that a close analysis of the discourse reveals. The earliest literature represents a Catholic culture under a perceived assault launched by what is most often referred to simply as "modern life." This literature makes it clear that living in America in the years after the First World War exposed Catholics to new attitudes toward sex. Perhaps as a last-ditch effort at deflecting the influence of these new attitudes, the prescriptive literature employed the culture of fear we've described above. But we found evidence that even as early as the 1920s Catholic literature did not rely on fear exclusively to mold behavior. We detected in some of the early literature a competing belief, probably based in modern psychology, that by the 1950s would become the ascendant ideology of American Catholics. (We discuss this competing ideology in the next section.)

Sometimes, though not often, the early behavior manuals explicitly threatened readers with hell. For example, the Jesuit Martin J. Scott, in his book *Marriage,* warns his readers not to divorce: "Catholics may disregard the Church of Christ, and contract marriage against her decrees, but they are defying God in so doing and must be prepared to stand the eternal consequences." The warning against birth control is just as explicit: "For Catholics it is enough to know that the Church of Christ forbids birth control under penalty of mortal sin." (This to a readership that knew that dying in a state of mortal sin sent one directly to hell for eternity.) To his credit, Scott describes neither the narrowness nor the stench nor the darkness nor any of the other imaginative attributes of hell, but in 1930 those descriptions did not lurk far behind his threats.[18]

But more interesting and probably more effective than such explicit threats are the colorful figures of speech that distinguish the literature in this period. The pages of these manuals teem with metaphors and analogies, and it is in these figures that the discourse of fear emerges. Despite their large number, most of the figures fall into only a few categories: business, disease, sports, agriculture, warfare, and travel. The last two—martial metaphors and metaphors of journey—occur most often. The martial metaphors present life as a gigantic battle. According to the preface to Scott's *You and Yours: Practical Talks on Home Life,* for example, "Modern life is making dreadful breeches in[to the home]. Church and state are threatened by this assault, for the home is the very heart of both." Elsewhere, modesty guards purity from the assaults of passion. Maidenly reserve and decency form a barricade. "[T]he great army of indifferentists . . . are drifting back to paganism." A Catholic who marries a non-Catholic must erect "every possible safeguard" to protect her faith.[19] In his preface to *Marriage*, Scott quoted a Protestant, the Reverend J. M. Lloyd Thomas, who waxed metaphoric:

> [The Catholic Church] whatever its past or present laxities of practice, is seen to be the one uncompromising corporate witness to that moral code of Christianity which preserves Western civilization from final collapse. It presents the last loyalty of the human race to its own highest moral standards. It is the iron bulwark of Christianity against the overwhelming invasion of the corrupting neopaganism of our times.[20]

In this world the good Catholic is a besieged citadel, and from every side—in the workplace, in advertisements, in movies, in books, in popular mores—that citadel is assaulted. The Catholic's codes of behavior form the walls of his citadel. Free thought and especially free love are the vanguard of the enemy.

Such figures of speech must have been all the more striking since they came on the heels of World War I, which would have provided an immediacy and vividness to what otherwise might have been clichéd comparisons. But they are hardly surprising, nor were they singular to Catholics. Comparing life to battle and comparing the virtuous life to a besieged city were popular with all moralists in the 1920s, whether they were Catholic or Protestant or anything else, and the 1920s produced more than its share of moralists. The war had liberalized many men and women, and conservatives lashed back with everything from Prohibition to film and book censorship. If not teetotalers, Catholics proved to be the best of censors, perhaps because they'd been conditioned by generations of such metaphors. The hierarchy had been vilifying "modern" attitudes, especially attitudes that diminished hierarchical authority in favor of personal conscience, since the pronouncement of papal infallibility at the First Vatican Council in 1870. Pope Leo XIII attacked modernism in 1899 with his *Testem Benevolentiae*, and Pius X did again in 1907.

The characterization of "modern life" as the enemy of salvation lasted at least into the 1960s, when William McManus, in his *Marriage Guide for Engaged Catholics*, discussed "the struggle between the Church and the World for the souls of men." "Every single, youthful, married couple," he warned, "leaves the altar rail on their wedding day to face the modern temptations almost alone and almost unsupported or protected."[21] Just a few years earlier, in 1958, George Kelly wrote, "[F]ostering the integrity and sanctity of Christian marriage is one of the most important missions of the Church, especially in our day when diabolical forces are at work to undermine the most fundamental of all human societies, the family."[22] These metaphors seem more clichéd than Scott's: Kelly's barely calls to mind an image of an army tunneling under the bulwark of a defense, and McManus's words—"facing" something "almost alone and almost unsupported or protected"—are so clichéd that probably they call no image to the common reader's mind at all. But the fact that they are clichés is telling in itself, because it means the discourse is nearly invisible. The practice of representing the world as a battle against evil forces had become such a habit that it seemed natural. The figures of speech are ready-made. Nevertheless, if the comparison to war did survive to the 1960s, it was not long for this world. Patrick Ryan, a decorated army veteran of World War II, found no occasion to make such comparisons in his 1963 book *A Soldier Priest Talks to Youth*. By the late 1960s, "modern life" no longer seemed to harbor "diabolical forces." As we'll discuss below, we think that the dropping off of these figures of speech indicates that American Catholics had nearly rejected the discourse of fear at least a decade before Vatican II.

We saw no decline in the use of travel figures. Metaphors and analogies that compare life to a journey will always be with us. They are as old as literature itself. Consider the opening lines of Dante's *Divine Comedy*, "In the middle of the journey of this life I found myself in a dark wood." Certainly they were prominent in the sixty years of prescriptive literature that we studied. The very longevity of the metaphor provides a unique opportunity to trace changes in ideology, because we can map how the character of the metaphors changes over the years. Here are a few examples from the early literature: "A good time [on a date], certainly, is not taboo — courtship is an oasis, one of the few in the desert of life. But why forget the journey ahead, in the short rest and refreshment possible on that tiny spot?"[23] "If God forbids something, it is not to tyrannize over man, but to benefit him. A hand-rail placed alongside a narrow footbridge over a deep chasm is not to hinder the traveler, but to save him from possible ruin."[24] "A Catholic girl should not be guided by the loose moral code of those who have no religion."[25] "The passion of love like every other passion will lead to disaster unless controlled."[26] "Twenty centuries of human experience ought to make the Church a safe guide even if she had not help from above."[27] Perhaps the most telling instance of these metaphors is Scott's extended version of a metaphor he had already called on once in his chapter "The True Nature of Marriage":

> The worst possible fallacy is to presume that God's laws are intended to hamper man. As well say that a guide over a dangerous and unknown tract hampers the wayfarer. The protecting railing of a narrow footbridge is not to restrict the liberty of the traveler, but in order to save him from a false step into the deadly chasm below. God's ordinances are for man's safe guidance over the perilous path to eternity.[28]

If life is a journey, the journey is a perilous one, for the world is a dangerous place. False guides will deliver you into all sorts of dangers. Missteps will tumble you over the precipice. We see the same emphasis on protecting one's self from danger that we saw in the martial metaphors. "The Commandment not to kill," Scott reasons, "protects man's life. The Commandment not to lie, protects man's character. The Commandment not to commit adultery, protects man's wife, mother, and daughter. . . . They are intended to safeguard mankind against passion and violence."[29]

According to these metaphors, the Catholic, with the aid of a proper guide, carries his or her virtue or soul through hostile territory. Life is a success if you arrive at death with your cargo intact, pure, inviolate. In a 1961 *Marriage Guide for Engaged Catholics*, marriage itself is the traveler "buffeted to and fro by the secular forces dominant in American society."[30] (Incidentally, among the winds that threaten marriage are the false beliefs that "The wife is just as much the head of the house as the husband," "God understands the sinner," "Incompatible couples are better off divorced," and "Understanding your child is more important than discipline.")[31] The 1955 *Guide to Catholic Marriage,* in a metaphor that calls to mind a traveler transporting a treasure through a gang of thieves, explained that receiving communion and confession frequently and "a strong devotion to the Blessed Virgin are the best guarantees of the preservation of purity or the regaining of it if it has unfortunately been lost."[32] The image is compatible with the martial metaphors discussed above. Indeed, the preserving, losing, and regaining of purity could as easily call to mind the fortunes of an army on the battlefield as a perilous journey. In either view, the various virtues (but especially sexual purity), faith, and even the soul itself are treasures to be guarded. The *Guide* invokes the images of "safeguards" and "danger" so often in its chapter "Mixed and Interracial Marriages" that it would be difficult to note each instance. (We should point out that the guide's writers indicate that interracial marriages pose no dangers. The many dangers they discuss derive from marrying outside the faith.)

This conception—that virtue and the soul are static things to be guarded from pressing dangers and thieves—corresponds to the figures of disease, which occurred less often. According to the 1955 *Guide,* "some 30 percent of Catholic mixed-marriage partners succumb to these [dangerous] influences and are lost to the faith"; here the self is compared to a body that falls ill.[33] Elsewhere, the *Guide* suggests that "the secularism and materialism of the day have infected many members of the Church," and "mixed marriage is another factor leading in this direction."[34] In this mixed metaphor we see again the villainous "modern life," this time represented as an infection, coupled with a journey metaphor—the false guide of mixed marriage leading the Catholic in the direction of disease. A few sentences later, the *Guide* characterizes mixed marriages as diseased cells that bring about the disintegration of the social body.[35] In these comparisons virtue still is assaulted, only more gradually than a city is overrun or a treasure stolen by highwaymen. Likewise, Kelly compares masturbation to "pollution," as if the soul were a body of pure water slowly fouled by sin.

In all these figures, whether they refer to warfare, journeys, or diseases, the successful life is a vigilant life. If you stop fearing dangers you will "succumb" to them. George Kelly's 1963 *Dating for Young Catholics* presents an extended metaphor that succinctly illustrates this conception of life:

> A favorite story of mine . . . concerns traveling conditions in the pioneer days out West. The first wagons that crossed the prairie naturally had to make their own roads. Then other wagons came along and found themselves in the grooves made by their predecessors. Finally the grooves turned into deep ruts. Things reached such a point that stagecoach companies warned their drivers: "Choose your ruts carefully. You'll be in them for twenty-five miles."
>
> Choosing your companions is like that. You'll be in their groove, following the path they follow. If their way leads to your sanctity, fine. But if you choose a group that travels along the path of easy morality, you'll find your road strewn with heartbreak and disaster.[36]

The chief characteristic of these metaphors is that the self is static—a treasure or a cargo. It is carried along in the stagecoach that could be assaulted by forces that would plunder your soul—Indians or swollen rivers, passion and sexual desire. The goal of life is to carry your soul safely to the journey's end. Fear is prudent if life is like this. These guides warned Catholics that they lived in a culture hostile to virtue and that they must avoid behaviors sanctioned by the larger culture lest they violate some aspect of the code—stray from the map, if you will—that leads to eternal salvation. And the gravest dangers were posed by birth control and divorce.

Curiously enough, Catholics in the decades before 1950 seemed headed toward convergence with non-Catholics in their reproductive behaviors and attitudes. Catholics entered the twentieth century with a significantly higher marital fertility rate than non-Catholics. Evidently, they used birth control less often than their Protestant and Jewish neighbors. This comports with the strong Catholic prescriptive literature that condemned birth control and threatened severe consequences to Catholics who used it. But in the years between 1920 and 1940 Catholic fertility rates began to converge with non-Catholic rates, suggesting that Catholics began to violate the proscriptions so prevalent throughout official Catholic writings on marriage and family life. By the middle of the 1940s, Catholic and non-Catholic marital fertility rates were nearly identical.[37] We hypothesize that as early as the 1920s Catholics had begun to reject the culture of fear, that they stopped experiencing life according to the terms we've analyzed above.

The Constructed Self

In fact, as early as 1929 some of the prescriptive literature began to offer Catholics a way of conceiving of their lives that made fear obsolete. Probably this alternative derived from the science of psychology, which supplied compelling new terms in which to think of the self. Paul Hanly Furfey, a sociologist and priest, relegated fear to a relatively minor role in the rearing of children. For him, it had no place in the development of the mature, adult conscience: "Punishment," he wrote, "should never play an important part in moral training. . . . Besides being good psychology this principle is also good theology. The fear of the Lord is indeed the beginning of wisdom; but the great saints attained to holiness through love rather than fear."[38] Basing his conclusions on recent studies of human development, Furfey suggested that "blind obedience" and the formation of "unreasoning habits" are proper only to the infant and preschool child. After children have reached the age of reason, they should be taught the reasons behind good behavior, so that they'll freely choose that behavior when they grow up and the threat of the rod has disappeared. Clearly Furfey swims against the current of the discourse of fear, which attempts to carry the threat of punishment even into adulthood. And Furfey agrees with pre–Vatican I doctrine, which, as we have seen, considered behavior influenced by fear to be only a little better than behavior physically coerced. In fact, as if he's aware of the mainstream Catholic doctrine, Furfey seems anxious to discredit the discourse of fear. Borrowing an analogy from the fifth- century church father John Chrysostom, Furfey emphasized that "the art of forming character in the child is far more excellent than the art of the painter or the sculptor. For whereas they work with paint or marble, he who has charge of the young, works with living flesh."[39] In this comparison we see an early instance of what will become, by the 1960s, the dominant figure in the prescriptive literature. You build the self. The moral and spiritual self or the soul, just like the psyche, develops as we live our lives. Fear of punishment might be equivalent to the first crude hackings at the marble. But if fear survives adolescence to remain the dominant moral force in adulthood, the soul will be crude and ill formed.

This idea of the developing self is reflected in the journey metaphors of some later guides, which revise the images we discussed above. For example, Mary Perkins's 1955 *Beginning at Home: The Challenge of Christian Parenthood* reduces the dangerous "modern world" of older tracts to "the foggy world of today." She retains the image of a journey, but gone are the snake pits and hostile Indians. "The family," she wrote, "has to start its members on the road to Christian perfection and teach them to walk."[40] The threat is not that you might get attacked along the way, but that you might not learn how to travel. The thing to fear, then, if "fear" is the right word, is not an external hostile assault that will steal your virtue, but undeveloped, immature limbs, an innate incapacity to move forward. The only thing to be feared is incompleteness.

The dynamic self became so prevalent that it even crept into the traditional guides of the 1950s. McManus, whom we cited above as a contributor to the discourse of fear, told engaged Catholics not to think of marriage as "a kind of shelter against the skepticism and futility which mark our time," but rather to "look upon your love as a door opening upon vast opportunities of dedication and service."[41] Elsewhere he insists that "a marriage will make progress when husband and wife accept each other's defects and encourage each other's strong points."[42] Clearly the type of journey he imagines here is not one in which a preexisting treasure—in this case a good marriage—is carried from one place to another and protected from thieves. Marriage is not a commodity to be safeguarded, but a treasure to be gathered coin by coin, and so the "progress" he referred to presupposes a dynamic relationship, one that improves through time. McManus's case is not unusual. What we have discovered in the literature of the 1950s is a strange mixture of two contradictory discourses—one encouraging obedience through fear and the other offering visions of a developing, improving, maturing soul. Some authors seemed to move between both worldviews even within the same presentation, suggesting that they were undergoing the change themselves, even as they wrote.

As early as 1930 Scott struggled to reconcile the traditional emphasis on fear of eternal misery with American Catholics' more immanent preoccupation with their existence on earth. He supplemented his threats of going to hell in the next world for breaking God's laws with tales of woe in this world for transgressing those of nature. For example, Scott wrote, "Outside wedlock, the gratification of [the sex] instinct interferes with nature's designs. The world is strewn with human wreckage as a consequence of unlawful sex relations."[43] He refers here not only to sexually transmitted diseases like syphilis (which was of great public concern in the early twentieth century), but also to "the chance of becoming an unmarried mother," which "means disgrace or abortion." [44] To hold that social disgrace is nature's vengeance is self-contradictory; nevertheless, no matter how awkwardly invoked, it is a threat.

This type of threatening continued into the 1950s. George Kelly contended in his *Dating for Young Catholics*, "the Church primarily wants you to save your soul when she warns you about the moral danger of mixed marriages. But she's also interested in your happiness on earth." And so he proceeds to spell out that "sad story" that "[m]ixed marriages tell . . . there [on earth], too." [45] Most often this train of reasoning devolved into threatening readers with social and ecclesiastical ostracism. Kelly attacked divorce on the grounds that female "divorcees [are] 'extra women' [who] creat[e] problems in entertaining that every hostess dreads. In most cases [of divorce] the number of invitations to social affairs dwindled gradually and finally stopped." [46] Patrick Ryan actually advises his readers to "steer clear" of people who are seeking annulments. [47] In the 1950s, these writers marshaled sociological data in an attempt to demonstrate how disobedience to the church's teachings leads to unhappiness in this life. The *Guide* warned readers that in mixed marriages the partners will find it "difficult to achieve that unity . . . which is desirable in all marriages" and that their "personalit[ies] may suffer." [48] George Kelly, arguing against the use of birth control, wrote in his 1958 *Catholic Marriage Manual*, "more attention should be paid to what Dr. John Kane, of Notre Dame, calls the 'almost unanimous conclusion' of sociological studies on marital happiness: 'Happiness in marriage is not associated with the presence or absence of children in the family, but with a strong desire to have children.' " [49] Threats of torture in the afterlife gave way to threats of the failure to achieve psychological fulfillment in this life.

This threat remained through the 1970s. For example, in 1979, David Knight counseled the young readers of *The Good News about Sex*, "Sometimes people have sex . . . just as an act of passion. They get carried away. They give in. When this happens to us, we have failed one test. We have failed to act as whole persons, with our emotions, intellects and wills. . . . We cannot do this without distorting our own value as persons." [50]

Nearly all the literature after 1950 (which is to say after the discourse of fear begins to die out) contains some version of this threat: the threat of incompleteness, personal unhappiness based on a dysfunctional or retarded psyche. But compared to threats of hell, this threat seems fairly benign—hardly something to fear at all. The reliance on such threats concedes the greater issue: the goal of life is not to transport yourself safely through a dangerous world, to pass through to the other side without incident, but to mature and develop within the world. The Vatican II statement on the church in the modern world, *Gaudium et Spes*, adopted on 7 December 1965, reflects this shift in ideology. The document is shot through with journey metaphors—Christians, guided by the Holy Spirit, "press onwards towards the kingdom of the Father," and the confusion of the modern world makes us uncertain "about how to plot our course"—that confirm heaven is the end of this life. Nevertheless, the weight of the document concerns itself with the here and now, as, for instance, in the following excerpt from the section "The Common Good": "Because of the closer bonds of human interdependence and their spread over the whole world, we are today witnessing a widening of the role of the common good, which is the sum total of social conditions which allow people, either as groups or individuals, to reach their fulfillment more fully and easily." [51] This section, like much of *Gaudium et Spes,* addresses the issues of social injustice that convulsed the 1960s. Explicit in this concern is the dynamic image of man—the notion that we construct or develop ourselves in this life. Note that in the passage quoted above, people are expected "to reach their fulfillment more fully and easily." Likewise, *Gaudium* claims that sin "brought man to a lower state, forcing him away from the completeness that is his to attain." [52] We should note that in places, such as in the section on sin, *Gaudium* does use the old martial metaphors—"the whole life of men, both individual and social, shows itself to be a struggle, and a dramatic one, between good and evil, between light and darkness." But even if "[m]an finds that he is unable of himself to overcome the assaults of evil," the result is a life "bound by chains"—that is, a life impeded from constructing itself fully.[53] The emphasis is always on fulfillment and completion. So the personal conscience is a "skill" by which man "secures for himself the means" of pressing "toward his goal" of "fully discover[ing] his true self." [54] Marriage is one of those "means," for through it men and women "increasingly further their own perfection and their mutual sanctification." [55] Sex is a tool given us by God: with it we enrich our spirit and ennoble ourselves. The proper use of this tool increases its power: "this love is actually developed and increased by the exercise of it." [56] Above all, the document conceives of marriage as an institution that is constructed and improved through time: "its nature . . . demand[s] that the mutual love . . . should grow and mature" (954). Because the family is imagined as a house or "a [place] where different generations come together and help one another to [grow wiser] and harmonize the rights of individuals with other demands of social life," the council called for "welfare legislation" that would provide everyone with such a structure that allows us to reach our fullest development (956). Despite a sprinkling of martial metaphors, *Gaudium et Spes* fully embraced the new discourse.

If the conservative writers conceded to a new discourse, the more liberal writers in the 1950s retained some of the old figures of fear. So we find Perkins, who mostly rejects fear, writing,

> In essentials, then, this sacramental way of living and thinking implies that we think of everything dynamically, in terms of the growth and perfecting of Christ's mystical Body, the building up and the victory of His kingdom. We see all history at once as a battle and as a work of construction, the battle of the City of God with the city of the devil, the perfecting of the City of God taking place somehow in and through the battle.
>
> We see also that the life, Passion, Death, and Resurrection of our Lord is, so to speak, the main plot or story-line or pattern of this battle as it should be waged in each life, as it is being fought out in the whole history of mankind; that this redemptive work of His is also the pattern for building up His City.
>
> We are preparing our children, then, to become Christ's soldiers and fellow workers, to share in the fellowship of all his sufferings with all their work, with all their

sufferings, in the joy of His companionship and of the victory that he has already won.
... This purpose implies that the children learn to see heaven and earth as full of God's
glory.[57]

We quote this passage at such length because in it we can see the transition from fear
taking place. The whole passage is a curious mixture of incompatible images. On one
hand, Christ is a general; Catholic children are his soldiers; from the holy citadel they
lob cannonballs at the fortress of the devil; ultimate victory is predicted. On the
other hand, Perkins insists on the dynamism of life and illustrates her point with an
organic metaphor—growth. (The organic metaphors used in the discourse of fear,
recall, depicted corruption—infection disintegrating its host body.) If the passage
keeps referring to battles and victories, it is difficult to imagine who loses those
battles. Who mans the battlements of the devil's fort? Already we've seen Perkins
characterize "modern life," that traditional foe, in rather benign terms as a fog,
hardly something you vanquish. And in this passage she declares that earth is "full of
God's glory." Despite all this talk of soldiers and battles, she fails to impress us with
much of a sense of fear.

The other extended metaphor in this passage—construction—dominates Perkins's book, which is why we've called her a more liberal moralist. In this passage we
see that life is not only a battle but a "work of construction." Christ's kingdom is
built up. Those soldiers are also "workers." The church militant marches side by side
with the church architectural. God is the master builder, who provides the plan of
our construction.[58] Consider this passage: "The training we try to give [children] in
acquiring skills of mind and body and in striving for skillful and charitable work-
manship in everything they do will prepare the way for their instruction, if and when
they come to be married, in the art of married life and the art of the marriage act
itself."[59]

Working with the aid of Christ, we construct ourselves according to a master plan,
until finally, near the end of our lives, we have made ourselves into a holy house, an
architectural work of art. Throughout the 1950s this figure competed with images of
battle. McManus, for example, warned against building up resentments, "which may
affect the entire structure of marriage."[60] The construction is slow, requires skill, and
is cumulative. Marriage is a part of that accumulation—a floor of the house, so to
speak—and building a marriage is an art. Even sexual intimacy is an art.

Significantly, this figure characterizes sex not as a potential peril or pitfall but as a
tool that can help our construction project. In the 1950s we see the writers begin to
treat sex as something that we use. "When we speak to children about sins against
the sixth commandment," Blaise Hettich wrote in the 1956 *You and Your Children*,
"we ought always to begin with the notion of God's plan for family love: that
Christian marriage is a pure and holy *use* of sex" (emphasis added).[61] To keep young
boys from looking at dirty pictures, Hettich suggests that "explanations are better
than warnings." The effective parent will explain that some people "use their bodies
wrongly. But we want to follow God's plan for a good marriage. That's why we must
not look at pictures that will stimulate us to misuse our powers of parenthood."[62]
We label this figure the power tool of sex: the "power of fatherhood" and the

"power of motherhood" are great tools that help construct marriage, which helps us construct ourselves, even as they allow us to work together "with God in the procreation of a child." [63] Without the power of sex we'd be struggling along with hand drills and handheld screwdrivers. McManus spoke of sex as having a power that can "fulfill you as a person," contribute "to your personal development," and bring about "the emotional and spiritual development of husband and wife." [64] In "Sex Education for Children," Blaise Hettich described sex as "the means of developing what is deepest in a personality." [65] The manuals strive to teach how to use the power tools correctly so the self will be better constructed.

There's not much room for fear in that metaphor. Actually, many of the books in the 1950s actively try to counteract the notion—to which Catholics raised in the discourse of fear are so prone—that sex is dirty and to be feared. Nearly all the literature after 1950, conservative and liberal alike, advocates that parents candidly discuss sex with their children, because if children are not taught how to use sex properly they will misuse it. Hettich openly attacked the discourse of fear when he wrote, "Among well-meaning parents who afflict their children with unreasonable suspicions of evil [about sex] are some whose ancestors recently came from the 'traditionally Catholic' nations of Europe." He admonished parents, "Do not arouse foolish fears." [66] Even writers who would be considered conservative, like Mihanovich, Schnepp, and Thomas, combat the "false conscience," the fearful attitude toward sex, that the discourse of fear produced. If there's anything to fear at all, it is only the misuse of this powerful tool.

It is true that some writers made clever use of the threat of misuse, which leads to fear of a sort, albeit less threatening than the fear of hell. For example, Mihanovich, Schnepp, and Thomas—three sociologists—succeeded in co-opting the new discourse Scott so fumbled with back in 1930:

> Many writers seem to think they are stating an obvious fact when they write that so far as reproduction is concerned, the institution of marriage is not necessary, since reproduction can follow a casual union of the sexes, and in no way implies stability. This is utterly to misunderstand the nature of man and the nature of human love. It will not do to segmentalize the operations of man as if to say that now he is acting on a purely physical level, and now he is acting as a rational being. . . . This is particularly true of the reproductive act, since, as we have pointed out, the property of sex exercises its consequential effects throughout the entire personality.[67]

To engage in sexual activity without a lifelong commitment to one's partner is to fail to experience sex properly, because the nature of sex includes an emotional dimension, and that dimension can be fully engaged only if the partners have made a lifelong commitment. Such a failure—casual sexual activity—skews the development of the personality. Sex without permanent commitment, then, causes unfulfillment. But skewed personality development as a means of inducing fear is a far cry from "a fire that is never going to be quenched" or "a gnawing worm that is never going to die."

Given the nature of the newer literature on marriage, sexual intimacy, and child rearing, and the lay movement in the earlier period away from the behavior the discourse of fear sought to instill, how did the laity act in this climate of the constructed self? More common and sophisticated surveys provide a fuller picture of Catholic behavior in this period than in the preceding decades. They reveal an interesting development. Catholic and Protestant marital fertility rates, which had moved closer together in the 1920s, 1930s, and early 1940s, began to diverge again. Both groups participated in the postwar baby boom, but Catholics did so far more enthusiastically. Their marital fertility rate soared while the non-Catholic rate rose at a far slower pace.[68] Perhaps Catholics had once again become fearful of practicing birth control.[69] Yet between 1955 and 1965, the end of the baby boom period, the percentage of Catholics who had never used any method of birth control declined from 43 percent to 22 percent. Moreover, the percentage of Catholics who practiced methods of birth control that the hierarchy explicitly condemned (church officials permitted abstinence and the rhythm method) rose from 30 in 1955 to 53 in 1965.[70] Catholic couples appear to have used birth control during this period to regulate the timing and spacing of their children's births even as they gave birth to more and more children. Despite their rising marital fertility rates, they did not respond favorably to the use of fear that a portion of the prescriptive literature continued to employ. At the close of Vatican II, then, nearly 78 percent of American Catholics were prepared to face the psychological dangers threatened by writers like George Kelly. By 1965, fear—whether fear of hell or fear of a misshapen psyche—was losing its influence on Catholic behavior.

The Personal Conscience

Within a generation, fear would be routed. The 1970s saw a return to the convergence of fertility rates between Catholics and non- Catholics and the first convergence of contraceptive use, despite a strongly worded papal encyclical condemning contraceptives.

That 1968 encyclical, Paul VI's *Humanae Vitae,* has defined the hierarchy's position on sex in marriage for the last generation. It was widely read and discussed by American Catholics and remains today at the center of any Catholic discussion of birth control. Though Paul VI released it in the 1960s, the encyclical, with its strange mix of the two discourses we discussed above, more reflects the period of transition of the 1950s.

To a degree, Paul VI seems influenced by the language and spirit of *Gaudium et Spes.* In a number of places he invokes the construction image of marriage. For example, "married persons are the free and responsible *collaborators* of God" in the work of transmitting human life (emphasis added).[71] Conjugal love increases "by means of the joys and sorrows of daily life, in such a way that a husband and wife . . . together attain their human perfection." [72] He states explicitly that one of the purposes of marriage is to work on the self: wielding the tool of periodic continence, for instance, "husband and wife fully develop their personalities." [73] He refers to sex as if it is a tool given us by God, which, if misused, will "contradict . . . the plan of God." [74] And he justifies his moral strictures—on fidelity, for example—by citing their ability to secure "profound and lasting happiness" in the here and now.[75] In one section the pope actually quotes *Gaudium et Spes* to suggest that God instituted marriage to help humans achieve his "design of love," marriage tends toward "personal perfection," and humans "collaborate with God" in creating and raising children.[76] Taken by themselves, these references would seem to indicate that Paul VI rejected the discourse of fear.

But these images hardly dominate the encyclical. In fact, they compete with figures that summon images of a dangerous world. He considers sex more a weapon than a tool. The rhythm method "helps both partners to drive out selfishness, the enemy of true love."[77] Similarly, it is legitimate to "use" sex during the wife's infertile periods "to safeguard . . . mutual fidelity."[78] Safeguards abound throughout the encyclical. "By safeguarding these essential aspects [of sex], the unitive and the procreative, the conjugal act preserves" mutual love and the "ordination" toward parenthood.[79] Paul VI calls on political "rulers . . . to safeguard moral customs."[80] Church law "defends the dignity of man and wife."[81] That dignity, presumably, is assaulted by modern conceptions of sex, for the modern world once again is characterized as the enemy. "[T]oo numerous are those voices—amplified by the modern means of propaganda—which are contrary to the voice of the Church."[82] The encyclical warns us of the "modern media of social communications" that lead to sexual arousal.[83] As in the discourse of fear, life is conceived of as a journey. The church and its doctrines are the best guides through the treacherous terrain of the modern world, and they are the best defense against a host of enemies. Not surprisingly, this view leaves little room for the personal conscience: "In the task of transmitting life, therefore, [men and women] are not free to proceed completely at will, as if they could determine in a wholly autonomous way the honest path to follow." They must instead follow the path "manifested by the constant teaching of the Church."[84] He attacked contraceptives because they would open a "wide and easy road" toward immorality.[85] Young people, he insisted, "must not be offered [this] easy means of eluding" moral law.[86] This image is a new twist on the journey metaphor: the narrow path doesn't keep us clear of danger so much as it facilitates our being rounded up and driven in whatever direction the authorities want us to go.

Such pastoral images—bishops as shepherds and the laity as sheep—have always been used to describe the church. But in this image of young men and women eluding authority by taking the easy road of contraception, Paul VI betrays an anxiety that seems to run just beneath the surface of the whole encyclical. The church has grown disobedient. The encyclical closes with calls for obedience: priests are reminded that "in the field of morals as well as in that of dogma, all should attend to the Magisterium of the Church."[87] Paul VI was aware that many good Catholics dissented from the morals he proposed in *Humanae Vitae*. In fact, the very commission first established by John XXIII and then expanded by Paul VI himself to study the issue of birth control advised the pontiff to relax the church's ban. The encyclical admits the commission "departed from the moral teaching on marriage proposed with constant firmness by the teaching authority of the Church."[88] So the priests are admonished that they must "all . . . speak the same language" if they want the laity to obey.[89] Explicit in this discussion is that obeying the magisterium is "necessary for salvation," though the encyclical never reverts to threatening readers with visions of hell.[90]

Paul VI's anxiety about obedience is one indication of how thorough was this shift toward personal conscience. Another indication is Catholic behavior. Despite *Humanae Vitae*, by 1975 fully three-quarters of American married Catholic women of childbearing age reported that they practiced some form of contraception.[91] This growing dissonance between official church teaching and lay Catholic belief and behavior derived at least in part from a widespread reliance on the formation of individual consciences over fear of church sanctions. George Gallup, Jr., and Jim Castelli reported that in 1987 fully 77 percent of Catholics said that they favored their own consciences rather than papal expression of church teachings to guide their moral decisions generally.[92] And only 12 percent of Catholics saw church leaders as the locus of final moral authority regarding the use of contraceptives.[93] It seems Catholics in the decades after the 1950s were not conditioned to fear, but rather were encouraged to develop mature personal consciences.

As late as 1955, the *Guide to Catholic Marriage* advised the young Catholic who "keeps company" with a non-Catholic to make sure her "confessor [is] kept informed of the progress of the friendship." If "the confessor deems it wise and necessary" to break off the friendship, the Catholic must do so.[94] Such admonitions to surrender your will to a confessor—in essence, to remain perpetually a child—disappeared after Vatican II. The new discourse abandoned fear in favor of persuasion, reflecting a conception of the world more closely aligned to the beliefs of the many Catholics who used birth control and married out of the faith. It typically sought to draw on theological developments and the reader's reasoning ability to shape individual consciences to embrace behavioral ideals rooted in love for other individuals and hope for social salvation. The world was not so much fraught with danger as full of possibilities for the fulfillment of Christian ideals.

Fear Redux

In recent years the hierarchical church has moved headlong back to the discourse of fear. Bishops have threatened prominent national politicians with eternal damnation for their positions on public issues, barred world-renowned Catholic theologians from teaching at Catholic universities (and driven others out of the priesthood altogether), and have even threatened to excommunicate lay Catholics who belonged to religious organizations that urge more open dialogue on fundamental church practices. The immediate results seem somewhat ominous for the church's future, as fewer and fewer Catholics choose to remain active members of a church whose clerical leaders embrace the juridical, fear-infused model of the early twentieth century. Though the ecclesiastical sanctions may be personally and collectively painful, Catholics appear to have permanently rejected the climate of fear once so powerfully exercised to keep them in line rather than violate their personal consciences.

This determination to resist the discourse of fear clearly places Catholics in the mainstream of late twentieth-century American emotional culture. Catholics seem very much immersed in a shared emotional ethos that rejects fear. Hierarchical efforts to bring American Catholics back into an emotionological ghetto provide a rare opportunity to observe the dynamic tension within an emotional subculture. Is the discourse of fear a forever lost or recoverable world? Whatever the outcome of the current conflict, the middle of the twentieth century saw a dramatic transformation in Catholic emotional culture from one of fear to one of reason and love.

NOTES

1. The sermon is quoted in Jay Dolan, *Catholic Revivalism: The American Experience, 1830–1900* (Notre Dame, IN, 1977), 96.

2. Dolan, *Catholic Revivalism*, 98.

3. Peter Stearns, *American Cool: Constructing a Twentieth-Century Emotional Style* (New York, 1995), 96. Stearns and Timothy Haggerty made essentially the same argument regarding fear in an earlier article: "The Role of Fear: Transitions in American Emotional Standards for Children, 1850–1950," *American Historical Review* 96 (February 1991): 63–94.

4. H. Gavin, "Fear," in *The New Catholic Encyclopedia* (Washington, DC, 1967), 863. People who experienced fear responded in two ways, according to the *New Catholic Encyclopedia,* one behavioral and the other physiological. In the first response, people in fear attempt "to avoid or escape the feared situation." In the physiological response, people experience a series of physical responses such as racing hearts, heightened muscular tension, and reduced somatic activity. The hierarchy concerned itself almost entirely with the behavioral response to fear, and set out to carefully assess the responsibility Catholics held for their actions when they behaved out of fear. We too focus on this behavioral aspect, and leave the physiological responses aside.

5. J. A. Oesterle, "Fear (Moral Aspect)", in *New Catholic Encyclopedia,* 864. The church did recognize that fear could be so overwhelming as to preclude rational action altogether. In these cases the actions "would not be voluntary at all," and the agent would not be responsible for the actions.

6. Ignatius of Loyola, *Spiritual Exercises of St. Ignatius,* trans. Anthony Mottoya (Garden City, NY, 1964), 59.

7. P. F. Mulhern, "Fear of the Lord," in *New Catholic Encyclopedia,* 864. Patrick O'Brien referred to this kind of fear as "Reverential fear" or "Reverential awe" in his treatise *Emotions and Morals: Their Place and Purpose in Harmonious Living* (New York, 1950), 203–4.

8. J. G. Chatham, "Force and Fear (Canon Law)," in *New Catholic Encyclopedia,* 1004.

9. Chatham, "Force and Fear," 1003. This kind of fear derived from Roman law, which the church adopted in its 1917 promulgation of canon law.

10. O'Brien, *Emotions and Morals,* 203–4.

11. Timothy Fry, O.S.B., ed., *The Rule of St. Benedict in English* (Collegeville, MN, 1982), 28.

12. Ignatius, *Exercises,* 59.

13. Jean Delumeau, *Sin and Fear: The Emergence of a Western Guilt Culture, 13th–18th Centuries* (New York, 1990). Delumeau notes largely the same origin for the culture of fear that we note for the American Catholic emphasis on fear, essentially a siege mentality that developed because of perceived threats from "Turks [substitute communism here for Americans], idolators, Jews, heretics, witches and so on" (xi).

14. Avery Dulles, S.J., *The Reshaping of Catholicism: Current Challenges in the Theology of Church* (San Francisco, 1988), 3.

15. Eugene Kennedy, *A Sense of Life, a Sense of Sin* (Garden City, NY, 1975), 15–16.

16. Theodore Hesburgh, C.S.C., *The Hesburgh Papers: Higher Values in Higher Education* (Kansas City, 1979), 179.

17. Eugene Kennedy, *The Now and Future Church: The Psychology of Being an American Catholic* (Garden City, NY, 1984), 54.

18. Martin J. Scott, S.J., *Marriage* (New York, 1930), 106, 187.

19. Martin J. Scott, S.J., *You and Yours: Practical Talks on Home Life* (New York, 1921), 148–49, 156, 158 n, 160.

20. Scott, *Marriage*, ix.

21. William J. McManus, *Marriage Guide for Engaged Catholics* (New York, 1961), 6.

22. Msgr. George Kelly, *The Catholic Marriage Manual* (New York, 1958), xv.

23. Scott, *Practical Talks*, 139.

24. Scott, *Marriage*, 4.

25. Scott, *Practical Talks*, 159.

26. Scott, *Marriage*, 6.

27. Scott, *Marriage*, 16.

28. Scott, *Marriage*, 91–92.

29. Scott, *Marriage*, 98.

30. McManus, *Marriage Guide*, 5.

31. McManus, *Marriage Guide*, 6.

32. Clement Simon Mihanovich, Brother Gerald J. Schnepp, and Rev. John L. Thomas, *A Guide to Catholic Marriage* (Milwaukee, 1955), 56.

33. Mihanovich, Schnepp, and Thomas, *Guide*, 163.

34. Mihanovich, Schnepp, and Thomas, *Guide*, 169.

35. Mihanovich, Schnepp, and Thomas, *Guide*, 169.

36. Msgr. George Kelly, *Dating for Young Catholics* (New York, 1963), 38.

37. Charles F. Westoff, "The Blending of Catholic Reproductive Behavior," in *The Religious Dimension: New Directions in Quantitative Research*, ed. Robert Wuthnow (New York, 1979), 236–38.

38. Rev. Paul Hanly Furfey, *You and Your Children: A Book for Parents, Priests and Educators* (New York, 1929), 44.

39. Furfey, *You and Your Children*, 51.

40. Mary Perkins, *Beginning at Home: The Challenge of Christian Parenthood* (Collegeville, MN, 1955), 8.

41. McManus, *Marriage Guide*, 17.

42. McManus, *Marriage Guide*, 38.

43. Scott, *Marriage*, 8.

44. Scott, *Marriage*, 8.

45. Kelly, *Dating*, 34.

46. Kelly, *Catholic Marriage Manual*, 156.

47. Patrick J. Ryan, *A Soldier Priest Talks to Youth* (New York, 1963), 192.

48. Mihanovich, Schnepp, and Thomas, *Guide*, 164. Paradoxically, the *Guide* concludes the section on mixed marriages by stating that "opposition to interracial marriages is a matter of expediency only and must be labeled un-Christian, unscientific, and undemocratic." Expediency could not be used as an excuse to discourage interracial marriage, but was sufficient to discourage interreligious marriages (180).

49. Kelly, *Catholic Marriage Manual*, 60.

50. David Knight, *The Good News about Sex* (Cincinnati, 1979), 145–46.

51. "The Pastoral Constitution on the Church in the Modern World (Vatican II, *Gaudium et Spes*)," in *Vatican Council II: The Conciliar and Post Conciliar Documents*, ed. Austin Flannery, O.P. (Collegeville, MN, 1975), 927.

52. Flannery, 914.

53. Flannery, 914.

54. Flannery, 917, 925.

55. Flannery, 951.

56. Flannery, 952.

57. Perkins, *Beginning at Home*, 146–47.

58. Perkins, *Beginning at Home,* 3.

59. Perkins, *Beginning at Home,* 137.

60. McManus, *Marriage Guide,* 40.

61. Blaise Hettich, "Sex Education for Children," in *You and Your Children,* ed. Eugene S. Geissler (Chicago, 1956), 47.

62. Hettich, "Sex Education," 51.

63. McManus, *Marriage Guide,* 48.

64. McManus, *Marriage Guide,* 42, 12, 45.

65. Hettich, "Sex Education," 32.

66. Hettich, "Sex Education," 36, 41.

67. Mihanovich, Schnepp, and Thomas, *Guide,* 52.

68. Westoff, "Blending of Catholic Reproductive Behavior"; Charles F. Westoff and Norman B. Ryder, *The Contraceptive Revolution* (Princeton, 1977), 24. Westoff and Ryder report slightly different percentages for Catholic contraception use, though they vary by only one or two percentage points from those reported in Westoff's other study. William D. Mosher, David Johnson, and Margorie C. Horn, "Religion and Fertility in the United States: The Importance of Marriage Patterns and Hispanic Origin," *Demography* 23 (August 1986): 369.

69. Gerhard Lenski reports that white Catholics in the Detroit area believed birth control to be morally wrong in greater numbers than white and black Protestants. Lenski did not examine fertility rates, so we cannot discern any connection between belief and behavior, nor can we determine whether Detroit followed the national trend in fertility noted elsewhere. *The Religious Factor: A Sociologist's Inquiry* (Garden City, NY, 1963), 166.

70. Leslie Aldridge Westoff and Charles F. Westoff, *From Now to Zero: Fertility, Contraception, and Abortion in America* (Boston, 1968), 193.

71. Paul VI, *Humanae Vitae: On the Regulation of Birth* (Washington, DC, 1968), 1. We refer in all future notes to this text to the paragraph number so that readers may locate the citation in any of the numerous versions of the encyclical.

72. *Humanae Vitae,* par. 9.

73. *Humanae Vitae,* par. 21.

74. *Humanae Vitae,* par. 13.

75. *Humanae Vitae,* par. 9.

76. *Humanae Vitae,* par. 8.

77. *Humanae Vitae,* par. 21

78. *Humanae Vitae,* par. 16.

79. *Humanae Vitae,* par. 12.

80. *Humanae Vitae,* par. 23.

81. *Humanae Vitae,* par. 18.

82. *Humanae Vitae,* par. 18.

83. *Humanae Vitae,* par. 22.

84. *Humanae Vitae,* par. 10.

85. *Humanae Vitae,* par. 17.

86. *Humanae Vitae,* par. 17.

87. *Humanae Vitae,* par. 28.

88. *Humanae Vitae,* par. 6.

89. *Humanae Vitae,* par. 28.

90. *Humanae Vitae,* par. 4.

91. Westoff, "Blending of Catholic Reproductive Behavior," 233.

92. George Gallup, Jr., and Jim Castelli, *The People's Religion: American Faith in the 90's* (New York, 1989), 18.

93. William V. D'Antonio, James D. Davidson, Dean R. Hoge, and Ruth A. Wallace, *Laity: American and Catholic: Transforming the Church* (Kansas City, 1996), 32.

94. Mihanovich, Schnepp, and Thomas, *Guide,* 170.

Twentieth-Century Emotional Standards and Emotional Experience
Class and Gender

Chapter Fourteen

Etiquette Books and Emotion Management in the Twentieth Century
American Habitus in International Comparison

Cas Wouters

Manners books (or etiquette books) are not an American invention. The reception of European manners books in eighteenth- and nineteenth-century America, particularly Lord Chesterfield's *Letters of Advice to His Son* (1775), launched the creation of American codes and ideals of behavior and emotion management. In close connection to the changing power structure, this revolutionary period saw the transition from a courtesy genre to an etiquette genre. In the latter genre, inherited status and class deference were no longer emphasized. As "the manners game was open to all who could compete," these were books for status-conscious social climbers.[1]

The present essay deals with changes in twentieth-century manners, comparing American, Dutch, English, and German etiquette books.[2] This comparison has revealed several significant national differences, with regard not only to a variety of specific topics but also to the genre as a whole. Here, a few of these differences will be discussed, particularly those that illuminate specifically American patterns of emotion management. Among them are different ways of addressing readers, differences in social dividing lines between private and public, formal and informal, introductions, reserve, snubbing, business etiquette, superlatives, and popularity. Other topics like "race," chaperonage, dating, and petting, in which there are significant differences, are part of the same overall emotional style, but will have to be discussed at a later time. International comparison is directed at presenting striking—and therefore illuminating—contrasts and placing them in the context of a wider framework of changes in both national *habitus* and national class structure. This framework needs to be outlined first.

As in earlier centuries, modern etiquette books generally express the codes of behavior and emotion management of established classes and their good society, functioning as a model for other social groups and classes. In 1890, Gabriel Tarde published his *Laws of Imitation,* an extensive study of this model function, capturing the "trickling" of codes and ideals "down" the social ladder in the metaphor of a water tower: "Invention can start from the lower ranks of the people, but its extention depends upon the existence of some lofty social elevation, a kind of social water-tower, whence a continuous waterfall of imitation may descend."[3] In his study of American etiquette books, the historian Arthur M. Schlesinger reported that

> The rules of etiquette were calculated, as an astronomer would say, for the meridian of the city, and even there it was "good society" that paid principal heed. Nevertheless the little candle threw its beams afar and as *time* toned down the differences between urban social classes and between country and town as well, something like a nationwide consensus of manners came about. (Italics added)

And in the 1960 edition of America's most famous etiquette book, first published in 1922, Emily Post also referred to the same process, relating it to growing prosperity: "What was once considered the tradition of gracious living of the few has in these times of plenty rightly become the heritage of us all."[4] The spread of "gracious living" and the "toning down of differences" in the development of "a nationwide consensus of manners" are undisputed developments, but their explanation in terms of a "social water-tower," "time," and "plenty" will have to be augmented. In the present essay, these developments will be analyzed in the wider framework of expanding and intensifying competition and cooperation, which operated as the main driving forces toward continued social differentiation and integration, a social interweaving in which networks of interdependence between various groups of people expanded and became denser and more multileveled. In one of Norbert Elias's formulations,

> The main line of this movement . . . , the successive rises of larger and larger groups, is the same in all Western countries, and incipiently so in increasingly large areas elsewhere. And similar, too, is the structural regularity underlying it, the increasing division of functions under the pressure of competition, the tendency to more equal dependence of all on all.[5]

It is this process of changing power and dependency relationships that is seen as the motor of changes in behavior, experience, values, emotions, and emotion management. On the whole, twentieth-century changes in power and dependency relationships can be interpreted as a process of social integration in which more and more groups of people came to be represented in the various centers of power. Their members increasingly adopted the same national code of behavior and feeling; thus the more extreme differences in power, ranking, behavior, and emotion management among all social groups diminished. In the same process, as larger and larger groups became interdependent, the people involved increasingly came to experience others as belonging to their own group or nation. This expanding group-feeling or widening identification has somewhat weakened the boundaries of class, religion, ethnic background, or race and provided a basis for a rising societal level of mutual trust and, correspondingly, a declining level of anxiety, mutual suspicion, and hatred. Thus, the process of social integration involves rising social constraints toward such self-restraints as reflection and consideration in controlling conflicts. The spectrum of accepted emotional and behavioral alternatives has expanded (with the important exception of feelings of superiority and inferiority); however, an acceptable and respectable usage of these alternatives implied a continued increase in the demands made on emotion management.[6] In this way, the successive ascent of larger and larger groups, their increasing status and power relative to other groups, has been reflected in the dominant codes and ideals of behavior and feeling, in an overall style of emotion management, in *habitus*.

In contrast to *individual* social ascent, the ascent of an entire social group involves a change in the whole shape and volume of the social water tower, to use Tarde's metaphor. It involves some form of mixing of the codes and ideals of the groups that have risen and those of the previously superior groups. My central hypothesis is that the way this mixing process has proceeded helps us understand, if not explain, particular changes in emotions and emotion management and the formation of a particular national habitus.[7] The sediments of this mixing process can be seen in longer-term changes in etiquette books: the "emotionology," or patterns of emotion management, of increasingly wider social groups is reflected in the rules of etiquette. In turn, major directional trends in these codes and ideals are indicative of changes in power relationships between all social groups—classes, sexes and generations— and changes in the level of integration in any particular society. Trends in manners are therefore indicative of trends in power relationships or class structures as well as in national habitus. It is in the light of these connections that this essay will focus on differences and changes in the abovementioned specifically American manners. Discussing manners as an integral part of dominant American patterns of behavior, ideals, and emotion management—conceptualized as habitus—will shed light on the development of a specifically American overall emotional style.

General Outline of National Developments

Since America was a "new nation" with an enormously varied population, ranging from black slaves to rich landowning and commercial patricians—but no aristoc- racy—its integration processes differed in many ways from those in "old nations." The lack of any hereditary ruling group is usually held to account for there being hardly any of the characteristics of a courtly civilization in the American national habitus. Yet the easygoing conduct that is so often portrayed as typically American can also be understood as a typical product of a court society and a courtly civilization: "While our rejection of the magnificent and the grandiose and our preference for ease and informality are probably influenced by leveling and demo- cratic ideas, the fact remains that the easy style was an invention of an aristocratic age and was meant to exalt its possessor above his fellows, not to bring him down to their level."[8] The easy style has remained a means for attaining success. As a 1992 book on success puts it, "Yes, there are little 'tricks of the trade' in meeting and greeting people and learning to become at ease and casual in social situations." This is a twentieth-century example of a process-continuity; it is in fact similar to the process that occurred in the late eighteenth century, when "the middling sort repudi- ated the basis of aristocratic power even as they seized the aristocratic armor of manners and remade it for their own purposes."[9] In each country under study (although only partially in Germany before 1871), appropriating the manners of superior groups has again and again facilitated the rise of subordinated groups.

Moreover, comparisons between new and old nations have often been ideologically inspired, to the extent that all old nations are lumped together after the model of England and France. Thus, the fact that countries like Germany and the Netherlands also have strong middle-class characteristics in their national habitus is generally neglected. In the Netherlands, rich merchants became the ruling class at a very early date. In 1581, their separatist movement succeeded in freeing the country from king and aristocracy. It has been reported that both the contents and history of the Dutch freedom charter, Het Plakkaat van Verlatinge (Declaration of Abandonment/ Desertion) of 1581, contain striking similarities to the American Declaration of Independence of 1776. Since 1581, merchant patricians have been the dominant class in the Netherlands; although this ruling group had come to function more or less as an aristocracy by the end of the seventeenth century, when they attempted to regard themselves "as equals of Crowned Heads," they continued to keep close ties to the world of commerce. Consequently, the Dutch national code of conduct and emotion management is highly permeated by middle-class characteristics. As early as the 1850s, the American historian John L. Motley compared the Dutch struggle for independence with that of the United States. The Dutch sociologist Johan Goudsblom thinks S. M. Lipset was wrong in calling the United States "the first new nation": "a further comparison of the early development of the two Republics along the lines suggested by Lipset would probably lead to some interesting analogies." [10]

In what was to become Germany, until the German unification in 1871, bourgeois classes and aristocratic circles remained highly segregated; accordingly, different habitus developed in the two groups. From 1871 until the Second World War, the bourgeois habitus amalgamated with certain elements of the aristocratic code into a German national habitus. However, lacking one central court and the development of a pacified courtly code like the ones in England or France, these elements were more directly related to an aristocratic warrior code than to an aristocratic courtly civilization. As Norbert Elias observed,

> it is military values which have once again grown deep roots in the German tradition of behaviour and feeling. In regard to his own honour, the honour of his country, his Kaiser, his Führer, the officer cannot make any compromises. . . . Complete determination, absolute loyalty to principles, uncompromising adherence to one's own convictions, still sound particularly good in German.

Since World War II, these warrior code elements have faded, and a "revised" middle-class habitus has turned into a German national habitus. A clear example of this process is found in an often reprinted etiquette book entitled *Good Manners Are Back Again (Mann benimmt sich wieder)*. It contains an open attack on an element of this warrior code: the feeling that to compromise is dishonorable and automatically brings loss of face, that is, loss of respect and self-respect:

> However, you can't and won't simply give up your claims altogether, because then you would lose face, and that . . . is completely ruled out. Therefore anyone who wants to "save face" has to be a skillful negotiator, . . . a *"typischer Kompromißler"* [typical compromiser]. This expression *"typischer Kompromißler"* is used deliberately because it

is taken to be a reproach in our country, whereas a "good compromiser" to most other people is a highly respected and very esteemed man, whose person and *"kompromiß-liche"* abilities are in demand and praised. As against what once used to be, we have to become clearly aware of this sharp contrast between German and foreign views on the importance attached to "partly giving in." We view, or used to view, rigid insistence on a total claim as proud, brave, and masculine, while the rest of the world views it as foolish and destructive, because it blocks any negotiation from ever producing results that are satisfying for both parties, while it generally rules out living together harmoniously.... The last war, and with it our present misery, was ignited by these contrasting views on "saving face."[11]

In England, throughout the nineteenth century, rich middle-class newcomers were allowed into the centers of power, including (high) society, provided they knocked at the appropriate doors in the appropriate ways. This way of integrating *nouveaux riches* helped make good society a unified and strong social and political center. Thus, the integration of new classes into society coincided with rather collective and nonconflicting changes in the English national code of conduct and affect-control:

In the making of this English code, features of aristocratic descent fused with those of middle-class descent—understandably, for in the development of English society one can observe a continuous assimilating process in the course of which upper-class models (especially a code of good manners) were adopted in a modified form by middle- class people, while middle-class features (as for instance elements of a code of morals) were adopted by upper-class people. Hence, when in the course of the nineteenth century most of the aristocratic privileges were abolished, and England with the rise of the industrial working classes became a nation state, the English national code of conduct and affect-control showed very clearly the gradualness of the resolution of conflicts between upper and middle classes in the form, to put it briefly, of a peculiar blend between a code of good manners and a code of morals.[12]

Etiquette Books in International Comparison

Public and Private: American and German Habitus Compared

Particularly in comparison with Germany, the American national habitus is characterized by an open and confident attitude toward the public (also political) arena, which has been widely penetrated by informality. In most social settings, "all were to avoid the extremes of formality and familiarity." In contrast, the Germans tend to distinguish rather sharply between public and private, formal and informal. In the words of Stephen Kahlberg, "the public realm is generally characterized by social distance and purely functional exchanges with only formal involvement. Conversely, all 'impersonal' values—... such as achievement, competition, and goal-attainment—are strictly banned from the private sphere."[13] In Germany, political power and the associated public sphere remained dominated by an aristocracy for about a century longer than in other Western countries. Representatives of the middle classes remained highly excluded and were obliged to either exhibit subservient behavior or adopt the aristocratic warrior code. Germans still behave rather formally in the public arena, as if they distrust it, particularly in the absence of a clear hierarchical setting with clearly designated superordinates and subordinates. In private, however, relationships tend to be experienced as highly personal and as "immediate, not domesticated by general rules, intent on honesty and profundity," which implies they may involve almost unlimited rights and obligations.[14] These characteristics can be interpreted as a process-continuity deriving from a distinction made by the bourgeois intelligentsia in eighteenth-century Germany. Blocked from the political centers of power, they emphasized their "depth of feeling," "honesty," and "true virtue" as against the "superficiality," "falsity," and "mere outward politeness" of the nobility.[15] A similar social inheritance of bourgeois habitus is evident in behavior in public, where a kind of formality is demanded that varies with hierarchical differences:

> the greater attentiveness and even, in some circumstances extreme sensitivity, to status of middle-class educated Germans erects obstacles to a free mixing from group to group, even if the social skills for doing so are present. This is the case simply because each new social situation requires an assessment of relative status and the assumption of either a posture of deference or leadership, an exercise that is far too stressful to be repeated frequently.[16]

Accordingly, in the public sphere, Germans tend to cling more strongly to hierarchically differentiated formal rules, whereas in private and in informal situations, they allow themselves to let go to a greater degree. Throughout this century, up to the present day, German etiquette books have contained questions like *Ehrlich oder höflich?* (honest or polite?—a chapter title)[17] as well as many warnings against getting too confidential and against *duzen* (using the informal you), for instance at office parties and trips. The next day at the office one will practically always regret this. In a more general formulation, "*Faith, not confidentiality, should be the basis of a friendship in which Du is used as an expression of a special bond. Whoever gives away this 'Du' lightheartedly forgets altogether that, together with this 'Du,' an obligation is to be accepted: to be a real friend, who will also prove himself as such in bad times.*"[18] Notwithstanding the informalization spurt of the 1960s and 1970s, when most social arbiters sincerely invited their readers to do away with uptight formalities, the formality-informality span of the Germans has remained much wider than that of the other countries.[19] It seems to be smallest in the United States, as the Americans tend to be relatively informal. From observations like "Americans invite people once to check them out; it's the second invitation which is a compliment,"[20] it follows that the American dividing line between private and public is less sharply drawn. The same goes for the boundaries of friendship. With regard to national symbols and ceremonies, however, Americans tend to be more formal. Moreover, many formal aspects of American behavior are not directly recognizable, for instance, the relatively strong pressure for conformity through a variety of social controls on individuals as members of communities and organizations.[21]

Manners and Class in England and America

In the nineteenth century the English developed a system of introductions, cards, and calling that functioned quite effectively to screen newcomers into good society and to close their ranks against others. In addition to this elaborate system, an important means of exclusion was the development and maintenance of "reserve." Until well into the twentieth century, most British manners books give the impression of having been written from a one-class perspective, as if the public of readers all belonged, or at least were on the verge of belonging, to society and as if all would participate in the events of the Season. Even at a time when many "new people" with "new money" were entering high society, as around 1900, this style of writing remained dominant. This process-continuity demonstrates that the system of gate-keeping functioned not only to identify and exclude undesirables, but also to ensure that the newly introduced would accommodate to the prevailing code of behavior and emotion management. As a whole, the existence of a strong, unified, and unifying center in combination with a gatekeeping system of introductions, cards, and calling and a habit of "reserve," might explain why discussions of problems connected with the social mingling of different classes are almost absent in British manners books, whereas they are openly and frequently discussed in manners books from other countries. The effective system of gatekeeping even allowed references to contact with lower classes to become scarce, and references to "lower instincts" (emotions related to bodily functions and body control, particularly sex and violence) to become taboo. In the nineteenth century, the latter came to be experienced as embarrassing and branded as vulgar: they would betray lower-class origin. But no such references are found in twentieth-century British etiquette books.

The degree of integration of English society and the effective gatekeeping of its good society may also explain why, as Curtin observed, "the requirement that a gentleman treat those he met in company on the basis of equality was one of the commonest and most frequently reiterated principles of etiquette."[22] An elaborate, highly formal, and hierarchically differentiated system of manners or rules operated to restrict "those he met in company." For example,

> If you are walking down the street in company with another person, and stop to say something to one of your friends ... do not commit the too common, but most flagrant error, of presenting such persons to one another.... If you should be so presented, remember that the acquaintance afterwards goes for nothing; you have not the slightest right to expect that the other will ever speak to you. But observe, that in all such cases you should converse with a stranger as if you knew him perfectly well; you are to consider him an acquaintance for the nonce.[23]

In other words, these rules helped identify situations in which the rules prescribed the practice of "reserve," that is, the avoidance of exactly the kind of emotion management required when one was "in company." Thus, the effective gatekeeping system of the English also helps explain why and how they developed a tendency to behave either with "reserve," which "implies that everyone is to be treated alike as a stranger,"[24] or "on the basis of equality," which implies that everyone "in company" is to be treated alike as an equal.

An unobtrusive insight into the significance of the elaborate and rather rigid system of manners can be derived from the following warning against the "visiting card trick," published in a 1906 British magazine:

> To bring this trick to a successful issue the beggar must be a man of respectable appearance and some address, for it is essential that he should gain access to your drawing room. . . . If he is fortunate enough to be admitted to the drawing room, he asks, before going, if you will oblige him with a glass of water. Should you leave him . . . he takes the opportunity to pocket any visiting cards he may see lying about. Presently one of the cards comes back to you. It is presented by another caller, and on the back you read: "Bearer is a thoroughly deserving man. He is on his way to (some distant town) to obtain work. I have given him ten shillings. Can you help?" . . . Some of the other stolen cards will be similarly presented to other friends of the people whose names they bear. Thus, the vicar's card will be presented to one of his churchwardens, the town councillor's to one of his collegues on the council, and so on. Visiting cards are a recognised article of commerce in some of the common lodging houses, where they are sold at prices ranging up to five shillings according to the supposed value of the card as a bait.[25]

This confidence trick demonstrates the importance of visiting cards and, at the same time, the high degree of seclusion and integration and the strength of the sense of belonging and protectedness that high society provided; without these, a con game like this could not have been successful. Only within such a protective environment could tact and consideration be developed more fully. The certainty of being more or less equals "in company" may also explain why many English, to this day, tend to behave in a rather easy and informal way in formal situations, whereas on the other hand, in informal situations where this certainty is lacking, they tend to cling to a relatively greater formality. In other words, when "in company" with each other, the English adhere to a code of conduct and emotion management characterized by a relatively small formality-informality span, but in informal situations outside this protected circle, traditional constraints of "reserve" toward "strangers" may operate.

The relatively high level of integration and seclusion of British high society may also explain, at least partly, why the British have developed a taste for understatements and self-mockery; this demonstrative "cool" is connected with a relatively strong inhibition of anger. "In company," some are more equal, of course, but by developing the custom of not accentuating these differences, the British prevent and contain tensions, conflicts, and loss of decorum. To a considerable extent, individual idiosyncrasies are allowed, but only if expressed within a rather strict social definition of modesty. Even with regard to dressing, "etiquette writers worried more about over-dressing than they did about under-dressing."[26] For example, "In the morning, before eleven o'clock, even if you go out, you should not be dressed. You would be stamped a *parvenue* if you were seen in anything better than a respectable old frock coat."[27] The development of relatively strict and effective rules for inclusion and exclusion, implying a relatively high degree of external social constraints on emotion management, corresponds to the development of a relatively high sensitivity to boundaries, fences, border lines, and gatecrashing. Taken together, these developments present an insight into the paradox that on the one hand the British have preserved a rather hierarchical class society, while on the other hand their national habitus—modeled after their best society—is characterized by a relatively high degree of tact, consideration, and tolerance. The latter implies an emotion management characterized by a relatively high level of mutually expected self-restraints and mutual identification.

In contrast, at the beginning of the twentieth century, American high society was far less integrated and secluded. American upper classes were more spread out and more strongly divided among themselves, the country being much larger and characterized by much greater differences between North, South, East, and West, without a unifying and dominant center like London. In such a setting, "those who felt they were eligible for entry on the basis of wealth and achievement but who were excluded on grounds of religion, ethnic background or race, formed their own Society."[28] To elaborate on Tarde's metaphor: there were many competing "social water towers" in the United States. In New York, for instance, there has been a more or less constant competition between "two Societies, 'Old New York' and 'New Society.' In every era, 'Old New York' has taken a horrified look at 'New Society' and expressed the devout conviction that a genuine aristocracy, good blood, good bone— themselves—was being defiled by a horde of rank climbers."[29] This high level of competition runs in tandem with a high degree of openness of high society (except for those excluded "on grounds of religion, ethnic background or race"). Often, America's openness is emphasized for ideological reasons, while the other side of the coin, its strong competitiveness, is downplayed. For instance, in the 1960s the author of a historical study of American manners claimed that "no other civilization can show so many orders, associations, fraternal lodges, . . . where it was possible to 'meet people,' 'make contacts' and find a place."[30] Of course, an open "frontier" and the absence of a landed aristocracy contributed to the relative openness of competition and, accordingly, to a less marked sensitivity for boundaries and fences, as these were likely to be more porous and changing. In the 1950s, Harold Nicolson, a British member of high society, portrayed Americans as having a

> curious indifference to, or disregard of, what to us is one of the most precious of human possessions, namely personal privacy. To them, . . . privacy denotes something exclusive, patronising, "un-folksey," and therefore meriting suspicion. Thus they leave their curtains undrawn at dusk, have no hedges separating their front gardens, and will converse amicably with strangers about private things.[31]

In America, the open competition between many best societies explains to a large extent why good society as a whole has had a weaker political significance than in England. Davidoff has pointed out that this "lack of access to real power through Society meant that its reward and entertainment function was stressed."[32] This is expressed in many ways, for instance, in the subtitle of Crowninshield's 1908 book *An Entrance Key to the Fantastic Life of the 400* and in American words like "the smart," "fashionable set," "jet set," and "socialites," words that are closely associated with "conspicuous consumption" and "showing off." In other words, whereas the British tend to tone down social differences, Americans tend to accentuate them. The weaker integration and seclusion of America's best society have also prevented a comparably advanced development of the British habit of keeping one's distance or "reserve." It made the dominant code of behavior and emotion management in America more universal than the British type, but at the same time, it prevented the American code from becoming as unified and yet subtly differentiated as the corresponding British code. The range of accepted behavior in the American code allowed for extremes that the British, according to their code, would experience as disgusting. A nineteenth-century example is spitting about the room; in 1859, an English author called this an American "national habit," and in 1884 an American author, addressing himself in a special preface to English readers, wrote that "Spitting upon the carpet naturally comes in for severe condemnation; and the authority of Dr. Wendell Holmes seems necessary to prove that a handkerchief should be used in blowing one's nose."[33] By the end of the nineteenth century, extremes like these had faded, but the differences in national codes and their perception of each other had remained, as this British example shows: "I should be glad to exhibit to the host of American *parvenues* their own broad, glittering cards—bearing upon them names reeking with plebeianism, sewgawed with some paltry title, the synonym and pass-port of insignificance—in contrast with the plain and modest cards of some of the highest peers of the British realm." This example also shows that national differences were experienced as class differences. However, hardly ever would a British author even address *parvenues* in his own country, let alone with strong words like these. Half a century earlier, Tocqueville had observed that "the English make game of the manners of the Americans."[34]

Differences in Introductions, in Snubbing, and in Ways of Addressing Readers

In contrast, many American authors of the early twentieth century explicitly presented the British code as an example: "If we could learn to treat the English people as they treat us in the matter of *introductions,* it would be a great advance. The English regard a letter of introduction as a sacred institution and an obligation which cannot be disregarded." Even when the British code was not explicitly mentioned, implicitly it was often there: "If not friend from childhood, acquaintance between young men and young women begins with an introduction, and this matter of introduction is one rather too lightly considered on our free American soil."[35] In this example, the authors start out to prescribe introductions in an almost command-ing tone, only to withdraw in the same sentence by appealing to the American dream. This quotation demonstrates a typical American ambivalence, to be found in most American etiquette books from around 1900. It is an ambivalence with regard to social usages like introductions and chaperonage, functioning to keep strangers and "intruders" at a distance. These were considered important by some authors and disputed by others, but many were just ambivalent. Taking the matter of introduc-tions "rather too lightly" implied that the ranks of American best society did not close as efficiently as those of English society. This also implied that protection against strangers or intruders was less efficient. This relatively weak protection from strangers, another aspect of America's rather open competition between many best societies, has kept these ranks more dependent on external social controls and has prevented the level of mutual trust from rising: "There are unfortunately many persons abroad in the land without proper social credentials, who seek new fields of adventure by the easy American manner of beginning a conversation." The ambivalence in etiquette books regarding introductions reflects yet another ambivalence: between trust and suspicion, or between the inclination to "converse amicably with strangers about private things" and the need to be evasive and keep a protective distance. This ambivalence might explain another difference:

> in fashionable London society a hostess takes it for granted that her guests understood that she would invite none but well-bred persons to her house, and that, therefore, they are safe in addressing strangers whom they encounter in her drawing-room. Americans, however, have not generally accepted this custom; and consider it better form for a hostess to introduce her guests.

Here, it is implied that Americans were not safe in addressing strangers whom they encountered in a drawing room and that they therefore had not accepted this custom. Instead, they preferred to leave the prime responsibility for new acquaintanceships to the hostess. This subtle difference was significant at that time, because around 1900, American "fashionable circles" still more or less tried to live up to the ideal that

> one individual introducing another becomes responsible for his good behavior, as if he should say, "Permit me to introduce my friend; if he cheats you, charge it to me." Such must be the real value of an introduction among all people who expect to take a place in good society. In the course of business, and under various circumstances, we form casual acquaintances, of whom we really know nothing, and who may really be anything but suitable persons for us to know. It would be wrong, therefore, to bring such characters to the favorable notice of those whom we esteem our friends.[36]

This ideal never died out completely, but it did fade considerably. In the revised 1937 edition of her etiquette book, Emily Post abandoned former, more formal claims by writing, "Under all informal circumstances the roof of a friend serves as an introduction." Her explanation reads, "Yesterday believed in putting the responsibility on the protector. . . . The idea of protection, as it existed then, is out of tune with the world of today."[37] The vanishing of protective rules of etiquette implies that these external social controls had to be taken over by self-controls: people increasingly expected each other to be able to protect themselves.

As social dividing lines in America were less sharply drawn, people wanting to cross these lines were accordingly presented with a much more direct kind of advice than anything to be found in the British sources. American advice such as "If a person is more prominent than ourselves, or more distinguished in any way, we should not be violently anxious to take the first step" or "Too much haste in making new acquaintances, however—'pushing,' as it is called—cannot be too much deprecated" would have sounded much too crude in the ears of British social arbiters of the same period.[38] They took the avoidance of such intruding manners more or less for granted. Consequently, British authors felt no need to point to the sanctions imposed on such conduct, as American advisors did: "there is the tyranny in large cities of what is known as the 'fashionable set,' formed of people willing to spend money. . . . If those who desire an introduction to this set strive for it too much, they will be sure to be snubbed; for this circle lives by snubbing."

This quotation demonstrates another characteristic difference: American authors of etiquette books regularly wrote from the perspective of outsiders—people wanting entrance into "smart circles," *Who's Who,* or the *Social Register.* In contrast, most British authors took their perspective rather exclusively from within best society:

> Years of mingling in good society are necessary to its full development, and though a delicate sense of what is due to others is of the very essence of tact, it is never quite perfect without a knowledge of the gentle art of snubbing. This is an accomplishment which some women never acquire. They cannot firmly repress the unduly officious or the over- eager without adopting harsh measures or losing their temper. Where they should simply ignore, they administer the cut direct.[39]

This British author's perspective reveals a confidence and a degree of identification with the established that is virtually absent in American manners books. A quotation like the last one can be read as another variation of "it takes three generations to make a gentleman," a maxim against which an American expert on how to behave had already protested in 1837: "This is too slow a process in these days of accelerated movement."[40] In this vein, many authors were quite explicit about the class and status gaps their readers were hoping to bridge. In 1905, for example, the introduction to an etiquette book addressed as its readers

> Men and women—women, in particular—to whom changed circumstances or re- moval from secluded homes to fashionable neighborhoods involved the necessity of altered habits of social intercourse; girls, whose parents are content to live and move in the deep ruts in which they and their forebears were born; people of humble lineage and rude bringing up, who yet have longings and tastes for gentlehood and for the harmony and beauty that go with really good breeding—these make up the body of our *clientèle.* Every page of our manual was written with a thought of them in our minds.[41]

Thus the identification of social arbiters with any particular "fashionable set" could only be halfhearted, balancing between an identification with rising outsiders and an identification with the established. A peculiar position was taken by Emily Post. Edmund Wilson contrasts her book to Lilian Eichler's successful etiquette book, published a year earlier (1921); Eichler, he wrote, "makes social life sound easy and jolly. But Mrs. Post is another affair." She "always assumes that the reader wants to belong to Society" and "to believe in the existence of a social Olympus"; moreover,

> What you get in Emily Post, for all her concessions to the age's vulgarization, is a crude version of the social ideal to which the mass of Americans aspired after the Civil War: an ideal that was costly and glossy, smart, self-conscious and a little disgusting in a period when even Mrs. Oldname reflected the lavish Gildings in stimulating her visitors to realize that the clothes she wore were "priceless" and her tableware and furniture museum pieces.[42]

This perspective may partly explain why Emily Post as late as 1922 still continued the attempt to gain greater acceptance for an elaborate system of introductions: a social

Olympus cannot be climbed without pull. Although she admits that "about twenty years ago the era of informality set in and has been gaining ground ever since," she remains rather strict in presenting specific shades and boundaries of introductions; for instance, "A lady who goes to see another to get a reference for a servant, or to ask her aid in an organization for charity, would never consider such a meeting as an introduction, even though they talked for an hour. Nor would she offer to shake hands in leaving." [43] And, according to Post, when people were introduced, this did not necessarily bring recognition: "if Mrs. . . . and Mrs. . . . merely spoke to each other for a few moments, in the drawing-room, it is not necessary that they recognize each other afterwards" (10). At the most, such a conversation could establish a "bowing acquaintanceship," but only if the lady of higher rank took that initiative. This was crucial to what the British called the "right of recognition." [44]

In her revised 1931 edition, this kind of advice was omitted. By that time, in all countries under study, such conduct was branded as too formal and artificial. This branding was typical of the 1920s, when the rise of whole social groups and an acceleration of processes of emancipation and integration were reflected in the shape and volume of the social water tower. The expansion of business and industry, together with an expansion of means of transportation and communication, gave rise to a multitude of new and more casual relationships. These made the old system of introductions too troublesome. It was an era in which many newly wealthy families were jostling for a place within the ranks of good society, bringing about a formidable spurt of informalization. It is then that the often observed American characteristic sometimes called social promiscuity was much more sharply profiled than elsewhere, not only in the eyes of foreign observers, but even by Emily Post. In her 1931 edition she writes, "Fashionable people in very large cities take introductions lightly; they are veritable ships that pass in the night. They show their red or green signals—which are merely polite sentences and pleasant manners—and they pass on again" (15). And in her revised edition of 1937, Post writes explicitly that "introductions in very large cities are unimportant" (16), while her new preface contains the observation that "In the general picture of this modern day the smart and the near-smart, the distinguished and the merely conspicuous, the real and the sham, and the unknown general public are all mixed up together. The walls that used to enclose the world that was fashionable are all down" (x–xi). The relatively modest importance and then further decline of formal rules for "getting acquainted" occurred in all countries under study. The trend implied the increased importance of individual social navigational abilities, the greater capacity to negotiate with ease and lack of friction the possibilities and limitations of relationships. This shift also implied that formal and external rules and constraints had to be taken more into individual custody. Social interweaving also exerted pressure toward an increased avoidance of conflicts, and in conflicts, to increased attempts at de-escalation through "role taking" and by using diplomacy and compromise, not anger, shouting, and ridicule. In the United States this trend was reinforced by studies like the "Hawthorne experiments" of Elton Mayo. An indication is the spread of industrial relations departments in American businesses; during the 1930s, 31 percent of all companies maintained such services. [45] This had spread much more widely in the United States than elsewhere. As to why this was, economic profitability is not likely to be the only explanation. An additional answer is related to the absence of a social class structure like the British in which a relatively high degree of tact, consideration, and tolerance was developed in its best society and had descended the social water tower. America's class system of open competition prevented a further rise in the societal level of mutual trust or mutually expected self-restraints, which made Americans more dependent on external social constraints. In this relational context, Americans developed "social engineering" into a kind of security system in order to control conflicts and the dangerous emotions involved. Industrial relations departments are such a form of external social control; they lubricate, supervise, and pacify, and it is this function of a social constraint toward self-restraint, lowering the level of insecurity, mutual fear, suspicion, and hatred, that helps explain why industrial relations departments spread so early and widely in the United States.

Superlatives and Popularity

The process-continuity of a variety of competing best societies and other groups also helps explain why Americans tend to use superlatives—overstatements, not only according to the British standard—and a relatively open display of feelings of superiority. More open competition and a stronger reliance on supervision and other forms of external social controls have formed a barrier to the development of lower-pitched or subtler forms of expression and negotiation; they continued to stimulate more pronounced and accentuated forms of impression management. "Bragging and boasting," "exaggeration," "national self-consciousness and conceit" appeared as generally recognized American characteristics in a 1941 review.[46] Cole Porter ironized this tradition in his lyric "Anything you can do, I can do better. I can do anything better than you." And in the late 1970s and again in the mid-1990s, Judith Martin did the same by calling her books *Miss Manners' Guide to Excruciatingly Correct Behavior* and *Miss Manners Rescues Civilization*. In some circles, media circles in particular, the use of superlatives in negotiations has reached levels at which the uncertainty about their meaning is pushed up so high that many are left with the question, "What's the bullshit degree?" This use of superlatives is symptomatic of uncertainty of rank, of porous and changing social dividing lines. In circles where social positions are more stable and established, the use of superlatives tends to diminish, as the example of British society demonstrates. Another example is the Republic of the Netherlands in the eighteenth century. In the first part of that century, it had become a civilized custom in Dutch society to outbid each other in mutual compliments. According to the Dutch historian Pieter Spierenburg, customs like these "reflect the fact that within the patriciate there was often no certainty about rank." In the second half of the eighteenth century, when this uncertainty had diminished, "the higher strata in the Republic dropped these forms of ceremonial altogether ... [and] the dropped habits came to be regarded as characteristic of the middle class."[47]

Open competition and its related status-striving may also explain why Americans are more directly and more openly concerned with social success in terms of popularity. In American etiquette books, manners and popularity are closely linked. The manners books from the other countries under study use the term "success" in the sense of gaining respect and appreciation, but the term "popularity" is completely absent. The close link in American books seems to be another symptom of relatively high status insecurity and status consciousness. In the antebellum period, Americans developed a high sensitivity to confidence men and a fear of hypocrisy that were countered by developing a system of "sincerity," as Karen Halttunen has vividly described. In her view, it "expressed the deep concern of status-conscious social climbers that they themselves and those around them were 'passing' for something they were not." After 1870, as she points out, "a new success literature was emerging that effectively instructed its readers to cultivate the arts of the confidence man in order to succeed in the corporate business world."[48] As the expansion of this world stimulated both status insecurity and the circuits in which confidence men could operate successfully, Americans more or less started to beat confidence men at their own game, a peculiar example of "if you can't beat them, join them." This change implies that the link between manners and popularity was established when Americans openly embraced social manipulation (or social engineering) as an art.[49] It was a transformation that can be interpreted as a conciliating mix of middle-class and aristocratic patterns of emotion management: middle-class "sincerity," "honesty," or "true virtue" was mixed with aristocratic "grace," "charm," or "outward politeness." This mix implied a higher level of awareness or reflection than the former, more or less automatic reliance on being principled and sincere. Book titles like *The Secret of Popularity: How to Achieve Social Success* are in themselves clear demonstrations of this embrace. The opening sentence of this book, published in 1904, states that it "has been written to the especial benefit of those men and women who wished to be liked and admired and are not," while its basic message is, "popularity, like charity, begins really at home," a clear attempt to give success striving a basis of sincerity.[50] In 1922, Emily Post also combined old-time sincerity with modern social manipulation. Focusing on young girls, she writes, "Instead of depending on beauty, upon sex-appeal, the young girl who is 'the success of to-day' depends chiefly upon her actual character and disposition. . . . secret of popularity? It is unconscious of self, altruistic interest, and inward kindliness, outwardly expressed in good manners" (287). Here, Post echoes the nineteenth-century demand to demonstrate "perfect sincerity" or "transparency of character." At the same time, the twentieth-century competitive "rating" aspect of popularity is quite outspoken: "In olden days and until a comparatively short while ago, a young girl's social success was invariably measured by her popularity in a ballroom. It was the girl who had the most partners, who least frequently sat 'against the wall' " (284). In 1937, Emily Post had written a whole new chapter on popularity with sections like "Popularity Analyzed," "Lasting or Transient Popularity," and "To Make Ourselves Liked." In the context of the "rating and dating complex," many discussions centered on petting: "The reason many teen-age girls pet is because 'everyone else does' and they're afraid of being unpopular, of missing out on good times! But petting is a high price to pay for popularity." In the 1960s, similar advice read, "Promiscuity isn't a short cut to authentic popularity. . . . You may say, 'Nobody needs to know.' But it never, never remains a secret that a girl is generally available."[51]

Dale Carnegie directly connected popularity and friendship to success in business, and he brought this out straightforwardly in his book's title, *How to Win Friends and Influence People* (1940). This open emphasis on social manipulation as an art, presenting its author as some sort of "charm school" director, seems typically American; in other countries such a title probably would have been banned as too embarrassing to be commercially sound. For instance, in the Netherlands, a translation of Carnegie's book was entitled *How to Make Friends and Establish Good Relations.* Earlier as well as later American book titles, for instance, *How to Make Friends and Deal Effectively in the Global Marketplace,* indicate a tradition of connecting friendship, popularity and business success.[52] In the countries under study, particularly in Germany, and also in France, this is often experienced as a tradition of insincerity and hypocrisy.[53] And indeed, in some cases this American tradition of wanting to be liked and to seek validation from everyone seems to go over the top. Take, for example, these introductory words:

> Too often many of us feel like Willy Loman did in Arthur Miller's classic play, *Death of a Salesman.* Willy said: "Oh, I'm liked, I'm just not *well* liked." We want to be well liked, we want to be able to meet new people without a trace of nervousness or a queasy stomach, we want to know how to be casual and friendly, know how to turn strangers into friends. In short how to unlock the "real you" and have people like you. That's what this book is going to do for you.[54]

Ironically, these lines are an example of exactly that American death-denying mentality—"Winning's not the most important thing, it's the only thing"—against which Miller's play is directed.

"Service" as Profitable and Pacifying

In the 1930s, the rise of "social promiscuity" in the United States, or, in other words, the declining importance of introductions and other such hierarchically differentiated ways of establishing relationships, coincided with an increasing concern for manners in the business world, that is, business etiquette. The Depression may have exerted pressure in this direction, but in the other countries under study, only a few translations from American books on this subject appeared. There, this concern reached comparable intensity only in the 1980s and 1990s, whereas in the United States a large number of sections and articles on the subject had already appeared in the 1930s. According to Deborah Robertson Hodges, author of an annotated bibliography of twentieth-century etiquette books, one of the authors of business etiquette, Joan Wing, "created a niche for herself by proving that improved manners among employees would mean improved efficiency in business."[55] Thus, what Emily Post had formulated rather casually about social navigation in fashionable society—"they show their red or green signals—which are merely polite sentences and pleasant manners"—was taken more seriously, adopted, and further developed in offices and other places of work. In the words of Schlesinger, "And so, by a strange juxtaposition of circumstances, stereotyped politeness, having been ejected from the drawing-room and the dance floor, found an unforeseen asylum in the marts of trade."[56] According to Hodges, "Even the railroads jumped on the courtesy bandwagon, as the [1937] article 'Smile School: Teaching Courtesy and Service to Railroaders, U.P. Trouble-Shooter's Job' would indicate. The trouble-shooter's job is 'instructing railroad employees on the best ways to avoid getting angry at finicky passengers."[57] A little later, via Dale Carnegie's famous book, the smile-school message was spread widely; it has been further developed in literature and campaigns ever since: "no 'attacking or defending' behaviors, please."[58] This literature describes the behavior Arlie Hochschild analyzed in *The Managed Heart* (1983); she has interpreted this kind of smiling and troubleshooting as a "commercial-ization of human feeling." A rival interpretation would see it as the commercializa-tion, or rather the "trickling down," of the pleasant manners of best society via the expansion of commercial classes. It was this "waterfall of imitation descending from the social water-tower" that has resulted in the type of civility for which Harold Nicolson expressed his deep admiration: "They call it 'service,' but we should de-scribe it as a universal gift for being unfailingly helpful, hospitable and polite. It is not a virtue confined to any class; it comes as naturally to a porter at a railway station as it does to the president of a fresh-water university."[59] This "public virtue" did not come naturally, of course, but resulted from the particular development of American society, in which good manners had a particularly important function. Until the present day, manners also have been more strongly emphasized than in the other countries; Americans take etiquette books and doing "the right thing" more seriously, in business and in politics. The latter is expressed in these typically American sentiments, published in 1946: "When manners break down, anarchy begins; and anarchy always ends eventually in force and tyranny of some kind. . . . Fascism and Nazism are modern examples."[60] A similarly serious appreciation of manners was demonstrated by President Bush when he used a term from the discourse of manners in formulating one of the arguments for ending the Gulf War; he said that it would have been "unchivalrous" to continue, for it would have only led to "unnecessary killing." In no other country is the pacifying function of man-ners—to avoid "unnecessary killing" and, of course, other humiliation—so heavily emphasized. The comparatively large overall importance attached to manners can be understood from their specific function in the integration process of a country with a quite open competition between best societies, businesses, and religious and ethnic groups.[61] A casual anecdote on snobs in *How to Be Happy Though Civil,* published in 1909, illuminates this function:

> The greatest snob is polite when he knows that it is safer or more to his interest to be so. "The idea of calling this the Wild West!" exclaimed a lady, travelling in Montana, to one of the old hands. "Why, I never saw such politeness anywhere. The men here all treat each other like gentlemen in the drawing-room!" "Yes, Marm, it's safer," laconi-cally replied the native, with a glance at his six-shooter.

Taken more broadly, this anecdote suggests that the waterfall of imitation was enforced by "American tough."[62] In the absence of specific rules of procedure for avoiding "strangers" and situations that might be dangerous (avoiding anger), both "American tough" and "have-a-nice-day" manners can be interpreted as functional successions to the protection provided by introductions, cards, and calling. The same goes for the multitude of American expressions like "take it easy," "no sweat," or "keep your shirt on." This "take-it-easy" custom has been interpreted (in 1943) as evidence of the desire of Americans "to avoid mental and physical irritation and the strain that follows it." In contrast to the tough-guy tradition, the "take-it-easy" and "have-a-nice-day" customs function not only to lubricate social intercourse but also to pacify it. They are another form of external social control, a kind of security system, preventing and containing conflicts and the dangerous emotions involved. They form a social constraint toward self-restraint through which the level of insecurity, mutual fear, suspicion, and hatred is lowered. In a country where so many "tough guys" of so many diverse groups are fiercely involved in open competition, where the state has rather incompletely monopolized the use of violence—where there are so many weapons around (that are used to kill and wound people)—the need "to avoid getting angry," not just at "finicky customers" but in all situations, has been quite pressing. This necessity illuminates Peabody's observations that "for Americans, a tradition of violence exists side by side with a desire to be liked by everyone" and that Americans in particular try to avoid public hostility and get "along with others without friction by smiling affably."[63]

In this chapter, I have attempted to describe developments in emotion management via changes in a few topics in manners books that stand out as specifically American. I have illuminated them mainly by placing them in a wider international comparative context, focusing on connections between differences and changes in national class structures and differences and changes in specific patterns of emotion management. The specific processes of social integration in each country, particularly the ways the ranks of the falling strata have been opened up by and to the rising strata, appear to have been decisive for the form and manner in which their distinctive patterns of emotion management influenced each other, and for the type of mixture that finally resulted as a national habitus. In other words, each national habitus emerged from the specific process of change in the relative power-chances of the rising and falling strata, from their specific forms and levels of competition and cooperation. National variations in these processes are reflected in the particular ways the courtesy genre of manners books developed into the etiquette genre. By comparative analysis of changes in ways of addressing readers, in the usage of social introductions and in social dividing lines between public and private, formal and informal, I have tried to illuminate the specifically American integration process, characterized by relatively open competition, a high level of (status) anxiety, and a comparatively strong reliance on external social controls. The development of a specifically American cultural structure—particularly the different importance of high society, its weaker protection against intruders, a rather high level of anxiety with regard to status, anger, and violence, and, correspondingly, a lower level of mutual trust—helps explain several aspects of the American habitus, such as a smaller formality-informality span, "American tough," "take-it-easy," and "have-a-nice-day" manners, the use of superlatives, a preoccupation with popularity, and social manipulation or engineering. In the description of these connections, the contours of the development of a specifically American overall emotional style have been outlined.

NOTES

My thanks to Johan Goudsblom, Richard Kilminster, Michael Schröter, Pieter Spierenburg, and Peter Stearns for valuable comments, as well as to Stephen Mennell, who revised my English.

1. The American transformation from the courtesy genre to the etiquette genre is solidly presented by C. Dallett Hemphill, "Middle Class Rising in Revolutionary America: The Evidence from Manners," *Journal of Social History* 30 (winter 1996): 317–44; this quotation, 333.

2. This chapter results from a larger comparative study; for earlier reports, see Cas Wouters, "Etiquette Books and Emotion Management in the 20th Century; Part One: The Integration of Social Classes," *Journal of Social History* 29 (1995): 107–24, and "Part Two: The Integration of the Sexes," *Journal of Social History* 29 (1995): 325–40.

3. Gabriel Tarde, *Laws of Imitation* (1903; original 1890), 221; see also Pitirim A. Sorokin, *Social and Cultural Mobility* (New York: Free Press, 1964), 549–640. The term "trickle effect" is from Lloyd A. Fallers, "A Note on the Trickle Effect," *Public Opinion Quarterly* 18 (1954): 314–21. There are many earlier formulations of this model function. De Tocqueville, for instance, distinguished between the copying of manners in aristocracies and copying in a democracy (America). In a democracy, he wrote, "manners are constantly characterized by a number of lesser diversities, but not by any great differences. They are never perfectly alike because they do not copy from the same pattern; they are never very unlike because their social condition is the same." *Democracy in America* (New York: Vintage, 1945), 2:229. An earlier such formulation can be read in the introduction to the Dutch translation of Freiherr von Knigge's famous courtesy book (1788):

> The courts, as they are the center to which everything flows, they are also the center or general source from which the mentality and way of life of nations is steadily springing and receiving its alterations. This goes in particular for the more civilized circuits; not only in the monarchical countries, although it is from there that everything spreads to nation after nation, at least in Europe . . . even those far away in the barren North, have tuned in.

J. H. Swildens, "Over den tegenwoordigen toestand der samenleving in onze republiek," in Knigge, *Over de verkeering met menschen* (Amsterdam, 1789), LXXXIX; quoted in Pieter Spierenburg, *Elites and Etiquette: Mentality and Social Structure in the Early Modern Northern Netherlands* (Rotterdam: Centrum voor Maatschappijgeschiedenis, Erasmus University, 1981), 9:28.

4. Arthur M. Schlesinger, *Learning How to Behave: A Historical Study of American Etiquette Books* (New York: Macmillan, 1946), 65–66; Emily Post, *Etiquette in Society, in Business, in Politics and at Home* (New York: Funk and Wagnalls 1922), xxvii. Revised editions were published in 1927, 1931, 1934, 1937, 1942, 1950, and 1960. Subsequent citations will specify the edition cited.

5. Norbert Elias, *The Civilizing Process* (Cambridge: Blackwell, 1994), 511.

6. See Wouters, "Integration of Social Classes"; idem, "Integration of the Sexes"; and idem, "On Status Competition and Emotion Management," *Journal of Social History* 24 (4) (1991): 699–717. See also Abram de Swaan, "Widening Circles of Social Identification: Emotional Concerns in Sociogenetic Perspective," *Theory, Culture and Society* 12 (1995): 25–39.

7. See Norbert Elias, *The Germans: Power Struggles and the Development of Habitus in the Nineteenth and Twentieth Centuries* (Cambridge: Polity Press, 1996), 459–60.

8. Michael Curtin, *Propriety and Position: A Study in Victorian Manners* (New York: Garland, 1987), 110.

9. Chet Cunningham, *How to Meet People and Make Friends* (Leucadia, CA: United Research Publishers, 1992), xi; Hemphill, "Middle Class Rising," 321.

10. J. P. A. Coopmans, "Het Plakkaat van Verlatinge (1581) en de Declaration of Independence

(1776)," *Bijdragen en Mededelingen betreffende de Geschiedenis der Nederlanden* 98 (1983): 540–67. The "process of aristocratization" (Spierenburg, *Elites and Etiquette*) was not unique to the Netherlands. In the United States too, after the decline of a "southern aristocracy" before and during the Civil War, ruling classes again attempted with some success to function as an aristocracy; see E. Digby Baltzell, *The Protestant Establishment: Aristocracy and Caste in America* (New Haven: Yale University Press, 1987, orig. 1964); Seymour Martin Lipset, *The First New Nation: The United States in Historical and Comparative Perspective* (Garden City, NY: Anchor Books, 1967, orig. 1963); Johan Goudsblom, *Dutch Society* (New York: Random House, 1967), 154.

11. Elias, *The Germans*, 296 (on compromising, 113, 133, 163, 199); Hans-Otto Meissner, *Man benimmt sich wieder* (Giessen: Brühlscher, 1951), 242–43.

12. Elias, *Civilizing Process*, 505–6.

13. Hemphill, "Middle Class Rising," 325; Stephen Kahlberg, "West German and American Interaction Forms: One Level of Structured Misunderstanding," *Theory, Culture and Society* 4 (1987): 603–18, here 608; see also Kurt Lewin, *Resolving Social Conflict* (New York: Harper and Row, 1948).

14. R. Dahrendorf, *Society and Democracy in Germany* (Garden City, NY: Doubleday, 1969), 300; Dean Peabody, *National Characteristics* (New York: Cambridge University Press, 1985), 113.

15. Elias, *Civilizing Process*, 13–21; De Tocqueville already observed a similar difference:

> In aristocracies the rules of propriety impose the same demeanor on everyone; they make all the members of the same class appear alike in spite of their private inclinations; they adorn and conceal the natural man. Among a democratic people manners are neither so tutored nor so uniform, but they are frequently more sincere. They form, as it were, a light and loosely woven veil through which the real feelings and private opinions of each individual are easily discernable. The form and substance of human actions, therefore, often stand there in closer relation. (*Democracy in America*, 2:230)

16. Kahlberg, "Interaction Forms," 616.

17. Gertrud Oheim, *Einmaleins des guten Tons* (Gütersloh: Bertelsmann, 1955), 29.

18. For recent warnings against *duzen* at office parties, see, for example, Sybil Gräfin Schönfeldt, *1 x 1 des guten Tons* (München: Mosaik Verlag, 1987; and Hamburg, 1991), 273; and Irmgard Wolter, *Der Gute Ton in Gesellschaft und Beruf* (Niedernhausen/Ts.: Falken Bücherei, 1990), 75–76; the quotation is from Oheim, *Einmaleins*, 133.

19. Elias, *The Germans*, 28; for examples of German informalization, see Wouters, "Integration of Social Classes."

20. Moyra Bremner, *Enquire Within upon Modern Etiquette and Successful Behaviour for Today* (London: Century, 1989), 20; see Lewin, *Resolving Social Conflict*, his illustrative drawings in particular.

21. David Riesman (with N. Glazer and R. Denney), *The Lonely Crowd* (New Haven: Yale University Press, 1969, orig. 1950); and Ralf Dahrendorf, *Die angewandte Aufklärung* (Frankfurt: Fischer, 1968). S. M. Lipset presents a connection between competition, status uncertainty, and conformity; he views the latter as resulting from status striving. *First New Nation*, 127–29.

22. Curtin, *Propriety and Position*, 121. An interesting comparison of English and Austrian habitus is Helmut Kuzmics, "Österreichischer und englisher Volkscharakter," in H. Nowotny and K. Taschwer, eds., *Macht und Ohnmacht im neuen Europa* (Vienna: WUV, 1993).

23. James Millar, *How to Be a Perfect Gentleman* (London: Rosters, 1897), 43–44.

24. Peabody, *National Characteristics*, 99.

25. Quoted in Cecil Porter, *Not without a Chaperone: Modes and Manners from 1897 to 1914* (London: New English Library, 1972), 24–25.

26. Curtin, *Propriety and Position*, 107.

27. Millar, *How to be a Perfect Gentleman*, 32; see the change in the meaning of "snob" in Wouters, "Integration of Social Classes."

28. Leonore Davidoff, *The Best Circles: Society, Etiquette and the Season* (London: Croom Helm, 1973), 102.

29. Tom Wolfe, *Radical Chic and Mau-Mauing the Flak Catchers* (New York: Farrar, Straus and Giroux, 1970), 35.

30. Gerald Carson, *The Polite Americans: A Wide-Angle View of Our More or Less Good Manners over 300 Years* (New York: William Morrow, 1966), 240. Carson views the "country club" as "an American improvisation, now about eighty years old, [which] provides a rough equivalent of the English weekend, adapted to American conditions" (244); see also Baltzell, *Protestant Establishment,* 123.

31. Harold Nicolson, *Good Behaviour: Studies of Certain Types of Civility* (London: Constable, 1955), 18.

32. Davidoff, *The Best Circles,* 102.

33. *Habits of Good Society: A Handbook of Etiquette* (London: James Hogg and Sons, 1859); Censor, *Don't: A Manual of Mistakes and Improprieties More or Less Prevalent in Conduct and Speech* (London: Field and Tuer, 1884), 5–6.

34. Millar, *How to Be a Perfect Gentleman,* 53. It is telling that rare exceptions in the British sources—sentences like "I have lunched in the house of a *nouveau riche* where they seemed to line the dining room with footmen and other servants, till it was positively oppressive" or "One occasionally meets vulgar people who seek to impress those around them with their own (supposed) superiority"—were deleted from a later edition. Flora Klickmann, *The Etiquette of To-day* (London, 1902), 33–48, (later edition was 1915); Tocqueville, *Democracy in America,* 2:229.

35. Mary E. W. Sherwood, *Manners and Social Usages* (New York: Harper, 1907), 359; Marion Harland and Virginia van de Water, *Everyday Etiquette: A Practical Manual of Social Usages* (Indianapolis: Bobbs-Merrill, 1905), 123.

36. Margaret Wade, *Social Usage in America* (New York: Thomas Crowell, 1924), 28; Emily Holt, *The Secret of Popularity: How to Achieve Social Success* (New York: McClure, Phillips, 1901), 9. Revised editions were published in 1904 and 1920; John Wesley Hanson, Jr., *Etiquette of To-Day: The Customs and Usages Required by Polite Society* (Chicago, 1896), 45.

37. Post, *Etiquette,* 1937 ed., 10, 353.

38. Hanson, *Etiquette,* 38; Sherwood, *Manners,* 2.

39. Hanson, *Etiquette,* 38–9; Mrs. C. E. Humphry, *Etiquette for Every Day* (London: Richards, 1897), 72. The "cut direct" is "to look directly at another and not acknowledge the other's bow . . . a direct stare of blank refusal." Post, *Etiquette,* 1940 ed., 30.

40. Quoted in Schlesinger, *Learning how to Behave,* 20.

41. Harland and de Water, *Everyday Etiquette.*

42. Edmund Wilson, "Books of Etiquette and Emily Post," in *Classics and Commercials: A Literary Chronicle of the Forties* (New York: Vintage, 1962), 375–81.

43. Post, *Etiquette,* 1922 ed., 81, 15. Mrs. Post was not that exceptional; Margaret Wade, in *Social Usage in America,* presented similarly strict rules for introductions.

44. Hanson, *Etiquette,* 38–39; Humphry, *Etiquette for Every Day,* 72; The "right of recognition" has found an optimal expression in the joke about the lady who refuses to "recognize" a man by saying, "sexual intercourse is no social introduction."

45. Peter N. Stearns, *American Cool: Constructing a Twentieth-Century Emotional Style* (New York: New York University Press, 1994), 125.

46. L. Coleman, "What Is American? A Study of Alleged American Traits," *Social Forces* 19 (1941): 492–99. A befriended businessman told me an amusing example of open display of feelings of superiority. Once, he was told, "You're a real pro; you can charm a monkey's balls! But there's a difference between you and me: I can do it *all* the time."

47. Spierenburg, *Elites and Etiquette,* 9:30.

48. Karen Halttunen, *Confidence Men and Painted Women* (New Haven: Yale University Press, 1982), xv, 198.

49. Another indication follows from a book on dating; in the 1958 edition a section headed "How to Be Popular" was changed to "Learning Social Skills" in the 1968 edition. Evelyn Millis Duvall with Joy Duvall Johnson, *The Art of Dating* (New York: Association Press, 1958, 1968), 17. It may also indicate that the traditional emphasis on popularity increasingly came to be experienced as embarrassingly direct and crude.

50. Holt, *Secret of Popularity*, 1904 ed., 241.

51. Willard Waller, "The Rating and Dating Complex," *American Sociological Review* 2 (1937), 727–34; Lilian Eichler Watson, *The Standard Book of Etiquette* (Garden City, NY: Garden City Publishing, 1948), 479; Elisabeth L. Post, *Emily Post's Etiquette*, 15th ed. (New York: HarperCollins, 1992), 152.

52. For example, Mary A. Hopkins, *Profits from Courtesy* (Garden City, NY: Doubleday, 1937); Cunningham, *How to Meet People;* Lennie Copeland and Lewis Griggs, *Going International: How to Make Friends and Deal Effectively in the Global Marketplace* (New York: Plume, 1986).

53. Raymonde Carroll, *Cultural Misunderstandings: The French-American Experience*, trans. Carol Volk (Chicago: University of Chicago Press, 1989).

54. Cunningham, *How to Meet People*, xi.

55. Deborah Robertson Hodges, *Etiquette: An Annotated Bibliography of Literature Published in English in the United States, 1900 through 1987* (Jefferson, NC: McFarland, 1989), 8.

56. Schlesinger, *Learning How to Behave*, 61.

57. Hodges, *Etiquette*, 8–9.

58. Stearns, *American Cool*, 310.

59. Arlie Russell Hochschild, *The Managed Heart: Commercialization of Human Feeling* (Berkeley: University of California Press, 1983); Nicolson, *Good Behaviour*, 16.

60. Struthers Burt, "Manners Maykth Man," *Ladies' Home Journal* 63 (May 1946), 6, quoted in Hodges, *Etiquette*, 9.

61. Before the 1950s, ethnic minority groups had been largely excluded from the "open" competition. From then on, African Americans had become sufficiently powerful to force white people to take their feelings and interests more into account. America's relatively high level of segregation on grounds of religion, ethnic background, or race had to be increasingly faced and its history of "open" competitiveness reconsidered. The tensions and conflicts involved in this process came to function as a barrier to further increases in the level of mutual trust and provided additional motives for avoiding public hostility and anger.

62. E. J. Hardy, *How to Be Happy Though Civil* (New York: Scribner's, 1909), 279; Rupert Wilkinson, *American Tough: The Tough-Guy Tradition and American Character* (Westport, CT: Greenwood, 1984).

63. John Whyte, *American Words and Ways Especially for German Americans* (New York: Viking, 1943), 131; Peabody, *National Characteristics*, 174–211.

Chapter Fifteen

Something Old, Something New
Romance and Marital Advice in the 1920s

David R. Shumway

In almost any bookstore today one can find a large section devoted to self-help books; among those, perhaps the largest category promises aid in improving intimate relationships. In one sense, such books could be understood to belong to a long-established genre, one that goes back at least to *The Art of Courtly Love* and would include various conduct books and seduction manuals of the seventeenth and eighteenth centuries and the guides to good health and moral hygiene of the Victorian era. In another sense, however, contemporary advice literature on relationships has a much more recent origin, dating to the 1910s and becoming common in the 1920s and 1930s. What distinguishes contemporary advice literature is precisely its focus on a new object, "the relationship" itself. Earlier advice literature taught individuals how to achieve their desired ends—the avoidance of pain, successful seduction, healthy offspring, and so on. What such literature didn't seek to do is teach people how to relate to each other. Relating was assumed to be natural, but also unteachable, and what's more, not terribly important. How having a good relationship came to be important is the subject of this essay.

My explanation will focus on two women whose writing reflects in different ways the beginning of the shift to the relationship. Though both women were British subjects, they were influential figures in America. Elinor Glyn first attained notoriety as the author of the salacious best-seller *Three Weeks* (1907), and by the 1920s she was well known to the American public as a writer of romantic novels and screenplays. She described herself as "a writer on psychological subjects which interest the average citizen" as well as a writer of romances.[1] Her book *The Philosophy of Love* (1923) collected essays published in popular magazines, and though it does not seem to have been a big seller, the original essays were available to a wide readership. Moreover, as we will see, *The Philosophy of Love* strongly reflects the ideology embodied in Glyn's popular fiction and screenplays. Marie Carmichael Stopes, a paleobotanist, sexologist, and birth-control crusader, wrote advice books that were best-sellers, and she is far better remembered as an author of such books. *Married Love* (1920) and *Enduring Passion* (1931) continued to sell into the 1950s, the former being the first book to successfully mediate sexology to a general audience.[2] For her trouble, Stopes was prosecuted for indecency; Glyn had also run afoul of English morals, having been excluded from society for *Three Weeks,* the stage version of which was refused permission for public performance. If both women were perceived as a threat to public morals, the character of their work differed greatly. Stopes's major concern is physical relations between a husband and wife, and the two books mentioned here are sex manuals. Glyn, on the other hand, never describes sexual acts in her advice literature or in *Three Weeks.* Her offense was not explicit language, but the supposed endorsement of an intentionally brief adulterous relationship.

While both authors were associated in the public mind with sex, their advice books are of interest for other reasons. What the advice literature of both authors has in common is the depiction of ideal marriage in terms taken from fictional romances, terms that had been explicitly applied not to marriage but rather to courtship or extramarital relations. My argument is that this explicit endorsement of romantic marriage marks a shift from nineteenth-century advice literature, which regarded romantic love with suspicion. In Glyn and Stopes, romance is no longer merely presented as fantasy or diversion, but rather is endorsed as an appropriate image of married life. By endorsing romance, however, Glyn and Stopes continue a discourse about love that had emerged in the Middle Ages and that had already had a strong impact on American culture through fiction. The effect of continuing this discourse was to perpetuate the construction of gender typical of the nineteenth century but also to make marriage as a relationship an object of discussion, and this discussion opened the door to the development of a postromantic vision of love that I call intimacy. It is my view that this change in the conception of love is at least as significant as the more frequently observed phenomenon of "sexualization."[3]

There is general agreement that the advice literature of this period represents an important shift from earlier, Victorian forms. The most frequently observed change is the increased importance of sex, which is seen as reflective of a "transformation in sexual mores . . . described as liberalization or modernization."[4] The main characteristic of this transformation is increased sexual activity on the part of women, especially middle-class women. A number of studies have interpreted this phenomenon as women having regained their sexual desire, of which Victorian mores had deprived them, and psychoanalysis is often cited as the chief source of this new way of thinking.[5] Steven Seidman titled his study of love in America *Romantic Longings,* but the major change he discusses in twentieth-century advice literature is that "sexual satisfaction . . . now assumes a primary role" in the foundation of a good marriage.[6]

Another change, however, involved the increasing importance of marriage as a source of individual happiness. Thus, as Francesca Cancian has observed, by the 1920s advice books assumed that "the highest personal happiness comes from marriage based on romantic love."[7] Elaine May argues that such rising expectations fueled the exponential rise in the divorce rate in post-Victorian America.[8] While not neglecting popular advisers, such as syndicated columnist Dorothy Dix, May attributes the spread of these rising expectations largely to the image of love presented in movies and in stories about the off-screen lives of movie stars. She argues that movies and other popular media presented a superficial conception of an ideal marriage, one that was likely to occur after equally superficial rituals of courtship

(69). She asks, "What followed the happy ending?" and reports that Hollywood stars like Mary Pickford and Douglas Fairbanks—who left their respective spouses to marry each other—seemed to realize the ideal marriage (75–76). May's account of the influence of film and other media representations is persuasive, but it leaves us wondering about the emergence of this new romantic conception of marriage. Where did it come from, and why were American audiences so ready to accept it? In order to answer these questions, we need to understand romantic love of the twentieth century in the context of the long history of the discourses of romance.

The term "romantic love" is sometimes used to describe love accompanied by sexual attachment, but I will use it here to describe a culturally specific discourse. Following Giddens, I hold that one can distinguish a more or less universally human capability, which he calls "passionate love," from "romantic love," a way of writing and thinking about love that is distinctive to the cultures of Western Europe.[9] This discourse has a definite history, having emerged in the late Middle Ages, when it appeared, according to Rougemont, as theology (the Catharist heresy), a new set of manners (courtly love), and a new form of literature (the medieval romance, for example, *Tristan*).[10] Rougemont's work makes clear the historical specificity of Western romantic love, but the conception of it he describes is different from the love described in the advice books that concern us here.[11] Rougemont claims that "Happy love has no history. Romance only comes into existence where love is fatal, frowned upon and doomed by life itself."[12]

This conception of romance is absent from the surface text of the advice books, however, which reflect a more recent conception of romance.[13] According to Niklas Luhmann, romantic love did not become firmly linked to marriage until the nineteenth century, when "passionate love [was proclaimed] to be the very principle upon which the *choice* of a spouse should be based—in other words, a love match."[14] While Rougemont's model assumes a fundamental incompatibility between romance and marriage, the romantic ideology of the nineteenth century assumed their inseparability. Thus, as Luhmann puts it, "the old thesis of the incompatibility of love and marriage had to be covered up; the end of the novel was not the end of life."[15] It is this later version of the romantic ideology that was dominant in America during the nineteenth century. American historical romances of the late nineteenth and early twentieth centuries—the most popular genre of fiction during this period—unite romantic love and marriage more explicitly than was typical of novels earlier in the nineteenth century. The characteristic version of the romantic ideology in the historical romance holds that there is a right man or woman for each person. It projects a life story that involves meeting that individual and living with him or her in marriage.

To illustrate this vision of romance, let us look at the conclusion to *The Crisis* (1901), Winston Churchill's best-selling novel of the Civil War. Though this novel touches on many of the major events and issues of the war, its central question is who its heroine, Virginia, will marry. The solution to this problem is delayed until the last chapter, where it is revealed that the hero, Stephen, and Virginia have loved each other all along, though she had "struggled against it." Both lovers admit that they dreamt of each other. Virginia agrees to marry Stephen the next day, saying, "I have no one but you—now." After they are married, Stephen tells Virginia, "some force that we cannot understand has brought us together, some force that we could not hinder. . . . when I first saw you, I had a premonition about you that I have never admitted until now even to myself." To which she replies, "Why, Stephen, . . . I felt the same way!"[16]

We find in these passages virtually the whole nineteenth- century discourse of romance in a nutshell. Love is tested against a series of obstacles. It leads inevitably to marriage, and both love and marriage are somehow foreordained. The marriage is not merely good or loving, but cosmically meant to be. The couple are defined against the rest of the world, including their own parents. They have only each other, but that is exactly what they should have. Other ties would merely interfere with their love. Though this novel has been set against a great social struggle, it ends with an absolutely private resolution, a retreat from social life to the promise of conjugal bliss and the creation of a nuclear family. However, the marriage itself is not depicted, and it is to the point that there are no other significant married characters. As *The Crisis* illustrates, novels now ended with marriage rather than death, but love inside marriage remained largely beyond description.

It is my hypothesis that fiction played the leading role in the dissemination of this nineteenth-century version of romantic love. We have evidence from such sources as letters and diaries that romantic love was indeed increasingly the dominant conception of the grounds for marriage during the nineteenth century.[17] Romantic love had long been the chief matter of extended fictional narratives, but the role and form of the novel in the nineteenth century were new. It is widely held that the novel as a genre emerges in the eighteenth century in the form of narratives that presented themselves as more realistic than earlier "romances." But in the nineteenth century, a new subgenre emerges, the romance novel, typified by the work of Scott and the Brontës. While such works are often today accused of a lack of realism, they claimed the same status as other novels. More important, perhaps, during the nineteenth century the novel became a medium of mass entertainment. The cost of production declined with advances in technology, and novels came to reach ever larger audiences. The habit of reading novels was regarded with suspicion, not so much on religious grounds, but out of a fear of their power to sway impressionable minds. Without questioning the ability of readers to distinguish novels as fiction, one can argue that it was the capacity of the novel to engender emotional involvement in the reader, especially in the form of identification, that made the novel so successful and so powerful. By living fictional romances vicariously, readers came to desire romantic love in their own lives. At the end of the nineteenth century, other media came to compete with the novel to entertain Americans, but mass-circulation magazines and movies continued to depend heavily on the discourse of romance, which circulated all the more widely as a result.

Because of the absence of marriage itself from the fictional discourse of romance, those who sought to explain what romantic marriage might mean could not discover an answer in novels. Novels and other fictional forms, however, were not all that modern lovers and their would-be advisers had to learn from. Nineteenth-century advice literature, however, seems to have conveyed mixed messages about romantic love. Many advice books claiming religious or medical authority, including Dr. J. H. Kellog's best-selling *Plain Facts for Young and Old,* seem to have rejected romantic love entirely.[18] These books "rarely mention affection or companionship" and claim that "a sound marriage is based on being religious, industrious, and healthy, and sex is for the purpose of procreation only."[19] On the other hand, most Victorian advice literature regards love as an essential element of a good marriage, and most assume that it will be the basis for the choice of a partner. Peter Stearns shows that the Victorians often extolled the virtues of passion, especially passionate love, but that they distinguished such "pure" love from "animal passion" or mere physical attraction. Victorian advisers often regarded love as a transcendent force that they understood in metaphysical terms: " 'True love ... appertains mainly to ... this cohabitation of soul with a soul. . . . It is this spiritual affinity of the mental masculine and feminine for each other.' Religiouslike intensity was love's hallmark."[20] Such intense love may seem to us "romantic," but, as Seidman argues, "The opposition between 'romantic' and 'true love' appeared prominently in middle class Victorian culture."[21] True love was spiritual and, as a result, it was constant; romantic love was fickle. As one nineteenth-century lover described it, romantic love is "a golden vagary, a self-created illusion, a spring-dream full of the flutter of doves wings."[22] As late as 1904, advisers could be heard asserting the need to "free the minds of young people from the romantic idea."[23] To avoid the illusions of romantic love required that "lovers had to know each other as thoroughly as possible," an injunction that in turn assumed "a norm of mutual self-disclosure."[24] This advice, of course, assumes the kind of reflective self-knowledge that would be seen in the twentieth century as blocked by the unconscious and compromised by power relations. In addition, such advice applied mainly to courtship; advisers were silent (except for repeating familiar religious formulas) on how spouses were to maintain transcendent love. Nineteenth-century advice books, then, failed as much as novels to translate their vision of courtship into a model of marriage that told people how to fulfill that vision.

Twentieth-century advice givers were driven to offer their instruction because marriage seemed not to be living up to its billing. In a larger sense, marriage no longer could be left to nature. As Glyn puts it in *The Philosophy of Love,* "Once upon a time Marriage was not considered a 'problem.' It was the natural course of events, and all in a day's work. But that was in the 'good old days' when a man was supreme master . . . and Woman was a chattel" (47). This corresponds to Luhmann's narrative in which the rise of romantic love is said to occur at the same time as the decline of male domination within the family. Under the old model the patriarch was morally enjoined to love all his property, including wife, children, and servants. In the regime of romance, love is established through the subjectivity of the beloved, and thus a wife cannot be mere property.[25] But as May points out, male dominance in society meant that "for women, finding and catching the right man was the key to personal fulfillment—the very essence of life" (71).[26] Men had other sources of fulfillment, but they too were disappointed by wives who did not live up to the romantic allure. With many marriages failing and many more failing to satisfy, one can see why advice about marriage would become such a hot commodity.

One course that advice givers might have taken would have been to provide readers with lower or at least different expectations of marriage, but this tack was not typical. More typical are the advice books under discussion here, which set very high expectations indeed. Some of these expectations derive from the Victorian advisers' spiritual conception of love with its religious intensity, but they also draw on romantic discourse about courtship and extramarital relations. *Married Love* depicts marriage as a "glorious unfolding" in which both partners are "transmuted" as in the chemical bonding of two elements to form a third.[27] Stopes's later book promised nothing less than *Enduring Passion.* Glyn envisions even more. *The Philosophy of Love* begins with a chapter titled "Ideal Love," which describes a "Perfect Love, ... a love so infinite that on neither side is there a shadow of difference in intensity. A perfect understanding, a holy meeting upon the planes of the soul, the brain, and the body. A complete trust, which is above outside influences. A physical satisfaction which sanctifies all material things. ... Such love is pure Heaven on earth" (14–15). Later, ideal marriage is described as "the infinite bliss of the mating of the soul in peace and freedom from anxiety" (62). Glyn acknowledges that few marriages meet this ideal, but she offers it as a possibility, a goal. We can recognize, I think, in Glyn's quasi-religious language a vision of intimacy, but as we will see, neither Stopes nor Glyn recognizes intimacy as the problem.

Since Marie Stopes's books were mainly concerned with physical relations, one might be surprised by my claim that her work depends on the discourse of romantic love. Seidman, for example, thinks that Stopes simply confuses "the language of love with the language of eroticism."[28] But as Lesley Hall has asserted, "in *Married Love* and its sequels [Stopes] was rewriting traditional narratives of marriage. ... *Married Love* propounded that far from being the end of romance and adventure, marriage was only the beginning."[29] It is apparent, I think, that Stopes's new narrative is rooted in the discourse of romance. *Married Love* begins, "Every heart desires a mate. For some reason beyond our comprehension, nature has so created us that we are incomplete in ourselves." Thus does Stopes naturalize not—or not merely—heterosexual desire, but monogamous marriage. The opening chapter of *Married Love* sounds very much like the vision of marriage at the end of romances like *The Crisis,* so that marriage is described as not merely a meeting of minds and bodies, but also a supernatural connection: "the innermost spirit of one and all so yearns as for a sense of union with another soul" (2). The descriptions of love Stopes uses would be regarded as excessive in any romantic novel: bodily differences are "mystical, alluring, enchanting in their promise"; lovers are "conscious of entering a new and glorious state. ... and see reflected in each other's eyes the beauty of the world ... a celestial intoxication"; "From the body of the loved one ... there springs ... the enlargement of the horizon of human sympathy and the glow of spiritual understanding which a solitary soul could never have attained alone" (3–8).

But the romantic vision presented in chapter 1 is, as chapter 2 tells us, too often unrealized—which is, of course, why Stopes wrote the book. Her explanation for the unhappiness of so many marriages—"there are tragically few which approach even humanly attainable joy"—is that most married couples remain ignorant of how to satisfy one another sexually (12). This affects both men and women, but differently:

in the early days of marriage the young man is often even more sensitive, more romantic . . . and he enters the marriage hoping for an even higher degree of spiritual and bodily unity than does the girl or woman. But the man is more quickly blunted, more swiftly rendered cynical. . . . On the other hand, the woman is slower to realise disappointment, and more often by the sex-life of the marriage is of the two the more *profoundly* wounded. (13, italics in original)

The "perfect happiness" envisioned in chapter 1 and expected by betrothed couples is possible, Stopes implies, but sexual failure prevents it.

Stopes does seem to reduce the intimate relationship to a sexual one, but the questions of interest to us are why she sees marriage in this way and why so many people seemed to find this picture of marriage helpful or enlightening. One obvious answer, *pace* Foucault, is that the Victorian era had repressed sexual knowledge. The traditional narrative of marriage had promised love, but it had not promised sexual satisfaction, which women were not even supposed to want and men were supposed to find elsewhere. As Stopes reports, "By the majority of 'nice' people woman is supposed to have no spontaneous sex-impulses" (37). Stopes not only provides practical knowledge about how to make sex more satisfying, but her new narrative depicts marriage as a relationship no longer dominated by men's needs. Creating a successful relationship is a matter of "mutual adjustment," as she titles one of her chapters. In Stopes's view, men and women have naturally different sexual needs, to which each partner must adjust, but she also holds that each couple must discover how they in particular can best satisfy each other: "it often takes several years for eager and intelligent couples fully to probe themselves to discover the extent and meaning of the immensely profound physiological and spiritual results of marriage" (77).

Stopes's books provided information that both men and women lacked and also a new conception of the role of sex in marriage that spoke powerfully to women, whose pleasure and desire had previously been ignored. But Stopes's advice is not offered merely in the service of greater pleasure or more equal relations, but rather in the quest to attain "marriage . . . as perfect, and hence as joyous, as possible" (158). Stopes's high expectations of marriage and the notion that they may be fulfilled by means of better knowledge about sex both derive from the discourse of romance. During the nineteenth century, marriage came increasingly to be seen as the promise of romantic love, a transcendent conclusion to the passionate adventure of courtship. Stopes accepts all that the discourse of romance invested in marriage, but she recognizes that most marriages did not pay off on that investment by living up to the promise of romance. In deciding that unsatisfactory sexual relations were the cause of this failure, Stopes located the problem where the discourse of romance told her to look for it. As Rougemont implies, romance has always been more about desire than about its satisfaction. Romantic discourse originally denied the possibility of satisfaction, but during the nineteenth century it came to be located in marriage— or at least in a courtship presumed to lead seamlessly to marriage. This connection is not made explicit by Stopes, but it is implicit in at least two places. In *Married Love*, the chapter "Modesty and Romance" urges couples not to become too familiar with each other, and if possible to maintain separate bedrooms. This advice is meant to avoid the problem that "woman . . . has been so thoroughly 'domesticated' by man that she feels too readily that after marriage she is all his. And by her very docility to his perpetual demands she destroys for him the elation, the palpitating thrills and surprises, of the chase" (96). What this advice does is bring the obstacle, which is indispensable to romance narratives, into marriage itself. As we will see, this tactic is central to Glyn's program.

The title of Stopes's later book, *Enduring Passion,* reveals its link to the discourse of romance, for passion is the characteristic state of the romantic subject, a state that was not previously understood to endure or to exist in marriage. The book is "Dedicated to all who are, might be, or should be *married lovers,*" a term that applies the model of romance to marriage.[30] Typical of her reductionism, Stopes relates the belief in the inevitable decline of marriage to a more fundamental but mistaken belief in the proverb "Post coitum omne triste" (3). The purpose of the book is "not only to challenge the desolating" proverb, but also "to show in detail how it is wrong, and how that wrong may be righted" (9). The proverb in her view is the result of "various physical faults commonly practiced," such that changing what happens in individual sex acts can change marriage itself. Stopes claims that "where the acts of coitus are rightly performed, the pair can disagree, can hold opposite views about every conceivable subject under the sun without any ruffling or disturbance of the temper, without any angry scenes or desire to separate" (21). But despite the mechanical explanation of passion's endurance or lack thereof, Stopes continues to understand passion itself as far more than physical desire. She coins a new term, "erogamic," to name "the mating and relation together of man and woman in all three planes—physical, mental and spiritual" (15). It is the discourse of romance that explains why it is "passion" that Stopes thinks must endure, and thus why sexual excitement becomes the guarantor of true love.

Stopes was a scientist, and it is plausible that her reductionism stems from habits of mind ingrained during her professional training. The very different form that Glyn gave to her advice also seems to stem from her work, writing romantic novels and screenplays. This experience explains why Glyn's advice much more explicitly reveals its connections to the discourse of romance. Glyn herself seems to be the perfect case study of the effects of that discourse on nineteenth-century women and girls. We know that Glyn was someone on whom romantic fictions had an early and lasting impact. Joan Hardwick titled her biography of Glyn *Addicted to Romance,* and she traces her subject's addiction all the way back to stories told by a grandmother in Glyn's early childhood.[31] Romance for the young Glyn came to be associated with marriage, and when she lived in France as a young woman she resisted the notion pervasive there that romance was to be found outside marriage. Her own courtship and marriage, however, failed to live up to her hopes for romance, and as Hardwick notes, her novels do not depict fairy-tale marriages: "Not all of Elinor's fictional marriages are depicted in [a] negative way, but the novels in which the couples do find sexual joy are those in which a union is achieved only after great difficulty and misunderstanding" (63).

The book for which Glyn was most famous was *Three Weeks,* a novel published in response to an unconsummated affair with a younger man some twelve years after her marriage. The young man served as the model for the book's hero, Paul, an innocent who leaves England for a tour of the Continent and there becomes involved passionately, but only for the eponymous three weeks, with a mysterious older woman going by the name Mme. Zalenska. Paul later learns that she is apparently the wife of an eastern European monarch, and she is most often referred to by the narrator as Paul's "lady." The novel is the quintessential romance of the older model wherein love and marriage are opposed rather than linked. Paul leaves behind in England Isabella, for whom he was "perfectly certain his passion . . . would last."[32] Isabella soon recedes far into the background, and Zalenska's husband is never more than a threatening but distant shadow. *Three Weeks,* then, makes much less of the triangular figure than most romances, but it still depicts an adulterous relationship. It is hard to miss the connection to medieval romances and lyrics: Paul's lover is "his lady," and his attitude toward her is appropriately worshipful. Perhaps in imitation of courtly love, the affair itself begins with the lady's prolonged teasing of Paul, delaying sexual consummation in spite of increasingly provocative gestures and poses on her part. The reader is also teased, since all he or she actually experiences are the preliminaries. After the affair is consummated, Paul quickly learns of the potential violence that his lady's husband might do to both of them. There are, thus, the typical range of obstacles to the lovers' happiness. Moreover, while the three weeks of the affair are experienced by both lovers as blissful, the brevity of the relationship is a cause of great pain to Paul, and his lady is described as suffering greatly during the year after their affair; she is murdered by her husband before she and Paul can meet again. Love and death are here linked, even if not so directly as in *Tristan.*

Although *Three Weeks* produced a scandal in England, its depiction of love is remarkable only in that an adulterous affair is not explicitly condemned—though, as Glyn was wont to point out, the lovers suffer greatly. The novel is of interest here because it exemplifies the romantic vision that *The Philosophy of Love* explicitly grafts on to a conception of marriage. Indeed, a great deal of Glyn's philosophy is already present in *Three Weeks.* Paul's lady is constantly teaching him, and she can be seen as a quite explicit example of that European institution, the older woman who initiates young men into sexual experience. Paul is explicitly a neophyte, as his lady's favorite term of endearment for him, "baby," emphasizes. But it is not just that Paul is young and inexperienced; his lack of wisdom is also at least implicitly a function of his gender. It would be hard to imagine the gender roles reversed, and not only because it would be unremarkable for a young woman to become passionately involved with an older man. What is taught in *Three Weeks* is not sexual technique—which a man might plausibly teach a younger woman—but lessons about the character of passionate love that would seem quite out of place in the mouth of a man. The lady provides not an *ars erotica,* but a philosophy of love. For example, his lady tells Paul that "The duration of love in a being always depends upon the loved one. I create an emotion in you, as you create one in me. You do not create it in yourself" (108–9), a point Glyn restates virtually verbatim in her *Philosophy.* In creating the character of the lady, Glyn presents us with a vision of the role she herself will later take on in her essays, a woman who has authoritative knowledge about love that men—and most women—lack.

The brevity and extramarital character of the romance in *Three Weeks* mean that the issue of preserving love in a long-term relationship need not be addressed. Indeed, the lady's philosophy seems to imply that love is not likely to last very long. Glyn herself believed in the possibility of romantic marriage, but she lived in a social milieu where marriages continued to be formed as alliances and where romance took place principally outside marriage. According to Hardwick, *Three Weeks* sprang from an "urgent need to put together on paper all the frustrated emotions of the last few years which had been suddenly set free by the love of Alistair Innes Ker" (117). Glyn said that "The book meant everything to me; it was the outpouring of my whole nature, romantic, proud, and passionate."[33] The paradox that marriage is supposed to be the goal and fulfillment of romance, but that romance is identified with brief, intense affairs is not merely a problem for Glyn; it is the legacy of the discourse of romance to Western culture. *The Philosophy of Love* should be understood as Glyn's attempt to resolve the paradox by explaining how marriage can be romantic.

It is worth recalling that *The Philosophy of Love* and Stopes's marriage manuals emerged into a culture that had been recently taught all manner of new and improved methods for doing things that had previously been thought to entail their own natural or inevitable processes. Frederick Taylor, for example, showed employers how workers' productivity might be greatly increased using methods of "scientific management." Advertisers were constantly explaining to the readers of magazines and newspapers how new products could make life easier or more pleasant. May notes that advertisements for products such as Pear's Soap claimed to be the means to youth, beauty, and finding a mate (63–67). It is as part of this regime of rationalization that the advice books under discussion here should be understood. *The Philosophy of Love* is an attempt to rationalize the basic assumptions of romantic love in order to make possible happy marriage. As Glyn explains, "Whether or no there is logic in love, we certainly cannot be so idiotic as to pretend that logic cannot be used in the management of it!" (214). Like those of Taylor and the advertisers, Glyn's method is primarily one of manipulation.

Manipulation is necessary because one of the fundamental assumptions of romance is that love is passionate in the sense that it is something to which the subject submits. Love is an experience to be undergone, rather than an act committed. My own love is always beyond my control, or, as Glyn puts it, *"no one can love or unlove at will"* (212, italics in original). In earlier times, the idea that love befell one led to the widespread association of passionate love with madness. But for Glyn, understanding that the other produces love in me gives me the opportunity to control the love of the other.

> Thus, realise that it is in yourself that the responsibility lies of keeping love. You ought to be very careful to use the right methods to accomplish this.
>
> When once two people feel certain that they love, their whole intelligence should be used to see if they can manage to remain in this blissful state. Every art of pleasing should be exercised by both, and every attraction polished. Selfishness should be curbed, and all habits likely to disillusionise the other. (213)

The love Glyn is describing and trying to teach her readers to preserve is not companionship but a "blissful state." Such a description certainly corresponds with May's notion of rising expectations of marriage, but its extremity reveals that these expectations are at least partly derived from a conception of love that was considered antithetical to marriage. Glyn herself seems aware of this contradiction, and thus makes avoiding "disillusionising the other" the central tenet of her advice. One wonders whether she ever thought about the idea, implicit in her position, that long-term lovers must be "illusionised," or, to put it more plainly, deluded. Producing love in the other seems on this reading like a magician's trick, and perhaps precisely so, since the other is moved in spite of his or her awareness that an illusion is being produced. We may seem close here to the cynicism Sloterdijk calls "enlightened false consciousness," but this clearly is not what Glyn intends.[34] That she remains a true believer in love's transcendence is revealed in the quotation above (it is asserted often enough elsewhere in the book) by her phrase "when once two people feel certain that they love," since this postulates an authentic, primary condition that the lovers will seek to perpetuate by the maintenance of mystery. Glyn's belief in the need for illusions, which corresponds to Stopes's advice about avoiding "domestication," is typical of other advice literature of the period. Newspaper columnist Dix, for example, explicitly urged married couples to "preserve illusions" by not being overly frank or inquiring too deeply.[35]

If the argument for the origins of this vision of marriage in the discourse of romance needs any more support, we may find it in her discussion of love outside marriage, which is focused on the figure of the mistress. Glyn's familiarity with the mistress stems from her own experience of Europe's ruling classes—she had by this time already played the role—but her privileging of it follows from the romantic ideology already apparent in *Three Weeks*. Glyn asserts that "often illicit unions are very happy, much happier while they last, than married ones. Why? Because both parties are showing the best side to the other, and the very knowledge that there is no tie, and that either can slip off if wearied, makes both take pains to be agreeable" (62). The relationship unbound by law exists at the pleasure of the parties involved, and it is the model for Glyn's conception of marriage. She remarks that "The wife can learn a great deal from the mistress: Continual attention to physical attraction; reviewing calmly what will be the best line to go upon with the particular man in case; and never nagging him, or wearying him" (69). Mistresses, in other words, are experts at avoiding disillusionising. Though wives have security that mistresses do not, wives must, it seems, continually fight against the ill effects of this state.

Glyn's views of marriage take for granted the gender roles of her day, but Glyn clearly sees herself as contributing to women's continuing emancipation. Her discussion of male and female roles in marriage demands a degree of equality unusual for her time. She urges both male and female partners to take responsibility for managing each other's love, where most authorities of this period regarded it as a woman's task to keep up illusions for the love's sake. Glyn's conceptions of gender serve as the grounds for much of her marital advice. Gender for Glyn is rooted in biology, which has given each sex a "fundamental nature," men being dominant and women subservient, men hunters, women mothers and wives. This biologism leads her to endorse the double standard. She counsels women involved with men in their twenties to "well past thirty" to tolerate some infidelity (68–69), while proclaiming that "For a woman married to a man and *living with him as his wife,* to deceive him, and give herself to another, sharing herself with them both, is a *supreme degradation,* a greater one for physiological and psychological reasons than for a man in like case" (61). Yet Glyn's biological notions of gender turn out not to be essentialist, and women are depicted as having changed significantly after having lived under "conditions of restraint and coercion . . . for thousands of years" (79). Women, in Glyn's view, now recognize their own rights and intelligence, and she predicts that in the future women may, like many men, regard love "as an ephemeral emotion, which comes and goes according to the physical attraction of the man calling it forth. The further emancipation goes . . . the more it is possible that women will look upon life more and more as men interpret it" (95). In an explicit rejection of essentialism, she asserts that "The woman of to-morrow will be in the melting-pot, where she will be reformed for the best use which evolution can make of her" (97). Stopes also believed, as *Enduring Passion* tells us, that human nature was in a constant process of change (12–13). Both authors, however, mainly take for granted the contemporary "fundamental natures" of men and women, and do not challenge the contemporary construction of gender.

These books' conceptions of gender doubtless contributed to the continuing emotional differentiation of men and women, but we also should observe that such emotional differentiation may account for their approach. Male advisers tended to present a more rational or scientific attitude.[36] It would be a mistake, then, to read the advice books by Glyn and Stopes as simply perpetuating traditional constructions of gender. While the degree to which twentieth-century advice literature continues the discourse of romance has often been misrecognized, the effects of this literature beyond sexualization have also not been well understood. This advice literature used the discourse of romance to conceive of marriage itself, imagining a new ideal, romantic marriage.[37] In their attempts to imagine such a marriage, Glyn and Stopes offer, I would argue, early instances of what Giddens calls the "pure relationship . . . a situation where a social relation is entered into for its own sake, for what can be derived by each person from sustained association with another; and which is continued only in so far as it is thought by both parties to deliver enough satisfactions for each individual to stay within it."[38] *The Philosophy of Love* and *Married Love,* typical of advice books of the period, regard marriage not as a religious or social obligation, but as a source of personal fulfillment. Moreover, they imagine the emotional life of marriage as more or less the equal responsibility of men and women.[39] Though neither Glyn nor Stopes is ready to abandon the privileging of marriage over other sexual relationships, they both define the ideal marriage in terms drawn from relationships outside marriage. If Giddens is right, books like these need to be understood as participating in the continuing transformation of intimacy. Though they perpetuated the discourse of romance, such books also paved the way for intimacy itself to become an object of inquiry and to be thus denaturalized. While the discourse of romance continues to have enormous power in Western culture, the discourse of intimacy, present mainly in self-help books and other nonfictional texts, has developed as an alternative. Whether this discourse is a satisfactory alternative is a matter for another occasion.

NOTES

1. Elinor Glyn, *The Philosophy of Love* (New York: Authors' Press, 1923), 197. Subsequent references cited parenthetically in the text.

2. Since the primary context of this essay is the United States, I've given the dates for publication in this country.

3. Steven Seidman, *Romantic Longings: Love in America, 1830–1980* (New York: Routledge, 1991), 65–91.

4. Pamela S. Haag, "In Search of 'The Real Thing': Ideologies of Love, Modern Romance, and Women's Sexual Subjectivity in the United States, 1920–40," *Journal of the History of Sexuality* 2 (1992): 548.

5. Haag, "In Search of 'The Real Thing,'" 549.

6. Seidman, *Romantic Longings*, 81.

7. Francesca M. Cancian, *Love in America: Gender and Self-Development* (Cambridge: Cambridge University Press, 1987), 34, quoting Ernest Burgess.

8. Elaine Tyler May, *Great Expectations: Marriage and Divorce in Post-Victorian America* (Chicago: University of Chicago Press, 1980). Subsequent references cited parenthetically in the text.

9. Anthony Giddens, *The Transformation of Intimacy: Sexuality, Love, and Eroticism in Modern Societies* (Stanford: Stanford University Press, 1992), 37–38. Giddens's terms are somewhat problematic since "passion" has a particular meaning and significance in the discourse of romance.

10. Denis de Rougemont, *Love in the Western World*, rev. ed., trans. Montgomery Belgion (New York: Harper, 1974 [1956]), 15.

11. Rougemont's history has become less influential of late in the wake of studies that argue for the universality of romantic love. See William Jankowiak, ed., *Romantic Passion: A Universal Experience?* (New York: Columbia University Press, 1995); and Helen Fisher, *Anatomy of Love: The Natural History of Monogamy, Adultery, and Divorce* (New York: Norton, 1992). But Rougemont's point is not that humans elsewhere lack the capacity to experience passion or that they never do so. Rather, he is arguing that the place that passionate love is given in Western culture and the specific form it has taken there are not universal, and this claim has certainly not been refuted.

12. Rougemont, *Love in the Western World*, 15.

13. It is this conception that Giddens, *Transformation of Intimacy*, 38–47, calls "romantic love." I wish to retain the longer historical frame of reference because I believe that the discourse of the modern period cannot rid itself of its inheritance from the medieval.

14. Niklas Luhmann, *Love as Passion: The Codification of Intimacy*, trans. Jeremy Gaines and Doris L. Jones (Cambridge: Harvard University Press, 1986), 129.

15. Luhmann, *Love as Passion*, 150.

16. Winston Churchill, *The Crisis* (New York: Grosset and Dunlap, 1927 [1901]), 509, 513.

17. See Ellen K. Rothman, *Hands and Hearts: A History of Courtship in America* (New York: Basic, 1984); and Karen Lystra, *Searching the Heart: Women, Men, and Romantic Love in Nineteenth-Century America* (New York: Oxford University Press, 1989) for such evidence.

18. J. H. Kellog, *Plain Facts for Young and Old* (New York: Arno, 1974 [1877]). See also Sylvester Graham, *A Lecture to Young Men on Chastity* (Boston: Charles Pierce, 1848); and Sylvannus Stall, *What a Young Man Ought to Know* (Philadelphia: Vir, 1904), which urges that a wife be selected on the grounds of her health and abilities as a housekeeper, and counsels, "Don't fall in love" (203).

19. Cancian, *Love in America*, 29.

20. Peter N. Stearns, *American Cool: Constructing a Twentieth-Century Emotional Style* (New York: New York University Press, 1994), 36–37, quoting Orson Fowler, *Love and Parentage* (1856).

21. Seidman, *Romantic Longings*, 47.

22. Byron Caldwell Smith, letter (1874), quoted in Seidman, *Romantic Longings,* 42.

23. Mary Wood-Allen, *What a Young Woman Ought to Know* (Philadelphia: Vir, 1905), 205.

24. Seidman, *Romantic Longings,* 50.

25. Luhmann, *Love as Passion,* 130.

26. A view that is often repeated in advice literature of the period. See, e.g., Laura Hutton, *The Single Woman and Her Emotional Problems* (Baltimore: William Wood, 1937 [1935]), 25.

27. Marie Carmichael Stopes, *Married Love: A New Contribution to the Solution of Sex Difficulties* (New York: Eugenics Publishing, 1931 [1918]), 160. Subsequent references cited parenthetically in the text.

28. Seidman, *Romantic Longings,* 84.

29. Lesley A. Hall, "Uniting Science and Sensibility: Marie Stopes and the Narratives of Marriage in the 1920s," in *Rediscovering Forgotten Radicals: British Women Writers, 1889–1939,* ed. Angela Ingram and Daphne Patai (Chapel Hill: University of North Carolina Press, 1993), 128.

30. Marie Carmichael Stopes, *Enduring Passion: Further New Contributions to the Solution of Sex Difficulties, Being the Continuation of "Married Love"* (London: Putnam, 1928), v. Subsequent references cited parenthetically in the text.

31. Joan Hardwick, *Addicted to Romance: The Life and Adventures of Elinor Glyn* (London: André Deutsch, 1994). Subsequent references cited parenthetically in the text.

32. Elinor Glyn, *Three Weeks* (New York: Macaulay, 1924 [1907]), 5–6.

33. Elinor Glyn, *Romantic Adventure,* quoted in Hardwick, *Addicted to Romance,* 117.

34. Peter Sloterdijk, *Critique of Cynical Reason,* trans. Michael Eldred (Minneapolis: University of Minnesota Press, 1987), 5.

35. Dorothy Dix quoted in May, *Great Expectations,* 70.

36. This is true of earlier advisers, such as Kellog and Stall as well as later ones, e.g., Ernest R. Groves, *Marriage* (New York: Holt, 1933).

37. By 1933, even a social scientist like Groves, *Marriage,* 18, had to concede the "romantic element" of courtship and marriage, since this "emotional attitude, now a convention in our culture, is too well established to be shaken by any sort of intellectual activity."

38. Giddens, *Transformation of Intimacy,* 58.

39. It is worth remembering, however, as Cancian, *Love in America,* 35–37, reminds us, that the actual course of most marriages during this period did not conform to the model that Glyn and Stopes proposed, and that a "family ideal" continued to be endorsed by many social scientists.

Chapter Sixteen

The Problem of Modern Married Love for Middle-Class Women

John C. Spurlock

The ideal of the modern companionate marriage that appeared around the turn of the twentieth century offered white middle-class men and women partnerships of warmth and affection. As in Victorian marriage, couples formed bonds of love in courtship that then became the basis for lifelong sharing and commitment. Both partners, but women in particular, expected to benefit from a more equal relationship, from the free play of sexual intimacy within marriage, and from disciplined consumption. Within marriage, however, women found their roles far more confusing, and their emotional rewards far more ambiguous, than they expected. The collision of earlier values with modern values and confusion over roles meant that middle-class women often experienced modern marriage as a failure of love and companionship.

While companionate marriage usually refers to the ideal of marriage that crystallized in the United States by the 1920s, the belief that marriage should be a loving companionship between husband and wife had been generally accepted by the middle class in the northeastern states by the middle of the nineteenth century. From about 1830 until late in the century the style of courtship in the middle class fostered romantic love—passionate and transcendent desire for another unique individual. Like antislavery crusaders Theodore Weld and Angelina Grimké, courting couples expected their love to create a "union of *heart* and *mind* and soul" that would last through marriage. Marriage advice literature in the nineteenth century dealt with disharmony in marriage by urging couples to find ways to foster greater commitment to the marriage and affection for one another. As William Alcott, a widely read writer on marriage, put it, "Mutual love is the only guide to connubial happiness."[1]

Passion as intense as romantic love could be depended on to fluctuate wildly. The distance between men and women, bridged during courtship, generally returned in marriage. The middle class that formed in the towns and cities of the young Republic created homes in which the father was frequently absent, at work in the countinghouse, the office, or the retail store. Men also created their own spheres of homosociality in fraternal organizations and recreational activities. Women assumed the most important role in child rearing, and the bonds between mother and child grew very strong. Women also maintained strong ties to female friends and relations. While the separate spheres provided supportive networks for the roles that women and men assumed in marriage, they could also make affectionate companionship difficult to achieve or maintain. Divorce, though generally a social disaster (especially for women), grew steadily through the late nineteenth century, while a gap between ideal and reality applied even more widely.[2]

From the perspective of the early twentieth century, Victorian marriages could appear very cold indeed. A social historian who supported a change toward greater companionship within marriage cited travel accounts that spoke of a coldness in relations between husbands and wives. By the turn of the century the separate spheres of Victorian marriage had eroded due to both social changes and shifting attitudes. A continuing decline in the birthrate, led by middle-class women, meant that wives had the care of far fewer children than their grandmothers had. This meant that women had more time for activities outside the home and, potentially at least, more time to spend with spouses. The separation of genders also declined, as women moved into the workplace in clerical positions and in growing numbers of professional positions. By the 1890s, high schools in many parts of the country extended schooling for both boys and girls. The sexes mixed in school and in the wide variety of social activities sponsored by the school. As new courtship styles emerged from adolescent and young adult socializing, the proportion of women who married rose and the age of marriage declined for women and men alike from 1890 until the 1920s.[3]

Social scientists, reformers, and popular writers had already begun to elaborate a new model of marriage. A broad range of intellectuals, from anarchist Emma Goldman to sex researcher Havelock Ellis and feminist Charlotte Perkins Gilman attacked the Victorian family for its stultifying effect on women, sexuality, or society as a whole. Many turn-of-the-century intellectuals questioned the transcendent value of the middle-class ideal of a closed, private marriage for life with complete sexual and emotional exclusiveness. By the early 1900s popular authors such as Ellen Key and Edward Carpenter had offered ideals of men and women freed from the nineteenth-century monogamous marriage for life. Purity crusaders joined other reformers in assaulting the sexual double standard and calling for open discussion of sex.[4]

Advocates of modern marriage understood it as a sharp break with the past. This may have owed as much to a misunderstanding of the past as to changes in social behavior in the early twentieth century. While supporters of modern marriage continued to hold up "mutual irresistible attraction," as one author called it, as a central value of marriage, they believed that the end of gendered spheres would allow marriage to become far more companionable. Supporters of modern marriage probably overstated the distance between husband and wife in Victorian marriage, and they expected extraordinary benefits from equality and companionship in marriage. They also took the casual sexual experimentation of the youth of the 1920s as evidence of freedom from sexual inhibitions. While youthful behavior contrasted sharply with the behavior of middle-class youth of a generation before, the new sexual freedoms of the 1920s may have meant less for married than for courting couples. Nevertheless, the widely accepted goals of greater openness and companionship for married couples, combined with frankness about sex and valuing of sexual pleasure, seemed to promise a new marriage relation. Technology and the fruits of the growing economy—including contraceptive and labor-saving devices—joined the delights of consumption to those of the flesh in support of the modern companionate marriage.[5]

The modern ideal found ready advocates among middle-class women. Women in the 1920s and 1930s actively sought marriages of companionship and love, good sex, and consumer enjoyment. For instance, Anne Morrow, fiancée and later wife of the aviator Charles Lindbergh, searched for examples of the "humdrum divinity" of married life in her travels before and after her own marriage. She wanted to see how women could be happily married and still "self-contained," how couples could work in equal partnership and maintain loving regard for one another. She also considered possessions—the flowers that women cultivated, how they furnished their homes— important expressions of the inner life of the couple. Like other middle-class women, Anne Morrow Lindbergh accepted that the "measure of success" of marriage, as described by sociologist Ernest Groves, was "the extent to which the relationship encourages the development of the character and personality of both husband and wife."[6]

Yet fulfillment through marriage proved elusive for middle-class women. With the breakdown of Victorian separate spheres and the growing popularity of an ideal of mutuality and partnership in marriage, married love no longer meant bridging a gendered divide. Instead, love would bind two people together, day in and day out. The difficulties of modern marriage proved extraordinarily complicated, and the duty of understanding and resolving these difficulties fell almost entirely to modern wives. In keeping house, a wife had to make do with her husband's income and provide a home free of clutter and household tensions for husbands who (in spite of the end of separate spheres) still spent relatively little time in the home. Decline of servanthood and increased consumer expectation changed the equation here, easily spilling over into emotional tensions that contradicted the companionate ideal. In physical love, the modern wife had to achieve a high level of satisfaction for herself to demonstrate her mental health and to encourage her husband's enjoyment. And in companionship with her husband, she had to find ways of managing her emotions as well as his to make married harmony possible.

Housekeeping and Consumption

A warning about the difficulties of modern marriage appeared in the image of the flapper wife. One woman strolling in Asbury Park, New Jersey, noted a sand painting depicting "the agonies of a man married to a flapper as he holds a small baby on his knee at the hour of two." A *Literary Digest* article warned of the "jazz-baby" who would soon tire of the "monotonies of matrimony." Part of Hollywood's stock in trade during its first two decades was the story of a married couple making a difficult adjustment from fun-loving singlehood to marriage.[7] The image of the flapper wife expressed anxieties felt by many in the roaring twenties that the public freedom of women, their new opportunities, and the breakdown of older systems of values might make women incapable of sacrificing themselves to marriage and child rearing. The recurring image also shows the strength of older ideals that women still recognized and respected and in many cases held firmly. Most middle-class women in the 1920s believed in modern marriage as an improvement over the image they held of Victorian marriage. In the image of the flapper wife, modern women received a warning that modern marriage could devolve into a parody of marriage, in which love, sex, companionship, and consumerism all worked against the happiness and contentment of the couple.

Beatrice Burton gave the flapper wife a name and a distinctly unpleasant personality in her 1925 novel. Gloria Gregory, on her wedding night, believes that she has the choice of becoming either a slave or a doll. "She would never be a household drudge," she resolves, "her hands shriveled with washing dishes. Her nails broken. Her dresses smudged with pastry flour." When her husband, Dick, insists that he doesn't make enough money to hire servants, Gloria becomes hysterical. In the end, she gets her way. This marriage, begun with such contrasting expectations, deteriorates rapidly. Dick wants children; Gloria finds the idea repulsive. Gloria wants to spend her days shopping and her nights dancing or going to parties. Dick complains of having too little money and too little energy. Gloria soon rekindles a romance with a former boyfriend and leaves Dick. But her life of freedom proves empty and lonely, and she returns to her hometown, takes work, and learns the skills of housekeeping. At the end of the novel Dick and the chastened Gloria reunite and look forward to a life together of domestic bliss.[8]

The commonest fear represented by the image of the flapper wife related to the consumer culture. Both social science and popular literature of the 1920s recognized the importance of "an adequate economic arrangement" as part of the complex set of relations, goals, and projects of modern marriage. By the early 1930s two-thirds of a family's income went to the purchase of retail goods. A prominent sociologist characterized the economic arrangement of most families as "making money and *buying* a 'living.'" Advertisers recognized women as the main consumers in the household and pitched their products to appeal to women's desire for a well-run and well-fed household. Legitimation for women's role as consumers appeared in ads and magazine articles touting women as household managers.[9]

Popular advice literature and advertisements stressed the emotional value of properly managed households. A well-run home would eliminate at least some of the sources of tension between husband and wife. As the wife became ever more competent as a housekeeper, she would gain greater self-esteem while her husband would accept her as a replacement for his mother. New products and new approaches would allow women to operate their homes more efficiently and give them more leisure, to gain a fuller life, and to raise their children better.[10]

Yet the affective goals of a well-run home and new products could easily collide with a family's budget and with older values of thrift and saving. Sociologist Robert Lynd recognized that emotional issues could flare up between husbands and wives over differences in the extent to which the partners had assimilated the new values around consumption. Differences in values appeared in popular culture as moral issues. An advice book for college youth about dating and courtship warned against mates who would be extravagant in spite of the limited means available to newlyweds (it gave two examples of extravagant wives, one of a spendthrift husband). One of *Good Housekeeping*'s "little lessons in married life" suggested that a "psychological expert" lecture prospective husbands and (especially) wives on the coming changes in their lives. "Realize, Mary," the expert tells the bride, "that you are still pretty much a strong-willed, egotistical, and selfish child." You think you will give up anything for John, but marriage will mean giving up one small thing after another for years to come. Live within your husband's income, a popular marriage guide commanded. "Every man has the right to expect that his wife will. . . . Women can be wonderful managers if they are loyal and honest, and if you aren't naturally a good manager you can learn to be." [11]

Social science linked the couple's finances to the success of their marriage in a 1929 study of married life. Couples in the study with the highest level of income were more satisfied than couples with lower levels, and couples that had saved money since marriage were more satisfied than those that had saved none. Most married couples, of course, lacked the income to both consume freely and save, thereby almost insuring that they would find themselves violating at least one important cultural value. Divorce proceedings during the 1920s reveal that the pressures of trying to provide material abundance could lead to marital problems. Women, as "the purchasing agent[s] of home and of society," found themselves vulnerable to the charge of mismanagement. William Ferris, for instance, told his mother that his wife, Margy, was "silly and extravagant." Mrs. Ferris accepted this as an adequate explanation for their divorce. [12]

The marriage of Winifred Willis shows the difficulties of meeting the shifting demands of consumption and savings. Winifred Willis married Lorin "Tommy" Thompson in 1924 after a short and romantic courtship. In spite of Tommy's well-to-do family and his job as a bond salesman, the couple still found themselves faced with financial stringency. When they sat down to go over finances after a few months of marriage, Winifred was shocked to realize that they spent twice what Tommy earned. Tommy, she recorded, knew this all along, but wanted to make her realize it without simply insisting on his way. Like Gloria Gregory in the novel, Winifred began as a spendthrift, but then quickly recognized the error of her spending habits and reformed. By seeking a frugal life that balanced the couple's desire for leisure and status with their financial means, Winifred believed that she had created the kind of cozy home that would allow affectionate companionship to thrive. "Now we go to plays, dine out occasionally, have laundry & house-cleaning done regularly (not by me!!) &, without being unduly extravagant, do pretty much as we please." She believed that this allowed her to become "a gay & happy companion with nothing on my mind—& very little in it." [13] Like the flapper wife, Winifred learned that love and harmony required a well-managed household.

The remaining years of their marriage showed that it was not a flapper mentality but images of a world of economic possibilities that created the major problems for Winifred and Tommy. The couple yearned to share more fully in the decade's prosperity. Tommy believed he deserved better than his sixty-dollar weekly salary, and the couple invested a sizeable gift from Tommy's father in oil and radio stocks. They dreamed of a home away from New York and a life of industrious comfort like the one Tommy's parents lived. In the coming years, however, the vagaries of the economy would rob them of even the frugal pleasures they had earned. Their investment of the gift from Tommy's father turned into a bad speculation; soon the couple had to move out of their own apartment and live with Winifred's mother. In the following year Tommy lost his job when his firm broke up, the couple began to move from one difficult living situation to another, and Tommy's fortunes apparently headed steadily downward. In November 1927 Winifred wrote that they had returned to New York "dead broke, no job as yet. My hands are full with child-care and housework." [14]

Winifred Willis noted the changes that economic circumstances brought in her relationship with her husband. During the early months of their marriage, after Tommy had begun a new job, he became engrossed in his work and had little time for emotional companionship. Later, when their fortunes had changed, Tommy became resentful of life with her mother and then sister and accused Winifred of being too dependent on him. Financial hardships took a heavy toll on the couple. Unemployed much of the time, Tommy spent his days looking for work. Winifred felt the distance growing between them as she spent more time caring for their son. Her marriage ended by 1930; her nervous collapse was partly a cause and partly a consequence. [15] The financial misfortunes of Winifred Willis and Tommy Thompson exemplified the problems many couples would face in the decade that followed. While prosperity and consumption were supposed to help love flourish, the impera- tive to consume could easily turn wives into bad managers or extravagant flappers, and financial woe could undermine affection and aggravate other shortcomings of married life.

Sexuality

While the flapper wife might prove too extravagant, it is hard to imagine her as failing to take a hearty interest in sex. Sex took on some of the significance of love for the modern marriage. "Making love" in the nineteenth century had referred to the verbal exchanges of courtship; by the 1920s it referred to the exchange of caresses on dates. A guide for college youth presented the period of courtship as a time of sexual exploration (not including intercourse) that would ease young men and women into a marriage of patiently nurtured sexual love. Marriage manuals from the nineteenth century onward urged husbands and wives to nurture loving relations. By the early twentieth century, marriage guides also assured women that if they made the effort to become sexually attractive, "you'll get a magnificent cooperation and appreciation by a husband who is inordinately grateful that you can meet him in his own bed and be a grand companion." As another marriage manual put it, "a successful marriage can hardly be expected where sexual attraction does not exist, or where the marital sex life is unsatisfactory and inadequate." [16]

The growing availability of artificial contraception and the growing respectability accorded to contraception by reformers and physicians seemed to make sexual pleasure even more available to the married couple. A study based on gynecological case histories noted that women typically reacted with shock to the first use of contraception but that the practice "gradually falls into routine like brushing the teeth." Studies of different middle-class populations from the late 1920s found large majorities of married couples using some form of contraception on a regular basis.[17]

The young middle-class women of the first decades of the twentieth century took some forms of sexual pleasure for granted, as the "loving up" or "spooning" of the generation born in the 1890s became the necking and petting of the generation born around 1900. Many young women recorded their pleasure in vamping men and spending time alone on outings with their beaux. Marjorie Kinnan could take delight in quoting to her fiancé that the "most correct honeymoon is an orgy of lust."[18] Winifred Willis identified the moment during their courtship that she realized she was in love with Tommy. After bringing her home from an evening on the town, Tommy sent the taxi away. He stayed at her apartment that night, and they slept together, as they would on many future nights, though without having sex. She wrote later, "When I lie back in his arms & give him my lips I forget everything else except the sweet, gentle, greedy feel of him."[19]

In spite of the broad agreement in American culture over the desirability of good married sex, and in spite of the desire of women to share fully in intimacy with their husbands, middle-class women experienced desire as a complicated and often ambiguous combination of motives and urges. While necking and petting seemed to turn into playful reality the culture's images of sexual desire, one advice columnist described it as "a combination of curiosity, natural instinct and an overwhelming yearning in the very young to establish once and for all time the truth that They Have Sex Appeal." Within the youth culture of the period, dating offered an objective standard for young women as to whether they had sex appeal and a gauge for their popularity. Adolescent and young adult women enjoyed the sex play that went with dating, but it came as part of a larger package of satisfactions. A college woman recorded her wish for a man in her diary in 1923 and went on to describe her desire "for companionship, for the thrill of it, for admiration, for self confidence, for show purposes, for an escort to take me places, for satisfaction of curiosity, and for surcease of Spring Fever!"[20]

Even though more women had what one study called "illicit sex" before marriage, middle-class women usually had intercourse first with the man they married. Chastity until marriage—or at least until engagement—remained a strongly held moral imperative for most. The eroticization of images in advertising and cinema coexisted with a continuing condemnation of unchastity for women. Jessamyn West tried to explain to her husband that a woman might delight in the attentions of a man but remain incapable of returning "that desire in kind"—"frank delight" might show "satiety." "The woman must appear to repulse and scorn."[21]

The revolution in attitudes toward sex had proceeded both quickly and unevenly in American society, leaving middle-class women with conflicting ideals about sex. To some observers it seemed that the civilized sexual morality that demanded chastity until marriage had become simply a hollow claim. Nevertheless, sexual repression played an important, and often a leading, role in married sex. In one study, only fourteen out of a hundred women recalled that "pleasure predominated" in their first experience of sex. Thirty-two felt disappointed, twenty-two experienced little or no pleasure, and eleven remembered it as painful. The anxiety and confusion that sex could inspire appear in the journal of a young woman in western Pennsylvania who found her self-assurance crumbling as marriage approached and she faced the prospect of giving up "her girlhood to become the possession of a man, his by every right, to cherish or to defile." On her wedding night she broke into sobs and pleaded with her husband to respect her person. He agreed. Only several weeks later did the couple have intercourse.[22]

Winifred Willis, whose passionate courtship with Tommy left many of her friends believing they were lovers as well as in love, also kept her virginity until marriage. When she finally surrendered to her husband, the result was "cold, sick, disappointment, the sense of failure, and of having failed him whom I loved." While couples generally worked out sexual issues in the early months of marriage, the problems that Winifred experienced in her first, unsatisfactory intercourse continued to plague her and led to further problems in her relationship with Tommy. Winifred placed the blame on the sexual morality that denied girls and young women "casual, sexual experiences" like those she believed men enjoyed. Another young woman described a friend whose problems sounded remarkably similar to Winifred's: "Said she was a virgin when she married and now wished she hadn't been."[23]

The sexual problems of young women moved one writer to hope "that some day the sexual training of these somewhat psychopathic and frigid girls can be taken largely out of the hands of psychopathic and man-hating mothers. What misery these mothers now hand on to their daughters through their evil and wrong- headed and vicious training!" As the advice writer shows us, women had to deal with not only conflicting cultural values about how to live their sex lives, but also with an insistence that they were the source of the problem. In both the popular and academic psychological literature of the 1920s, female sexuality appeared as a complicated mix of emotions, desires, and drives. Frigidity became the summary term for any problem in the psychological or medical lives of women that robbed them or their husbands of sexual pleasure. Wilhelm Stekel, whose two volumes on the topic appeared in 1926, asserted that "the most frequent of the sex-diseases of women is frigidity." He concluded that 40 to 50 percent of women suffered from it. One of the earliest scientific studies of marriage placed frigidity within a broader range of sexual problems for women characterized by inadequate orgasm. Almost half of the women in the study fell into the category. The author concluded that "Unless the sex act ends in a fully releasing, fully terminate climax in at least 20 percent of copulations there is likely to be trouble ahead." The marriage, of course, may suffer. The women themselves will likely experience restlessness and tension; of the forty-six women considered inadequate in orgasm, twenty had been diagnosed at some time as "seriously psychoneurotic."[24]

Women believed that within marriage they had to feel and inspire sexual longing, and when they could not, they had to face the judgment that they had a serious problem. Like Gladys Bell, they might wonder if sexual failure meant a physical deformity requiring surgery. Like Dorothy Dushkin, they might seek psychotherapy to allow them to experience sexual desire as something other than "slightly repulsive."[25] Or they might conclude, with Winifred Willis, that sexual failure contributed to the failure of their marriages.

Companionable Emotions

While physical love apparently required more passion by the 1920s, the emotional experience of married love looked more like friendship than romantic love. Both cautious consumption and sexual pleasure were to support an affectionate companionship between husband and wife, "a partnership deal between individuals of equal personality," as one woman in the 1910s termed it. Between 1890 and 1920 a "democratic" model of marriage, in which husband and wife shared equally in the cares of the household, became popular among middle-class families. Just as more women found professional possibilities outside the home by the turn of the century, some suburban men became attracted to an ideal of "domestic masculinity" that valued time spent at home with wife and children rather than among male friends and business associates. For men and women alike, the ideal of modern marriage offered friendship as well as affection, emotional expressiveness as well as physical pleasure.[26]

Both in prospect and practice, women happily embraced this key facet of the companionate ideal. "We're so intensely *individualistic*," Marjorie Kinnan wrote to her fiancé; "it just happens that our individualities cuddle down in the same box together like two halves of a pecan." Dorothy Thompson considered her wedding vows to Sinclair Lewis a commitment to a "life- ideal." "In the end," she wrote Lewis, "it is as my friend that I think of you clearest, love you best." Both Lella Secor, a reformer and journalist, and Gladys Bell, a rural schoolteacher, could reflect on their early years of marriage as times of "wonderful growth and development," to use Secor's phrase.[27]

While some women could report that for at least some period their marriages worked wonderfully well, a large body of popular and scientific literature from the 1920s onward found that marriage often failed to realize the companionate ideal so widely accepted in American culture. In Middletown the Lynds found "little spontaneous community of interest" in marriage and a lack of honesty between husbands and wives. G. V. Hamilton's study of marriage placed most of the marriages he examined in categories ranging from "doubtful success" to separation and divorce. Dorothy Dix, one of the most widely read advice columnists in the early decades of the century, warned that the differences due to sex, heredity, and upbringing could threaten the companionship in companionate marriage. Like other guides to marriage, Dix wrote that couples marry an image of one another as much as they marry the real person, but once they begin to live together "they find out that they have married ordinary human beings instead of angels and motion-picture heroes. Comes the clash of personalities."[28]

As with financial crisis and sexual failure, women often bore the responsibility for the failure of companionship. "I like to go to dances and parties," a young flapper wife wrote to Margaret Sanger, "and have innocent flirtations. I like pretty clothes and admiration. My husband cannot understand why at my age I am so frivolous." Novelist Elinor Glyn mourned "young men under thirty tied and bound to impossible young women" because they could not muster the will to "resist the passion in its first stages." A *Good Housekeeping* article pointed out that marriage gave women everything they want in life, that is, a home and children, while men lost their independence and even their personal space.[29]

Advice literature frequently gave women the responsibility for making the ideal work or making it fit the reality of married life. Margaret Sanger believed that women had to "keep romance alive in spite of the influence of the prosaic demands of everyday life." Another advisor offered detailed instructions on saving romance, along with tips on sexual attractiveness and household finances. Columnist Anne Hirst believed that the man you marry may not be the man you thought you were marrying. If so, then "adapt yourself to this new being and make for him the kind of home he wants. If you do, he'll stay in it." Adaptation included becoming skilled at managing one's own and one's husband's emotions. "If your husband seems to be unreasonable," wrote Hirst, "put yourself in his place before you sass him back, and perhaps you'll find he has a perfect right to ask what he does." Dorothy Dix also recommended that women make adaptations, both in their own behavior and in the companionate ideal. To manage husbands, she recommended that women use strategic dishonesty. Men want to be "treated as good fellows," she wrote, but they also "enjoy being bamboozled by women who turn out a nice artistic job." Spouses should be good to one another but they also must observe limits. Otherwise they will encourage weakness and selfishness in the other. Dix considered a delusion the idea that "any man or woman . . . can supply another individual's whole need of human companionship."[30]

Most middle-class women began marriage, at least, with more faith in the companionate ideal than Dix had. But whether they believed in bamboozling their husbands or in providing the perfect domestic situation for them, women found themselves responsible for the success of companionate marriages and yet dependent on husbands who often lacked a clear understanding of their own companionate roles. Women in widely varied social settings found themselves distressed at the behavior of their husbands. Ione Robinson, who returned with her husband to their New York apartment after their wedding, felt "as if I'm sitting in heaven and just starting my real life." Yet two weeks later she had begun to feel "that I am nothing." Her husband, Joe, an ardent communist, discussed politics with guests at dinner while Ione spent the time "setting the table, cooking the dinner, and washing the dishes as though I were not present, as far as the others are concerned." Before her marriage, Gladys Bell imagined she would control her husband through her womanly wiles. She also took for granted that most situations turned on her own emotional responses, and believed that she could shape these through her willpower. Yet in the years following her marriage, she discovered that her wiles and her emotional strategies offered little help in the face of her husband's absences and their frequent misunderstandings. Dorothy Thompson, still yearning for a romantic partnership, despaired of the vagaries of Sinclair Lewis's behavior. She wrote in one of her letters to him that she wanted to express her love, "but I can't. . . . it would be like writing to someone imaginary. Do you exist, and are you you, and what *is* you? I have known so many yous." [31]

The marriage of Allen Tate and Caroline Gordon showed the importance of companionship and individual fulfillment, as well as confusion over roles within modern marriage. Though both would become identified with southern regional writing, they met in Greenwich Village, where they married in 1924. They supported one another with their encouragement and criticism and with the occasional publisher's advance. Yet even this marriage of committed artists left most of the housework in Caroline Gordon's hands (though Tate did the ironing). In letters to a friend she complained repeatedly of her inability to do enough writing. "Yes, you must have plenty of servants to abandon yourself to your emotions, even to what mind you have. I can't write when I'm doing scullery work because when I get the time my mind won't take hold of any problem." Modern women, deprived of a distinctive sphere as in Victorian life, still found themselves with many of the same duties as their grandmothers and little gain in opportunities. While men had the duty of providing goods for the household, their roles within the households, and within marriage, remained limited and probably confusing for most men. [32]

Like Dorothy Dix, many experts on marriage encouraged a shift toward lower expectations for married companionship and for emotional fulfillment. Psychologist Elton Mayo considered love "an ailment of adolescence" and warned that it "must be got over" before the real marriage can begin. "Persons become attached to dogs, cats, furniture and what not," wrote one physician. Marriage had less to do with love than with "admiration, respect, association, mutual interests, reciprocal assistance, attachment and becoming accustomed to each other." [33]

The diaries and letters from middle-class women in the 1920s and 1930s suggest—inevitably impressionistically—a range of gaps between marital reality and emotional expectations. To some extent, these gaps perpetuated an older rift, derived from the ideals of Victorian love. But the emotional standards of the companionate marriage raised new issues, particularly when juxtaposed with changes in housekeeping, consumerism, and sexuality. The companionate goal of an emotional linkage between determinedly individualistic partners was itself elusive. The combined result, obviously, could be considerable disappointment, even a sense of emotional void.

Just as a rising divorce rate seems to have accompanied the rising expectations placed on the emotional content of Victorian marriage, divorce continued to grow as a resolution to marriages that fell short of the companionate ideal. Gladys Bell contemplated divorce, though she remained married. Many of the women whose writings have allowed us to look inside the modern marriage resorted to divorce, including Ione Robinson, Dorothy Thompson, Marjorie Kinnan Rawlings, and Winifred Willis. The Gordon-Tate marriage suggests the emotional complexity of personal fulfillment in modern marriage. The couple divorced in 1946, only to soon remarry and then divorce again in 1959. Perhaps trial marriage, the idea behind the term "companionate marriage" as coined by Judge Ben Lindsey, has always been implicit in a relation ideally founded on affection alone. V. F. Calverton, a harsher critic of marriage than Lindsey, noted that divorce had taken the place that Lindsey contemplated for companionate marriage.[34]

While the experience of marriage often fell short of the hopes that middle-class women held for it, the ideal that two people could become perfect emotional complements to one another continued to flourish. With the continuing shift in the economy and the transformation or undermining of most institutions in the early twentieth century, property and duty held less and less power to shape marriage. Emotional satisfactions, bolstered by desire and consumption, remained the most important ingredients of modern marriage. The difficulty of negotiating emotional satisfaction in marriage also continued. Emotional management—especially a therapeutic approach to personal relationships—would become twentieth-century America's replacement for the intense passion of Victorian love. Like trial marriage, marital therapeutics were implicit in an ideal marriage of mutuality and companionship. Married love in the twentieth century increasingly became a complicated package of romance, friendship, and carefully scrutinized communication.

NOTES

I wish to thank John Gillis, Jan Lewis, Cynthia Magistro, James Reed, and Peter Stearns, who generously read earlier versions of this essay and offered many valuable suggestions.

1. Gilbert H. Barnes and Dwight L. Dumond, eds., *Letters of Theodore Dwight Weld, Angelina Grimké and Sarah Grimké, 1822–1844* (New York: D. Appleton-Century, 1934), 2:561; Karen Lystra, *Searching the Heart: Women, Men and Romantic Love in Nineteenth-Century America* (New York: Oxford University Press, 1989), 192–94; William A. Alcott, *The Moral Philosophy of Courtship and Marriage* (Boston: John P. Jewett, 1857), 43–44; James Reed, *The Birth Control Movement and American Society: From Private Vice to Public Virtue* (Princeton: Princeton University Press, 1984), 20–33.

2. Carroll Smith-Rosenberg, "The Female World of Love and Ritual: Relations between Women in Nineteenth-Century America," *Signs: Journal of Women in Culture and Society* 1 (autumn 1975): 1–29; E. Anthony Rotundo, *American Manhood: Transformation in Masculinity from the Revolution to the Modern Era* (New York: Basic Books, 1993), 239–40; William L. O'Neill, *Divorce in the Progressive Era* (New Haven: Yale University Press, 1967), 20.

3. Arthur W. Calhoun, *A Social History of the American Family*, vol. 2, *From Independence through the Civil War* (New York: Barnes and Noble, 1918), 83; Peter N. Stearns, "Girls, Boys, and Emotions: Redefinitions and Historical Change," *Journal of American History* 80 (June 1993): 61–69; Reed Ueda, *Avenues to Adulthood: The Origins of the High School and Social Mobility in an American Suburb* (Cambridge: Cambridge University Press, 1987), 119; John Modell, *Into One's Own: From Youth to Adulthood in the United States, 1920–1975* (Berkeley: University of California Press, 1989), 77; Steven Mintz and Susan Kellogg, *Domestic Revolutions: A Social History of American Family Life* (New York: Free Press, 1988), 108–9.

4. O'Neill, *Divorce*, 98–99, 108–11; John C. Burnham, "The Progressive Era Revolution in American Attitudes toward Sex," *Journal of American History* 59 (March 1973): 885–908.

5. M. V. O'Shea, *The Trend of the Teens* (Chicago: Frederick J. Drake, 1920), 122; Sophonisba P. Breckinridge, *Women in the Twentieth Century: A Study of Their Political, Social and Economic Activities* (New York: McGraw Hill, 1933), 101; V. F. Calverton, *The Bankruptcy of Marriage* (New York: Macauley, 1928), 61–62. For recent evaluations of the sexual changes of the early twentieth century, see Carl N. Degler, "What Ought to Be and What Was: Women's Sexuality in the

Nineteenth Century," *American Historical Review* 79 (December 1974): 1467–90; and Rosalind Rosenberg, *Beyond Separate Spheres: Intellectual Roots of Modern Feminism* (New Haven: Yale University Press, 1982), 179, 185, 204.

6. Anne Morrow Lindbergh, *Hour of Gold, Hour of Lead: Diaries and Letters of Anne Morrow Lindbergh, 1929–1932* (New York: Harcourt Brace Jovanovich, 1973), 53, 64, 69; Ernest R. Groves and others, *The Family and Its Relationships* (Chicago: J. B. Lippincott, 1932), 165, 174.

7. Viola C. White, *Partridge in a Swamp: The Journals of Viola C. White, 1918–1941* (Taftsville, VT: Countryman Press, 1979), 88; "The Rocky Road from the Altar," *Literary Digest* 77 (February 26, 1927): 31–32; Lary May, *Screening Out the Past: The Birth of Mass Culture and the Motion Picture Industry* (New York: Oxford University Press, 1980), 109–46.

8. Beatrice Burton, *The Flapper Wife* (New York: Grosset and Dunlap, 1925), 8, 344.

9. Christina Simmons, "Modern Sexuality and the Myth of Victorian Repression," in Kathy Peiss and Christina Simmons, eds., *Passion and Power: Sexuality in History* (Philadelphia: Temple University Press, 1989), 165–66; the quotations come from Hannah M. Stone and Abraham Stone, *A Marriage Manual: A Practical Guide-Book to Sex and Marriage*, rev. ed. (New York: Simon and Schuster, 1935), 155, and Robert Lynd, "Family Members as Consumers," *Annals of the American Academy of Political and Social Science* 160 (March 1932): 87–89; William H. Chafe, *The Paradox of Change: American Women in the Twentieth Century* (New York: Oxford University Press, 1991), 111–15.

10. Clara Savage Littledale, "Adam at Home," *Good Housekeeping* 75 (August 1922): 49 +; Anne Hirst, *Get Your Man—and Hold Him* (New York: H. C. Kinsey, 1937), 84–88; Christine Frederick, *Selling Mrs. Consumer* (New York: Business Bourse, 1929), 29–31; Susan Strasser, *Never Done: A History of American Housework* (New York: Pantheon, 1982), 203, 244–48, 263–64.

11. Lynd, "Family Members as Consumers," 89; Grace Elliott Loucks and Harry Bone, *The Sex Life of Youth* (New York: Association Press, 1929), 94; Clara Savage Littledale, "Living Happily Ever After," *Good Housekeeping* 74 (March 1922): 15, 154; Hirst, *Get Your Man*, 94.

12. G. V. Hamilton, *A Research in Marriage* (New York: Medical Research Press, 1929), 97, 101; Elaine Tyler May, *Great Expectations: Marriage and Divorce in Post-Victorian America* (Chicago: University of Chicago Press, 1980), 138; Christine Frederick, *The New Housekeeping: Efficiency Studies in Home Management* (Garden City: Doubleday, Page, 1912), 103; quote from diary of Edna St. Claire Ferris (November 6, 1929) in E. H. Mallory II, ed., "Good Life and Hard Times," facsimile in Huntington Library, San Marino, CA.

13. Winifred Lockhart Willis Papers (MC 369), Schlesinger Library, Radcliffe College, box 1, folder 2, August 2, 1924, January 27, 1925 (hereafter, Willis Papers).

14. Ibid., box 1, folder 3, February 23, 1925, May 15, 1925; box 2, folder 10, November 13, 1927.

15. Ibid., box 1, folder 4, June 11, 1926; box 1, folder 3, May 15, 1925; box 2, folder 10, June 1930 (p. 281).

16. Loucks and Bone, *Sex Life of Youth*, 16–17; Hirst, *Get Your Man*, 116; Stone and Stone, *Marriage Manual*, 155; Sheila M. Rothman, *Woman's Proper Place: A History of Changing Ideals and Practice, 1870 to the Present* (New York: Basic Books, 1978), 179–80; Peter N. Stearns, *American Cool: Constructing a Twentieth-Century Emotional Style* (New York: New York University Press, 1994), 273.

17. Reed, *Birth Control Movement*, 143–93; Robert Latou Dickinson and Lura Ella Beam, *A Thousand Marriages: A Medical Study of Sex Adjustment* (Baltimore: Williams and Wilkins, 1931), 67; Modell, *Into One's Own*, 115; Katherine Bement Davis, *Factors in the Sex Life of Twenty-two Hundred Women* (New York: Harper and Brothers, 1929), 12.

18. Malcolm Cowley, *Exile's Return: A Literary Odyssey of the 1920s* (New York: Viking, 1934), 22; Marjorie Kinnan Rawlings, *Selected Letters of Marjorie Kinnan Rawlings*, ed. Gordon E. Bigelow and Laura V. Monti (Gainesville: University of Florida Press, 1983), 27.

19. Willis Papers, box 1, folder 2, November 26, 1923 and March 11, 1924.

20. Hirst, *Get Your Man*, 12; Marion Taylor Papers (A86), Schlesinger Library, Radcliffe College, box 1, folder 4, February 20, 1923.

21. Hamilton, *Research in Marriage*, 346–47; Robert S. Lynd and Helen Merrell Lynd, *Middle-*

town: A Study in American Culture (New York: Harcourt, Brace, 1929), 112; May, *Great Expectations,* 101; Jessamyn West, *Double Discovery: A Journey* (New York: Harcourt Brace Jovanovich, 1980), 229.

22. Hamilton, *Research in Marriage,* 204; Daniel Scott Smith, "The Dating of the American Sexual Revolution: Evidence and Interpretation," in *The American Family in Social-Historical Perspective,* ed. Michael Gordon (New York: St. Martin's, 1973), 321–35; Papers of Gladys Bell Penrod, Indiana County (PA) Historical and Genealogical Society, April 28, 1925, May 23, 1925 (hereafter, Penrod Papers).

23. Willis Papers, box 2, folder 10, May 1, 1928; Ruth Raymond Papers (81-M18), Schlesinger Library, Radcliffe College, box 1, volume 11, January 19, 1933.

24. I. M. Hotep, *Love and Happiness: Intimate Problems of the Modern Woman* (New York: Knopf, 1938), 46; Wilhelm Stekel, "Frigidity in Mothers," in *The New Generation,* ed. V. F. Calverton and Samuel Schmalhausen (New York: Macauley, 1930), 247; Jeffrey Weeks, "Movements of Affirmation: Sexual Meanings and Homosexual Identities," in *Passion and Power,* ed. Peiss and Simmons, 169–70; Hamilton, *Research in Marriage,* 543.

25. Penrod Papers, April 28, 1925; Papers of Dorothy Dushkin, Sophia Smith Collection, Smith College, box 3, folder 2, December 31, 1926.

26. Papers of Azalia Peet, Sophia Smith Collection, Smith College, August 23, 1914; Margaret Marsh, "Suburban Men and Masculine Domesticity, 1870–1915," *American Quarterly* 40 (June 1988): 165–88; Paula S. Fass, *The Damned and the Beautiful: American Youth in the 1920s* (New York: Oxford University Press, 1977), 93; Francesca Cancian, *Love in America: Gender and Self-Development* (Cambridge: Cambridge University Press, 1987), 34; Mintz and Kellogg, *Domestic Revolutions,* 113–14.

27. Rawlings, *Selected Letters,* 26; Vincent Sheehan, *Dorothy and Red* (Boston: Houghton Mifflin, 1963), 87; Lella Secor, *Lella Secor: A Diary in Letters, 1915–1922,* ed. Barbara Moench Florence (New York: Burt Franklin, 1978), 164; Penrod Papers, April 25, 1926.

28. Lynd and Lynd, *Middletown,* 118–20; Hamilton, *Research in Marriage,* 82; Dorothy Dix, *Dorothy Dix — Her Book: Every-day Help for Every-day People* (New York: Funk and Wagnalls, 1926), 306.

29. Margaret Sanger, *Happiness in Marriage* (Elmsford, NY: Maxwell Reprint, 1969 [1926]), 30; Elinor Glyn, *The Philosophy of Love* (New York: Authors' Press, 1923), 177; Littledale, "Adam," 49.

30. Sanger, *Happiness,* 177; Hirst, *Get Your Man,* 104, 106; Dix, *Dorothy Dix,* 8–9, 39, 53–54.

31. Kevin White, *The First Sexual Revolution: The Emergence of Male Heterosexuality in Modern America* (New York: New York University Press, 1993), 148, 173–79; Cancian, *Love in America,* 37; Ione Robinson, *A Wall to Paint On* (New York: Dutton, 1946), 122–24; Penrod Papers, April 23, 1925, April 19, 1926, March 3, 1927; Sheehan, *Dorothy and Red,* 167.

32. Sally Wood, ed., *The Southern Mandarins: Letters of Caroline Gordon to Sally Wood, 1924–1937* (Baton Rouge: Louisiana State University Press, 1984), 52 and introduction for biographical material. John Gillis, in corresponding with me about this essay, stressed the role played by the separate spheres of the Victorians and the problems created for married companionship when these spheres disappeared.

33. Stearns, *American Cool,* chap. 8; Elton Mayo, "Should Marriage Be Monotonous?" *Harper's Monthly* 151 (September 1925): 427; Don Cabot McCowan, *Love and Life: Sex Urge and Its Consequences* (Chicago: Pascal Covici, 1928), 172.

34. Wood, introduction to *Southern Mandarins;* Ben B. Lindsey and Wainwright Evans, *The Revolt of Modern Youth* (New York: Boni and Liveright, 1925), 139; Calverton, *Bankruptcy of Marriage,* 150.

Chapter Seventeen

The New Man and Early Twentieth-Century Emotional Culture in the United States

Kevin White

Scholars in the history of the emotions have described the strict limitations on emotional expression of the nineteenth century as giving way to an informalization of controls in the twentieth century. Historians of sexuality have to date produced work that has seemed to fit this pattern. Victorian repression therefore lives in the popular image of frigid virgins and covered table legs, in part because Victorian rhetoric around sexuality stressed its spiritual aspects in reverential tones. This seems alien, as do the ritual and self-control practiced by both men and women. Victorian repression lives, too, in the image of American women that women's historians have created: the pious, pure, domesticated, and submissive woman who adhered to the "cult of true womanhood" and exemplified Nancy Cott's justly celebrated account of the "passionlessness" that dominated expectations of women's sexuality.[1]

Studies on the developments in the early twentieth-century "revolution in morals," or sexual revolution, have tended to emphasize a clear contrast with Victorianism that seems to confirm a repression versus liberation dichotomy. Kinsey's stunning statistic from his 1953 report *Sexual Behavior in the Human Female* that women born between 1900 and 1910 were two and a half times as likely to have experienced premarital sexual intercourse as women born between 1890 to 1900 remains the benchmark evidence of early twentieth-century change. Daniel Scott Smith has found complementary evidence that the percentage of brides who were pregnant at marriage rose from the late nineteenth century into the twentieth century.[2] These figures suggest that the Victorian double standard of morality by which men could consort with prostitutes before marriage while women remained virgins was being replaced by a less repressive single standard for both men and women that permitted some limited preconjugal sexual activity. Yet contemporary evidence points to even wider changes in the direction of sexual liberation. As more and more young people of both sexes began to work before marriage, they had spare cash to date and enjoy all the pleasures of a growing heterosocial leisure world in the cities of America. In amusement parks, dance halls, movie theaters, and automobiles, young Americans enjoyed greater freedom to explore one another's sexuality away from parents than any previous generation. Here the flapper, the "Charity Girl," the New Woman debated how far to go with her boyfriend. All the way? Or perhaps not.[3] In need of advice, the couple could turn to an industry of romance stories, advice columns, and sex and marriage manuals that increasingly recommended that they go all the way and advised how to do so in ever more explicit detail. Although we are hardly yet in the heady days of the sexual liberation of the 1960s–1970s generation, "nice girls did" forty years before Helen Gurley Brown, and their boyfriends gladly went along. The era of what D'Emilio and Freedman have dubbed "sexual liberalism" had arrived, in sharp contrast to the preceding era of repression.[4]

Or so goes the current historical orthodoxy, which celebrates the growth of heterosexual pleasure as birth control freed women to plan their families and as declining fears of disease permitted sexual laxity and a retreat from propriety. There have been scholars who differ. Michel Foucault famously challenged the "repressive hypothesis" of Victorianism, and many historians have come to see Victorianism as, if not exactly Bacchanalian, then at least entailing enjoyment of orgasmic sex within the context of marriage. Most influentially, Christina Simmons has identified the creation of a "myth of Victorian repression" that has fooled scholars ever since about Victorians' capacity for erotic fulfillment.[5] Yet in American history, so often rooted anyway in Progressive meliorism, even with the doubts about Victorianism, the onset of AIDS has hardly yet dented the overwhelming view of a shift from nineteenth-century repression to twentieth-century party, with, perhaps, a brief interlude of neo-Victorianism in the 1950s.

Most of this work, however, has focused on women. There is much evidence that the emergence of a New Woman in the early twentieth century represented a genuine freeing of women in all kinds of areas of their lives, from the world of work to their erotic experience. Out with the stifling and confining world of separate spheres and the cult of true womanhood, and on with the brave new world of dating and companionate marriage. But how far is this image of sexless women suddenly liberated relevant to men? Men appear in these accounts either as also-rans or as patriarchs spoiling the fun. Yet as historians of masculinity begin to establish new paradigms to take us beyond the limitations of feminist scholarship, it is surely time that we asked whether the conceptual framework of repression/liberation is appropriate to the experience of American men. Did the early twentieth century see the emergence of a New Man?[6]

Scholars of emotions offer us little help with this problem. The dominant paradigms among emotions' theorists seem to support unquestioningly the fairly simplistic repression versus liberation dichotomy. Norbert Elias has famously talked of a "civilizing process" that began in the eighteenth century to rein in powerful and intense passions in order to better facilitate the pursuit of reason. Individuals were expected to pursue "emotional self-control."[7] In a valuable study, John Kasson has recently applied this schema to the United States. Citing Arlie Hochschild, he argues that "feeling rules ... formed a deep level of etiquette governing social relations among the middle classes." From the eighteenth century, a "decisive shift in notions of appropriate behavior, including a new stress upon emotional control," developed along with an "urban industrial capitalist society."[8] Dutch sociologist Cas Wouters, among others, has argued that an "informalization" of external emotional controls occurred in the twentieth century as a system of "emotional self-restraint" that placed the onus of control onto the self gained ground. Wouters has recently entered the field of the history of sexuality in support of the repression/liberation dichotomy. As he puts it, in a study of British, Dutch, and American etiquette books, "the process may have been experienced as slow or fast, but the direction was undisputed; it went towards greater freedom to control the dynamics of their own relationships, whether romantic or not, and to decide about the respectability of meeting places and conditions." Moreover, "greater freedom ran in tandem with greater intimacy and a chance of friendship and camaraderie between the sexes." There was also a "diminishing social and psychic distance between the sexes." Informalization did not mean the ending of controls over emotions; rather, control was left to the individual. Yet this did involve what he describes rather clumsily as "a collective controlled decontrolling of controls over emotions, especially those that before were considered to be too dangerous and/or degrading to allow."[9] He thus confirms his view of a loosening of mores. Wouters's work neatly complements that of American sociologist Francesca Cancian. In her book *Love in America* she has argued that growing democracy and sexual opportunities in relationships facilitated "intimacy in marriage" and eventually gave a chance for "individual self-development" to complement this intimacy.[10] Theorists of emotions from the field of sociology have therefore generally tended to accept uncritically the female-biased repression/liberation dichotomy in their forays into the history of sexuality.

When we look at the evidence from the male experience, however, another view is possible. This study aims to show that, if we see the changes of the early twentieth-century sexual revolution from the perspective of shifting male sexual emotions, a very different interpretation can be advanced, and the repression/liberation dichotomy can be turned on its head. Victorians had rules around sexuality. But this only served to emphasize the reverence with which they regarded it. Victorian men therefore experienced the greatest intensity of emotion in the deep passion of romantic love that could be experienced with both men and women. They were not emotionally repressed. Thus, as the new sexual culture of the early twentieth century emerged, the result was not liberation. As British sociologist Anthony Giddens has suggested, the new world of youth and amusements heralded a fresh and uncharted sexual and emotional culture. In this era of what he has wittily dubbed "plastic sexuality," the breaking down of controls around male sexuality exposed its "compulsive character," which resulted in the creation of an "emotional abyss . . . between the sexes."[11] Far from informalization, therefore, leading to men and women having more emotional freedom, it distanced them from one another. "Plastic sexuality" implied, too, a sexuality that, having been unleashed from the constraints imposed by sex's connection to reproduction, seemed actually artificial on account of its revolutionary remoteness from perceived traditional and familiar morality. As evidence from the new mass popular culture of movies, ads, sex confession magazines, and marriage manuals will show, when love became sexualized in the early twentieth century, higher, deeper love was subsumed and buried in a compulsive search for sexual gratification. This was superficially more exciting but ultimately vastly less fulfilling, as men experienced a sense of unreality and emotional numbing. In the twentieth century, love and passion seemed to become less remarkable as the mystery and transcendence that Victorians had built around these emotions eroded. Evidence from a wide range of sources that delineate actual experience will show how the New Woman confused for men lust and love on the path to marriage. And I will show how the stress on sex, greater democracy, and easier divorce in marriage undermined the transcendent experience of love. Further, the breaking down of formal enforced rules of etiquette, that is, the "civilizing process," actually created chances for more subtle yet insidious and more compelling forms of social control that stressed lust over love and hence stunted, rather than freed, male emotions. Informalization therefore led not to liberation but entrapment.

On the face of it, Victorians fit perfectly into the model for the history of the emotions established by Norbert Elias. Victorians believed in "civilized morality." In a production- oriented economy, gratification ought to be delayed until the future because of the need for hard work in the present. Leisure, self-indulgence, and the exotic were discouraged by the best people in favor of temperance and self-control. But above all, the attainment of "character" involved the cultivation of "morals." Men of character controlled their primitive urges in order to build up America; hence the "civilizing process" that Elias has identified could make headway. Such men followed a single standard of purity for themselves as well as for women. Victorian marriage manuals lauded the advantage of celibacy. Indeed, men were to be very "athletes of continence." [12] Dutifully accepting this idea, Theodore Roosevelt famously wrote in his diary before marrying his first wife, "Thank God I am perfectly pure." [13]

Procreation was the only justification for sexual intercourse. On that account some writers went to considerable lengths to refer to sex as an "unfortunate necessity." Health reformer Sylvester Graham asserted that men should not "spend" their semen for fear that they would lose valuable energy. [14]

Of course, this massive attempt to assert reason over passion can be seen as an appropriate conservation of energy in an expanding economy. But equally, as Gertrude Himmelfarb has pointed out, it reflected Victorian fears that America was a society adrift from its moorings, and that young men increasingly independent from their parents might take advantage of women and cause illegitimacy and divorce rates to rise. [15] In this context must be seen the emergence around 1830 of the celebrated Victorian ideology of "passionlessness" that urged women to stay free of desire in order to help check, tame, and control overardent males. Pure women symbolized for men their highest spiritual ideals and the possibility of transcendence. At all costs, civilization and the "civilizing process" must be maintained.

This stress on sexual control somewhat ironically explains, too, the peculiar strength in Victorian times of the ancient double standard of sexual morality. Men could relieve their primitive desires and urges by having sex before and even after marriage with lower-class prostitutes. [16] As late as the 1920s, Judge Lindsey surmised that 50 percent of men in Denver had consorted with prostitutes. A study of seven hundred California couples in 1938 by psychologist Lewis Terman suggested that of people born before 1900, three times as many middle-class men as women had experienced premarital sexual intercourse, which confirms the pervasiveness of the double standard at the same time that it implies that some of the sex might have been with working-class prostitutes.[17] The presence of prostitutes in the large cities was given "tacit acceptance" so long as it was contained in the red-light districts that sprang up beside the business areas.[18] Of course, this widespread phenomenon meant sexual indulgence, not control. But in fact, in a long tradition going back to St. Augustine, Victorians saw prostitution as necessary to civilization and the protection of middle-class women: uncontrolled and rampant male sexuality could be channeled off into red-light districts, where the coarser sexual emotions belonged.

Victorians further established in the public world an elaborate conspiracy of silence around sexuality. Marriage manuals were given titles such as *Plain Talks on Avoided Subjects*.[19] British visitor Captain Marryat in the 1830s observed the covering of table legs for fear they suggested female legs.[20] There is much evidence that many Victorians actually balked at the subject of sex. The Reverend Philip Moxon of the White Cross Purity League wondered in a speech, "How shall I put this fitly and plainly say what need to be said without revolting those who hear from a subject which everyone of us would gladly drop into oblivion?"[21] Discussion of sex was strictly taboo. Michel Foucault has famously suggested that the conspiracy of silence only served to make sex more exciting and to make Victorians obsessed with the subject.[22] This is unconvincing. Actually, the conspiracy helped keep lust under control so that romantic love could be the stronger, and in order to maintain the "civilizing process." In this guise, it appears as a key part of the Victorian system of morality.

The rhetoric of control that pervaded public discourse entered into elaborate Victorian courtship rituals. This private arena, as much as the public world, served to check male sexuality. Strict decorum and formal "feeling rules" were essential. The memoirist Henry Seidl Canby recalled in 1934 how men saw courtship at the turn of the century: "We tried to see our girls as romantic beauties and ourselves as gentlemen who lived by honor." An elderly man interviewed in *Middletown* in the mid-1920s who had been a "young buck about town in the 80s" said, "the fellows nowadays don't seem to mind being seen on the streets with a fast woman, but you bet we did then." If the codes were not always as rigid as James Thurber's mother had experienced—"Why, when I was a girl, you didn't dare walk with a man after sunset, unless he was your husband, and even then there was talk"—they were still pretty strict.

As John Kasson has recently shown, the purpose here was not merely the control of sexuality but "preserving public dignity." For a husband and wife there was "no better rule . . . than that they should treat each other, in all outward forms, and in all true respect and courtesy, as if they were not married." Americans prided themselves on the fact that they did not kiss socially—"a reprehensible custom," for it was "not well-bred to kiss any one on the street, even a baby."[23]

The upper and middle classes in the cities in the 1880s relied on the convention of the "call." A gentleman gave his card to a servant at the door, requesting to see the young lady in whom he was interested. If he was frequently received he knew that he had her favor, but if she turned him down, he knew equally where he stood. This was a female-controlled ritual, a consequence of women's power in the domestic sphere. Once the young couple saw each other a few times, they would be allowed out together, traditionally with a chaperone. For the time being, however, the affair must yet remain relatively sedate and unexciting. And sexuality was kept mysterious.

But not for long. Here lay the great irony of Victorian sexual morality. All the stress on reason over passion, the protection of women, fears of sexual anarchy, of youth out of control and the conspiracy of silence did not belie the extraordinarily positive view of sex that Victorians held, provided sex was set in the context of a relationship of romantic passion and love. Victorians were somehow saving the best for last. Stiff formality in public should not therefore be confused with repression. This "civilizing process" ensured that Victorian times were veritably the era "when passion reigned," so long as sex was kept in the private sphere.[24]

As a couple got to know one another and as they developed a relationship, they could spend time alone and build a physical intimacy. They could kiss. They could pet. They could even, once engaged, have full sexual intercourse so long as they cultivated the attitude of "romantic love." In a culture steeped in Christian imagery, yet where Christianity was slowly losing its hold on people, "romantic love" became a central focus of young men's and women's aspirations for happiness and fulfillment. People increasingly lacked the faith that happiness, if not attainable here on earth, could be gained in the next life, but they strove ever harder to ensure that they could be happy in this world.

Romantic love became infused with religious language. To be in love was to be reborn. By the 1830s, the object of "romantic love" had become effectively a challenge to God as the individual's main symbol of purpose and transcendence. Even more significant, sex as the major expression of romantic love became the great sacrament of this new religion, which meant that the act of sex gained importance beyond anything it had before. Although the procreative role of sexuality remained vital, especially in an era of only primitive birth control, sexuality became respectable in the context of "romantic love." Indeed, as a sacramental act, love was celebrated as a spiritual and transcendent experience. Given that sex was permissible only in marriage or in a relationship that was close to marriage and that recreational sex was strictly taboo, sex in love became a wondrous high point in the lives of Victorians, buoyed in the mystery in which it was surrounded.

No wonder the letters Victorian couples wrote to one another reveal an intensity of emotion that is embarrassing in our time. The highest, the very civilizing aspirations of a young man focused on the love object. One man, Albert Janin, wrote to a friend that "my whole emotional being seems merged in yours; robbed of you I should be poor indeed." Another lover wrote of his love for his girlfriend,

> And when I have reasoned it all out, and set bounds for your love that it may not pass, lo, a letter from Clara, and in one sweet, ardent, pure, Edenic page, her love overrides my boundaries as the sea sweeps over rocks and sands alike, crushes my barriers into dust out of which they were builded, over whelms me with its beauty, bewilders me with its sweetness . . . loses me in its great shoreless immensity.

This seems like melodrama. Yet Victorian men and women often felt "romantic love" so intensely that they thought themselves combined in one another. One midwestern farmer wrote to his fiancée that "I look forward with much more pleasing anticipation when we may be united and enjoy all the pleasure of two loving soles *(sic)* joined in one and engulphed *(sic)* in each others arms and swim in a sea of pleasure." Clearly, the years of control were worth the wait. For Victorians, for whom divorce was relatively rare and for whom cohabitation was not a realistic option, the key relationship that led to marriage became all the more important and perhaps even more pleasurable as a result. In a producer-oriented economy, gratification may have been delayed, but when it arrived, how sweet it was. Accordingly, Lester Frank Ward wrote of his fiancée that "We lay with our faces together. I unfastened my shirt and put her tender little hands on my bare breast, and . . . she gave me her heart and her body." Another man wrote to his fiancée, "I could not help saying a few words . . . would that I could kiss you all over and then eat you up." These letters confirm that Victorian times represented, perhaps, an all-time peak of heterosexual experience; for this evidence suggests that in Victorian America, it was truly great to be straight.[25]

Ironically, perhaps, it may also have been a heyday for homoeroticism too. Victorian men, perhaps on account of the lengthy time before they met their wives, formed their own world of intimacy and "romantic friendship." These relationships may or may not have been sexual. But they certainly confirm the capacity for intense feeling and passion that boosted Victorians: "It is not friendship merely that I feel for him, or it is friendship of the strongest kind. It is a heart-felt, a manly, a pure, deep, and fervent love," wrote one young man to another. He described his "deep and burning affection" for his friend. One man described another as "so handsome," and he wrote of their embracing in bed: "How sweet to sleep with him, to hold his beloved form in embrace, to have his arms about my neck, to imprint upon his face sweet kisses." In this environment, Walt Whitman could sleep with his friend John Burroughs, who could comment that "He kissed me as if I were a girl. . . . He bathed today while I was there — such a handsome body. I told him he looked good enough to eat." Yet there was no homoerotic implication. Whether these friendships were actually genital is quite irrelevant. What is significant is that men could and did have intense and passionate relationships with other men without any suspicion that there was a sexual component involved. Walt Whitman could therefore make long lists of young men, without any erotic connotations. Depth and intensity of passion among men who would describe each other with epithets like "Lonely Boy" or "Dearly Beloved" was therefore a socially accepted part of Victorian culture.[26]

Hence the stress on sexual control can surely be seen not as indicative of sexual repression, but as enhancing sexual intensity and passion within the context of "romantic love." Lust, the blandest of sexual emotions, was stifled or kept in its place. This served to make love, the highest of sexual emotions, all the better. As Karen Lystra has suggested, "the public constraints on sexual expression actually encouraged the growth and intensified the experience of private eroticism."[27] So a view of the "civilizing process" that emphasizes erotic regulation is a misreading of Victorian America. Sexual control enabled the "civilizing process" to advance by ensuring that sex took place in the context of "romantic love" and by enforcing the virtues of a production-oriented economy. Victorian "civilized morality" hence appears as the very opposite of repression; rather, it represents the attainment of the greatest intensity and passion of our civilization. Victorians understood that that which could be delayed could be most savored.

But by the turn of the century the Victorian moral system had begun to unravel. The fundamental shifts in American society are well known. As the process of industrialization got under way, a new middle class of managers, bureaucrats, and salesmen appeared in the large corporations of urban America.[28] Lacking the autonomy and independence of Victorian self-made men, and bored by the dullness of the routine of their jobs, this new middle class sought therapy and relief in the advice of an army of experts—doctors, clergy, advertisers who more and more disparaged Victorianism as repressive—and in a vibrant and growing leisure world of movie theaters, dance halls, and new amusements that sprang up in the city as the site of a new American sexual culture. By the 1920s the dating system had developed. An ethos of leisure, pleasure, instant gratification, and fulfillment was diffusing into this world as women, with a little money from work, freed more and more from fears about pregnancy by the availability of birth control, relinquished their role as controllers and checkers of male sexuality. A major paradigm shift was clearly under way in the social relations between the sexes.[29]

Men's experience of love and sexuality was indeed profoundly altered in the new erotic culture. A process of "informalization" got under way with the challenge to the conspiracy of silence. In 1913 the *St. Louis Mirror* famously declared that it was "sex o'clock" in America. Agnes Repplier noted the "repeal of reticence" as a flood of sex books, sex films, sex plays, and sex articles breached the conspiracy. John D'Emilio and Estelle Freedman have depicted the beginnings of a trend toward "sex on display" at this time. By the 1920s there was widespread discussion of sex in American society as sexuality became more visible. Before the onset of censorship in the 1930s, silent films could be relatively open. The first female sex symbols of the movies, Theda Bara and Mary Pickford, had their personal lives raked over in press tittle-tattle. The attention given to male movie stars like Douglas Fairbanks, Sr., and Rudolph Valentino was no less intense. In the theater, Antoine Briand's *Damaged Goods* caused a great scandal in the teens, setting off a genre of plays concerned with venereal disease that, ostensibly aiming to educate, in fact titillated. But this was nothing compared to Mae West's antics as she adopted a prostitute persona for the stage and in films like *She Done Him Wrong* in the 1920s. Further, an entire group of novels about youth caused scandal because of their relative sexual explicitness. The furor aroused by works like Percy Marks's *Plastic Age* was often merely because of the lingering description of kisses. But more usually it was the decadent portrayal of young Americans in works like Warner Fabian's *Flaming Youth* that raised the ire of moralists. Most shocking of all at the time was James Branch Cabell's *Jurgen,* which, although mellowed by its medieval setting, was all the same semipornographic.[30]

Popular journalism, too, breached earlier codes of decorum. To be sure, the *Police Gazette* had been notorious for years. But now it was joined by the likes of the publications of "physical culture" guru Bernarr Macfadden. In particular, his *New York Evening Graphic* featured voyeuristic composites of scenes from contemporary divorce cases. Publications like *True Story* and *Physical Culture* featured scantily clad women in efforts to extend their mass readership. But even relatively respectable magazines like *Munsey's* and *Cosmopolitan* did this too. Of course, there was true pornography in the 1920s, which was not on public display as it is today. But there was a whole genre of relatively risqué material that was: *Art Studies, Art Poses, Art Models,* and *Art Albums* justified the baring of female breasts in the name of art, while *Hot Dog, Hi-Jinks, Whizz Bang, Happy Howls,* and *Paris Nights* served the lowest common denominator. It is significant that all of the above were notorious rather than mainstream. But it's a plausible hypothesis to see in these works the precursors of magazines such as *Playboy* and *Penthouse* that from the 1950s and 1960s heralded the compulsive sexuality of the "sexualized society." Yet the breaching of the conspiracy of silence was no frivolous matter: the whole edifice of Victorian sexuality that had depended on it was undermined by the new public encouragement of unrefined, rawer sexual emotion.

In this context, a new and sexualized set of masculine ideals and images appeared. A fantasy world very different from Victorian public ideals developed for men. Advertisements, innocent by today's standards, offered the prize of sexual satisfaction by encouraging people to purchase the products of mass production. Sexual release or relief was the carrot that substituted for the loss of autonomy that "character" had given the Self-Made Man. Hence advertisements already played overtly on male fears of sexual inadequacy. "He could be so attractive," declared an advertisement in *Colliers* in 1926, but when girls would "look him over carefully" they would "just as carefully overlook him" because of his "grimy-looking skin spotted with blackheads and dull in appearance." The solution to this dilemma was Pompeian Massage Cream. Similarly, cigarette ads accentuated sex appeal. Milano pipes were advertised as "rakish and distinctive." A 1926 *Collier's* ad used a quotation from a student at the University of California who had been converted to pipes when his girlfriend declared them to be "more manly than cigarettes." In one ad in *Physical Culture,* a woman was pictured next to her male dancing partner, thinking, "A good dancer but. . . . No excuse now for perspiration odor — just wash and bathe with the hygienic toilet soap that keeps pores purified." But this stress on bodily attractiveness focused on the carnal, not the spiritual. And new advertising, by arousing male desires insidiously, subliminally, and surreptitiously, gave greater importance to sexuality rather than romance. It stirred up the rawer instincts, sexualized ideals of maleness, and hence contributed to the undermining of the Victorian consensus around sexuality.[31]

These changes were perhaps most clearly exemplified in the sexualization of love itself that occurred in literature and marital advice manuals. Instead of being ethereal and spiritual, love became overtly sexualized. This phenomenon is prevalent in the literature of the youth culture. In Marks's novel *The Plastic Age,* the hero, Hugh, is "lashed by desire, burning with curiosity" at the prospect of meeting his lover. In Fabian's *Flaming Youth,* one young man is described as feeling about his lover that "the terrible fiery desire seized him to claim her then and there, to bid her leave everything for love and go with him to the ends of the earth, to overwhelm her with the force of his desire."[32] Such an aggressive approach to love contrasted sharply with Victorian refinements.

Also significant were the sex confession magazines pioneered by Bernarr Macfadden, among others. Although these stories often preserved the veneer and rhetoric of "romantic love," they veered from Victorianism in their focus on sexual sensation. In one story, "The Fickleness of Men," the hero seizes the heroine: "I snatched her into my arms and held her as in a vise. I smothered her face with my kisses. I was madly infatuated beyond vision or hope. I could hold bounds no longer, nor did I want to. I thrust her from me, tingling in every atom of my being." Similarly, in "A Midnight's Memories," the heroine is swept away by the hero's passion. The author describes how "lower and lower the man's face dropped, while the woman waited in suspenseful bliss for the touch of his lips. They brushed her softly." The sex confession magazines were no less cynical in their commercialization of sex than were advertisers and filmmakers. Their reduction of "romantic love" to crass thrill seeking only continued what other artifacts of the consumer culture had begun: greater value was given to less refined sexual emotions.[33]

But it was in sex and marriage manuals that the sexualization of love was most evident. Hence Samuel Schmalhausen asked, "What in truth is the meaning of marriage if it is not sexual felicity?" Likewise, William Fielding wondered, "But what is love, even in its noblest form, but the supreme refinement of the sexual impulse?" Marriage counselor Ira Wile wrote that while "sex communion possesses esthetic and spiritual attributes . . . this does not, however, mean that the physical side of sex life is not of tremendous importance."[34] The sex manuals of the 1920s encouraged not the brisk, passionate lover of Victorian times, but a robotic sexual automaton. Men were expected to perform in bed. They were to be masterly. Every young husband had to learn that "to be the master of his passion instead of its slave is the first essential rule in love etiquette." He must juggle "passion with compassion." A "magic male manipulation" of women was the secret of the success of the sex act. But while being masterly, he was also supposed to display "tenderness" and "gentle manhood." He should thus be extra careful "not to permit the weight of his body to hold down his wife." The husband's caresses should be likened to the gentle touches of a "composer whose fingers begin an improvisation on a keyboard of his piano." He should "take plenty of time," "avoid hurry," "avoid violence," and "remember that true strength may and should express itself gently." Not all the experts brought out the contradictions in the ideal as clearly as Sanger, who at one point called for "aggressive gentleness."[35]

The first manual to elaborate extensively on sexual technique, Van de Velde's *Ideal Marriage*, first appeared in the United States in 1930. This work brought components of the biology textbook into the American home and accelerated the trend toward what sociologists Brissuet and Lewis have called "sex as work," most clearly illustrated in what Michael Gordon has dubbed "the cult of the mutual orgasm." An interest in women's involvement in the act pervaded these works. For Paul Popenoe, "Sexual intercourse plays fully as large a part in the life of the average wife as it does in that of the average husband." Poet and sex manual writer Clement Wood feared a "passion that leaves the woman unsatisfied." Marriage expert Sherwood Eddy asked whether the sex act was "mutual or one-sided and does it mean the same thing to both parties." For the Binkleys, the central part of the entire "artistry of marriage" was the mutual orgasm: "If the man reaches the orgasm too quickly the woman will fail to experience it at all. The man who understands the physiology of sex can often correct such disharmonies by taking pains more amply to stimulate the tumescent process in the woman, while restraining the process in himself, thus compensating for physiological differences."[36]

The manuals, along with ads, books, and films that increasingly encouraged sexual expression and the informalization of "feeling rules" broke down the elaborate controls around male sexuality. This could all too easily blur for men the distinction between sex and love; here was "plastic sexuality" writ large, a sexuality divorced from higher emotions that reduced love to the level of physical mechanics. Lust could be satisfied, but the deeper fulfillments of love became more elusive. By emphasizing sexual mechanics and techniques, the sex manuals actually succeeded in removing much of the mystery and hence excitement from love. For all the good intentions of some of these writers, these works, like the other artifacts of the mass culture, did not encourage young men's deepest emotional aspirations.

One of the most striking characteristics of the 1920s "revolution in morals" provoked this trend further. Fifteen years ago Barbara Ehrenreich identified a "revolt from commitment" among men in the 1950s.[37] But there is no question that this phenomenon existed in the 1920s too. Popular magazines voyeuristically preyed on the private lives of movie stars, which were every bit as complex as they are today. Whether it was the marriage of Douglas Fairbanks, Sr., and Mary Pickford, the sexual shenanigans of Charlie Chaplin, or the erotic peccadilloes of Rudolph Valentino, the papers loved to write about it. In the process, however, they helped create a fantasy of ideal male behavior that was freewheeling, even permissive, and a long way from Victorian monogamy. To be sure, there was nothing new in a flight from domesticity. Leslie Fiedler, for example, has observed this as a phenomenon in Victorian writing that he terms the "evasion of love": in *Moby-Dick,* he notes, the crew of the *Pequod* experience their last happiness in their encounter with the whaler, *Bachelor.*[38] But a belief in respectability kept this theme firmly in its place and beneath the surface of the public dominance of "romantic love." Now, however, in the emergent mass culture, the flight became a part of the new male ideal.

This tendency was transmitted to American culture by another route, too. From 1910 bohemian groups—the descendants of nineteenth-century free lovers—began to make a mark on the American mainstream. Influenced by the British writers Edward Carpenter and Havelock Ellis and the Swedish marriage expert Ellen Key, they emphasized not merely the sexual aspects of love but also the pleasures of serial monogamy, even of multiple relationships—"varietism," as they rather euphemistically called it. These bohemian groups advocated both polygamy and polyandry in New York's Greenwich Village and on Chicago's East Side. They often disparaged marriage. In the teens, these groups were vilified and spoofed mercilessly in conservative magazines like *Life.* But by the 1920s several of the bohemians wrote works that became texts of the emergent youth and college culture. Two authors in particular expressed and articulated the new morality. Floyd Dell, in a series of intriguing autobiographical novels, *The Moon-Calf* (1920), *The Briary Bush* (1921), and *Janet March* (1923), examined his younger self: he had dabbled in a series of relationships before finally settling into a permanent and very successful marriage with B. Marie Gage. He discussed men's period of "play-need," of experimentation, in which in a series of temporary "relationships" his hero, Felix Fay, considers whether he is in love enough to move on to a long-term relationship: "Yet, even erect and proud, as he thought of her, his mind braced itself, would not quite surrender to the profound restfulness of happiness, but held itself erect and proud as though indeed his soul perceived a beautiful and sweet antagonism." By the time of *An Unmarried Father* in 1925, he was ready to declare that the hero's distrust of marriage was because "he [has] not quite grown up." Ultimately, Dell was a conformist, but one who looked on youthful serial monogamy, even varietism, with affection. Yet because of his advocacy of a series of short, sweet relationships—as he put it memorably, he was looking for a "girl who could be talked to and be kissed"—he represented a clear break from the male ideals of Victorianism.[39]

Harry Kemp's work, best exemplified by *Tramping on Life* (1922) and *More Miles* (1926), made an even sharper break. Imitating Jack London's *Vagabondia*, Kemp advocated the life of the tramp or hobo moving from town to town and girl to girl. He shifted from one brief fling to another, and his work contains long harangues against marriage. But the distance that Kemp felt with women was most strongly depicted in the violence of his relationships. When he first kissed one girl he reveled in her "shrill exclamation of virginal fright, not at me, but at my abrupt, hungry masculinity." Another girl he wooed by declaring, "I love you and I'll kill you—or myself—or both of us—you've got to become my sweetheart." Such work then heralded not just a retreat from deeper intensities as love and sex became confused, but also sexual hostility and a distancing between the sexes. This surely seems more like retrogression than opportunity.[40]

Sex confession magazines also included stories of the antics of Don Juans and Greenwich Village bohemians. Ostensibly, they mocked such a lifestyle, but because the stories were evidently meant to titillate, they represented the further diffusion of the new morality into the middle classes. In "How Life's Lessons Came to Me," the heroine is warned by a friend not to marry a bohemian: "If Allan marries again, he will be faithful to his wife for a while: but the lure to intimate associations with more than one woman will be too strong."

In "Renee Finds a Link," the heroine moves to the Village only to find that "offers of marriage in the village were few." *True Story* in fact delineated for a largely female audience the traps set by the New Man. The magazine warned women of the dangers of predatory bosses, "Stage Door Johnnies," "Lady Bugs," and "Rolling Stones." In "Can a Woman Come Back?" the heroine neatly summarized how this new male ideal differed in his emotional life from his Victorian forebears: "As time went on, I found that love had indeed no deeper meaning to him. He seemed utterly incapable of seeing its spiritual aspect. Openly he boasted to me of his affairs with other women before we were married." Here then was a new model for men: a fantasy world created by popular culture that encouraged a retreat from the deep emotional intensities of committed love and an encouragement of brief, shallow, sex-based relationships of emotional distance that brought temporary, not long-term, fulfillment. By provoking this informalization, popular culture encouraged a profound erosion of private life and spread its own subtle controls that further limited emotional expression.[41]

While this trend was widely noted and remarked on in the America of the 1920s, this "revolt against Victorianism" was not yet respectable. It still competed with powerful traditional forces that worked hard to express their message to the young. Yet a full understanding of the extent of the shift in the male experience of the sexual emotions cannot be had unless some attempt is made to gauge the influence of this "revolt" on middle-class youth. Common sense should tell us that in some regards intimate life remains essentially the same, uninfluenced by social fluxes and forces. Yet considerable evidence—especially in our period—points to a massive shift in male emotional culture that, albeit with some significant cultural lag, had a very real impact.

Most of the work in the history of the emotions has focused on heterosexuality. But much of the most compelling evidence of a growing social control is in two relatively uncharted and understudied areas. One of the oft-cited characteristics of Victorian marriage manuals was an obsession with masturbation, "the solitary vice." Manual writers warned men of the loss of virility that would be entailed if they indulged and, famously, threatened them with various alarming medical conse- quences. Winfield Scott Hall wrote that the "natural process of development from youth to manhood could be seriously interfered with by the act of self-abuse." Indeed, if he continued to practice it, "the youth might almost have no testicles." Further, according to sex educator E. B. Lowry, "older boys who are masturbating usually get a sallow look and have a hang-dog expression." This injunction had a social function; sex was officially appropriate only in the context of "romantic love." Masturbation was understood as substandard and emotionally stunting. But in some manuals from the turn of the century there were signs of liberalization. Social hygienist Frederic Gerrish in his book *A Talk to College Boys* admitted that "in general the health is not ruined, as is alleged in the quack adverts that deface and disgrace some journals." Still, he opposed onanism; "the fact remains that the practice is low, filthy, bestial and degrading." W. J. Robinson, the leading liberalizer, was relatively enthusiastic, however: "The evil results of masturbation have been shamefully and stupidly exaggerated. In the vast majority of cases masturbation leads to no disastrous results and it is better for a man who cannot satisfy his sex instinct naturally to indulge in occasional masturbation." W. F. Robie was even more pragmatic: "Occasional masturbation is for many single people a necessity to prevent marital disorders or the moral contamination of promiscuous sex relations." And in a strikingly modern mood he continued, "Practically all young people masturbate at one time or another." These writers here established the roots of the strong encour- agement of masturbation in contemporary advice.[42]

Certainly men still worried about masturbation. A young man wrote in to Lindsey that on account of past masturbation habits, he was "ashamed to look a girl in the face." Another young man pleaded that he "would rather be a eunoch than continue this way. Oh, please help me!" But a more pragmatic older man noted that the "practice is not harmful when practiced with restraint." He continued, "I know from twenty five years experience. I married; we have one son, who is now away at college. I advise him to practice it when the appetite troubles him. I know that it does not weaken the enjoyment of intercourse with a woman and does not debase in any way.

All the supposed experts who advise to the contrary are liars, parasites who are exploiting the young people." [43] Various sex surveys at the time established that a large percentage of people were concerned about masturbation, but that a substantial percentage were unconcerned, as well. However, the trend toward greater liberalization is clear. This relative tolerance in some ways epitomized the new pragmatic—yet plastic, bland, rather numbing, and controlling—attitude toward sexual emotions.

Even more intriguing was the changing approach to homoeroticism. In Victorian male middle-class culture, love between men was not sexualized. Hence strong emotional attachments to other men were often an important part of male development. But now doctors and experts, drawing on lower-class models, identified a distinctive homosexual type of person. This identification drew a cloud of ambiguity into love between men, from which it has never recovered. In *The Doctor Looks at Love and Life* (1926), a highly popular manual, Joseph Collins devoted one-third of its space to homoeroticism and cast direct suspicion on the Victorian world of "romantic friendship" between men. "There are persons who indulge in unnatural sexual relations who are not homosexuals. They are real degenerates. There are many potential and actual homosexuals whose intercourse with persons of their own sex is confined to emotional and intellectual contact; to establish romantic friendship with them." Alarmingly, this homosexual was difficult to identify. He was not really a man "of broad hips and mincing gait, who vocalizes like a lady and articulates like a chatterbox, who likes to sew and knit, to ornament his clothing and decorate his face." "Strangely enough," there were "husky, articulate, self-opinionated and even domineering ones. Indeed, most of them ... have what is known as a superiority complex which they conceal." Such a man could be your best friend. [44]

Equally as undermining of male romantic friendship was the identification of widespread homosexual feeling in adolescence. This was a genuinely new perspective. Bohemian manual writer Clement Wood noted that at puberty 30 percent of male sexual feeling was homosexual, down from 50 percent in a boy of twelve. There is plenty of evidence that the experts' recognition of this feeling caused actual anxiety. In *A Research in Marriage,* Gilbert Hamilton asked one hundred married men about their attitudes toward homoeroticism in the late 1920s. He found that "the majority of American adult males probably fear all the other tabooed components of the human reactive equipment taken together." Forty-seven percent of the men he interviewed said that it made them "uncomfortable to have a person of their own sex put his arm about [him] or make other physical demonstrations." Bromley and Britten's 1930s study of college men noted that "over half of the men condemned the practice, some more severely than others." Some declared that homosexuals "should be hung" and that they would not even speak to "queers, pansies and fruits." If new attitudes on masturbation offered men a bland alternative to sex with another person, it seems that attitudes toward homosexuality actually blocked off one whole previous area of emotional experience. Homosexuality, surveys of early twentieth-century men suggest, was quite prevalent. In Hamilton's study of theater people, 57 percent of the men interviewed claimed to have experienced some kind of homo-erotic activity during their lives, while 17 percent had practiced after the age of eighteen. Kinsey famously found that 37 percent of American men had had experience to orgasm. This is probably much too high, as is his oft-quoted claim that 10 percent of American men had had mainly homosexual experiences over at last three years. But George Chauncey, Jr., examining recent studies from Britain and Europe that imply a figure for recent gay experience of around 2.5 percent, has compellingly suggested that opportunities for the homoerotic alternative really have been reduced: "the pre-war sexual regime would have made it easier for men to engage in casual homosexual behavior in the 1930s than in the 1980s, when such behavior would have ineluctably marked them out as homosexual."[45]

The same phenomenon may have subverted the path to heterosexual adjustment as well. The 1920s heralded two new approaches to American courtship and marriage—the dating system and companionate marriage. The dating system was in some ways a much lighter, less serious business than Victorian courtship. It gave opportunity for middle-class men to have relationships of varying intensity with middle-class women, from casual dating to "going steady" to Victorian-style engagement. The dating system epitomized the informalization of "feeling rules" identified by Wouters because it took courtship away from the rigid, if flexible, system controlled by home and family—and into the peer-led youth culture, where it was subject to the whims of fad and fashion, and where a system of "emotional self-restraint" took hold.

Dating helped create and provoke a growing emotional distance between men and women. In his classic 1937 article of sociological analysis, "The Rating and Dating Complex," Willard Waller described the style of dating among young people in the 1920s and 1930s as very different from the Victorian practice of "calling." Dating was, according to Waller, a "competitive game" between men and women. To be valued as a male, one had to cultivate a "line." This "line" was a "conventional attempt on the part of the young man to show that he had already at this early stage fallen seriously in love with her . . . a sort of exaggeration, sometimes a burlesque of coquetry." Not only was the "line" crucial in starting the relationship, but it also was of importance to its continuation. It was vital to "invite the other to rapid sentiment formation— each encourages the other to fall in love by pretending that he has not already done so." The purpose of the game was to cause one or the other to "rise to the bait," that is, actually to fall in love. Waller famously emphasized the "principle of least interest," whereby the one who had less invested in the continuation of the affair controlled the relationship. Hence "the rating and dating complex" introduced a rather cynical and competitive element into the previously ethereal and ritualized process of falling in love.[46]

Waller also believed that the dating system involved mutual exploitation for the attainment of "thrills" rather than any long-term commitment or a serious search for love. There is evidence for this shift from popular culture. The movies helped establish kissing as an essential "thrill" that did not especially provoke controversy. All the same, such animated discussion of this subject was quite new at the time. One young man in a study of the effect of the movies on youth declared that "I found that I, the pure virgin, actually conceived of kissing a girl, and actually enjoying it, too." A white Jewish sophomore confessed that the movies caused him to "want to kiss and fondle any young lady that happens to be with me." The movies were a central resource for the mores of the peer-led youth culture. They could determine that at least "kissing" was an acceptable "thrill" on a date. Indeed, "kissing" became a part of contemporary dating.[47]

Petting, however, was another matter. The question of how to pet, when to pet, even "why they pet" was constantly being discussed in the 1920s. One of the characteristics of the flapper was her willingness to pet. Yet the flapper who petted represented a departure and clouded the distinction between a good and a bad woman. Much Victorian mystery and excitement disappeared. As women under the dating system were encouraged to be more sexually expressive, so men became confused as to appropriate behavior. Cas Wouters has talked of the rise of "emotional self-restraint," but when was it necessary to hold back and when should one express? Young men commented on the "many codes" available to them in the 1920s. Sociologist Ernest Groves noted that "the question for all thoughtful youth . . . is what type and degree of physical-emotional intimacy, if any, is advisable before the more definite mutual commitment of one man and one woman to each other in engagement?" Numerous social commentators observed the confusion over changing mores. Theodore Newcomb discussed these contradictions: "It is expected by both boys and girls that men should prefer virginity in girls, but don't insist"; "Boys do not particularly want the Victorian conception of purity in the girl they marry"; "it is right and decent to have intimate relations with the person you love, but you mustn't be promiscuous—that's cheap and vulgar." Indeed, writing in the mid-1930s, he concluded that the codes were united only by an aversion to "marital infidelity and premarital promiscuity." In their study *Middletown* in 1929 the Lynds noted that "a heavy taboo, supported by law and by both religion and popular sanctions, rests on sexual relations between persons who are not married." But by 1937, when they returned to Middletown for their update, *Middletown in Transition,* they could observe that "the range of sanctioned choices is wider, the definition of the one 'right way' less clear." Ultimately, Newcomb wrote, "If there is a 'typical' attitude of college youth today, it is presumably one of conflict between codes which diverge in greater or lesser degree in respect to the point beyond which one may not go." Dating involved informalization. Floyd Dell's period of "play-need" had been institutionalized. But the stress on "thrill seeking" and the competitive game confused the path to love by blurring the distinction between lust and "romantic love."[48]

Hence it was the definition of sexual boundaries that preoccupied youth in the 1920s. The informalization of rules, far from bringing men and women closer together, actually drove them further apart, because the young who looked to their peers for advice about "emotional self-restraint" would learn merely through trial and error. Wouters is optimistic about this. He writes that "both sexes will have to rely on experience as well as experimenting, searching for new balances between ways and means of intimacy and distance, between the quest for attachment and the fear of avoiding the emotional extremes of emotional wildness and emotional numbness." But Wouters is, perhaps, too hopeful here: young men simply held on to older values. They lacked the time, luxury, or savoir faire to re-create gender roles in their relations with women. The New Woman elicited a great deal of distrust because it was acceptable to defile a bad woman, but not a good woman. Which was she? To defile a good woman was shameful: "Dear God. That I had to do this to her . . . she of all girls whom I cared for alone, she who had been so pure and sweet—blasted by my own damned uncontrollable passion." But not to know if a future wife was a virgin was worse: "in all this time I have not dared ask her as to her physical standing, and neither have I told her as to mine and all that, but I would like to know frankly just what is what." Men still held to the double standard. It had not created hostility between the sexes in Victorian times because a woman's virginity was assumed, as now it could not be. The 1930 Katz/Allport report on undergraduate adjustment found that men had "a keener consciousness of moral propriety when contemplating the behavior of women than when judging themselves." They described the conundrums that men faced: "Most codes are that a fellow will not if he knows it seduce a virgin, but any advances on their part will be accepted. But the sad part with most boys is, that if a good girl permits this, he thinks she has conducted herself the same as when this is not the case and they will not believe her." And there is intriguing evidence from Kinsey that the number of men who wanted to marry virgins actually was increasing: 41.6 percent of the forty-six or older group at the time of interview wished for their brides to be virgins, compared to 50.7 percent of those aged between adolescence and twenty-five at the time of interview. The new freedom therefore clearly blurred the distinction between good and bad women so essential to Victorians and hence confused for men the crucial distinction between lust and love.[49]

However, it went beyond this: purity in a woman for men raised in this way symbolized their higher aspirations for emotional and spiritual transcendence. Anything less seemed to threaten their sense of right and wrong and seemed to challenge their very capacity to love. Hence men reacted in more and more vehement and less savory ways to the emotional confusion that the ambiguous codes represented. They publicly flaunted their disrespect for women. In a YMCA in-house journal a writer wrote of an upcoming dance, "Bring your favorite skirt with you—wife, sweetie, friend, acquaintance, or the other bloke's girl. If you're a poor bum and you can't get a chicken, remember you're coming to a pilot's affair." Movie starlets were described as "beautiful but dumb." In *The Plastic Age,* young college men discussed their motives for talking dirty, as they had been doing to their "dates." Sociologist Ernest Burgess noted that sex was now an "open subject for repartee and discussion among mixed groups." Eleanor Wembridge said it best: "The sex manners of the large majority of uncultivated and uncritical people have become the manners for all."[50]

Many men did not worry over the finer points of the shifting codes and insisted on attaining whatever thrills they wished. "Plastic sexuality" was, as Giddens indicated, "compulsive." Some girls complained that "we are non-petters. So far we have upheld our views but we are becoming desperate. Every young man we have found to be inclined towards petting." A girl quoted by sociologists Blanchard and Manasses complained that she "was not popular" for she had "yet to find [a man] who does not want a girl to pet the first time he meets her." But men complained about women, too. "Gold-digger" became a commonly used expression for a woman who spent a man's money. In the *American* magazine in September 1924, a man noted that he had spent five thousand dollars on courting in the previous five years, and now he was going to declare a "one-man buyer's strike." Needless to say, men were hesitating to marry because of the costs: "Get married. Why I can't even afford to go with the sort of girls with whom I would wish to associate." Another young man wrote to Martha Carr of the *St. Louis Post-Dispatch* that (he thought) "the modern girl is too calculating. If she is a young girl with an eye to matrimony she coolly sits down and figures it out. What am I going to get? Where will I have to live?"[51] Therefore, young men and women were very far from the active agents negotiating the balance between "emotional wildness and emotional numbness" that Wouters has described; rather, a battle had ensued between the sexes in which "emotional numbness" soon became ascendant.

No wonder magazines praised bachelorhood. Men openly declared that they preferred the company of other men. An article in *Collier's* noted that "the general opinion seems to be that the young men of today do not wish to marry." Magazine articles reveled in the "joys of single blessedness" with renewed vigor. If a young man remained free, he "could take a blonde to dinner in a Bohemian restaurant," "dance on a table with her," and "vamp three other women" at the same time. Psychologist Beatrice Hinkle confirmed that this was not new behavior: "the disinclination of men towards marriage is not a recent development." But its cause had changed: "their former attitude was more of an egoistic unwillingness to give up the pleasures of bachelor freedom or to assume the responsibility and obligations of a family," whereas the situation now was different, being "frankly one of fear and uncertainty regarding women." This was not liberation; rather, it confirms Giddens's view of a "growing emotional abyss between men and women" as men abandoned committed relationships.[52]

Marriage was hardly free from these developments either. One landmark was Lindsey's book *The Companionate Marriage* (1927). With the aid of birth control, the arrival of children could be delayed so that the married couple could determine their suitability for one another and, if necessary, obtain an easy divorce should they decide they were incompatible. Lindsey was describing a precursor to the 1970s trial marriage. But his ideas are important because they represent the trend and direction of marriage in the period—toward more divorce, a greater emphasis on sex, and more democratic roles for men and women. Lindsey well understood that marriage was becoming a less momentous event. In 1924, there was one divorce for every 6.9 marriages, as compared to one for every 17.1 marriages in 1890. As the Lynds put it in *Middletown in Transition*, "Marriage need not be final since divorce is no longer a serious disgrace." Hence marriage lacked the make or break, once in a lifetime element that had perhaps better facilitated the development of deeper feelings and emotions for the Victorians, that had indeed made engagement and marriage so exciting. Even marriage could be temporary, if intense.[53]

There is much evidence that sex was becoming more significant in marriage. Lindsey's stress on the importance of compatibility included sexual suitability. The studies of the Chicago sociologists and the popularity of marriage manuals all confirm this. Kinsey's figures do not, however, suggest that men were having more sex in marriage. But the most tantalizing evidence is from Lewis Terman's 1938 study *Psychological Factors in Marital Happiness*. He argued that men and women were becoming more capable of enjoying sex. He proposed that "the fault of excessive modesty is rapidly disappearing among women of the populations sampled by our group. The proportion of husbands reporting the wife to be overmodest or prudish decreased from 21.9% for husbands born before 1890 to 12.3% for those born after 1909." Even more suggestive is evidence that men actually spent more time performing the sex act. The amount of time involved having sex itself increased by around 30 percent from those born before 1880 to those born after 1909. This Terman attributed to "the effects upon young people themselves of the widely popular literature dealing with sex technique." But the emphasis on sex could distance men and women. As one Chicago man wrote to Marie Stopes in London, "She, you would classify as 'cold' . . . I am the other extreme unfortunately and crassly stupid. And in my ignorance I ask her if there is some mode of caressing that might be happily preparatory. . . . No—if I could tell you would probably go through your lesson in a mechanical (?) way and all the element of surprise and pleasure would be lacking." Writing of England, Lesley Hall has delineated a vast amount of anxiety over sexuality in marriage in letters to Marie Stopes. Similarly, Elaine Tyler May, in her study of California and New Jersey divorce cases, has demonstrated how greater expectations of sexual felicity influenced marriage at this time. One husband in her survey of 1920 Los Angeles and New Jersey divorce cases called his wife a "God damn whore" because he was impotent. But many men were "deeply suspicious" of wives' sexual desires: one husband described his wife as a "lewd and dissolute" person because of her desires. Still, the evidence about sexuality in marriage remains ambiguous, suggesting the perils of transition.[54]

Marriage did become more democratic. Lindsey argued that companionate marriage could be fostered by "communication." Francesca Cancian has argued that this change provided an opportunity for extended "emotional intimacy," as "self-development and enduring love can be mutually reinforcing." This conclusion, too, is debatable. Many articles appeared that proposed that men's adjustment to their working wives was difficult. In "We Both Had Jobs," "progressive" husband "Jerry" still felt that the "instinct was strong to be what his father had been—sole provider for the family." In the 1920s, the genre of the "neurotic husband" gained currency. Psychiatrist Abraham Myerson detected a "nervousness, a kind of neurosis normally associated with housewives" that was spreading to men; it entailed "in both, the same fatigue, easily arising and hard to dispel—changes in mood, loss of desire for food, restlessness." As writer Smiley Blanton put it, man "with his unconscious feeling of superiority, his ignorance of women's subtle sex life, his repression and shame at the art of love, his insistence on domination by force or by infantile methods, is undergoing a severe emotional strain that is causing him to break down with an actual neurosis." Further, when faced with divorce, men complained. One man wrote of his divorce, "There is a feeling of wounded pride here in my breast, and it hurts as much as though I had been dealt a stiff blow." Men sought to free themselves from the New Woman. Marcus Ravage wondered in the *American Monthly* why his "Wife Won't Let Me Be a Gypsy." Joseph Hergesheimer asked in the *Pictorial Review* of 1926 whether it was now possible to be "married and free." He went on: "Where once he had been in control, now he must explain to unsympathetic ears just why he supposes he is a Moses." It is therefore at the very least an exaggeration to stress as Cancian does that modern marriage gives the chance to enhance "psychic intimacy."[55] This chance, such as it was, was all too often squandered in squabbles, mutual hostility, and growing divorce. Cancian is therefore overoptimistic about modern love. Much of the evidence suggests there was an emotional emptiness about many modern marriages: democratic marriage all too often involved a decline in commitment to the institution as the individual saw the relationship only as a means of fulfilling short-term needs. "Self-development" without social responsibility made "enduring love" all the harder.

What is clear is that from the early twentieth century men faced a sexual and emotional culture in the United States that was indifferent and worse to the deep intensities of sexual passion and "romantic love." The artifacts of mass culture titillated by stressing less refined sexual emotions; they worked against the religious and secular ideals of "romantic love" on which the "civilizing process" had depended. Ads, movies, and popular literature all set an appropriate fantasy image for American men to attain, one that was highly sexualized and attractive to women, yet that was also self-absorbed and liable to provoke emotional distancing from women. Sex and marriage manuals grafted on to this image the idea of men as performers in bed: the Victorian "athlete of continence" became the twentieth- century sexual athlete as love became sexualized. Less rarified emotions—lust—were mixed in with higher emotions. Victorians had stifled, or at least confined, less-refined emotions to make romantic love better. But moderns, by confusing the two, actually stunted the higher. This confusion was reflected in the growing informalization or casualization of private life. The dating system encouraged "thrill seeking" and game playing as peer-led youth culture stressed "emotional self-restraint." But it also hopelessly confused the difference between lust and love. Far from enhancing male-female relationships and intimacy, the dating system and companionate marriage actually worked against intimacy between men and women because the resulting confusion of emotions aggravated distrust. Informalization therefore did not mean liberation but the actual undermining of "romantic love" in its highest, most intense form. The capacity to love was impeded and restrained. No wonder men increasingly revolted against marriage and commitment and, unable to love as intensely, sought out short, sharp, sweet, and fleeting relationships. Social commentator Theodore Newcomb noted that "there is considerable evidence that among some groups at least the newer codes . . . were actually compulsive, that individuals in considerable numbers felt themselves in danger of losing caste if the new freedom was not explored."[56] The undermining of transcendent and higher love left many men aimlessly searching for substitutes in the world of leisure and pleasure for the deeper satisfactions—even the better orgasms— that the Victorians had had. Moreover, informalization, ironically, did not just mean the replacement of liberation for something a good deal less ethereal, but rather the setting up of subtly coercive controls that promised excitement and thrills but that actually delivered emotional distancing and numbing. Such was modern love.

It would all the same be naive to assume that men and women, men and men, or women and women did not still fall deeply, meaningfully, and passionately in love with one another as they have always done. Love could conquer all, even the social construction of emotions. But American culture actually worked against it doing so and made it harder for love to succeed in the long term. This was indeed a "plastic sexuality" divorced from older procreative imperatives and set adrift from older moral constraints. In this way a focus on male emotions exposes the female-biased repression/liberation dichotomy of historical change from the nineteenth to the twentieth centuries and turns it on its head. Wouters and Cancian's view of shifts in the sexual emotions in this period is challenged as overly optimistic and as also reflecting female bias; Victorian women do seem to have been confined and the dating system does seem to have given them greater freedom to enhance intimacy. But these scholars' heavy reliance on female-written etiquette books does not help us particularly to understand the male experience. Equally, the history of the emotions' paradigm of "informalization" needs to be evaluated in the light of findings in the particular fields in which it applies: in view of the cooling and distancing that informalization and casualization have wrought in the area of sexuality, have we in our abandonment of "civilizing" controls lost out and become decentered and disconnected from one another? Are we losing the capacity for emotional intimacy itself? Are we paying too high a price for modern love?

NOTES

1. Barbara Welter, "The Cult of True Womanhood," *American Quarterly* 18 (March 1966); Nancy Cott, "Passionlessness: An Interpretation of Victorian Sexual Ideology," *Signs* 4 (Autumn 1978): 219–36.

2. Alfred Kinsey, *Sexual Behavior in the Human Female* (New York: W. B. Saunders, 1953), 299; Daniel Scott Smith, "The Dating of the American Sexual Revolution: Evidence and Interpretation," in Michael Gordon, ed., *The American Family in Socio-Historical Perspective* (New York: St. Martin's, 1973), 321–35.

3. On the New Woman, see Carroll Smith-Rosenberg, "The New Woman as Androgyne," in *Disorderly Conduct: Visions of Gender in Victorian America* (New York: Knopf, 1985); and Estelle Freedman, "The New Woman: Changing Views of Women in the 1920s," *Journal of American History* 64 (March 1974): 398–411; Kathy Peiss, *Cheap Amusements: Working Women and Leisure in Turn of the Century New York* (Philadelphia: Temple University Press, 1986).

4. John D'Emilio and Estelle Freedman, *Intimate Matters: A History of Sexuality in America* (New York: Harper and Row, 1988).

5. Michel Foucault, *The History of Sexuality,* vol. 1, *An Introduction* (New York: Pantheon, 1978); Christina Simmons, "Modern Sexuality and the Myth of Victorian Repression," in Kathy Peiss and Christina Simmons, eds., *Passion and Power* (Philadelphia: Temple University Press, 1989), 57–77. The liberationist argument is epitomized by the likes of Beth Bailey, *From Front Seat to Backseat: Courtship in Twentieth Century America* (Baltimore: Johns Hopkins University Press, 1988).

6. Historians have shown little interest in twentieth- century male sexuality. Except Kevin White, *The First Sexual Revolution: The Emergence of Male Heterosexuality in Modern America* (New York: New York University Press, 1993); and Peter Stearns and Mark Knapp, "Men and Romantic Love: Pinpointing a Twentieth Century Change," *Journal of Social History* 26 (summer 1993): 769–97.

7. Norbert Elias, *The Civilizing Process: The History of Manners,* trans. Edmund Jephcott (New York: Urizen, 1978).

8. John Kasson, *Rudeness and Civility: Manners in Nineteenth Century Urban America* (New York: Hill and Wang, 1990), 147; Arlie R. Hochschild, "Emotion Work, Feeling Rules, and Social Structure," *American Journal of Sociology* 85 (1979): 551–75.

9. Cas Wouters, "Etiquette Books and Emotion Management in the Twentieth Century: Part Two—The Integration of the Sexes," *Journal of Social History* 29 (winter 1995): 325–41.

10. Francesca Cancian, *Love in America* (New York: Oxford University Press, 1987), 29.

11. Anthony Giddens, *The Transformation of Intimacy* (London: Polity, 1992), 2, 3.

12. Charles Rosenberg, "Sexuality, Class and Social Role in Nineteenth Century America," in Joseph H. Pleck and Elizabeth H. Pleck, eds., *The American Man* (Englewood Cliffs, NJ: Prentice Hall, 1980), 224.

13. Quoted in John Burnham, "The Progressive Era Revolution in American Attitudes towards Sex," in *Paths into American Culture* (Philadelphia: Temple University Press, 1988), 151.

14. Sylvester Graham, *A Lecture to Young Men* (Providence, RI: Weeden and Cory, 1834), 17, 33; Ben Barker Benfield, *The Horrors of the Half-Known Life: Male Attitudes towards Women and Sexuality in Nineteenth Century America* (New York: Harper and Row, 1976).

15. Gertrude Himmelfarb, *The De-Moralisation of Society: From Victorian Virtues to Modern Values* (London: IEA Health and Welfare Unit, 1995).

16. Judge Ben B. Lindsey, *The Revolt of Modern Youth* (New York: Boni and Liveright, 1925), 56.

17. Lewis M. Terman, *Psychological Factors in Marital Happiness* (New York: McGraw Hill, 1938), 321.

18. Neil Larry Shumsky, "Tacit Acceptance: Respectable Americans and Segregated Prostitution, 1870 to 1910," *Journal of Social History* 19 (fall 1986): 664–79.

19. F. A. David, *Plain Talks on Avoided Subjects* (Philadelphia, 1899).

20. Captain Marryat, *A Diary in America* (London: Orme, Brown, Green, and Longman's, 1839), 2:244–47.

21. Reverend Philip Moxon, *The White Cross Purity League* (New York: YMCA, 1888).

22. Foucault, *History of Sexuality*, 3–13.

23. Henry Seidl Canby, "Sex and Marriage in the Nineties," *Harper's* 169 (June–November 1934): 427–36; Robert Lynd and Helen Lynd, *Middletown: A Study in American Culture* (New York: Harcourt, Brace, Jovanovich, 1929), 112; James Thurber, *Alarms and Diversions* (New York: Harper and Brothers, 1957), 99; Kasson, *Rudeness and Civility*, 162.

24. Patricia Anderson, *When Passion Reigned: Sex and the Victorians* (New York: Basic, 1995).

25. Karen Lystra, *Searching the Heart: Men, Women and Romantic Love in Victorian America* (New York: Oxford University Press, 1989), 45, 176; Ellen Rothman, *Hands and Hearts: A History of Courtship in America* (New York: Basic, 1985), 139, 134, 128.

26. Anthony Rotundo, *American Manhood: Transformations in Masculinity from the Revolution to the Modern Era* (New York: Basic, 1993), 81, 82; Philip Callow, *Walt Whitman: From Noon to Starry Night* (London: Alison and Busby, 1992), 257.

27. Rom Harre, "An Outline of the Social Constructionist Viewpoint," in Rom Harre ed., *The Social Construction of Emotions* (New York: Oxford University Press, 1986), 5 states that lust is not an emotion, but "a bodily agitation." This indeed is my point; it is no more than this; this is why emotions are stunted and stifled; Lystra, *Searching the Heart*, 91.

28. Robert Wiebe, *The Search for Order* (New York: Hill and Wang, 1967).

29. John Modell, *Into One's Own: From Youth to Adulthood in the United States, 1920 to 1975* (Berkeley: University of California Press, 1989).

30. Agnes Repplier, "The Repeal of Reticence," *Atlantic* (March 1914): 297–304; D'Emilio and Freedman, *Intimate Matters*, 277–88; Percy Marks, *The Plastic Age* (New York: Grosset and Dunlap, 1924); Warner Fabian, *Flaming Youth* (New York: Macaulay, 1923); James Cabell, *Jurgen* (New York: Crown, 1919).

31. *Collier's*, August 14, 1926, 33; *Life*, May 20, 1925, 29; *Collier's*, July 3, 1926, 38; *Physical Culture*, June 1927, 67.

32. Marks, *Plastic Age*, 165; Fabian, *Flaming Youth*, 205.

33. "The Fickleness of Men," *True Story* 13, no. 3 (1925): 135; "A Midnight's Memories," *True Story* 7, no. 6 (1922): 112.

34. Samuel Schmalhausen, *Why We Misbehave* (New York: Macaulay, 1928), 14; William Field-

ing, *Man's Sexual Life* (Girard, KS: Haldeman-Julius, 1925), 156; Ira Wile, *Marriage in the Modern Manner* (New York: Century, 1929), 57.

35. Quotes from Margaret Sanger, *Happiness in Marriage* (New York: Blue Ribbon, 1926); Schmalhausen, *Why We Misbehave*; H. W. Long, *Sane Sex Life and Sane Sex Living* (New York: Eugenics, 1919); Wile, *Marriage in the Modern Manner*.

36. Theodore Van de Velde, *Ideal Marriage: Its Physiology and Technique* (New York: Random House, 1934); Michael Gordon, "From an Unfortunate Necessity to a Cult of Mutual Orgasm: Sex in Marital Education Literature, 1840–1940," in James Henslin, ed., *The Sociology of Sex* (New York: Schocken, 1978), 53–67; Paul Popenoe, *Modern Marriage: A Handbook* (New York: Macmillan), 157; Clement Wood, *Manhood: The Facts of Life Presented to Men* (Girard, KS: Haldeman-Julius, 1924), 3; Sherwood Eddy, *Sex and Youth* (New York: Doubleday, Doran, 1928), 55; Robert Binkley and Frances Binkley, *What Is Right with Marriage? An Outline of Domestic Theory* (New York: Appleton, 1929), 242.

37. Barbara Ehrenreich, *The Hearts of Men: American Dreams and the Flight From Commitment* (New York: Doubleday, 1983).

38. Leslie Fiedler, *Love and Death in the American Novel* (New York: Stein and Day, 1966), 369–88.

39. Floyd Dell, *Moon-Calf* (New York: Knopf, 1920), 322; idem, *An Unmarried Father* (New York: Knopf, 1925), 30; idem, *Moon-Calf*, 293.

40. Harry Kemp, *More Miles: An Autobiographical Novel* (New York: Boni and Liveright, 1926), 213.

41. "How Life's Lessons Came to Me," *True Story* 2, no. 3 (1919): 23; "The Little Cloud," *True Story* 3, no. 2 (1920): 23; "Renee Finds a Link," *True Story* 4, no. 3 (1921): 79; "Can a Woman Come Back?" *True Story* 10, no. 4 (1923): 73–74.

42. Winfield Scott Hall, *Sexual Knowledge* (Philadelphia: Winston, 1918), 106; E. B. Lowry, *Himself* (Chicago: Forbes, 1916), 65; Frederic Gerrish, *A Talk to College Boys* (Boston: Gorham, 1917), 30; W. J. Robinson, *Sex Morality* (New York: Critic and Guide, 1919), 65; W. F. Robie, *Sex and Life* (New York: Rational Life Publishing, 1924), 23.

43. Letter to Lindsey, April 14, 1925, box 351, Judge Ben B. Lindsey Papers, Library of Congress, Washington, DC; letter to Lindsey, January 8, 1925, Lindsey Papers; Cyrus H. to Lindsey, December 12, 1926, Lindsey Papers.

44. Joseph Collins, *The Doctor Looks at Love and Life* (New York: Doran, 1926), 73, 74, 65.

45. Gilbert Hamilton, *A Research in Marriage* (New York: Boni, 1929), 478; Dorothy Bromley and F. L. Britten, *Youth and Sex: A Study of Thirteen Hundred College Students* (New York: Harper and Brothers, 1938), 210–12; George Chauncey, Jr., *Gay New York: Gender, Urban Culture and the Making of the Gay Male World, 1890–1940* (New York: Basic, 1994), 71 n.

46. Willard Waller, "The Rating and Dating Complex," *American Sociological Review* 2 (1937): 727–34.

47. Herbert Blumer, *Movies and Conduct* (New York: Macmillan, 1933), 154, 113.

48. Ernest W. Burgess, "Sociological Aspects of the Sex Life of the Unmarried Adult," in Ira Wile, ed., *Sex Life of the Unmarried Adult*, 125; Theodore Newcomb, "Recent Changes in Attitudes toward Sex and Marriage," *American Sociological Review* 2 (1937): 659–66, 663; Lynd and Lynd, *Middletown*, 112; idem, *Middletown in Transition* (New York: Harcourt, Brace, Jovanovich, 1927), 175; Newcomb, "Recent Changes," 663.

49. Letter to Lindsey, November 6, 1926, Lindsey Papers; 11 W 115th. Street to Lindsey, January 7, 1926, Lindsey Papers; Wouters, "Etiquette Books and Emotion Management," 336; Daniel Katz and Floyd Allport, *Student Attitudes: A Report of the Syracuse University Reaction Study* (Syracuse: Craftsman, 1931), 253; Alfred Kinsey, *Sexual Behavior in the Human Male* (Philadelphia: W. B. Saunders), 364.

50. "West Side Men," New York West Side YMCA, April 5, 1929, 1; Percy Marks, *The Plastic Age* (New York: Grosset and Dunlap, 1924), 155; Burgess, "Sociological Aspects of the Sex Life of the Unmarried Adult," 133; Eleanor Rowland Wembridge, "Petting and the Campus," *Survey* 34 (1925): 39.

51. Doris Blake, *New York Daily News,* September 7, 1926; Phyllis Blanchard and Carolyn Manasses, *New Girls for Old* (New York: Macaulay, 1930), 64; "The Too High Cost of Courting," *American,* September 1924; "Why Men Won't Marry the New Woman," *Collier's,* March 14, 1925, 22–23; *St. Louis Post-Dispatch,* March 30, 1931.

52. "Why Men Won't Marry"; *Life,* January 1920, 903; Beatrice Hinkle, "Chaos of Marriage," *Harper's,* December 1925, 7; Anthony Giddens, *The Transformation of Intimacy,* 3.

53. Judge Ben B. Lindsey, *The Companionate Marriage* (New York: Boni and Liveright, 1927); figure from Paul H. Jacobson, *American Marriage and Divorce* (New York: Rinehart, 1959), 21; Lynd and Lynd, *Middletown in Transition,* 152.

54. Kinsey, *Human Male,* 368; Terman, *Psychological Factors in Marital Happiness,* 310, 296; University Club of Chicago to Marie Stopes, August 10, 1931, MAC:PP/MCS/A.63, Wellcome Institute for the History of Medicine, London; Lesley Hall, *Hidden Anxieties: British Male Sexuality, 1900 to 1950* (London: Pluto, 1991); Elaine Tyler May, *Great Expectations: Marriage and Divorce in Post-Victorian America* (Chicago: University Of Chicago Press, 1980), 109, 111.

55. Cancian, *Love in America,* 31; Ernest Groves, "Marriage," *American Youth,* January 1920, 24; "We Both Had Jobs," *Women's Home Companion,* April 1928, 130; Abraham Myerson, "Nervous Husband," *Ladies' Home Journal,* September 1, 1921; Smiley Blanton and Woodbridge Riley, "Shell Shocks of Family Life," *Forum,* November 1929, 287; "End of the Trail," *Sunset,* April 1923, 40; Marcus Ravage, "My Wife Won't Let Me Be a Gypsy," *American Monthly,* January 10, 1926, 47; Joseph Hergesheimer, "Can You Be Married and Free?" *Pictorial Review,* June 1927, 203–4.

56. Newcomb, "Recent Changes."

Chapter Eighteen

"Another Self"?

Middle-Class American Women and Their Friends, 1900–1960

Linda W. Rosenzweig

The popular contemporary novel *Beaches* portrays the centrality and significance of late twentieth-century sisterhood in the lives of two dissimilar but devoted friends whose paths cross first in childhood. Their lives take very different routes, but despite periodic conflict and misunderstanding, the bonds between them remain strong. Eventually the more conventional of the two women suffers a terminal illness. Her brash and spirited comrade, now a celebrated entertainer, rises to the occasion as a devoted caregiver and finally as the guardian of her friend's daughter. In the film version of this story, the appealing if somewhat maudlin signature theme, "The Wind beneath My Wings," highlights and reiterates the central role of female friendship in the lives of the main characters.[1]

While the song's message and the novel's plot may strike a critical listener or reader as overly sentimental, the theme of female friendship as an essential, sustaining influence in women's lives has a familiar cultural resonance. Over the past three decades, discussions ranging from the idealistic visions of "sisterhood" that emerged in the early years of the contemporary feminist movement to more academic, analytic examinations of the relationship have asserted that female friends play a vital role in one another's survival. Frequently this discourse has also suggested that women have a special aptitude for making and keeping friends, and that they excel in this regard. Thus their relationships, as opposed to male friendships, embody the highest ideals of true friendship expressed in a distinctive emotional friendship style. However, this cultural affirmation of the value of female friendship is a relatively recent phenomenon.

Although discussions of both the concept and the experience of friendship pervade Western cultural tradition, most literary and cultural representations of this fundamental yet elusive form of interpersonal connection have stressed its importance in the public world of men. Traditional definitions and prescriptive images of the relationship have identified examples of comradeship and loyalty between ancient heroic warriors or modern soldiers as models of the essence of friendship. In contrast, relationships between women typically have been characterized as shallow, insincere, temporary, and insignificant. The intensity and recurrence of these contrasting images reflect the pervasive privileging of men within the patriarchal tradition as well as the importance attributed to friendship in Western society.

The cultural significance of the relationship has been emphasized consistently, from Aristotle's vision of a friend as another self to current social scientific and psychological analyses of friendship. In the context of the growing recognition of the validity of women's lives and experiences, recent empirical studies have generated a range of interesting data about American women's friendships specifically as well as contemporary friendship more generally.[2] But this research does not analyze concrete experiences or cultural representations of the relationship in historical context, nor does it examine the issue of linkage between the two.

The emergence and advancement of emotions history offer substantial support for the idea that friendship between women is a historical experience rather than a universal ahistorical occurrence. Historical studies of emotion also point to the existence of a connection between actual experiences and cultural images of friendship. The growing body of research on emotional standards and experience in the past has revealed substantial change over time in both cultural expectations about emotion and the expression of various emotions. Some studies also suggest that changes in these areas may have altered the nature of people's actual emotional experiences as well.[3] Friendship is not a single emotion, but rather an affectional experience incorporating various emotions—love, anger, jealousy, guilt, sadness, grief, for example. Hence evidence of change over time in the individual emotions that constitute the interpersonal interaction we describe as friendship raises intriguing questions about the historicity of that interaction in general, and about change and continuity in the specific context of American women's friendships.

Social historians have not engaged in extensive research on friendship, but several studies have generated a baseline of information from which such questions can be more fully investigated. The most focused of these, Carroll Smith-Rosenberg's classic examination of nineteenth-century middle-class American women's relationships, describes intense, long-lasting, often physically demonstrative female friendships that sometimes competed in importance with male-female relationships. In this "female world of love and ritual," friends provided companionship, love, and emotional support for one another. They frequently expressed their devotion in extravagantly affectionate terms that resemble the language typically found in love letters between men and women. Other studies corroborate Smith-Rosenberg's contention that devoted and supportive friendships played a central role in the lives of American women in the past.[4]

This research suggests that many white eighteenth- and nineteenth-century women experienced intimate, mutually supportive friendships. They were drawn together by their common social condition; by shared biological moments, most frequently childbirth; by other distinctly female rituals as the domestic sphere became increasingly separate from the public world of men; by geographic isolation from family members; and also by mutual commitment to unconventional roles. In their letters to one another, such women often articulated a self-conscious recognition of the significance of their relationships with female friends and a passionate commitment to the preservation of these bonds.[5] This pattern of strong, emotionally expressive female friendship has a rich history in Western society more generally and in other traditions also. While a complete analysis of its origins remains beyond the scope of the present discussion, it seems plausible to suggest that women's subordinate status and economic dependency and the concomitant disempowerment contributed to the development of intense same-sex attachments and an emotional friendship style.

Correspondence represents only one tangible expression of the esteem in which women in the past held their female friends. Many recorded their affection for one another in autograph albums, which grew very popular during the 1830s. Between 1840 and 1875, the friendship quilt provided another vehicle for the expression of similar sentiments. Like autograph albums, friendship quilts served as keepsakes and reminders of treasured friendships. Quilt patterns varied; they incorporated biblical and secular verses as well as personalized information such as friends' names, significant dates, addresses, bits of advice, and so forth. Often designed as going-away presents for women who were moving west, friendship quilts were also exchanged by friends locally and by sisters. These gifts were carefully preserved by their recipients, displayed decoratively, or handed down through families as part of the female inheritance. As concrete symbols of women's regard for one another, friendship quilts offer durable evidence of nineteenth-century sisterhood; in some cases they also provide the only record of a woman's existence other than a gravestone or a notation in a family Bible.[6]

The endurance of close female friendships and their tangible manifestations in the form of affectionate letters, autograph albums, and friendship quilts reflect the development of a characteristic Victorian emotional culture. Recent reexaminations of the image of Victorian restraint have revised the traditional portrayal of emotional repressiveness as a distinguishing feature of the period. Beginning around 1820, a Victorian emotional style that stressed the management and appropriate use of emotions rather than their systematic suppression emerged. Succeeding decades witnessed the further evolution of a mature Victorian approach that stressed loving family relationships, particularly between mothers and their children, and supported a conception of intense, enduring, spiritual love between men and women. The intensity with which Victorian culture treated love in general and the emphasis on self-disclosure as a symbol of intimacy and closeness fostered both the development of affectionate female friendships and the use of extravagantly romantic language to express that affection. Thus, for example, nineteenth-century publications such as *Godey's Lady's Book and Magazine* romanticized the idea of female friendship, publishing poems and verses for women to copy into friends' autograph albums and friendship quilt blocks.[7]

This Victorian emotional ethos created a climate in which physical contact between same-sex friends was permissible. Nineteenth-century gender ideology also supported intense female friendships through its portrayal of women as frivolous and asexual. Thus close friendships between them could be viewed as unimportant, transient components of the interval between girlhood and marriage. In this context, physically demonstrative relationships could be accepted temporarily and even considered a form of preparation for eventual adjustment to the marriage relationship.

Moreover, while nineteenth-century middle-class women did not necessarily experience the separation and isolation from men implied by the ideology of true womanhood and the doctrine of separate spheres, the beliefs represented by these concepts offered further cultural validation for a romanticized idea of female friendship. Nineteenth-century physically demonstrative friendships and women's explicit references to such relationships, then, clearly reflect a specific historical context.

It is impossible to document the exact nature of physical contact between women in the past and its meaning to specific individuals. Furthermore, the physical dimension represents only one factor in a relationship. Hence the analysis of these romantic friendships poses a difficult task for the historian. Contemporary scholars disagree with regard to the appropriateness of designating such relationships homosexual or lesbian in the sense that the terms are currently construed. However, the effort to categorize particular nineteenth-century women's friendships in terms of a contemporary construction of lesbian identity seems less important than the need to acknowledge a physical dimension as integral to some friendships, to describe it sensitively, and to recognize its pertinence in the framework of Victorian emotional culture.[8]

Victorian emotionology remained dominant in American culture throughout the nineteenth century and in the early decades of the twentieth century, although some discussions in the prescriptive literature hinted at changing views. For example, the volume of advice literature devoted to emotional standards declined between 1900 and 1920, and the treatment of some specific emotions suggested revisionism. Coverage of the topic of female friendship during these decades included both positive and negative commentary about women's capabilities and performances as friends.[9]

Despite the advent of major changes in women's lives between 1880 and 1920, actual female friendships, like the dominant emotionology, continued to resemble the characteristic Victorian model for at least three reasons. Victorian emotional standards were widely disseminated from early childhood on, and they found unqualified acceptance in mainstream middle-class society. In addition, the emphasis on intensity in these standards gave the emotionology power. Nevertheless, occasional suggestions of a transition in the nature of women's friendships are discernible, as in the case of prescriptive literature. Yet even for so-called new women, who took advantage of the growing opportunities for more education, new kinds of work outside the home, and participation in a wide range of clubs and women's associations, as for their more conventional peers, female friends played an important role.[10]

Women who chose not to marry and assume traditional family roles frequently relied on friendship—either with or without a physical component—as the central relationship and the fundamental source of emotional support in their lives. Such relationships, referred to as Boston marriages, often endured throughout the lives of a couple who combined their resources and shared a home. Indeed, the ability to rely on a community of female friends for companionship, affirmation, and sometimes intimacy enabled women to make unconventional choices and assert personal independence.[11]

Friends remained central in the lives of more conventional turn-of-the-century women also. Adolescents and young adults cared deeply about their friendships. On her twentieth birthday, Mary Pratt Sears reminisced poignantly about a close friend who had died several years earlier. "In forty minutes I shall really be twenty! It will be my fourth number that Fanny never had, but as I grow older, she seems to grow older too," Mary wrote to her cousin. "I remember her writing to me on my fifteenth birthday about its being the first birthday we had ever had apart, and now there have been four. Do you suppose she has thought about it at all today?"[12]

While Mary Pratt Sears wondered wistfully about her deceased confidante, the concerns of other young women often focused on the fear of being excluded by their friends. Extravagantly affectionate language and explicit references to apparently physical expressions of love in letters suggest the continued presence of intimate relationships and "crushes" among adolescents, although some correspondence reflects a transition in these friendships to a more social, heterosexual orientation. Adolescent friendships could provoke anxiety, but they also formed the basis of lasting, valued relationships.[13]

Turn-of-the-century college friendships, particularly among students at women's colleges, also exhibited characteristics similar to the Victorian model. The phenomenon of "crushes" or "smashes," typically based on a younger woman's admiration for an older student and occasionally involving an older student and a faculty member, either with or without an erotic component, was common at Vassar and Smith, for example. The experience of romantic friendships was particularly prevalent in the women's college setting, where the intensity of living close together and the emphasis on dormitory life appear to have fostered stronger emotional bonds than those between women who attended coeducational institutions. A survey of 2,200 women, most of whom had graduated from college around the turn of the century, revealed that intense same-sex friendships were common in coeducational and women's colleges, but more prevalent in the latter. While strong bonds developed within the female communities at both types of institutions, social and economic differences could create friction in either setting.[14] Nevertheless, for many young women, the establishment of close friendships represented a major benefit of higher education, and female friendship remained important as they moved beyond the college years.[15]

Friends played a very central though perplexing role for Azalia Emma Peet, a Smith graduate who found it particularly difficult to sort out her feelings about the various young women with whom she socialized and to cope with their feelings of jealousy as well as her own. Her relationship with one individual involved a special intensity: "In my heart of hearts," Azalia confided to her diary, "I fear I covet her love and *all* of it. . . . she has been a friend when I sorely needed friendship. And too she has intuitively denied me the physical part of friendship which in the past has been disastrous." The dimensions of this relationship are difficult to ascertain. The diary reveals that the two young women "slept together" on several occasions and that Azalia "craved Patty's demonstrative love." It also records Azalia's dismay over the fact that a severe headache prevented her friend from accompanying her to a party, but the affliction miraculously vanished when a young man and his "auto" arrived.[16]

This particular diary entry juxtaposes clear evidence of continuity in the intensity and importance of female friendships with an indication of the impending transition to a stronger emphasis on heterosexual relationships. Azalia Peet's observations foreshadow the dominance of new, twentieth-century standards regarding women's relationships with one another while they also preserve the flavor of nineteenth-century values. In addition, her enigmatic references to the physical dimension of her relationship with Patty graphically illustrate the challenging nature of the task of interpreting historical evidence concerning romantic friendships during this transitional era as well as earlier.

Strong and intense friendships between young adult women during this period did not necessarily involve a physical dimension. Anita Pollitzer and Georgia O'Keeffe, who met in 1914 as students in the School of Practical Arts at Teachers College, Columbia University, discussed their teachers, their peers, their commitment to art, their hopes and aspirations, and their efforts to understand the meaning of life. Their shared artistic vision gave this relationship a special quality. Overwhelmed by the impact of a series of drawings Georgia sent to her, Anita described her reaction vividly: "I tell you I felt them! . . . They've gotten past the personal stage into the big sort of emotions that are common to big people—but it's your version of it." These young women, like many of their peers, shared less traditional concerns than those typically encountered by their Victorian predecessors, but the importance of female friendship in their lives links the generations.[17]

Mature women's friendship experiences at the turn of the century suggest a similar continuity with those of their nineteenth-century counterparts. Conventional wives and mothers as well as individuals whose lives followed less traditional paths might share their deepest personal interests and values with female friends, rely on them for financial and moral support of various kinds, and maintain close contact over many years. Yet these women could also be dilatory correspondents for whom friendship took second place to family relationships.[18] Obviously many factors, including the disparity between the responsibilities of a wife and mother and those of an independent single woman, determine the course of any long-term friendship. But various clues, such as intimations of a more casual attitude toward friendship and hints of ambivalent feelings about the physical demonstration of affection, provide evidence of impending change and herald the emergence of different expectations and priorities.

These expectations and priorities began to crystallize in the 1920s as a new emotional culture that stressed more cautious emotional management took form. Although Victorian emotionology had maintained that certain negative emotions should be controlled, love was not among them. Intense expressions of love and affection, between mothers and their children, men and women, and same-sex friends (especially female), had remained acceptable, and indeed had been encouraged. The twentieth-century revision of emotional norms resulted in a culture that stressed restraint in all emotional areas, including those that Victorian culture had defined as positive, such as familial love. This revision also encompassed a reduction of emphasis on gender difference in emotional socialization. Thus women as well as men were expected to manage their feelings now.[19]

Prescriptions for friendship changed in this context. Prescriptive literature in general became less philosophical and more expertise-oriented. Periodicals contained fewer articles on friendship than in prior decades. Where magazines and advice books addressed the topic, they often linked it with new concerns about the importance of conforming to group norms and cultivating a pleasing personality. The importance of friendship might be acknowledged, but the dangers of intense emotional attachment were emphasized. Parents of adolescents were instructed on the importance of peer acceptance and approval for the future well-being of their offspring.[20] Both the tone and quantity of this literature, then, reflect the broader cultural effort to replace emotional intensity with moderation and restraint. This new emotional culture, along with other major influences, fostered significant changes in the experience of female friendship as the twentieth century advanced.

For example, the dissemination and popularization of Freudian ideology produced a heightened cultural emphasis on heterosexual relationships and a concomitant stigmatization of passionate same-sex attachments. Companionate marriage was expected to provide the emotional support and companionship that women (and men also) had found previously with members of their own sex. Furthermore, from the 1920s on, the amount of time women spent with men increased. In this context, close female ties began to appear old-fashioned, if not abnormal, to women themselves as well as to the wider society.[21]

Several other trends in mature industrial society also contributed to alterations in women's friendships in the post-1920 period. The proliferation of women's organizations around the turn of the century reflects the impact of a general trend toward impersonality and organization. This development also produced a major new venue for middle-class female friendship. While the intimate sororal relationships of the nineteenth century were anchored primarily in the domestic setting, women's interactions increasingly occurred in a broader context of shared intellectual interests and social commitments, which may have moderated the tendency toward fervent self-disclosure.[22] Additional influences such as the growth of geographic and social mobility and the availability of the telephone resulted in decreased face-to-face visiting between friends; the latter development obviously facilitated communication at another level, although long-distance phone calls were not the ordinary occurrence they are now.

A final category of change specifically affected young women as the rise of a strong youth culture displaced adult influences in important ways. At both the high school and college levels, the lives of white middle-class students were structured according to a system governed informally but rigorously by peer oversight and centered on heterosexual dating.[23] On coeducational college campuses, fraternities and sororities formed the center of this peer social structure. This culture stressed conformity, submerged individuals into the group, and downplayed commitments and interests that failed to serve group needs. Sororities, which proliferated on college campuses during the 1920s, socialized a significant number of young women to these standards and encouraged them to devote large quantities of time and energy to the pursuit of activities that would equip them to be successful wives and companions. Belonging to the "right" sorority facilitated encounters with appropriate young men. Hence affiliation might be sought as much for prestige and conformity as for the opportunity to build friendships. In addition, the interactions of sorority "sisters" frequently consisted mainly of activities related to planning heterosexual encounters: arranging dates for one another, discussing hairstyles, cosmetics, clothing, and appropriate sexual conduct, and sharing the details of the ensuing experiences. Sororities were not present in women's colleges, but a strong emphasis on heterosexual conquests, which often took precedence over female friendships, also characterized this setting.[24]

The relationships of young women in the post-1920 period distinctly reflect the combined influences of the new emotional culture, the rise of a powerful peer culture, and the strong emphasis on heterosexuality. Adolescent friendships often centered on discussions about "boys" and dates, and the necessity of conforming to peer group standards could determine how young women treated one another. Diaries suggest that concerns about personal appearance and emerging sexuality rather than those pertaining to affection for female friends consumed much of the energy of girls in their teens, although friendship remained significant, particularly for younger adolescents.[25] Friends still played a major role in women's college experiences also, but a less intense type of interaction linked with a strong emphasis on heterosexual relationships typified the relationship in the post-1920 period. "I have met some very nice girls and of course some pills," Wellesley freshman Jane Shugg wrote breezily to her parents. "The social life on the floor has been dull as dull can be," she noted on another occasion, so "to keep ourselves from getting too low, we have had numerous birthday parties and just parties."[26] Earlier college women had looked forward to dormitory parties as special occasions for fun and friendship, but now such events apparently served more to console and amuse female students in the absence of dates or heterosexual gatherings. Other evidence also suggests that though close female friends definitely enhanced college life, heterosexual social life tended to represent a higher priority. One student, whose diary consistently reiterates her enjoyment of female friends and her regard for a particularly "swell" individual, still concluded, "It isn't college not to go out and have dates."[27] Not all young women shared this view completely, however. For example, Margaret Mead and her friends at Barnard agreed among themselves to an explicit rule against canceling plans with a female friend in order to go out with a man. Nevertheless, for many college women the pursuit of "sisterhood" was decisively displaced by the competition for dates.[28]

Relationships with female friends could be complicated by additional factors. Earlier young women (and men) who pursued higher education had generally shared similar social backgrounds, but increased social mobility and immigration resulted in a more heterogeneous student population in the decades following 1920. Disparaging allusions to the racial, ethnic, and religious backgrounds of peers of both genders suggest that social prejudice influenced the choice of female friends as well as male companions for at least some college women during this period. Apparently the social selectivity of the sorority system also contributed to this situation: according to one dean of women, "A very deplorable practice in sororities is to select girls who dress well and rate well with men."[29]

As the preceding examples suggest, distinctly new twentieth-century features characterized post-1920 college women's friendships. Yet these relationships might still incorporate vestiges of earlier patterns. Martha Lavell, a freshman at Mills College in

1927, enjoyed a "Baby Party" at which students dressed in costumes and played children's games, an event reminiscent of gatherings also enjoyed by earlier generations of college women. She especially valued the friendship of one thoughtful and articulate young woman to whom she attributed her own mental awakening. Their conversations ranged from serious intellectual and philosophical questions to the distinctly twentieth-century issue of "whether there were any boys who didn't insist on petting." This relationship resembled earlier close friendships to some extent, but it manifested an unmistakably modern tone at the same time. Like her turn-of-the-century predecessors, Martha Lavell worried about having friends. She compared her "happy times" at Mills with the isolation she felt after she transferred to the University of Minnesota. When she found it easier to make friends as a graduate student at Smith, she pondered her newfound ability to conquer what she described in distinctly twentieth-century terms as the "crushing feeling of inferiority" that had troubled her previously. Eventually she consciously decided to "become aggressive" because she could not "endure another year with no men companions."[30]

Mature women's friendships also reflect the impact of social and cultural changes after 1920, but the accent on change seems less pronounced than in the case of adolescents and young adults. While the friendship choices and priorities of younger women unequivocally mirrored the new emotional culture, particularly the dominant heterosexual imperative, friendships of women past the stage where dating typically defined the crucial *raison d'être* manifested a more textured quality. The category of post-1920 mature women encompasses individuals who came of age in the first two decades of the century, when Victorian culture still prevailed, as well as those who matured after 1920. Female friendships remained important to women in both groups, although shades of difference, for example, nuances of language, distinguish the relationships of the two generations. This discrepancy in generational style represents a potential source of confusion and misunderstanding for the historian, as recent discussion about the nature of Eleanor Roosevelt's friendships illustrates.[31]

Not surprisingly, friends continued to play an important role in the lives of single women in midlife and beyond. As one aging woman observed, "The road seems long as one draws near the end, long and a bit lonely. It is good to have footsteps chiming with one's own, and to know that a friend in whom one has a deep and abiding trust is on the same track, moving toward the same goal." Friendships that were interrupted by marriage and the accompanying home and family duties might resume when these responsibilities lessened. One woman, born in 1924, remembered that although her high school friends were too busy to get together more than a few times a year while they were raising their families, later "these same girls (now women)" became "closer than ever" and their friendship was "a precious blessing." The advent of the "empty nest" phenomenon, then, helped shape mature women's friendship experiences after 1920, as did the gender gap in longevity, which had a similar effect.[32]

Round-robin letters exchanged by women who graduated from college both before and after 1920 and regular reunions of high school friends over long periods of time provide clear evidence that despite the pressures of the heterosexual imperative, friendships formed in the adolescent and college years remained strong over the years. Mature women valued opportunities to share both good and bad personal and family news and to enjoy one another's company in person. While their expressions of regard projected a less emotional tone than the language used by earlier women, they reiterated the importance of long-term, supportive female friendship.[33] Not all women enjoyed renewing old ties, however; Frida Semler Sebury's comments on this subject suggest that at least some found the notion of an enduring network of college friends unpalatable. "Something in me has a horror of female gatherings," she observed in 1933. "I went to our last 1908 breakfast and ran away after the second course. . . . If I had known I would have to keep telling the story of my life, I would not have gone to college."[34]

Long-term friendships in the post-1920 period often blended traditional and modern qualities. A woman who was born in 1917 attributed the endurance of a friendship of more than seven decades to "our love of reading & our imaginations" but also to the fact that her husband and her friend's husband "found common grounds & so even tho [sic] we were 300 miles apart we could maintain contacts with no problem." Moreover, she observed, "this was really unusual for girlhood friends as they easily drifted apart due to their husbands' boredom." Such an observation would have appeared virtually incomprehensible in a Victorian context. Her emphasis on the role of husbands in the maintenance of female friendship clearly reflects the influence of twentieth-century culture, but this woman's reaction to the death of her friend conveys a distinctly timeless quality that would have evoked instant recognition in earlier periods: "I feel as if part of my life has gone," she commented. "We were good friends for over 70 years & that cannot ever be replaced."[35]

Even where strong ties endured over time, friendships could be fraught with tension. Initially, Dorothy Thompson's long relationship with Rose Wilder Lane resembled earlier female friendships in its closeness and in its importance to both women. While their confidential exchanges focused on distinctly modern concerns — love affairs, failed marriages, and their work — Thompson assured her friend, "Your letters are the chief joys of my life." However, conflict and misunderstanding, triggered by Thompson's lengthy silences (often the result of her involvement with a new man) and by intellectual and political disagreements, caused irreparable damage to the friendship, although they were eventually partially reconciled. The intensity of the friendship between Georgia O'Keeffe and Anita Pollitzer also cooled in the post-1920 period as their lives and careers developed in different directions. Finally a bitter disagreement over Pollitzer's effort to publish a laudatory biography of her eminent friend effectively destroyed the remaining trust between them.[36]

Female friendships fulfilled both personal and more utilitarian public functions for one particular subset of mature women after 1920, the increasing number of professional women. This group, which included veterans of earlier Progressive reform movements as well as their younger counterparts, drew vital emotional as well as practical support from female mentors and peers as they pursued their goals. The mutually supportive relationships of the women who played active roles in the New Deal offer a classic example in this category.[37]

Such friendships were not limited to women in politics or to those in the early stages of their careers. As a middle-aged woman, Margaret Sanger relied on Dorothy

Brush for financial backing for her work in family planning and also for companionship and understanding. On one occasion, Sanger, who was engaged in a casual six-year affair with a much younger man, confided to her friend in an informal, distinctly twentieth-century manner that he was fun but "not for keeps." Hannah Arendt and Mary McCarthy also confided in each other; they shared personal and marital concerns, exchanged gossip, discussed literary and philosophical issues, and provided mutual encouragement and advice for twenty-five years. As Arendt's literary executor, McCarthy devoted three years to editing and annotating her friend's last manuscript at the expense of her own work. Ayn Rand and Isabel Paterson discussed substantive intellectual issues in their letters too. Rand was delighted to have a personal friend with whom she could examine "important and abstract subjects." "I suppose you will never believe how much Frank and I love you, so there," she wrote to Paterson in anticipation of a forthcoming visit. Despite their shared interests, a conflict ended this relationship after a few years. For other women with common intellectual concerns, however, long-term female friendships provided a vital source of reciprocal support and sustenance, and sometimes served to mitigate the effects of exclusion by male colleagues.[38]

The history of Heterodoxy, a Greenwich Village club for "unorthodox women," many of whom had active professional careers, offers an interesting example of enduring friendship while it also suggests the impact of new cultural influences after 1920. Founded in 1912, Heterodoxy existed until 1942. Its 103 members included married and divorced women, free-love advocates, and single women, some of whom shared their lives with female partners. During the organization's most active years, these women met biweekly for lunch and discussions of a wide range of issues. This setting fostered the development of warm personal friendships that lasted throughout the lives of club members. Yet few new members joined Heterodoxy after the mid-1920s, suggesting that in the context of the dominant cultural ambiance, younger women may have found both the idea of community among women and the concept of "heterodoxy" less appealing than their early twentieth-century predecessors had.[39]

One final category of post-1920 female friendship remains to be considered. Strong romantic friendships endured in this era despite pervasive cultural condemnation of intimacy between women. Because same-sex liaisons were no longer socially acceptable, participants undoubtedly grew more circumspect about the ways they defined and revealed themselves than their nineteenth-century counterparts had been. In turn, this reticence imposed constraints on the nature of the data that document their relationships. Furthermore, although lesbian culture existed by the post-1920 period, and some women identified unequivocally as lesbians, others whose primary commitment in adult life was also to women did not choose this identity. This distinction further increases the difficulty of the task of interpreting friendships in this category.[40]

Nevertheless, the evidence indicates that members of both groups enjoyed strong, devoted, supportive friendships, often with the women they loved (occasionally while they remained married to men) and also with female friends who were not their intimate partners. In the former case, couples continued to express their attachments in terms reminiscent of the emotional intensity of the Victorian period, as for example in a letter from Janet Flanner to Natalia Danesi Murray: "My darling love, Thank you for the most beautiful and complete love letter I have ever known in my life. . . . I cannot in any way express my love for you in an equality of discovery and appreciation." Similar expressions of romantic affection, such as "I love you and love you and love you, my own other soul" and "I love you with all my heart," appear frequently in correspondence as women who lived together for many years and also those who found one another in mature adulthood declared their love in language comparable to that of both their Victorian predecessors and heterosexual couples.[41] At the same time, they enjoyed and valued congenial friendships with colleagues and other single and married women as well. While they might express warm regard for these friends, however, they reserved ardently affectionate language for situations in which romantic attachment and friendship were combined.[42]

The foregoing examples suggest that although the displacement of Victorian emotional culture and values, along with other social and cultural changes, produced a new friendship model in the twentieth century, the relationships of woman-committed women and their partners contrasted sharply with those of their hetero-sexually oriented peers and paralleled nineteenth-century female friendships in their intensity and ardor. Despite the challenges of a new emotionology and powerful social norms that mitigated against such continuity, then, the friendships of these women preserved earlier traditions in a very specific manner that distinguished them definitively from their post-1920 peers.

The years between 1900 and 1960 define an era of significant change in the history of female friendship. As the preceding discussion illustrates, clear evidence of modera-tion in the intensity of white middle-class American women's relationships with one another distinguishes this period. With the emergence of a distinctive twentieth-century emotional culture, a new friendship style supplanted earlier, more effusive emotional displays between women and probably also reflected changes in their actual feelings about one another. While evidence of change in emotional standards and emotional expression can be relatively accessible to the historian, transforma-tions in individuals' real personal experiences of emotion typically prove far more difficult to capture. Thus, the paucity of extravagant expressions of affection between female friends after 1920 does not necessarily mirror a significant change in their emotional experiences. However, emotions historians increasingly discern potential meaning in silences, particularly when the absence of emotional display in a specific period contrasts significantly with evidence from other periods, as it does in this case. Evidence of diminished intensity in other aspects of women's emotional experi-ences also points to a change in their feelings about friends as well in the emotional culture surrounding friendship in the post-1920 decades.[43]

Yet continuity as well as change characterized women's relationships with one another during the first half of the twentieth century. Several factors help explain the abiding role of friendship in their lives generally and the persistence of intense romantic friendships against the background of twentieth-century emotional stan-dards and social and cultural influences. First, women's continuing socioeconomic subordination and dependency perpetuated the need for the empathy and mutuality of female friendship. Second, despite the general trends toward gender similarity in socialization patterns and restraint and management in emotional expression after 1920, women's emotional culture continued to stress love and romantic imagery. This emotional frame of reference undoubtedly influenced friendship patterns as well as relations with husbands and children. Third, even in the context of revised emotional standards and cultural stipulations about the centrality of heterosexual relationships, women remained agents of their own lives; they did not necessarily succumb to patriarchal prescriptions where female friendship was concerned. Individuals' personal histories, as well as their cultural milieux, shape their emotional experiences, including the nature of their friendships.[44] Furthermore, it is also possible that strong romantic friendships represent a translation of twentieth-century cultural prescriptions for heterosexual relationships into a framework and setting more compatible with the inclinations of some women.

Finally, contemporary research on relational development suggests that female bonding functions as a vehicle of self-definition and identity formation. Hence women's friendships may serve an important and necessary developmental psychological function. While historians must exercise extreme caution in using ahistorical generalizations derived from late twentieth-century data to explain historical phenomena, this theory may also apply to the experiences of middle-class American women in the first half of the century (and even earlier). Thus it may help account for those aspects of female friendship that endured after the displacement of Victorian emotional culture.[45]

The data on middle-class American women's friendships during the first half of the twentieth century clearly confirm the historicity of the relationship. An intricate blend of change and continuity marks the years between 1900 and 1960 as a unique period in the history of middle-class American female friendship. New emotional standards and other social and cultural changes altered earlier versions of sisterhood after 1920. The legitimacy of close relationships between women was rejected. Heterosexual interactions often took precedence over female friendship, although they did not supplant it completely. This pattern varied in accordance with age and life stage, but it generally defined the experience of middle-class American women until the late twentieth-century feminist movement, with its valorization of sisterhood, ushered in a new period in the history of women's friendships. Further research will be necessary to determine whether the special claims regarding female friendship in recent decades reflect a major change as women find new reasons to draw together, a disguised nostalgia, or perhaps a response to a cultural reauthorization of close female relationships.

NOTES

1. Iris Rainer Dart, *Beaches* (New York: Bantam, 1985).
2. *Nichomachean Ethics,* quoted in D. J. Enright and David Rawlinson, eds., *The Oxford Book of Friendship* (New York: Oxford University Press, 1991), 7. For a comprehensive overview of recent research pertaining to women's friendships, see Pat O'Connor, *Friendships between Women: A Critical Review* (New York: Guilford, 1992). On friendship generally, see the essays in Valerian J.

Derlega and Barbara A. Winstead, eds., *Friendship and Social Interaction* (New York: Springer-Verlag, 1986); and Clyde Hendrick, ed., *Close Relationships* (Newbury Park, CA: Sage, 1989).

3. For discussions of the relationship between emotional standards and actual emotions, see Shula Sommers, "Understanding Emotions: Some Interdisciplinary Considerations," in Carol Z. Stearns and Peter N. Stearns, eds., *Emotion and Social Change: Toward a New Psychohistory* (New York: Holmes and Meier, 1988), 23–38; and Margaret S. Clark, "Historical Emotionology: From a Social Psychologist's Perspective," in Andrew E. Barnes and Peter N. Stearns, eds., *Social History and Issues in Human Consciousness: Some Interdisciplinary Connections* (New York: New York University Press, 1989), 262–69.

4. Carroll Smith-Rosenberg, "The Female World of Love and Ritual: Relations between Women in Nineteenth-Century America," *Signs* 1 (1975):1–29. Anthony E. Rotundo has described similarly intense, physically demonstrative friendships between young men in "Romantic Friendship: Male Intimacy and Middle Class Youth in the Northern United States, 1800–1900," *Journal of Social History* 23 (1989): 1–26; and idem, *American Manhood: Transformations in Masculinity from the Revolution to the Modern Era* (New York: Basic Books, 1993). See also Karen V. Hansen, " 'No *Kisses* Is Like Youres': An Erotic Friendship between Two African-American Women during the Mid-Nineteenth Century," *Gender and History* 7, 2 (August 1995): 153–82; Nancy F. Cott, *The Bonds of Womanhood: "Woman's Sphere" in New England, 1780–1835* (New Haven: Yale University Press, 1977); Terri L. Premo, *Winter Friends: Women Growing Old in the New Republic, 1785–1835* (Urbana: University of Illinois Press, 1990); and Marilyn Ferris Motz, *True Sisterhood: Michigan Women and Their Kin* (Albany: State University of New York Press, 1983).

5. *The Journal of Esther Edwards Burr, 1754–1757*, ed. Carol F. Karlsen and Laurie F. Crumpacker (New Haven: Yale University Press, 1984); Carol Lasser, " 'Let Us Be Sisters Forever': The Sororal Model of Nineteenth-Century Female Friendship," *Signs* 14 (autumn 1988): 158–81; Smith-Rosenberg, "Female World of Love and Ritual"; Cott, *Bonds of Womanhood;* Premo, *Winter Friends;* Motz, *True Sisterhood.* Recent work by Karen V. Hansen suggests that female friendships played fundamental roles in the lives of less affluent women as well as their middle-class counterparts. *A Very Social Time: Crafting Community in Antebellum New England* (Berkeley: University of California Press, 1994), 52–53, 65.

6. Linda Otto Lipsett, *Remember Me: Women and Their Friendship Quilts* (San Francisco: Quilt Digest Press, 1985); Mary Hunt, *Fierce Tenderness: A Feminist Theology of Friendship* (New York: Crossroad, 1991), 58–59.

7. Peter N. Stearns, *American Cool: Constructing a Twentieth-Century Emotional Style* (New York: New York University Press, 1994), 16–94; Karen Lystra, *Searching the Heart: Women, Men, and Romantic Love in Nineteenth-Century America* (New York: Oxford University Press, 1989), 33; Lipsett, *Remember Me,* 18–19.

8. Lillian Faderman, *Surpassing the Love of Men: Romantic Friendship and Love between Women from the Renaissance to the Present* (New York: William Morrow, 1981); idem, *Odd Girls and Twilight Lovers: A History of Lesbian Life in Twentieth-Century America* (New York: Penguin, 1991); Liz Stanley, "Feminism and Friendship," in *The Auto/Biographical I: The Theory and Practice of Feminist Auto/Biography* (Manchester, England: Manchester University Press, 1992); and Leila J. Rupp, " 'Imagine My Surprise': Women's Relationships in Mid-Twentieth Century America," in Martin B. Duberman et al., eds., *Hidden from History: Reclaiming the Gay and Lesbian Past* (New York: New American Library, 1989), 395–410.

9. Stearns, *American Cool,* 97–100. On women and friendship, see William Garland, "Friendship between the Sexes," *Westminster Review* 153 (March 1900): 30–32; and L. Keith Stibbard's reply, 154 (November 1900): 583–85; Margaret E. Sangster, "Talks on Friendship: I. Of Woman and Woman," *Harper's Bazar* 33 (November 10, 1900): 1784–85; Mary A. Jordan, "On College Friendships," *Harper's Bazar* 35 (December 1901): 722–27; Rafford Pyke, "What Women Like in Women," *Cosmopolitan* 34 (November 1902): 35–40; Judith Lloyde, "In and after Business Hours," *Ladies' Home Journal* 22 (June 1905): 24; Albert Bigelow Paine, "Of Friendship among Women," *North American Review* 183 (November 16, 1906): 1082–84; Anne Bryan McCall, "Friendship in a Girl's Life," *Woman's Home Companion* 38 (January 1911): 27; Harrie Brunkhurst, "Danger of a Girl's 'Intimate'

Friend," *Ladies' Home Journal* 28 (May 15, 1911): 10; Anne Bryan McCall, "Our Ideals of Friendship," *Woman's Home Companion* 42 (September 1915): 22; Virginia Blair, "Adventures in Girlhood: The Quest for Friends," *Good Housekeeping* 61 (November 1915): 610–14; and E. Aria, "Concerning Companionship," *Living Age* 295 (October 6, 1917): 36–40.

10. Lisa M. Fine, "Between Two Worlds: Business Women in a Chicago Boarding House, 1900–1930," *Journal of Social History* 19, 3 (spring 1986): 511–19.

11. Faderman, *Surpassing the Love of Men;* idem, *Odd Girls and Twilight Lovers;* Patricia A. Palmieri, *In Adamless Eden: The Community of Women Faculty at Wellesley* (New Haven: Yale University Press, 1995).

12. Mary Pratt Sears to Edith Paine, August 21, 1884, Book of Letters, 1864–1928, in Ella Lyman Cabot Papers, Schlesinger Library, Radcliffe College.

13. Ida Sophia Scudder Papers and Maida Herman Solomon Papers, Schlesinger Library; Rachel McClelland Sutton Papers, Pittsburgh Regional History Center.

14. Nancy Sahli, "Smashing: Women's Relationships before the Fall," *Chrysalis* 8 (1979); Helen Lefkowitz Horowitz, "Smith College and Changing Conceptions of Educated Women," in Ronald Story, ed., *Five Colleges: Five Histories* (Amherst: Five Colleges, Inc. and Historic Deerfield, Inc., 1992), 79–102; Katharine Bement Davis, *Factors in the Sex Life of Twenty-two Hundred Women* (New York: Harper and Brothers, 1929); Lynn D. Gordon, *Gender and Higher Education in the Progressive Era* (New Haven: Yale University Press, 1990), 105–8; Palmieri, *In Adamless Eden*, 203–4.

15. Dorothy Reed Mendenhall Papers and Elizabeth Kimball Papers, Smith College Archives; Jane Cary Papers, Wellesley College Archives; Maida Herman Solomon Papers.

16. Diary of Azalia Emma Peet, June 19, 1916, January 17, March 13, April 15, September 17, and April 8, 1915, in Penelope Franklin, ed., *Private Pages: Diaries of American Women, 1830s–1970s* (New York: Ballantine, 1986), 267, 256, 258, 262.

17. Anita Pollitzer to Georgia O'Keeffe, January 1, 1916, in *Lovingly, Georgia: The Complete Correspondence of Georgia O'Keeffe and Anita Pollitzer* (New York: Simon and Schuster, 1990), 116.

18. See, for example, "Frances Crane Lillie: A Memoir by Mary Prentice Lillie Barrows," Ellen Gates Starr Papers, Sophia Smith Collection, Smith College; Ellen Chesler, *Woman of Valor: Margaret Sanger and the Birth Control Movement in America* (New York: Simon and Schuster, 1992); and correspondence between Anna Lee Allan Tracy and Mary Helen Humphrey, Anna Lee Allan Tracy Papers, Schlesinger Library.

19. Stearns, *American Cool*, 139–92.

20. See, for example, Robert Bridges, "Affection," *Forum* 69 (June 1923): 1649–50; Walter B. Pitkin, "Add Friends, Multiply Opportunity," *Rotarian* 53 (October 1938): 34–36; "Wanted: Friendship Spreaders," *Scholastic* 33 (September 17, 1938): 2; Ruth Fedder, *A Girl Grows Up*, 2d ed. (New York: McGraw-Hill, 1948), 83–87, 98–109; idem, *You, the Person You Want to Be* (New York: Whittlesey House, 1957), 123–40; and Jean Schick Grossman, *Do You Know Your Daughter?* (New York: Appleton-Century, 1944), 45.

21. Sara N. Evans, *Born for Liberty: A History of Women in America* (New York: Free Press, 1989), 175–96; Rosalind Rosenberg, *Divided Lives: American Women in the Twentieth Century* (New York: Hill and Wang, 1992), 93. Child-rearing literature also stressed the centrality of heterosexual relationships. See, for example, Bernard Glueck, "The Family Drama" and Ernest R. Groves, "Loosening Family Ties," both in Dorothy Canfield Fisher and Sidonie M. Gruenberg, eds., *Our Children: A Handbook for Parents* (New York: Viking, 1932), 169–81 and 257–65.

22. Carl Degler, *At Odds: Women and the Family in America from the Revolution to the Present* (New York: Oxford University Press, 1980), 150–51; Robert S. Lynd and Helen Merrell Lynd, *Middletown: A Study in American Culture* (New York: Harcourt Brace Jovanovich, 1929), 272–81; Sheila M. Rothman, *Woman's Proper Place: A History of Changing Ideals and Practices, 1870 to the Present* (New York: Basic Books, 1978), 64–74; Theodora Penny Martin, *The Sound of Our Own Voices: Women's Study Clubs, 1860–1910* (Boston: Beacon Press, 1987), 128–33.

23. John Modell, *Into One's Own: From Youth to Adulthood in the United States, 1920–1975* (Berkeley: University of California Press, 1989), esp. chap. 3; Beth Bailey, *Front Porch to Back Seat* (Baltimore: Johns Hopkins University Press, 1988); Paula S. Fass, *The Damned and the Beautiful:*

American Youth in the 1920s (New York: Oxford University Press, 1977); Lynd and Lynd, *Middletown*, 133, 135–36, 143, 162–63, 522–23.

24. Fass, *The Damned and the Beautiful*, 139–67, 191–221; Horowitz, "Smith College"; Rothman, *Woman's Proper Place*, 181–84. It is interesting to note that among African American women, sororities have fulfilled broader functions than just the structuring of social life. See, for example, Susan L. Smith, "Sharecroppers and Sorority Women: The Alpha Kappa Alpha Mississippi Health Project," in Susan L. Smith, *Sick and Tired of Being Sick and Tired: Black Women's Health Activism in America, 1890–1950* (Philadelphia: University of Pennsylvania Press, 1995).

25. See journals of Beth Twiggar Goff, Adele Mongan Fasick diary, June Calender diaries, and Yvonne Blue diaries, all in Schlesinger Library, and Helen Laprovitz diary, quoted in Joan Jacobs Brumberg, "Coming of Age in the 1920s: The Diaries of Yvonne Blue and Helen Laprovitz," in Susan Ware, ed., *New Viewpoints in Women's History: Working Papers from the Schlesinger Library Fiftieth Anniversary Conference, March 4–5, 1994* (Cambridge, MA: Schlesinger Library, Radcliffe College, 1994).

26. Jane Shugg to her family, September 25, 1936, January 26, 1939, unprocessed collection, Wellesley College.

27. October 26, November 9, 1933, January 2, March 10, July 22, 1934, February 14, 1935, Helen Snyder diary, in author's possession.

28. Margaret Mead, *Blackberry Winter: My Earlier Years* (New York: Morrow, 1972), 109; Nancy Woloch, *Women and the American Experience: A Concise History* (New York: McGraw-Hill, 1996), 262.

29. Virginia Durr, *Outside the Magic Circle: The Autobiography of Virginia Foster Durr*, ed. Hollinger F. Barnard (Birmingham: University of Alabama Press, 1985), 59; Jane Shugg correspondence; Yvonne Blue Skinner diaries, Schlesinger Library; Ethel Chase, "Some Concrete Problems Facing the Dean," *Sixteenth Yearbook*, National Association of Deans of Women (1929), 109, quoted in Rothman, *Woman's Proper Place*, 182.

30. Diary of Martha Lavell, September 26, 1926, October 3, 1927, January 8, May 4, 1928, July 12, 1930, in Franklin, ed., *Private Pages*, 191, 192–93, 197, 202, 212.

31. See Lillian Hellman's observations about the gap between women who matured after 1920 and those in the previous generation in *An Unfinished Woman: A Memoir* (Boston: Little Brown, 1969), 29–30. On the issue of Eleanor Roosevelt's friendships, see the contrasting interpretations offered in Doris Faber, *The Life of Lorena Hickock: E.R.'s Friend* (New York: William Morrow, 1980); and Blanche Wiesen Cook, *Eleanor Roosevelt*, vol. 1, *1884–1933* (New York: Penguin, 1992).

32. Margaret Sherwood to Elizabeth Kendall, December 2, 1945, Elizabeth Kendall Papers, Wellesley College Archives, quoted in Palmieri, *In Adamless Eden*, 257; Elsie Frances Hagemann Noetzel to her daughter, December 12, 1995, in author's possession.

33. See, for example, William Plummer and Sandra Gurvis, "After 58 Years, a Round-Robin Letter Keeps on Delivering," *People Weekly* 31, 2 (January 16, 1989): 99–100; Susan Schindette and Barbara Wegher, "Six Texas Pals, Class of '44, Still Share Lunch, Life and Laughter," *People Weekly* 30, 8 (August 22, 1988): 52–54; Round Robin Letters, Class of 1943, Wellesley College Library.

34. Dolores Avelleyra Murphy, comp., *In Red Hats, Beads, and Bags: 1908 Graduates Sharing Their Lives through Letters* (Morrison, CO: Cassiopeia Press, 1990), 73.

35. Personal letters to author, February 22, 1993, January 1994.

36. Dorothy Thompson to Rose Wilder Lane, July 15, 1921, in William Holtz, ed., *Dorothy Thompson and Rose Wilder Lane: Forty Years of Friendship: Letters, 1921–1960* (Columbia: University of Missouri Press, 1991), 12; *Lovingly, Georgia*.

37. Susan Ware, *Beyond Suffrage: Women in the New Deal* (Cambridge: Harvard University Press, 1981); Frances M. Seeber, "Eleanor Roosevelt and Women in the New Deal: A Network of Friends," *Presidential Studies Quarterly* 20, 4 (fall 1990): 707–17. See also Leila J. Rupp, "The Women's Community in the National Woman's Party, 1945 to the 1960s," *Signs* 10, 4 (summer 1985): 715–40.

38. Margaret Sanger to Dorothy Brush, January 14, 1947, quoted in Chesler, *Woman of Valor*, 406; Carol Brightman, ed., *Between Friends: The Correspondence of Hannah Arendt and Mary*

McCarthy 1949–1975 (New York: Harcourt Brace, 1995); Ayn Rand to Isabel Paterson, October 10, 1943, July 4, 1945, February 28, April 11, May 17, 1948, in Michael S. Berliner, ed., *Letters of Ayn Rand* (New York: Dutton, 1995), 173, 185, 197, 205–6, 215–17; Sally Wood, ed., *The Southern Mandarins: Letters of Caroline Gordon to Sally Wood, 1924–1937* (Baton Rouge: Louisiana State University Press, 1984); Elizabeth Bishop, "Efforts of Affection: A Memoir of Marianne Moore," in Robert Giroux, ed., *The Collected Prose: Elizabeth Bishop* (New York: Farrar, Straus, Giroux, 1984), 121–56; Eudora Welty, "My Introduction to Katherine Anne Porter," in Rosemary M. Magee, ed., *Friendship and Sympathy: Communities of Southern Women Writers* (Jackson: University Press of Mississippi, 1992), 120–35.

39. Judith Schwarz, *Radical Feminists of Heterodoxy: Greenwich Village, 1912–1940* (Lebanon, New Hampshire: New Victoria, 1982).

40. Martha Hodes, "Romantic Love across the Color Line: White Women and Black Men in Nineteenth-Century America," in Ware, ed., *New Viewpoints in Women's History;* Leila Rupp, "Imagine My Surprise: Women's Relationships in Historical Perspective," *Frontiers* 5, 3 (fall 1980); Stephen Seidman, *Romantic Longings: Love in America, 1830–1980* (New York: Routledge, 1991), 112–14. Lillian Faderman has argued that in the context of explicit societal condemnation of lesbians, only very naive women could continue to see themselves as romantic friends. *Surpassing the Love of Men,* 411–12.

41. December 31, 1958, in Janet Flanner, *Darlinghissima: Letters to a Friend,* ed. Natalia Danesi Murray (New York: Harcourt Brace Jovanovich, 1985), 235; Frances Perry to Winnifred Wygal, March 15, 1932, box 1, Winnifred Wygal Collection, Schlesinger Library; Geraldine Thompson to Miriam Van Waters, April 2, 1936, box 7, folder 267, Miriam Van Waters Collection, Schlesinger Library.

42. Susan Ware, *Partner and I: Molly Dewson, Feminism, and New Deal Politics* (New Haven: Yale University Press, 1987); Martha Freeman, ed., *The Letters of Rachel Carson and Dorothy Freeman, 1952–1964* (Boston: Beacon Press, 1995); Frieda Segelke Miller Papers and Mary Elizabeth Dreier Papers, both in the Schlesinger Library.

43. Linda W. Rosenzweig, *The Anchor of My Life: Middle-Class American Mothers and Daughters, 1880–1920* (New York: New York University Press, 1993).

44. Peter N. Stearns, "Girls, Boys, and Emotions: Redefinitions and Historical Change," *Journal of American History* 80, 1 (June 1993): 66–69; Stanley, "Feminism and Friendship"; John C. Spurlock and Cynthia A. Magistro, " 'Dreams Never to Be Realized': Emotional Culture and the Phenomenology of Emotion," *Journal of Social History* 28, 2 (winter 1994): 295–310.

45. Elizabeth Abel, "(E)Merging Identities: The Dynamics of Female Friendship in Contemporary Fiction by Women," *Signs* 6, 3 (spring 1981): 413–35.

Emotion and the Consumer Economy

Chapter Nineteen

Frocks, Finery, and Feelings
Rural and Urban Women's Envy, 1890–1930

Susan J. Matt

In 1835 Alexis de Tocqueville noted that envy was widespread in the United States: "in America I never met a citizen too poor to cast a glance of hope and envy towards the pleasures of the rich or whose imagination did not snatch in anticipation good things that fate obstinately refused to him."[1] Sixty years later, Americans found even more cause for envy.

The dramatic growth of the consumer economy between 1890 and 1930 unquestionably multiplied the occasions for envy. Luxury goods were displayed more publicly than ever before. In department store windows, catalogs, advertisements, and movies, Americans came face to face with a vast array of the tantalizing items that factories were producing at unprecedented rates.[2] Yet despite the new abundance and visibility of luxurious clothing, hats, lamps, pianos, mirrors, and the like, these articles often remained out of the financial reach of many who viewed them. Such a situation frequently produced envy and desire in those who saw with new clarity and detail what they could not possess.[3]

Bourgeois Americans who felt envy in the consumer economy expressed it in distinctive ways. While envy in many societies has been accompanied by resentment and malice, among the American middle class, envy was commingled with hope.[4] Bourgeois men and women aspired to move up the social ladder and attain a lifestyle equal to those they envied. The aspirational envy of the American bourgeoisie may be attributed both to their position in the capitalist system and the specific nature of the system itself. As members of the middle class, they had a stake in the existing economic order and believed the capitalist means of distributing goods to be just. They were convinced that they might one day be able to gain the wealth and status of those they envied. Rather than wishing for the downfall of the rich, middle-class Americans hoped to move up the social ladder and join them.

The consumer economy itself produced conditions that made the middle class aspire to, rather than resent, the position and privileges of the upper classes. Anthropologist George Foster has posited that envy is a powerful presence in cultures that have an "image of the limited good," where "one player's advantage is at the expense of the other." In such a setting, resentment, rather than hope, is an understandable response to another's good fortune, for the fact that the envied possesses something means that there is less for the envious to possess. By the late nineteenth century, such conditions of scarcity were disappearing in the United States. The consumer economy and the mass production on which it was based were creating an expanding rather than finite pool of goods. The new abundance banished the notion of the "limited good" from the minds of middle-class men and women; consequently they felt little resentment at another's good fortune and instead tried to attain it for themselves.[5]

Bourgeois Americans often expressed this aspirational envy by emulating the wealthy. Between 1890 and 1930 the expanding consumer economy, while providing new occasions for envy, also offered envious men and women unprecedented opportunities for emulation. Prior to 1890, members of the middling and lower classes had envied the possessions of the elites but had far fewer ways to act on the emotion. By the end of the nineteenth century, however, they might avail themselves of the mass-produced imitation luxury goods that flooded the market. Such goods made it easier to emulate the rich. The consumer revolution thus offered new remedies for envy as well as new provocations.

While much scholarly attention has been paid to this consumer revolution of the late nineteenth and early twentieth centuries, little notice has been given to the ways these new institutions affected middle-class Americans' social and emotional lives. William Leach, T. J. Lears, and Roland Marchand have ably described the finance capitalists, advertisers, and merchants who created the stores, catalogs, window displays, factories, and advertising campaigns at the turn of the twentieth century. These historians, however, have ignored the way these institutions affected everyday people. In *When Ladies Go A-Thievin'*, Elaine Abelson has examined the experiences of consumers within the department store; yet she has done so in a fairly limited way. Although she has begun to recover the experiences of bourgeois women as they encountered new enticements and alluring objects, she focuses on only a small minority's extreme and deviant responses to these temptations.[6]

In contrast, this essay explores the emotional responses of people who saw the luxurious abundance of the expanding consumer economy but who could not always possess it. In particular, it focuses on the envy that middle-class women, both urban and rural, felt as they compared their possessions to those of wealthier women. While only a few women made explicit confessions of their envy, they left other testimony to their emotions. In records of their consumer behavior, patterns of emulative purchasing can be clearly read. Moralists and cultural leaders at the turn of the century also left behind heated discussions of women's behavior in the consumer marketplace. They observed the acquisitive and emulative activity of middle-class women and believed such activity to be symptomatic of envy. These diverse sources offer us a way of understanding the emotions of bourgeois women who saw about them an emerging culture of abundance and felt entitled to its fruits.

While the American middle class had long been eager consumers, enviously aware of upper-class styles, the economic conditions of the late nineteenth century heightened their awareness and their desires.[7] The expansion of the consumer economy between

1890 and 1930 multiplied occasions for bourgeois envy. As mass-circulation magazines, newspapers, and eventually movies spread across the country, Americans of all classes gained greater knowledge of the high fashions, luxurious household furnishings, and elaborate entertainments of the upper classes.

The growth of urban department stores also allowed middling folk to have new knowledge of the comforts of the elites. As Daniel Boorstin has pointed out, before the emergence of department stores, "common citizens might spend their lives without ever seeing a wide array of the fancy goods that they could not afford."[8] With the spread of department stores in the late nineteenth century, however, members of all classes could see luxury items that previously had been the exclusive domain of the wealthy. Mail-order catalogs, which emerged in the 1870s and 1880s, also made desirable consumer goods more visible, as did alluring magazine advertisements. They were instrumental in making the rural middle class aware of the consumer society's luxurious bounty and they increased opportunities for envy.[9]

Not only did the enviable possessions of the wealthy become more visible, the new consumer culture made them more central as standards of taste, as well. Across the nation, women in cities, towns, and farms paged through issues of mass-circulation magazines like the *Ladies' Home Journal, Woman's Home Companion,* and the *American Magazine,* studying their often extensive fashion and home decor features and advertisements. They frequently flipped through the same catalogs. In the early twentieth century, women across the country were entranced by the same film stars and glamorous images projected on the silver screen. These diverse media instructed women from Montana to Massachusetts about what was fashionable and current. This widely disseminated consumer culture standardized their tastes: it led women separated by vast geographical distances to measure themselves and their possessions against the same ideals and it prompted them to long for similar goods. In the midst of the emerging commercial culture, middle-class women in metropolis and hamlet and on the open range were united in their consumer desire and envy.

While these women felt pangs of envy when they observed the houses, carpets, carriages, and later the cars of upper-class women, their words and their consumer behavior indicate that they focused even greater attention on the apparel of the wealthy. The tailored dresses, fine laces, expensive jewelry, gracefully plumed hats, fur stoles, and other accessories of elite women excited envy among their bourgeois sisters. Rural and urban women alike came to view these items as extremely desirable, believing that such goods would establish and elevate their social status.

Although consumer institutions unified these women's tastes, they nevertheless led to sharply differentiated lifestyles. While the promotional vehicles of the consumer society—ads, movies, magazines, and radios—infiltrated even the remotest parts of the nation, the actual retail establishments did not spread as rapidly or as far. This uneven development led some women to feel deprived and envious as they contrasted their circumstances with those of women with greater access to consumer goods.

Geography as well as class therefore shaped women's emotional lives. City women found it easier than their country cousins to satisfy their desire for fine apparel because they had greater access to fashionable tailors and well-stocked stores that offered items in a variety of price ranges. Surrounded by shops and department stores that sold imitation luxury goods, city women might easily find high-fashion gowns rendered in more affordable fabrics, inexpensive shirtwaists styled to resemble costly ones, and cheap "knock-offs" of elegant jewelry. Such imitations made it easy for them to express their envy through emulation. Their ability to appear stylishly dressed despite limited means provoked sharp pangs of envy among their rural sisters. Without the same array of stores, country women had to rely on handmade clothing or turn to general stores, which often were understocked and sold out-moded, overpriced garments. For a time, they found a solution in mail-order catalogs; by the 1920s, however, catalog clothing had become all too recognizable as such and was disparaged as typical country garb.[10]

As a result, the contrast between urban and rural consumer opportunities led city and country women to act on their envy and desire for high fashions in different ways. Urban women, with access to a wide choice of goods in a variety of price ranges, developed strategies of emulative consumption in order to resolve their envy of upper-class women's wardrobes. Rural women, however, with only home-sewn garments or unsatisfying ready-to-wear, found it more difficult to faithfully emulate urban styles. Their discontent at their limited opportunities and inferior circum-stances was widely recognized. They felt a gap not only between their own appear-ances and those of upper-class women, but also between their lives and those of their urban bourgeois sisters who were surrounded by so many alluring goods. Rural women's envy, therefore, was often directed as much at other members of the middle class as it was toward the upper class.

Not only did women's experiences of envy vary across space, they varied across time as well. Between 1890 and 1915, moralists condemned women's emulative behav-ior. Because emulation was based on envy, it was considered a sin. Ministers, editors, columnists, and reformers claimed that there was a divinely ordained social order and sacred laws governing marketplace behavior. Women who expressed envy threat-ened to disrupt this order. These moralists therefore harshly condemned and hoped to restrain women's emulation in order to maintain social stability and a moral marketplace. After World War I, however, a new generation of cultural leaders disputed the conventional understanding of envy as a dangerous sin and upheld a secular understanding of the emotion and its role in the social and economic order. They encouraged women to act on their envy, recognizing the emotion as a valuable economic stimulant.

Urban Women's Envy and Emulative Consumption

The nature of turn-of-the-century city life led women to search for goods that would eloquently communicate their status and aspirations to all who viewed them. Possessions, particularly clothing, became crucial markers of class in urban America because judgments about people's background, position, and prospects gradually came to depend less on close acquaintance and more on appearances. Thorstein Veblen, in his *Theory of the Leisure Class*, explained how the anonymity of the city made consumer purchases more important as signals of social standing:

The exigencies of the modern industrial system frequently place individuals and house-holds in juxtaposition between whom there is little contact in any other sense than that of juxtaposition. One's neighbors ... often are socially not one's neighbors, or even acquaintances; and still their transient good opinion has a high degree of utility. The only practicable means of impressing one's pecuniary ability on these unsympathetic observers of one's everyday life is an unremitting demonstration of ability to pay.[11]

In a society filled with strangers ignorant of each others' true economic circumstances, a woman might wear particular styles in order to signal a higher social status than she actually possessed. As a *Saturday Evening Post* columnist observed in 1913, "people try, by appearance and the possession of mere things, to give themselves fictitious social values." It was because of their perceived usefulness in creating social identities that articles of dress gained new importance for women.[12]

Between 1890 and 1930 bourgeois women, through their words and their purchases, frequently and eloquently expressed their faith in the power of clothing to provide social mobility and resolve their envy. In 1905 a twenty-eight-year-old woman reported to psychologist G. Stanley Hall that when she was well dressed, "I feel equal to meeting anyone." A twenty-year-old claimed that with the right attire she "mingle[d] more freely with others," while a nineteen-year-old reported that "I feel able to meet any person" when well dressed. In contrast, when poorly dressed, a nineteen-year-old reported, she felt "as though somebody else were better dressed," while an eighteen-year-old girl worried that "I am afraid people will think less of me" when poorly attired.[13]

In 1912, reformer Ida Tarbell criticized such beliefs as she explained the relationship of envy and fashion to social advancement in a democratic society. "[W]hole bodies of women place their chief social reliance on dress.... If you look like the women of a set, you are as 'good' as they, is the democratic standard of many a young woman." She added that "the folly of woman's dress ... lies in the pitiful assumption that she can achieve her end by imitation, that she can be the thing she envies if she look [sic] like that thing."[14] Tarbell astutely observed that many American women expressed their envy and aspirations through emulation.

Emulation was indeed an important strategy for those women who wanted symbols of an elevated class position but who could not afford the actual goods that the upper class possessed. Women sometimes purchased imitation goods and sometimes tried to create them by hand. Machine-made imitations were increasingly accessible as a result of the new technologies of mass production. Women could buy imitation silk instead of real silk, machine-made laces that were reproductions of costly hand-made lace, rhinestones marketed as substitutes for diamonds, and cheap furs made to resemble sealskin or mink. Such faux luxury goods came to have an increasingly central role in establishing class identities and signaling social aspirations.

Contemporary observers recognized the important role emulation played in establishing a social identity and concluded that envy was its primary cause. Envy dictated the prevailing fashions among the middle class, causing some styles to catch on and gain popularity. Columnist Juliet Virginia Strauss confided that she, like many women, felt envy. "The oldest and plainest and 'sensiblest' of us," she wrote, experienced "the quick envy of other women's clothes" and the "determination to have something as fine or as pretty or as stylish as her neighbors. It is a great system of imitation, this dress business." [15]

Many commentators concluded that such imitation was futile and would not lead to social advancement. A columnist in the *Ladies' Home Journal* reported that she saw evidence of envy all about her: "I see feathers and laces and embroideries and garments rich or trying to seem so, worn by graceful young women who are in [narrow] circumstances." Such attire, however, failed to change the wearer's status. She reminded readers, "To envy the rich . . . does not bring us one step closer to the fulfillment of our desires." [16]

Nevertheless, bourgeois women continued to array themselves after the fashion of elites. The imitative clothing they left behind is perhaps the most interesting evidence of their envy. Ida Tarbell described how the fashion industry spread styles to all classes and how these garments were altered to meet the budgets of middle- and lower-class women. She claimed that the rich imported their fashions from Europe and introduced them to American society. Other classes quickly demanded similar styles. She traced the route of a dress as it spread through New York's shopping districts and class system.

> The French or Viennese mode, started on upper Fifth Avenue, spreads to 23rd st., from 23rd st., to 14th st. to Grand and Canal. Each move sees it reproduced in material a little less elegant and durable, its colors a trifle vulgarized, its ornaments cheapened, its laces poorer. By the time it reaches Houston st. the $400 gown in brocaded velvet from the best looms in Europe has become a cotton velvet from Lawrence or Fall River, decorated with mercerized lace and glass ornaments from Rhode Island. . . . The very shop window where it is displayed is dressed and painted and lighted in imitation of the uptown shop. The same process goes on inland. [17]

Women's envy left a trail of gowns as silent witnesses.

It was not only dress styles, however, that started out in elite circles and trickled down. Upper-class luxury items with little utility except as social symbols spread to the middle and lower classes, demonstrating how envy could be a powerful spur for consumption. Over the span of two decades, all classes of American women came to wear what had once been a symbol of privilege and luxury: silk stockings.

At the turn of the century, only members of the elite wore silk stockings. As David Cohn pointed out in his history of the Sears catalog, silk hosiery was not even offered in the 1905 catalog. Instead, most American women wore "black cotton or lace stockings," while only wealthy women wore silk hose. [18]

By 1912, however, middle-class women deemed silk stockings highly desirable and began to emulate the habits of upper-class women. This sartorial change alarmed some:

> I have been especially interested during the last year in silk stockings. I've seen so many of them on exhibition on the legs of women climbing off and on the street cars. I have seen young women whose husbands were working on low salaries—arrayed in silk stockings and pumps. Now this was merely the effort to carry out somebody else's ideal. Some other woman, whom these girls envied or whose way of living embodied their ambition, wore silk stockings and pumps. [19]

Although silk stockings started out as "somebody else's ideal," they quickly became an item to which middle-class and some working-class women felt entitled. Between 1914 and 1923 the desirability and the consumption of silk or "artificial-silk" stockings (made of rayon and "mixed fibers") increased dramatically. Silk hosiery production rose 26 percent and artificial silk hosiery production increased 417 percent. Cotton hose, meanwhile, gradually but decisively fell out of favor.[20]

Indeed, by 1920, not only middle-class women but working-class women came to see silk or pseudo-silk stockings as a necessity. Albert Atwood, a writer for the *Saturday Evening Post,* reported that all the girls in a New York canning factory wore silk hose, "though any sense of fitness and desire to get the most wear out of a garment would have abolished silk stockings from such a place."[21] Working women laboring at a cannery but clad in silk provided poignant proof that merely imitating the attire of the elites would not bring a higher class position. Women, buying on the basis of envy and hoping for advancement, ended up with the stockings but not the status.

Yet these urban women, while they might not succeed in changing their actual social status, nevertheless managed to assuage their pangs of envy through emulation. By dressing "up" and imitating the fine fashions of upper-class ladies, urban women found a way to act on their discontent and lessen their sense of inferiority and deprivation.

The Country Cousin

Lulu Rutenber Bartz, born in 1901 in Tacoma, New York, recalled her envy of other girls' skirts and her inability to dress similarly. Like many rural young women, she relied on her own or her mother's handiwork for clothes, and these garments often proved unfashionable. "When I went to school, Mother made all our clothes, and I had but one dress to wear. That was kinda hard for me. We were from the farm, and some of those village kids wore those broomstick skirts that were so pretty."[22] Lulu and rural women like her found it more difficult to resolve their envy than city women did. There were fewer opportunities for country women to participate in the fashion parade; instead they felt they could only be spectators who watched hungry-eyed as the procession of the stylishly dressed marched past.

It was "kinda hard" on Lulu to see others wear fashionable skirts and to be unable to do so herself, for she felt excluded. Wearing stylish clothes, such as broomstick skirts, conferred membership in a group. Lulu was not the only young woman to recognize the shortcomings of homemade dresses and to envy those with store-bought or tailor-made garments. A columnist in *Rural Manhood,* a YMCA journal, observed in 1915 that it was important to teach rural girls the value of " 'home-made' things, especially clothes, which in many communities are scorned, 'bought' clothes being considered far more stylish and popular."[23]

Many young women, however, clearly remained unconvinced of the value of homemade clothes. They tried to buy clothing that resembled the apparel of sophisti-cated urban women. And if money did not permit, they often attempted to make their own replicas of urban styles. Their buying and sewing habits offer testimony to their strong desires for high fashion. Margaret Slattery, author of several books on girls' development, described the efforts of two country girls who tried to leave country ways behind by transforming themselves into urban sophisticates. The girls had run away to Boston. Upon their arrival in the city, "their dress showed attempts to copy newspaper interpretations of the fall styles, their eyes were bright with excitement."[24]

With the advent of the automobile, some fortunate, affluent rural women found new ways to resolve their envy. They began to travel to the city to shop or ordered from city stores. Mary Meek Atkeson reported in her 1924 book *The Woman on the Farm,*

> The desire of the American country woman is to dress so much like her city sisters that she can mingle in the city crowds without an added glance in her direction. . . . the only way to look exactly like the city woman is to wear exactly the same kind of clothes. . . . For this reason many of the farm women whom I know buy their clothes by mail from the shops on Fifth Avenue, New York rather than from the local stores or the general mail-order which cater particularly to the country trade.

Atkeson reported that not only did rural women want to emulate urban dress, they also desired to be part of the "silk stocking" class. Like their urban middle-class sisters, they were convinced that they should wear silk hose, long the exclusive privilege of economic elites. Atkeson reported that for special occasions and for trips to town, farm women wore silk stockings, despite their impracticality. She observed that many country women cared more about social acceptance than practicality. "Cotton stockings are more sensible for general country wear because they are not damaged so easily by briars and weeds. . . . but who wants to be sensible to the extent of wearing cotton when every other woman is wearing silk!"[25]

Rural women envied the silk stockings and broomstick skirts so popular and accessible in cities and towns. In their longings for urban styles and their distaste for their own handiwork, we can see the rise of a national, homogenizing culture. Rural women looked to large cities rather than to their own communities to discover what was fashionable and current. The taste for silk stockings and urban styles had become national tastes.

The Apostles of Contentment, 1890–1915

Although urban and rural women's experiences differed, the criticism they faced from moral leaders was almost identical. Between 1890 and 1915 women in city and country constantly heard that envy and emulation were sinful. Moralists told women to be content with what they had rather than coveting what they did not. Envious women should feel guilt, and rural women in particular should resist envy because they bore the added responsibility of maintaining a threatened way of life. Only after World War I, as these moral leaders lost prominence and authority in the market-place and a new generation of secular leaders gained influence, would women's envy be greeted with anything but disapproval.

Between 1890 and 1915, ministers, editors, columnists, and rural reformers propagated a doctrine of contentment. In sermons, secular and religious journals, and popular literature, these moralists condemned envy and praised contentment, which they considered envy's opposite. They told women that to envy was to question God's wisdom, for he had ordained the social positions that all were destined to occupy. Moralists invoked Saint Paul, who had taught that whatever condition one found oneself in, whatever one possessed, "therewith to be content." [26]

The apostles of contentment reassured their audience that the earthly economic differences that caused envy were irrelevant. What truly mattered was an individual's condition in the hereafter. As a columnist in the Methodist-Episcopal journal the *Christian Advocate* wrote in 1890, "Be content with such things as ye have. Some people have better things, others have worse; then be content with what you have. ... learn the lesson of contentment, and wait on God for brighter days, for richer fruits, for purer joys." [27]

Moralists told women that they should not desire more than they had. In 1891 Edward Bok, editor of the *Ladies' Home Journal,* wrote, "I do not want you, my dear woman, to be envious of the possessions ... of one woman in this world, be she rich or poor. To say 'Oh, I wish I were rich' is to express discontent with the judgement and dispensation of an All-wise creator, who knows far better what is good for you than you do." That year the *Saturday Evening Post* offered the same lesson with a story of parents who tried to inculcate contentment in their daughter. Mary wanted diamond earrings, which her father, "a man in moderate circumstances," decided to give her, hoping that "she'd soon find that happiness does not consist in fine jewelry, but in a contented and cheerful spirit." After realizing that her earrings brought only temporary satisfaction and that she was prone to envy, Mary announced that she wished to return them:

> It isn't what we wear that makes us happy; it is the contented mind within. . . . I find now ... that I was unhappy, not because I had no diamonds, but because I was daily breaking the tenth commandment, and guilty of covetousness. . . . So, if you please, I'll do without them, and be content with [my] old ones, which are more appropriate to your means, dear papa.

At this both parents cried, happy that their daughter had found the way to serenity and contentment.[28]

Ministers and columnists who encouraged contentment also urged their readers to be "sincere" in their self-presentation, that is, to restrain their emulative instincts. To the moralists, a sincere woman was one whose clothing accurately reflected her true social status. Such sincerity sprang from contentment. A contented city woman would not dress "up" in order to pass for a member of a higher class. Similarly, a contented rural woman would not adopt city styles unsuited to her daily life. The contented woman—on farm or city avenue—would embrace her true status and the material symbols appropriate to it.

Moralists assumed that urban women might easily be caught up in the whirl of city social life and try to emulate the styles of high-society women by purchasing imitation goods. Women who wore such imitations of high fashion, fake jewelry, and cheap laces faced accusations of "insincerity." Edward Bok piously intoned, "I can conceive nothing so well fitted to the term disagreeable as a woman who pretends to be what she is not, to clothe and carry herself in a manner unbecoming to her circumstances . . . spoiling herself for her family and friends by being a sham." Such imitative dressing was not only dishonorable, it was futile. "Instead of trying to cover your real position with sham, why not adorn it and make yourself envied for your own qualities if not for your possessions. . . . To strive to be what you are not, is as unworthy of you as it is useless." [29]

In the moralists' eyes, dishonesty in appearance was no different from dishonest words. Women who emulated were trying to deceive the world. In the *Christian Advocate* in 1904, Orison Swett Marden scolded envious young women:

> Dressing or living beyond one's means is nothing less than absolute dishonesty. . . . If your jewelry, your carriages, your furs, and your costly gowns tell me that you are rich, when you live in a poverty-stricken home, and when your mother is obliged to make all sorts of sacrifices to enable you to make this false display, you lie just as surely as you would if you try to deceive me by your words.[30]

Rural girls also were warned against envy and emulation and encouraged to adorn themselves in a "sincere" manner, suited to their environment. Country girls should suppress their envy of city girls' wardrobes and should realize that such attire was inappropriate for their life circumstances. Ruth Ashmore, a regular *Ladies' Home Journal* columnist, warned that visits from city cousins bearing details of the latest urban fashions should not be occasions for envy. The country girl might legitimately ask about city ways, but she should be careful not to become discontented with her own life in the process: "Talk about frocks if you like . . . but if you feel the little demon of envy biting at your heartstrings, change the subject right away."

Further, it would be wrong for a country girl to respond to the "demon of envy" and try to dress like a city girl. What was true for city girls was also true for country girls: a young woman's dress should correspond to her place—social or geographical—in society. Ashmore warned rural girls that if they imitated urban modes they would look silly and insincere:

> That country girl is wise who, remembering that the blue of the skies and the green of the trees form her background, elects that during the summer she wears pretty cottons daintily made, and wide-brimmed, somewhat fantastic straw hats. She would be entirely out of place in stuffy woolens or elaborate silks, and yet each one of you knows that this mistake is sometimes made. . . . She is unwise in imitating her city cousin, who nine times out of ten looks overdressed. I know it is in the heart of every girl to long for pretty gowns, and a much-betrimmed lace silk frock may look very charming to the girl who has not one, while to the unprejudiced observer it seems absolutely out of place.

Ashmore realized that country girls might easily feel inferior if they compared themselves to city girls. In an essay entitled "The Girl in a Small Community," she wrote, "When she [the city cousin] comes it seems to you as if your gowns were shabby and as if you knew nothing." Despite these feelings, the envious girl should not try to make herself over in her city cousin's image. "Any attempt on your part to make your gown look like hers will result in a failure, for undoubtedly a dressmaker, knowing her trade well, designed and made that one you so admire."[31] Country women, like their city sisters, must not emulate the wealthy or try to be what they were not.

The idea that a dress could tell a lie, that clothing must reflect a woman's actual economic conditions rather than her aspirations, reveals the prevailing conceptions of feminine identity. A woman's self was not a self she constructed and presented to society; rather, it was an unchanging, unchangeable set of qualities with which she was born. While most of these moralists were comfortable with liberal notions of the self that stressed the idea of self-creation for males, such a model seemed unsuitable for women, idealized as moral and submissive beings.

Not only did moralists believe that women's envy might lead to insincerity in self-presentation, they also believed that the emotion might have grave consequences for America's social and moral order. Some argued that envy of city lifestyles was the cause of the rural exodus that was emptying the countryside. These observers worried that the mass migration to the cities might erode the civic order and upset the social balance of the nation. Other reformers worried about the hazards of urban social life and the driving need to spend in order to keep up with the dominant classes. In both cases, moralists concluded that envy, because it often prompted individuals to act on their sense of entitlement, was a serious threat to the prevailing social order.

Many observers of country life, alarmed by the exodus of rural youth at the turn of the century, concluded that envy of city fashions and amenities led the rising generation to desert the farm. They deplored the fact that so many young people were leaving the moral purity of the countryside for the corrupting, materialistic environment of the American city. As the number of rural dwellers declined, from 71 percent of the population in 1880 to 60 percent in 1900, and to only 48 percent of the population in 1930, many sociologists, editorialists, and extension workers became convinced that women's discontent with farm life lay at the bottom of the mass migration. Sociologists noted that more young women than men were leaving the farm.[32] Some observers argued that this led to an instability in rural social life, for without women, how could rural society continue? President Theodore Roosevelt, trying to redress rural discontent, noted that "there is too much belief among all our people that the prizes of life lie away from the farm." He proposed that "whatever will brighten home life in the country and make it richer and more attractive for the mothers, wives and daughters of families should be done promptly, thoroughly, and gladly."[33]

Many, however, were unsympathetic to rural women's envy and discontent. They portrayed it as unfounded and blamed it for dissolving agrarian life. In 1913, for example, the "Country Contributor" wrote in the *Ladies' Home Journal* that too many rural residents suffered from the "common delusion" that urban socialites were inherently superior. She claimed that "This [mistaken belief] causes considerable envy and unrest" among farmers and often caused them to leave the farm. "This is because the wife and daughters keep hankering after that sophisticated town sense which they imagined they could absorb." [34] Such commentators believed that rural women's envy was illegitimate and was dissolving rural society. It therefore needed to be suppressed.

Women's envy not only threatened rural life, it also endangered the morality of urban society. Many writers who urged women to control their envy reminded readers of their economic dependency on men. If a bourgeois woman envied an article of clothing and hoped to purchase it, she generally would have to turn to a man for the money to do so. Reliance on men for money could easily bring financial ruin on the man and the whole household, or cause the moral ruin of the woman herself.

Commentators often maintained that women were the main impetus behind spending in a household. These authors repeatedly reminded readers that it was a wife or daughter's desire to keep up with a neighbor's consumption that led to dreaded debt and eventually the financial downfall of a household. A *Journal* columnist presented such an argument in 1894:

> Many a business man can trace his downfall to the diamond earrings for which his wife or daughter begged so hard. And then a woman is so seldom satisfied with just one bit of prettiness. So, my dear girl, unless you know your father can afford it, don't even hint to him that you would like a bracelet, or a locket, or a brooch.[35]

Mrs. Amelie E. Barr, writing in the *North American Review,* agreed, reminding her readers of the folly of "discontented wives, who goad their husbands into extravagant expenditure, and urge them to projects from which they would naturally recoil." [36]

Not just financial ruin, but moral ruin awaited envious women, according to these commentators. Turning to men for resources to assuage envy might exact another price. Moralists implied that women might have sex, and even become prostitutes, in exchange for finery. In most of the scenarios which moralists provided for their middle-class readers, it was single working or working-class women who lost their virtue, but the cautionary tales still served to show the middle class just where unchecked envy could lead.

Laura Smith, writing in the *Ladies' Home Journal,* warned young girls not to accept gifts from men. "Above all, never allow a man to make you a present of articles of clothing, no matter how plausible his reason seems to you or how badly you want the article." She did not say explicitly where such actions could lead, but others were more blunt. Ida Tarbell informed her audience outright of the evils caused by accepting gifts from men. " 'I wanted the money,' I heard a girl arrested on her first street soliciting tell the judge. 'Have you no home?' 'Yes.' 'A good home?' 'Yes.' 'For what did you want the money?' 'Clothes.' " The girl's story was all too common, Tarbell noted. " 'Gee, but I felt as if I would give anything for one of them willow plumes,' a pretty young sixteen-year old told the police matron who had rescued her after leaving home with a man, because he promised her silk gowns and hats with feathers." Tarbell believed that these girls' experiences represented a larger social evil: "This ugly preoccupation with dress does not begin with the bottom of society . . . it exists at the top and filters down."

Because the "ugly preoccupation" with fashion existed at all levels of society, some held the enviable upper classes to blame for the moral ruin of the lower classes. In 1912, columnist Juliet Virginia Strauss speculated on how the sight of rich women's opulent fashions affected poor women. The rich woman attending the theater, "costumed to the limit ... her hair elaborately dressed, her fine wrap slipping from her shoulders, the grand hat nodding its trailing plumes," was unaware of the effects of her display on poor young girls who observed her:

> That very hat, that very opera cloak may tonight turn the balance against that young girl's virtue. She may decide that the world is well lost if only she may look, for once in her life, like that rich woman in the box. . . . while custom may make a woman safe in ornamenting her body conspicuously and presenting it to the public gaze . . . the effect upon general moral conditions of so much noticeable dressing is decidedly bad, and has much more to do with prevailing evils than any of us even dream.[37]

As long as women were dependent on men for a large part of their spending money, they would be vulnerable. Moralists hoped that if women knew the dangers inherent in their envy of finery they would be more prudent in acting on their longings.

Between 1890 and 1915 the attacks on envy were multifaceted and directed toward women of all social classes. Moralists expressed deep anxiety at women's attempts to obfuscate their true social position and to cross class boundaries. They encouraged women to accept their circumstances—if they were on farms, to remain there; if they were in modest financial straits, to accept them. As they condemned the envy that they thought caused social disorder, they reinforced the traditionally feminine virtues of piety and submissiveness, both to God's will and to man's will. They hoped that by reinvigorating these values they might preserve the distinctions that separated classes.

A Revolution in Mores, 1915–1930: The Acceptance of Envy

This moral vision of the marketplace, with its strong prohibitions against envy, lost power after World War I. In the years between 1915 and 1930, American women—both rural and urban—witnessed a revolution in mores. The influence and prominence of the apostles of contentment waned as a new generation of diverse voices came to powerfully and publicly endorse envy and emulation in the marketplace. Less concerned with preserving a traditional and hierarchical social order, the new generation of cultural leaders discarded the virtue of contentment and instead embraced discontent, envy, and the emulative actions these emotions might inspire.

After World War I, a new generation of secular opinion makers began to make their voices heard in middle-class society. Some were editorialists, some were fashion writers or advice writers, some economists. They were joined by a large and ever increasing number of advertisers. Despite their diverse backgrounds and perspectives, many of these individuals articulated a similar viewpoint: envy, discontent, and consumer desire were legitimate instincts. Although there continued to be a number of conservative voices who espoused the doctrine of contentment, it was this new generation, and their successors, whose views would ultimately carry the day. After 1915, their opinions about market behavior became dominant and helped redefine women's roles in economic and commercial life. These advocates of envy argued that women should have what they wanted, whether or not an object was conventionally understood as appropriate to their class position or geographical location.

Rural women, for instance, encountered new acceptance of their envy and discontent. In the period after the war, rural leaders publicly recognized emulation as a legitimate social instinct and offered country girls new institutional support in the hope of alleviating the causes of the rural exodus. Agricultural extension programs and reformers involved in the Country Life movement came to recognize that the ideology of contentment was ineffectual in stopping discontent and the migrations it often motivated. Instead, these social leaders realized that only by confronting envy, and bringing the much desired amenities of city life to the country, might they stem the flow of migrants to the city.

Rural girls who tried to keep up with city fashions received new encouragement. For example, a 1914 pamphlet entitled *The Young Woman on the Farm* argued that women who kept their children stylishly attired might keep them content with rural life. In it a farmer's wife stated, "I would dress the boys and girls as well as my means would allow and in no way different from the young people in town." [38]

Some rural girls and their mothers were lucky to have agricultural extension programs to turn to for help as they sought to copy city styles. Such programs offered them practical advice about how to dress fashionably. For instance, the December 1918 *Cornell Junior Extension Bulletin,* entitled "Elementary Garment Making," taught extension workers how to help farm girls make desirable garments like kimonos, bloomers, middy blouses, shirtwaists, and other city fashions that they might long for. The Cornell Extension Program also offered lectures and demonstrations to countywide or district groups. The most popular lecture in 1924 was entitled "The Well Dressed Woman." Twenty-nine counties participated in the program; 4,597 women attended from across the state. Other programs that drew hundreds and sometimes thousands of women included "How to Buy Ready-Mades," "Accessories—Their Use and Abuse," and "Successful Homemade Clothes." Social leaders condoned the country girl's longing for stylish, chic apparel. [39]

The increasing acceptance of rural women's envy was symptomatic of a larger shift in mores. Women across the United States, in cities as well as on farms, encountered far less criticism and far more encouragement of their envy. Repudiating the traditional wisdom, which held that women who dressed above their station were insincere, imprudent, and immoral, many of the new generation of opinion makers argued just the opposite. An early advocate of this philosophy was Dr. Woods Hutchinson, a physician who popularized health and hygiene issues. In 1911 he urged women to attire themselves fashionably. In a piece he wrote for the *Saturday Evening Post* entitled "The Sin of Homeliness, the Duty of Every Woman to Be Well Dressed," he argued that women should indulge their tastes for elite fashions. He sought to dispel the fear that such emulative spending might bring moral and financial ruin on a household. He proclaimed,

Every woman ought to be dressed just as beautifully as she can possibly afford to be, without risking bankrupting her husband—and she need not worry too much about this latter consideration. The number of men, with the right kind of brains, whose business was in sound condition, that have been bankrupted by their wives' extravagance is about as great as the number of those who die in poverty from having given too much to the poor. "Ruined by my wife's extravagance" is chiefly a belated echo of the old whine in the Garden of Eden.[40]

In 1913 economist Simon Patten also encouraged women to strive to get what they envied, arguing that women who dressed above their station displayed virtue, not vice. He rejected the common belief that well-dressed women of moderate means were immoral and sexually promiscuous, claiming, "It is no evidence of loose morality when a stenographer, earning eight or ten dollars a week, appears dressed in clothing that takes nearly all of her earnings to buy. It is a sign of her growing moral development." Dressing "up" could help a woman advance; it was now a canny and practical way of bettering her position.[41]

By 1923 the once conservative editorial staff of the *Ladies' Home Journal* was congratulating American women for dressing so well:

> Whatever their background, they seem all to be inspired with what we are told is a typical and standardized American desire to "look like a million dollars." Some of it may be stupid vanity, some of it may be decadent or degenerate vanity, but justly weighed and charitably considered, isn't most of it innocent vanity—wholesale ambition to look one's best, to achieve beauty and distinction, to assert good taste and cultivated selection in clothes?[42]

To try to look "like a million dollars" regardless of one's background was a goal the previous generation of moralists had strongly condemned. But in this new era, women no longer had to wear clothes that matched their incomes. Striving to look like a fashionable neighbor was acceptable, and perhaps even necessary.

Women also found further encouragement of their envy in the advertisements of the time. Copywriters came to preach much the same gospel in their ads as the editors and extension workers did in their publications and classrooms. Advertisers embraced envy with particular vigor because they recognized that it could be a powerful spur to consumption.

Between 1915 and 1930 advertising began to take on its modern form and gained new influence in American culture. The size, color, and style of ads during this period gave them new prominence in magazines and newspapers. Even more important to the history of envy was the changing tenor of the ads. In the years before the war, ads merely sold the product; after the war they came to focus on the attendant social and psychic benefits of the item. Envious women had long believed what this new generation of advertisers emphatically told them: material things had a larger social meaning. A dress was not merely a dress, it was a symbol and a signal. It was these social connotations that made an object enviable. Ads of the late teens and 1920s took advantage of this already existing belief as they tried to attach a desirable social meaning to virtually all products.[43] Ads also came to focus on the implications of

392 SUSAN J. MATT

not having something desirable, the high cost of not having the correct car or sweet breath or a clear complexion. They lavished attention on social handicaps, hoping to manipulate envy and inspire spending.

In order to sell goods, advertisers after World War I repeatedly legitimated envy, discontent, and a desire to change one's self and one's status. Their copy encouraged readers to act on these feelings and make a purchase. Quick cures for envy abounded in the ad pages. "Don't Envy Beauty—Use Pompeiian and have it." Similarly, Colgate extolled the charms of "gleaming teeth," confiding that "there is nothing mysterious about these enviable results. The men and women fortunate to secure them did nothing that you cannot easily do yourself." [44] Such ads argued that what women wanted but did not have they could easily and legitimately purchase. There was no moral problem with straining after what one lacked, no modern-day sumptuary law constricting the range of purchases.

In fact, advertisements went further and encouraged women to make themselves enviable. "The Envied Girl—Are you one? Or are you still seeking the secret of charm?" asked Palmolive. Another ad queried, "Do Other Women Envy You? Or do you envy them? The woman who gets what she wants out of life—the woman other women envy and copy—never depends on youth alone, or a pretty face, or brains." Such a woman had "charm," "poise," and used Houbigant Perfume. [45] There was no trace of the old fear that inciting envy might lead others to moral or financial ruin. After World War I, if a woman was envied, she was successful.

The history of envy illustrates the changing images of the idealized capitalist actor. Until World War I, moralists denied that women had or should have desires. In doing so, they upheld women's exclusion from the liberal capitalist marketplace. Market activity required individuals to be competitive, ambitious, acquisitive, and, indeed, envious. In contrast, women were perceived to be naturally religious, self-sacrificing, without desire or envy, and therefore contented. Accordingly, they had no need to participate in the market economy—without desires or drive they had no impetus for the restless, struggling behavior endemic to capitalism.

By 1930 journalists, social commentators, merchants, advertisers, and women themselves had redefined the boundaries of acceptable female behavior. The new behavioral model affirmed women's right to consume, to handle money (if not to earn it), and to pursue the objects they desired. Businessmen, writers, and advertisers admitted what women themselves had long known: women had longings and in-stincts that might lead them to participate in the economy. Cultural leaders began to acknowledge, accept, and sometimes literally capitalize on women's envy. As cultural proscriptions on their envy relaxed, women were given a somewhat wider space for action in the economy.

The changing experience and social meaning of envy also illustrate how the previously excluded rural classes were brought into the consumer economy and how the differences between rural and urban cultures were slowly effaced. Rural women's envy of city styles reveals just how successful the promoters of consumer culture were in spreading word of their goods and infiltrating the culture of the countryside, even from afar. Rural women envied because they were learning ever more about the commercial culture centered in America's cities and were coming to feel as entitled to its bounty as their city sisters. They came to regard the slower pace of rural existence as inferior and longed to take part in the glittering life of the cities.

Those who attempted to restrain rural women's envy were concerned with both defending traditional codes of morality and preserving the distinctiveness of country life. Rural reformers believed (as many had before them) that rural culture was noncommercial and uncorrupt, and they sought to protect it from the commercial influences of city culture.[46] In their eyes, rural women's envy and emulation of city styles menaced the purity of country life with the contagion of capitalist values.

After World War I, a new generation of rural reformers and cultural leaders recognized that the consumer ethos had spread irreversibly to the countryside. Rural dwellers felt entitled to consume on an equal basis with their city peers. They no longer wanted to maintain the divide between rural and urban life, but instead demanded equal access to the new and alluring consumer society. Reformers no longer sought to turn back the threatening influences of city culture, but instead welcomed elements of city culture into rural communities across the nation, realizing that this was the only viable way of solving the problem of envy.

The new consumer society, with its abundance in clear and tantalizing sight of all, broke down traditional ideologies and boundaries. Rural cultures fell under the sway of a national and homogenizing urban culture as farmers' daughters attempted to dress like financiers'. Women from remote farms and from Fifth Avenue found new acceptance of their limited participation in the economy, as cultural leaders and entrepreneurs came to recognize that women had longings and desires that, if properly channeled, might prove quite profitable. Women's envy, once regarded as a grave sin and the first step on the road to ruin, came to be seen as a powerful economic stimulant and as a "natural" part of femininity in twentieth-century America.

This view of envy as a legitimate and potentially profitable emotion, which arose in the teens and the twenties, has continued to influence the emotional lives of women of succeeding generations as they confront the enticements of consumer society. Since the twenties women have become less circumspect in articulating and acting on their envy, and have encountered little disapproval when they have done so. Bourgeois Americans today accept envy as a natural response to the unequal distribution of consumer goods and believe that in a market full of mass-produced imitations, emulation is a sensible and harmless way to resolve these feelings. The emotion that nineteenth- century moralists condemned as destructive of the social order, twentieth-century Americans now accept as a central pillar of the consumer society.

NOTES

1. Alexis de Tocqueville, *Democracy in America,* trans. George Lawrence (New York, 1969), 531.

2. William Leach, *Land of Desire: Merchants, Power, and the Rise of a New American Culture* (New York, 1993), 16.

3. As historian Elaine Tyler May has argued, the rise of the corporate and consumer economy

"offered abundance and leisure. The tragedy, however, was that the aspiration for affluence was more widespread than the luxurious life itself." Elaine Tyler May, *Great Expectations: Marriage and Divorce in Post-Victorian America* (Chicago, 1980), 142. May sees the new desires the consumer revolution produced as a source of marital discord. When wives' material aspirations outstripped their husbands' salaries, domestic strife might ensue.

4. George Foster, "Interpersonal Relations in Peasant Society," *Human Organization* 19, no. 4 (winter 1960–61): 174–78; Helmut Schoeck, *Envy: A Theory of Social Behavior*, ed. Michael Glenny and Betty Ross (New York, 1969), 46–61.

5. George Foster, "The Anatomy of Envy: A Study in Symbolic Behavior," *Current Anthropology* 13, no. 2 (April 1972): 167–68; see also John Kenneth Galbraith, *The Affluent Society* (Boston, 1958).

6. See Leach, *Land of Desire*; T. J. Jackson Lears, "From Salvation to Self Realization: Advertising and the Therapeutic Roots of the Consumer Culture, 1880–1930," in *The Culture of Consumption*, ed. Richard Wightman Fox and T. J. Jackson Lears (New York, 1983); idem, *Fables of Abundance: A Cultural History of Advertising in America* (New York, 1994); Roland Marchand, *Advertising the American Dream: Making Way for Modernity, 1920–1940* (Berkeley, CA, 1985); Elaine Abelson, *When Ladies Go A-Thievin': Middle-Class Shoplifters in the Victorian Department Store* (New York, 1989).

7. See, for instance, Karen Halttunen, *Confidence Men and Painted Women: A Study in Middle-Class Culture in America, 1830–1870* (New Haven, 1982), 61–62.

8. Daniel Boorstin, *The Americans: The Democratic Experience* (New York, 1973), 107.

9. Leach, *Land of Desire*, 20–21; Boorstin, *The Americans*, 101–9, 118–29; David Cohn, *The Good Old Days: A History of American Morals and Manners as Seen through the Sears Roebuck Catalogs, 1905 to the Present* (New York, 1940), 538–39.

10. See, for instance, Mary Meek Atkeson, *The Woman on the Farm* (New York, 1924), 134. See also Cohn, *The Good Old Days*, in which he describes the embarrassment some country dwellers felt about the Sears labels in their clothing. Historian Joan Severa, in her recent book *Dressed for the Photographer: Ordinary Americans and Fashion, 1840–1900* (Kent, OH, 1995) easily picks out mail-order dresses from tailor-made fashions; see, for example, 377.

11. Thorstein Veblen, *Theory of the Leisure Class* (New York, 1953), 71. See also Paul Boyer, *Urban Masses and Moral Order in America, 1820–1920* (Cambridge, MA, 1978), 4–5.

12. Veblen also noted the particular value of clothing as a symbol of pecuniary power. "Expenditure on dress has this advantage over most other methods, that our apparel is always in evidence and affords an indication of our pecuniary standing at first glance." *Theory of the Leisure Class*, 118–19. "Getting Good Value in New York: How to Move Safely Round the Big Spending Machine," *Saturday Evening Post*, February 15, 1914, 12.

13. Louis W. Flaccus, "Remarks on the Psychology of Clothes," *Pedagogical Seminary* 13, no. 1 (March 1906): 76, 77. Flaccus, a "sometime fellow" at Clark University, based his study in part on responses to a questionnaire that G. Stanley Hall had designed and circulated.

14. Ida Tarbell, "A Woman and Her Raiment," *American Magazine*, August 1912, 472, 474.

15. Juliet Virginia Strauss, "When a Man Thinks of a Woman as a Pretty Fool, The Third of the Series: The Woman Who Frets over Things," *Ladies' Home Journal* 29, no. 1 (January 1912): 16.

16. Mrs. James Farley Cox, "The Council Chamber: A Special Talk with Girls," *Ladies' Home Journal* 20, no. 7 (June 1903): 18.

17. Tarbell, "A Woman and Her Raiment," 470–71.

18. Cohn, *The Good Old Days*, 355.

19. "The Ideas of a Plain Country Woman," *Ladies' Home Journal* 29, no. 1 (January 1912): 32.

20. Cohn, *The Good Old Days*, 356.

21. Albert Atwood, "Are We Extravagant?" *Saturday Evening Post*, January 3, 1920, 116.

22. "Lulu Rutenber Bartz," in Anne McCall and Mary Jane Henderson, *Fragments of Yesterday: A Collection of Childhood Memories in Delaware County from 1892–1929* (Deposit, NY, 1994), 60.

23. Helen A. Ballars, "The Country Girl—Your Ally," *Rural Manhood*, November 1915, 382.

24. Margaret Slattery, *The American Girl and Her Community* (Boston, 1918), 27.

25. Atkeson, *The Woman on the Farm*, 134.

26. Philippians 4:11 King James Version.

27. "Be Content," *Christian Advocate*, June 12, 1890, 379.

28. Edward W. Bok, "At Home with the Editor," *Ladies' Home Journal* 8, no. 5 (April 1891): 10; "An Early Lesson," *Saturday Evening Post*, December 11, 1897, 5.

29. Edward Bok, "At Home with the Editor," *Ladies' Home Journal* 8, no. 10 (September 1891): 10.

30. Orison Swett Marden, "Keeping Up Appearances," *Christian Advocate*, November 19, 1904, 181.

31. Ruth Ashmore, "The Country Girl," *Ladies' Home Journal* 10, no. 7 (July 1893): 10; idem, "The Girl in a Small Community," *Ladies' Home Journal* 12, no. 3 (March 1895): 16.

32. Pitirim Sorokin and Carle C. Zimmermann, *Principles of Rural-Urban Sociology* (New York, 1929), 546; J. H. Kolb and E. des Brunner, *A Study of Rural Society* (Boston, 1940), 222.

33. Theodore Roosevelt to Liberty Hyde Bailey, August 10, 1908, Liberty Hyde Bailey Collection, Cornell University Archives, Collection #21/2/400, box 4, folder 2.

34. "The Ideas of a Plain Country Woman," *Ladies' Home Journal* 30, no. 2 (February 1913): 32.

35. Ruth Ashmore, "The Small Faults of Girls," *Ladies' Home Journal* 12, no. 1 (December 1894): 26. It is clear that these fears about women's supposedly frivolous and potentially ruinous spending habits have a long history; Stuart Blumin in *The Emergence of the Middle Class: Social Experience in the American City* (Cambridge, 1989), 185–86, describes similar mid-nineteenth-century concerns about women's spending habits.

36. Amelie E. Barr, "Discontented Women," *North American Review* 162 (February 1896): 203.

37. Laura A. Smith, "The Girl in the Small Town: How She Can Best Succeed in the City," *Ladies' Home Journal* 23, no. 11 (October 1906): 24; Tarbell, "A Woman and Her Raiment," 469; Strauss, "When a Man Thinks of a Woman as a Pretty Fool," 16.

38. Martha Foote Crow, *The Young Woman on the Farm, The Cornell Reading Courses*, vol. 3, no. 63, Rural Life Series, no. 8, May 1, 1914, 211, Cornell University Archives Collection, #23/2/749, box 46.

39. *Cornell Junior Extension Bulletin*, no. 2 (December 1918), "Elementary Garment Making: A Manual for Junior Extension Workers in Clothing," Cornell University Archives, Collection #23/2/749, box 46; Extracts from Annual Report, 1924, Extension Service in Home Economics, New York State College of Agriculture at Cornell University, School of Home Economics, Cornell University Archives, Collection #23/2/749, box 24, folder 1.

40. Woods Hutchinson, "The Sin of Homeliness, the Duty of Every Woman to Be Well Dressed," *Saturday Evening Post*, March 25, 1911, 45.

41. "Extravagance as a Virtue," *Current Opinion* 54, no. 1 (January 1913): 51–52. Patten's speech sparked a heated debate.

42. *Ladies' Home Journal* 40, no. 1 (January 1923): 24.

43. Roland Marchand explores this issue in some depth in his chapter "Advertisements as Social Tableaux" in *Advertising the American Dream*, 194 et seq.

44. *Ladies' Home Journal* 36, no. 6 (June 1919): 153; *Ladies' Home Journal* 45, no. 7 (July 1928): 6.

45. *Saturday Evening Post*, November 19, 1921, 49; *Ladies' Home Journal* 42, no. 11 (November 1925): 132.

46. For evidence of both the prevalence of this myth and its essentially fictional nature, see, for instance, Richard Hofstadter, *The Age of Reform: From Bryan to F.D.R.* (New York, 1955), 37–40; Joyce Appleby, "Commercial Farming and the 'Agrarian Myth' in the Early Republic," *Journal of American History* 68, no. 4 (March 1982): 833–49.

Chapter Twenty

Consumerism and Childhood
New Targets for American Emotions

Peter N. Stearns

Individual emotional repertoires often include intense attachments to material objects or, more generally, to a process of acquisition. Children cherish a doll or blanket from babyhood and suffer genuine grief if the object is lost. Adults "must have" this or that item, sought with an emotional fervor that may rival love. They distract themselves from emotional stress in other facets of life by indulging themselves in a spree at the local mall. While certain emotional uses of consumerism are associated particularly with women, intense attachment to specific objects can be male as well, like the genuine grief or anger experienced when a cherished new car gets its first scratch or dent. Children and adults alike, of both genders, may develop vivid envy over a possession flaunted by an acquaintance and feel emotionally deprived as a result of their lack. Charles Foster Kane's attachment to his sled "Rosebud" in the classic movie *Citizen Kane* graphically illustrated the emotions associated with things. Advertisers, of course, play on and surely enhance the emotional life devoted to things by building up the need for certain items as a means of avoiding undesirable emotions (preventing disgust, fear, or of course envy) or assuring pleasurable ones (enhancing love or joy, provoking envy in others). Yet the emotions-consumerism link has not been systematically explored, particularly from the emotions side. One crucial aspect of this topic is changes in the emotional socialization of children.

To be sure, the direction of emotions toward material objects is not an invention of modern history. Men and women alike in preindustrial times could develop emotional attachment to cherished tools or weapons, and in more affluent classes emotions might connect to household items or fashions as well. But it is highly likely that the emotional importance of things has increased in modern times; more emotional energy is expended on wanting and at least initially enjoying things, and the process of acquisition is more likely to distract from emotional or other setbacks. Through these changes, in turn, envy of other people's material items—rather than their power—has become an increasing issue for social and emotional management. In fact, a definition of modern consumerism—along with the sheer increase in the availability and display of objects and the use of consumption to establish personal and social status—might be, very simply, a stage in the history of emotions in which the feelings devoted to consumer items and acquisition play a significant role in overall emotional life.

Consumerism is only now developing an extensive historical literature, however, and the history of emotions is even newer as a field.[1] So an understanding of the evolution of emotions into consumerist expressions has not received a great deal of attention. Nevertheless, it is possible to trace the emergence of growing connections by the early twentieth century in the United States; this is one of the really significant changes in more general emotional life.

Several interrelated symptoms suggest how the acquisition of things was developing new emotional salience. Boredom, an emotionally related state, became an active concept only in the eighteenth century, in association with consumerism's first phase. Increasingly abundant home furnishings—the form of consumerism most acceptable to the Victorian middle class—surely helped link emotions of home with specific objects, though not necessarily with the process of acquisition itself. More elaborate emotional associations began to emerge by the late nineteenth century. The emergence of kleptomania from the 1870s onward in the United States and Western Europe was, of course, a deviant development, but a case in which deviance simply extended normal passions.[2] The surge of kleptomania reflected a number of broader changes: the confinement of middle-class housewives, for some of whom kleptomania could be a rebellion against powerlessness; the growth of department stores where goods were lavishly arrayed and could be directly handled; and the increasing leisure interest in strolling past enticing display windows and through the aisles of the munificent urban emporiums. Here were both new motives and new means for the development of a compulsive theft of goods not needed for survival. Kleptomania also denoted, however, the growth of passionate longing for things.

At the same time, and of more general import, advertisements began to take on a more explicitly emotional quality. While the idea of appealing to the senses through signs and store arrangements was not new—studies of eighteenth-century consumerism, particularly in England, have shown how alert shopkeepers innovated in these areas—most media advertisements had remained fairly dry stuff before 1900. They might at most be spiced by status appeals or humor; sex and overt emotion were noticeably absent. The general format was a closely written newspaper paragraph, made to look as much like a standard news item as possible, and stressing the availability and utilitarian qualities of the objects advertised. Silks goods, for example, were still being described in terms of value and utility in newspaper product lists in the 1890s. But then the tone changed. Daily papers by 1900 were touting silk items as "alluring," "bewitching"; "to feel young and carefree, buy our silk." The association of material goods and acquisition with emotions obviously continued to escalate from this point onward. Soaps, given huge advertising boosts in the 1920s, appealed to "rational" hygiene concerns but also an emotional desire for beauty and avoidance of disgust. The association of soap commercials with highly emotional radio dramas in the 1920s also signaled the deliberate linkage of goods with affective release.[3]

Another revealing link between emotion and consumerism occurred with the transformation of Christmas giving, beginning in the 1890s. Previous gift exchanges had featured simple homemade items, designed to express friendship or familial ties without, however, drawing great emotional attention to the goods themselves. Now, Americans bought most of the items they gave, and the process of associating new emotional expectations with holiday commercialism began its steady ascent.[4]

Changes in children's emotional relationships to material objects were particularly significant in these crucial turn-of-the-century decades in American consumerist and emotional history. The implications were twofold. First, adults were now sufficiently comfortable with the emotional salience of consumer items to introduce children to the same connections, using goods to help shape emotional life. Second, early exposure to consumer items used as emotional targets helped socialize individuals to the ongoing emotional validity of consumerism, not only in childhood but in adult life.

Adult use of goods to guide children emotionally won explicit attention in the 1920s, as a new generation of popularized child-rearing expertise gained ground. Formal psychological discussions in the behaviorist school of John Watson; a new spate of scientifically inspired middle-class manuals, whose number and sales suggested a growing parental audience for novel kinds of advice; and the emergence of the first widely popular child-rearing periodical, *Parents' Magazine,* all embodied the consumerist approach, even though no one explicitly noted the change in direction that was occurring.

Parental manuals in the nineteenth century (a new series of guidance efforts had taken shape from the 1820s onward) paid little attention to things. The emphasis was on internal character development and relations with others, beginning with appropriate behavior toward parents and siblings. Children's stories, similarly, focused primarily on moral uplift and relations with other people, urging emotions such as love and affection (particularly for girls, but also for boys in relation to their mothers), bravery (for boys), and righteous, appropriately targeted anger (for boys again). There was no consumerist intermediary. Indeed, there were abundant warnings against investing emotions in things. Lydia Child explicitly told mothers to teach children to share their toys. Louisa May Alcott made a similar point in *Little Women,* by having the girls give away some of their possessions or accept the destruction of cherished toys. The message was clear: one should not become too attached to things, on pain of vanity. And while stories were designed to entertain, their moral purposes robbed them of explicit escapist content; children's stories themselves were not mere consumerist items for their young readers.[5] None of this is to argue that consumer goods for middle-class children did not exist (in fact, there was a growing, highly criticized escapist literature for boys by the last third of the nineteenth century), but consumerism was not part of adult discussion of how children should be treated.

Not so in the generation of popularized expertise emerging in the 1920s. Acquisition was now designed to ease emotional relationships with people, or possibly in some instances to substitute for these relationships, in a number of specific contexts.

Fear, for example, came in for new comment in the 1920s and 1930s. New psychological research demonstrated that young children developed a variety of fears for no particular reason. Behaviorist psychologists, a bit more systematic, argued that generalized fears developed from unwise treatment of two basic anxieties, but they too agreed that fear was a frequent problem. Children now needed to be shielded from fear-provoking situations (Victorian invocations of stiff-upper-lip courage were too risky in this new climate) and at the same time manipulated around fears that did develop. This is where a new emotional consumerism came in.[6]

Beyond avoidance of fights and affectionate reassurance, the most widely recommended strategy involved the use of material objects to persuade children to overcome their fears in return for a tangible reward. One popular manual after another repeated the behaviorist advice. Take a child afraid of the dark. Every evening, place a bit of candy or a sought-after toy in a darkened room. Start with the object right at the door, and each night move it a bit farther in. Each night, the toddler would presumably weigh fear against proto-consumerist appetite and find the latter triumphant. At the end of the process, the fear would be gone, banished by the lure of acquisition. Similar strategies could be used to overcome fear of a strange adult or of animals. None of the literature presented these exercises as part of a larger consumerism. Indeed, the very matter-of-factness in the assumption that children wanted new things and would go to some lengths to gain them suggested a solid commitment to consumer values.[7]

Certainly parents were open to the strategy. They were increasingly concerned about children's fears, as they dealt more directly with infants during the night without the help of live- in maids. They were receptive to expert persuasion that fear could easily get out of hand and that careful material strategies made sense to compensate. By the 1930s parents were proudly writing to journals like *Parents' Magazine* about how they used material inducements to deal with fears of darkness, strangers, and other targets.[8]

An even more interesting use of things arose in conjunction with a second new category of adult anxiety, sibling jealousy. Beginning at least by the 1920s, middle-class parents began to worry, or were told to worry, about a problem that had barely warranted mention during the nineteenth century: the intense resentment of a new baby by a toddler, on grounds of rivalry for parental affection.[9] A series of psychological studies in the 1920s and 1930s purported to demonstrate that the vast majority of toddlers displayed signs of jealousy. The classic jealousy scenario involved reactions to a new baby: the sibling would worry that he or she was losing love and would vent this worry on the new arrival. The jealousy of young children, in turn, was a twofold problem. First, it jeopardized family harmony, even the safety of a new baby, in the short term. Jealous children were potential murderers. Second, if left untended or badly handled it could fester, creating a jealous personality in later life who would be incapable of mature relationships in family or in business. Adult jealousy in turn was attributed to "emotional immaturity," an acute emotional issue that had been improperly treated in early life.[10]

Sibling rivalry commanded extended treatment in virtually all manuals on child rearing, from the 1920s through the 1950s. The problem's advent resulted from new expert findings conjoined with an equally acute expert desire to gain new attention from parents. Jealousy received particular notice in a context in which demands for group harmony were increasing and in which adult men and women were socializing more extensively and openly; intense jealousy would have been a glaring hazard amid youth dating and new kinds of adult parties. The attack on sibling jealousy reflected, finally, the daily concerns of parents dealing more directly than before with young children, who themselves may have become more rivalrous for parental attention as the size of the sibling cohort diminished thanks to more rigorous birth control. Hence the abrupt, if novel, conclusion: sibling rivalry "indelibly stamps personality and distorts character."[11]

Fortunately there were strategies at hand to cope with the problem, including the provision of clearly marked things for the young child. If a new baby is on the way, give the existing child his or her own room if at all possible—and it would repay the extra expense on this, given the dire alternative of jealousy. (Dr. Spock, who became the Thomas Aquinas of twentieth-century American child-rearing advice givers, specifically noted in 1945 that it would be worth "a lot of effort" to distract from sibling rivalry.)[12] Make sure to mark all toys, to minimize disputes over ownership. Give the existing child some new toys when the baby arrives, to distract him from the potential threat. If the baby is to receive some hand-me-downs, such as outgrown clothing, dye the clothing (or repaint the baby furniture). Finally, explain to visitors, especially grandparents, the need to bring presents to the young child when they made their offerings to the new baby. And this practice, so the experts urged, should continue. At a birthday, provide presents for the other child as well as the celebrant—a practice that did indeed become increasingly widespread in American middle-class homes—when dealing with children younger than six or eight.[13]

Material distractions did not exhaust the anti-jealousy tactics; compensatory attention and affection were also urged. But the implications of the procedures concerning toys and other items were fascinating, particularly as they coincided with the new approach to fear and other disturbing emotions. Teach children, so the implicit message read, that when they are upset they should expect to find solace in things, including newly acquired items. Associate their individual identity with things, which can be carefully marked and protected as one's own (though of course the consumerist assumption was that this association was natural; parental tactics only acknowledged it). Distract children from siblings, in essence by urging them to invest in things. Love and consumer objects, in turn, should be directly linked.

Parents seem to have eagerly picked up these messages. Parental concern about jealousy ranked high in polls concerning problems with children. More to the point, in letters to *Parents' Magazine* and other outlets, mothers proudly cited their ability to distract children with presents, avoiding the emotional problems that could spoil childhood. By the 1940s, testimonies to the power of material diversions, in creating a viable context for the celebration of a birthday, for example, became almost routine.[14]

The lure of consumer items was applied to other emotional categories as well. Children might harmlessly take out their anger on objects, like punching bags. Children might also be distracted from potentially damaging grief by devoting attention to a new doll, pet, or similar item. The general points were clear: purchased objects should be provided to children in some abundance not simply because they were educational (though that rationale persisted), but because they would provide explicit emotional focus. They would help defuse young children's potentially dangerous emotional relationships with other members of the family, or with friends, through compensatory attachments to the consumer objects. This strategy developed at a time when popularized advice was impressing on parents not only the potential seriousness of emotional issues among young children, but also the need to damp down their own emotional displays. Mothers, especially, were advised to cool the kind of maternal ardor that had become popular in the nineteenth century. "Mother love is a dangerous instrument," argued the most extreme, behaviorist camp, while even more balanced advice literature argued that "parents have to guard against smothering the child's developing tendencies in a too vehement love, and thus preventing his ever attaining independence."[15] No one, to be sure, advocated directly substituting things for maternal love. It was revealing, nevertheless, that the attack on potential emotional excess extended to one of the central emotional bastions of nineteenth-century family life at the same time that casual assumptions about the validity and importance of young children's attachments to consumer items were gaining ground. Priorities were shifting; acquisition played a growing emotional role.

Obviously, this argument invites further study of actual acquisition patterns in the crucial transition decades of the 1920s and even the 1930s. While evidence for parental acceptance of emotional warnings and consumerist stratagems is solid, and specific behaviors (like compensatory birthday gifts) did become increasingly common, the overall implementation of consumer surrogates for emotional intensity warrants additional investigation. So of course does the explicit impact on children, for there is danger in extrapolating from adult evidence despite the plausibility of a new level of childhood investment in consumerism. At the same time, it requires no sophisticated psychological model to suggest that young children encouraged to depend on acquisition might cling to that source of meaning later in life.

Another key change that complemented the consumerist child-rearing advice was the association of early childhood with attachments to material objects. This shift, too, depended on adult revisions, but could have major impact not only on children but also on the goals they would retain in their own adulthood. The idea of introducing an array of material objects to the cribs and playpens of infants took hold even a bit before the alteration of child-rearing advice, and may in some senses have prepared this wider redefinition of the uses of purchases for children. Linking babies and consumerism was related to other new parental approaches. Experts were urging that all the early stages of childhood were more difficult and emotionally risky than nineteenth-century parents had been led to believe. Faith in childish innocence declined, bringing the need for new kinds of distractions and safeguards. More prosaic changes in parent-child relations also entered in. Bribing toddlers with goods had something to do with the decline of assistance in the care of children, as parents (particularly mothers) increasingly lacked hired help, and as older siblings and resident grandparents also became less available thanks to changes in birth rates and in geriatric residence patterns. Putting an abundance of objects around babies, before they could in any conscious sense want them, was also designed to aid parents by distracting offspring, hopefully reducing their resort to crying and other attention-getting ploys; it also accompanied a dramatic shift in sleeping arrangements. But the consumerist construction of infancy, coming relatively early in the emotional retooling of consumerism, occasioned a certain amount of debate, ultimately resolved in favor of the benign properties of store-bought objects.

Around 1900, middle-class parents began to develop a taste for a new kind of manufactured doll, different from both the homemade items previously emphasized and the main type of crafted (often fairly expensive) dolls marketed for older girls in the later nineteenth century. The new item, cuddly, factory-made dolls designed for babies rather than older children, clearly expressed the interest of manufacturers in expanding potential sales and the new technologies and marketing techniques available for such consumer products. The result, however, was not simply a new set of items, but a line of products directly designed to receive the love and affection of the very young—to receive, in other words, an emotional commodity that had been highly touted in the Victorian family when directed toward parents and siblings. It was small wonder that the creation of lovable objects set off some anguished soul-searching among middle-class family experts. The result of the discussion, however, clearly pointed toward a new kind of emotional commodification, and with this a new step in forming consumerist personalities in the American middle class.

Dolls, again, were no innovation of the turn-of-the-century decades. During most of the nineteenth century, however, dolls had been designed primarily for older children. Their functions, while not divorced from emotion, were defined primarily in terms of utility and aesthetics.[16] Dolls were intended to teach various kinds of learning and developmental skills and (particularly after the Civil War) an appreciation for fashion, the latter especially for the younger girls. By the 1890s an emotional role for dolls began to be suggested; comments were made to the effect that dolls might serve as objects of attachment to replace fathers absent at work. It was at this point also that girls were urged to use dolls for training in grief; doll funerals and other rituals were encouraged, as were such objects as doll coffins. Still, however, most purchased dolls remained stiff, fragile creatures destined more for admiration and role playing than for deep affection, and the fascinating effort at grief involvement was designed for middle childhood, not the impressionable early years.

This situation changed in part because of new technology that allowed American manufacturers to displace European importers and to provide a succession of soft, cuddly creatures, including the famous American teddy bear, that were directed at infants of both sexes. By preventing German exports, World War I furthered the process of converting doll production to domestic centers and to products designed for physical contact rather than fragile items designed for aesthetic admiration. Rag dolls of all sorts proliferated, and the conversion to dolls that looked like children (or young animals) rather than adults was completed.[17]

At the same time dolls for older children, increasingly varied and numerous, became enmeshed in a variety of fantasy productions. Children's stories supplemented the use of dolls by providing settings in which dolls expressed and received a variety of emotions. Children were encouraged to display attachment to dolls, and on their own they might also turn dolls into objects of rage or jealousy. Above all, dolls were increasingly designed to act as surrogate children or siblings amid the declining real birth rate, with their child owners being encouraged to feel parental or sisterly emotion toward them.

Not surprisingly, in this new climate dolls began for the first time to receive comment from child-rearing authorities and popularizers. Some objected to the kinds of fantasies that dolls stimulated: "Why foster a craving for novelty and variety that life cannot satisfy?" A minister blasted teddy bears as substitute objects of affection that corrupted the maternal instinct. More observers, however, commented on the positive roles dolls could play in emotional life. Thus teddy bears "may have robbed childhood of one of its terrors"—the fear of animals.[18] The importance of the new dolls' cuddly qualities was emphasized, both because they facilitated girls' acquisition of maternal instincts and, more generally, because they provided infants of both sexes with a concrete, reliable focus for attachments. A 1931 observer in *Hygeia* put the point directly, though stiffly: "With the realization of the psychologic importance of the child's early years, there has arisen a new need, that of definite toys of peace and a technic of presenting play material that will furnish the right background and associations for feelings."[19] Or, in an article of 1914: "Children's affections [have] come to center around the toys with which they have lived and played." For infants, parents were advised to "choose a soft animal; the affections as yet are very physical, and this is known as the 'cuddling' age."[20] The link between dolls and other toys and children's emotions, though not an invention of the twentieth century, was almost certainly expanding.

One of the key reasons for the new interest in dolls and other objects for babies, in addition to general expert advice about the importance and emotional difficulty of early childhood and the desire for parent-saving distractions, involved the change in sleeping arrangements that also took shape in the decades around 1900. Until the 1890s, infants were characteristically lodged in cradles for sleep, near an adult, whether parent or nursemaid, who could rock the infant easily if it stirred. Adult activities in evenings, focused on family and on tasks like darning or knitting that could be accomplished near an infant, were compatible with this kind of attention. But in the 1890s the practice began to shift; infants were placed in separate bedrooms, and in cribs rather than the less structured cradles, early on. Cribs, with their elaborate fencing, began to proliferate shortly before 1900; many designs were patented. By 1915 cradles were being advertised as nostalgia items—"the very plainest cradle possesses a subtle sense of soul"—and soon as outright antiques. Cribs, in contrast, were widely and approvingly discussed in the family magazines, touted for their safety, their contributions to good posture, their conduciveness to sleep. And after infancy, when nineteenth-century parents had placed children together, often in the same beds (if the children were of the same sex), children now graduated to a regular bed, but they still slept alone. All the experts agreed that, wherever possible, children should have their own rooms (and with this, of course, their own proliferating possessions).[21]

These changes in sleep habits reflected new concerns about childhood sexuality, particularly homosexuality. They expressed a new interest in making children robust individuals. And they also followed from changes in parental habits, including more spousal socializing and a new desire to see the evenings devoted to adult entertainments, such as radio programs or card parties, in which the presence of a cradled infant would be an encumbrance. But for all the admitted and unacknowledged reasons for change, the fact was that children were now put to sleep with far less human companionship than before. They lacked the assurance of a loving adult presence to rock the cradle, and then they slept independent of the raucous but often affectionate contact with siblings. This was the context in which a new array of sleep toys, beginning with cuddly dolls, made particularly good sense in providing surrogate, intensely emotional contact with things.

By the 1920s, then, middle-class children began encountering implicit consumerism almost literally from birth. Parents expected things to do a good bit of emotional work, an expectation extended by the child-rearing advice on dealing with fear, jealousy, or grief during the interwar decades and beyond. Along with new adult behaviors and new advertising pitches, providing greater emotional rewards for acquisition, this redefinition of childish emotions toward greater dependence on the contiguity and profusion of material objects set a major new stage in consumerism's affective basis and its affective role.

For children, of course, this dramatic shift was confirmed and maintained by ongoing opportunities for contacts with the emotional lures of consumption. Children could be appealed to, by the decades around 1900, as a market of their own, thanks to novel media and a new if modest purchasing power obtained by the innovation of the allowance. During the earlier stages of modern consumerism, most purchases for children were clearly mediated through adults, who had to do the buying; and of course this remained true for the very young. Adults, in turn, were wooed primarily by arguments of utility: items would benefit children's health and education. Now, however, with children newly won to the charms of consumerism by their own experience as infants and toddlers, and possessed of some spending money of their own, appeals could shift to the same enhanced emotionality that defined adult advertisements. And, thanks to reading matter purchased directly by children (such as staple comic books, many of which carried advertisements by the 1930s) and due even more to the rise of radio programming targeted at children, pitchmen could now reach a child audience without parental mediation. Thus comics played up special offers for cheap items like magical rings that would give children particular powers; ads often stressed the importance of being the first kid on the block to have one—that is, being the target of desirable childish envy. Radio shows, available even to the preliterate, directly urged emotional pressure on parents to buy the latest cereal or toy. The assumption here was that parents would recognize the validity of a child's passionate yearning for some item—having helped to create the yearning in the first place. The theme of emotionally meaningful consumerism, in other words, spread to children as to adults through advertising, all the more readily in that the affective basis had already been set.

New emotional attachments to things, finally, created a fascinating chapter in adult-child consumer interaction that also opened up during the 1920s and 1930s. Concerned about children's growing interests in commercial amusements outside the home, a variety of experts, in *Parents' Magazine* and elsewhere, began urging parents to establish playrooms and backyard playgrounds at home. The effort was reminiscent of earlier consumer interests, in that the settings were presumed to be more educational than outside venues. But the spaces were to be crammed with things, places where parents and children could agree on the new importance of material objects in children's lives. As playrooms or recreation rooms began to be built into new middle-class housing, particularly after World War II, children could literally graduate from crib to entire room with emotional orientations toward consumer goods. [22]

The intensification of emotions associated with consumer activity, visible in adult behavior and solicitation and in child-rearing and childhood experience, raises two further questions. The first involves causation: why did this change in emotional and consumer history occur at this time? The second, applicable particularly in the context of further explorations in the history of emotion, involves impact: how did the shift alter the larger contours of emotional life?

The most obvious cause of the new emotional uses of acquisition and material items was the previous buildup of consumerism itself, which made investments in the process seem increasingly normal and morally valid. One of the great gains in recent historical research is the discovery of the origins of modern consumerism in the late seventeenth and eighteenth centuries. New shops, new interests in goods, new ploys to attract buyers all denoted a heightened valuation of things well before industrialization. This means that by the late nineteenth century, several generations of Americans had been schooled in substantial consumerist behavior. This background does not distract from the important changes in the phenomenon during the turn-of-the-century decades, when intensification and emotional signification went hand in hand, but it helps explain the changes themselves.[23] Furthermore, again with time, some earlier scruples about consumerism declined. Mainstream American Protestants, for example, who could still fulminate against material lures into the 1840s, by the 1870s were beginning to accept fashion and material acquisition as part of the good life acceptable to the Christian. Now the message was "enjoy the present . . . the blessings of this day if God sends them." While it was true that the new stage of consumerism around 1900 generated fervent protests, both in the United States and Europe—protests that denoted indeed the importance of the change that was occurring even in an established behavior pattern—they were less grounded in traditional religion, and on the whole easier to shrug off or accommodate to, than previous moralism had been.[24]

Earlier consumerism itself had emotional overtones, again helping to prepare the fuller unions of the early twentieth century, including the greater incorporation into child rearing. Consumer interests in the eighteenth century had focused on items for the family—better furnishings, table settings more conducive to family meals—and on personal apparel. Family items obviously had emotional connotations, helping indeed to prepare the belief in the family as a sanctified refuge from the world while reflecting the early stages of this belief. Purchase of tableware that would be part of family rituals, or the nineteenth-century middle-class fascination with pianos as centers of family solidarity, obviously had emotional meaning. The family context also encouraged the first generation of new consumer purchases for children, including the production of explicitly (and suitably uplifting) children's books. Clothing, an expression of personal identity, clearly began to focus intense emotional strivings.

Thus clothing purchases increased, but so did thefts of items not necessary to subsistence—an eighteenth-century indication of emotional need. New precision about consumer items in wills, particularly those left by women, suggests emotional investment in both clothing and family items on another front. Women, particularly, were increasingly careful to mark a particular dress or piece of furniture for a friend or child as a special sign of affection. While the picture of the first 150 years of modern consumerism is still not fully drawn, it is clear that the emotional shifts in consumerism after 1870 occurred in part because they had been well prepared by previous middle-class experience.[25]

By the late nineteenth century, alterations in the consumer apparatus helped build on previous attachments to acquisition. Advancing industrialization generated this framework. New printing and illustrative technology facilitated new kinds of advertisements. The department stores consolidated merchants' appeals. Increased purchasing power and growing leisure time contributed. Novel, more emotional consumerism was not solely a response to capitalist lures, but it was that in part, particularly for middle-class Americans schooled by several prior generations of eager if selective consumerists.[26]

Changes on the emotional front, however, also contributed to the new marriage between passion and acquisition. Prior consumerist history remains the most important factor, but by itself it did not assure the turn toward greater emotional signification. Three related emotional shifts helped set the stage. First, work was becoming less satisfying emotionally. What had long been true for the working class began to apply to the middle groups. Opportunities for independent entrepreneurship or professional life were increasingly turning into the thralldoms of middle management or corporate offices. Lower-middle-class people faced increasingly routine jobs amid typewriters and regimentation, and it was no wonder that they showed some of the leading consumerist interest in faddish items such as cigarettes and radios. Women's work may not have become less rewarding, but it was certainly becoming clearer to women, better educated than their mothers, that housework had its drawbacks as personal expression. Though obviously impossible to chart precisely, emotional investments that had once focused on work were available for other interests and a need for new meanings.[27]

Second, emotional culture itself began to change, away from Victorian emphases on carefully defined but intense contacts with friends and family, toward a more measured emotional approach across the board. Vivid grief, recommended as part of a loving family life in the 1880s, was attacked by the 1920s as antiquated and dangerous; people should be able to bounce back from loss without major emotional detours. Jealousy, as we have seen, was now derided as childish and intrusive. Guilt, an acknowledged staple of nineteenth-century emotional enforcement, was now criticized as dangerous to fragile psyches—not surprisingly, for in a heightened consumerist atmosphere too much guilt would be risky. Motherlove, as we have seen, came in for resounding attack, and while this moderated by the 1940s, maternal emotion never recovered the sanctification granted in Victorian emotional culture. Smooth, controlled emotional contacts—as one employment manual urged, "impersonal, but friendly"—now set the tone, appropriate for ordered interactions in an economy dominated by service work and management hierarchies. Personal emotions management became in some respects more demanding. In this context, diversions of some emotional energy toward acquisition became positively useful in helping avoid embarrassing interpersonal outbursts; this was one reason for the use of consumerist strategies in the emotional socialization of children. At the same time, new constraints over Victorian intensities may have created greater needs for material surrogates. At the risk of projecting greater precision than can be proved: when mothering became more problematic, more mothers went shopping. Or, because the change was gendered only to a degree: when legitimate outbursts of male anger at work became taboo, more men turned to symbolic displays in the professional sports that became a growing part of American consumer life.[28]

One explicit sign of the emotional replacement process involved changes in the culture of love, at least from the masculine side. Victorian conventions, urged on men and women alike in nineteenth-century prescriptive literature and mirrored in many men's letters about their love, had emphasized a soaring, transcendent passion, religious-like in its intensity. New outlets such as *Esquire*, founded in 1933 and aimed at middle-class men, explicitly attacked this conception. As a 1934 article put it, the older ideal of "a pair of passion-oozing souls merg[ing] into a mystical unity" was "a dream conceived in fallacy and proposed by childish desires." Intense love, in other words, needed the same kind of reconsideration that prescriptive authors were giving to fear, grief, maternal affection, and jealousy in the child-rearing literature. For several years, virtually every issue of the widely selling periodical contained blasts against the Victorian love ideal as outdated, sickly, a potential trap for the independent modern man. The attack raised the question, of course, of what standards should replace the older conventions. *Esquire* defined a new kind of relationship that would emphasize shared leisure, companionship, and sexuality—a definition of heterosexual love the marriage counseling experts were also urging on the middle-class public during the same decades. Shared leisure included, of course, mutual interests as consumers. A couple, no longer entwined by ethereal passion, would build on the pleasure of joint acquisitions. But *Esquire* pushed further still. After several years of exploration of what modern love should be about, *Esquire* underwent a metamorphosis after the mid-1930s. Material on love began to dwindle, then disappear, initially in the heat of coverage of World War II. Travel and leisure interests began to predominate, in addition to war reporting, along with pictorials on Hollywood starlets and "Varga" girls. In 1950 the magazine announced a new philosophy, promising to be "dedicated more than ever to what men are interested in." And this meant that, replaced by pictures of women, travel, automobiles, and fashion, discussion of love or other explicit emotional issues virtually vanished. Implicitly, then, *Esquire*, a bellwether magazine for up-to-date middle-class men until the advent of *Playboy*, did to love what parenting manuals urged with regard to other emotions: it surrounded it with new caution and then provided consumerist alternatives.[29]

This was, of course, a shift in one cultural outlet, and its ramifications should not be exaggerated. Love did not die, and the emotional lives of actual men, varied as they surely were, were not confined to consumerism alone. But the shift in guidelines, in a magazine that tried to be extremely attentive to audience interests, was revealing, suggesting a new set of priorities at the cognitive-emotional level, with acquisition providing increasing competition to Victorian emotional interests. The man who seemed to love his car more than his wife, a recurrent lament of advice to the lovelorn after World War II, was foreshadowed by the 1930s–40s transition in representations, a major outgrowth in turn of the larger transition in emotional culture in which consumerism met new needs.

Finally, key features of the novel emotional uses of consumerism responded to yet another set of emotional changes, a new level of parental self-doubts and unacknowledged guilts. The late nineteenth century seemed to see an apotheosis of Victorian images of the child: innocent, worthy, and as one author has put it, truly "priceless."[30] Yet growing valuation created adult vulnerabilities: how could such esteemed objects ever be treated as they deserved? Further, actual adult recreational interests were, as we have seen, turning somewhat away from time spent with children, as separate entertainments in the home or opportunities for recreation outside the home—the movies, for example—became more popular. Above all, the birth rate was falling precipitously, and while this facilitated greater attention to individual children and made all sorts of economic sense, it created guilts as well.[31] A number of changes thus made it increasingly possible for parents to worry that they were not doing right by their children—not having enough of them, not paying enough attention, not responding adequately to a public culture that continued to emphasize child-centeredness in what had been billed, revealingly but inaccurately, as "the century of the child." This context, in turn, combined with some of the prosaic alterations of family life: the reduction of maid service, the lesser availability of older siblings to help with care, the withdrawal of live-in grandparents, and the new recommendations about sleep. The result was a setting in which new needs for inducing children to place more emotional reliance on dolls and toys were supplemented by a new desire to try to demonstrate parental worthiness by showering presents. These connections, of course, would intensify further as the twentieth century wore on, as the increasingly frantic gift-getting at Christmas annually demonstrated. Parental guilts themselves would escalate further, thanks, for example, to new work patterns for mothers. But the base emerged early, and provided the final ingredient for the marriage of consumerism and emotional support.

How far did this marriage go, in actual emotional life? Here, surely, questions exceed the answers yet available, as we begin the exploration of the new roles of consumer behavior in the twentieth century. Did the new devotion to things reduce the emotional reservoirs available in personal relationships? Granting individual variations, a number of observers have claimed to note a diminution in the emotional intensity of friendship in the twentieth century. A nineteenth-century pattern of vibrant, expressive intimacies among young adult men, for example, seems to have disappeared as a norm by the 1920s, just as male conversational staples turned increasingly to cars and spectator sports. Even women, though claiming greater expressiveness, shifted the language used with friends toward a cooler vocabulary. These changes remain to be fully plumbed, and of course if valid they have several causes, including the growing twentieth-century concern about homosexuality. But a new emotional equation between people and things might play a role. The same could hold for marital emotions, as successful middle- class marriages increasingly focused on shared consumer interests and activities, along with sexuality, in contrast to the more directly emotional norms of Victorian culture.[32]

Emotionally invested consumerism surely affected the role of envy in American life, though here again a key passion is just beginning to receive the kind of attention it deserves. Envy was not explicitly countenanced in American middle-class emotional culture in the twentieth century. It could be reproved as a sign of the same insecurity that was held to cause jealousy and other dysfunctional emotions. Historians of American advertising have noted that (in partial contrast to Europe) direct appeals to envy were downplayed in favor of a more democratic approach that urged the availability of consumer rewards to anyone who worked hard. Nevertheless, envy had two obvious new appeals as a result of the equation of consumerism and emotion that developed during the early twentieth century. First, it expressed the strength of the identification with things as a means of avoiding jealousy or anger or excessive maternal affection; some of the power of these emotions could now feed a desire to acquire what others already had. Studies of the professed values of older American children and adolescents in the 1930s demonstrated a pronounced desire to avoid any taint of jealousy of other people, whether siblings or friends, but a concomitant tendency to envy possessions or qualities (nice hair or a new bicycle, for example) of classmates.[33] Envy was thus not approved, but seemed safer and more relevant than some of the emotions more clearly designated as inappropriate. The same heightened investment in envy fed other familiar staples of American middle-class culture, such as the attention to "keeping up with the Joneses," which surfaced amid the suburban surge of the late 1940s and 1950s. Interestingly, marketing directed toward children appealed more openly to envy than adult advertisements did, with the suggestions of being the "first kid on the block" to have this or that. The very strategies designed to use things to distract children from fear or jealousy assumed that some envy was normal, if not desirable; hence the stratagems to give distracting presents on the occasion of another sibling's birthday and the careful arrangements urged to designate a child's inviolable private consumer property. Revealingly, at all ages, Americans began to call envy jealousy from the 1930s onward, suggesting how attachments to things began to evoke new intensity. If another individual has things that I envy, I am thereby somehow diminished, which means in turn that jealousy more properly conveys my sense of loss and the vigor of my reactions. Envy became more complex and almost surely more ascendant—exactly what one would expect in a new stage of emotional consumerism.[34]

The attachment of greater emotional stakes to consumerism continued to feed both facets of personal experience. American emotional patterns began to be distinguished by an unusually clear ability to distinguish between good and bad emotions on the basis of their pleasurability, and a reluctance to believe that any utility could be constructed from the bad (in contrast, for example, to Chinese cultural interest in using difficult emotions to improve character). This was not a Victorian distinction, for in the nineteenth century good and bad had been defined differently and both assessed in terms of their contribution to personal development. Consumer attachments, however, made it more sensible to designate an unquestionably unpleasant emotion like guilt "bad" and try to avoid it.[35]

Emotional dependence on consumerism surely encouraged a growing interest in being able to buy appropriate emotional surrogates, particularly through the means of commercial entertainments. Though permitted by new technologies such as television and videos, the desire to have purchasable choices that could make one vicariously feel happy, sad, nostalgic, or loving—depending on a particular mood or whim at the time—followed from the logic of the consumerist emotions that had developed earlier in the twentieth century. One should be able to purchase responses to emotional needs. In his provocative study of the changes in American character, David Riesman argued that consumerism replaced manners as a means of interpersonal relationships, with intricate, emotionally invested discussions of acquisitions becoming a conversational staple in ways unimaginable in the nineteenth century. Again, new childhood introductions both reflected and prepared this kind of change in life's currency.[36] Did this shift, in the process, worsen the actual quality of emotional life, making it more dependent on the representations of others, more superficial and bland? These judgments go beyond purely historical analysis, but they deserve attention as part of the further exploration of this aspect of modern emotional change.

And there is a transnational angle to explore as well. Other societies entered what might be termed, analogously with industrialization, a mature consumerist phase in the twentieth century, though a bit later than the United States. Western Europe showed all the signs by the 1950s and 1960s, Japan about a decade later, complete with massive department stores that served as leisure centers. Did the consumerist evolution have emotional implications similar to those in the United States, or did different emotional traditions, including different attitudes toward children, lead to a distinctive configuration? Consumerism and emotion always relate in some fashion, and consumerist escalations surely have emotional implications, if not necessarily emotional causes of the sort that prodded the American equation. Love of things, with its attendant vulnerability to envy and distractions from other emotional targets, is an important topic in the evaluation of a host of contemporary cultures.

Certainly, the ever intensifying association of American childhood with emotion-laden processes of acquisition has constituted a distinguishing feature of twentieth-century life. Consumerism has come to serve a very real role in emotional experience. Emotional spurs help explain behaviors such as high levels of installment buying, where impulse satisfaction takes precedence over personal financial stability. They even contribute to political tendencies to judge candidates increasingly in terms of the ups and downs of acquisitive opportunities. In acquiring, many Americans directly recall emotional strategies they learned when young. The lessons have become powerful.

NOTES

1. Colin Campbell, *The Romantic Ethic and the Spirit of Modern Consumerism* (London, 1989); Neil McKendrick, Colin Brewer, and J. H. Plumb, *The Birth of a Consumer Society: The Commercialization of Eighteenth-Century England* (Bloomington, IN, 1982); John Brewer and Roy Porter, eds., *Consumption and the World of Goods* (London, 1993); Lorna Weatherhill, *Consumer Behavior and Material Culture in England, 1600–1760* (London, 1988); T. H. Breen, " 'Baubles of Britain': The American and Consumer Revolutions of the Eighteenth Century," *Past and Present* 119 (1988).

2. Elaine S. Abelson, *When Ladies Go A-Thieving: Middle-Class Shoppers in the Victorian Department Store* (New York, 1989).

3. Francis G. Couvares, *The Remaking of Pittsburgh: Class and Culture in an Industrializing City, 1877–1919* (Albany, NY, 1984); Roland Marchand, *Advertising the American Dream: Making Way for Modernity, 1920–1940* (Berkeley, 1985); Vincent Vinikas, *Soft Soap, Hard Sell: American Hygiene in an Age of Advertisement* (Ames, IA, 1992); T. J. Jackson Lears, *Fables of Abundance: A Cultural History of Advertising in America* (New York, 1994).

4. William Waits, *The Modern Christmas in America* (New York, 1993).

5. Joseph M. Hawes and N. Ray Hiner, eds., *American Childhood* (Westport, CT, 1985); Anthony Rotundo, *American Manhood: Transformations in Masculinity from the Revolution to the Modern Era* (New York, 1993); J. H. Plumb, "The New World of Children," *Past and Present*, May 1975. Lydia Child, *The Mother's Book* (Boston, 1831), 28–32; Louisa May Alcott, *Little Women* (1868–69) (New York, 1946), 93–98.

6. Peter N. Stearns and Timothy Haggerty, "The Role of Fear: Transitions in American Emotional Standards for Children, 1850–1950," *American Historical Review*, February 1991, 63–94.

7. William Byron Forbush, *The Character Training of Children* (New York, 1919), 2:157–63; John B. Watson, *Psychological Care of Infant and Child* (1928; rpt., New York, 1972), 45–88.

8. "Childhood Problems" section in *Parents' Magazine* 21 (March 1946): 34; 21 (May 1946): 46; 22 (October 1947): 35; 23 (May 1948): 34; 23 (July 1948): 42; "Now This Is What I'd Do," *Parents' Magazine* 4 (January 1929): 24. See also Children's Welfare Federation of New York City, *Child Care Questions and Answers* (New York, 1948), 103–7.

9. Peter N. Stearns, *Jealousy: The Evolution of an Emotion in American History* (New York, 1989); D. A. Thom, *Child Management* (Washington, DC, 1925), 9–12; see also U.S. Department of Labor, Children's Bureau, *Are You Training Your Child to Be Happy?* (Washington, DC, 1930), 31.

10. Allan Fromme, *The Parents Handbook* (New York, 1956), 93; Sidonie Gruenberg, *We the Parents* (New York, 1939), 90; Dorothy Baruch, *New Ways in Discipline* (New York, 1949), 124; idem, *Understanding Young Children* (New York, 1949), 41; John C. Montgomery and Margaret Suydam, *America's Baby Book* (New York, 1951), 123; Daniel M. Levy, *Maternal Overprotection* (New York, 1943), 22–23.

11. Luella Cole and John J. B. Morgan, *Psychology of Childhood and Adolescence* (New York, 1947); Edmund Zilmer, *Jealousy in Children: A Guide for Parents* (New York, 1949).

12. Benjamin Spock, *The Common Sense Book of Baby and Child Care* (New York, 1945).

13. Montgomery and Suydam, *Baby Book*, 123–25; "Family Clinic," *Parents' Magazine* 30, no. 6 (June 1955): 26 and passim, 1954–59; Spock, *Common Sense*, 272–79; Fromme, *Parents Handbook*, 251.

14. Arthur T. Jersild et al., *Joys and Problems of Childrearing* (New York, 1949), 28–30, 87, 94.

15. Peter N. Stearns, *American Cool: The Creation of a Twentieth-Century Emotional Style* (New York, 1994), chaps. 4 and 5; Lillian Evelyn Gilbreth, *Living with Our Children* (New York, 1928), 106–7; Anna W. M. Wolf, *The Parents' Manual: A Guide to the Emotional Development of Young Children* (New York, 1941), 81; Ernest R. Groves and Gladys Groves, *Wholesome Childhood* (Boston, 1931), 12–13, 98–101.

16. Miriam Formanek-Brunell, "Sugar and Spice: The Politics of Doll Play in Nineteenth-Century America," in Elliott West and Paul Petrik, eds., *Small Worlds: Children and Adolescents in America, 1850–1950* (Lawrence, KS, 1992), 107–24.

17. Inez McClintock and Marshall McClintock, *Toys in America* (Washington, DC, 1961), 212;

Janet Pagter, *The Fascinating Story of Dolls* (New York, 1941); Max von Boehm, *Dolls and Puppets* (Boston, 1956), 156, 191–92.

18. John Burroughs, "Corrupting the Innocents," *Independent* 61 (December 1906): 1424; "The Ethics of Toys," *Nation* 85 (September 1907): 224–25; see also Angelo Patri, *Child Training* (New York, 1922), 21–22.

19. Ruth Frankel, "Choosing the Right Toys," *Hygeia*, December 1931, 1106; see also Marian Faegre, "Playthings That Help Children Grow," *Ladies' Home Journal* 50 (December 1933): 38; Jane Franklin, "A Grandmother Talks about Picking Toys," *American Magazine* 114 (December 1932): 86.

20. Patty Smith Hill and Grace Brown, "Avoid the Gifts That Over-Stimulate," *Delineator* 85 (December 1914): 22–23; Sarah Canstock, "The Significance of Playthings," *Good Housekeeping* 69 (December 1918): 35.

21. Peter N. Stearns, Perrin Rowland, and Lori Giarnella, "Children's Sleep: Sketching Historical Change," *Journal of Social History* 30 (1996): 345–66; Morris Fishbein, "The Tired Child," *Hygeia*, 1926, 406–7.

22. Lisa Jacobson, "Revitalizing the American Home: Children's Leisure and the Revaluation of Play, 1920–1940," *Journal of Social History* (1997): 581–96.

23. See note 1. See also Carole Shammas, *The Pre-Industrial Consumer in England and America* (Cambridge, 1990); Beverly Lemire, *Fashion's Favourite: Cotton Trade and the Consumer in Britain, 1660–1800* (New York, 1991); Hoh-Cheung Mui and Lorna H. Mui, *Shops and Shopkeeping in Eighteenth-Century England* (Ontario, 1989).

24. *Presbyterian Banner,* June 3, 1874, July 28, 1875.

25. Beverly Lemire, "The Theft of Clothes and Popular Consumerism in Early Modern England," *Journal of Social History* 24 (1990): 255–76; Maxine Berg, "Women's Consumption and the Industrial Classes of Eighteenth-Century England," *Journal of Social History* 30 (1996): 415–34.

26. John Benson, *The Rise of Consumer Society in Britain, 1880–1980* (London, 1994); Gary Cross, *Time and Money: The Making of a Consumer Culture* (London, 1993), ix and passim; Grant McCracken, ed., *Culture and Consumption* (Bloomington, IN, 1988); Michael Miller, *The Bon Marché: Bourgeois Culture and the Department Store, 1869–1920* (Princeton, 1981).

27. Richard Fox and T. J. Jackson Lears, eds., *The Culture of Consumption: Critical Essays on American History, 1880–1980* (New York, 1983), 1–38; Abelson, *When Ladies;* Lizabeth Cohen, *Making a New Deal: Industrial Workers in Chicago, 1919–1939* (New York, 1990).

28. Stearns, *American Cool,* chaps. 4 and 5; Carl Renz and Mildred Renz, *Big Problems on Little Shoulders* (New York, 1934); Cas Wouters, "On Status Competition and Emotion Management," *Journal of Social History* 4 (1991): 699–717; Jürgen Gerhards, "The Changing Culture of Emotions in Modern Society," *Social Science Information* 28 (1989).

29. Karen Lystra, *Searching the Heart: Women, Men and Romantic Love in Nineteenth-Century America* (New York, 1989); Henry Morton Robinson, "This Brave New Love," *Esquire*, February 1934, 56; G. T. Sweeter, "A Note from the Publisher," *Esquire*, January 1950, 6.

30. Viviana Zelizer, *Pricing the Priceless Child* (Newport, 1986).

31. Rudolph Binion, "Fiction as Social Fantasy: Europe's Domestic Crisis of 1879–1914," *Journal of Social History* 27 (1994): 679–99. The "birth rate guilt" phenomenon needs careful handling, but in the United States it clearly entered into the subsequent baby boom surge.

32. Lillian Ruben, *Just Friends: The Role of Friendship in Our Lives* (New York, 1985); E. Anthony Rotundo, "Romantic Friendship: Male Intimacy and Middle-Class Youth in the Northern United States," *Journal of Social History* 23 (1989): 1–25; Robert Lynd and Helen M. Lynd, *Middletown: A Study in Contemporary American Culture* (New York, 1929); Barbara Ehrenreich, *Hearts of Men: American Dreams and the Flight from Commitment* (New York, 1984).

33. Marchand, *Advertising the American Dream;* Peter Salovey, ed., *The Psychology of Jealousy and Envy* (New York, 1991); Arnold Gesell, Francis Ilg, and Laura Ames, *Youth: The Ages from Ten to Sixteen* (New York, 1956).

34. Peter Salovey and Judith Rodin, "Coping with Envy and Jealousy," *Journal of Social and Clinical Psychology* 7 (1988): 15–33; Richard H. Smith, Suyng Hee Kim, and W. Gerrod Parrott, "Envy and Jealousy: Semantic Problems and Experimental Distinctions," *Personality and Social*

Psychology Bulletin 14 (1988): 401–9; Shula Sommers, "Adults Evaluating Their Emotions: A Cross-Cultural Perspective," in Carol Z. Malatesta and Carroll Izard, eds., *Emotion in Adult Development* (Beverly Hills, CA, 1984); Abram de Swaan, "The Politics of Agoraphobia: On Changes in Emotional and Relational Management," *Theory and Society* 10 (1981); Gerhards, "Changing Culture"; Wouters, "On Status Competition."

35. Sommers, "Adults."

36. David Riesman, *The Lonely Crowd: A Study of the Changing American Character* (New Haven, 1961).

Emotion and Individual Experience
in the Twentieth Century

Chapter Twenty-One

Toward a Psychohistory of Late-Life Emotionality

W. Andrew Achenbaum

No substantial psychohistory of late-life emotionality yet exists. Behavioral scientists have generated many postulates concerning human growth and development, but most of these focus on the early stages of life. Although gerontology has matured as a field of inquiry since World War II, psychologists and other researchers on aging have not made the study of motivation and affect in later years a top priority. The several competent histories of old age available rarely probe the inner lives of men and women in past times. So there are many opportunities to do good work in this area: little is known about when, how, or the extent to which older people's feelings changed over time.

The historiographic challenge is deciding where to begin. Thus far research by contemporary scholars has set the terms of investigation. This tack makes sense— given the paucity of hard evidence. Experts usually prefer to build knowledge on a foundation of solid data rather than develop a set of hypotheses that are not grounded in real-life experiences. Furthermore, not knowing whether late-life emotions *really* differ in quality and range from those manifested in younger persons inhibits inquiries. Since few gerontologists qualify for AARP cards, they must use their imagination and take risks in order to test their hunches about what it feels to be old. Just as historians recover the voices of women, minorities, and ordinary folk in order to capture the richness of the human condition in times past, so too this endeavor rests heavily on useful insights from aged experts. Hence I start with an anonymous essay in the January 1921 issue of the *Atlantic Monthly.*

"Now I am divorced from my world, and there is nothing more to be said of me save the exact date of my death."[1] The writer claimed that he had planned for his retirement and groomed successors to take over his positions. Despite his preparation, the author found himself sinking into depression due to the "painful renunciation" of past activities. In his forced solitude, however, came inspiration for a new *raison d'être:* he would survey the socioeconomic aspects of old age and the elderly's inner lives from every conceivable angle. A year later the nameless correspondent to the *Atlantic* revealed himself to be G. Stanley Hall, at age seventy-five still one of the major intellectual figures of his era. He hoped that his latest book, *Senescence,* would transform popular attitudes and scholarly assumptions about the second half of life.

At minimum it offers a window into late-life emotionality at a critical moment in U.S. history.

Granville Stanley Hall was a pioneer in several senses. Born in western Massachusetts in 1846, he attended Williams College and Union Theological Seminary before studying with Wilhelm Wundt, a German experimental psychologist, and earning his Ph.D. at Harvard under William James. By the age of forty Hall had already made his reputation at Johns Hopkins for contributions to the behavioral sciences. During the next three decades he advanced the fields of educational psychology, psychological testing, and child development; served as first president of the American Psychological Association; and started four scholarly journals that conjoined basic and applied research at the interface of psychology, education, and theology.

In 1888 Hall was invited to become the first president of Clark University, a small research university that he would head for the next thirty-two years.[2] Administrative responsibilities did not diminish Hall's scholarly productivity. Clark University under his aegis became an internationally renowned center in the behavioral sciences; there, Hall trained key figures in the next generation of experimental researchers, including the child psychologist Arnold Gessell and methodologist Lewis Terman. He also wrestled with metaphysical questions: in *Jesus, The Christ, in the Light of Psychology* (1917), Hall explored the "greatest of all oscillations that the psychic world has ever known or can know, from the deepest ebb tide of dysphoria or the highest flood of euphoria."[3]

G. Stanley Hall's *vita* suggests that he was an energetic, productive scholar whose research and personal interests had remained fairly constant (not to mention eclectic) over his intellectual career. Perhaps Hall could look forward to the blessings of a good old age; that would have been consistent with the continuities that had characterized his accomplishments in youth and middle age. But perhaps not: viewing "life as a binomial curve," he knew that the years between forty-five and sixty-five were filled with the "most wreckage"; they were full of "emulsive tendencies."[4] So on a certain level Hall anticipated that his would not be an easy transition to retirement.

Old age was a distinctive stage of life, his *Atlantic* essay declared, with its own set of emotional dynamics that were shaped by internal and external factors. Hall moreover was conscious of "incipient infirmities"—he had problems with his eyesight and digestion—and soon concluded that physicians did not know much about how to maintain healthfulness in their elderly patients. As he took stock of his own options, Hall was not unmindful of the pleasures afforded by increased time to travel, to garden, to read, and to join in family activities. Still, he admitted that "no program that I can construct out of such possibilities seems entirely satisfactory."[5] Having acknowledged that "I am really and truly old," Hall realized that he had to come to terms with death. He prepared his will, which "should have been done long ago but I have been withheld from this duty, partly by preoccupation but far more by the instinctive reluctance all feel to thus anticipate their own death."[6] At this juncture, he decided to use a lifetime's worth of acquired skills to make sense of the *terra incognita* on which he had landed.

Hall's *Senescence: The Last Half of Life* (1922) usually is compared (unfavorably) to his two-volume study *Adolescence* (1904). *Adolescence* is a scholarly, definitive text;

Senescence, in contrast, is a self-indulgent, rambling jeremiad. The book, nevertheless, has great value in establishing a baseline from which to gauge continuities and changes in the history of late- life emotionality. In *Senescence* we observe a patriarchal scientist wrestling with his own fears and hopes as he mines the treasure trove of knowledge, ancient and modern, to grasp what it means and what it feels like to grow older. "I will not accept the subtle but persistently intrusive suggestion that it will do no good or that former colleagues whom I esteem, and whose judgment I greatly prize, will ignore it because other old men have written fatuously," Hall declared in his introduction. "I can, at least, speak more honestly than I have ever dared to do before, and if I am never read or even venture into print, I shall have the satisfaction of having clarified and unified my own soul."[7] Hall freely interjected his own biases, ideas, and "scientific" evidence in *Senescence.*

Not surprisingly, the pessimistic tone of Hall's confessional *Atlantic Monthly* essay colors the opening pages of *Senescence.* "Youth is an exhilarating, age a depressing theme. Both have their zest but they are as unlike as the mood of morning and evening, spring and autumn," Hall asserted. "An old man devoting himself for many months to the study of senectitude and death has a certain pathetic aspect, even to those nearest to him."[8] Hall affirmed that his late life was darkened by a mood different from any he had experienced earlier in life. Furthermore, even potentially productive older people (like himself) found themselves segregated:

> Resent, resist, or ignore it as we will, the fact is that when we are once thought of as old, whether because of mental or physical signs or by withdrawal from our wonted sphere of activities, we enter a class more or less apart and by ourselves. We can claim, if we will, certain exemptions, privileges, immunities, even demand allowances; but, on the other hand, we are liable to feel set aside by, or make room for, younger people, and find that even the new or old services we have a new urge to render may be declined.[9]

Isolation in old age exacerbated late-life depression.

Was Hall's dark mood unusual? Was there something unique about the way he or his particular birth cohort felt and was being treated? Or had old age always been a period of physical and emotional decline? To answer such questions, Hall devoted more than a quarter of *Senescence* to synthesizing humanistic perspectives on aging. He began with prehistorical artifacts, interspersed with anthropological case studies of the treatment of old age among "existing savage tribes." Particular attention was paid to the range of attitudes about age and aging and to transgenerational interactions among biblical peoples and the ancient Greeks and Romans. Highlighting gender differences, Hall focused on the role of older women in witchcraft during the Middle Ages. He recounted the views of well-known savants from Bacon to H. G. Wells, and quoted from late works by Tolstoy, Ruskin, Gogol, and lesser U.S. writers.

From Hall's analysis emerged a central theme: the emotional lives of older persons, past and present, have been and continue to be extraordinarily diverse. Some were loved and respected, because (like Nestor) they remained useful or (like Cato) were stoic in their suffering. Other characters in classical and medieval literature were portrayed as cruel and loathsome; a few, morbid or suicidal. Still others in their later years displayed a mix of emotional states. No single image, favorable or unfavorable, prevailed.

In the middle section of *Senescence*, Hall turned to the sciences: "It is to biology, not to theology or philosophy, that we must look for our most authoritative and normative ideas of both life and death." [10] Like Harvard cytologist Charles Sedgwick Minot, Hall believed that cell differentiation caused the physiological changes and pathological decline associated with growing older. Only glandular implantation or some endocrinological injections, he reckoned, might ease the vicissitudes of age and, ideally, postpone death. [11] In the absence of any viable biomedical intervention, Hall considered psychology the next best source of insight into the nature of senescence: "Now psychology teaches not only that there are certain determining tendencies that always, in part at least below the threshold of consciousness, direct the course of thought, slowly build up centers of apperception and interest . . . [but also that these] have a secondary anagogic value in great efficacy." [12] The study of psychology, which Hall believed was a *via media* between the humanities and the sciences, prompted greater self-knowledge.

Psychology was "anagogic," Hall contended, because the field could not yet specify mysterious links between the body, mind, and emotions. That connections existed was taken for granted in *Senescence;* variations in linkages were manifest in the elderly's physical, mental, and emotional conditions:

> Old age dulls conscience, may bring vanity and new ambitions, petulance, irritability, misanthropy, and slows down activity. But the best average barometer of mental failure is memory, the loss of which comes as an advance guard of many symptoms. . . . The old are particularly prone to flush under very slight emotional strain and cannot throw off care or control patience. . . . There is an unhealthy tendency to force decline by overtaxing the body and the nerves. [13]

Hall, like most of his contemporaries, considered the physiological and pathological manifestations of advancing years to be more pronounced than emotional decline. When "vitality" did wane, changes in affect could be traced back to an organic cause. Thus in keeping with earlier practices, Hall recommended that doctors check their aged patients' blood pressure, eating habits, and alcohol consumption.

Perturbations in mental health were most apparent among the oldest of the old. "While the process of senile involution rests apparently on the defective nutrition of cell tissues," Hall observed, "we usually do not think of our somatic state until some discomfort compels us to do so." [14] Following tradition, Hall distinguished between premature and advanced stages of senility. "There is often a change of temperament into egoism, perverseness, peevishness, loss of ambition, religiosity, inability to bear slight discomforts and depression. . . . Our mental attitude is simply resignation to the inevitable." [15]

So as to verify his own impressions and experts' opinions, Hall prepared a questionnaire that he distributed to residents of nursing homes, eminent contemporaries, friends, and elderly people who wrote him in response to his *Atlantic* essay. Among other things, he asked subjects when they first acknowledged the coming of age, if they experienced an " 'Indian summer' of renewed vigor before the winter of age began," and whether they relied more now than formerly on clergy and/or physicians. Hall also probed their emotional states, querying what old or new temptations they felt.[16] Many respondents expressed regrets over earlier mistakes, dissatisfactions about the ways they interacted with people, or a "corroding sense of sexual errors in their past that may have impaired the quality of all their family relations." While his survey revealed "no tragic remorse of either the old classic or theological kind," Hall deduced that "old people to-day are just as fond of acting as mentors for the young as they were in ancient Greece, though now it takes the very form of propensity to give advice and warnings."[17]

The questionnaire confirmed Hall's personal distaste for the negative aspects of growing older: "Each decade the circle of the Great Fatigue narrows around us, restricting the intensity and endurance of our activities."[18] It also validated his own depressive state in old age. Pessimism seemed to grip most of Hall's contemporaries; serenity and "disciplined tranquillity" were rare. Feeling superfluous or unloved made some elders egocentric or hysterical. Yet the survey suggested that new elements were affecting the emotional texture of later years. Again, Hall was struck by gender differences. Physically and sexually, women as a group sensed the coming of age sooner than men; they more often found themselves incapable of altering their sense of powerlessness. Hence it seemed to follow that later in life women were more likely than men to become selfish as their spheres of interest and influence diminished. This tendency was apparent especially among females in the uneducated classes who suffered from impaired health or needed more money.[19]

Gender differences notwithstanding, Hall recognized that shifting historical contexts altered how the elderly related to others and what they thought about themselves. New institutions affected power relations, family ties, and economic patterns. "Our retirement, even if gradual and not dated, calls attention to our age, and to our little world we grow old a decade the day it learns that we have stepped aside while to ourselves we may and ought to feel that we grow young that day by yet more."[20]

Old age, G. Stanley Hall concluded, was different from what he had expected it to be, from what younger persons imagined it to be, and from what he observed in both humanistic and scientific literature. "We feel that we have made landfall on a new continent where we must not only disembark but explore and make new departures and institutions and give a better interpretation to human life."[21] The plural pronoun is revealing. Hall recognized that he was part of a vanguard of elders whose added years were to affect all aspects of American society, including its emotional tenor.

> Now that the average length of human life is increased and there are more and more old people, a fact that marks the triumph of science and civilization, there is more need of studying them ... for medically, at least after the climacteric, they constitute a class in the community that is somewhat alien, its intrinsic nature but little known, and the services it was meant to render but little utilized.[22]

Since the publication of Hall's *Senescence,* and especially after World War II, research into the psychology of aging has been booming. The American Psychological Association established Division 20 on Maturity and Old Age in 1946.[23] Behavioral scientists from the start have been major architects and prime movers in the field of gerontology. Multivolume handbooks of aging invariably include a separate book devoted exclusively to research in psychology. About 15 percent of the current members of the Gerontological Society of America are psychologists, roughly the same percentage as physicians.

Because the first generation of gerontologists tended to focus on *problems* of aging, the first postwar publications dealt with various mental health issues, such as whether intelligence declined with age. Psychologists investigated genetic aspects, physiological changes, nutritional factors, and environmental conditions; unlike Hall, they paid more attention to variations in race, ethnicity, and class than in gender. Representative of the genre was Oscar J. Kaplan's *Mental Disorders in Later Life* (1945), a compendium of psycho-geriatrics that offered case studies on neuroses, involutional psychoses, presenile dementias, and senile atrophy, as well as analyses of the adverse effects of long hospitalization and cerebral arteriosclerosis. "Although we are only at the threshold of our understanding of these puzzling conditions," Kaplan wrote, "we are moving from work that is primarily descriptive to inquiries concerned essentially with etiology."[24] Current handbooks of mental health in aging, following Kaplan, emphasize the severity of depression and psychoses among the elderly.

The (re)discovery of old-age diseases has galvanized scientific and popular attention to the emotional woes of the elderly. It has been a commonplace among researchers in aging during the past two decades to investigate patterns of "normal" aging unaffected by pathological involution. This has been especially so in efforts to unravel the causes, and to reverse the effects, of Alzheimer's disease. First identified in 1906, Alzheimer's was generally associated with presenile dementia; its victims suffered from rapid mental deterioration, delirium, and confusion. In the mid-1970s, however, scientists linked the malady to the existence of structural abnormalities found in the brains of dead people who had lost their memory at advanced age. By the late 1980s, Alzheimer's disease accounted for 60 percent of all cases of senile dementia, and was considered the fourth largest cause of death among the elderly.[25] The federal National Institute on Aging now devotes more research dollars to studying this disease than any other budget item; a nationwide network of caregivers, local support groups, and fundraisers exists.

Most of the research within the psychology of aging over the past seventy-five years, however, has not dealt with the relationship between mental and pathological disorders or with the emotional states of people afflicted with Alzheimer's disease. Instead, investigators have focused on older people's mental health, cognitive changes with advancing age, and the effect of living environments on the elderly's well-being. Such research is indispensable, of course, but it does not directly address the nature and dynamics of late-life emotionality. According to a current leader in the field, "psychologists know comparatively little about motivation and emotion in the aged, and many textbooks do not even have special chapters devoted to this topic; instead, phenomena *related* to motivation or emotion are often indexed under special terms (e.g., life satisfaction)."[26] Most researchers interested in personality changes investigate the development of emotion in the early years of human growth. Developmental psychologists who study the latter stages of life generally have been preoccupied with disentangling age, cohort, and period effects in both longitudinal and cross- sectional samples.

That said, behavioral scientists generally concur that there *is* a class of emotions and affect associated with old age. Indeed, psychologists have generated at least two sets of findings that are indispensable for reconstructing the history of old-age emotions.[27] First, consistent with Hall's suggestion that biology shadows psychology, scientists have attributed to organic factors various alterations in late-life emotional states in terms of level of arousal, duration, and localizability. Age- specific differences, they hypothesize, are related to neuronal changes, such as the loss of synapses and the appearance of organic anomalies, that govern regulatory effectiveness. Dementia, for instance, seems to be correlated with certain alterations in the structure and composition of the brain. Reduced levels of noradrenaline and/or serotonin are associated with high rates of depression.

Second (just as Hall supposed), psychologists do not relate all changes in emotional states during the latter stages of life to biological causes. Feelings are relative, researchers acknowledge. What, for example, is the basis of comparison in describing an emotion as fundamental as love? To the ways one expressed passion in youth? To the standards senior citizens might be expected to uphold in exchanges of affection among peers, as well as among youth? Do the same types of events elicit similar emotional experiences over time? Or do thresholds change with age? Is love better the second time around, as the popular song has it, or does it become more bittersweet, less euphoric with advancing years? Current research indicates that people's basic emotional "machinery" may remain intact, but it is deployed in new ways. Some elders might appear less emotional than other members of their cohort or than middle-aged people because of the tactics they have learned over their lives. Others may choose novel strategies to control and express their emotions.

Erik Erikson (1902–94) was probably the postwar psychologist who achieved the greatest fame for his explorations into the emotional choices humans made at various stages of their lives. In *Childhood and Society* (1950), he elaborated with his wife. Joan, a "conceptual itinerary" of human development. "Each successive stage and crisis had a special relation to one of the basic elements of society, and this for the simple reason that the human life cycle and man's institutions have evolved together."[28] As the Eriksons grew older, they delved into the last stages. Like G. Stanley Hall, the couple "had no intention of (or capacity for) imagining ourselves as really old." Yet, once old, they found themselves amazed by their capacity for wisdom, for the sensual, "in maintaining some order and meaning in the dis-integration of body and mind."[29]

Taking cues from disciplinary mentors and peers, historians and other experts in the humanities have greatly enriched our understanding of ideal-types by exploring the milieu in which biblical and classical archetypes and myths of late-life emotionality have arisen and been reworked over time. The Genesis account of Sarah and Abraham, for instance, shows that the aging couple remained faithful to their covenant with God until death. Amid ever changing opportunities and crises, however, this highly individuated pair experienced joy, grief, anguish, surprise, and doubts—a wide range of emotions at advanced ages.[30] Theologians also have rediscovered aspects of the past that previous generations forgot or chose to ignore. Hence, in reviving the image of Sophia as a Goddess of Wisdom in both Hebrew and Hellenic traditions, feminist theologians have squarely challenged masculine notions of the Godhead. Their reinterpretations of the Book of Job and Proverbs, among other works in the Wisdom literature, have transformed scholars' understanding of the relationship between divine and private uses of power in ancient households. Still other scholars debunk tradition itself: Solomon, contrary to what we learned in Sunday school, was not an elder when his cognitive genius was most evident; Solon, the first architect of Athenian citizenship, did not associate growing wisdom with advancing years.[31]

Besides correcting false impressions about times past, historians have laid the groundwork for writing a contemporary history of late-life emotions by delineating the varieties of human experiences from womb through tomb. The portrait of the past is incomplete: more is understood about the past circumstances of white, gainfully employed males who lived north of the Equator in ancient times and since 1700 than is known about others in different places and times. Nonetheless, U.S. and European historians during the past two decades have demonstrated that particular phases of the life course have their own distinctive features. History shapes every stage of life: as they age, people adapt, react, and respond to prevailing social mores, cultural attitudes, political forces, economic imperatives, and demographic exigencies.[32]

Great divisions exist within age groups. People who happen to be the same age at a given time and place do not inevitably act, think, and feel in similar ways. This "truth" matters greatly in the reconstruction of the history of age relations—especially among the elderly, because old age's chronological boundaries are both wider and less clear-cut than markers at earlier stages. "Age" has been, and is, a key sociohistorical indicator, but not all-important. Except for brief (some might say revolutionary)[33] historical episodes, age has remained secondary to the ways that race, gender, and class affected ordinary persons' lives in past times. Like psychologists, therefore, historians must be sensitive to individual diversity and the dynamics of cultural pluralism as they sort out age, cohort, and period effects.

Most of the standard monographs that trace continuities and changes in the meanings and experiences of old age in U.S. and European history since 1600 do not dwell on the emotional lives of the elderly. They are more concerned with mapping out major shifts in older people's economic and social status, analyzing twists in popular and professional attitudes toward the aged, and tracing the messy evolution of national and local policies to prevent old-age indigence and to provide a range of social support and health care services for the old.[34]

There are a few noteworthy exceptions. First, gender differences matter. Terri Premo's *Winter Friends* and Laurel Ulrich's *A Midwife's Tale* extend an argument originally set forth in Nancy Cott's *Bonds of Womanhood* (1977): older women provided a resilient network by sharing their often frayed emotions and their resources in day-to-day exchanges. They could count on support in times of sickness and tragedy as well as moments of joy. "The enhanced domestic purview of women's sphere responded very closely to many of the needs and special concerns of women facing old age," Premo observes, "one that encompassed a fuller identity with the world while enabling them to face the singular reality of their own supersession. As age advanced, women looked further inward through reading, reminiscence, and reflection to gain direction along the final path they would be walking alone." [35]

Second, some historians are sensitive to the importance of age in shaping historical memory and consciousness. Peter N. Stearns, for instance, referred to the aged's emotional state in his pioneering *Old Age in European History* (1977). His attention to late-life issues continues as he explores the history of emotionality. In *American Cool* (1994), he cites evidence from the Victorian period to support the psychologists' suggestion that emotions dampen in later years. [36] The evidence is used as provocatively as possible in the absence of a conceptual framework to gird a history of old-age emotionality.

Stearns and his associates have over the past decade provided useful guidelines for writing histories of emotion. Three approaches have been recommended: (1) linking the history of emotions to the history of familial relationships, (2) establishing the norms for particular emotions during specific periods, and (3) relating emotional patterns to broader cultural styles. Each has its merits. The first approach prompts scholars to look for gender-specific differences in emotions, which the first wave of historical literature amply documents. The second enables historians to enter uncharted territory in as cautious and straightforward a manner as possible: as long as they are accurate in reporting what they find, they are bound to make a contribution. The third tack invites grand synthesis, for it relates cultural, social, and political history: "A new emotional culture, even when its interaction with direct emotional experience is incomplete, characteristically has important institutional consequences, if only because the kinds of thinking and expertise that help formulate standards also affect other public norms." [37] In the last section of this essay, I make additional suggestions for proceeding.

Beginning this survey of late-life emotionality with G. Stanley Hall's *Senescence* turns out to have been shrewder than first imagined. It just so happens that Hall was thinking about old age in the very decade judged pivotal in transforming the socialization and expression of other emotions such as anger, jealousy, and fear. "The early part of the twentieth century [was] a time of significant alterations in the American emotional climate," Peter Stearns asserts.

> Several emotions . . . summoned up new strategies of avoidance and social manipulation as both Victorian intensity and Victorian gender differentiations were downplayed. Here, at least on the suppressive side, was the emotional counterpoint to the construction of new American personality values, suitable (or so it was deemed) for a new, secular consumer culture and a managerial organizational and economic structure. [38]

As a longtime student of human development and of the dramatic changes wrought in higher education by his nation's new urban- industrial order, Hall was well positioned to sense major changes under way. In *Senescence* he suggested several themes that are worth pursuing.

First, Hall was convinced that members of his cohort had to assume new social roles. Far from being obsolescent, America's aged had a unique opportunity to help rising generations realize their potential. "Intelligent and well-conserved senectitude has very important social and anthropological functions in the modern world not hitherto utilized or even recognized. The chief of these is most comprehensively designated by the general term synthesis, something never so needed as in our very complex age of distracting specializations," Hall observed. "There is, thus, a kind of harvest-home effort to gather the fruitage of the past and to penetrate further into the future."[39] Relying on the elderly's experiences had ample precedent in U.S. history: in the early years of the Republic, older people showed where and how to plant the crops, and they offered all sorts of advice in the shop and in the kitchen. *Senescence*'s novelty, however, lies in Hall's claim that age must counterbalance youth's temptation to be narrow and unduly specialized by affording them a synthetic overview of the "big picture."

Hall's "well-conserved senectitude," to be sure, sounds like biblical "wisdom" as reworked in Montaigne's and Franklin's essays. Yet in modern psychological and philosophical circles at least, "wisdom" was falling out of vogue—precisely when Hall was urging its cultivation. If behavioral research was to be judged a "pure" science like physics, its practitioners had to be positivists, faithful to empirical methods. "Whereas science was being established epistemologically and institution-ally, wisdom vanished and reappeared as an irrepressible shadow or uncanny ghost of science."[40] Our renewed interest in wisdom may thus be an indication that the current pursuit of knowledge has entered the postmodern era.

During the past fifteen years psychologists have made important contributions to our current understanding of wisdom. Researchers have taken great pains to establish problem domains—to determine when a problem is specific to a particular stage of development and set of life circumstances—and to differentiate between practical and expert knowledge. They have constructed measures by which to identify older people who might be considered wise on the basis of their words and deeds.[41] Significantly, much of this research corresponds to what has been learned in gender studies about age-changes over the life course. As men and women grow wiser, they seem to become more androgynous—more comfortable with their "other" side.[42] Historians should build on this literature, working with psychologists in stipulating the emotional conditions that seem to lie at the interstices of people's attempts to integrate their thoughts, feelings, and actions in coming to terms with their strengths and weaknesses, in interacting with significant others, and in dealing on human terms with global issues.[43]

If the desire to grow wiser does indeed become more pronounced with advancing years, then historians must be very sensitive to the way they contextualize the process across cohorts. It hardly suffices to note that the connection between age and wisdom is age-old. Historians should seize on a central paradox: the elderly's search for an all-embracing wisdom may have further marginalized them in modern times, when their contemporaries put greater faith in technology and social control. Yet it was precisely lessons learned on the quest itself that gave older men and women something distinctive to transmit to rising generations.

If I am interpreting trends plausibly, Hall's plea for a "well-conserved senectitude" was a real gamble. Older persons, especially those in physical decline and those who had retired from work or withdrawn from social circles, might have been wiser *not* to accentuate the extent to which they no longer conformed to (or were constrained by) midlife ideals. Rather than bemoaning their aches or chiding others, Hall and his cohort might have found greater acceptance by suppressing unpleasant emotions—both to demonstrate their ongoing capacity for conforming to the cult of youth and to fit into an emotional culture increasingly intolerant of "negativity" in affect.[44]

In addition to dealing with changing contexts for wisdom, scholars interested in reconstructing the history of late-life emotionality should take note of the emphasis paid to death in *Senescence*. Significantly, Hall put his chapter on "the psychology of death" *after* the chapter in which he proffered "some conclusions." Hall's exploration of thanatology ranges from the Egyptians and Pauline Christianity to Kant, Schopenhauer, Royce, and Durkheim. Interspersed are data from a survey on middle-aged and elderly people's fears of dying that he conducted around the turn of the century. At times Hall is platitudinous—"We come into life buoyant and happy but before leaving it have to pay for all the joy by pain enough to compensate"[45]—and sentimental: he closes his tome with Tennyson's "Crossing the Bar." Nevertheless, some of Hall's valedictory insights into fears of dying and hopes for immortality follow from his belief that old age should be a time of intense introspection and mentoring: "The fear of death and forms of mitigating this fear are chiefly because man still dies young. If we had experienced and explored senescence fully we should find that the lust of life is supplanted later by an equally strong counterwill to die."[46]

Hall wrote in the midst of a demographic revolution. Three- quarters of all gains in life expectancy at birth have occurred since 1900. There have also been increases in life expectancy at age forty, more notable for women than men. Significant social changes affected how people could use these added years. Workers no longer expected to die on the job; they could look forward to retirement. Whereas men and women once struggled to have the resources to age in place, the new middle-class old were increasingly on the road, heading south or to second homes. Advancing age, moreover, brought a concatenation of acute diseases and chronic maladies, which means that their added years put the elderly at increased risk for disablement.[47] By the 1920s the old were the group most likely to face death. Hence Hall's hypothesis that people's attitudes toward dying and death may be affected not only by their own growing sense of finitude but by prevailing historical circumstances merits serious attention.

Psychologists have done more than historians in analyzing the connection between old age and death in the twentieth century. They have produced imaginative studies of "terminal decline," constructed "purpose-in-life" tests, and surveyed the dying and older people in term care. Still, behaviorists concede that it is difficult to trace the developmental thread through adult years. "The combined power of science and social policy has issued a fresh if implicit invitation to trivialize and compartmentalize death," claims Robert Kastenbaum, arguably the nation's leading gerontologist/ thanatologist. "Just as the future of developmental psychology has required its extension into later adulthood, so the new life-span psychology perhaps requires the willingness to revise and expand our conceptual horizons by considering the human relationship to death on its own terms rather than through the limitations of current theory and method."[48] Death is not a "hot" topic among U.S. social or cultural historians. Splendid studies of mortality in colonial times have been done by demographic historians such as Daniel Scott Smith and Maris Vinovskis; others have written on funeral practices and cemeteries.[49] Death figures in existing histories of the elderly, but authors usually treat the subject as if it were a separate topic.

Recent events may be remaking history. In hospitals and nursing homes across the nation, families and doctors negotiate the most appropriate (and least detectable) way to hasten an end to prolonged suffering. Advocates as different as former Colorado governor Richard Lamm and bio-ethicist Daniel Callahan now are suggesting that men and women over sixty-five should consider dying, since they can no longer make a claim for economic or medical support from public sources. And some older people are taking matters into their own hands: they join euthanasia societies, seek assistance from Jack Kevorkian, or quietly commit suicide. What motivates these emotions and actions? What in our contemporary culture promotes and impedes suicide and euthanasia at advanced age? Hall speculated about such matters in the 1920s. To write a full survey of late-life emotionality will require scholars to take account of recent developments and to ascertain whether they represent a new turning point in that history.

NOTES

1. "Old Age," *Atlantic Monthly* 127 (January 1921): 23–24.

2. W. Andrew Achenbaum and Daniel M. Albert, *Profiles in Gerontology: A Biographical Dictionary* (Westport, CT: Greenwood, 1995), 151–52. For a different interpretation of Hall's views of old age, see Thomas R. Cole, *The Journey of Life* (New York: Cambridge University Press, 1992), chap. 10.

3. G. Stanley Hall, *Jesus, The Christ, in the Light of Psychology* (Garden City, NY: Doubleday, Page, 1917), xii.

4. G. Stanley Hall, *Senescence: The Last Half of Life* (New York: D. Appleton, 1922) 1, 25.

5. Ibid., xiii.

6. Ibid., xii, xxi.

7. Ibid., xxi.

8. Ibid., viii.

9. Ibid., viii–ix.

10. Ibid., 314.

11. Ibid., 317. For more on biomedical ideas about senescence prevailing from Minot to transplanters such as Serge Voronoff, see W. Andrew Achenbaum, *Old Age in the New Land* (Baltimore: Johns Hopkins University Press, 1978), 119–20.

12. Hall, *Senescence,* 314.

13. Ibid., 206–7.

14. Ibid., 219.

15. Ibid.

16. Ibid., 319. Although Hall acknowledged his "subjective bias" in a sample that presented "somewhat heterogeneous data" (322), he chose not to differentiate responses from old-age–home residents, friends, and correspondents.

17. Ibid., 329, 341.

18. Ibid., 366.

19. Ibid., 335, 387–92.

20. Ibid., 381.

21. Ibid., 382.

22. Ibid., xvi–xvii.

23. The division's name was later changed to Adult Development and Aging. See W. Andrew Achenbaum, *Crossing Frontiers* (New York: Cambridge University Press, 1995), 147.

24. Oscar J. Kaplan, preface to Oscar J. Kaplan, ed., *Mental Disorders in Later Life* (Stanford: Stanford University Press, 1945), vii. The statistics on the incidence of mental disease come from Benjamin Malzberg's essay, "A Statistical Review of Mental Disorders in Later Life," in the second edition (Stanford University Press, 1956), 17, 24.

25. Stephen Fuller, "Alzheimer's Disease," *Journal of Nervous and Mental Disease* 39 (1912):207–19; A. F. Jorm, *The Epidemiology of Alzheimer's Disease and Related Disorders* (London: Chapman and Hall, 1990); Henry Gruetzner, *Alzheimer's: A Caregiver's Guide and Sourcebook* (New York: John Wiley, 1992).

26. Sigrun-Heide Filipp, "Motivation and Emotion," in James E. Birren and K. Warner Schaie, eds., *Handbook of the Psychology of Aging*, 4th ed. (San Diego: Academic Press, 1996), 218.

27. Most of the information in this and the following paragraphs comes from Richard Schulz, "Emotion and Affect," in James E. Birren and K. Warner Schaie, eds., *Handbook of the Psychology of Aging*, 2d ed. (New York: Van Nostrand Reinhold, 1985), 531–43 and from Filipp, "Motivation and Emotion."

28. Erik Erikson, "Eight Ages of Man," in *Childhood and Society* (New York: Norton, 1963 [1950]), 250. The phrase "conceptual itinerary" appears on 17.

29. Erik H. Erikson, *The Life Cycle Completed* (New York: Norton, 1985), 62, 64, respectively.

30. I choose this example because Stephen Modell and I drew explicit parallels in the pathways of wisdom taken by Abraham and Sarah and by Joan and Erik Erikson. The essay will appear in Eugene Thomas and Susen Eisenhandler, eds., *Religion, Spirituality, and Aging* (New York: Springer, forthcoming).

31. Thomas M. Falkner and Judith de Luce, "A View from Antiquity: Greece, Rome, and Elders," in Thomas R. Cole, David D. Van Tassel, and Robert Kastenbaum, eds., *Handbook of the Humanities and Aging* (New York: Springer, 1992), 3–39.

32. Several historiographic surveys of the literature exist. For a recent overview, see Carole Haber and Brian Gratton, *Old Age and the Search for Security* (Bloomington: Indiana University Press, 1994), introduction and chap. 6.

33. This is the thesis of David Hackett Fischer, *Growing Old in America* (New York: Oxford University Press, 1977), chap. 2, who claims that the elderly lost their gerontocratic sway in the American Revolution. Older men and women actually enjoy a moment of glory at the height of the French Revolution, according to David Troyansky, *Old Age in the Old Regime: Image and Experience in Eighteenth-Century France* (Ithaca: Cornell University Press, 1989).

34. Here, I refer mainly to Fischer, *Growing Old in America;* Achenbaum, *Old Age in the New Land;* idem., *Shades of Gray* (Boston: Little, Brown, 1983); William Graebner, *A History of Retirement* (New Haven: Yale University Press, 1980); Carole Haber, *Beyond Sixty-Five* (New York: Cambridge University Press, 1983); Brian Gratton, *Urban Elders* (Philadelphia: Temple University Press, 1985); Jill Quadagno, *The Transformation of Old Age Security* (Chicago: University of Chicago Press, 1988); Cole, *Journey of Life;* and Theda Skocpol, *Protecting Soldiers and Mothers* (Cambridge: Harvard University Press, 1993).

35. Terri Premo, *Winter Friends: Women Growing Old in the New Republic, 1785–1835* (Urbana: University of Illinois Press, 1990), 105. See also Laurel Ulrich, *Midwife's Tale* (New York: Random, 1990).

36. For references to avarice among French elders, see Peter N. Stearns, *Old Age in European History* (New York: Holmes and Meier, 1977), 30, 38. For references to late-life emotionality in U.S. history, including the emotional impact of associating the coming of age with the inevitability of death, see Stearns, *American Cool: Constructing a Twentieth-Century Emotional Style* (New York: New York University Press, 1994), 150, 161.

37. Peter N. Stearns and Timothy Haggerty, "The Role of Fear: Transitions in American Emotional Standards for Children, 1850–1950," *American Historical Review* 96 (1991): 91. The three approaches to writing the history of emotionality appear in Stearns, *American Cool*, 5.

38. Stearns and Haggerty, "The Role of Fear," 86.

39. Hall, *Senescence*, 405–6.

40. Aleida Assmann, "Wholesome Knowledge: Concepts of Wisdom in a Historical and Cross-Cultural Perspective," in David L. Featherman, Richard M. Lerner, and Marion Perlmutter, eds., *Life-Span Development and Behavior* (Hillsdale, NJ: Lawrence Erlbaum Associates, 1994), 12:202. See also Stephen G. Holliday and Michael J. Chandler, *Wisdom: Explorations in Adult Competence* (Basel: Karger, 1986); and Ronald J. Manheimer, "Wisdom and Method: Philosophical Contributions to Gerontology," in Cole et al., eds., *Handbook of the Humanities and Aging*, 426.

41. In the growing literature, see Robert Sternberg, ed., *Wisdom* (New York: Cambridge University Press, 1990); Jacqui Smith and Paul Baltes, "Wisdom-Related Knowledge," *Developmental Psychology* 26 (1990): 494–505; Paul Baltes, Jacqui Smith, and Ursula M. Staudinger, "Wisdom and Successful Aging," in Theo B. Sonderregger, ed., *Nebraska Symposium on Motivation* (Lincoln: University of Nebraska Press, 1991), 125–48; and for a philosopher's views, John Kekes, "Wisdom," *American Philosophical Quarterly* 20 (1983): 277–86.

42. David Gutmann, *Reclaimed Powers* (New York: Basic Books, 1987); Douglas H. Heath, *Fulfilling Lives* (San Francisco: Jossey-Bass, 1991).

43. W. Andrew Achenbaum and Lucinda Orwoll, "Becoming Wise," *International Journal of Aging and Human Development* 32 (1991): 21–39.

44. Peter N. Stearns, "Suppressing Unpleasant Emotions: The Development of a Twentieth-Century American Style," in Andrew E. Barnes and Peter N. Stearns, eds., *Social History and Issues in Human Consciousness* (New York: New York University Press, 1989), 230–61.

45. Hall, *Senescence*, 461.

46. Ibid., 514.

47. For more on this, see Alan Pifer and Lydia Bronte, eds., *Our Aging Society* (New York: Norton, 1986); and Lois M. Verbrugge and Alan M. Jette, "The Disablement Process," *Social Science Medicine* 38 (1994): 12.

48. Robert Kastenbaum, "Dying and Death: A Life Span Approach," in Birren and Schaie, eds., *Handbook of the Psychology of Aging*, 2d ed. (1985), 640.

49. See Maris Vinovskis, "Death," in Mary Kupiec Cayton, Elliott J. Gorn, and Peter W. Williams, eds., *Encyclopedia of American Social History* (New York: Scribner's, 1993), 3: 2063–70. For more specialized treatments, see also Philippe Aries, *Western Attitudes toward Death* (Baltimore: Johns Hopkins University Press, 1974); and Jan Lewis, *The Pursuit of Happiness* (New York: Cambridge University Press, 1983).

Chapter Twenty-two

Reuben Davis, Sylvia Plath, and Other American Writers
The Perils of Emotional Struggle

Bertram Wyatt-Brown

And then a Plank in Reason, broke,
And I dropped down, and down—
And hit a World, at every plunge,
And Finished knowing—then—
　　—Emily Dickinson, "I Felt a Funeral, in My Brain"

The main subjects of the remarks to follow are a study in sharp contrasts. In 1953 Reuben Davis, a novelist and short-story writer, published the novel *Shim,* named for the young hero, whose growing up in a desolate Mississippi clearing bears a relationship to the author's early life.[1] Determined to reveal little of himself in his writing, Davis transcribed personal trauma into the safeguarded framework of fiction. There, damage to the psyche could be explored without the embarrassment and threat of personal exposure. Reviewers were positive, but *Shim* was soon forgotten. In the winter of 1962–63 Sylvia Plath wrote *Ariel.* Like her single novel, *The Bell Jar,* these poems of her despair were as openly confessional as Davis's novel was autobiographically restrained. Unlike Davis, who died in 1966 virtually unknown to the literary world, Plath, whose brief career ended in early 1963, quickly became a cult figure. Since then, her career has engaged no fewer than seven biographers. Davis has had none to resurrect his life. Thus Davis's literary achievements were undervalued, while the breakup of Plath's marriage and the dramatic manner of her death have sometimes diverted attention from the universality and freshness of her poetic insights.[2]

How different could two writers be? Davis belonged to the world of southern rurality, even frontier wilderness. As a youngster at the turn of the century, he had watched as his beloved home county in Mississippi changed from unspoiled terrain of canebrakes and timber stands with scattered farms to corporate lumbering operations, feeding the industries of the New South. The rape of the forest filled him with dismay and a deep soreness of soul, but it inspired his work. Born in 1932 in

Massachusetts, Sylvia Plath anticipated a major change in the way Americans, especially women, thought of themselves. Coming of age before the dawn of a new wave of feminism, she was a child of economic depression and war. These conditions had reinforced in her parents' generation a social conservatism of a Victorian sort. Though a rebel at heart, Sylvia Plath had not secured a distance from those years of genteel penny-scraping and world conflict. In her poems and her single novel, she explored her doubts and anger about her constant struggle between a commitment to her poetic talent and her role as the wife of Ted Hughes, the English poet.

What could possibly lead to a pairing of these disparate figures of the mid-twentieth-century United States—one, a countryman who never graduated from college, the other a sophisticated young woman who attended the finest schools of America and England? The answer is central to this exploration. Davis and Plath were not just gloomy harbingers of a changing world. Rather, they both suffered from a profound melancholy that informed their writing, admittedly in ways hard to grasp in a completely satisfying fashion. This unifying factor is vital for understanding the relationship of art to life and the intermixture of environment, cultural history, and personal, medical factors in fashioning both the themes and thrust of the literature produced. The chemistry of the brain, a trauma in childhood, a family environment of tension and gloom, an intellectual's sense of apartness from the workaday world—these are factors that must all be examined. The lives and work of Reuben Davis, Sylvia Plath, and others who suffered from the malady illustrate this complex set of artistic conditions.

In dealing with such subtle and even speculative concerns, the historian, whose work is ordinarily grounded in concrete data, is clearly taking a risk. A modest connection with both writers inspired my choices. Yet the most significant reason for conjoining a southern fiction writer with a poet from New England is the opportunity to demonstrate the need for fresh perspectives on how emotions have affected events and people in the past. Sensitive to the cultural circumstances in which past lives flourished, the historian is particularly qualified to draw on a range of sources and disciplines even when the subject is the wellspring of literary creativity. By such means the scholar can unveil the whole tapestry in which the artist's life, art, and emotions are woven. Examples from the lives of Conrad Aiken, William Styron, and others—in addition to Davis and Plath—broaden the basis for this analysis.

There is room in historical studies for new approaches. Too often historians, along with other skeptical scholars, complain that in the humanistic fields the use of psychological expertise has led to reductionism and Freudian oversimplification. Any effort to rely simply on old psychological clichés should be justly criticized. Clinical work in psychiatry, however, has advanced enormously since the days of the Viennese progenitor. In addition, medical advances have been made in understanding the functions and dysfunctions of the brain, especially with regard to such illnesses as alcoholism, schizophrenia, depression, and manic-depression. These are matters that the historian who seeks understanding of the emotions ignores at peril. Thus, the findings emerging from both clinical practice and neurological and genetic research have a very significant bearing on the interpretation of motives in the lives of any historical figure.

Examples of depressed writers include such different practitioners as Jack London, Tennessee Williams, J. D. Salinger, Richard Wright, Langston Hughes, John Kennedy Toole, and, in most recent years, Tracy Thompson, Vivian Gornick, Wilfred Sheed, and William Styron, among others.[3] Among novelists both here and abroad, the range of creative depression runs from Lawrence Sterne and Charles Dickens to Joseph Conrad and Marcel Proust, from Mark Twain, who spoke of "sudden changes of mood ... from deep melancholy to half-insane tempests and cyclones," to the often despairing Paul Auster.[4] Each artist was afflicted—and inspired by that affliction—in separate but still proximate ways. Examples could be drawn from various American regions and times, since depression and creativity are bound by neither chronology nor locale.

As a writer whose youth bridged the worlds of the old plantation South and the advent of a more commercialized region, Reuben Davis offers a poignant example of trauma and uncanny literary skill. Davis's tale of sublimated rage and hidden class and racial tensions has a special relevance to the fiction writing of other depressed American writers. The novel employs one of the most persistent plot lines in American and especially southern letters—the anger and grief of a boy for a missing or inadequate father and the substitution of another fatherlike guide who helps the youth on his path to adulthood. It is a theme Leslie Fiedler explored in *Love and Death in the American Novel.*[5] That story, often told as an adventure tale throughout Western countries—Charles Dickens's *Oliver Twist* and *Great Expectations* spring to mind—bears examination as a clue to the history of the author himself.

The literary example of Mark Twain also encouraged the use of the orphaned boy narrator embarking on life's journey. His story of Huck Finn and slave Jim provided his American successors with precedent and guidance. For later authors as well, the employment of the device grows out of the often flawed relationship between real fathers and sons. In this case, the story has special relevance for an inheritor, as Davis was, of southern culture. In a regional society with deeply implanted notions of familial loyalty and patriarchal values, the maturing of a preadolescent boy who must gird on the armor of honor resonates with particular vitality. From a storyteller's point of view, the trope of the preadolescent *bildungsroman* immediately engages the reader. The naive vulnerability of the youth, the imperfections of the father, and the contrasting heroism and magnetism of the surrogate parent, set in the midst of perilous quests, carry the anticipation of a happy outcome.

To borrow a phrase from the title of a book about the Irish poet Brenden Kennelly, writers like Davis drew out their "dark fathers" into the glaring "light" of fiction or autobiography.[6] Disillusioned by the literal or figurative absence of the natural father, each young hero in the youth novel seeks an adult proxy of some kind to advise, command, and love him. Popular writers like John Grisham and Pat Conroy have adopted the formula, which obviously has had much cinematic appeal—in *The Client* and *Prince of Tides* most notably.[7] Reuben Davis's *Shim* contains all the ingredients of violence, narrow escape, and excitement that make the genre so well adapted to imaginative representation, whether serious or light.

The son of Louvica Ann and Reuben Davis, Sr., born on December 22, 1888, in Tallahatchie County, Davis grew up in an underpopulated corner of the Mississippi

Delta. In a short memoir Davis recalled, "I was born on a plantation in the delta section of Mississippi in the days when the timber was virgin, the hunting good, and work was something somebody else did."[8] Set in the middle of canebrakes and thick forests, the Davises' plantation oasis was a mile from the nearest white family. The railroad depot was fifteen miles away. His sole playmates were the black tenants' children, who taught him how to hunt small game. At twelve, he recalled, "I was a steady hunter, shooting coons out of trees at night wearing a headlight, hunting deer and bear and panthers with the men, both black and white."[9]

His father died when Davis was nine. As the youngest child in the family, he took the loss extremely hard. Often wandering through the woods by himself, he did not flourish at school and lasted only one semester at Mississippi College. The aimless rambling continued. Davis crossed the country riding empty boxcars until the American entry into the Great War sent him to the French battle front with the Twentieth Engineers. Severely wounded in some way that has not yet come to light, he was in various government hospitals from 1918 to 1924. His gradual recovery owed much to Helen Dick of Greenwood, Mississippi, whom he married in 1926. A Phi Beta Kappa from the University of Wisconsin, she was instrumental in starting his writing career while rearing their two children on a Delta farm near Carter, Mississippi. With money from the publication of several short stories about plantation blacks, Davis bought additional Mississippi farmland but had to relinquish it for unpaid taxes in 1935.[10]

Amid the troubles of the Depression, he must have been especially gratified with the favorable reaction to his first novel, *Butcher Bird* (1936). In it, he demonstrated an uncommonly keen ear for black speech patterns and gestures. His editors at Little, Brown doubtless expected great things from his spare, vigorous prose, but nothing was forthcoming until the appearance of his second and last novel, *Shim*, seventeen years later.

Shim, like *Butcher Bird*, won accolades in the popular press. Harnett Kane in the *New York Times*, for instance, declared, "It presents sharply, vividly, often with moving eloquence, a vanished Southern world of nature." In the story, the timber industry is invading, Kane continued, but Davis had recaptured "a place complete in color and fragrance and mutations—the 'dark dreggy water' of the lakes, the cypress knees at the swamp edges, the 'rich, sweet smell of wood smoke.'"[11] Meeting deadlines after a quick reading, reviewers failed to suspect the underlying structure of the work and interpreted it as a boy's story with a simple message about the inevitability of social and economic change in the South. Their view was not wrong, merely incomplete.

We cannot guess if Davis really understood his own motives in writing the story. But this much is certain: he intended no artist-tells-all confession. In a sketch designed for publicity, he contended that, for someone with the ordinary "instinct" for "privacy," it was repellent "to reveal personal thoughts and experience" in a book that "any Tom, Dick or Harry" might "pick up." In fact, "revealing yourself is the one thing you can't do, no matter how hard you try. I'll be, as unknown to you," Davis promised, "as your wife, your husband, your child, your parents—or for that matter, yourself, at the end of the book as at the beginning." Such authorial announcements cannot be taken at face value. Mark Twain taught us that with his notice in *Huckleberry Finn:* "Persons attempting to find a motive in this narrative will be prosecuted; persons attempting to find a moral in it will be banished." William Faulkner similarly found it distressing to have reporters probe for autobiographical materials to gratify the curiosity of readers. As historian Joel Williamson puts it, "When forced to emerge into public view against his will, he often stood behind a shield of impeccably correct manners and a reticence approaching taciturnity."[12] In his Faulkner-like hostility toward the inquiring reader who would like to peel back the layers of defenses, Davis wryly admitted that no words of his could prevent speculation. "In this lifelong scuffle of trying to figure out what makes a man tick, you can't win for losing. From eavesdropper to psychiatrist, from Peeping Tom to philosopher, it's the same, primary absorption of us all." Although not intending to universalize his point, he had exposed a basic tension in American and particularly southern letters—the contradiction between the compulsion to tell stories and the desire to preserve the pride and privacy of the self and family under siege. The narrative tradition necessarily feeds on gossip, but at the same time exposure threatens the fragile crust of community order and family protectiveness.[13]

Regardless of the warning, Davis's *Shim* hints at deeply emotional factors behind its composition. But first, a brief sketch of the contents. The hero of the story, thirteen-year-old Shim Govan, seems estranged from his father, who appears as a distant, opaque figure. Instead, the boy idolizes Henry, the plantation's black major domo, who is neither a replication of Twain's Jim nor Faulkner's mythic and mystical Sam Fathers, the proxy father for Ike McCaslin, in the famous story "The Bear." Davis's Henry is fiercely self-reliant, and his motives and complexities have no bearing on his relationship with his worshipful white apprentice. Henry is a natural leader, and neither Shim nor his older brothers ever question his judgment. In fact, one recognizes Henry's race only by his dialect, since Davis never alludes to Henry's color or condition as presumably a former slave. In the Mississippi that the author knew, racial distinctions could be assumed. On their hunts in the woods, however, a meritocracy designated mentors and followers in reality as in fiction. As Davis portrays Henry, he tolerates the lad and instructs him in the lore of forest and swamp. Yet the tenant farmer is clearly aware that Shim's adoration will soon pass— when boy becomes man. Besides, Henry is more concerned with Kiz, his childless wife's youthful niece and the expert cook for the plantation household. As her surrogate father, Henry loves the bright-eyed adolescent girl as intensely as Shim loves him, his father substitute. But Kiz rebels against her uncle's guardianship and naively seeks sexual adventure with an itinerant black, who turns out to be insane. He seduces her and abducts her into the swamp. Finally aware of his madness, she vainly tries to return home; the crazed lover kills her but remorsefully remains at her side. Running down his prey in the forest, Henry slays the murderer in aggrieved revenge. In the tale, the law does not intervene in that remote locale.

The plot proceeds from that tragedy to the dramatic conclusion, a far better close than the one that Twain fashioned for Huck Finn. Henry, still mourning his loss, organizes a panther hunt that he secretly intends to be his parting gift to the boy. Shim differs from Faulkner's Chick Mallison in *Intruder in the Dust.* In that story of growing up southern, Chick's relationship to the independent-minded Lucas Beauchamps (Beecham) is highly conflicted. Instead, Davis's Shim is grateful and not humiliated when the black farmer Henry saves the boy's honor by retrieving his weapon, which he had accidentally dropped in deep water. Skipping school some days later, Shim drops by to converse with his old friend but finds his cabin deserted and forlorn. Carved on a wooden porch step are the words "I LEAVES IT WITH YOU. Suddenly the fresh morning air was choking to breathe."[14] The child imagines that his friend has disappeared like a ghost far into the wilderness — "farther back in the woods, far away from outsiders."[15] Shim realizes that not only did he fail to know his friend and the pain he was suffering with the loss of Kiz, but he was also not even aware that Henry could read and write.

At one time Henry, we had learned earlier, had owned his own farm but had relinquished it, he told Shim, to save himself trouble. "I moved here with the Captain [Shim's father] and lets him do the worrying," he claims. But disfranchised, poor, and unorganized, Henry, like so many others of his class and color, resentfully could never speak up; it was wiser to sell out. Like the journalist W. J. Cash in *The Mind of the South*, Davis recognized that, for all their boasting, whites could not read their black neighbors' minds at all. In this case, it is slave Jim who "lights out for the territory," not Huck Finn. Instead, Davis has the boy grieving and left solitary in a world without trust or meaning.

In the typical self-centeredness of the young, Shim naively assumes a romantic departure into the deep forests for his hero, but the reader may interpret the situation in a different light. Henry might have had enough of backwoods plantation folk. His overwhelming sense of lost independence and vulnerability to misfortune had finally become unbearable during his time of grief. Earlier we learn that banks refused him loans during the hard times of the late 1880s and early 1890s, when cotton prices fell to record lows and drove thousands of independent black Delta farmers like Henry from their land. The tenant farmer's problems with white oppression thus had long preceded this episode. Maybe he headed for the train depot and the city, but that possibility, of course, is outside the story's frame. Rather, it is Henry's sense of aloneness that Davis dramatically renders as he has Shim ride into the yard and see nothing "but emptiness." Yet with the artist's commanding discipline, he turns from sentimentality by remarking simply in the novel's last line: "He rode out the gate and down the turnrow toward home."[16] The reader is not permitted to enter the sense of bereavement that the writer intended for Shim to feel, but we suspect it with a rush of consternation.

The story resolutely stands by itself. It would make a superb film. But its implications become clearer when we know more about the author himself. The character Shim's boyish attitude toward his mother and father — Capt'n Govan and Miss Cherry — reflected what Davis himself, reclusive and troubled, would like to have been true of his own experience. But the difference between the fancy of the novel and the actuality of his emotional life was enormous. Like Twain's *Huckleberry Finn*, *Shim* is more dream than reality despite its seemingly natural evocation of a vanished time and place. The brisk, compelling stories of fights with bears, panthers, alligators, snakes — and murderers, white and black — move the story at a quickening pace chapter by chapter. It is a most exciting story. Nonetheless, the reader completes the work with a sense of foreboding. Just as Huck's flight to the wilderness at the end of Twain's novel seems almost purposeless, we wonder why at the end of *Shim* we feel poised on the edge of an abyss. Davis seems to have described a loss far greater than a yearning for a return to youthful days hunting in the forest shadows. His sense of loss for the departure of his African American elder is too extreme, or so it seems to a reader thoroughly caught up in the feelings attributed to the boy.

Not long ago I wrote an introduction for the University Press of Mississippi's republication of *Shim*. JoAnne Pritchard, the editor for the reprint, sent a copy to Reuben Davis's son, Nicholas Davis, a professor of architecture at Auburn University. He wrote me with particular regard to the curious sense of sadness and troubled loss that I thought the novel evoked. Professor Davis explained that his father's early life could account for the atmosphere of overwhelming grief that runs through the narrative like a low booming of kettledrums in a symphony.

Reuben Davis had not merely lost his father at age nine: he had witnessed his murder. Before his young eyes, Reuben's two half-brothers had shot their father to death at that plantation deep in the forest. They did so because Reuben, Sr., abusive in his drunkenness, had come to kill his wife. In real life, as in the story, the law did not intervene in the wild fastnesses of the Delta. As blood kin to both the victim and the killers, the novelist Davis had to shoulder a terrible burden of guilt, confusion, and anger thereafter. His half-brothers were guilty of liquidating his father in order to save their mother. Reuben Davis's son Nicholas told me recently that he remembers when his father had said to him, "If they had not killed him, I would have." The episode might have been an ancient Greek legend depicted on a Sophoclean stage. "Daddy's feelings of sorrow, alienation, and even guilt sent him off on long flips alone, mostly hoboing all over the U.S.A.," Nicholas Davis explained. "Though he did not help shoot his father, he belonged to the family who did, and this *might* have created bad feelings against him. All of this is to point out that he felt an outcast from his own fatherland for about twenty years, and this probably intensified his feelings for the entire contents of SHIM."[17] Reuben Davis hoped that no one outside the family would ever learn of these events. Nor could he even write about it directly. He confided to his wife, Helen, that by age eleven, "I was more a man than I am now—I could protect myself from any danger; I could get a peaceful living from fields and woods; I could rest."[18] Rest is not usually what a boy looks for or a man remembers of his youth. Thus the hunting in what he remembered as a lost Eden was not just a matter of fresh delight. The encounters with wild animals that he made so dramatic in *Shim* had been his early means of self-defense—against perils in a wilderness of human betrayal and unpredictability. Exploring the canebrakes and hammocks of pine and water oak also served as a diversion from terrifying memories. What thoughts would pass through his mind as he tracked rabbits, snakes, and bears?

The reticence with which Reuben Davis wrote *Shim* actually served its author well—as it often does. Emily Dickinson once noted in a poem, "Tell all the Truth but tell it slant—/ Success in Circuit lies."[19] Davis fulfilled that sentiment. A personal acquaintance with tragedy led him to create in fiction a tentatively more hopeful story, bleak though the conclusion is. Davis sought to separate his private life from his art, a common yearning analogous to that of William Faulkner's attempt to shield his inner life. "It is my ambition," Faulkner wrote Malcolm Cowley in 1949, "to be as a private individual, abolished and voided from history, leaving it markless, no refuge save the printed books."[20] That desire for fame on the one hand and freedom from close scrutiny on the other were marks of a style that Reuben Davis also shared as a member of a close-knit if troubled family. But there is also the writer's need and burden of silence itself—what John Keats called *agonie ennuyeuse*—the tedious agony—out of which, Tillie Olsen contends, may come sterility but, if overcome, greatness of achievement.[21]

Instead of confessing the story in autobiographical form, Reuben Davis wrote a tale of considerably less calamity than the one he had endured. He could not fully suppress the horror of that event. The tension between the life he lived and the one he splendidly transformed into a boy's adventure story gave his work a texture that places it alongside the most moving work in the genre of boys' literature.

Parental loss as prelude to depression and subsequent creativity was by no means a rare occurrence in the annals of twentieth-century writers. Recently Paul Auster, the New York author of *City of Glass* and *Moon Palace,* novels of gothic complexity, observed,

> I think my work has come out of a position of intense personal despair, a very deep nihilism and hopelessness about the world, the fact of our own transience and mortality, the inadequacy of language, the isolation of one person from another. And yet, at the same time, I've wanted to express the beauty and extraordinary happiness of feeling yourself alive, of breathing in the air, the joy of being alive in your own skin.

Sam Auster, the writer's father, experienced a tragedy when he was only nine years old: his mother murdered her husband, Sam's father, with a pistol. Acquitted on grounds of insanity, she was afflicted with "acute mania," according to the family physician's testimony at her trial. The calamity had a devastating impact on the boy and, in turn, on his son, Paul Auster, who was reared by a troubled parent whose wife had left him early in their marriage. The grand house in New Jersey, with leaded windows and slate roof, in which Paul and his father lived was haunted by an almost Poe-like curse. The novelist did not learn the truth about his family's violent history until a short while before Sam Auster's death.[22]

Certainly the impulse to write out of a need to express the inexpressible from one's past was evident in Auster's life. It affected earlier writers as well, most particularly the poet Conrad Aiken, who was originally from Savannah before tragedy sent the child to New England, where his grandparents lived. His life of imagination, like that of Reuben Davis, filled a spiritual chasm. (The story is partially represented in the recent best-seller *Midnight in the Garden of Good and Evil* by John Berendt.)[23] His father, William Ford Aiken, a Harvard-trained physician who had established a practice in Savannah, Georgia, suffered from psychotic manic-depression. In his moments of madness, he accused his wife of betraying the marriage bed and ranted incoherently in other paranoid frenzies, sometimes directed at his petrified children. Though brilliant in his studies and eager to win his father's praise,

Conrad could never please the unpredictable parent, and he early felt that his mother, Anna, rejected him. "I was cruelly beaten. I was humiliated. My pride and will were broken before I had come to my seventh year. I was in a state of continual terror." [24]

Early on February 27, 1901, when Conrad was eleven years old, he heard the report of two quick shots coming from his parents' bedroom. Hurrying into the chamber, he found both father and mother dead. At that abrupt moment Conrad, like Reuben Davis under similar circumstances, became older than his years. After taking charge of the household servants and his younger brother and sister, he ran to the police and explained the tragedy in cool detail.[25] At the time of the tragedy, relatives and friends thought silence on such horrors was the best and most convenient means for wiping out memories in children. We can imagine that for reasons of law as well as family pride, the Davises had likewise kept tight silence on the tragic event. Reticence, however, drove Aiken's sense of guilt deeper into himself. Children ordinarily blame themselves for such traumas. In their natural self-absorption, they have very little perspective on the adult world. At the same time, the murder and suicide shaped his extraordinary art. Malcolm Cowley once called Aiken "the buried giant of twentieth-century writing." [26] As critic James Wheeler remarks, "It was a wonderful irony, of course, that the very oedipal wound which killed his parents, became the driving force of the son's poetic act, and through it, of his salvation." In the 1920s Aiken thought of doing away with himself more than once but each time managed to regain his equilibrium—and continued to produce some of the most remarkable verse in the American idiom.[27] Yet, as in all these instances of almost numbing horrors, tragedy was translated into beauty just as in Davis's *Shim.* Aiken's "Silent Snow, Secret Snow," a short story, revealed his understanding of a child's descent into fantasy and madness with chilling effect.

Yet he never acknowledged that his poetry or short stories had any relationship to his own life.[28] No less than Reuben Davis, Aiken had no intention of self-exposure even though admitting that his concerns were egocentric. He told Malcolm Cowley that autobiography cast in the third person, as in his work *Blue Voyage,* was more "honest" than a "straight confession" because it made possible his intention "to give myself *away.*" Poets like himself are "the most private" and individualistic of people and find that through an "extreme privacy of awareness they become themselves *universals.*" Aiken protected the details of his life and personality apart from their expression in fiction and poetry, which were under his full control. He chastised the psychoanalytic critic Jay Martin for interpreting his work as simply drawn from his personal experience.[29]

Loss of parents, either by death or by "lack of sufficient sympathy," the historian Arnold Toynbee declared, robs the child of an opportunity to imitate the values they could convey. That "voluntary legacy," he maintained, is no less significant than biologically inherited characteristics. The source of depression often has seemed to lie in this kind of deprivation, in which later tragic events in life can reactivate the same feelings of loss experienced in childhood.[30] The following authors, when relatively young, also lost one or both parents: Edgar Allan Poe, Edmund Ruffin, Kate Chopin, Katherine Anne Porter, Shelby Foote, James Agee, John Kennedy Toole, Walker Percy, Gail Godwin, Kaye Gibbons, Truman Capote, Harry Crews, and

William Styron. Many more felt emotionally abandoned by absconding or unmindful fathers, dejected mothers, or sometimes dead brothers and sisters. Among writers affected by such circumstances were Langston Hughes, Richard Wright, Jean Toomer, Ellen Glasgow, Evelyn Scott, Carson McCullers, Thomas Wolfe, William Faulkner, Eugene O'Neill, Tennessee Williams; and on it goes.

Sometimes suicide in a family deeply affected children who later became both artists and victims of the familial and genetic curse as well. Ernest Hemingway was a young man when his father shot himself to death, an act his son would repeat in his own old age. Anne Sexton, who later followed the same path to the grave, lost both her sister and an aunt to self-inflicted death, and her father was an alcoholic. John Berryman's father, like his son, also committed suicide; so did Berryman's aunt on his father's side. The poet's anger did not wholly mask his sense of an irretrievable love: "I spit upon this dreadful banker's grave / who shot his heart out in a Florida dawn / O ho alas alas / When will the indifference come." [31]

William Styron, for instance, is convinced that his still lingering struggles with depression stem from "the death of my mother when I was thirteen" from cancer. According to the psychiatric literature, Styron continues, a disaster at that age is "sometimes likely to create nearly irreparable emotional havoc." Equally important in Styron's case was the clinical depression of his father, who "battled the gorgon for much of his lifetime and had been hospitalized in my boyhood after a despondent spiraling downward that in retrospect I saw greatly resembled mine." [32]

So repressed were Styron's feelings about these events that he had once claimed that his novels dealt solely with "human institutions: humanly contrived situations which cause people to live in wretched unhappiness." [33] He had no conception that they concerned themes with which he was subconsciously wrestling. Once he had faced his own madness and recovered, however, he began rereading his own works. In those parts of his published novels "where my heroines have lurched down pathways toward doom," he writes in his autobiographical sketch, *Darkness Visible,* "I was stunned to perceive how accurately I had created the landscape of depression in the minds of these young women. . . . Thus depression, when it finally came to me, was in fact no stranger, not even a visitor totally unannounced; it had been tapping at my door for decades." Moreover, Styron's portrayal of Nat Turner, the Southampton rebel, gives the protagonist all the characteristics of chronic depression. Contemporary critics, however, failed to notice the emotional affinity between author and subject in their haste to condemn Styron's alleged racism. [34] Having rediscovered his own psychic history, Styron, in his most recent work, the semi-autobiographical *Tidewater Morning,* like Reuben Davis's *Shim,* centered the action on himself as a boy facing the crises of parental death. Styron, however, is much more willing to explore his own feelings directly than was Davis, who belonged to the earlier, more reticent generation. [35] As Styron suggests, these emotional traumas assisted writers in entering the lives of characters quite different from themselves in terms of sex, age, or color: Davis's Henry, the black tenant farmer; Styron's suicidal Sophie in *Sophie's Choice* and his melancholy Nat Turner, the slave rebel; Faulkner's Caddy, Quentin Compson's troubled sister, in *The Sound and the Fury.* The fragmentation of the artist's personality that melancholia and grief seem to entail makes such imaginative antinomies possible.

Thus, depression of a severe nature has been paradoxically the source of both artful creation and irremediable injury in twentieth-century American writers. It is the wellspring of personal agony and sometimes even self-destructive inclinations. But on the whole, if an artist's goal is to gain some purchase over death by living on in print, they were the literary victors, regardless of how they lived or died. "I believe you have to discover your true self through ordeal," the late Walker Percy once said. "It helps enormously when a person can make a friend with her terror, plumb the depths of her depression. 'There's gold down there in the darkness,' said Dr. Jung." Percy, himself the son and grandson of suicides, had reason to know whereof he spoke.[36]

The evidence of melancholy as the source of creativity that Percy discerned is especially clear in the writing of poetry. The incidence of depression and potential or realized suicide among poets (whether by birth English or American), even when compared with novelists, is astonishing. English psychoanalyst Felix Brown has concluded from a pioneering study that some 70 percent of the poets in the *Oxford Book of English Verse* lost one or both of their parents before the artistic child reached the late teens. "In one study death of either parent before 15 is almost twice as frequent in these depressive cases [among poets] as in the general population," Brown observes.[37] Among the American ranks of poets the number who had to be hospitalized for depressive disorders included such figures as T. S. Eliot, Robert Lowell, Edna St. Vincent Millay, Delmore Schwartz, and Ezra Pound. Those poets who killed themselves included Hart Crane, John Gould Fletcher, Randall Jarrell, John Berryman, Anne Sexton, and Vachel Lindsay.[38]

With this record in mind, the task remains to explore the career of Sylvia Plath, who fled down the corridors of episodic madness and, sadly, came to an end that Reuben Davis, her counterpart in these pages, escaped. Women's experiences with depression and art in midcentury America shared some of the characteristics of such male representatives as Davis, Aiken, and Styron. But there were differences as well. From the era of Jane Austen, writing poetry and fiction was something "ladies" of an independent bent had been permitted—so long as their pens did not cross the boundaries of delicacy.[39] Brave spirits like the melancholy Charlotte Brontë in some measure challenged convention. The constraints, however, gave way only slowly. No American writer better exemplifies the discouragements facing female writers than Plath, a poet whose husband's fame and brilliance overshadowed her own strivings during her lifetime. Yet she also demonstrates the accuracy of Percy's comment about the rich vein of inner experience which the writer ought to mine. As a woman writer who had to confront a male-dominated empire of letters, she also reveals the role that depression and childhood struggle have played in the creation of a feminine literary tradition. After all, she was scarcely the first woman writer in the United States to brave the problem of melancholia and configure it into art. Among her predecessors were Emily Dickinson, Henry James's suicidal friend Constance Fenimore Woolson, James's younger sister Alice, Kate Chopin, Ellen Glasgow, Zelda

Fitzgerald, Dorothy Parker, Shirley Jackson, Jean Stafford, Anne Sexton, and more recently, the manic best-selling author Patricia Cornwell and two contemporary southern novelists, Gail Godwin and Kaye Gibbons.[40]

In all these cases there is good reason to suspect that genetic factors, rather than just troubled childhoods alone, played a substantial role in both the melancholy and the talents that these women shared. Of course, the neurobiological elements can scarcely be proved beyond a doubt, at least not until DNA tests are more sophisticated than they are now. Nonetheless, reports in the national media indicate how fast the medical advances have recently progressed for an understanding of the brain's neural systems and mental disorders that arise from their malfunctioning. Elliot S. Gershon, a leading expert at the National Institutes of Health, concludes that "affective disorders" like those Plath and others, male or female, experienced "are familial, since the rate in relatives of patients is consistently about two or three times the rate in relatives of appropriately chosen case controls."[41]

Sylvia Plath's parental history is lost behind the veils of family reticence. Aurelia Plath, her mother, never quite acknowledged her daughter's mental problems, much less any possibility of familial precedents for them. Because of its very severity, Sylvia Plath's manic-depressive condition of violent mood swings had to have arisen from genetic as well as environmental factors. In any event, the death of her father, a distinguished professor of entomology at Boston University, in 1940, had a devastating impact on his eight-year-old daughter. Years later Plath, in a powerful poem, mourned, "Daddy, I have had to kill you. / You died before I had time."[42] In her fictionalized autobiography, *The Bell Jar,* she recalls that in adulthood she realized when she burst into tears at the sight of her father's gravestone that she had never cried over his death before. So, she continues, "I laid my face to the smooth face of the marble and howled my loss into the cold salt rain." Writing in verse and prose were the means for expressing her grief and anger at his sudden departure. Indeed, her remembrance of how neither she nor her mother had wept at the time was accurate. Her mother believed in adopting the cheerful approach. Her daughter, however, reacted to the news of the tragedy by dully remarking in her profound resentment, "I'll never speak to God again." Then the little girl trudged off to school in untearful grief and unreconcilable misery.[43]

A precocious child, Sylvia Plath was thereafter terrified of abandonment. As she grew up, Sylvia sought to ward off pain by throwing herself with abandon into everything she did: biking, intent study, group projects at school, tennis—and writing. Nonetheless, her father's death had obliterated her self-confidence. School activities of all sorts became a way to shore up a fear of losing respect and a means to evade the sense of inner void. She strove with increasing fervor for fame, even as a youngster, but earned success chiefly with school authorities, not with her peers. In the ninth grade she lost a hard-fought election for class secretary and remarked in her diary, "Perhaps I was doomed always to be on the outside."[44]

As Anne Stevenson records in her biography, in these years Sylvia won prizes—including a college scholarship from Olive Higgins Prouty, inspiration for the long-running radio soap opera *Stella Dallas*—but captured no popularity contests at Smith College. Yet despite her increasing promise as a published writer and winner of awards and high grades and her almost desperate concern to keep ever busy, she could be sarcastic, arrogant, and sullen. Such behavior masked a sense of insecurity. It suggests that she was judging herself by impossible standards, and so she scrutinized others with an equally critical eye. Those who knew her were well advised to keep their distance at times. She had a biting tongue, and her sometimes mean-spirited self-centeredness could be exasperating.[45]

Behind this behavior was her mental illness. It was not merely a set of neurotic tendencies, which are subject to some degree of self-control, but an unmanageable psychosis that rose or fell according to its own arbitrary imperatives.[46] Indeed, during her college days at Smith, Sylvia Plath's manic-depressive illness was coming so fast upon her that even encouraging letters from publisher Harold Straus, impressed by a short story she had written, failed to give her much solace. She veered uncontrollably from mania to despair. In her journal in 1952, she pondered her internal plight with these words, "It is like lifting a bell jar off a securely clock-worklike functioning community, and seeing all the little people stop, gasp, blow up, and float in the inrush (or rather outrush) of the rarified scheduled atmosphere—poor little frightened people, flailing impotent arms in the aimless air." She felt that she was "running madly, in a crowded schedule, in a squirrel cage of busy people."[47] Though prompted by her emotional dismay, her remarks are particularly acute for so young an observer of the human condition. Her words show an affinity with David Riesman, whose book *The Lonely Crowd* criticized the contemporary impulse for conformity.

Like Edgar Allan Poe and Robert Lowell, both victims of manic-depression, Sylvia dreaded most this very possibility: loss of reason. In the summer before her junior year at Smith, she recorded in her diary how she walked under the shade trees of Wellesley's residential streets and imagined herself living in the body of one inhabitant or another—anyone's but her own frightening flesh and bone. Of course, as mentioned earlier, poets and writers like Plath must cultivate a skill for imagining others' lives and hearing a variety of voices—conceptualizations that are essential in the creative process. For instance, an early poem, "Temper of Time," deals with the emotional wraiths that had hunted her down: "Black birds of omen," she wrote, "Now prowl on the bough" while "tall skeletons walk." The poem ends with the lines, "There's a hex on the cradle / And death in the pot."[48] The poem is interesting less for its inherent merit than its indication of her themes and direction so early in her writing career.

In her emerging creativity she was beginning to find a way to express the mysterious sources of her solitary wretchedness: "So I pressed thumb-down-on-latch and step up into the light, into tomorrow, into people known by sight, by sound, by touch, by smell, by flavor ... and the door closes behind me, and I turn the lock with a click that shuts out the disturbing wasteland of sleeping streets and fenceless acres of night."[49] However effectively she translated the emotions of the illness, the disease itself remained always a source of mortification and sense of disgrace. Robert Graves observed of his own experience that after the "intoxication" of manic feelings passed, "my chief emotional reaction is shame and disgust with myself, and a wonder that my fear of death could be so wonderfully and idiotically twisted. That the facing humiliation, of despair, or deprivation should produce a desire for death is quite natural."[50] Plath could have echoed his sentiments.

Her most critical biographer, Anne Stevenson, concludes that "her gift was for romantic self-aggrandizing" as she found herself "trapped in her story, condemned to telling it again and again to whoever would listen." Although that might seem plausible, one must remember that those cursed with a genetic and, at that time, medically untreatable mental disorder struggled with emotions too wild to be vanquished. Plath confessed in her diary that "with groggy sleepless blood dragging through my veins," she was not far from choosing death over the persistence of pain in life. Successes in her senior year did nothing to relieve her misery, rigidly hidden from the outside world. "I feel behind my eyes a numb, paralyzing cavern, a pit of hell, a mimicking nothingness," she grieved. "I want to kill myself, to escape from responsibility, to draw back into the womb. I do not know who I am, where I am going."[51]

For such problems of identity as these, the parent, not the victim, is often blamed. Aurelia Plath, a woman of intelligence and great intensity, had tried to please her austere, patriarchal, European husband, who stubbornly rejected her advice to see a doctor despite his illness from cancer. As a widow, she had reared Sylvia and her son with the attention, discipline, and self-sacrifice that women of her day were expected to employ. One can too readily overanalyze and thus morally condemn her. Just as a mother might be overly protective of a child with a severe physical handicap, so too, Aurelia Plath confronted moods and conduct in her daughter that would defy both the soothing and the authoritative approaches of the best of mothers. The analyst D. W. Winnicott has called such women as Aurelia Plath "good enough mothers." He refers to normal circumstances in which mothers encourage the child's sense of selfhood. But the term could well be used to describe abnormal situations in which the mother, with the usual imperfections of the human species, must find means to compensate for elements missing in the child. Love is necessary, of course, but can it alone suffice, meeting all the complexities that childish tendencies leading toward insanity can generate? The child rearing of "good enough mothers," no matter how caring, simply cannot supply the deficiencies in mentally afflicted children's ego development.[52] With a daughter who could plunge herself into the very depths of despondency, what could a mother like Aurelia Plath do but be forever cheerful while trying to show her daughter the brighter, gentler side? She was not consigned merely to being a mother but a psychiatric nurse of sorts to a patient whose eventual cure was at best problematic. In 1961, during a visit to Sylvia and Ted Hughes in London, Aurelia Plath exclaimed after a lifetime of frustration, "Everything I do is *wrong;* I can't seem to do anything right." Breaking with her usual optimism about Sylvia, she added, "I just don't know how Ted stands it."[53]

Sylvia Plath could barely stand it herself. Like Virginia Woolf, another woman writer who chose the option of death, Sylvia Plath early learned that her uncontrollable sense of emptiness that rose and fell so rapidly had only two resolutions—the temporary but exhilarating act of creating art and the temptation of suicide. Writing, claimed Sylvia Plath, was the only way to "get rid of the accusing, never satisfied gods who surround me like a crown of thorns." The language is remarkable in its poetic resonance and its self-dramatization. Both Woolf and Plath were victims of unsettled childhoods. Equally if not possibly more significant, however, was the second factor of biological dysfunction in the very seat of consciousness. Referring to Virginia Woolf, literary critic Thomas Caramagno notes, "Suicide is at once a personal and an impersonal event, an intended act—at the very least, it is an attempt to escape one's pain—but it is also one that occurs when . . . conditions may have undermined the intention-mediating neural circuits in the brain."[54] So it was with Sylvia Plath. An imbalance of serotonin, dopamine, and other chemicals that move thought through the synapses creates the conditions for melancholia. In some instances, chemical malfunctioning of a similar nature may be a significant factor in the frantic drive of the victim to kill all consciousness by dying.

One expert calls depression "a biological storm in the brain." After lengthy investigation, psychiatrist Kay Redfield Jamison, who has eloquently told the story of her own college-age distress with both mania and depression, affirms that the mental disorder has a biological component. Neither she, Sylvia Plath, nor any other victim has much if any control over these devastating neurological conditions. That state of wandering through the labyrinth of isolation was particularly hard to bear in the era before the current array of antidepressants became available.[55] Earlier in the century Emil Kraepelin and other psychiatric authorities had begun to recognize the disease as a physical as well as emotional disorder.[56] In Sylvia's time, however, the illness was still considered in the lay world a terrible stigma, a signal of unforgivable moral failure, and few indeed believed in the efficacy of psychotherapy, however defective it might have been.

Sylvia Plath's mental health deteriorated precipitously in 1953. A symptom of her descent into mental hell was her intense identification with the plight of the Rosenbergs, about to be executed for treason. It seemed as if she imagined herself strapped in the electric chair. In *The Bell Jar*, she explained, "I couldn't help wondering what it would be like, being burned alive all along your nerves. I thought it must be the worst thing in the world." Their Jewishness also drew them to her. It was as if her father's Germanic roots had been responsible for the Holocaust and other forms of anti-Semitic persecution.[57] Aurelia Plath's fragile health was also a factor, but still worse was Sylvia's rejection for a seminar in fiction writing at Harvard under Frank O'Connor's direction. She scolded herself unmercifully. The decision against her admission signified, she felt, a complete annihilation of her existence. Meeting famous members of the New York intelligentsia while working for *Mademoiselle* did nothing to lift her spirits, and she entered what St. John of the Cross called "the dark night of the soul." In a climactic outburst, she cried out, "Oh, Mother, the world is too rotten! I want to die!" Alarmed, Aurelia Plath put her daughter under the care of an inexpert physician, who ordered the torture of shock treatments without any prior discussion or follow-up with the distraught patient. He then went on vacation! Soon after, diving into the maelstrom of mental confusion, Sylvia swallowed a bottle of sleeping pills and crept into a crawl space under the house. There, unconscious, she remained curled up for two days. Frantic over her disappearance, Aurelia Plath called the police, and soon officers, friends, and news reporters were scouring the neighborhood. A low moan from her hiding spot finally revealed her location. Sylvia was hospitalized "more dead than alive," said a nurse at the Newton-Wellesley Hospital. Yet while at first still suicidal, she recovered eventually and returned for her final year at Smith.[58]

Full of honors and enjoying a rising reputation for her published short stories, Sylvia graduated and looked forward to two years abroad. "If only I get accepted at Cambridge!" she exclaimed to her mother. "My whole life would explode in a rainbow."[59] How seldom do lives explode in rainbows. For Sylvia, however, the prospect represented release, a door to possible independence and maybe an escape from the blue devils, as melancholia once was called, that might follow her across the seas. Furthermore, like other manic-depressives, Sylvia had a desperate need for external validation. High grades, prizes, special notice of the Manhattan intelligentsia, acceptance into prestigious summer writing programs were supposed to fill the empty vessel within. As a recipient of a Fulbright scholarship, she felt vindicated and triumphant when she was accepted into Newnham College in 1955. That was also the year I went to King's College and first met her.

As it happened, I was affiliated with a group of poets who put together a slim but handsome journal during the winter of 1956. The *St. Botolph's Review*, as it was impiously dubbed, contained Ted Hughes's first published poems. Sylvia bought a copy from me and raced off on her bicycle. Having read the poems, hours later she found me a second time and asked how she could meet Ted Hughes, whose poems she had already memorized.[60] Astonished at her almost off-putting effervescence, I invited her to attend a celebration for the *Review* at the Cambridge Women's Union in Falcon Yard that evening. She did so, and immediately fell in love with him. Ted Hughes struck her as the ideal masculine intellectual—handsome, brilliant, a combination of virile protector and poetic genius. "Sylvia had always, in her way, gushed and gone on and been very public about all the men she . . . was spending time with," recalls Jane Baltzell, one of Sylvia's housemates at Whitstead Cottage, a Newnham College lodging, where they were living. But, Jane continued, "this was not so with Ted. I remember thinking she was serious about Ted because she didn't talk about him, had absolutely nothing to say about him."[61]

Yet for all the romance of those days, Sylvia had to encounter the ambivalence of her fellow students, an attitude that she had generated against herself, consciously or not. At Whitstead, there had been mild trouble. Jane Baltzell (now Jane Kopp), a brilliant Marshall Fellow and poet from Pembroke College, Brown University, re-members that Sylvia was not well liked by the other residents. They were a rather prissy lot, as I recall. Some disliked Sylvia's supposedly vulgar American ways. She raved effusively over things the English thought unremarkable. Once the authorities at Whitstead scolded her for allowing a young male visitor to use an upstairs bathroom, where he might see forbidden feminine things.[62] (In those days, the university rules governing parietal hours and similar regulations for both men and women were, by today's standards, ludicrous. Many of us were military veterans, and women like Sylvia and Jane were already college graduates, senior to the other inmates at Whitstead.)

Sylvia thought of Jane as her "Doppelgänger"—her double, a second identity.

Baltzell grew very exasperated with the role of double that Sylvia wanted her to play. It "gave [me] the creeps," Jane once exclaimed. In truth, however, they were somewhat alike in appearance though not in temperament. Both were striking blonds, strong-limbed, with glowing cheeks and shining teeth in a very northern European way. Subject to odd spells of envy, Sylvia resented Jane's intelligence, sensitivity, and self-control. Jane also played the classical piano with considerable talent. She was unquestionably gifted in her own right. Sylvia once told her "double" that "Cambridge wasn't big enough for both of us" and, though laughing, "she sort of meant it," as Jane later confided to a biographer. After one vacation, Jane explained to me how she and Sylvia had had a big quarrel in Paris. Sylvia had been consumed with rage because Jane, exhausted from a stormy channel crossing, had inadvertently locked her out of the hotel room and slept on through her frantic banging on the door. To be sure, Sylvia had reason for grievance, but her fury was extraordinary. Despite Sylvia's erratic moods, Jane proved a loyal friend. Although she hinted at some other problems with her hotel roommate, she was too discreet to gossip to me or any other man about Sylvia's lovemaking with "Richard S" on that expedition, as biographers have later recounted.[63] Baltzell did, however, complain once in a while about the way Sylvia would appropriate clothing from Jane's closet without a by-your-leave.

If Sylvia had trouble getting along with even so temperate a friend as Jane Baltzell, her associations with the poets who were Ted's friends were also problematic. Consisting of a dozen or so young men with shared interests in poetry, the group generally met in the afternoons or evenings at the Anchor on Silver Street overlooking the Cam. They had not known Plath before her dramatic evening at the Women's Union, but weeks before had read her poems and ephemera in *Granta* and other Cambridge papers that remained inaccessible to their own work. They judged her poetry shallow and phony. Besides, she published in American magazines like the *Ladies' Home Journal* and *Mademoiselle,* in which male poets would scarcely deign to appear. Lucas Myers was an American friend of Hughes and prominent figure in the preparation of the *St. Botolph's Review* for publication. On one occasion, Myers contended that her ambition shone through her poems, "or so we thought, and we thought it was not legitimate to write poetry which should come down on the poet somewhere, out of sheer will."[64] With these penetrating opinions we were all in agreement, but smugly unaware that her talent might later mature.

The attitude of Ted Hughes's Cambridge friends did not help make the path of courtship and love smooth and cheering. Also at the beginning Hughes himself may not have been as enthusiastic about the marriage as Sylvia was. She could press very hard for something she desperately wanted. Sylvia earnestly believed that Ted could be her salvation and free her from her own worst compulsions. He would help her achieve fresh knowledge of herself and enhance her drive toward poetic greatness. At the beginning of a courting, any such conviction would certainly place strains on the relationship unless the other party welcomes the prospect of becoming a personal therapist. In any event, on June 16, 1956, at the Church of St. George the Martyr in Bloomsbury, London, Hughes did marry her "against his better judgment." At the start of their love life Ted Hughes "fundamentally felt apologetic," Myers remembers, at least when they were around the Cambridge poets.[65] I recall our unhappy surprise to hear the news.

An element in this tense situation was something those living through that period did not consciously recognize. The St. Botolph's crowd, as Ted's friends might be called, represented a certain Anglo-American male attitude toward female writers. At that time Ernest Hemingway and William Faulkner dominated the literary landscape like great, virile colossi, however tarnished the image has lately become. To compete against such reputations must have been discouraging for a female writer like Sylvia Plath. One of her early sponsors, Stephen Spender, who had little use for any of the Botolph clique, took a typically English swipe at the supposedly female source of Sylvia's creativity. He pointed out that, while Wilfred Owen's message "came out of the peculiar circumstances of the trenches" of the Great War, the case with Plath was different. "Her femininity is that her hysteria comes completely out of herself," Spender pontificated, implying that hysteria was purely a female problem. During World War I, William Halse Rivers Rivers, senior alienist (with a curiously repetitive middle name), and his colleagues had treated such shell-shock victims as the poets Owen and Siegfried Sassoon at Craiglockhart Hospital for Officers in Scotland. Contrary to Spender's remarks, the hospital physicians concluded that hysteria was very much an internal problem with deep childhood roots for men. In some cases homosexual or bisexual inclinations added another burden of shame and remorse, as any sort of attraction to other men was a taboo no less condemned than cowardice or desertion at the front. Spender's prejudice that women's experiences were by the nature of things less dramatic, less "poetic" than those of Lord Byron dying at Missolonghi, Shelley sailing to his death off the coast of Leghorn, or Owen in a rat-infested dugout on the Western Front in the last week before the Armistice was typical of male artists of the time. What women did, even in art, did not matter—that seemed to be Spender's prognosis.[66]

In retrospect, Sylvia's early work, as the Cambridge crowd claimed, was indeed unformed. The very ambition that had set the male poets' teeth on edge, however, helps explain Ted Hughes's early successes. For all her emotional difficulties, Sylvia Plath was the ideal literary agent—efficient, knowledgeable, and persuasive as she carried a briefcase of Ted's poems on her visits to editors' offices. On the other hand, he had the poet's disdain for self-promotion, preferring to let her stoop to conquer.[67] For his part, though, Ted served as a most constructive critic, and she learned much about poetry writing from him. "Ted had a unique way of helping, stimulating, encouraging writer friends," Lucas Myers reports; "after spending an afternoon with him, they could come out with a batch of new poems from parts of themselves that had been dormant."[68]

Far from being frivolous or merely pretty, Sylvia Plath's mature verse grew out of patience, discipline, hard work, determination, and an ever deeper exploration of herself that Spender dismissed as a source of inspiration. After her marriage to Ted Hughes in 1956—and certainly partially as a result of Ted's literary help—her poetry began to assume a self-confident, probing, and serious character. She boldly reached down into her own depths, as Walker Percy later advised artists to do. Critic Richard

Blessing observes how remarkably she touches the reader's emotions. John Berryman, he points out, once observed that he sought "to terrify and comfort." So did Plath. Even though never far from death or even cruelty, the notion of comfort is evident in her poem "Kindness," written on February 1, 1963, only ten days before she died. After describing how "Dame Kindness . . . glides about my house," she ends it with the lines "here you come, with a cup of tea" and "hand me two children, two roses." Yet even in this poem, there's another, compulsive note about the creative role that has a somewhat angry edge: "The blood jet is poetry / There is no stopping it." It is as if she thought of her verse as a life stream spilling out into the world and leaving her drained and dying. In like manner, there's something infinitely sad about her lines in "Morning Song": "I'm no more your mother / Than the cloud that distills a mirror to reflect its own slow / Effacement at the wind's hand."[69]

Her late poems strike hammer blows, driven as they were by her manic state before her final decision. That period in the emotional cycle is often a time of special peril for the suicide who fears losing the inspiration of the moment and again entering into the dark shadows of madness. The verses deal with subjects that could run from the mordant to the seemingly commonplace. Yet whatever the subject, the language is dramatic and immediately arrests the reader's concern in the fashion of Coleridge's Ancient Mariner. In her poems about her dead father she reveals how, even as an adult, she still misses him and still hates him for abandoning her by dying. In "Daddy" she writes,

> I was ten when they buried you
> At twenty I tried to die
> And get back, back, back to you.

Again at thirty she would try once more, she promises, and oddly counts his death as the last of three episodes of her own suicidal efforts, as if a part of her has been buried with him. In the same poem, she inspects a picture of her father standing before a blackboard and notices "A cleft in your chin instead of your foot / But no less a devil for that"—as if her father had Satan's cloven hoof.[70]

The ordinary duties of motherhood, the exasperation with children who demand and demand in their ravenous need for love, the monotonous tasks of cleaning, feeding, shopping, and washing—these topics were then regarded as subjects unworthy of poetic notice. In the hands of Sylvia Plath, though, they become sources of madness themselves. As she interprets her experience, they stifle the creative impulse and, in a circular way, divert her from the very preoccupations with insanity and death into which domesticity seemed, in her fright, to lead her. Children's tears and "cries are hooks that catch and grate like cats." She finds herself at "the center of an atrocity" and comes to hate "babies." In "Three Women: A Poem for Three Voices," she tries to master the situation. Yet the effort is a failure, as she confesses in a prefiguring of her suicidal plans. "I am calm. I am calm. It is the calm before something awful." Hope has fled, life has no joy or meaning, only remembrances of a dead father, memories dulled in repressed fury. "I am dumb and brown. I am a seed about to break. / The brownness is my dead self, and it is sullen. / It does not wish to be more, or different."[71]

It is not surprising that throughout her life, but especially in her later years, she was most attuned to poets whose work sought, as Theodore Roethke put it, to create verse that took "the shape of the psyche itself, in times of great stress[;] that is what I wanted to write."[72] Sylvia Plath, Robert Lowell, John Berryman, Roethke, and above all, her soul-mate Anne Sexton, were kindred souls. They were united in the same preoccupation with the hovering presence of mortality that Plath knew so well. Like her, they provided death—that inevitability most of us deny—with imagery, drama, and fresh insights as if by dressing Father Death in fine literary apparel they could tame him. In the introduction to Plath's collection *Ariel,* Robert Lowell wrote perceptively about his one-time student and compatriot in the domain of despair, "Dangerous, more powerful than man, machinelike from hard training, she herself is a little like a racehorse, galloping relentlessly with risked, outstretched neck, death hurdle after death hurdle topped."[73]

Plath was also among the handful of brilliant female poets who questioned the feminine proprieties, especially those conventional demands for a delicacy that seemed to suffocate the artistic temperament. Like Adrienne Rich or Anne Sexton, Plath, in her poem "The Disquieting Muses," closes on a bitter note. The poet protests to her mother that the "kingdom" of ovaltine, piano lessons, absent father, and vigilant aunts that she presented her is not her style at all: "Mother, mother. But no frown of mine / Will betray the company I keep."[74]

In one of Plath's most arresting poems, "The Moon and the Yew Tree" (1961), the reader enters the sunless, "cold and planetary" inner realm—the desperation of one living in a world that offers no hope or succor. The setting is a churchyard at night. "Fumy, spiritous mists inhabit this place," the narrator exclaims. "How I would like to believe in tenderness." An effigy of Mary is supposed to offer that gift of compassion, but instead, "her blue garments unloose small bats and owls." Richard Blessing claims that the reference to the virtues of affection, opposite to hopelessness, creates a tension, a "motion rocking back and forth between these emotional poles." Yet there is no self-adjusting spinning on an emotional axis, but rather an ultimate denial of salvation, a repudiation of love. The gyre is hurtling downward end over end. Unlike the melancholy Walker Percy, who, in his novel *Lancelot* provides a tentative "yes" to the possibility of redemption, Plath arrives at the bleakest conclusion possible. Her poem makes the point emphatically in the last lines: The moon, she writes, is blind to the gentler facets of humanity. "She is bald and wild. / And the message of the yew tree is blackness—blackness and silence."[75] Art alone, one might guess, is the only solace that makes living worthwhile in Plath's world of imagination, but even that resource is not a cornucopia. The ache of mental exhaustion can empty the soul.

During her Cambridge years, Sylvia's black moods were usually hidden from the view of outsiders. The Botolph crowd had come to respect this brilliant addition to the group, whom Ted Hughes was almost proud to have won. With Ted Hughes's support, Sylvia was probably happier and more carefree then than at any other time in her brief life. That idyllic interlude in her life at Cambridge did seem to fulfill her dream of an exploding rainbow, particularly in the company of Ted Hughes. As the years went by, and the pair tried to cope with academic life in New England and then in London and Devonshire, the pleasant days were not to last. Domesticity, as British culture then expected it to be in those prefeminist years, left Sylvia little time for her own work. With two small ones, Frieda and Nicholas, to care for, she had to rise at five to enjoy a silent period in which to write. Moreover, she could be easily frustrated by impish behavior that male poets then seemed to think appropriate to their romantic calling. Once, when the couple was living in a cramped London flat, she was preparing dinner when she asked Ted and their guest, Lucas Myers, to get something for the meal and return quickly. Instead, they spent too long at a nearby pub and returned much, much later than Sylvia thought right. She was understandably furious. Despite their protestations of remorse and compliments for the meal, she refused to speak to the pair and forced them to eat a congealed supper—half-filled bowls of clam chowder—in tense silence.[76]

Yet Sylvia Plath could give as good as she ever got. On a weekend at a French château at Fons, owned by the well-known English anthropologist Julian Pitt-Rivers, Sylvia Plath's behavior was so outrageously selfish and even vicious that Ted had to take her away early to save themselves and their hosts further embarrassment. According to Dido Merwin, Sylvia's jealousy of Margot Pitt-Rivers, a brave fighter in the Spanish Civil War and an accomplished anthropologist in her own right, was the ostensible reason for her rudeness. But a second pregnancy, then in the third month, might also have frightened her into a nearly psychotic state.[77]

The growing strains of the marriage and estrangement and separation need not detain us. Let it simply be said that, compelled to devote so much energy to battling madness, Sylvia had few inner resources for dealing with married life's complications. Who was more to blame for Sylvia's mental collapse and suicide— Ted Hughes or Sylvia herself? Needless to say, those driven to near suicide are not generally very companionable. Their habits become maddeningly erratic. They require a degree of understanding and imposed discipline that becomes extremely taxing, sometimes to the edge of endurance. Clinical findings demonstrate that those nearest someone in the throes of mania or melancholy find themselves by turn worried, angry, repelled, appalled, or stubbornly, blindly unwilling to recognize the obvious. They might pretend that all is well when clearly it is not. Paul Auster recalls that "when my sister suffered a series of debilitating nervous breakdowns, my father continued to believe there was nothing wrong with her." All that was needed was a change of scene, meeting new people, getting a job, as if it simply were a matter of insufficient moral courage and willpower. But, Auster notes, the worst of it was the sense of helplessness that such illness elicits from the apprehensive onlooker. Kindness is rejected and efforts to control or discipline simply lead to recrimination. His father, hiding his grief beneath a rigid mask, tried to accept what could not be changed, but, Auster observes, "the more you accept it, the greater your despair becomes."[78]

Although subjected to these varying emotions, Ted Hughes loyally tried to be Sylvia's caregiver as best he could. For his part Ted Hughes, to adapt Winnicott's characterization, might be called a "good enough husband," neither the best nor worst of that customarily flawed species. Little serious guidance or knowledge of the affective disorder, however, was available to him in the early sixties, before the advent of lithium. That drug and others would later be combined with medical and psychological therapies—to imperfect but at least ameliorative effect. Dido Merwin, Ted's friend, once asked him why he did not show more authority in dealing with her. He wisely replied, "it would only make things worse; . . . she couldn't be helped that way."[79] Dido Merwin agreed: "How can you dissuade or even warn someone who is incapable of accepting that they might be wrong?" The answer to Merwin's rhetorical question is indisputable, but she was assuming that Plath had a hold on reality. The fact was that she did not.[80] To be sure, Ted's infidelity—perhaps inevitable under the circumstances—doubled Sylvia's lifelong sense of insecurity and fear of abandonment. Her agonized bereavement over the marital collapse was a second loss that grievously compounded the anguish that she had never resolved after the death of her father years before.

In the final analysis, no one should take the blame for her death, save the hooded Fates who preside over who should suffer and learn to create from the abundance of that suffering. Winston Churchill called his onslaughts of the malady "the black dog." Walker Percy entitled his "the sweet beast of catastrophe." Sylvia Plath named her illness "the demon of negation" and "the groveling image of the fearful beast within myself." For all of them as well as many others so afflicted, depression had to be fought "minute by minute" with a "stoic face" and "a position of irony," as Plath reminded herself in her journal. "I cannot ignore this murderous self; it's there. I smell it and feel it, but will not give it my name. . . . When it says you shall not sleep . . . I shall go on anyway, knocking its nose in."[81] Brave, sad words.

Fear of imperfection pursued her all her life. She strove to be the perfect daughter, student, wife, mother, and, most of all, perfect poet. Her letters to her mother tended to be so overly cheery that the reader would scarcely know how often the center was not holding. Her mother's false light-heartedness was a natural response to Sylvia's mordancy, but it did lead to an inauthentic relationship between them. Aurelia's repression of grief and worry set an example before her daughter, who replied with even greater false happiness to assure her mother that all was well. The result was that, in keeping with the times, Aurelia Plath believed that her daughter's illness was at most a temporary thing. Admission of helplessness had to be a matter of familial shame. Chronic and irremediable despondency was something to be hidden as much as possible from public knowledge.[82]

Sylvia Plath knew her goals were impossible. Always an admirer of Virginia Woolf, she took her standards of achievement from the great Bloomsbury novelist. Sylvia, however, was a married woman of the 1950s. When she and Ted Hughes settled for a while in America in the late 1950s, Hughes received the most attention. His *Hawk in the Rain* established him as a major poet. She rejoiced when he won a poetry prize; it had been judged by Marianne Moore, W. H. Auden, and, ironically, Stephen Spender. She was thrilled and declared, "it is as if [Ted] is the perfect male counterpart of my own self."[83] Yet when she was relegated to being known simply as Ted's wife, she soon promised herself to outdo Woolf—and also, perhaps, match her husband's fame.

In 1957, while working at a clerical job at a psychiatric clinic in the Massachusetts General Hospital in Boston, Sylvia Plath pledged to write down her observations, the stories told her by other women, and her own "passing thoughts," just as Woolf had done. But "I will be stronger" than she was, Sylvia determined. "I will write until I begin to speak my deep self, and then have children, and speak still deeper. The life of the creative mind first, then the creative body." [84] It was a noble aim, and she was beginning to sort out her priorities. Sylvia joined Robert Lowell's Boston University seminar, returned to psychotherapy, and had long martini afternoons with Anne Sexton at the Ritz Carlton off the Boston Commons. The poet Adrienne Rich, who did not know of Sylvia's fragile mental health, nonetheless tried to advise her not to try too much. Like Rich herself, she might become savagely torn between motherhood and the urge to write, Rich warned. [85]

Yet the burden of conflicting aims—all to be mastered with equal efficiency and dispatch—became too much of a strain. Poems and babies followed, but the nemesis of perfection never faded. In one of her last poems, she recognized the danger of her lifelong obsession: "Perfection is terrible, it cannot have children. / Cold as snow breath, it tamps the womb." [86] How hard it was, though, to resist the impulse. Perhaps she thought that striving toward empyrean heights was the indispensable source of her imaginative powers. The latter gift had kept her alive to her thirtieth year. The afflictions of the brain, the sleeplessness, the distracted thoughts and imagined horrors, however, had become unbearable. For Sylvia, writing was not just a vocation, disciplined and professional though she was. Composing verse was an exercise of quite a different dimension. For her, the creative impulse, she once wrote, *"breaks open the vaults of the dead and the skies behind which the prophesying angels hide.* The mind makes and makes, spinning its web." [87]

Like Sylvia, Virginia Woolf had tried to kill herself once before she succeeded. She had known that same downward vortex of mind into which Sylvia was sucked. Neither Woolf's loyal husband, Leonard, nor Ted Hughes could prevent them from slipping into incurable psychosis and suicide, whether the surviving spouse was faithful or not. Before Virginia put stones in her pockets and waded out to sea, she wrote Vanessa Bell, "I feel I have gone too far this time to come back again. . . . I am always hearing voices, and I know I shan't get over it now." [88] Sylvia, however, apparently wrote no one of her intention, perhaps out of fear that they might stop her. Elizabeth Hardwick, Robert Lowell's wife, observed that although Sylvia sought to be "both heroine and author, when the curtain goes down, it is her own dead body there on the stage, sacrificed to her own plot." [89] In light of more recent findings about the afflictions of the mind, that reading seems shallow and almost contemptuous. Yet it does point to the histrionic, narcissistic aspect of her desperation.

Leaving behind two babies motherless, she might seem to have been unconscionably callous to indulge herself in this way. But the suicide feels bereft of choices. The purpose of the act is to end a crashing cascade of intolerable mental agony. Sylvia Plath was prompted to die, stalked by fears and terrifying whispers in her mind similar to those that haunted Virginia Woolf. Sylvia Plath's psychiatrist, John Horder, had argued that an accumulation of personal disappointments and an artist's "irresponsibility" by no means could be the causes of so tragic an act. The wildness of her swings of mood, he wisely guessed, were "so excessive that a doctor inevitably thinks in terms of brain chemistry."[90] If the leading expert on the subject, Edwin Shneidman, is accurate, the deed arises from a form of psychosis that must be understood as something apart from even so ostensibly similar a state as clinical depression. Schizophrenics and alcoholics, he points out, may also open the door to a beckoning death. In recent years, biochemists have discovered that there is an indisputable relationship between self- elimination and a serotonin metabolite called CSF5-HIAA. The research has been replicated in autopsies of suicidal patients in whose brains the affected receptors have been located. In more familiar terms, it is safe to say that the feelings of low self- esteem, anger, emotional numbness, and sense of lovelessness, which psychological depression arouses, sometimes tempt the manic-depressive to seek a permanent closure on pain, perhaps prompted by the disarray of these chemical compounds.[91]

Thus, Sylvia Plath died of an illness, that, in a sense, still has no name. Suicidal psychosis, if that is the nearest term for it, is as mysterious in its biological complexity as the cause of cancer and no less elusive. Neurologists, geneticists, and biochemists have located some of the elements involved but are still searching for its eradication. Rather than being the source of anguish, the neurological factors could perhaps arise from the emotional effects of stress, or possibly psychological and somatic dysfunctions are interconnected, even joined together. The addition of a physiological element does not by any means simplify the whole problem of mental cause and effect. Instead, it makes her doleful pilgrimage into the Valley of the Shadow of Death all the more confounding. None of Plath's biographers has dealt with the neurological sources of her malady, and indeed, too little is yet known about the medical aspect to settle the question beyond all doubt.[92]

Yet amazingly, Sylvia Plath's creative spirit did not desert her. In a matter of weeks after her separation from Ted Hughes in 1962, she wrote her masterpiece, the collection of poems published posthumously in *Ariel*. Hughes remarks that "she knew with a great certainty that she had made the leap. As she wrote her mother on October 16, in the middle of her extraordinary month: 'I am a genius of a writer: I have it in me. I am writing the best poems of my life; they will make my name.' "[93] Six days before her death she composed one of the most moving of all the pieces in her enduring testament, "Edge." "The woman is perfected. / Her dead / Body wears the smile of accomplishment, / The illusion of Greek necessity." She re-enfolds her "dead children" into her flesh like a rose whose petals curl at a time when "odors bleed" in the garden. The moon, like a paid mourner dressed in funereal garb, is indifferent: "She is used to this sort of thing. / Her blacks crackle and drag."[94]

Alone, having refused the company of her solicitous friends, she turned on the gas in the oven of her London flat and died on February 11, 1963. Her babies upstairs were spared the fumes, as she had carefully planned. Yet they were never to know thereafter either the warm breath or the unbearable desolation of their mother. Their chief comfort would have to be gratitude for the literary inheritance that Sylvia Plath's dark torment bequeathed. The same sentiment applies as well to so many other writers, Reuben Davis among them. Their art and lives were shaped by a condition about which much has yet to be unearthed. In any case, we are the beneficiaries of their sadness and their ecstasy.

NOTES

I am grateful to Anne M. Wyatt-Brown for her critical contributions to this essay and especially for her insights into this interpretation of Sylvia Plath's art and life, and to Natalie Wyatt-Brown, Jane Kopp, Robert Zieger, and Lucas Myers for additional, substantive suggestions. Jan Lewis's superb editing is also deeply appreciated.

1. Reuben Davis, *Shim* (1953; Jackson: University Press of Mississippi, 1995).

2. I owe this section to Richard Allen Blessing, "The Shape of the Psyche: Vision and Technique in the Late Poems of Sylvia Plath," in Gary Lane, ed., *Sylvia Plath: New View on the Poetry* (Baltimore: Johns Hopkins University Press, 1979), 59. Plath's conflicted relation to Dickinson is discussed in Steven Gould Axelrod, *Sylvia Plath: The Wound and the Cure of Words* (Baltimore: Johns Hopkins University Press, 1990), 126–30. The epigraph by Dickinson is taken from Thomas H. Johnson, ed., *Final Harvest: Emily Dickinson's Poems* (Boston: Little, Brown, 1951), 43.

3. See Arnold Rampersad, *The Life of Langston Hughes*, 2 vols. (New York: Oxford University Press, 1986); Margaret Walker, *Richard Wright, Daemonic Genius: A Portrait of the Man and a Critical Look at His Work* (New York: Warner, 1988); Walker Percy, foreword, in John Kennedy Toole, *A Confederacy of Dunces* (Baton Rouge: Louisiana State University Press, 1980), v–vii; Lyle Leverich, *Tom: The Unknown Tennessee Williams* (New York: Crown, 1995); Tracy Thompson, *The Beast: A Reckoning with Depression* (New York: Putnam's, 1995); Wilfrid Sheed, *In Love with Daylight: A Memoir of Recovery* (New York: Simon and Schuster, 1995); William Styron, *Darkness Visible: A Memoir of Madness* (New York: Random House, 1990).

4. A. Alvarez, *The Savage God: A Study of Suicide* (New York: Random House, 1972); Kay Redfield Jamison, *Touched with Fire: Manic-Depressive Illness and the Artistic Temperament* (New York: Basic Books, 1993); Michael Reynolds, *The Young Hemingway* (New York: Blackwell, 1986); on Proust, see Arnold M. Ludwig, *The Price of Greatness: Resolving the Creativity and Madness Controversy* (New York: Guilford, 1995), 99, 103; and Albert Rothenberg, *Creativity & Madness: New Findings and Old Stereotypes* (Baltimore: Johns Hopkins University Press, 1990), 104, 115; Paul Auster, *The Invention of Solitude* (1982; London: Faber and Faber, 1988); Walter Schonau, "Fantasy Structures in Paul Auster's *New York Trilogy*," in *Proceedings of the Ninth International Conference on Literature and Psychology* (Lisbon: Instituto Superior de Psicologica Aplicada, 1993), 233–41; Justin Kaplan, *Mr. Clemens and Mark Twain: A Biography* (New York: Touchstone, 1966), 123 (quotation).

5. Leslie A. Fiedler, *Love and Death in the American Novel* (Cleveland: World, 1962).

6. Richard Pine, ed., *Dark Fathers into Light: Brenden Kennelly* (Newcastle upon Tyne: Bloodaxe, 1994).

7. In the film, *The Client,* the woman lawyer is not a nurturing figure but rather a guide and counselor, a more paternal than motherly role.

8. Reuben Davis, statement on dustjacket of *Shim* (Indianapolis: Bobbs-Merrill, 1956).

9. Reuben Davis, "Autobiography," copy of typescript, l, University Press of Mississippi files, Jackson.

10. Ibid., 2. Some authorities record that Helen Dick was from Memphis rather than Greenwood. See Helen Dick's correction of Frank Smith's column, *Jackson Clarion-Ledger,* December 21, 1986.

11. Harnett T. Kane, review, *New York Times Book Review,* October 18, 1953, photocopy, files of the University Press of Mississippi, Jackson.

12. Mark Twain, *The Adventures of Huckleberry Finn* (New York: Penguin, 1987), 10; Joel Williamson, *William Faulkner and Southern History* (New York: Oxford University Press, 1993), 4.

13. Unpublished Miscellaneous Autobiography, c. 1950–51, University Press of Mississippi files, Jackson.

14. Davis, *Shim,* 282.

15. Davis, *Shim,* 282.

16. Davis, *Shim,* 282, 283.

17. Nicholas Davis to author, November 28, 1995, in author's possession. Cited with the permission of the writer.

18. Reuben Davis, as reported by his wife, Helen Dick, from her journal (probably early 1950s), Davis collection, University Press of Mississippi, Jackson.

19. Richard B. Sewall, *The Life of Emily Dickinson* (New York: Farrar, Straus and Giroux, 1980), 1:3.

20. Faulkner quoted in Richard Gray, *The Life of William Faulkner: A Critical Biography* (Oxford: Blackwell; New York: Cambridge University Press, 1994), 1.

21. Tillie Olsen, *Silences* (New York: Delta/Seymour Lawrence, 1978), 6.

22. Mark Irwin, "Memory's Escape: Inventing The Music of Chance—A Conversation with Paul Auster," *Denver Quarterly* 28 (winter 1984): 118; Dennis Barone, ed., *Beyond the Red Notebook: Essays on Paul Auster* (Philadelphia: University of Pennsylvania Press, 1995), 13; Auster, *Invention of Solitude*, 7, 35–51.

23. John Berendt, *Midnight in the Garden of Good and Evil* (New York: Random House, 1994).

24. Edward Butscher, *Conrad Aiken: Poet of White Horse Vale* (Athens: University of Georgia Press, 1988), 21, 35, 92, 93, 112, 113; Seymour L. Gross, "The Reflection of Poe in Conrad Aiken's 'Strange Moonlight,' " *Modern Language Notes* 72 (March 1972): 186(quotation).

25. Butscher, *Conrad Aiken*, 21.

26. Cowley quoted in Sanford Pinsker, "The Artist and the Art Novel: A Reappraisal of Conrad Aiken's *Blue Voyage*," *Southern Quarterly* 21 (fall 1982): 29.

27. James L. Wheeler, "The Ushant Dream of Conrad Aiken," *Southern Quarterly* 21 (fall 1982): 97 n. 3. See Jennifer Aldrich, "The Deciphered Heart: Conrad Aiken's Poetry and Prose Fiction," *Sewanee Review* 75 (summer 1967): 485–519. She offers an interesting interpretation that does not take account of his biography.

28. Conrad Aiken, "Silent Snow, Secret Snow," in *The Short Stories of Conrad Aiken* (New York: Duell, Sloan, and Pearce, 1950), 234–35. Aiken did not consider "Silent Snow" to contain autobiographical revelations. See Conrad Aiken to Jay Martin, October 8, 1961, in Joseph Killorin, ed., *Selected Letters of Conrad Aiken* (New Haven: Yale University Press, 1978), 310.

29. Joseph Killorin, introduction to Killorin, ed., *Selected Letters of Conrad Aiken,* xiii–xiv; Aiken to Martin, October 8, November 12, 1961, in ibid., 309–10, 311–12.

30. Arnold Toynbee, "History," in R. W. Livingston, ed., *The Legacy of Greece* (London: Oxford University Press, 1922), 291; Felix Brown, "Bereavement and Lack of a Parent in Childhood," in E. Miller, ed., *Foundations of Child Psychiatry* (London: Pergamon, 1968), 436.

31. Diane Middlebrook, *Anne Sexton: A Biography* (Boston: Houghton Mifflin, 1991); John Berryman, "The Marker Slants," in *The Dream Songs* (New York: Farrar, Straus and Giroux, 1969), 406.

32. Styron, *Darkness Visible*, 79.

33. Styron quoted in Lewis A. Lawson, "William Styron," in Louis D. Rubin, Jr., et al., eds., *The History of Southern Literature* (Baton Rouge: Louisiana State University Press, 1985), 481.

34. Styron, *Darkness Visible*, 78–79. Cf. Albert E. Stone, *The Return of Nat Turner: History, Literature, and Cultural Politics in Sixties America* (Athens: University of Georgia Press, 1992).

35. William Styron, *A Tidewater Morning: Three Tales from Youth* (New York: Random House, 1993).

36. Robert Cubbage, "A Visitor Interview: Novelist Walker Percy and His Subversive Message," in Lewis A. Lawson and Victor A. Kramer, eds., *More Conversations with Walker Percy* (Jackson: University Press of Mississippi, 1993), 187.

37. Brown, "Bereavement and Lack of a Parent in Childhood," in 435–55. One American poet to lose his father at an early age was Robert Frost, but there were many more. See William H. Pritchard, *Frost: A Literary Life Reconsidered* (New York: Oxford University Press, 1984), 31–35.

38. Jamison, *Touched with Fire*, 267–68, John Unterecker, *Voyager: A Life of Hart Crane* (New York: Farrar, Straus and Giroux, 1969); Peter Ackroyd, *T. S. Eliot: A Life* (New York: Simon and Schuster, 1984), 113–15; Eileen Simpson, *Poets in Their Youth: A Memoir* (New York: Random House, 1982), 244–45 (Delmore Schwartz), 157–59, 248–49, 252–53 (John Berryman), 221–22 (Theodore

Roethke); Ian Hamilton, *Robert Lowell: A Biography* (New York: Random House, 1982); Ben F. Johnson III, *Fierce Solitude: A Life of John Gould Fletcher* (Fayetteville: University of Arkansas Press, 1994); William H. Pritchard, *Randall Jarrell: A Literary Life* (New York: Farrar, Straus and Giroux, 1990); Diane Wood Middlebrook, *Anne Sexton.*

39. See Joanna Russ, *How to Suppress Women's Writing* (1982; Austin: University of Texas Press, 1992).

40. Elizabeth Gaskell, *The Life of Charlotte Brontë,* ed. Alan Shelston (New York: Penguin, 1985); Mary Wells, "Was Emily Dickinson Psychotic?" *American Imago* 28 (winter 1962): 309–21; Sewall, *Life of Emily Dickinson,* 1:3–11; Jean Strouse, *Alice James: A Biography* (Boston: Houghton Mifflin, 1980), esp. 177–90; Per Seyersted, *Kate Chopin: A Critical Biography* (1969; Baton Rouge: Louisiana State University Press, 1980); Cheryl B. Torsney, *Constance Fenimore Woolson: The Grief of Artistry* (Athens: University of Georgia Press, 1989); J. R. Raper, *Without Shelter: The Early Career of Ellen Glasgow* (Baton Rouge: Louisiana State University Press, 1971); Ann Hulbert, *The Interior Castle: The Art and Life of Jean Stafford* (New York: Knopf, 1992); Judy Oppenheimer: *Private Demons: The Life of Shirley Jackson* (New York: Fawcett, 1988); Diane Wood Middlebrook, *Anne Sexton: A Biography* (Boston: Houghton Mifflin, 1991); Peter D. Kramer, "How Crazy Was Zelda?" *New York Times Magazine,* December 1, 1996, 106–8; Mary Cantwell, "How to Make a Corpse Talk: Patricia Cornwell's Grim Fascinations," *New York Times Magazine,* July 14, 1996, 15–17; Dannye Romine Powell, ed., *Parting the Curtains: Interviews with Southern Writers* (Winston-Salem, NC: John F. Blair, 1994), Kaye Gibbons, 115–34; Gail Godwin, 135–56.

41. Frederick K. Goodwin and Kay Redfield Jamison, *Manic-Depressive Illness* (New York: Oxford University Press, 1990), 379. This is an indispensable volume.

42. "Daddy," in Sylvia Plath, *Collected Poems,* ed. Ted Hughes (New York: Harper and Row, 1981), 222.

43. Sylvia Plath, *The Bell Jar* (New York: Bantam, 1972), 137; Linda Wagner-Martin, *Sylvia Plath: A Biography* (New York: Simon and Schuster, 1987), 28.

44. Wagner-Martin, *Sylvia Plath,* 40.

45. Stevenson, *Bitter Fame: A Life of Sylvia Plath* (Boston: Houghton Mifflin, 1989), 25. Author's conversations with Amy Gardner of Eaglesmere, PA, and Cynthia Parsons of Cockeysville, MD, November 29, 1996. These two friends of Sylvia at Smith College concur with that conclusion.

46. Goodwin and Jamison, *Manic-Depressive Illness,* 31–35. Admittedly this is a very controversial area in the study of affective disorder, and it was only at very troubled times that Plath succumbed to the full range of classic symptoms of psychosis—delusional and disoriented thinking, hallucinations, and prolonged insomnia.

47. July 11, 1952, entry in Ted Hughes and Frances McCullough, eds., *The Journals of Sylvia Plath* (New York: Dial Press, 1982), 51.

48. "Temper of Time," in *Collected Poems,* 336.

49. Sylvia Plath's Smith College journal quoted by Stevenson, *Bitter Fame,* 32.

50. Goodwin and Jamison, *Manic-Depressive Illness,* 19.

51. Stevenson, *Bitter Fame,* 32; November 3, 1952, entry in Hughes and McCullough, eds., *Plath Journals,* 59; last quotation from Wagner-Martin, *Sylvia Plath,* 89.

52. D. W. Winnicott, *The Family and Individual Development* (1965; London: Tavistock/ Routledge, 1989), 17–19. There is no reason to think that Aurelia Plath was a deficient mother rather than a brave and enterprising widow who managed to keep things together as well as one could expect. See Wagner-Martin, *Sylvia Plath,* 15–30; Stevenson, *Bitter Fame,* 9–12. For an inappropriately critical view, see Ronald Hayman, *The Death and Life of Sylvia Plath* (London: Heineman, 1991), 30–42. Blaming everyone else for her condition as much as she blamed herself, Sylvia, in *The Bell Jar* and some of her poems, lashed out at her mother cruelly and quite irrationally.

53. Aurelia Plath quoted in Dido Merwin, "Vessel of Wrath: A Memoir of Sylvia Plath," appendix 2 in Stevenson, *Bitter Fame,* 332.

54. Stevenson, *Bitter Fame,* 166 (quotation); Thomas Carmelo Caramagno, "Suicide and the Illusion of Closure: Aging, Depression, and the Decision to Die" (unpublished paper); idem, *The Flight of the Mind: Virginia Woolf's Art and Manic-Depressive Illness* (Berkeley: University of

California Press, 1992); "Biochemical Models," in Goodwin and Jamison, *Manic-Depressive Illness,* 402–15; Elliot S. Gershon et al., "The Inheritance of Affective Disorders," in A. G. Steinberg et al., eds., *Progress in Medical Genetics,* (Philadelphia, Saunders, 1977), 2:101–64.

55. Edwin Shneidman, *Suicide as Psychache: A Clinical Approach to Self-Destructive Behavior* (Northvale, NJ: Jason Aronson, 1993), 55 (quotation). See Kay Redfield Jamison, *The Unquiet Mind: A Memoir of Moods and Madness* (New York: Knopf, 1995).

56. Emil Kraepelin, *Manic-Depressive Insanity and Paranoia,* trans. R. M. Barclay, ed. G. M. Roberston (1921; New York: Arno Press, 1976); Goodwin and Jamison, *Manic-Depressive Illness,* 25; Stanley W. Jackson, *Melancholia and Depression; From Hippocratic Times to Modern Times* (New Haven: Yale University Press, 1986), 207–11.

57. Plath, *Bell Jar,* 1.

58. F. Scott Fitzgerald, *The Crack-Up* (New York: New Directions, 1956), 75 (quotation); Wagner-Martin, *Sylvia Plath,* 92–105 (103, 105, quotations); Hayman, *Death and Life of Sylvia Plath,* 56.

59. Wagner-Martin, *Sylvia Plath,* 120.

60. The poems by Ted Hughes were "Fallgrief's Girlfriends," "When Two Men Meet," "Whenever I Am under My Gravestone," and "If I Should Touch Her," *St. Botolph's Review,* 1956, 16–19. The other poems were by Daniel Weissbort, Daniel Huws, E. Lucas Myers, and David Ross; three short sketches were written by Than Minton, E. Lucas Myers, and Daniel Weissbort. When I spoke with Sylvia on the day of the *Review*'s publication, she was particularly struck by Hughes's "Fallgrief's Girlfriends" and Luke Myers's "Sestina of the Norse Seaman," ibid., 8. Daniel Huws of the National Library of Wales, Aberystwyth, has since published his poems under the title *Noth* (London: Secker and Warburg, 1972). Daniel Weissbort, formerly of London, now professor of English and comparative literature and director of the Translation Workshop at the University of Iowa, has recently published his fifth book of poetry in a collection entitled *Lake: New and Selected Poems* (Riverdale-on-Hudson, NY: Sheep Meadow Press, 1992).

61. Edward Butscher, *Sylvia Plath: Method and Madness* (New York: Simon and Schuster, 1977), 202.

62. Jane Baltzell Kopp, " 'Gone, Very Gone Youth': Sylvia Plath at Cambridge, 1955–1957," in Edward Butscher, ed., *Sylvia Plath: The Woman and the Work* (New York: Dodd, Mead, 1977), 63–65; Butscher, *Sylvia Plath: Method and Madness,* 184–85.

63. See Butscher, *Sylvia Plath: Method and Madness,* 185–92, 187 (quotation), 202 (quotation). Butscher is not very accurate with the facts: he calls Botolph's a priory; I am identified as Bart Wyett-Brown; he names Jane Baltzell as Jane Kopp, her name after marriage some years after the Cambridge interlude; and he misspells Whitstead Cottage.

64. Myers, "Ah Youth: Ted Hughes and Sylvia Plath at Cambridge and After," appendix 1 in Stevenson, *Bitter Fame,* 312.

65. Stevenson, *Bitter Fame,* 90.

66. Richard Slobodin, *W. H. R. Rivers* (New York: Columbia University Press, 1978), 59–66; Paul Fussell, *The Great War and Modern Memory* (New York: Oxford University Press, 1975), 101, 102; but more to the point is the detailed account of Rivers and his patients, especially Graves, in Miranda Seymour, *Robert Graves: Life on the Edge* (New York: Henry Holt, 1995), 65–70, 105–7, 115–17. See also Anne M. Wyatt-Brown, "Headhunters and Victims of War: W. H. R. Rivers and Pat Barker," in *Proceedings of the Twelfth International Conference on Literature and Psychology* (Lisbon: Instituto Superior de Psicologica Aplicada, 1997); Russ, *How to Suppress Women's Writing,* 44.

67. Myers, "Ah, Youth," 314.

68. Myers, "Ah, Youth," 315.

69. Blessing, "Shape of the Psyche"; "Kindness," in Sylvia Plath, *Ariel* (New York: Harper and Row, 1965), 82. "Morning Song," in *Ariel,* 1.

70. "Daddy," in *Ariel,* 50, 51.

71. Plath, "The Detective," in *Winter Trees* (New York: Harper and Row, 1972), 13–14; "Daddy," in *Ariel,* 51; "Lady Lazarus," in *Ariel,* 6; "Three Women: A Poem for Three Voices," in *Collected*

Poems, 179. This section owes much to Norman H. Holland, "Literary Suicide: A Question of Style," *Psychocultural Review,* summer 1977, 299.

72. Blessing, "Shape of the Psyche," 57, 58.

73. Robert Lowell, foreword to Plath, *Ariel,* vii.

74. Sylvia Plath, *The Colossus and Other Poems* (1962; New York: Random House, 1968), 60; Middlebrook, *Anne Sexton,* 109–10.

75. Blessing, "Shape of the Psyche," 63; Plath, "The Moon and the Yew Tree," in *Collected Poems,* 172–73.

76. Recalling the incident in a memoir, Myers claims they were only forty minutes late but acknowledges that memories of embarrassing moments can be tricky: see Myers, "Ah, Youth," 307–21.

77. Merwin, "Vessel of Wrath," 337–41.

78. Auster, *Invention of Solitude,* 25–26.

79. Stevenson, *Bitter Fame,* 217.

80. Merwin, "Vessel of Wrath," 341.

81. October 1, 1957, entry in Hughes and McCullough, eds., *Plath Journals,* 177; Stevenson, *Bitter Fame,* 114–15; Anthony Storr, *Churchill's Black Dog, Kafka's Mice and Other Phenomena of the Human Mind* (New York: Ballantine, 1988), 76.

82. Sylvia Plath, *Letters Home: Correspondence, 1950–63,* ed. Aurelia Schober Plath (1976; New York: Bantam, 1977). Olwyn Hughes, Ted's sister, wrote Janet Malcolm quite convincingly that "Mrs. Plath was ashamed of the mental illness" and shrank from recognizing "just how very ill Sylvia was with her first breakdown." See Janet Malcolm, *The Silent Woman: Sylvia Plath and Ted Hughes* (New York: Random House, 1994), 29.

83. February 25, 1957, entry in Hughes and McCullough, eds., *Plath Journals,* 154.

84. July 17, 1957, entry in Hughes and McCullough, eds., *Plath Journals,* 165.

85. Middlebrook, *Anne Sexton,* 103–4, 111.

86. "The Munich Mannequins," in *Collected Poems,* 262.

87. July 17, 1957, entry in Hughes and McCullough, eds., *Plath Journals,* 165.

88. Virginia Woolf to Vanessa Bell, March 23, 1941, in Nigel Nicholson and Joanne Trautman, eds., *The Letters of Virginia Woolf,* 6 vols. (New York: Harcourt Brace Jovanovich, 1980), 6:485.

89. Harding quoted in Stevenson, *Bitter Fame,* 298.

90. Horder quoted in Stevenson, *Bitter Fame,* 298; Shneidman, *Suicide as Psychache,* 33–34.

91. Goodwin and Jamison, *Manic-Depressive Illness,* 493. On the same page Goodwin and Jamison also have noted "increased postsynaptic serotonin receptors . . . and decreased presynaptic auto-receptors"—both signals of a slowing of neurotransmissions. There are, they say, curious variations in the data that are related to alcoholism, homicide, aggressive behavior, manic- depression—variables that "need to be explored more systematically in future studies." See Shneidman, *Suicide as Psychache,* 55, passim.

92. Plath's biographers, including those already cited, are Stevenson, *Bitter Fame;* Wagner-Martin, *Sylvia Plath;* Malcolm, *Silent Woman;* Butscher, *Sylvia Plath: Method and Madness;* Eileen Aird, *Sylvia Plath: Her Life and Work* (New York: Harper and Row, 1973); Paul Alexander, *Rough Magic: A Biography of Sylvia Plath* (New York: Viking, 1991); Hayman, *Death and Life of Sylvia Plath.* As Malcolm notes, A. Alvarez's biographical sketch of Plath in *The Savage God,* cited earlier, makes her the victim of an unfeeling husband, as if living with someone subject to violent swings of mood and an almost constant self-preoccupation or narcissism presents only minor vexations. See Malcolm, *Silent Woman,* 23.

93. Hughes and McCullough, eds., *Plath Journals,* 357.

94. Plath, "Edge," in *Collected Poems,* 272–73.

Contributors

W. Andrew Achenbaum is a professor of history at the University of Michigan and the deputy director of its Institute of Gerontology. Author of several works on the history of old age, he is currently doing research on "wisdom" in contemporary society.

Michael Barton is an associate professor of American studies and history at Penn State Harrisburg, Capital College. His field is national character studies, and his major publications have been on Civil War soldiers' values and personalities.

Mary H. Blewett is a professor of history at the University of Massachusetts at Lowell and teaches graduate students at Amherst. She specializes in the social history of industrialization in New England; her current work in progress is *Constant Turmoil: The Politics of Industrial Life in Nineteenth-Century New England.*

Hasia R. Diner is the Paul S. and Sylvia Steinberg Professor of American Jewish History at New York University, where she holds a joint appointment in the department of history and the Skirball Department of Hebrew and Judaic Studies. She is the author of *In the Almost Promised Land: American Jews and Blacks, 1915–1935; Erin's Daughters in America: Irish Immigrant Women in the Nineteenth Century;* and *A Time for Gathering, 1820–1880: The Second Migration,* which is the second volume in the Johns Hopkins University series The Jewish People in America.

Otniel E. Dror, M.D., is a doctoral candidate in the department of history, Princeton University. He is currently working on his dissertation, "The Emotional Perspective: The Study of Emotions in Physiology, Psychology and Medicine, 1880–1950."

Kenneth J. Gergen is the Mustin Professor of Psychology, Swarthmore College. Coordinator for the Interpretation Theory concentration at Swarthmore, Gergen is the author of *Toward Transformation in Social Knowledge, The Saturated Self,* and *Realities and Relationships.* He is also a founder of the Taos Institute, an organization devoted to exploring the relationships between social constructionist theory and societal practice.

R. Marie Griffith holds a Ph.D. in the study of religion from Harvard University and is currently a Mellon Postdoctoral Fellow in the Humanities at Northwestern University. She is the author of *God's Daughters: Evangelical Women and the Power of Submission.*

C. Dallett Hemphill received her doctorate from Brandeis University and is currently an associate professor of history at Ursinus College. She is completing a book-length study of the history of manners in early America.

Dolores Janiewski is Senior Lecturer in History at Victoria University of Wellington in New Zealand where she teaches U.S. history.

Joseph Kelly is a literary critic whose work has appeared in such journals as the *James Joyce Quarterly, Joyce Studies Annual,* and *Studies in Short Fiction.* His book, *Our Joyce: A History of James Joyce's Literary Reputation,* is forthcoming. He is an assistant professor of English at the College of Charleston in Charleston, South Carolina.

Timothy Kelly is a social historian whose work focuses primarily on American Catholics. His "Suburbanization and the Decline of Catholic Public Ritual" appeared in the *Journal of Social History.* He has collaborated with Joseph Kelly on a number of projects, including "Searching the Dark Alley: New Historicism and Social History," which also appeared in the *Journal of Social History.* He is an assistant professor of history at Saint Vincent College in Latrobe, Pennsylvania.

Jan Lewis is a professor of history at Rutgers University, Newark, and author of *The Pursuit of Happiness: Family and Values in Jefferson's Virginia.*

Susan J. Matt received her Ph.D. from Cornell University in 1996. She is a visiting assistant professor at Clark University, where she teaches American cultural, social, and women's history.

Lucia McMahon is a Ph.D. candidate in history at Rutgers University. She is working on a dissertation on gender, individualism, and society in the early Republic.

Kimberley L. Phillips teaches at the College of William and Mary. Her research has focused on the social and cultural history of the African American working class.

Linda W. Rosenzweig is a professor of history at Chatham College. She is the author of *The Anchor of My Life: Middle-Class American Mothers and Daughters, 1880– 1920* and is working on a book on the friendship experiences of middle-class American women between 1900 and 1960.

David R. Shumway is an associate professor of English and literary and cultural studies, Carnegie Mellon University. He is the author of *Michel Foucault* and *Creating American Civilization: A Genealogy of American Literature as an Academic Discipline,* and he is currently working on a book on the discourses of romantic love (film, fiction, songs, self-help, etc.) in twentieth-century America.

John C. Spurlock is an associate professor of history at Seton Hill College. He is the author of *Free Love: Marriage and Middle- Class Radicalism in America.* His current work deals with women's emotions and American culture in the 1920s and 1930s.

Peter N. Stearns is the dean of the College of Humanities and Social Sciences, Carnegie Mellon University, and editor of the *Journal of Social History*. He has written on various aspects of the history of emotions and its interdisciplinary connections. He also recently published a book on the comparative history of dieting in the United States and France.

Jeffrey Steele is a professor of English at the University of Wisconsin-Madison. He is the author of *The Representation of the Self in the American Renaissance; The Essential Margaret Fuller* (a *Choice* "Outstanding Academic Book"); and numerous articles on Margaret Fuller, Walt Whitman, and other nineteenth-century American writers. He is completing book-length studies on the emergence of Margaret Fuller and on the politics of mourning.

Kevin White has taught history and American studies at the University of Sussex and Ohio State University, where he received his Ph.D. in history. He is the author of *The First Sexual Revolution: The Emergence of Male Heterosexuality in Modern America* and *The Revolt against Victorian Sexual Morality in the Twentieth Century United States*.

Cas Wouters is a researcher at the Faculty of Social Sciences, Utrecht University, Netherlands. His research project is titled "Informalization and the Civilizing of Emotions in the Netherlands, Germany, England and the USA, since the 19th Century." He has published numerous articles and books on emotions, women, and dying.

Bertram Wyatt-Brown is the Richard J. Milbauer Professor of History at the University of Florida. He is the author of several works in American antebellum history and recently published *The House of Percy: Honor, Melancholy and Imagination in a Southern Family* and *The Literary Percys: Family History, Gender and the Southern Imagination*.

Index